# PORTUGUESE ENGLISH

## DICTIONARY • DICIONÁRIO

# INGLÊS PORTUGUÊS

## Berlitz Dictionaries

| | |
|---|---|
| **Dansk** | Engelsk, Fransk, Italiensk, Spansk, Tysk |
| **Deutsch** | Dänisch, Englisch, Finnisch, Französisch, Italienisch, Niederländisch, Norwegisch, Portugiesisch, Schwedish, Spanisch |
| **English** | Danish, Dutch, Finnish, French, German, Italian, Norwegian, Portuguese, Spanish, Swedish, Turkish |
| **Español** | Alemán, Danés, Finlandés, Francés, Holandés, Inglés, Noruego, Sueco |
| **Français** | Allemand, Anglais, Danois, Espagnol, Finnois, Italien, Néerlandais, Norvégien, Portugais, Suédois |
| **Italiano** | Danese, Finlandese, Francese, Inglese, Norvegese, Olandese, Svedese, Tedesco |
| **Nederlands** | Duits, Engels, Frans, Italiaans, Portugees, Spaans |
| **Norsk** | Engelsk, Fransk, Italiensk, Spansk, Tysk |
| **Português** | Alemão, Francês, Holandês, Inglês, Sueco |
| **Suomi** | Englanti, Espanja, Italia, Ranska, Ruotsi, Saksa |
| **Svenska** | Engelska, Finska, Franska, Italienska, Portugisiska, Spanska, Tyska |

# PORTUGUESE ENGLISH

## DICTIONARY · DICIONÁRIO

# INGLÊS PORTUGUÊS

with mini grammar section
com secção de mini-gramática

Library of Congress Catalog Card Number: 78-78080

Revised edition — 1st printing 1994
Printed in Switzerland

# Contents

# Índice

# Preface

In selecting the 12.500 word-concepts in each language for this dictionary, the editors have had the traveller's needs foremost in mind. This book will prove invaluable to all the millions of travellers, tourists and business people who appreciate the reassurance a small and practical dictionary can provide. It offers them—as it does beginners and students—all the basic vocabulary they are going to encounter and to have to use, giving the key words and expressions to allow them to cope in everyday situations.

Like our successful phrase books and travel guides, these dictionaries—created with the help of a computer data bank—are designed to slip into pocket or purse, and thus have a role as handy companions at all times.

Besides just about everything you normally find in dictionaries, there are these Berlitz bonuses:

- imitated pronunciation next to each foreign-word entry, making it easy to read and enunciate words whose spelling may look forbidding

- a unique, practical glossary to simplify reading a foreign restaurant menu and to take the mystery out of complicated dishes and indecipherable names on bills of fare

- useful information on how to tell the time and how to count, on conjugating irregular verbs, commonly seen abbreviations and converting to the metric system, in addition to basic phrases.

While no dictionary of this size can pretend to completeness, we expect the user of this book will feel well armed to tackle foreign travel with confidence. We should, however, be very pleased to receive comments, criticism and suggestions that you think may be of help in preparing future editions.

# Prefácio

Ao seleccionarem as 12.500 referências em cada língua para este dicionário, os editores pensaram sobretudo nas necessidades dos viajantes. Este livro será de um valor inestimável para os milhões de turistas e homens de negócios que apreciarão a confiança que lhes pode dar um pequeno e prático dicionário. O dicionário oferece-lhes, assim como aos principiantes e estudantes, todo o vocabulário de base que vão encontrar e que deverão utilizar, e as palavras-chave e expressões que lhes permitirão enfrentar situações correntes.

Como os nossos apreciados livros de frases e guias de viagem, estes dicionários – criados com a ajuda de um banco de dados de computador – são feitos de maneira a caberem facilmente no bolso ou no saco de mão e a serem prontamente acessíveis em qualquer momento.

Para além de quase tudo o que normalmente se encontra num dicionário, estão incluídas as seguintes vantagens da edição Berlitz:

- a pronúncia simulada que aparece junto a cada vocábulo na língua estrangeira, o que torna fácil a leitura e a enunciação de palavras com uma ortografia complicada

- um único e prático glossário destinado a simplificar a leitura da ementa de um restaurante estrangeiro e a tornar compreensíveis os nomes misteriosos e complicados das iguarias e os termos indecifráveis que nela aparecem

- informação útil sobre a maneira de dizer as horas e de contar, sobre a conjugação de verbos irregulares e abreviaturas mais comuns, para além das frases de base.

Embora nenhum dicionário deste tamanho possa ter a pretensão de ser completo, esperamos que o leitor se sinta preparado para enfrentar com confiança as suas viagens ao estrangeiro. Teríamos o maior prazer, no entanto, em receber comentários, críticas e sugestões que o leitor julgue úteis à preparação de edições futuras.

portuguese-english

português-inglês

# Abbreviations

| | | | |
|---|---|---|---|
| *adj* | adjective | *n* | noun |
| *adv* | adverb | *nAm* | noun (American) |
| *Am* | American | | |
| *art* | article | *num* | numeral |
| *Br* | Brazilian | *p* | past tense |
| *conj* | conjunction | *pl* | plural |
| *f* | feminine | *plAm* | plural (American) |
| *fBr* | feminine (Brazilian) | | |
| *fpl* | feminine plural | *pp* | past participle |
| *fplBr* | feminine plural (Brazilian) | *pr* | present tense |
| | | *pref* | prefix |
| *m* | masculine | *prep* | preposition |
| *mBr* | masculine (Brazilian) | *pron* | pronoun |
| *mpl* | masculine plural | *v* | verb |
| *mplBr* | masculine plural (Brazilian) | *vAm* | verb (American) |
| | | *vBr* | verb (Brazilian) |

# Introduction

This dictionary has been designed to take account of your practical needs. Unnecessary linguistic information has been avoided. The entries are listed in alphabetical order, regardless of whether the entry is printed in a single word or in two or more separate words. As the only exception to this rule, a few idiomatic expressions are listed alphabetically as main entries, according to the most significant word of the expression. When an entry is followed by sub-entries, such as expressions and locutions, these are also listed in alphabetical order.

Each main-entry word is followed by a phonetic transcription (see guide to pronunciation). Following the transcription is the part of speech of the entry word whenever applicable. If an entry word is used as more than one part of speech, the translations are grouped together after the respective part of speech.

Irregular plurals are given in brackets after the part of speech.

Whenever an entry word is repeated in irregular forms or sub-entries, a tilde ( ~ ) is used to represent the full word. In plurals of long words, only the part that changes is written out fully, whereas the unchanged part is represented by a hyphen (-).

| Entry word: | Plural |
|---|---|
| abre-latas *m* (pl ~) | abre-latas |
| actual *adj* (pl -ais) | actuais |

An asterisk (*) in front of a verb indicates that it is irregular. For more details, refer to the list of irregular verbs.

The dictionary is based on the Portuguese written and spoken in Portugal. All words and uses of words that are exclusively Brazilian have been marked as such.

# Guide to Pronunciation

Each main entry in this part of the dictionary is followed by a phonetic transcription which shows you how to pronounce the words. This transcription should be read as if it were English. It is based on Standard British pronunciation, though we have tried to take account of General American pronunciation also. Below, only those letters and symbols are explained which we consider likely to be ambiguous or not immediately understood.

The syllables are separated by hyphens, and stressed syllables are printed in *italics*.

Of course, the sounds of any two languages are never exactly the same, but if you follow carefully our indications, you should be able to pronounce the foreign words in such a way that you'll be understood. To make your task easier, our transcriptions occasionally simplify slightly the sound system of the language while still reflecting the essential sound differences.

## Consonants

| | |
|---|---|
| **bh** | an indistinct **b**-sound, slightly like a **v** |
| **dh** | an indistinct **d**-sound, slightly like **th** in **th**is |
| **g** | always hard, as in **go** |
| **ǥ** | an indistinct **g**-sound, like a soft, voiced version of **ch** in Scottish lo**ch** |
| **lʸ** | like **lli** in mi**lli**on |
| **ng** | as in si**ng**, not as in fi**ng**er (no **g**-sound!) |
| **ñ** | as in Spanish se**ñ**or, or like **ni** in o**ni**on |
| **r** | like Scottish **r** (rolled with the tip of the tongue) |
| **rr** | a strongly rolled **r** |
| **s** | always hard, as in **so** |
| **zh** | a soft, voiced **sh**, like **s** in plea**s**ure |

## Vowels and Diphthongs

| | |
|---|---|
| **ah** | a short version of the **a** in car, i.e. a sound between **a** in cat and **u** in cut |
| **eh** | like **e** in get |
| **er** | more or less as in oth**er**, without any **r**-sound |

| i | like **i** in b**i**t |
|---|---|
| **igh** | as in h**igh** |
| o | always as in h**o**t (Standard British pronunciation) |
| **oa** | as in r**oa**d (but a *pure* vowel, i.e. the lips and tongue don't move while you're pronouncing it) |
| **oo** | as in r**oo**t |
| **ou** | as in l**ou**d |

1) Portuguese vowels are fairly short.

2) Raised letters (e.g. **er**<sup>ee</sup>, <sup>y</sup>**oo**) should be pronounced only fleetingly.

3) Portuguese contains nasal vowels, which we transcribe with a vowel symbol plus **ng** (e.g. **ahng**). This **ng** should *not* be pronounced, and serves solely to indicate nasal quality of the preceding vowel. A nasal vowel is pronounced simultaneously through the mouth and the nose. It can calso be part of a diphthong (e.g. **erng**<sup>w</sup>).

## Brazilian Pronunciation

Brazilian Portuguese differs from the Portuguese spoken in Portugal in several important respects. The Brazilian pronunciation is slower and the words are less linked together than in Portugal. Unstressed vowels sound clearer when spoken by Brazilians, while in Portugal they are rapidly slurred over; s and z at the end of a syllable tend to be pronounced like s in sit and z in razor (rather than like **sh** in shut or s in pleasure). Vowel groups or diphthongs are often simplified.

# A

**a** (er) *pron* her; *prep* to, at; on

**abadia** (er-bher-*dhee*-er) *f* abbey

**abaixar** (er-bhigh-*shahr*) *v* lower

**abaixo** (er-*bhigh*-shoo) *adv* over; down

**abaixo-assinado** (er-bhigh-shoo-er-see-*nah*-dhoo) *m* the undersigned

**abajur** (er-bher-*zhoor*) *m* lampshade

**abalroamento** (er-bhahl-rrwer-*mayngn*-too) *m* collision

**abanar** (er-bher-*nahr*) *v* \*shake

**abandonar** (er-bhernɡn-doo-*nahr*) *v* \*leave, abandon, desert; \*leave behind

**abastado** (er-bhersh-*tah*-dhoo) *adj* well-to-do, well-off

**abastecimento** (er-bhersh-ter-see-*mayngn*-too) *m* supply

**abatido** (er-bher-*tee*-dhoo) *adj* down, discouraged

**abcesso** (erbh-*seh*-soo) *m* abscess

**abelha** (er-*bhay*-lYer) *f* bee

**abençoar** (er-bhayng-*swahr*) *v* bless

**aberração** (er-bhee-rrer-*serngʷ*) *f* (pl -ções) aberration

**aberto** (er-*bhehr*-too) *adj* open

**abertura** (er-bherr-*too*-rer) *f* overture; opening

**abibe** (er-*bhee*-bher) *m* pewit

**abismo** (er-*bheezh*-moo) *m* abyss

**abóbada** (er-*bho*-bher-dher) *f* vault; arch

**\*abolir** (er-bhoo-*leer*) *v* abolish

**aborrecer** (er-bhoo-rrer-*sayr*) *v* annoy

**aborrecido** (er-bhoo-rrer-*see*-dhoo) *adj* boring; unpleasant; bored; annoyed

**aborrecimento** (er-bhoo-rrer-see-*mayngn*-too) *m* annoyance

**aborto** (er-*bhoar*-too) *m* abortion; miscarriage

**abotoaduras** (er-bhoo-twer-*dhoo*-rersh) *fpl/Br* cuff-links *pl*

**abotoar** (er-bhoo-*twahr*) *v* button

**abraçar** (er-bhrer-*sahr*) *v* hug, embrace

**abraço** (er-*bhrah*-soo) *m* embrace, hug; grip

**abrandar** (er-bhrerngn-*dahr*) *v* slow down

**abre-garrafas** (ah-bhrer-ger-*rrah*-fersh) *m* (pl ~) bottle opener

**abre-latas** (ah-bhrer-*lah*-tersh) *m* (pl ~) tin-opener, can opener

**abreviatura** (er-bhrer-vYer-*too*-rer) *f* abbreviation

**abrigar** (er-bhree-*gahr*) *v* shelter

**abrigo** (er-*bhree*-goo) *m* cover, shelter

**Abril** (er-*bhreel*) April

**abrir** (er-*bhreer*) *v* open; unlock; turn on

**absolutamente** (erbh-soo-loo-ter-*mayngn*-ter) *adv* absolutely

**absoluto** (erbh-soo-*loo*-too) *adj* sheer; total

**absolvição** (erbh-soal-vee-*serng*ʷ) *f* (pl -ções) acquittal

**abstémio** (erbhsh-*teh*-mʸoo) *m* teetotaller

***abster-se de** (erbhsh-*tayr*-ser) abstain from

**abstracto** (erbhsh-*trah*-too) *adj* abstract

**absurdo** (er-bher-*soor*-dhoo) *adj* absurd; foolish

**abundância** (er-bhoongn-*derng*-sʸer) *f* plenty, abundance

**abundante** (er-bhoongn-*derngn*-ter) *adj* plentiful, abundant

**abuso** (er-*bhoo*-zoo) *m* abuse; misuse

**abutre** (er-*bhoo*-trer) *m* vulture

**acabado** (er-ker-*bhah*-dhoo) *adj* over, finished; ~ **de** just

**acabar** (er-ker-*bhahr*) *v* finish; stop, end

**academia** (er-ker-dher-*mee*-er) *f* academy; ~ **das belas-artes** art school

**acalmar** (er-kahl-*mahr*) *v* calm down; **acalmar-se** calm down

**acampamento** (er-kerngm-per-*mayngn*-too) *m* camp

**acampar** (er-kerngm-*pahr*) *v* camp

**acaso** (er-*kah*-zoo) *m* chance; **ao** ~ at random; **por** ~ by chance

**acção** (ah-*serng*ʷ) *f* (pl acções) action, deed; share; **acções** stocks and shares

**aceder** (er-ser-*dhayr*) *v* grant; consent

**aceitar** (er-say-*tahr*) *v* accept

**acelerador** (er-ser-ler-rer-*dhoar*) *m* accelerator

**acelerar** (er-ser-ler-*rahr*) *v* accelerate

**acenar** (er-ser-*nahr*) *v* wave

**acender** (er-sayngn-*dayr*) *v* *light; turn on

**acento** (er-*sayngn*-too) *m* accent

**acentuar** (er-sayngn-*twahr*) *v* stress, emphasize

**acepipe** (er-ser-*pee*-per) *m* delicacy; **acepipes** hors-d'œuvre

**ácer** (*ah*-sehr) *m* maple

**acerca de** (er-*sayr*-ker) about

**acertar** (er-serr-*tahr*) *v* *hit; adjust

**acessível** (er-ser-*see*-vehl) *adj* (pl -eis) accessible; attainable

**acesso** (er-*seh*-soo) *m* access; entrance, approach

**acessório** (er-ser-*so*-rʸoo) *adj* additional; **acessórios** accessories *pl*

**achaque** (er-*shah*-ker) *m* ailment

**achar** (er-*shahr*) *v* consider; *find; **achados e perdidos** lost and found

**acidentado** (er-see-dhayngn-*tah*-dhoo) *adj* hilly; bumpy

**acidental** (er-see-dhayngn-*tahl*) *adj* (pl -ais) accidental

**acidente** (er-see-*dhayngn*-ter) *m* accident

**ácido** (*ah*-see-dhoo) *m* acid

**acima** (er-*see*-mer) *adv* up

**aclamar** (er-kler-*mahr*) *v* cheer

**aclarar** (er-kler-*rahr*) *v* clarify

**acne** (*ahk*-ner) *f* acne

**aço** (*ah*-soo) *m* steel; ~ **inoxidável** stainless steel

**acolher** (er-koo-*lʸayr*) *v* welcome; lodge

**acolhimento** (er-koo-*lʸee*-*mayngn*-too) *m* welcome; reception

**acomodação** (er-koo-moo-dher-*serng*ʷ) *f* (pl -ções) accommodation

**acomodar** (er-koo-moo-*dhahr*) *v* accommodate

**acompanhar** (er-kawngm-per-*ñahr*) *v* accompany; conduct, escort

**aconchegado** (er-kawng-sher-*gah*-dhoo) *adj* cosy

**aconselhar** (er-kawng-sɪ-*lʸahr*) *v* advise; recommend

**acontecer** (er-kawngn-ter-*sayr*) *v* happen, occur

**acontecimento** (er-kawngn-ter-see-mayngn-too) *m* event; happening

**acordado** (er-koor-*dhah*-dhoo) *adj* awake

**acordar** (er-koor-*dahr*) *v* \*awake; \*wake; wake up

**acordo** (er-*koar*-doo) *m* agreement; settlement; **de acordo!** okay!

**acostumar** (er-koosh-too-*mahr*) *v* accustom

**acreditar** (er-krer-dhee-*tahr*) *v* believe

**acrescentar** (er-krish-sayngn-*tahr*) *v* add; increase

**acta** (*ah*-ter) *f* minutes

**actividade** (ah-tee-vee-*dhah*-dher) *f* activity

**activo** (ah-*tee*-voo) *adj* active

**acto** (*ah*-too) *m* act

**actor** (ah-*toar*) *m* actor

**actriz** (ah-*treesh*) *f* actress

**actuação** (ah-twer-*serng*ᵂ) *f* (pl -ções) appearance, performance

**actual** (ah-*twahl*) *adj* (pl -ais) topical; present

**actualmente** (ah-twahl-*mayngn*-ter) *adv* now; at present

**actuar** (ah-*twahr*) *v* operate

**açúcar** (er-*soo*-kahr) *m* sugar

**acusação** (er-koo-zer-*serng*ᵂ) *f* (pl -ções) charge

**acusado** (er-koo-*zah*-dhoo) *m* accused

**acusar** (er-koo-*zahr*) *v* accuse, charge; blame

**adaptador** (er-dahp-ter-*dhoar*) *m* adaptor

**adaptar** (er-dahp-*tahr*) *v* adapt; ~ **a** suit

**adega** (er-*dhay*-ger) *f* wine-cellar

**adepto** (er-*dhehp*-too) *m* supporter

**adequado** (er-dher-*kwah*-dhoo) *adj* appropriate

**\*aderir a** (er-dher-*reer*) join

**adesivo** (er-dher-*zee*-voo) *m* adhesive tape

**adestrar** (er-dhish-*trahr*) *v* train; drill

**adeus** (er-*dhay*ᵒᵒsh) *m* farewell; **adeus!** good-bye!

**adiamento** (er-dhʸer-*mayngn*-too) *m* delay; postponement

**adiantadamente** (er-dhʸerngn-tah-dher-*mayngn*-ter) *adv* in advance

**adiantado** (er-dhʸerngn-*tah*-dhoo) *adj* advanced

**adiantamento** (er-dhʸerngn-ter-*mayngn*-too) *m* advance

**adiantar** (er-dhʸerngn-*tahr*) *v* advance

**adiante** (er-*dhʸerngn*-ter) *adv* before; onward, forward; ~ **de** ahead of

**adiar** (er-*dhʸahr*) *v* postpone; adjourn, delay, \*put off

**adição** (er-dhee-*serng*ᵂ) *f* (pl -ções) addition

**adicional** (er-dhee-sʸoo-*nahl*) *adj* (pl -ais) additional

**adicionar** (er-dhee-sʸoo-*nahr*) *v* add

**adivinha** (er-dher-*vee*-ñer) *f* riddle

**adivinhar** (er-dher-vee-*ñahr*) *v* guess

**adjectivo** (er-jeh-*tee*-voo) *m* adjective

**administração** (erdh-mer-neesh-trer-*serng*ᵂ) *f* (pl -ções) administration; direction

**administrar** (erdh-mer-neesh-*trahr*) *v* manage; administer

**administrativo** (er-dh-mer-neesh-trer-*tee*-voo) *adj* administrative

**admiração** (erdh-mee-rer-*serng*ᵂ) *f* (pl -ções) admiration; wonder

**admirador** (erdh-mee-rer-*dhoar*) *m* fan

**admirar** (erdh-mee-*rahr*) *v* admire

**admissão** (erdh-mee-*serng*ᵂ) *f* (pl -sões) admission

**admitir** (erdh-mer-*teer*) *v* admit; acknowledge

**adoçar** (er-dhoo-*sahr*) *v* sweeten

**adolescente** (er-dhoo-lish-*sayngn*-ter) *m* teenager

**adoptar** (er-dho-*tahr*) *v* adopt

**adorar** (er-dhoo-*rahr*) v worship

**adorável** (er-dhoo-*rah*-vehl) adj (pl -eis) adorable

**adormecer** (erdh-dhoor-mer-*sayr*) v *put to sleep; *fall asleep

**adormecido** (erdh-dhoor-mer-*see*-dhoo) adj asleep

**adquirir** (erdh-ker-*reer*) v acquire; *buy

**adulto** (er-*dhool*-too) adj adult, grown-up; m adult, grown-up

**advérbio** (erdh-*vehr*-bhʸoo) m adverb

**adversário** (erdh-verr-*sah*-rʸoo) m opponent

**adverso** (erdh-*vehr*-soo) adj averse

***advertir** (erdh-verr-*teer*) v caution, warn

**advogado** (erdh-voo-*gah*-dhoo) m solicitor, barrister, attorney, lawyer

**advogar** (erdh-voo-*gahr*) v plead

**aéreo** (er-*eh*-rʸoo) adj airy; **correio ~** airmail

**aeroporto** (er-eh-roo-*poar*-too) m airport

**afastado** (er-fersh-*tah*-dhoo) adj out of the way

**afável** (er-*fah*-vehl) adj (pl -eis) friendly

**afecção** (er-fehk-*serng*ʷ) f (pl -ções) affection

**afectado** (er-feh-*tah*-dhoo) adj affected

**afectar** (er-feh-*tahr*) v affect

**afectuoso** (er-feh-*twoa*-zoo) adj affectionate

**afeição** (er-fay-*serng*ʷ) f (pl -ções) affection

**afiado** (er-*fʸah*-dhoo) adj sharp

**afiar** (er-*fʸahr*) v sharpen

**afinal** (er-fee-*nahl*) adv finally; at last

**afirmar** (er-feer-*mahr*) v claim

**afirmativo** (er-feer-mer-*tee*-voo) adj affirmative

**aflição** (er-flee-*serng*ʷ) f (pl -ções) grief

**afligir-se** (er-flee-*zheer*-ser) v worry

**afluente** (er-flwayngn-ter) m tributary

**afogador** (er-foo-ger-*dhoar*) mBr choke

**afogar** (er-foo-*gahr*) v drown; **afogar-se** *be drowned

**afortunado** (er-foor-too-*nah*-dhoo) adj fortunate; lucky

**África** (*ah*-free-ker) f Africa; **África do Sul** South Africa

**africano** (er-free-*ker*-noo) adj African; m African

**afrouxar** (er-froa-*shahr*) v slow down

**afugentar** (er-foo-zhayngn-*tahr*) v chase

**afundar-se** (er-foongn-*dahr*-ser) v *sink

**agarrar** (er-ger-*rrahr*) v seize, grip, grasp, *catch; *take; **agarrar-se** *hold on

**agência** (er-*zhayng*-sʸer) f agency; **~ de colocação** employment exchange; **~ de informações** information bureau; **~ de turismo** tourist office; **~ de viagens** travel agency

**agenda** (er-*zhayngn*-der) f diary; notebook; agenda

**agente** (er-*zhayngn*-ter) m agent; **~ de viagens** travel agent; **~ imobiliário** house agent

**ágil** (*ah*-zheel) adj (pl ágeis) supple

**agir** (er-*zheer*) v act

**agitação** (er-zhee-ter-*serng*ʷ) f (pl -ções) unrest

**agora** (er-*go*-rer) adv now; **até ~** so far; **de ~ em diante** henceforth

**Agosto** (er-*goash*-too) August

**agradar** (er-grer-*dhahr*) v please

**agradável** (er-grer-*dhah*-vehl) adj (pl -eis) agreeable, nice, pleasant, enjoyable, pleasing

**agradecer** (er-grer-dher-*sayr*) v thank

**agradecido** (erg-rer-dher-*see*-dhoo) *adj* thankful

**agrafo** (er-*grah*-foo) *m* staple

**agrário** (er-*grah*-rʸoo) *adj* agrarian

***agredir** (er-grer-*dheer*) *v* attack, assault

**agressivo** (er-grer-*see*-voo) *adj* aggressive

**agrião** (er-grʸerng*ʷ*) *m* (pl -iões) watercress

**agrícola** (er-*gree*-koo-ler) *adj* agrarian

**agricultor** (er-gree-kool-*toar*) *m* farmer

**agricultura** (er-gree-kool-*too*-rer) *f* agriculture

**agrupar** (er-groo-*pahr*) *v* arrange; group

**água** (*ah*-gwer) *f* water; ~ **corrente** running water; ~ **doce** fresh water; ~ **do mar** sea-water; ~ **gasificada** soda-water; ~ **gelada** iced water; ~ **mineral** mineral water; ~ **oxigenada** peroxide; ~ **potável** drinking-water

**aguaceiro** (er-gwer-*say*-roo) *m* downpour, shower

**água-forte** (ah-gwer-*for*-ter) *f* etching

**aguarela** (er-gwer-*reh*-ler) *f* water-colour

**agudo** (er-*goo*-dhoo) *adj* acute; pointed

**aguentar** (er-gwayngn-*tahr*) *v* *hold up, *put up with

**águia** (*ahg*-ʸer) *f* eagle

**agulha** (er-goo-lʸer) *f* needle; spire

**aí** (er-*ee*) *adv* there

**ainda** (er-*eengn*-der) *adv* yet, still; ~ **agora** just now, a moment ago; ~ **assim** nevertheless; ~ **bem** fortunately; ~ **que** though

**aipo** (*igh*-poo) *m* celery

**ajoelhar** (er-zhwi-*lʸahr*) *v* *kneel

**ajuda** (er-*zhoo*-dher) *f* assistance, aid

**ajudante** (er-zhoo-*dherngn*-ter) *m*

helper

**ajudar** (er-zhoo-*dhahr*) *v* help, aid

**ajustar** (er-zhoosh-*tahr*) *v* adjust

**ajuste** (er-*zhoosh*-ter) *m* settlement

**alabote** (er-ler-*bo*-ter) *m* halibut

**alargar** (er-lerr-*gahr*) *v* widen

**alarido** (er-ler-*ree*-dhoo) *m* racket

**alarmar** (er-lerr-*mahr*) *v* alarm

**alarme** (er-*lahr*-mer) *m* alarm; ~ **de incêndio** fire-alarm

**alavanca** (er-ler-*verngñ*-ker) *f* lever; ~ **das mudanças** gear lever

**albergue** (ahl-*bhehr*-ger) *m* hostel; ~ **de juventude** youth hostel

**álbum** (*ahl*-bhoong) *m* album

**alcachofra** (ahl-ker-*shoa*-frer) *f* artichoke

**alcançar** (ahl-kerng-*sahr*) *v* reach; achieve

**alcance** (ahl-*kerng*-ser) *m* reach, range

**alçapão** (ahl-ser-*perng*ʷ) *m* (pl -pões) hatch

**alcatrão** (ahl-ker-*trerng*ʷ) *m* tar

**alce** (*ahl*-ser) *m* moose

**álcool** (*ahl*-kwol) *m* (pl -ois) alcohol; ~ **desnaturado** methylated spirits; **lamparina de** ~ spirit stove

**alcoólico** (ahl-*kwo*-lee-koo) *adj* alcoholic; *m* alcoholic

**alcunha** (ahl-*koo*-ñer) *f* nickname

**aldeia** (ahl-*day*-er) *f* village

**aldeola** (ahl-dʸo-ler) *f* hamlet

**alegrar** (er-ler-*grahr*) *v* cheer up

**alegre** (er-*leh*-grer) *adj* joyful, merry, gay, cheerful

**alegria** (er-ler-*gree*-er) *f* joy, gaiety; gladness

**aleijado** (er-lay-*zhah*-dhoo) *adj* crippled

**além** (er-*lerng*ʸ) *adv* beyond; ~ **de** past, beyond; besides; ~ **disso** besides; furthermore, moreover; **mais** ~ further

**Alemanha** (er-ler-*merng*-ñer) f Germany

**alemão** (er-ler-*merng*ᵂ) adj (f -mã; pl -ães) German; m German

**alergia** (er-lerr-*zhee*-er) f allergy

**alfabeto** (ahl-fer-*bheh*-too) m alphabet

**alface** (ahl-*fah*-ser) f lettuce

**alfaiate** (ahl-fer-ᵞah-ter) m tailor

**alfândega** (ahl-*ferng*-der-ger) f Customs pl

**alfinete** (ahl-fee-*nay*-ter) m pin; ~ **de segurança** safety-pin; **prender com alfinetes** pin

**alforreca** (ahl-foo-*rreh*-ker) f jellyfish

**algarismo** (ahl-ger-*reezh*-moo) m figure; number; digit

**álgebra** (ahl-*zher*-bhrer) f algebra

**algemas** (ahl-*zhay*-mersh) fpl handcuffs pl

**algibeira** (ahl-zhee-*bhay*-rer) f pocket

**algo** (ahl-goo) adv somewhat, a little; pron something, anything

**algodão** (ahl-goo-*dherng*ᵂ) m (pl -dões) cotton; cotton-wool; **de ~** cotton

**alguém** (ahl-*gerng*ᵞ) pron someone, somebody

**algum** (ahl-*goong*) pron some; any

**alguns** (ahl-*goongsh*) adj some

**alho** (ah-lᵞoo) m garlic

**ali** (er-*lee*) adv over there; **para ~** there

**aliado** (er-lᵞah-dhoo) m associate

**aliança** (er-lᵞerng-ser) f alliance; wedding-ring

**alicate** (er-lee-*kah*-ter) m pliers pl

**alicerce** (er-lee-*sehr*-ser) m base, foundation

**alimentação** (er-lee-mayngn-ter-*serng*ᵂ) f (pl -ções) fare, food

**alimentar** (er-lee-mayngn-*tahr*) v *feed; adj alimentary; **intoxicação ~** food poisoning

**alimentício** (er-lee-mayngn-*tee*-sᵞoo) adj nourishing

**alimento** (er-lee-*mayngn*-too) m food

**alínea** (er-*lee*-nᵞer) f paragraph

**aliviar** (er-lee-vᵞahr) v relieve

**alívio** (er-*lee*-vᵞoo) m relief

**alma** (ahl-mer) f soul

**almanaque** (ahl-mer-*nah*-ker) m almanac

**almirante** (ahl-mee-*rerng*-ter) m admiral

**almoçar** (ahl-moo-*sahr*) v lunch

**almoço** (ahl-*moa*-soo) m dinner, lunch, luncheon; **pequeno ~** breakfast

**almofada** (ahl-moo-*fah*-dher) f pillow; cushion; ~ **eléctrica** heating pad

**almofadão** (ahl-moo-fer-*dherng*ᵂ) m (pl -dões) pillow

**almofadinha** (ahl-moo-fer-*dhee*-ñer) f pad

**alocução** (er-loo-koo-*serng*ᵂ) f (pl -ções) speech

**alojamento** (er-loo-zher-*mayngn*-too) m accommodation, lodgings pl

**alojar** (er-loo-*zhahr*) v accommodate

**alongar** (er-lawng-*gahr*) v lengthen

**alperche** (ahl-*pehr*-sher) m apricot

**alpinismo** (ahl-pee-*neezh*-moo) m mountaineering

**altar** (ahl-*tahr*) m altar

**alteração** (ahl-ter-rer-*serng*ᵂ) f (pl -ções) alteration

**alterar** (ahl-ter-*rahr*) v alter

**altercar** (ahl-terr-*kahr*) v dispute

**alternado** (ahl-terr-*nah*-dhoo) adj alternate

**alternativa** (ahl-terr-ner-*tee*-ver) f alternative

**altifalante** (ahl-tee-fer-*lerngn*-ter) m loud-speaker

**altitude** (ahl-tee-*too*-dher) f altitude

**altivo** (ahl-*tee*-voo) adj haughty

**alto** (ahl-too) adj tall, high; loud; m

lump; **alto!** stop!

**altura** (ahl-*too*-rer) *f* height

**alugar** (er-loo-*gahr*) *v* lease, rent, hire, *let; **para** ~ for hire

**aluguer** (er-loo-*gehr*) *m* letting; ~ **de carros** car hire

**alumiar** (er-loo-*m*Y*ahr*) *v* illuminate

**aluno** (er-*loo*-noo) *m* pupil, scholar

**alvará** (ahl-ver-*rah*) *m* patent

**alvo** (*ahl*-voo) *m* target; mark

**âmago** (er-mer-goo) *m* heart

**amaldiçoar** (er-mahl-dee-*swahr*) *v* curse

**amamentar** (er-mer-mayngn-*tahr*) *v* nurse

**amanhã** (ah-mer-*ñerng*) *adv* tomorrow

**amanhecer** (ah-mer-ñer-*sayr*) *m* daybreak

**amante** (er-*merngn*-ter) *m* lover; *f* mistress

**amar** (er-*mahr*) *v* love

**amarelo** (er-mah-*reh*-loo) *adj* yellow

**amargo** (er-*mahr*-goo) *adj* bitter

**amarrotar** (er-mer-rroo-*tahr*) *v* crease '

**ama-seca** (er-mer-say-ker) *f* nurse

**amável** (er-*mah*-vehl) *adj* (pl -eis) amiable, kind

**âmbar** (*erngm*-bahr) *m* amber

**ambicionar** (erngm-bee-sYoo-*nahr*) *v* wish, *strive for

**ambicioso** (erngm-bee-sYoa-zoo) *adj* ambitious

**ambiente** (erngm-bYayngn-ter) *m* atmosphere

**ambíguo** (erngm-*bee*-gwoo) *adj* ambiguous

**ambos** (*erngm*-boosh) *pron* either, both

**ambulância** (erngm-boo-lerng-sYer) *f* ambulance

**ameaça** (er-mYah-ser) *f* threat

**ameaçador** (er-mYer-ser-*dhoar*) *adj* threatening

**ameaçar** (er-mYer-*sahr*) *v* threaten

**ameixa** (er-*may*-sher) *f* plum; ~ **passada** prune

**amêndoa** (er-*mayngn*-dwer) *f* almond

**amendoim** (er-mayngn-*dweeng*) *m* peanut

**América** (er-*meh*-ree-ker) *f* America; ~ **Latina** Latin America

**americano** (er-mer-ree-*ker*-noo) *adj* American; *m* American

**ametista** (er-mer-*teesh*-ter) *f* amethyst

**amianto** (er-mYerngn-too) *m* asbestos

**amiga** (er-*mee*-ger) *f* friend

**amígdalas** (er-*meeg*-der-lersh) *fpl* tonsils *pl*

**amigdalite** (er-*meeg*-dher-lee-ter) *f* tonsilitis

**amigo** (er-*mee*-goo) *m* friend

**amimar** (er-mee-*mahr*) *v* *spoil; fondle

**amistoso** (er-meesh-*toa*-zoo) *adj* friendly

**amizade** (ah-mee-*zah*-dher) *f* friendship

**amnistia** (er-mnersh-*tee*-er) *f* amnesty

**amoníaco** (er-moo-*nee*-er-koo) *m* ammonia

**amontoar** (er-mawngn-*twahr*) *v* pile

**amor** (er-*moar*) *m* love; darling; **meu** ~ sweetheart

**amora** (er-*mo*-rer) *f* mulberry; ~ **silvestre** blackberry

**amortecedor** (er-moor-ter-ser-*dhoar*) *m* shock absorber

**amostra** (er-mosh-trer) *f* sample; specimen

**ampliação** (erngm-plYer-*serng*W) *f* (pl -ções) extension; enlargement

**ampliar** (erngm-*plYahr*) *v* enlarge; extend

**amplo** (*erngm*-ploo) *adj* extensive; broad

**amuleto** (er-moo-*lay*-too) *m* charm

**analfabeto** (er-nahl-fer-*bheh*-too) *m* illiterate

**analisar** (er-ner-lee-*zahr*) *v* analyse;

\*break down

**análise** (er-*nah*-lee-zer) *f* analysis

**analista** (er-ner-*leesh*-ter) *m* analyst

**análogo** (er-*nah*-loo-goo) *adj* similar

**anamnese** (er-nerm-*neh*-zer) *f* history of a disease

**ananás** (er-ner-*nahsh*) *m* pineapple

**anão** (er-*nerng*ᵂ) *m* (*f* anã; pl anões) dwarf

**anarquia** (er-nerr-*kee*-er) *f* anarchy

**anatomia** (er-ner-too-*mee*-er) *f* anatomy

**anca** (*erngñ*-ker) *f* hip

**anchova** (erng-*shoa*-ver) *f* anchovy

**ancinho** (erng-*see*-ñoo) *m* rake

**âncora** (*erng*-koo-rer) *f* anchor

**andaime** (erngn-*digh*-mer) *m* scaffolding

**andar** (erngn-*dahr*) *v* \*go, walk, step; *m* pace, gait; floor, storey; apartment *nAm*; ~ **com** associate with; ~ **térreo** *Br* ground floor

**andorinha** (erngn-doo-*ree*-ñer) *f* swallow

**anedota** (er-ner-*dho*-ter) *f* joke

**anel** (er-*nehl*) *m* (pl anéis) ring; ~ **de noivado** engagement ring

**anemia** (er-ner-*mee*-er) *f* anaemia

**anestesia** (er-nɪsh-ter-*zee*-er) *f* anaesthesia

**anestésico** (er-nɪsh-*teh*-zee-koo) *m* anaesthetic

**anexar** (er-nehk-*sahr*) *v* annex

**anexo** (er-*nehk*-soo) *m* enclosure, annex

**ângulo** (*erng*-goo-loo) *m* angle

**animado** (er-nee-*mah*-dhoo) *adj* crowded; lively

**animal** (er-ner-*mahl*) *m* (pl -ais) animal; beast; ~ **de estimação** pet; ~ **de rapina** beast of prey

**animar** (er-nee-*mahr*) *v* cheer up

**aniversário** (er-nee-verr-*sah*-rᵞoo) *m* anniversary

**anjo** (*erng*-zhoo) *m* angel

**ano** (er-*noo*) *m* year; ~ **bissexto** leap-year; **Ano Novo** New Year

**anoitecer** (er-noi-ter-*sayr*) *m* dusk

**anónimo** (er-*no*-nee-moo) *adj* anonymous

**anormal** (er-noor-*mahl*) *adj* (pl -ais) abnormal

**anotar** (er-noo-*tahr*) *v* note; \*write down

**ansiedade** (erng-sᵞay-*dhah*-dher) *f* anxiety

**ansioso** (erng-sᵞoa-zoo) *adj* anxious

**antecedente** (erngn-ter-ser-*dhayngn*-ter) *adj* former

**antecipadamente** (erngn-ter-see-pah-dher-*mayngn*-ter) *adv* in advance

**do anteguerra** (doo erngn-ter-*geh*-rer) pre-war

**antena** (erngn-*tay*-ner) *f* aerial

**anteontem** (erngn-ter-*awngn*-terngᵞ) *adv* the day before yesterday

**antepassado** (erngn-ter-per-*sah*-dhoo) *m* ancestor

**anterior** (erngn-ter-rᵞoar) *adj* previous; prior

**anteriormente** (erngn-ter-rᵞoar-*mayngn*-ter) *adv* formerly

**antes** (*erngn*-tish) *adv* before; rather, sooner; ~ **de** before; ~ **que** before

**antibiótico** (erngn-tee-*bh*ᵞo-tee-koo) *m* antibiotic

**anticongelante** (erngn-tee-kawng-zher-*lerngn*-ter) *m* antifreeze

**antigamente** (erngn-tee-ger-*mayngn*-ter) *adv* formerly

**antigo** (erngn-*tee*-goo) *adj* former; antique; ancient

**antiguidade** (erngn-tee-gwee-*dhah*-dher) *f* antiquity; antique

**antipatia** (erngn-tee-per-*tee*-er) *f* dislike, antipathy

**antipático** (erngn-tee-*pah*-tee-koo) *adj* unfriendly, nasty

**antiquado** (er̃gn-tee-*kwah*-dhoo) *adj* quaint, old-fashioned, ancient

**antiquário** (er̃gn-tee-*kwah*-rʸoo) *m* antique dealer

**antisséptico** (er̃gn-tee-*sehp*-tee-koo) *m* antiseptic

**antologia** (er̃gn-too-loo-*zhee*-er) *f* anthology

**anual** (er-*nwahl*) *adj* (pl -ais) annual; yearly

**anualmente** (er-nwahl-*mayŋgn*-ter) *adv* per annum

**anuário** (er-*nwah*-rʸoo) *m* annual

**anular** (er-noo-*lahr*) *v* cancel

**anunciar** (er-noong-sʸahr) *v* announce

**anúncio** (er-*noong*-sʸoo) *m* announcement; advertisement; commercial

**anzol** (er̃g-*zol*) *m* (pl anzóis) fishing hook

**apagado** (er-per-*gah*-dhoo) *adj* dull

**apagar** (er-per-*gahr*) *v* extinguish; *put out

**apaixonado** (er-pigh-shoo-*nah*-dhoo) *adj* in love; passionate

**apalpar** (er-pahl-*pahr*) *v* *feel

**apanhar** (er-per-*ñahr*) *v* *catch; pick up

**aparafusar** (er-*pah*-rer-foo-*zahr*) *v* screw

**apara-lápis** (er-pah-rer-*lah*-peesh) *m* (pl ~) pencil-sharpener

**aparar** (er-per-*rahr*) *v* trim

**aparecer** (er-per-rer-*sayr*) *v* appear

**aparelho** (er-per-*ray*-lʸoo) *m* apparatus; appliance

**aparência** (er-per-*rayŋg*-sʸer) *f* appearance; look, semblance

**aparentado** (er-per-rayŋgn-*tah*-dhoo) *adj* related

**aparente** (er-per-*rayŋgn*-ter) *adj* apparent

**aparentemente** (er-per-rayŋgn-ter-*mayŋgn*-ter) *adv* apparently

**aparição** (er-per-ree-*serŋg*ʷ) *f* (pl -ções) apparition

**apartamento** (er-perr-ter-*mayŋgn*-too) *m* flat; suite; apartment *nAm*

***apear-se** (er-pʸahr-ser) *v* *get off

**apelido** (er-per-*lee*-dhoo) *m* surname; family name; *mBr* nickname; ~ **de solteira** maiden name

**apelo** (er-*pay*-loo) *m* appeal

**apêndice** (er-*payŋgn*-dee-ser) *m* appendix

**apendicite** (er-payŋg-dee-*see*-ter) *f* appendicitis

**aperceber** (er-perr-ser-*bhayr*) *v* perceive

**aperitivo** (er-per-ree-*tee*-voo) *m* aperitif; **aperitivos** appetizer

**apertado** (er-perr-*tah*-dhoo) *adj* narrow, tight

**apertar** (er-perr-*tahr*) *v* tighten; **apertar-se** tighten

**aperto** (er-*payr*-too) *m* clutch, grasp; ~ **de mão** handshake

**apesar de** (er-per-*zahr* der) despite, in spite of

**apetecer** (er-per-ter-*sayr*) *v* *feel like

**apetite** (er-per-*tee*-ter) *m* appetite

**apetitoso** (er-per-tee-*toa*-zoo) *adj* appetizing

**apinhado** (er-pee-*ñah*-dhoo) *adj* crowded

**apito** (er-*pee*-too) *m* whistle

**aplanar** (er-pler-*nahr*) *v* level

**aplaudir** (er-plou-*dheer*) *v* clap; cheer

**aplausos** (er-*plou*-zoosh) *mpl* applause

**aplicação** (er-plee-ker-*serŋg*ʷ) *f* (pl -ções) application; diligence

**aplicado** (er-plee-*kah*-dhoo) *adj* diligent

**aplicar** (er-plee-*kahr*) *v* apply; **aplicar-se a** apply to

**apogeu** (er-poo-*zhay*ᵒᵒ) *m* peak; height, zenith

**apoiar-se** (er-poa-ʸahr-ser) *v* *lean

apólice (er-*po*-lee-ser) f policy

apontador (er-pawngn-ter-*doar*) mBr pencil-sharpener

apontamento (er-pawngn-ter-*mayngn*too) m note

apontar (er-pawngn-*tahr*) v point, point out; ~ para aim at

aposta (er-*posh*-ter) f bet

apostar (er-*posh*-tahr) v *bet

apreciação (er-prer-sʸer-*serng*ʷ) f (pl -ções) appreciation

apreciar (er-prer-sʸ*ahr*) v appreciate

apreender (er-prʸayngn-*dayr*) v impound

aprender (er-prayngn-*dayr*) v *learn

apresentação (er-prer-zayngn-ter-*serng*ʷ) f (pl -ções) introduction

apresentar (er-prer-zayngn-*tahr*) v present, introduce; apresentar-se report; appear

apressadamente (er-prer-sah-dher-*mayngn*-ter) adv in a hurry

apressado (er-prer-*sah*-dhoo) adj hasty

apressar-se (er-prer-*sahr*-ser) v rush, hurry, hasten

apropriado (er-proo-prʸah-dhoo) adj suitable, convenient, proper, fit, appropriate

aprovação (er-proo-ver-*serng*ʷ) f (pl -ções) approval

aprovar (er-proo-*vahr*) v approve; consent

aproveitar-se (er-proo-vay-*tahr*-ser) v profit; *take advantage of

aproximadamente (er-pro-see-mah-dher-*mayngn*-ter) adv approximately; about

aproximado (er-pro-see-*mah*-dhoo) adj approximate

aproximar-se (er-pro-see-*mahr*-ser) v approach

aptidão (erp-tee-*dherng*ʷ) f (pl -dões) faculty

aquecedor (er-keh-ser-*dhoar*) m heater; ~ de imersão immersion heater

aquecer (er-keh-*sayr*) v warm, heat

aquecimento (er-keh-see-*mayngn*-too) m heating; ~ central central heating

aquele (er-*kay*-ler) adj that; pron that, that one; aqueles those

aqui (er-*kee*) adv here; ~ está here you are

aquilo (er-*kee*-loo) pron that

aquisição (er-ker-zee-*serng*ʷ) f (pl -ções) acquisition

ar (ahr) m sky, air; ao ~ livre outdoors; ~ condicionado air-conditioning; corrente de ~ draught

árabe (ah-rer-bher) adj Arab; m Arab

Arábia Saudita (er-*rah*-bhʸer sou-*dee*-ter) Saudi Arabia

arado (er-*rah*-dhoo) m plough

arame (er-*rer*-mer) m wire

aranha (er-*rer*-ñer) f spider; teia de ~ cobweb, spider's web

arbitrário (err-bhee-*trah*-rʸoo) adj arbitrary

árbitro (*ahr*-bhee-troo) m umpire

arborizado (err-bhoo-ree-*zer*-dhoo) adj wooded

arbusto (err-*bhoosh*-too) m shrub; bush

arca (*ahr*-ker) f chest

arcada (err-*kah*-dher) f arcade

arcebispo (err-ser-*bheesh*-poo) m archbishop

archote (er-*sho*-ter) m torch

arco (*ahr*-koo) m arch, bow

arco-íris (ahr-koo-*ee*-reesh) m (pl ~) rainbow

arder (err-*dayr*) v *burn

ardil (err-*deel*) m (pl -is) ruse

ardósia (err-do-zʸer) f slate

área (*ahr*-ʸer) f area

areia (er-*ray*-er) f sand

arejamento (er-rer-zher-*mayngn*-too) *m* ventilation

arejar (er-rer-*zhahr*) *v* air, ventilate

arenoso (er-rer-*noa*-zoo) *adj* sandy

arenque (er-*rayngng*-ker) *m* herring

Argélia (err-*zheh*-l<sup>Y</sup>er) *f* Algeria

argelino (err-zher-*lee*-noo) *adj* Algerian; *m* Algerian

Argentina (err-zhayngn-*tee*-ner) *f* Argentina

argentino (err-zhayngn-*tee*-noo) *adj* Argentinian; *m* Argentinian

argila (err-*zhee*-ler) *f* clay

argumentar (err-goo mayngn-*tahr*) *v* argue

argumento (err-goo-*mayngn*-too) *m* argument

árido (*ah*-ree-dhoo) *adj* arid

arinca (*ah*-reeng-ker) *f* haddock

aritmética (er-reet-*meh*-tee-ker) *f* arithmetic

arma (*ahr*-mer) *f* arm, weapon

armação (err-mer-*serngʷ*) *f* (pl -ções) frame

armadilha (err-mer-*dhee*-l<sup>Y</sup>ah) *f* trap

armado (err-*mer*-dhoo) *adj* armed

armador (err-mer-*dhoar*) *m* shipowner

armadura (err-mer-*dhoo*-rer) *f* armour

armar (err-*mahr*) *v* arm

armarinho (ahr-mah-*ree*-ñoo) *m Br* haberdashery

armário (err-*mah*-r<sup>Y</sup>oo) *m* closet, cupboard

armazém (err-mer-*zerngʸ*) *m* warehouse; depository, store-house, depot; department store

armazenagem (err-mer-zer-*nah*-zherngʸ) *f* storage

armazenar (err-mer-zer-*nahr*) *v* store

armazenista (err-mer-zer-*neesh*-ter) *m* wholesale dealer

aroma (er-*roa*-mer) *m* aroma

arqueado (err-k<sup>Y</sup>*ah*-dhoo) *adj* arched

arquejar (err-kı-*zhahr*) *v* pant

arqueologia (err-k<sup>Y</sup>oo-loo-zhee-er) *f* archaeology

arqueólogo (err-k<sup>Y</sup>o-loo-goo) *m* archaeologist

arquitecto (err-kee-*teh*-too) *m* architect

arquitectura (err-kee-teh-*too*-rer) *f* architecture

arquivo (err-*kee*-voo) *m* archives *pl*; file

arrancar (er-rrerng-*kahr*) *v* extract

arranha-céus (er-rrer-ñer-*seh*-oosh) *m* (pl ~) skyscraper

arranhão (er-rrer-*nerngʷ*) *m* (pl -hões) graze, scratch

arranhar (er-rrer-*ñahr*) *v* scratch

arranjar (er-rrerng-*zhahr*) *v* arrange; **arranjar-se com** *make do with

arrastar (er-rrersh-*tahr*) *v* drag, haul

arrecadação (er-rrer-ker-dher-*serngʷ*) *f* (pl -ções) shed

arredondado (er-rrer-dhawngn-*dah*-dhoo) *adj* rounded

arredores (er-rrer-*dhoa*-rısh) *mpl* surroundings *pl*, environment; outskirts *pl*

arreliar (er-rrer-l<sup>Y</sup>*ahr*) *v* tease; annoy

arremessar (er-rrer-mer-*sahr*) *v* toss

arrendamento (er-rrayngn-dah-*mayngn*-too) *m* lease

arrendar (er-rrayngn-*dahr*) *v* rent; lease

arrependimento (er-rrer-payngn-dee-*mayngn*-too) *m* repentance

arrepio (er-rrer-*pee*ᵒᵒ) *m* shiver

arriscado (er-rreesh-*kah*-dhoo) *adj* risky

arriscar (er-rreesh-*kahr*) *v* risk

arrogante (er-rroo-*gerngn*-ter) *adj* snooty

arrojado (er-rroo-*zhah*-dhoo) *adj* bold

arroz (er-*rroash*) *m* rice

arruinar (er-rrwee-*nahr*) *v* ruin

arrumador (er-rroo-mer-*dhoar*) *m* usher

**arrumadora** (er-rroo-mer-*dho*-rer) *f* usherette

**arrumar** (er-rroo-*mahr*) *v* tidy up

**arte** (*ahr*-ter) *f* art; **artes e ofícios** arts and crafts

**artéria** (ahr-*teh*-r<sup>Y</sup>er) *f* artery; ~ **principal** thoroughfare

**artesanato** (ahr-ter-zer-*nah*-too) *m* handicraft

**articulação** (ahr-tee-koo-ler-*serng*<sup>W</sup>) *f* (pl -ções) joint

**artificial** (err-ter-fi-s<sup>Y</sup>*ahl*) *adj* (pl -ais) artificial

**artifício** (err-ter-*fee*-s<sup>Y</sup>oo) *m* artifice

**artigo** (err-*tee*-goo) *m* article, item; **artigos de toalete** toiletry

**artista** (err-*teesh*-ter) *m* artist; *f* artist

**artístico** (err-*teesh*-tee-koo) *adj* artistic

**árvore** (*ahr*-voo-rer) *f* tree; ~ **de cames** camshaft

**asa** (*ah*-zer) *f* wing

**ascendência** (ersh-sayngn-*dayng*-s<sup>Y</sup>er) *f* origin

**ascender** (ersh-sayngn-*dayr*) *v* ascend

**ascensão** (ersh-sayng-*serng*<sup>W</sup>) *f* (pl -sões) ascent

**ascensor** (ersh-sayng-*soar*) *m* lift

**asfalto** (ersh-*fahl*-too) *m* asphalt

**Ásia** (er-z<sup>Y</sup>er) *f* Asia

**asiático** (er-z<sup>Y</sup>*ah*-tee-koo) *adj* Asian; *m* Asian

**asilo** (er-*zee*-loo) *m* asylum

**asma** (*ahzh*-mer) *f* asthma

**asneira** (erzh-*nay*-rah) *f* rubbish; blunder; mistake

**aspas** (*ahsh*-persh) *fpl* quotation marks

**aspecto** (ersh-*peh*-too) *m* aspect; look

**áspero** (*ahsh*-per-roo) *adj* rough, harsh

**aspirador** (ersh-pee-rer-*dhoar*) *m* vacuum cleaner

**aspirar** (ersh-pee-*rahr*) *v* aim at, aspire; hoover; ~ **a** aim at

**aspirina** (ersh-pee-*ree*-ner) *f* aspirin

**assaltar** (er-sahl-*tahr*) *v* burgle

**assalto** (er-*sahl*-too) *m* assault, attack

**assar** (er-*sahr*) *v* roast

**assassinar** (er-ser-see-*nahr*) *v* murder

**assassínio** (er-ser-*see*-n<sup>Y</sup>oo) *m* assassination

**assassino** (er-ser-*see*-noo) *m* murderer

**assaz** (er-*sahsh*) *adv* enough, sufficiently; rather

**asseado** (er-s<sup>Y</sup>*ah*-dhoo) *adj* neat; tidy

**assegurar** (er-ser-goo-*rahr*) *v* assure

**assembleia** (er-sayngm-*blay*-er) *f* assembly, meeting

**assemelhar-se** (er-ser-mi-l<sup>Y</sup>*ahr*-ser) *v* resemble

**assento** (er-*sayngn*-too) *m* seat; chair

**assim** (er-*seeng*) *adv* so; thus; ~ **como** as well as; ~ **por diante** and so on; ~ **que** as soon as

**assinalar** (er-see-ner-*lahr*) *v* indicate

**assinante** (er-see-*nerng*-ter) *m* subscriber

**assinar** (er-see-*nahr*) *v* sign

**assinatura** (er-see-ner-*too*-rer) *f* signature; subscription; ~ **de temporada** season-ticket

**assistência** (er-seesh-*tayng*-s<sup>Y</sup>er) *f* attendance; assistance, relief

**assistente** (er-seesh-*tayngn*-ter) *m* assistant

**assistir** (er-seesh-*teer*) *v* assist; ~ **a** assist at; attend

**assobiar** (er-soo-bh<sup>Y</sup>*ahr*) *v* whistle

**associação** (er-soo-s<sup>Y</sup>er-*serng*<sup>W</sup>) *f* (pl -ções) association; club, society

**associar** (er-soo-s<sup>Y</sup>*ahr*) *v* associate; **associar-se a** join

**assoprar** (er-soo-*prahr*) *v* \*blow

**assunto** (er-*soongn*-too) *m* matter; theme, concern, affair, subject, business

**assustado** (er-soosh-*tah*-dhoo) *adj*
frightened; afraid

**assustador** (er-soosh-ter-*dhoar*) *adj*
scary; creepy

**assustar** (er-soosh-*tahr*) *v* frighten;
scare; **assustar-se** \*be frightened

**astronomia** (ersh-troo-noo-*mee*-er) *f*
astronomy

**astuto** (ersh-*too*-too) *adj* clever; sly

**atacador** (ah-tah-ker-*dhoar*) *m* shoe-
lace, lace

**atacar** (er-ter-*kahr*) *v* attack, assault;
\*strike

**atalho** (er-*tah*-lʸoo) *m* trail

**ataque** (er-*tah*-ker) *m* attack, fit;
stroke

**atar** (er-*tahr*) *v* tie; bundle, \*bind, attach, fasten; ~ **num molho** bundle

**atarefado** (er-ter-rer-*fah*-dhoo) *adj*
busy

**até** (er-*teh*) *prep* till; until, to; ~ **a-
gora** so far; ~ **que** till

**atenção** (er-tayng-*serng*ʷ) *f* (pl -ções)
attention; notice, consideration;
**prestar** ~ mind; **prestar** ~ **a** attend to; \*pay attention to, mind

**atencioso** (er-tayng-sʸoa-zoo) *adj* considerate; thoughtful

**atender** (er-tayng-*dayr*) *v* attend on

**atento** (er-*tayng*-too) *adj* attentive

**aterrador** (er-ter-rrer-*dhoar*) *adj* terrifying

**aterrar** (er-ter-*rrahr*) *v* land

**aterrorizar** (er-ter-rroo-ree-*zahr*) *v* terrify

**atestado** (er-tɪsh-*tah*-dhoo) *adj* full up;
*m* certificate; ~ **de saúde**
health certificate

**atestar** (er-tɪsh-*tahr*) *v* fill up

**ateu** (er-*tay*ᵒᵒ) *m* (f ateia) atheist

**atingir** (er-teeng-*zheer*) *v* attain; \*hit

**atirar** (er-tee-*rahr*) *v* \*throw, \*cast

**atitude** (er-tee-*too*-dher) *f* attitude;

position

**Atlântico** (ert-*lerng*-tee-koo) *m* Atlantic

**atleta** (ert-*leh*-ter) *m* athlete

**atletismo** (ert-ler-*teezh*-moo) *m* athletics *pl*

**atmosfera** (ert-moosh-*feh*-rer) *f* atmosphere

**atómico** (er-*to*-mee-koo) *adj* atomic

**átomo** (*ah*-tuu-muu) *m* atom

**atordoado** (er-toor-*dhwah*-dhoo) *adj*
dizzy, giddy

**atormentar** (er-toor-mayng-*tahr*) *v*
torment

**atracar** (er-trer-*kahr*) *v* moor

**atracção** (er-trah-*serng*ʷ) *f* (pl -ções)
attraction

**atractivo** (er-trah-*tee*-voo) *m* attraction

**atraente** (er-trer-*ayng*-ter) *adj* attractive

\***atrair** (er-trer-*eer*) *v* attract

**atrás** (er-*trahsh*) *adv* behind; back; ~
**de** behind

**atrasado** (er-trer-*zah*-dhoo) *adj* late;
overdue

**atrasar** (er-trer-*zahr*) *v* delay

**atraso** (er-*trah*-zoo) *m* delay

**através** (er-trer-*vehsh*) *adv* across,
through; ~ **de** through

**atravessar** (er-trer-ver-*sahr*) *v* cross,
pass through; \*go through

**atrevido** (er-trer-*vee*-dhoo) *adj* bold

\***atribuir** (er-tree-*bhweer*) *v* allot
~ **a** assign to

**átrio** (*ah*-trʸoo) *m* lobby

**atroz** (er-*trosh*) *adj* horrible

**atum** (er-*toong*) *m* tuna

**audácia** (ou-*dhah*-sʸer) *f* nerve

**audiência** (erᵒᵒ-*dhʸayng*-sʸer) *f* audience

**auditório** (erᵒᵒ-dhee-*to*-rʸoo) *m* auditorium

**audível** (ou-*dhee*-vehl) *adj* (pl -eis)

audible

**aula** (*ou*-ler) *f* lesson

**aumentar** (ou-may̆ngn-*tahr*) *v* increase; raise

**aumento** (ou-*may̆ngn*-too) *m* increase; rise; raise *nAm;* ~ **de salário** raise *nAm*

**aurora** (ou-*ro*-rah) *f* dawn

**auscultador** (oush-kool-ter-*dhoar*) *m* receiver; stethoscope

**ausência** (ou-*zay̆ng*-s<sup>y</sup>er) *f* absence

**ausente** (ou-*zay̆ngn*-ter) *adj* absent; away

**Austrália** (oush-*trah*-l<sup>y</sup>er) *f* Australia

**australiano** (oush-trer-*l<sup>y</sup>er*-noo) *adj* Australian; *m* Australian

**Áustria** (*oush*-tr<sup>y</sup>er) *f* Austria

**austríaco** (oush-*tree*-er-koo) *m* Austrian, *adj* Austrian

**autêntico** (ou-*tay̆ngn*-tee-koo) *adj* authentic; original

**autocarro** (ou-too-*kah*-rroo) *m* coach, bus

**auto-estrada** (ou-tŏŏ<sup>ee</sup>sh-*trah*-dher) *f* motorway; highway *nAm*

**automático** (ou-too-*mah*-tee-koo) *adj* automatic; **distribuidor** ~ **de selos** stamp machine

**automatização** (ou-too-mer-tee-zer-*say̆ng*<sup>w</sup>) *f* (pl -ções) automation

**automobilismo** (ou-too-moo-bhee-*leezh*-moo) *m* motoring

**automobilista** (ou-too-moo-bhee-*leesh*-ter) *m* motorist

**automóvel** (ou-too-*mo*-vehl) *m* (pl -eis) automobile; motor-car; **andar de** ~ *ride

**autonomia** (ou-too-*noo*-mee-er) *f* self-government

**autónomo** (ou-too-*no*-moo) *adj* independent, autonomous

**autópsia** (ou-*top*-s<sup>y</sup>er) *f* autopsy

**autor** (ou-*toar*) *m* author

**autoridade** (ou-too-ree-*dhah*-dher) *f*

authority

**autoritário** (ou-too-ree-*tah*-r<sup>y</sup>oo) *adj* authoritarian

**autorização** (ou-too-ree-zer-*say̆ng*<sup>w</sup>) *f* (pl -ções) permission, authorization, permit; ~ **de residência** residence permit; ~ **de trabalho** work permit; labor permit *Am*

**autorizar** (ou-too-ree-*zahr*) *v* license; ~ **a** allow to; *estar autorizado *be allowed

**auto-serviço** (ou-too-serr-*vee*-soo) *m* self-service

**auxiliar** (ou-see-*l<sup>y</sup>ahr*) *v* assist, aid

**avalanche** (er-ver-*lay̆ng*-sher) *f* avalanche

**avaliação** (er-ver-l<sup>y</sup>er-*say̆ng*<sup>w</sup>) *f* (pl -ções) appreciation

**avaliar** (er-ver-*l<sup>y</sup>ahr*) *v* value; appreciate, evaluate

**avançar** (er-vay̆ng-*sahr*) *v* *get on, advance; *go ahead, *go on

**avanço** (er-*vay̆ng*-soo) *m* lead; advance

**avante** (er-*vay̆ngn*-ter) *adv* forward

**avarento** (er-ver-*ray̆ngn*-too) *adj* avaricious

**avaria** (er-ver-*ree*-er) *f* breakdown

**avariado** (er-ver-*r<sup>y</sup>ah*-dhoo) *adj* out of order, broken

**avariar-se** (er-ver-*r<sup>y</sup>ahr*-ser) *v* *break down

**ave** (*ah*-ver) *f* bird; ~ **marinha** seabird; **aves de criação** poultry, fowl

**aveia** (er-*vay*-er) *f* oats *pl*

**avelã** (er-ver-*lay̆ng*) *f* hazelnut

**avenida** (er-ver-*nee*-dher) *f* avenue

**avental** (er-vay̆ngn-*tahl*) *m* (pl -ais) apron

**aventura** (er-vay̆ngn-*too*-rer) *f* adventure; affair

**aventurar** (er-vay̆ngn-too-*rahr*) *v* venture

**aversão** (er-verr-*say̆ng*<sup>w</sup>) *f* (pl -sões)

dislike, aversion

**do avesso** (doo er-*veh*-soo) inside out

**avestruz** (er-vish-*troosh*) *f* ostrich

**avião** (er-v*Yerng*ᵂ) *m* (pl aviões) aeroplane; aircraft, plane; airplane *nAm*; ~ **a jacto** jet

**avisar** (er-vee-*sahr*) *v* caution, warn; notify

**aviso** (er-*vee*-zoo) *m* warning; notice

**avistar** (er-veesh-*tahr*) *v* \*see

**avó** (er-*vo*) *f* grandmother; **avozinha** grandmother

**avô** (er-*voa*) *m* grandfather; granddad; **avós** grandparents *pl*; **avozinho** grandfather

**à-vontade** (ah-vawngn-*tah*-dher) *m* at ease, ease

**azáfama** (er-*zah*-fer-mer) *f* bustle

**azar** (er-*zahr*) *m* bad luck; chance

**azedo** (er-*zay*-dhoo) *adj* sour

**azeite** (er-*zay*-ter) *m* olive oil

**azeitona** (er-zay-toa-ner) *f* olive

**azia** (er-*zee*-er) *f* heartburn

**azinhaga** (er-zee-*ñah*-ger) *f* lane

**azoto** (er-*zoa*-too) *m* nitrogen

**azul** (er-*zool*) *adj* (pl azuis) blue

**azulejo** (er-zoo-*lay*-zhoo) *m* tile

# B

**bacalhau** (ber-ker-*lᵞou*) *m* cod

**bacia** (ber-*see*-er) *f* basin

**baço** (*bah*-soo) *adj* mat, dull, dim

**bacon** (bay-*kern*) *m* bacon

**bactéria** (berk-*teh*-r*Yer*) *f* bacterium

**baga** (*bah*-ger) *f* berry

**bagageira** (ber-ger-*zhay*-rer) *f* luggage rack

**bagagem** (ber-*ger*-zherng*ᵞ*) *f* baggage, luggage; ~ **de mão** hand luggage; hand baggage *Am*

**baía** (ber-*ee*-er) *f* bay

**bailado** (bigh-*lah*-dhoo) *m* ballet

**baile** (*bigh*-ler) *m* ball

**bainha** (ber-*ee*-ñer) *f* hem

**bairro** (*bigh*-rroo) *m* district, quarter; ~ **pobre** slum

**baixa-mar** (bigh-sher-*mahr*) *f* low tide

**baixar** (bigh-*shahr*) *v* lower

**baixo** (*bigh*-shoo) *adj* short; low; *m* bass; **em** ~ below; downstairs; **para** ~ down; downwards, downstairs

**bala** (*bah*-ler) *f* bullet

**balança** (ber-*lerng*-ser) *f* scales; weighing-machine

**balançar** (ber-lerng-*sahr*) *v* \*swing; **balançar-se** \*swing

**balancé** (ber-lerng-*seh*) *m* seesaw

**balanço** (ber-*lerng*-soo) *m* balance; *mBr* swing

**balão** (ber-*lerng*ᵂ) *m* (pl balões) balloon

**balas** (*bah*-lersh) *fplBr* sweets

**balaustrada** (ber-loush-*trah*-dher) *f* rail

**balbuciar** (bahl-boo-s*Yahr*) *v* falter

**balcão** (bahl-*kerng*ᵂ) *m* (pl -cões) counter; circle

**balde** (*bahl*-der) *m* bucket, pail

**balé** (bah-*leh*) *mBr* ballet

**baleia** (ber-*lay*-er) *f* whale

**baliza** (ber-*lee*-zer) *f* goal

**balofo** (ber-*loa*-foo) *adj* flaccid

**baloiçar** (ber-loi-*sahr*) *v* rock

**baloiço** (ber-*loi*-soo) *m* swing

**bambu** (berngm-boo) *m* bamboo

**banana** (ber-*ner*-ner) *f* banana

**banco** (*berng*-koo) *m* bench; bank

**banda** (*berng*-der) *f* band

**bandeira** (berngn-*day*-rer) *f* flag

**bandido** (berngn-dee-dhoo) *m* bandit

**banhar-se** (ber-*ñahr*-ser) *v* bathe

**banheira** (ber-*ñay*-rer) *f* bathtub

**banheiro** (ber-*ñay*-roo) *mBr* bathroom

**banho** (*ber*-ñoo) *m* bath; ~ **turco**

Turkish bath; **tomar** ~ bathe; **tomar um ~ de sol** sunbathe; **touca de ~** bathing-cap; **traje de ~** *Br* bathing-suit

**banquete** (berng-*kay*-ter) *m* banquet

**baptismo** (bah-*teezh*-moo) *m* christening, baptism

**baptizar** (bah-tee-*zahr*) *v* christen, baptize

**bar** (bahr) *m* saloon, bar; public house

**baralhar** (ber-rer-*lʸahr*) *v* shuffle

**barato** (ber-*rah*-too) *adj* cheap, inexpensive

**barba** (*bahr*-ber) *f* beard; **\*fazer a ~** shave

**barbaridade** (berr-ber-ree-*dhah*-dher) *f* barbarity

**\*barbear-se** (berr-*bʸahr*-ser) *v* shave

**barbeiro** (berr-*bay*-roo) *m* barber

**barco** (*bahr*-koo) *m* boat; **~ a motor** launch, motor-boat; **~ a remos** rowing-boat; **~ a vapor** steamer; **~ à vela** sailing-boat

**barítono** (ber-*ree*-too-noo) *m* baritone

**barómetro** (ber-*ro*-mer-troo) *m* barometer

**barquinho** (berr-*kee*-ño-o) *m* dinghy

**barra** (*bah*-rrer) *f* bar; rail

**barraca** (ber-*rrah*-ker) *f* shed

**barragem** (ber-*rrah*-zhernɡᵛ) *f* dam

**barreira** (ber-*rray*-rer) *f* barrier; **~ de protecção** crash barrier

**barrete** (ber-*rray*-ter) *m* cap

**barrica** (ber-*rree*-ker) *f* keg

**barriga** (ber-*rree*-ger) *f* stomach; **~ da perna** calf

**barril** (ber-*rreel*) *m* (pl -is) cask; barrel

**barro** (*bah*-rroo) *m* terracotta

**barroco** (ber-*rroa*-koo) *adj* baroque

**barulho** (ber-*roo*-lʸoo) *m* noise

**base** (*bah*-zer) *f* basis, base

**\*basear** (ber-z*ʸahr*) *v* base

**basebol** (*bayz*-bhol) *m* baseball

**basílica** (ber-*zee*-lee-ker) *f* basilica

**bastante** (bersh-*terngn*-ter) *adj* sufficient, enough; *adv* quite, rather, pretty, fairly

**bastar** (bersh-*tahr*) *v* \*do, suffice

**bastardo** (bersh-*tahr*-dhoo) *m* bastard

**bata** (*bah*-ter) *f* smock

**batalha** (ber-*tah*-lʸer) *f* battle

**batata** (ber-*tah*-ter) *f* potato; **batatas fritas** chips

**batedeira** (ber-ter-*dhay*-rer) *f* mixer

**bater** (ber-*tayr*) *v* \*beat; whip, bump, knock, tap, smack, \*strike, slap, \*hit; **~ as palmas** clap

**bateria** (ber-ter-*ree*-er) *f* battery

**baton** (bah-*tawng*) *m* lipstick

**baú** (ber-*oo*) *m* trunk

**baunilha** (bou-*nee*-lʸer) *f* vanilla

**bêbado** (*bay*-bher-dhoo) *adj* drunk

**bebé** (beh-*bheh*) *m* baby; **alcofa de ~** carry-cot; **carrinho de ~** pram; baby carriage *Am*

**beber** (ber-*bhayr*) *v* \*drink

**beberete** (ber-bher-*ray*-ter) *m* cocktail

**bebida** (ber-*bhee*-dher) *f* beverage, drink; **~ não alcoólica** soft drink; **bebidas alcoólicas** spirits, liquor

**beco** (*bay*-koo) *m* alley; **~ sem saída** cul-de-sac

**bege** (behzh) *adj* beige

**beijar** (bay-*zhahr*) *v* kiss

**beijo** (*bay*-zhoo) *m* kiss

**beira** (*bay*-rer) *f* bank; **à ~ de** on the edge of

**beira-mar** (bay-rer-*mahr*) *f* seashore; shore

**beira-rio** (bay-rer-*rree*ᵒᵒ) *f* riverside

**belas-artes** (beh-lerz-*ahr*-tɪsh) *fpl* fine arts

**belbutina** (behl-boo-*tee*-ner) *f* velveteen

**beleza** (ber-*lay*-zer) *f* beauty

**belga** (*behl*-ger) *adj* Belgian; *m* Belgian

**Bélgica** (behl-zhee-ker) f Belgium

**beliche** (ber-lee-sher) m bunk, berth

**beliscar** (ber-leesh-kahr) v pinch

**belo** (beh-loo) adj fine, beautiful; handsome

**bem** (berngᵞ) adv well; **bem!** well!; **está bem!** all right!

**bem-estar** (berngᵞ-ish-tahr) m comfort; welfare

**bênção** (bayng-serngʷ) f (pl ~s) blessing

*bendizer (berngᵞ-dee-zayr) v bless

**beneficiar** (ber-ner-fee-sᵞahr) v benefit

**beneficiário** (ber-ner-fee-sᵞah-rᵞoo) m payee

**benefício** (ber-neh-fee-koo) m benefit, profit

**bengala** (bayngng-gah-ler) f cane; walking-stick

**bengaleiro** (bayngng-ger-lay-roo) m hat rack

**bens** (bayngeesh) mpl possessions; goods pl, belongings pl

**benvindo** (berngᵞ-veengn-doo) adj welcome

**berço** (bayr-soo) m cradle

**beringela** (ber-reeng-zheh-ler) f eggplant

**berlinde** (berr-leengn-der) m marble

**berma** (behr-mer) f roadside

**berrar** (ber-rrahr) v yell

**berro** (beh-rroo) m yell

**betão** (ber-terngʷ) m concrete

**beterraba** (ber-ter-rrah-bher) f beet; beetroot

**bétula** (beh-too-ler) f birch

**bexiga** (ber-shee-ger) f bladder; **bexigas doidas** chicken-pox

**bíblia** (bee-bhlᵞer) f bible

**biblioteca** (bee-bhlᵞoo-teh-ker) f library

**bicha** (bee-sher) f queue; *fazer ~ queue

**bicho** (bee-shoo) m worm; animal

**bicicleta** (ber-see-kleh-ter) f cycle, bicycle; ~ **a motor** moped; motorbike nAm

**bico** (bee-koo) m point; nozzle; beak

**bicudo** (bee-koo-dhoo) adj pointed

**biela** (bᵞeh-ler) f piston-rod

**bife** (bee-fer) m steak

**bifurcação** (bee-foor-ker-serngʷ) f (pl -ções) road fork, fork

**bifurcar** (bee-foor-kahr) v fork

**bigode** (bee-go-dher) m moustache

**bilha** (bee-lᵞer) f pitcher

**bilhar** (bee-lᵞahr) m billiards pl

**bilhete** (bee-lᵞay-ter) m ticket; ~ **de gare** platform ticket; ~ **gratuito** free ticket; ~ **postal** postcard

**bilheteira** (bee-lᵞer-tay-rer) f box-office; ~ **automática** ticket machine; ~ **de reservação** box-office

**bilheteria** (bee-lᵞer-ter-ree-er) fBr box-office

**bilião** (bee-lᵞerngʷ) m (pl -iões) billion

**bilíngue** (bee-leeng-gwer) adj bilingual

**bílis** (bee-leesh) f bile; gall; **vesícula biliar** gall bladder

**binóculo** (bee-no-koo-loo) m binoculars pl; field glasses

**biologia** (bᵞoo-loo-zhee-er) f biology

**biombo** (bᵞawngm-boo) m screen

**biscoito** (beesh-koi-too) m biscuit; cookie nAm

**bispo** (beesh-poo) m bishop

**bloco** (blo-koo) m block; ~ **de notas** writing-pad; pad; ~ **de papel** writing-pad; ~ **habitacional** house block Am

*bloquear (bloo-kᵞahr) v block

**blusa** (bloo-zer) f blouse

**boate** (bwaht) f nightclub

**bobagem** (boa-bhah-zherngᵞ) fBr rubbish

**bobina** (boo-*bhee*-ner) f spool; ~ **de ignição** ignition coil

**boca** (*boa*-ker) f mouth

**bocadinho** (poa-koo-*shee*-ñoo) m bit

**bocado** (boo-*kah*-dhoo) m bite; fragment; morsel, part, lump

**bocejar** (boo-sı-*zhahr*) v yawn

**bode** (bo-*dher*) m goat; ~ **expiatório** scapegoat

**bofetada** (boo-fer-*tah*-dher) f slap

**boi** (boi) m ox

**bóia** (bo-Yer) f buoy

**boina** (*boi*-ner) f beret

**bola** (bo-ler) f ball; ~ **de futebol** football

**bolacha** (boo-*lah*-sher) f waffle; ~ **de baunilha** wafer

**bolbo** (*boal*-bhoo) m bulb

**boletim** (boo-ler-*teeng*) m bulletin; ~ **meteorológico** weather forecast

**bolha** (*boa*-lYer) f bubble; blister

**Bolívia** (boo-lee-vYer) f Bolivia

**boliviano** (boo-lee-vYah-noo) adj Bolivian; m Bolivian

**bolo** (*boa*-loo) m cake

**bolor** (boo-*loar*) m mildew

**bolorento** (boo-loo-*rayngn*-too) adj mouldy

**bolota** (boo-*lo*-ter) f acorn

**bolsa** (*boal*-ser) f pouch, bag; stock market, exchange, stock exchange; ~ **de estudos** scholarship; ~ **de valores** stock exchange

**bolso** (*boal*-soo) m pocket

**bom** (bawng) adj (f **boa**; pl **bons**) good; kind; well; nice; **é boa!** indeed!

**bomba** (*bawngm*-ber) f bomb; pump; ~ **de água** water pump; ~ **de gasolina** petrol pump; fuel pump Am; *dar à ~ pump

*****bombardear** (bawngm-berr-dYahr) v bomb

**bombazina** (bawngm-ber-*zee*-ner) f corduroy

*****bombear** (bawngm-bYahr) v Br pump

**bombeiros** (bawngm-bay-roosh) mpl fire-brigade

**bombom** (bawngm-*bawng*) m chocolate

**bombordo** (bawngm-*boar*-dhoo) m port

**bonde** (*boan*-der) mBr tram, streetcar nAm

**bondoso** (bawngn-*doa*-zoo) adj good-natured; kind

**boné** (boo-*neh*) m cap

**boneca** (boo-*neh*-ker) f doll

**bonito** (boo-*nee*-too) adj pretty; nice, fair, good-looking

**boquilha** (boo-kee-lYer) f cigarette-holder

**borboleta** (boor-boo-*lay*-ter) f butterfly

**borbulha** (boor-boo-lYer) f pimple

**borda** (*bor*-dher) f verge, edge, brim, border, rim

**bordado** (boor-*dah*-dhoo) m embroidery

**bordar** (boor-*dahr*) v embroider

**bordel** (boor-*dehl*) m (pl -déis) brothel

**a bordo** (er *bor*-doo) aboard

**borracha** (boo-*rrah*-sher) f rubber; eraser

**borrão** (boo-*rreng*ʷ) m (pl -rões) blot

**borrego** (boo-*rray*-goo) m lamb

**bosque** (*boash*-ker) m wood

**bota** (*bo*-ter) f boot; **botas de esqui** ski boots

**botânica** (boo-*ter*-nee-ker) f botany

**botão** (boo-*terng*ʷ) m (pl **botões**) button; push-button; bud; ~ **de colarinho** collar stud; **botões de punho** cuff-links pl; **casa de ~** buttonhole

**boutique** (boo-*tee*-ker) f boutique

bowling (*boa*-leeng) *m* bowling

braço (*brah*-soo) *m* arm; **de ~ dado** arm-in-arm

brado (*brah*-dhoo) *m* cry

braguilha (brer-*gee*-lᵞah) *f* fly

bramir (brer-*meer*) *v* roar

branco (*brerng*-koo) *adj* white; **em ~** blank

brando (*brerngn*-dhoo) *adj* tender, soft; smooth

Brasil (brer-*zeel*) *m* Brazil

brasileiro (brer-zee-*lay*-roo) *adj* Brazilian; *m* Brazilian

brecha (*breh*-sher) *f* breach; gap

breve (*breh*-ver) *adj* brief; **dentro em ~** shortly; **em ~** soon

brevemente (breh-ver-*mayngn*-ter) *adv* shortly, soon

bridge (breej) *m* bridge

briga (*bree*-ger) *f* quarrcl, dispute

brilhante (bree-*lᵞerngn*-ter) *adj* brilliant; *m* diamond

brilhar (bree-*lᵞahr*) *v* *shine; glow

brilho (*bree*-lᵞoo) *m* glare; glow

brincar (breeng-*kahr*) *v* play

brinco (*breeng*-koo) *m* earring

brinde (*breeng*-der) *m* toast

brinquedo (breeng-*kay*-dhoo) *m* toy

brioche (*bree*-osh) *m* bun

brisa (*bree*-zer) *f* breeze

britânico (bree-*ter*-nee-koo) *adj* British; *m* Briton

broca (*bro*-ker) *f* drill

brocar (broo-*kahr*) *v* bore; drill

broche (*bro*-sher) *m* brooch

brochura (broo-*shoo*-rer) *f* brochure

bronquite (brawng-*kee*-ter) *f* bronchitis

bronze (*brawng*-zer) *m* bronze; **de ~** bronze

bronzeado (brawng-*zᵞah*-dhoo) *adj* tanned

bruços (*broo*-soosh) *mpl* breaststroke; **de ~** face downwards

bruma (*broo*-mer) *f* haze

brutal (broo-*tahl*) *adj* (pl -ais) brutal

bruto (*broo*-too) *adj* gross; *m* brute

bruxa (*broo*-sher) *f* witch

bufete (boo-*fay*-ter) *m* buffet

bule (*boo*-ler) *m* teapot

Bulgária (bool-*gah*-rᵞer) *f* Bulgaria

búlgaro (*bool*-ger-roo) *adj* Bulgarian; *m* Bulgarian

buraco (boo-*rah*-koo) *m* hole

burguês (boor-*gaysh*) *adj* middleclass, bourgeois

burla (*boor*-ler) *f* swindle

burlão (boor-*lerng*ʷ) *m* (pl -lões) swindler

burlar (boor-*lahr*) *v* swindle

burocracia (boo-roo-krer-*see*-er) *f* bureaucracy

burro (*boo*-rroo) *m* ass, donkey

busca (*boosh*-ker) *f* search

buscar (boosh-*kahr*) *v* look for; *ir ~** fetch; collect

bússola (*boo*-soo-ler) *f* compass

busto (*boosh*-too) *m* bust

buzina (boo-*zee*-ner) *f* horn; hooter

buzinar (boo-zee-*nahr*) *v* hoot

búzio (*boo*-zᵞoo) *m* winkle

## C

cá (kah) *adv* here

cabana (ker-*bher*-ner) *f* cabin; hut

cabeça (ker-*bhay*-ser) *f* head; **~ do motor** cylinder head

cabeçalho (ker-bher-*sah*-lᵞoo) *m* headline

cabeçudo (ker-bhay-*soo*-dhoo) *adj* head-strong

cabedal (ker-bher-*dhahl*) *m* (pl -ais) leather

cabeleireiro (ker-bay-lay-*ray*-roo) *m* hairdresser

**cabelo** (ker-*bhay*-loo) *m* hair; ~ **postiço** hair piece

**cabeludo** (ker-bher-*loo*-dhoo) *adj* hairy

\***caber** (ker-*bhayr*) *v* \*be contained in; fit in

**cabide** (ker-*bhee*-dher) *m* hanger; coat-hanger

**cabina** (ker-*bhee*-ner) *f* booth, cabin; ~ **telefónica** telephone booth

**cabo** (*kah*-bhoo) *m* handle; cape; cable

**cabra** (*kah*-bhrer) *f* goat

**caça** (*kah*-ser) *f* chase, hunt; game

**caçador** (ker-ser-*dhoar*) *m* hunter

**caçar** (ker-*sahr*) *v* hunt; ~ **furtivamente** poach

**caçarola** (ker-ser-*ro*-ler) *f* saucepan

**cacete** (ker-*say*-ter) *m* club, cudgel

**cachimbo** (kah-*sheengm*-boo) *m* pipe

**cada** (*kah*-dher) *adj* each, every; ~ **um** everyone

**cadáver** (ker-*dhah*-vehr) *m* corpse

**cadeado** (ker-dhʸ*ah*-dhoo) *m* padlock

**cadeia** (ker-*dhay*-er) *f* chain; gaol

**cadeira** (ker-*dhay*-rer) *f* chair; ~ **de braços** armchair; ~ **de lona** deck chair; ~ **de rodas** wheelchair

**cadela** (kah-*dheh*-ler) *f* bitch

**café** (ker-*feh*) *m* coffee; café

**cafeína** (ker-feh-*ee*-ner) *f* caffeine

**cafetaria** (ker-fer-ter-rʸer) *f* cafeteria

**cafeteira** (ker-fer-*tay*-rer) *f* coffee-pot; ~ **de filtro** percolator

**cãibra** (*kerng*ʸm-brer) *f* cramp

\***cair** (ker-*eer*) *v* \*fall; **deixar** ~ drop

**cais** (kighsh) *m* wharf, quay, dock

**caixa** (*kigh*-sher) *f* box; pay-desk; cashier; *m* carton; cashier; ~ **automática** cash dispenser, ATM; ~ **de cartão** carton; ~ **de ferramenta** tool-box; ~ **de fósforos** match-box; ~ **de papelão** *Br* carton; ~ **de primeiros socorros** first-aid kit; ~ **de tintas** paint-box; ~ **de**

**velocidades** gear-box; ~ **económica** savings bank

**cal** (kahl) *f* lime

**calado** (kah-*lah*-dhoo) *adj* silent; \***estar** ~ \*be silent

**calafrio** (kah-ler-*free*ᵒᵒ) *m* chill

**calamidade** (kah-ler-mee-*dhah*-dher) *f* calamity

**calar** (ker-*lahr*) *v* silence: **calar-se** \*keep quiet

**calçada** (kahl-*sah*-dher) *f* causeway

**calçado** (kahl-*sah*-dhoo) *m* footwear

**calcanhar** (kahl-ker-*ñahr*) *m* heel

**calcar** (kahl-*kahr*) *v* stamp

**calças** (*kahl*-sersh) *fpl* slacks *pl*, trousers *pl*; pants *plAm*; ~ **de esqui** ski pants; ~ **de ganga** jeans *pl*

**calcinhas** (kahl-*see*-ñersh) *fpl* knickers *pl*, panties *pl*

**cálcio** (*kahl*-sʸoo) *m* calcium

**calções** (kahl-*sawng*-ish) *mpl* shorts *pl*; briefs *pl*; ~ **de banho** swimming-trunks *pl*; ~ **de ginástica** gym-trunks

**calculadora** (kahl-koo-ler-*dhoarer*) *f* calculator

**calcular** (kahl-koo-*lahr*) *v* calculate, reckon

**cálculo** (*kahl*-koo-loo) *m* calculation; ~ **biliar** gallstone

**calendário** (ker-layngn-*dah*-rʸoo) *m* calendar

**calista** (kah-*leesh*-ter) *m* chiropodist

**calmante** (kahl-*merngn*-ter) *m* tranquillizer

**calmo** (*kahl*-moo) *adj* calm, quiet; sedate

**calo** (*kah*-loo) *m* callus; corn

**calor** (ker-*loar*) *m* warmth, heat

**caloria** (ker-loo-*ree*-er) *f* calorie

**calúnia** (ker-*loo*-nʸer) *f* slander

**calvinismo** (kahl-vee-*neezh*-moo) *m* Calvinism

**cama** (*ker*-mer) *f* bed; ~ **de acampa-**

**mento** camp-bed; cot *nAm*; ~ **e mesa** room and board; **duas camas** twin beds

**camada** (ker-*mah*-dher) *f* layer

**camafeu** (ker-mer-*fay*$^{oo}$) *m* cameo

**câmara municipal** (*ker*-mer-rer moo-ner-see-*pahl*) town hall

**camarada** (ker-mer-*rah*-dher) *m* comrade

**câmara-de-ar** (ker-mer-rer-*dhahr*) *f* inner tube

**camarão** (ker-mer-*rerng*$^w$) *m* (pl -rões) shrimp; ~ **grande** prawn

**cambiante** (kerngm-b$^y$*erngn*-ter) *m* nuance

**câmbio** (*kerngm*-b$^y$oo) *m* exchange rate; **casa de** ~ money exchange, exchange office

**cambota** (kerngm-*bo*-ter) *f* crankshaft

**camelo** (ker-*may*-loo) *m* camel

**camião** (ker-m$^y$*erng*$^w$) *m* (pl -iões) lorry; truck *nAm*

**caminhar** (ker-mee-*ñahr*) *v* step, walk

**caminho** (ker-*mee*-ñoo) *m* way; **a** ~ **de** bound for; **a meio** ~ halfway; **beira do** ~ wayside

**caminho-de-ferro** (ker-mee-ñoo-der-*feh*-roo) *m* railway; railroad *nAm*

**camisa** (ker-*mee*-zer) *f* shirt; vest; ~ **de dormir** nightdress

**camiseta** (ker-mee-*zay*-ter) *f Br* undershirt

**camisola** (ker-mee-*zo*-ler) *f* sweater, jumper; *f Br* nightdress; ~ **interior** undershirt

**campainha** (kerngm-per-*ee*-ñer) *f* bell; ~ **da porta** doorbell

**campanário** (kerngm-per-*nah*-r$^y$oo) *m* steeple

**campanha** (kerngm-*per*-ñer) *f* campaign

**campeão** (kerngm-p$^y$*erng*$^w$) *m* (pl -eões) champion

**campismo** (kerngm-*peezh*-moo) *m*

camping; **parque de** ~ camping site

**campista** (kerngm-*peesh*-ter) *m* camper

**campo** (*kerngm*-poo) *m* field; country, countryside; ~ **de aviação** airfield

**camponês** (kerngm-poo-*naysh*) *m* peasant

**camurça** (ker-*moor*-ser) *f* suede

**cana** (*ker*-ner) *f* cane; reed

**Canadá** (ker-*nah*-dher) *m* Canada

**canadiano** (ker-ner-d$^y$er-noo) *adj* Canadian; *m* Canadian

**canal** (ker-*nahl*) *m* (pl -ais) channel; canal; **Canal da Mancha** English Channel

**canalizador** (ker-ner-lee-zer-*dhoar*) *m* plumber

**canário** (ker-*nah*-r$^y$oo) *m* canary

**canção** (kerng-*serng*$^w$) *f* (pl -ções) song; ~ **popular** folk song

**cancela** (kerng-*seh*-ler) *f* barrier; gate

**cancelamento** (kerng-ser-ler-*mayngn*-too) *m* cancellation

**cancelar** (kerng-ser-*lahr*) *v* cancel

**cancro** (*kerng*-kroo) *m* cancer

**candeeiro** (kerngn-d$^y$*ay*-roo) *m* lamp; ~ **de mesa** reading-lamp

**candelabro** (kerngn-der-*lah*-bhroo) *m* candelabrum

**candidato** (kerngn-dee-*dhah*-too) *m* candidate

**candidatura** (kerngn-dee-dhah-*too*-rer) *f* application

**caneca** (ker-*neh*-ker) *f* mug

**canela** (ker-*neh*-ler) *f* cinnamon; shinbone

**caneta** (ker-*nay*-ter) *f* pen; ~ **de tinta permanente** fountain-pen; ~ **esferográfica** ballpoint-pen

**canga** (*kerng*-ger) *f* yoke

**canguru** (kerng-goo-*roo*) *m* kangaroo

**cânhamo** (*ker*-ñer-moo) *m* hemp; canvas

**canhão** (ker-*ñerng*ᵂ) *m* (pl -hões) gun

**canhoto** (ker-*ñoa*-too) *adj* left-handed

**canil** (ker-*neel*) *m* (pl -is) kennel

**canivete** (ker-nee-*veh*-ter) *m* pocket-knife, penknife

**cano** (*ker*-noo) *m* pipe; tube

**canoa** (ker-*noa*-er) *f* canoe

**cansaço** (kerng-*sah*-soo) *m* tiredness

**cansado** (kerng-*sah*-dhoo) *adj* weary, tired

**cansar** (kerng-*sahr*) *v* tire

**cantar** (kerng*n*-*tahr*) *v* *sing

**canteiro** (kerng*n*-*tay*-roo) *m* flowerbed

**cantina** (kerng*n*-*tee*-ner) *f* canteen

**canto** (*kerng*-too) *m* singing; corner

**cantor** (kerng*n*-*toar*) *m* singer

**cantora** (kerng*n*-*toa*-rer) *f* singer

**cão** (kerng*ᵂ*) *m* (pl cães) dog; ~ **de cego** guide-dog; **casota do** ~ kennel

**caos** (*koush*) *m* chaos

**caótico** (ker-o-tee-koo) *adj* chaotic

**capa** (*kah*-per) *f* cape; cover; jacket; sleeve; ~ **de chuva** *Br* raincoat, mackintosh

**capacete** (ker-per-*say*-ter) *m* helmet

**capacidade** (ker-per-see-*dhah*-dher) *f* capacity; ability; faculty

**capataz** (ker-per-*tahsh*) *m* foreman

**capaz** (ker-*pahsh*) *adj* able, capable; *ser ~ **de** *be able to

**capela** (ker-*peh*-ler) *f* chapel

**capelão** (ker-per-*lerng*ᵂ) *m* (pl -ães) chaplain

**capelista** (ker-per-*leesh*-ter) *m* haberdashery

**capital** (ker-pee-*tahl*) *adj* (pl -ais) capital; *f* capital; *m* capital

**capitalismo** (ker-pee-ter-*leez*-moo) *m* capitalism

**capitão** (ker-pee-*terng*ᵂ) *m* (pl -ães) captain

**capitulação** (ker-pee-too-ler-*serng*ᵂ) *f* (pl -ções) capitulation

**capricho** (ker-*pree*-shoo) *m* fancy, whim, fad

**cápsula** (*kahp*-soo-ler) *f* capsule

**captura** (kerp-too-rer) *f* capture

**capturar** (kerp-too-*rahr*) *v* capture

**capuz** (ker-*poosh*) *m* hood

**caqui** (ker-*kee*) *m* khaki

**cara** (*kah*-rer) *f* face

**caracol** (ker-rer-*kol*) *m* (pl -cóis) snail; curl

**carácter** (ker-*rah*-tehr) *m* character

**característica** (ker-rer-ter-*reesh*-tee-ker) *f* characteristic; quality; feature

**característico** (ker-rer-ter-*reesh*-tee-koo) *adj* characteristic; typical

**caracterizar** (ker-rer-ter-ree-*zahr*) *v* mark, characterize

**caramelo** (ker-rer-*meh*-loo) *m* caramel; toffee

**caranguejo** (ker-rerng-*gay*-zhoo) *m* crab

**caravana** (kah-rah-*ver*-ner) *f* caravan; trailer *nAm*

**carburador** (kerr-boo-rer-*dhoar*) *m* carburettor

**carcaça** (kerr-*kah*-ser) *f* wreck

**carcereiro** (kerr-ser-*ray*-roo) *m* jailer

**cardápio** (kahr-*dhahp*-Yoo) *mBr* menu

**cardeal** (kerr-dhᵞ*ahl*) *m* (pl -ais) cardinal; *adj* cardinal

**cardo** (*kahr*-doo) *m* thistle

**careca** (ker-*reh*-ker) *adj* bald

**carecer de** (ker-rer-*sayr*) lack

**carência** (ker-*rayngs*ᵞer) *f* shortage, lack, want

**careta** (ker-*ray*-ter) *f* grin

**carga** (*kahr*-ger) *f* cargo, freight; charge

**cargo** (*kahr*-goo) *m* office, duty, function

**caridade** (ker-ree-*dhah*-dher) *f* charity

**caril** (ker-*reel*) *m* curry

**carimbo** (ker-*reengm*-boo) *m* stamp

**Carnaval** (kerr-ner-*vahl*) *m* (pl -ais) carnival

**carne** (*kahr*-ner) *f* flesh; meat; ~ **de carneiro** mutton; ~ **de porco** pork; ~ **de vaca** beef

**carneiro** (kerr-*nay*-roo) *m* sheep, ram

**caro** (*kah*-roo) *adj* dear, expensive; precious

**caroço** (ker-*roa*-soo) *m* pip; stone

**carpa** (*kahr*-per) *f* carp

**carpinteiro** (kerr-peengn-*tay*-roo) *m* carpenter

**carrasco** (ker-*rrahsh*-koo) *m* executioner

**carregador** (ker-rrer-ger-*dhoar*) *m* porter

**carregamento** (ker-rrer-ger-*mayngn*-too) *m* cargo, charge, load

**carregar** (ker-rrer-*gahr*) *v* charge, load; press; ~ **em** press

**carreira** (ker-*rray*-rer) *f* career

**carreiro** (ker-*rray*-roo) *m* path

**carrilhão** (ker-rree-*lYerngᵂ*) *m* (pl -hões) chimes *pl*

**carro** (*kah*-rroo) *m* car; **carrinho de mão** wheelbarrow; ~ **de desporto** sports-car

**carroça** (ker-*rro*-ser) *f* cart

**carroçaria** (ker-rroo-ser-*rree*-er) *f* body-work

**carro-esporte** (kah-rroo-ish-*por*-ter) *m Br* sportscar

**carrossel** (ker-rroo-*sehl*) *m* (pl -séis) merry-go-round

**carruagem** (ker-rrwah-*zherngʸ*) *f* coach, carriage

**carruagem-cama** (ker-rrwah-zherngʸ-*ker*-mer) *f* sleeping-car, Pullman

**carruagem-restaurante** (ker-rrwah-zherngʸ-rrish-tou-*rerngn*-ter) *f* dining-car

**carta** (*kahr*-ter) *f* letter; ~ **de condução** driving licence; ~ **de crédito** letter of credit; ~ **de jogar** playing-card; ~ **de recomendação** letter of recommendation; ~ **registada** registered letter; ~ **verde** green card

**cartão** (kerr-*terngᵂ*) *m* (pl -tões) cardboard; card; ~ **de crédito** credit card; charge plate *Am*; ~ **de visita** visiting-card; **de** ~ cardboard

**cartaz** (kerr-*tahsh*) *m* placard; poster

**carteira** (kerr-*tay*-rer) *f* wallet, pocket-book; bag; desk; ~ **de escola** desk; ~ **de motorista** *Br* driving licence

**carteiro** (kerr-*tay*-roo) *m* postman

**cárter** (*kahr*-terr) *m* crankcase

**cartilagem** (kerr-tee-*lah*-zherngʸ) *f* cartilage

**cartucho** (kerr-*too*-shoo) *m* cartridge

**carvalho** (kerr-*vah*-lYoo) *m* oak

**carvão** (kerr-*verngᵂ*) *m* coal; ~ **de lenha** charcoal

**casa** (*kah*-zer) *f* house; ~ **de banho** bathroom; ~ **de campo** cottage, country house; ~ **de repouso** rest-home; ~ **flutuante** houseboat; **dentro de** ~ indoors; **dona de** ~ housewife; mistress; **em** ~ at home; **em** ~ **de** with; **lida da** ~ housekeeping, housework; **para** ~ home

**casacão** (ker-zer-*kerngᵂ*) *m* (pl -cões) coat; cloak

**casaco** (ker-*zer*-koo) *m* coat; jacket; ~ **de malha** cardigan; ~ **de peles** fur coat; ~ **desportivo** sports-jacket; blazer

**casa-forte** (kah-zer-*for*-ter) *f* vault

**casal** (ker-*zahl*) *m* (pl -ais) farm-house; married couple

**casamento** (ker-zer-*mayngn*-too) *m* marriage; wedding

**casar-se** (ker-*zahr*-ser) *v* marry

**casca** (*kahsh*-ker) *f* bark; peel, skin;

shell; ~ **de noz** nutshell
**cascalho** (kersh-*kah*-lʸoo) *m* gravel
**casco** (*kahsh*-koo) *m* hoof
**caseiro** (ker-*zay*-roo) *adj* home-made
**casino** (ker-*zee*-noo) *m* casino
**caso** (*kah*-zoo) *m* case; instance, event; ~ **que** in case; **em ~ algum** by no means; **em ~ de** in case of; *****fazer ~ de** *****pay attention to
**caspa** (*kahsh*-per) *f* dandruff
**casquilho** (kersh-*kee*-lʸoo) *m* socket
**cassino** (kah-*see*-noo) *mBr* casino
**castanha** (kersh-*ter*-ñer) *f* chestnut
**castanho** (kersh-*ter*-ñoo) *adj* brown; ~ **claro** fawn; ~ **encarniçado** auburn
**castelo** (kersh-*teh*-loo) *m* castle
**castigar** (kersh-tee-*gahr*) *v* punish
**castigo** (kersh-*tee*-goo) *m* penalty, punishment
**casto** (*kahsh*-too) *adj* chaste
**castor** (kersh-*toar*) *m* beaver
**casual** (ker-*zwahl*) *adj* (pl -ais) casual
**catacumba** (ker-ter-*koom*-ber) *f* catacomb
**catálogo** (ker-*tah*-loo-goo) *m* catalogue
**catarro** (ker-*tah*-rroo) *m* catarrh
**catástrofe** (ker-*tahsh*-troo-fer) *f* calamity, disaster, catastrophe
**catedral** (ker-ter-*dhrahl*) *f* (pl -ais) cathedral
**categoria** (ker-ter-goo-*ree*-er) *f* category; sort
**categórico** (ker-ter-*go*-ree-koo) *adj* explicit; downright
**católico** (ker-to-lee-koo) *adj* catholic; Roman Catholic
**catorze** (ker-*toar*-zer) *num* fourteen
**caução** (kou-*serng*ʷ) *f* (pl -ções) guarantee, bail
**cauda** (*kou*-dher) *f* tail
**causa** (*kou*-zer) *f* reason, cause; case; ~ **judicial** lawsuit; **por ~ de** be-

cause of, for; on account of
**causar** (kou-*zahr*) *v* cause
**cautela** (kou-*teh*-ler) *f* caution
**cavaco** (ker-*vah*-koo) *m* chat
**cavala** (ker-*vah*-ler) *f* mackerel
**cavaleiro** (ker-ver-*lay*-roo) *m* horseman, rider; knight
**cavalheiro** (ker-ver-*l*ʸ*ay*-roo) *m* gentleman
**cavalho-de-batalha** (ker-vah-loo-der-ber-*tah*-lʸer) *m* hobby-horse
**cavalo** (ker-*vah*-loo) *m* horse; ~ **de corridas** race-horse
**cavalo-vapor** (ker-vah-loo-ver-*poar*) *m* horsepower
*****cavaquear** (ker-ver-kʸ*ahr*) *v* chat
**cavar** (ker-*vahr*) *v* *****dig
**cave** (*kah*-ver) *f* basement; cellar
**caverna** (kah-*vehr*-ner) *f* cavern; cave
**caviar** (ker-vʸ*ahr*) *m* caviar
**cavidade** (kah-vee-*dhah*-dher) *f* cavity
**cavilha** (ker-*vee*-lʸer) *f* bolt
**caxemira** (ker-sher-*mee*-rer) *f* cashmere
**cebola** (ser-*bhoa*-ler) *f* onion; bulb
**cebolinho** (ser-bhoo-*lee*-ñoo) *m* chives *pl*
**ceder** (ser-*dhayr*) *v* indulge, *****give in
**cedo** (*say*-dhoo) *adv* early
**cegar** (ser-*gahr*) *v* blind
**cego** (*seh*-goo) *adj* blind
**cegonha** (ser-*goa*-ñer) *f* stork
**ceia** (*say*-er) *f* supper
**ceifa** (*say*-fer) *f* harvest
**ceifar** (*say*-fahr) *v* harvest
**celebração** (ser-ler-bhrer-*serng*ʷ) *f* (pl -ções) celebration
**celebrar** (ser-ler-*bhrahr*) *v* celebrate
**celebridade** (ser-ler-bhree-*dhah*-dher) *f* celebrity
**celeiro** (ser-*lay*-roo) *m* barn
**celibatário** (ser-lee-bher-tah-rʸoo) *m* bachelor
**celibato** (ser-lee-*bhah*-too) *m* celibacy

**celofane** (ser-loo-*fer*-ner) *m* cellophane

**célula** (*seh*-loo-ler) *f* cell

**cem** (serng<sup>v</sup>) *num* hundred

**cemitério** (ser-mee-teh-r<sup>y</sup>oo) *m* cemetery, churchyard, graveyard

**cena** (*say*-ner) *f* scene

**cenário** (ser-*nah*-r<sup>y</sup>oo) *m* setting

**cenoura** (ser-*noa*-rer) *f* carrot

**censura** (sayng-*soo*-rer) *f* censorship; reproach; blame

**censurar** (sayng-soo-*rahr*) *v* reproach; blame; censor

**centavo** (sayng-*tah*-voo) *m* 1/100 of an escudo or a cruzeiro

**centena** (sayng-*tay*-ner) *f* some hundred

**centímetro** (sayngn-*tee*-mer troo) *m* centimetre

**central** (sayngn-*trahl*) *adj* (pl -ais) central; ~ **eléctrica** power-station; ~ **telefónica** telephone exchange

**centralizar** (sayngn-trer-lee-*zahr*) *v* centralize

**centro** (*sayngn*-troo) *m* centre; ~ **comercial** shopping centre; ~ **da cidade** town centre; ~ **de saúde** health centre; ~ **recreativo** recreation centre

**cera** (*say*-rer) *f* wax

**cerâmica** (ser-*rer*-mee-ker) *f* pottery, ceramics

**cerca** (*sayr*-ker) *f* fence; ~ **de** about

**cercar** (serr-*kahr*) *v* surround; encircle

**cerco** (*sayr*-koo) *m* siege

**cereal** (ser-r<sup>y</sup>*ahl*) *m* (pl -ais) grain; **cereais** cereals *pl*

**cérebro** (*seh*-rer-bhroo) *m* brain

**cereja** (ser-*ray*-zher) *f* cherry

**cerimónia** (ser-ree-*mo*-n<sup>y</sup>er) *f* ceremony; **sem** ~ informal

**certamente** (sehr-ter-*mayngn*-ter) *adv* surely, naturally

**certeza** (serr-*tay*-zer) *f* certainty; **com** ~ of course

**certidão** (serr-tee-*dherng*<sup>w</sup>) *f* (pl -dões) certificate

**certificado** (serr-ter-fee-*kah*-dhoo) *m* certificate

**certificar** (serr-ter-fee-*kahr*) *v* certify; **certificar-se de** ascertain

**certo** (*sehr*-too) *adj* sure, certain; correct; **certos** some

**cerveja** (serr-*vay*-zher) *f* ale, beer; **fábrica de** ~ brewery; **fabricar** ~ brew

**cervejaria** (serr-vɪ-zher-*ree*-er) *f* pub

**cessar** (ser-*sahr*) *v* quit, stop, discontinue, cease

**cesta** (*saysh*-ter) *f* hamper

**cesto** (*saysh*-too) *m* basket; ~ **dos papéis** wastepaper-basket

**cetim** (ser-*teeng*) *m* satin

**céu** (seh<sup>oo</sup>) *m* heaven, sky

**cevada** (ser-*vah*-dher) *f* barley

**chá** (shah) *m* tea; **salão de** ~ tea-shop

**chalé** (shah-*leh*) *m* chalet

**chaleira** (sher-*lay*-rer) *f* kettle

**chama** (*sher*-mer) *f* flame

**chamada** (sher-*mah*-dher) *f* call; ~ **interurbana** trunk-call; ~ **local** local call; ~ **telefónica** telephone call

**chamar** (sher-*mahr*) *v* cry, call; name; recall; **chamar-se** *be called

**chaminé** (sher-mee-*neh*) *f* chimney

**champanhe** (sherngm-*per*-ñer) *m* champagne

**champô** (sherngm-*poa*) *m* shampoo

**chantagem** (sherngn-*tah*-zherng<sup>v</sup>) *f* blackmail; *fazer ~ blackmail

**chão** (sherng<sup>w</sup>) *m* (pl ~s) floor

**chapa** (*shah*-per) *f* sheet; plate; ~ **da matrícula** registration plate

**chapéu** (sher-*peh*<sup>oo</sup>) *m* hat; **chapeleira de senhoras** milliner

**charco** (*shahr*-koo) *m* puddle

**charlatão** (shahr-ler-*terng*ʷ) *m* (pl -ães) quack

**charneca** (shahr-*neh*-ker) *f* heath; moor

**charuto** (sher-*roo*-too) *m* cigar

**chassi** (sher-*see*) *m* chassis

**chatear** (*shah*-tʸahr) *v* annoy, bother (someone)

**chave** (*sher*-ver) *f* key; ~ **de parafusos** screw-driver; ~ **de porcas** spanner; ~ **de trinco** latchkey

**chave-inglesa** (shah-ver-eeng-*glay*-zer) *f* wrench

**chávena** *f* cup; ~ **de chá** teacup

**checo** (*sheh*-koo) *adj* Czech; *m* Czech

**chefe** (*sheh*-fer) *m* chief; boss, leader, manager; chieftain; ~ **de estação** station-master; ~ **de estado** head of state; ~ **de mesa** head-waiter

**chegada** (sher-*gah*-dher) *f* arrival, coming

**chegado** (sher-*gah*-dhoo) *adj* near

**chegar** (sher-*gahr*) *v* arrive

**cheio** (*shay*-oo) *adj* full

**cheirar** (shay-*rahr*) *v* *smell; ~ **mal** *stink, *smell

**cheiro** (*shay*-roo) *m* smell; **mal cheiroso** smelly

**cheque** (*sheh*-ker) *m* cheque; check *nAm*; **livro de cheques** cheque-book; check-book *nAm*

**chicote** (shee-*ko*-ter) *m* whip

**chifre** (*shee*-frer) *m* horn

**Chile** (*shee*-ler) *m* Chile

**chileno** (shee-*lay*-noo) *adj* Chilean; *m* Chilean

**China** (*shee*-ner) *f* China

**chinês** (shee-*naysh*) *adj* Chinese; *m* Chinese

**chocante** (shoo-*kerng*-ter) *adj* revolting, shocking

**chocar** (shoo-*kahr*) *v* shock; bump, collide; ~ **com** knock against

**chocolate** (shoo-koo-*lah*-ter) *m* chocolate

**choque** (*sho*-ker) *m* shock; crash, collision

**chorar** (shoo-*rahr*) *v* *weep, cry

**chover** (shoo-*vayr*) *v* rain

**chumbo** (*shoongm*-boo) *m* lead

**chupar** (shoo-*pahr*) *v* suck

**churrasqueira** (shoo-rrah-*shkay*-rer) *f* grill-room

**chuva** (*shoo*-ver) *f* rain; ~ **miudinha** drizzle

**chuvada** (shoo-*vah*-dher) *f* cloud-burst

**chuvoso** (shoo-*voa*-zoo) *adj* rainy

**cicatriz** (see-ker-*treesh*) *f* scar

**ciclista** (see-*kleesh*-ter) *m* cyclist

**ciclo** (*see*-kloo) *m* cycle

**cidadania** (see-dher-dher-*nee*-er) *f* citizenship

**cidadão** (see-dher-*dherng*ʷ) *m* (pl ~s) citizen

**cidade** (see-*dhah*-dher) *f* town, city

**ciência** (sʸ*ayng*-sʸer) *f* science; **ciências naturais** physics

**ciente** (sʸ*ayng*-ter) *adj* aware

**científico** (sʸ*ayngn*-*tee*-fee-koo) *adj* scientific

**cientista** (sʸ*ayngn*-*teesh*-ter) *m* scientist

**cigano** (see-*ger*-noo) *m* gipsy

**cigarreira** (see-ger-*rray*-rer) *f* cigarette-case

**cigarro** (see-*gah*-rroo) *m* cigarette

**cilindro** (see-*leengn*-droo) *m* cylinder

**cima** (*see*-mer) *m* summit; **em** ~ above; up; overhead, upstairs; **em** ~ **de** on top of; **para** ~ up, upwards; upstairs; **por** ~ over; **por** ~ **de** over

**cimento** (see-*mayngn*-too) *m* cement

**cimo** (*see*-moo) *m* top

**cinco** (*seeng*-koo) *num* five

**cinema** (see-*nay*-mer) *m* pictures, cinema

**cinquenta** (seeng-kwayngn-ter) num fifty

**cinta** (seengn-ter) f girdle

**cintilante** (seengn-tee-lerngn-ter) adj sparkling

**cinto** (seengn-too) m belt; ~ **de ligas** suspender belt; ~ **de segurança** safety-belt, seat-belt

**cintura** (seeng-too-rer) f waist

**cinza** (seengn-zer) f ash

**cinzeiro** (seeng-zay-roo) m ashtray

**cinzel** (seeng-zehl) m (pl -zéis) chisel

**cinzento** (see-zayngn-too) adj grey

**circo** (seer-koo) m circus

**circuito turístico** (seer-kooee-too too-reezh-tee-koo) tour

**circulação** (seer-koo-ler-serngw) f (pl -ções) circulation

**círculo** (seer-koo-loo) m ring, circle; club; ~ **eleitoral** constituency

**circundar** (seer-koongn-dahr) v circle

**circunstância** (seer-koongsh-terng-sYer) f circumstance; condition

**cirurgião** (see-roor-zhYerngw) m (pl -iões) surgeon

**cisne** (seezh-ner) m swan

**cistite** (seesh-tee-ter) f cystitis

**citação** (see-ter-serngw) f (pl -ções) quotation

**citadino** (see-ter-dhee-noo) m townspeople pl

**citar** (see-tahr) v quote

**ciúme** (sYoo-mer) m jealousy

**ciumento** (sYoo-mayngn-too) adj envious, jealous

**cívico** (see-vee-koo) adj civic

**civil** (see-veel) adj (pl -is) civil, civilian; m civilian

**civilização** (see-ver-lee-zer-serngw) f (pl -ções) civilization

**civilizado** (see-ver-lee-zah-dhoo) adj civilized

**clareira** (kler-ray-rer) f clearing

**claro** (klah-roo) adj bright, light, clear; plain

**classe** (klah-ser) f class, form; ~ **média** middle class; ~ **turística** tourist class

**clássico** (klah-see-koo) adj classical

**classificar** (kler-ser-fee-kahr) v classify; sort, grade, assort

**cláusula** (klou-soo-ler) f clause

**clavícula** (kler-vee-koo-ler) f collarbone

**clemência** (kler-mayng-sYer) f mercy

**clérigo** (kleh-ree-goo) m clergyman

**cliente** (klYayngn-ter) m customer, client

**clima** (klee-mer) m climate

**clínica** (klee-nee-ker) f clinic

**cloro** (klo-roo) m chlorine

**clube** (kloo-bher) m club; **automóvel** ~ automobile club; ~ **náutico** yacht-club; ~ **nocturno** cabaret

**coador** (kwer-dhoar) m strainer

**coagular** (kwer-goo-lahr) v coagulate

**cobarde** (koo-bhahr-der) adj cowardly; m coward

**cobertor** (koo-bherr-toar) m blanket

**cobiçar** (koo-bhee-sahr) v desire

**cobrador** (koo-bhrer-dhoar) m conductor

**cobre** (ko-bhrer) m copper

***cobrir** (koo-bhreer) v cover

**coçado** (koo-sah-dhoo) adj threadbare

**cocaína** (koo-ker-ee-ner) f cocaine

***fazer cócegas** (fer-zayr ko-ser-gersh) tickle

**coche** (koa-sher) m coach, carriage

**coco** (koa-koo) m coconut

**côdea** (koa-dhYer) f crust

**código** (ko-dhee-goo) m code; ~ **postal** zip code Am

**codorniz** (koo-dhoor-neesh) f quail

**coelho** (kway-lYoo) m rabbit

**coerência** (kwer-rayng-sYer) f coherence

**cofre-forte** (ko-frer-*for*-ter) *m* safe

**cogumelo** (koo-goo-*meh*-loo) *m* mushroom; toadstool

**coincidência** (kweeng-see-*dhayng*-s*Y*er) *f* concurrence, coincidence

**coincidir** (kweeng-see-*dheer*) *v* coincide

**coisa** (*koi*-zer) *f* thing; **alguma ~** something; **entre outras coisas** among other things; **qualquer ~** anything

**cola** (*ko*-ler) *f* glue, gum

**colaborador** (koo-ler-bhoo-rer-*dhoar*) *adj* co-operative; *m* collaborator

**colar** (koo-*lahr*) *v* paste; *stick; *m* beads, necklace

**colarinho** (koo-ler-*ree*-ñoo) *m* collar

**colcha** (*koal*-sher) *f* quilt; counterpane

**colchão** (koal-*sherng*ᵂ) *m* (pl -hões) mattress

**colecção** (koo-leh-*serng*ᵂ) *f* (pl -ções) collection; **~ de obras de arte** art collection

**coleccionador** (koo-leh-s*Y*oo-ner-*dhoar*) *m* collector

**coleccionar** (koo-leh-s*Y*oo-*nahr*) *v* gather, collect

**colectivo** (koo-leh-*tee*-voo) *adj* collective

**colector** (koo-leh-*toar*) *m* collector

**colega** (koo-*leh*-ger) *m* colleague; **~ de classe** *Br* class-mate; **~ de turma** class-mate

**colégio** (koo-*leh*-z*Y*oo) *m* college; **~ interno** boarding-school

**coleira** (koo-*lay*-rer) *f* collar

**cólera** (*ko*-ler-rer) *f* anger

**colete** (koo-*lay*-ter) *m* waistcoat; vest *nAm;* **~ salva-vidas** life jacket

**colheita** (koo-*lᵞay*-ter) *f* crop, harvest

**colher**[1] (koo-*lᵞayr*) *f* spoon; **~ de chá** teaspoon; **~ de sopa** soup-spoon, tablespoon

**colher**[2] (koo-*lᵞayr*) *v* pick; gather

**colherada** (koo-lᵞer-*rah*-dher) *f* spoonful

**colidir** (koo-lee-*dheer*) *v* collide, crash

**colina** (koo-*lee*-ner) *f* hill

**colisão** (koo-lee-*zerng*ᵂ) *f* (pl -sões) collision

**collants** (koo-*lerngsh*) *mpl* tights *pl*

**colmeia** (koal-*may*-er) *f* beehive

**colocar** (koo-loo-*kahr*) *v* *put; *lay, place

**Colômbia** (koo-*lawng*-bᵞer) *f* Colombia

**colombiano** (koo-lawng-bᵞer-noo) *adj* Colombian; *m* Colombian

**colónia** (koo-*lo*-nᵞer) *f* colony; **~ de férias** holiday camp

**colorido** (koo-loo-*ree*-dhoo) *adj* colourful

***colorir** (koo-loo-*reer*) *v* colour, paint

**coluna** (koo-*loo*-ner) *f* pillar, column; **~ de direcção** steering-column

**com** (kawng) *prep* with

**coma** (*koa*-mer) *m* coma

**comandante** (koo-merngn-*derngn*-ter) *m* commander, captain

**comandar** (koo-merngn-*dahr*) *v* command

**comando** (koo-*merngn*-doo) *m* order

**combate** (kawngm-*bah*-ter) *m* battle, struggle, combat

**combater** (kawngm-ber-*tayr*) *v* combat; *fight, battle

**combinação** (kawngm-bee-ner-*serng*ᵂ) *f* (pl -ções) combination

**combinar** (kawngm-bee-*nahr*) *v* combine

**comboio** (kawngm-*boi*-oo) *m* train; **~ correio** stopping train; **~ de mercadorias** goods train; **~ de passageiros** passenger train; **~ directo** through train; **~ nocturno** night train; **~ rápido** express train; **~ suburbano** local train

**combustível** (kawngm-boosh-*tee*-vehl) *m* (pl -eis) fuel

**começar** (koo-mer-*sahr*) *v* *begin, commence, start

**começo** (koo-*mer*-soo) *m* start

**comédia** (koo-*meh*-dh<sup>Y</sup>er) *f* comedy; ~ **musical** musical comedy

**comediante** (koo-mer-dh<sup>Y</sup>erngn-ter) *m* comedian

**comemoração** (koo-mer-moo-rer-*serng*<sup>w</sup>) *f* (pl -ções) commemoration

**comentar** (koo-mayngn-*tahr*) *v* comment

**comentário** (koo-mayngn-*tah*-r<sup>Y</sup>oo) *m* comment

**comer** (koo-*mayr*) *v* *eat

**comercial** (koo-merr-s<sup>Y</sup>*ahl*) *adj* (pl -ais) commercial

**comerciante** (koo-merr-s<sup>Y</sup>*erngn*-ter) *m* merchant, tradesman, trader

**comércio** (koo-*mehr*-s<sup>Y</sup>oo) *m* commerce; business, trade; ~ **a retalho** retail trade

**comestível** (koo-mersh-*tee*-vehl) *adj* (pl -eis) edible

**cometer** (koo-mer-*tayr*) *v* commit

**comichão** (koo-mee-*sherng*<sup>w</sup>) *f* (pl -hões) itch; *ter ~ itch

**cómico** (*ko*-mee-koo) *adj* comic; *m* comedian

**comida** (koo-*mee*-dher) *f* food; fare; ~ **congelada** frozen food

**comigo** (koo-*mee*-goo) with me

**comissão** (koo-mee-*serng*<sup>w</sup>) *f* (pl -sões) commission; committee

**comissário** (koo-mee-*sahr*-Yoo) *m* commissioner; ~ **de bordo** steward

**comité** (koo-mee-*teh*) *m* committee

**como** (*koa*-moo) *conj* as, like; *adv* how; ~ **se** as if

**comoção cerebral** (koo-moo-*serng*<sup>w</sup> ser-rer-*bhrahl*) concussion

**cómoda** (*ko*-moo-dher) *f* chest of drawers; bureau *nAm*

**comodidade** (koo-moo-dhee-*dhah*-dher) *f* comfort

**cómodo** (*ko*-moo-dhoo) *adj* convenient, easy

**comover** (koo-moo-*vayr*) *v* move

**compacto** (kawngm-*pahk*-too) *adj* compact

**compaixão** (kawngm-pigh-*sherng*<sup>w</sup>) *f* sympathy

**companheiro** (kawngm-per-*ñay*-roo) *m* companion; associate

**companhia** (kawngm-per-*ñee*-er) *f* company; society; ~ **de aviação** airline; ~ **de navegação** shipping line

**comparação** (kawngm-per-rer-*serng*<sup>w</sup>) *f* (pl -ções) comparison

**comparar** (kawngm-per-*rahr*) *v* compare

**compartimento** (kawngm-perr-tee-*mayngn*-too) *m* compartment; ~ **para fumadores** smoker; smoking-compartment

**compatriota** (kawngm-per-tr<sup>Y</sup>o-ter) *m* countryman

**compêndio** (kawngm-*payngn*-d<sup>Y</sup>oo) *m* textbook

**compensação** (kawngm-payng-ser-*serng*<sup>w</sup>) *f* (pl -ções) indemnity, compensation

**compensar** (kawngm-payng-*sahr*) *v* compensate; *pay; *make good

**competência** (kawngm-per-*tayng*-s<sup>Y</sup>er) *f* capacity, competence

**competente** (kawngm-per-*tayngn*-ter) *adj* qualified, expert, competent

**competição** (kawngm-per-tee-*serng*<sup>w</sup>) *f* (pl -ções) competition

**competir** (kawngm-per-*teer*) *v* compete

**compilar** (kawngm-pee-*lahr*) *v* compile

**completamente** (kawngm-pler-ter-

*mayngn*-ter) *adv* completely; quite, wholly

**completar** (kawngm-pler-*tahr*) *v* complete

**completo** (kawngm-*pleh*-too) *adj* complete; utter, total, whole

**complexo** (kawngm-*pleh*-ksoo) *adj* complex; *m* complex

**complicado** (kawngm-plee-*kah*-dhoo) *adj* complicated

***compor** (kawngm-*poar*) *v* *make up, compose

**comporta** (kawngm-*por*-ter) *f* sluice, lock

**comportamento** (kawngm-poor-ter-*mayngn*-too) *m* behaviour

**comportar-se** (kawngm-poor-*tahr*-ser) *v* act

**composição** (kawngm-poo-zee-*serng*ᵂ) *f* (pl -ções) composition; essay

**compositor** (kawngm-poo-zee-*toar*) *m* composer

**compra** (*kawngm*-prer) *f* purchase; ***fazer compras** shop

**comprador** (kawngm-prer-*dhoar*) *m* buyer, purchaser

**comprar** (kawngm-*prahr*) *v* *buy, purchase

**compreender** (kawngm-prᵞayngn-*dayr*) *v* *understand; *take, conceive, *see; comprise; ~ **mal** *misunderstand

**compreensão** (kawngm-prᵞayng-*serng*ᵂ) *f* (pl -sões) insight; understanding

**compreensivo** (kawngm-prᵞayng-see-voo) *adj* sympathetic, understanding

**comprido** (kawngm-*pree*-dhoo) *adj* long

**comprimento** (kawngm-pree-*mayngn*-too) *m* length; ~ **de onda** wavelength

**comprimido** (kawngm-pree-*mee*-dhoo)

*m* pill; ~ **para dormir** sleeping-pill

**comprometer-se** (kawngm-proo-mer-*tayr*-ser) *v* engage

**compromisso** (kawngm-proo-*mee*-soo) *m* compromise; engagement

**computador** (kawngm-poo-ter-*dhoar*) *m* computer

**comum** (koo-*moong*) *adj* common; plain

**comuna** (koo-*moo*-ner) *f* commune

**comunicação** (koo-moo-nee-ker-*serng*ᵂ) *f* (pl -ções) information, communication

**comunicar** (koo-moo-nee-*kahr*) *v* inform, communicate

**comunidade** (koo-moo-nee-*dhah*-dher) *f* community; congregation

**comunismo** (koo-moo-*neezh*-moo) *m* communism

**comunista** (koo-moo-*neesh*-ter) *m* communist

**conceber** (kawng-ser-*bhayr*) *v* conceive

**conceder** (kawng-ser-*dayr*) *v* extend, grant

**conceito** (kawng-*say*-too) *m* idea

**concentração** (kawng-sayngn-trer-*serng*ᵂ) *f* (pl -ções) concentration

**concentrar** (kawng-sayngn-*trahr*) *v* concentrate

**concepção** (kawng-sehp-*serng*ᵂ) *f* (pl -ções) conception

**concerto** (kawng-*sayr*-too) *m* concert

**concessão** (kawng-ser-*serng*ᵂ) *f* (pl -sões) concession

**concha** (*kawng*-sher) *f* sea-shell, shell

**conciso** (kawng-*see*-zoo) *adj* concise

**conclusão** (kawng-kloo-*zerng*ᵂ) *f* (pl -sões) conclusion; end, issue

**concordar** (kawng-koor-*dahr*) *v* agree; ~ **com** approve of

**concorrência** (kawng-koo-*rrayng*-sᵞer) *f* rivalry, competition

**concorrente** (kawng-koo-*rrayngn*-ter)

*m* competitor

**concreto** (kawng-*kreh*-too) *adj* concrete; *mBr* concrete

**concurso** (kawng-*koor*-soo) *m* contest; quiz

**condenação** (kawng-der-ner-*serng*ʷ) *f* (pl -ções) conviction

**condenado** (kawng-der-*nah*-dhoo) *m* convict

**condenar** (kawng-der-*nahr*) *v* sentence; condemn; disapprove

**condição** (kawng-dee-*serng*ʷ) *f* (pl -ções) condition; term; **à ~** on approval

**condicionador de cabelos** (kawng-dee-s*Ɏ*oo-ner-*dhoar* der ker-*bhay*-loosh) *m* conditioner

**condicional** (kawng-dee-s*Ɏ*oo-*nahl*) *adj* (pl -ais) conditional

**condimentado** (kawng-dee-mayngn-*tah*-dhoo) *adj* spiced

*****condizer** (kawng-dee-*zayr*) *v* fit; **~ com** match

*****condoer-se de** (kawng-*dwayr*-ser) pity

**conduta** (kawng-*doo*-tah) *f* conduct

**condutor** (kawng-doo-*toar*) *m* driver

*****conduzir** (kawng-doo-*zeer*) *v* carry, conduct; *****drive

**confederação** (kawng-fer-dher-rer-*serng*ʷ) *f* (pl -ções) union

**confeitaria** (kawng-fay-ter-*ree*-er) *f* sweetshop

**confeiteiro** (kawng-fay-*tay*-roo) *m* confectioner

**conferência** (kawng-fer-*rayng*-s*Ɏ*er) *f* conference; lecture; **~ de imprensa** press conference

*****conferir** (kawng-fer-*reer*) *v* check; award

**confessar-se** (kawng-fer-*sahr*-ser) *v* confess

**confiança** (kawng-f*Ɏ*erng-ser) *f* confidence; trust, faith; **de ~** reliable;

**digno de ~** trustworthy; **indigno de ~** unreliable; untrustworthy

**confiante** (kawng-f*Ɏ*erngn-ter) *adj* confident

**confiar** (kawng-f*Ɏ*ahr) *v* commit; entrust; **~ em** trust

**confidencial** (kawng-fee-dhayng-s*Ɏ*erl) *adj* (pl -ais) confidential

**confirmação** (kawng-feer-mer-*serng*ʷ) *f* (pl -ções) confirmation

**confirmar** (kawng-feer-*mahr*) *v* confirm

**confiscar** (kawng-feesh-*kahr*) *v* confiscate

**confissão** (kawng-fee-*serng*ʷ) *f* (pl -sões) confession

**conflito** (kawng-*flee*-too) *m* conflict

**conforme** (kawng-*for*-mer) *adv* according to; in accordance with; *adj* conform

**confortar** (kawng-foor-*tahr*) *v* comfort

**confortável** (kawng-foor-*tah*-vehl) *adj* (pl -eis) comfortable

**conforto** (kawng-*foar*-too) *m* comfort

**confundir** (kawng-foongn-*deer*) *v* confuse; *****mistake

**confusão** (kawng-foo-*zerng*ʷ) *f* (pl -sões) confusion; muddle

**confuso** (kawng-*foo*-zoo) *adj* confused; obscure

**congelador** (kawng-zher-ler-*dhoar*) *m* deep-freeze

**congelar** (kawng-zher-*lahr*) *v* *****freeze

**congratular** (kawng-grer-too-*lahr*) *v* congratulate

**congregação** (kawng-grer-ger-*serng*ʷ) *f* (pl -ções) congregation

**congresso** (kawng-*greh*-soo) *m* congress

**conhaque** (ko-*ñah*-ker) *m* cognac

**conhecedor** (koo-ñer-ser-*dhoar*) *m* connoisseur

**conhecer** (koo-ñer-*sayr*) *v* *****know

**conhecido** (koo-ñer-*see*-dhoo) *adj*

well-known; *m* acquaintance

**conhecimento** (koo-ñer-see-*mayngn*-too) *m* knowledge; acquaintance

**conjectura** (kawng-zheh-*too*-rah) *f* guess

**conjuntamente** (kawng-zhoongn-ter-*mayngn*-ter) *adv* jointly

**conjunto** (kawng-*zhoon*-too) *adj* joint; *m* a whole

**conjura** (kawng-*zhoo*-rer) *f* plot

**connosco** (kawng-*noash*-koo) with us

**conquista** (kawng-*keesh*-ter) *f* conquest

**conquistador** (kawng-keesh-ter-*dhoar*) *m* conqueror

**conquistar** (kawng-keesh-*tahr*) *v* conquer

**consciência** (kawngsh-s*Yayng*-s*Y*er) *f* consciousness; conscience

**consciente** (kawngsh-s*Yayngn*-ter) *adj* conscious

*****conseguir** (kawng-ser-*geer*) *v* obtain; manage, succeed in

**conselheiro** (kawng-ser-l*Yay*-roo) *m* counsellor; councillor

**conselho** (kawng-*say*-l*Y*oo) *m* advice; council, counsel; board

**consentimento** (kawng-sayngn-tee-*mayngn*-too) *m* consent

*****consentir** (kawng-sayngn-*teer*) *v* agree, consent; allow

**consequência** (kawng-ser-*kwayng*-s*Y*er) *f* consequence; issue, result; **em ~ de** as a result of

**consequentemente** (kawng-ser-kwayngn-ter-*mayngn*-ter) *adv* consequently

**consertar** (kawng-serr-*tahr*) *v* repair, mend

**conserto** (kawng-*sayr*-too) *m* repair

**conservação** (kawng-serr-ver-*serng*ʷ) *f* (pl -ções) preservation

**conservador** (kawng-serr-ver-*dhoar*) *adj* conservative

**conservar** (kawng-serr-*vahr*) *v* preserve; maintain

**conservas** (kawng-*sehr*-versh) *fpl* tinned food; **~ em vinagre** pickles *pl*; *****pôr em conserva** preserve

**conservatório** (kawng-serr-ver-*to*-r*Y*oo) *m* music academy

**consideração** (kawng-see-dher-rer-*serng*ʷ) *f* (pl -ções) consideration

**considerar** (kawng-see-dher-*rahr*) *v* regard, consider, count, reckon

**considerável** (kawng-see-dher-*rah*-vehl) *adj* (pl -eis) considerable

**consigo** (kawng-*see*-goo) with you

**consistir em** (kawng-seesh-*teer*) consist of

**consolação** (kawng-soo-ler-*serng*ʷ) *f* (pl -ções) comfort

**consolar** (kawng-soo-*lahr*) *v* comfort

**conspiração** (kawngsh-pee-rer-*serng*ʷ) *f* (pl -ções) plot

**conspirar** (kawngsh-pee-*rahr*) *v* conspire

**constante** (kawngsh-*terngn*-ter) *adj* constant; even, steadfast

**constatar** (kawngsh-ter-*tahr*) *v* ascertain; note, diagnose

**constipação** (kawngsh-tee-per-*serng*ʷ) *f* (pl -ções) cold

**constipar-se** (kawngsh-tee-*pahr*-ser) *v* *****catch a cold

**constituição** (kawngsh-tee-twee-*serng*ʷ) *f* (pl -ções) constitution

**construção** (kawngsh-troo-*serng*ʷ) *f* (pl -ções) construction

*****construir** (kawngsh-*trweer*) *v* *****build, construct

**cônsul** (*kawng*-sool) *m* (pl ~es) consul

**consulado** (kawng-soo-*lah*-dhoo) *m* consulate

**consulta** (kawng-*sool*-ter) *f* consultation; appointment

**consultar** (kawng-sool-*tahr*) *v* consult

**consultório** (kawng-sool-to-rᵞoo) m surgery

**consumidor** (kawng-soo-mee-dhoar) m consumer

*consumir** (kawng-soo-meer) v use up

**conta** (kawngn-ter) f account; bill; bead; check nAm; ~ **bancária** bank account

**contactar com** (kawngn-ter-tahr) contact

**contacto** (kawngn-tah-too) m contact; touch

**contador** (kawngn-ter-dhoar) m meter

**contagioso** (kawngn-ter-zhᵞoa-zoo) adj contagious

**contanto que** (kawngn-terngn-too ker) provided that

**contar** (kawngn-tahr) v count; relate, *tell; ~ **com** rely on

**contemporâneo** (kawngn-tayngm-poo-rer-nᵞoo) adj contemporary; m contemporary

**contente** (kawngn-tayngn-ter) adj happy, glad, joyful

*conter** (kawngn-tayr) v contain; comprise; restrain

**contestar** (kawngn-tish-tahr) v dispute

**conteúdo** (kawngn-tᵞoo-dhoo) m contents pl

**contextura** (kawngn-tish-too-rer) f texture

**contigo** (kawngn-tee-goo) with you

**contíguo** (kawngn-tee-gwoo) adj neighbouring

**continental** (kawngn-tee-nayngn-tahl) adj (pl -ais) continental

**continente** (kawngn-tee-nayngn-ter) m continent

**continuação** (kawngn-tee-nwer-serngʷ) f (pl -ções) sequel

**continuamente** (kawngn-tee-nwer-mayngn-ter) adv continually, all the time

**continuar** (kawngn-tee-nwahr) v carry

on, continue; *keep on; *go on, *go ahead

**contínuo** (kawngn-tee-nwoo) adj continuous; continual

**conto** (kawngn-too) m tale

**contornar** (kawngn-toor-nahr) v bypass

**contorno** (kawngn-toar-noo) m contour, outline

**contra** (kawngn-trer) prep versus, against

*contrabandear** (kawngn-trer-bherngn-dᵞahr) v smuggle

**contraceptivo** (kawngn-trer-seh-tee-voo) m contraceptive

**contraditório** (kawngn-trer-dhee-to-rᵞoo) adj contradictory

*contradizer** (kawngn-trer-dhee-zayr) v contradict

*contrair** (kawngn-trer-eer) v contract

**contralto** (kawngn-trahl-too) m alto

**contrário** (kawngn-trah-rᵞoo) adj opposite, contrary; m reverse, contrary; **ao** ~ the other way round; **pelo** ~ on the contrary

**contraste** (kawngn-trahsh-ter) m contrast

**contratar** (kawngn-trer-tahr) v engage

**contrato** (kawngn-trah-too) m agreement, contract; ~ **de arrendamento** lease

**contribuição** (kawngn-tree-bhwee-serngʷ) f (pl -ções) contribution

**controlar** (kawngn-troo-lahr) v control

**controle** (kawngn-troa-ler) m control

**controverso** (kawngn-troo-vehr-soo) adj controversial

**contudo** (kawngn-too-dhoo) conj however, yet

**contusão** (kawngn-too-zerngʷ) f (pl -sões) bruise

**convencer** (kawng-vayng-sayr) v convince; persuade

**conveniente** (kawng-ver-nᵞayngn-ter)

*adj* convenient

**convento** (kawng-*vayngn*-too) *m* cloister, convent; nunnery

**conversa** (kawng-*vehr*-ser) *f* talk, discussion, conversation; chat

**conversação** (kawng-verr-ser-*serng*ᵂ) *f* (pl -ções) conversation

**conversar** (kawng-verr-*sahr*) *v* chat

**converter** (kawng-verr-*tayr*) *v* convert

**convés** (kawng-*vehsh*) *m* deck; **camarote de** ~ deck cabin; ~ **principal** main deck

**convicção** (kawng-veek-*serng*ᵂ) *f* (pl -ções) conviction, persuasion

**convidado** (kawng-vee-*dhah*-dhoo) *m* guest

**convidar** (kawng-vee-*dhahr*) *v* invite; ask

**\*convir** (kawng-*veer*) *v* suit

**convite** (kawng-vee-ter) *m* invitation

**convocação** (kawng-voo-ker-*serng*ᵂ) *f* (pl -ções) summons

**convulsão** (kawng-vool-*serng*ᵂ) *f* (pl -sões) convulsion

**cooperação** (kwoa-per-rer-*serng*ᵂ) *f* (pl -ções) co-operation

**cooperador** (kwoa-perrer-*dhoar*) *adj* co-operative

**cooperativa** (kwoa-per-rer-*tee*-ver) *f* co-operative

**cooperativo** (kwoa-per-rer-*tee*-voo) *adj* co-operative

**coordenação** (kwoar-der-ner-*serng*ᵂ) *f* (pl -ções) co-ordination

**coordenar** (kwoar-der-*nahr*) *v* co-ordinate

**cópia** (*ko*-pᵛer) *f* copy

**copiar** (koo-pᵛ*ahr*) *v* copy

**copo** (*ko*-poo) *m* glass; tumbler; **copinho para os ovos** egg-cup

**coquetel** (ko-ker-*tehl*) *mBr* cocktail

**cor** (koar) *f* colour; **de** ~ coloured; by heart; **de** ~ **fixa** fast-dyed

**coração** (koo-rer-*serng*ᵂ) *m* (pl -ções) heart; core; **ataque de** ~ heart attack

**coragem** (koo-*rah*-zhemgᵛ) *f* courage; guts

**corajoso** (koo-rer-*zhoa*-zoo) *adj* brave, courageous

**coral** (koo-*rahl*) *m* (pl -ais) coral

**corante** (ko-*rerngn*-ter) *m* colourant

**corar** (ko-*rahr*) *v* blush

**corda** (*kor*-der) *f* rope; cord; **\*dar** ~ **\*wind**

**cordão** (koor-*derng*ᵂ) *m* (pl -dões) string, cord

**cordeiro** (koor-*dhay*-roo) *m* lamb

**cordel** (koor-*dehl*) *m* (pl -déis) string

**cor-de-laranja** (koar-der-ler-*rerng*-zher) *adj* orange

**cor-de-rosa** (koar-der-*rro*-zer) *adj* pink

**cordial** (koor-dᵛ*ahl*) *adj* (pl -ais) cordial, amiable

**cordilheira** (koor-dee-lᵛ*ay*-rer) *f* mountain range

**coro** (*koa*-roo) *m* choir

**coroa** (koo-*roa*-er) *f* crown

**coroar** (koo-*rwahr*) *v* crown

**coronel** (koo-roo-*nehl*) *m* (pl-néis) colonel

**corpete** (koor-*pay*-ter) *m* corset

**corpo** (*koar*-poo) *m* body

**corpulento** (koor-poo-*layngn*-too) *adj* corpulent; stout

**correcção** (koo-rreh-*serng*ᵂ) *f* (pl -ções) correction

**correcto** (koo-*reh*-too) *adj* correct; right

**corredor** (koo-rrer-*dhoar*) *m* corridor

**correia** (koo-*rray*-er) *f* strap; ~ **de relógio** watch-strap; ~ **de ventoinha** fan belt

**correio** (koo-*rray*-oo) *m* post, mail; **caixa do** ~ letter-box; pillar-box; mailbox *nAm;* ~ **aéreo** airmail; **correios** postal service; post-office; **deitar no** ~ post; **\*pôr no** ~ mail

**corrente** (koo-*rrayngn*-ter) *adj* current; regular; *f* stream, current; chain; ~ **alterna** alternating current; ~ **contínua** direct current; **\*pôr ao** ~ inform

**correr** (koo-*rrayr*) *v* \*run; stream, flow

**correspondência** (koo-rrısh-pawngn-*dayng*-sᵛer) *f* correspondence; connection

**correspondente** (koo-rrısh-pawngn-*dayngn*-ter) *m* correspondent

**corresponder** (koo-rrısh-pawngn-*dayr*) *v* correspond

**corretor** (koo-rrer-*toar*) *m* broker; ~ **de apostas** bookmaker

**corrida** (koo-*rree*-dher) *f* race; ~ **de cavalos** horserace; **pista de corridas** race-course, race-track

**corrigir** (koo-rree-*zheer*) *v* correct

**corrimão** (koo-rree-*merng*ᵂ) *m* (pl ~s) banisters *pl*

**corromper** (koo-rrawngm-*payr*) *v* corrupt

**corrupção** (koo-rroo-*serng*ᵂ) *f* (pl -ções) corruption

**corrupto** (koo-*rroop*-too) *adj* corrupt

**corta-papel** (kor-ter-per-*pehl*) *m* paper-knife

**cortar** (koor-*tahr*) *v* \*cut; \*cut off, chop

**corte**[1] (*kor*-ter) *m* cut; ~ **de cabelo** haircut

**corte**[2] (*koar*-ter) *f* court

**cortejo** (koor-*tay*-zhoo) *m* procession

**cortês** (koor-*taysh*) *adj* courteous

**cortina** (koor-*tee*-ner) *f* curtain

**corvo** (*koar*-voo) *m* raven

**coser** (koo-*zayr*) *v* \*sew

**cosméticos** (koozh-*meh*-tee-koosh) *mpl* cosmetics *pl*

**costa** (*kosh*-ter) *f* coast; **costas** back

**costela** (koosh-*teh*-ler) *f* rib

**costeleta** (koosh-ter-*lay*-ter) *f* cutlet, chop

**costumado** (er-koosh-too-*mah*-dhoo) *adj* accustomed, customary

**costume** (koosh-*too*-mer) *m* custom; **como de** ~ as usual; **costumes** morals; **\*ter por** ~ \*be in the habit of

**costura** (koosh-*too*-rer) *f* needlework; seam; **sem** ~ seamless

**cotovelo** (koo-too-*vay*-loo) *m* elbow

**cotovia** (koo-too-*vee*-ah) *f* lark

**couro** (*koa*-roo) *m* leather

**couve** (*koa*-ver) *f* cabbage; **couve-de-bruxelas** sprouts *pl*; **couve-flor** cauliflower

**cova** (*ko*-ver) *f* pit, hole

**coxa** (*koa*-sher) *f* thigh

**\*coxear** (koo-*sh*ᵛ*ahr*) *v* limp

**coxo** (*koa*-shoo) *adj* lame

**cozer** (koo-*zayr*) *v* cook, boil, bake

**cozinha** (koo-*zee*-ñer) *f* kitchen; **livro de** ~ cookery-book

**cozinhar** (koo-zee-*ñahr*) *v* cook; ~ **no forno** bake

**cozinheiro** (koo-zee-*ñay*-roo) *m* cook

**cozinheiro-chefe** (koo-zee-ñay-roo-*sheh*-fer) *m* chef

**crânio** (*krer*-nᵛoo) *m* skull

**cratera** (krer-*teh*-rer) *f* crater

**cravo** (*krer*-voo) *m* harpsichord; carnation

**creche** (*kreh*-sher) *f* nursery

**creditar** (krer-dhee-*tahr*) *v* credit

**crédito** (*kreh*-dhee-too) *m* credit

**credor** (kreh-*dhoar*) *m* creditor

**crédulo** (*kreh*-dhoo-loo) *adj* credulous

**creme** (*kreh*-mer) *m* cream; *adj* cream; ~ **de base** foundation cream; ~ **de beleza** face-cream; ~ **de noite** night-cream; ~ **hidratante** moisturizing cream; ~ **para a barba** shaving-cream; ~ **para a pele** skin cream; ~ **para as mãos** hand cream; ~ **para o cabelo** hair

cream
**cremoso** (krer-*moa*-zoo) *adj* creamy
**crença** (*krayng*-ser) *f* belief
**crepúsculo** (krer-*poosh*-koo-loo) *m* twilight
***crer** (krayr) *v* believe
**crescer** (krish-*sayr*) *v* *grow; increase
**crescimento** (krish-see-*mayngn*-too) *m* growth
**criada** (*krYah*-dher) *f* maid; ~ **de quarto** chambermaid
**criado** (*krYah*-dhoo) *m* servant; valet, boy, waiter; ~ **de café** waiter; ~ **de quarto** valet
**criança** (krYerng-ser) *f* child, kid; ~ **de peito** infant; ~ **pequena** tot; ~ **pequenina** toddler
**criar** (krYahr) *v* create; *bring up, rear; raise, *breed
**criatura** (krYer-*too*-rer) *f* creature
**crime** (*kree*-mer) *m* crime
**criminal** (kree-mee-*nahl*) *adj* (pl -ais) criminal
**criminalidade** (kree-mee-ner-lee-*dhah*-dher) *f* criminality
**criminoso** (kree-mee-*noa*-zoo) *adj* criminal; *m* criminal
**críquete** (*kree*-kert) *m* cricket
**crise** (*kree*-zer) *f* crisis
**cristal** (kreesh-*tahl*) *m* (pl -ais) crystal; **de** ~ crystal
**cristão** (kreesh-*terngw*) *adj* (pl ~s) Christian; *m* Christian
**Cristo** (*kreesh*-too) Christ
**crítica** (*kree*-tee-ker) *f* criticism; review
**criticar** (kree-tee-*kahr*) *v* criticize
**crítico** (*kree*-tee-koo) *adj* critical; *m* critic
**crocodilo** (kroo-koo-*dhee*-loo) *m* crocodile
**crómio** (*kro*-mYoo) *m* chromium
**crónico** (*kro*-nee-koo) *adj* chronic
**cronológico** (kroo-noo-*lo*-zhee-koo) *adj* chronological
**cru** (kroo) *adj* raw
**crucificação** (kroo-ser-fee-ker-*serngw*) *f* (pl -ções) crucifixion
**crucificar** (kroo-ser-fee-*kahr*) *v* crucify
**crucifixo** (kroo-ser-*feek*-soo) *m* crucifix
**cruel** (krwehl) *adj* (pl cruéis) harsh, cruel
**cruz** (kroosh) *f* cross
**cruzada** (kroo-*zah*-dher) *f* crusade
**cruzamento** (kroo-zer-*mayngn*-too) *m* crossroads; junction
**cruzar** (kroo-*zahr*) *v* cross
**cruzeiro** (kroo-*zay*-roo) *m* cruise; *mBr* Brazilian monetary unit
**Cuba** (*koo*-bher) *f* Cuba
**cubano** (koo-*bhah*-noo) *adj* Cuban; *m* Cuban
**cubo** (*koo*-bhoo) *m* cube
**cuco** (*koo*-koo) *m* cuckoo
**cuecas** (*kweh*-kersh) *fpl* pants *pl*, drawers, briefs *pl*; shorts *plAm*
**cuidado** (kwee-*dhah*-dhoo) *m* care; *ter ~ beware, look out; **tomar** ~ watch out
**cuidadoso** (kwee-dher-*dhoa*-zoo) *adj* careful
**cuidar** (kwee-*dahr*) *v* tend; ~ **de** *take care of; look after
**culpa** (*kool*-per) *f* fault, blame; guilt
**culpado** (kool-*pah*-dhoo) *adj* guilty
**culpar** (kool-*pahr*) *v* blame
**cultivar** (kool-tee-*vahr*) *v* raise, cultivate; *grow
**culto** (*kool*-too) *adj* cultured; *m* worship
**cultura** (kool-*too*-rer) *f* culture
**cume** (*koo*-mer) *m* peak
**cumeada** (koo-*mYah*-dher) *f* ridge
**cúmplice** (*koongm*-plee-ser) *m* accomplice
**cumprimentar** (koongm-pree-*mayngn*-tahr) *v* greet; compliment

**cumprimento** (koongm-pree-*mayngn*-too) *m* compliment

**cumprir** (koongm-*preer*) *v* perform

**cunha** (*koo*-ñer) *f* wedge

**cunhada** (koo-*ñah*-dher) *f* sister-in-law

**cunhado** (koo-*ñah*-dhoo) *m* brother-in-law

**cupão** (koo-*perng*ʷ) *m* (pl cupões) coupon

**cupidez** (koo-pee-*dhaysh*) *f* greed

**cúpula** (*koo*-poo-ler) *f* dome

**cura** (*koo*-rer) *f* cure; recovery

**curandeiro** (koo-rerngn-*day*-roo) *m* quack

**curar** (koo-*rahr*) *v* cure; heal; **curar-se** recover

**curiosidade** (koo-rʸoo-zee-*dhah*-dher) *f* curiosity; curio

**curioso** (koo-rʸoa-zoo) *adj* curious; inquisitive

**curso** (*koor*-soo) *m* course; ~ **intensivo** intensive course

**curto** (*koor*-too) *adj* short

**curto-circuito** (koor-too-seer-*koo*ee-too) *m* short circuit

**curva** (*koor*-ver) *f* turn, bend; turning, curve

**curvado** (koor-*vah*-dhoo) *adj* curved

**curvar** (koor-*vahr*) *v* *bend; **curvar-se** *bend down

**curvatura** (koor-ver-*too*-rer) *f* bend

**curvo** (*koor*-voo) *adj* curved; bent

***cuspir** (koosh-*peer*) *v* *spit

**cuspo** (*koosh*-poo) *m* spit

**custar** (koosh-*tahr*) *v* *cost

**custo** (*koosh*-too) *m* cost

**custódia** (koosh-*to*-dhʸer) *f* custody

# D

**dactilógrafa** (dahk-tee-*lo*-grer-fer) *f* typist

**dactilografado** (dahk-tee-loo-grer-*fah*-dhoo) *adj* typewritten

**dactilografar** (dahk-tee-loo-grer-*fahr*) *v* type

**dado** (*dah*-dhoo) *m* data *pl*

**daltónico** (dahl-*to*-nee-koo) *adj* colour-blind

**dança** (*derng*-ser) *f* dance; ~ **folclórica** folk-dance

**dançar** (derng-*sahr*) *v* dance

**danificar** (der-ner-fee-*kahr*) *v* damage

**dano** (*der*-noo) *m* damage; mischief; harm

***dar** (dahr) *v* *give; donate

**data** (*dah*-ter) *f* date

**de** (der) *prep* from; of; out of; with; off

**debaixo** (der-*bigh*-shoo) *adv* below, underneath, beneath; ~ **de** below, under; beneath

**debate** (der-*bhah*-ter) *m* debate, discussion

**debater** (der-bher-*tayr*) *v* discuss

**débito** (*deh*-bhee-too) *m* debit

**debruçar-se** (der-bhroo-*sahr*-ser) *v* *lean out; *bend down

**decência** (der-*sayng*-sʸer) *f* decency

**decente** (der-*sayngn*-ter) *adj* decent

**decepcionar** (der-seh-sʸoo-*nahr*) *v* *be disappointing

**decerto** (der-*sehr*-too) *adv* certainly

**decidido** (der-see-*dhee*-dhoo) *adj* resolute

**decidir** (der-see-*dheer*) *v* decide

**décimo** (*deh*-see-moo) *num* tenth; ~ **nono** nineteenth; ~ **oitavo** eighteenth; ~ **primeiro** eleventh; ~ **quarto** fourteenth; ~ **quinto** fifteenth; ~ **segundo** twelfth; ~ **sétimo** seventeenth; ~ **sexto** sixteenth; ~ **terceiro** thirteenth

**decisão** (der-see-*zerng*ʷ) *f* (pl -sões) decision

**declaração** (der-kler-rer-*serng*ᵂ) *f* (pl -ções) declaration; statement

**declarar** (der-kler-*rahr*) *v* declare; state; ~ **culpado** convict

**declive** (der-*klee*-ver) *m* incline

**decoração** (der-koo-rer-*serng*ᵂ) *f* (pl -ções) decoration

**decorar** (der-koo-*rahr*) *v* memorize; decorate

**decorativo** (der-koo-rer-*tee*-voo) *adj* decorative

**dedal** (der-*dhahl*) *m* (pl -ais) thimble

**dedicado a** (der-dhee-*kah*-dhoo er) attached to, devoted to

**dedicar** (der-dhee-*kahr*) *v* devote, dedicate

**dedo** (*day*-dhoo) *m* finger; ~ **do pé** toe; ~ **mínimo** little finger

**\*deduzir** (der-dhoo-*zeer*) *v* subtract, deduct; infer, deduce

**defeito** (der-*fay*-too) *m* fault

**defeituoso** (der-fay-*twoa*-zoo) *adj* defective, faulty

**defender** (der-fayngn-*dayr*) *v* defend

**defensor** (der-fayng-*soar*) *m* advocate, champion

**defesa** (der-*fay*-zer) *f* defence; plea

**défice** (*deh*-fee-ser) *m* deficit

**deficiência** (der-fee-sᵞ*ayng*-sᵞer) *f* deficiency

**definição** (der-fer-nee-*serng*ᵂ) *f* (pl -ções) definition

**definido** (der-fer-*nee*-dhoo) *adj* definite

**definir** (der-fer-*neer*) *v* define; determine

**deformado** (der-foor-*mah*-dhoo) *adj* deformed

**defraudar** (der-frou-*dhahr*) *v* cheat

**defronte de** (der-*frawngn*-ter der) facing

**degelar** (der-zher-*lahr*) *v* thaw

**degelo** (der-*zhay*-loo) *m* thaw

**degrau** (der-*grou*) *m* step

**deitar** (day-*tahr*) *v* \*throw; pour; **deitar-se** \*lie down, \*go to bed; **\*estar deitado** \*lie

**deixar** (day-*shahr*) *v* \*leave, \*let

**delapidado** (der-ler-pee-*dher*-dhoo) *adj* dilapidated

**delegação** (der-ler-ger-*serng*ᵂ) *f* (pl -ções) delegation

**delegado** (der-ler-*gah*-dhoo) *m* delegate

**deleite** (der-*lay*-ter) *m* delight

**deles** (deh-*lish*) their; of them

**delgado** (dehl-*gah*-dhoo) *adj* slim

**deliberação** (der-lee-bher-rer-*serng*ᵂ) *f* (pl -ções) deliberation

**deliberado** (der-lee-bher-*rah*-dhoo) *adj* deliberate

**deliberar** (der-lee-bher-*rahr*) *v* deliberate

**delicado** (der-lee-*kah*-dhoo) *adj* tender, delicate; gentle; sheer; polite

**delícia** (der-*lee*-sᵞer) *f* delight

**deliciar** (der-lee-sᵞ*ahr*) *v* delight

**delicioso** (der-lee-sᵞ*oa*-zoo) *adj* delicious, delightful; wonderful, lovely

**delinquente** (der-leeng-*kwayngn*-ter) *m* criminal

**demais** (der-*mighsh*) *adv* besides, moreover; ~ **a mais** moreover; **os** ~ the rest, the others

**demasiado** (der-mer-zᵞ*ah*-dhoo) *adv* too, too much

**demência** (der-*mayng*-sᵞer) *f* madness

**demente** (der-*mayngn*-ter) *adj* mad

**demissão** (der-mee-*serng*ᵂ) *f* (pl -sões) resignation

**demitir-se** (der-mee-*teer*-ser) *v* resign

**democracia** (der-moo-krer-*see*-er) *f* democracy

**democrático** (der-moo-*krah*-tee-koo) *adj* democratic

**demolição** (der-moo-lee-*serng*ᵂ) *f* (pl -ções) demolition

**\*demolir** (der-moo-*leer*) *v* demolish

**demonstração** (der-mawngsh-trer-*serng*ʷ) f (pl -ções) demonstration

**demonstrar** (der-mawngsh-*trahr*) v prove, demonstrate; \*show

**demora** (der-*mo*-rer) f delay

**demorar-se** (der-moo-*rahr*-ser) v \*be late; \*be long; linger

**denegar** (der-ner-*gahr*) v deny

**denso** (*dayng*-soo) adj dense

**dentadura** (dayngn-ter-*dhoo*-rer) f denture; false teeth

**dente** (*dayngn*-ter) m tooth

**dente-de-leão** (*dayngn*-ter-der-lᵛerngʷ) m dandelion

**dentista** (dayngn-*teesh*-ter) m dentist

**dentro** (*dayngn*-troo) adv inside; in; ~ de inside; into, in, within; **para** ~ inwards; **por** ~ inside, within

**deparar com** (der-per-*rahr*) run into

**departamento** (der-perr-ter-*mayngn*-too) m department

**depenar** (der-per-*nahr*) v \*bleed, extort money from; pluck

**dependente** (der-payngn-*dayngn*-ter) adj dependant

**depender de** (der-payngn-*dayr*) depend on

**depois** (der-*poish*) adv afterwards; then; ~ de after; ~ que after

**depositar** (der-poo-zee-*tahr*) v deposit; bank

**depósito** (der-*po*-zee-too) m deposit; ~ **da gasolina** petrol tank; ~ **de bagagens** left luggage office; ~ **de gás** gasworks; ~ **de objectos perdidos** lost property office

**depressa** (der-*preh*-ser) adv fast, quickly

**depressão** (der-prer-*serng*ʷ) f (pl -sões) depression

**deprimente** (der-pree-*mayngn*-ter) adj depressing

**deprimido** (der-pree-*mee*-dhoo) adj blue, low, depressed

**deprimir** (der-pree-*meer*) v depress

**deputado** (der-poo-*tah*-dhoo) m deputy; Member of Parliament

**derramar** (der-rrer-*mahr*) v \*shed; \*spill

**derrapar** (der-rrer-*pahr*) v skid

**derreter** (der-rrer-*tayr*) v melt

**derrota** (der-*rro*-ter) f defeat

**derrotar** (der-rroo-*tahr*) v defeat

**derrubar** (der-rroo-*bhahr*) v knock down

**desabitado** (der-zer-bhee-*tah*-dhoo) adj uninhabited

**desabotoar** (der-zer-bhoo-*twahr*) v unbutton

**desacostumado** (der-zer-koosh-too-*mah*-dhoo) adj unaccustomed

**desafiar** (der-zer-*f*ᵛ*ahr*) v dare; challenge

**desafio** (der-zer-*fee*ᵒᵒ) m challenge; match

**desagradar** (der-zer-grer-*dhahr*) v displease

**desagradável** (der-zer-grer-*dhah*-vehl) adj (pl -eis) disagreeable; unpleasant, nasty; unkind

**desajeitado** (der-zer-zhay-*tah*-dhoo) adj clumsy

**desalinhado** (der-zer-lee-*ñah*-dhoo) adj untidy

**desaparafusar** (der-zer-per-rer-foo-*zahr*) v unscrew

**desaparecer** (der-zer-per-rer-*sayr*) v disappear; vanish

**desaparecido** (der-zer-per-rer-*see*-dhoo) adj lost; m missing person

**desapertar** (der-zer-perr-*tahr*) v loosen

**desapontar** (der-zer-pawngn-*tahr*) v disappoint

**desaprender** (der-zer-prayngn-*dayr*) v unlearn

**desaprovar** (der-zer-proo-*vahr*) v disapprove

**desarrazoado** (der-zer-rrer-*zwah*-dhoo)

*adj* unreasonable

**desarrolhar** (der-zer-rroo-*lYahr*) *v* un-cork

**desassossego** (der-zer-soo-*say*-goo) *m* unrest

**desastrado** (der-zersh-*trah*-dhoo) *adj* awkward

**desastre** (der-*zahsh*-trer) *m* disaster; accident; ~ de aviação plane crash

**desastroso** (der-zahsh-*troa*-zoo) *adj* disastrous

**desatar** (der-zer-*tahr*) *v* untie

**desavergonhado** (der-zer-verr-goo-*ñah*-dhoo) *adj* impudent

**desbotar** (dɪzh-bhoo-*tahr*) *v* fade

**descafeinado** (dɪsh-ker-fay-*nah*-dhoo) *adj* decaffeinated

**descansar** (dɪsh-kerng-*sahr*) *v* rest

**descanso** (dɪsh-*kerng*-soo) *m* rest

**descarado** (dɪsh-ker-*rah*-dhoo) *adj* bold; shameless

**descarregar** (dɪsh-ker-rrer-*gahr*) *v* discharge, unload

**descascar** (dɪsh-kersh-*kahr*) *v* peel

**descendente** (dɪsh-sayngn-*dayngn*-ter) *m* descendant

**descer** (dɪsh-*sayr*) *v* descend; *get off

**descida** (dɪsh-*see*-dher) *f* descent

**descoberta** (dɪsh-koo-*bhehr*-ter) *f* discovery

**descoberto** (dɪsh-koo-*bhayr*-too) *adj* bare

***descobrir** (dɪsh-koo-*bhreer*) *v* discover; detect

**descolagem** (dɪsh-koo-*lah*-zherngᵞ) *f* take-off

**descolar** (dɪsh-koo-*lahr*) *v* *take off

**descolorir** (dɪsh-koo-loo-*reer*) *v* discolour; bleach

**desconcertar** (dɪsh-kawng-serr-*tahr*) *v* overwhelm

**desconfiado** (dɪsh-kawng-f ᵞ*Yah*-dhoo) *adj* suspicious

**desconfiança** (dɪsh-kawng-f ᵞ*Yerng*-ser) *f* suspicion

**desconfiar** (dɪsh-kawng-f ᵞ*Yahr*) *v* mistrust; suspect

**desconfortável** (dɪsh-kawng-foor-*tah*-vehl) *adj* (pl -eis) uncomfortable

**descongelar** (dɪsh-kawng-zher-*lahr*) *v* thaw

**desconhecido** (dɪsh-koo-ñer-*see*-dhoo) *adj* unknown; unfamiliar

**descontar** (dɪsh-kawngn-*tahr*) *v* cash

**descontente** (dɪsh-kawngn-*tayngn*-ter) *adj* discontented

**desconto** (dɪsh-*kawngn*-too) *m* discount; rebate, reduction

**descontracção** (dɪsh-kawngn-trah-*serng*ᵂ) *f* (pl -ções) relaxation

**descontraído** (dɪsh-kawngn-*trer*-ee-dhoo) *adj* easy-going

***descontrair-se** (dɪsh-kawngn-trer-*eer*) *v* relax

**descrever** (dɪsh-krer-*vayr*) *v* describe

**descrição** (dɪsh-kree-*serng*ᵂ) *f* (pl -ções) description

**descuidado** (dɪsh-kwee-*dhah*-dhoo) *adj* careless; slovenly

**descuidar** (dɪsh-kwee-*dhahr*) *v* neglect

**desculpa** (dɪsh-*kool*-per) *f* excuse; apology; **pedir ~** apologize

**desculpar** (dɪsh-kool-*pahr*) *v* excuse; **desculpar-se** apologize; **desculpe!** sorry!

**desde** (*dayzh*-dher) *prep* since; as from; ~ **então** since; ~ **que** since

**desdém** (dɪzh-*dherng*ᵞ) *m* contempt

**desdobrar** (dɪzh-dhoo-*bhrahr*) *v* unfold

**desejar** (der-zɪ-*zhahr*) *v* desire, wish; want; long for

**desejável** (der-zɪ-*zhah*-vehl) *adj* (pl -eis) desirable

**desejo** (der-*zay*-zhoo) *m* desire; wish, longing

**desejoso** (der-zay-*zhoa*-zoo) *adj* eager

**desembarcar** (der-zayngm-berr-*kahr*) *v*

land, disembark

**desembrulhar** (der-zayngm-broo-*lYahr*) *v* unwrap

**desempacotar** (der-zayngm-per-koo-*tahr*) *v* unpack

**desempenhar** (der-zayngm-per-*ñahr*) *v* perform; execute

**desempregado** (der-zayngm-prer-*gah*-dhoo) *adj* unemployed

**desemprego** (der-zayngm-*pray*-goo) *m* unemployment

**desencaminhar** (der-zayngng-ker-mee-*ñahr*) *v* \*mislay

**desenhar** (der-zı-*ñahr*) *v* \*draw; sketch, design

**desenho** (der-*zay*-ñoo) *m* sketch, drawing; pattern; **banda desenhada** comics *pl*; **caderno de ~** sketch-book; **~ animado** cartoon

**desenvolver** (der-zayng-voal-*vayr*) *v* develop; expand

**desenvolvimento** (der-zayng-voal-vee-*mayngn*-too) *m* development

**desertar** (der-zerr-*tahr*) *v* desert

**deserto** (der-*zehr*-too) *adj* desert; *m* desert

**desesperado** (der-zısh-per-*rah*-dhoo) *adj* hopeless, desperate

**desesperar** (der-zısh-per-*rahr*) *v* despair

**desespero** (der-zısh-*pay*-roo) *m* despair

**desfalecido** (dısh-fer-ler-*see*-dhoo) *adj* faint

**desfavorável** (dısh-fer-voo-*rah*-vehl) *adj* (pl -eis) unfavourable

**\*desfazer** (dısh-fer-*zayr*) *v* \*undo; **\*desfazer-se de** discard

**desfiar** (dısh-*fYahr*) *v* fray

**desfiladeiro** (dısh-fee-ler-*dhay*-roo) *m* mountain pass

**desfile** (derz-*fee*-ler) *m* parade

**desfrutar** (dısh-froo-*tahr*) *v* enjoy

**desgostar** (dısh-goosh-*tahr*) *v* dis-

please

**desgosto** (dısh-*goash*-too) *m* grief, sorrow; **\*ter desgosto** grieve

**desgostoso** (dısh-goosh-*toa*-zoo) *adj* sad

**desgraça** (dısh-*grah*-ser) *f* disaster

**desgraçado** (dısh-grah-*sah*-dhoo) *adj* unfortunate

**designação** (der-zee-gner-*serngw*) *f* (pl -ções) denomination

**designar** (der-zeeg-*nahr*) *v* designate; appoint

**desigual** (der-zee-*gwahl*) *adj* (pl -ais) uneven, unequal

**desiludir** (der-zee-loo-*dheer*) *v* \*let down; disappoint

**desilusão** (der-zee-loo-*zerngw*) *f* (pl -sões) disappointment

**desinfectante** (der-zeeng-feh-*terngn*-ter) *m* disinfectant

**desinfectar** (der-zeeng-feh-*tahr*) *v* disinfect

**desinteressado** (der-zeeng-ter-rer-*sah*-dhoo) *adj* unselfish

**desistir** (der-zeesh-*teer*) *v* \*give up

**desligar** (dızh-lee-*gahr*) *v* disconnect; switch off

**deslizar** (dızh-lee-*zahr*) *v* \*slide, slip

**deslize** (dızh-*lee*-zer) *m* slide

**deslocado** (dısh-loo-*ker*-dhoo) *adj* dislocated

**deslocar** (dızh-loo-*kahr*) *v* move

**deslumbrante** (dızh-loongm-*brerngn*-ter) *adj* glaring

**desmaiar** (dızh-mer-*Yahr*) *v* faint

**desmantelado** (dızh-merngn-ter-*lah*-dhoo) *adj* ramshackle

**desmobilado** (dızh-moo-bhee-*lah*-dhoo) *adj* unfurnished

**desmoronar-se** (dızh-moo-roo-*nahr*-ser) *v* collapse

**desnecessário** (dızh-ner-ser-*sah*-rYoo) *adj* unnecessary

**desocupado** (der-zoa-koo-*pah*-dhoo)

*adj* unoccupied

**desodorante** (dı-zo-dhoa-*rerng*-ter) *mBr* deodorant

**desodorizante** (der-zoo-dhoo-ree-*zerngn*-ter) *m* deodorant

**desolado** (der-zoo-*lah*-dhoo) *adj* sorry; desolate

**desonesto** (der-zoo-*nehsh*-too) *adj* dishonest; crooked

**desonra** (derz-*awng*-rrer) *f* disgrace; shame

**desordem** (derz-*or*-derng<sup>Y</sup>) *f* disorder, mess; riot

**desossar** (der-zoo-*sahr*) *v* bone

**despachar** (dısh-per-*shahr*) *v* despatch; **despachar-se** hurry

**despedida** (dısh-per-*dhee*-dher) *f* parting; departure

**\*despedir** (dısh-per-*dheer*) *v* dismiss; fire

**despenhar-se** (dısh-per-*ñahr*-ser) *v* crash

**despensa** (dısh-*payng*-ser) *f* larder

**desperdiçar** (dısh-perr-dee-*sahr*) *v* waste

**desperdício** (dısh-perr-*dee*-s<sup>Y</sup>oo) *m* waste

**despertador** (dısh-perr-ter-*dhoar*) *m* alarm-clock

**despertar** (dısh-perr-*tahr*) *v* wake up; \*awake

**despesa** (dısh-*pay*-zer) *f* expense; expenditure; **despesas de viagem** travelling expenses

**despido** (dısh-*pee*-dhoo) *adj* bare; naked

**\*despir-se** (dısh-*peer*-ser) *v* undress

**desportista** (dısh-poor-*teesh*-tah) *m* sportsman

**desporto** (dısh-*poar*-too) *m* sport; **desportos de inverno** winter sports

**desposar** (dısh-poo-*zahr*) *v* marry

**desprender** (dısh-prayngn-*dayr*) *v* loosen; unfasten

**despreocupado** (dısh-pr<sup>Y</sup>oo-koo-*pah*-dhoo) *adj* carefree

**desprezar** (dısh-prer-*zahr*) *v* despise; scorn

**desprezo** (dısh-*pray*-zoo) *m* contempt; scorn

**despropositado** (dısh-proo-poo-zee-*tah*-dhoo) *adj* misplaced

**desprotegido** (dısh-proo-tı-*zhee*-dhoo) *adj* unprotected

**destapar** (dısh-ter-*pahr*) *v* uncover

**destinar** (dısh-tee-*nahr*) *v* destine

**destinatário** (dısh-tee-ner-*tah*-r<sup>Y</sup>oo) *m* addressee

**destino** (dısh-*tee*-noo) *m* fate, destiny, lot; destination

**destro** (*dehsh*-troo) *adj* skilful

**destruição** (dısh-trwee-*serng*<sup>W</sup>) *f* (pl -ções) destruction

**\*destruir** (dısh-*trweer*) *v* destroy; wreck

**desusado** (der-zoo-*zah*-dhoo) *adj* unusual

**desvalorização** (dızh-ver-loo-ree-zer-*serng*<sup>W</sup>) *f* (pl -ções) devaluation

**desvalorizar** (dızh-ver-loo-ree-*zahr*) *v* devalue

**desvanecer** (dızh-ver-ner-*sayr*) *v* fade

**desvantagem** (dızh-verngn-*tah*-zherng<sup>Y</sup>) *f* disadvantage

**desviar** (dızh-v<sup>Y</sup>ahr) *v* avert; hijack; **desviar-se** deviate

**desvio** (dızh-*vee*<sup>oo</sup>) *m* detour; diversion

**detalhado** (der-ter-l<sup>Y</sup>ah-dhoo) *adj* detailed

**detalhe** (der-*tah*-l<sup>Y</sup>er) *m* detail

**detective** (der-tehk-*tee*-ver) *m* detective

**detenção** (der-tayng-⊗oo) *f* (pl -ções) custody

**detergente** (der-terr-*zhayngn*-ter) *m* detergent; ~ **em pó** washing-powder

**deteriorável** (der-ter-r<sup>Y</sup>oo-*rah*-vehl) *adj* (pl -eis) perishable

**determinar** (der-terr-mee-*nahr*) *v* determine; define; **determinado** definite

**detestar** (der-tısh-*tahr*) *v* hate, dislike

**detido** (der-*tee*-dhoo) *m* prisoner

**deus** (day<sup>oo</sup>sh) *m* god

**deusa** (day<sup>oo</sup>-zer) *f* goddess

**dever** (der-*vayr*) *v* \*have to (\*must); owe; *m* duty

**devido** (der-*vee*-dhoo) *adj* due; proper; ~ **a** owing to

**devolver** (der-voal-*vayr*) *v* \*bring back; \*send back

**dez** (dehsh) *num* ten

**dezanove** (der-zer-*no*-ver) *num* nineteen

**dezasseis** (der-zer-*saysh*) *num* sixteen

**dezassete** (der zer-*seh*-ter) *num* seventeen

**Dezembro** (der-*zayngm*-broo) December

**dezena** (der-*zay*-ner) *f* ten, about ten

**dezoito** (der-*zoi*-too) *num* eighteen

**dia** (*dee*-er) *m* day; **bom dia!** hello!; **de** ~ by day; ~ **de semana** weekday; ~ **dos anos** birthday; ~ **útil** working day; **por** ~ per day; **qualquer** ~ some day

**diabetes** (d<sup>Y</sup>er-*bheh*-tersh) *f* diabetes

**diabético** (d<sup>Y</sup>er-*bheh*-tee-koo) *m* diabetic

**diabo** (d<sup>Y</sup>ah-bhoo) *m* devil

**diabrura** (d<sup>Y</sup>er-*bhroo*-rer) *f* mischief

**diagnosticar** (dee-erg-noosh-tee-*kahr*) *v* diagnose

**diagnóstico** (dee-erg-*nosh*-tee-koo) *m* diagnosis

**diagonal** (dee-er-goo-*nahl*) *adj* (pl -ais) diagonal; *f* diagonal

**diagrama** (dee-er-*grah*-mer) *m* diagram

**dialecto** (dee-er-*leh*-too) *m* dialect

**diamante** (d<sup>Y</sup>er-*merngn*-ter) *m* diamond

**diante de** (d<sup>Y</sup>erngn-ter der) in front of; before

**diário** (d<sup>Y</sup>ah-r<sup>Y</sup>oo) *adj* daily; *m* diary; daily

**diarreia** (d<sup>Y</sup>er-*rray*-er) *f* diarrhoea

**dicionário** (dee-s<sup>Y</sup>oo-*nah*-r<sup>Y</sup>oo) *m* dictionary

**dieta** (d<sup>Y</sup>eh-ter) *f* diet

**diferença** (dee-fer-*rayng*-ser) *f* difference; contrast, distinction

**diferente** (dee-fer-*rayngn*-ter) *adj* different; unlike

**\*diferir** (dee-fer-*reer*) *v* vary, differ

**difícil** (dee-*fee*-sıl) *adj* (pl -ceis) difficult; hard

**dificuldade** (dee-fee-kool-*dhah*-dher) *f* difficulty; pains

**\*digerir** (dee-zher-*reer*) *v* digest

**digestão** (dee-zhersh-*terng*<sup>w</sup>) *f* digestion

**digestivo** (dee-zhersh-*tee*-voo) *adj* digestible

**digital** (dee-zhee-*tahl*) *adj* digital

**digno de** (*dee*-gnoo der) worthy of

**\*diluir** (dee-*lweer*) *v* dissolve; dilute

**dimensão** (dee-mayng-*serng*<sup>w</sup>) *f* (pl -sões) extent, size

**diminuição** (dee-mee-nwee-*serng*<sup>w</sup>) *f* (pl -ções) decrease; subtraction

**\*diminuir** (dee-mee-*nweer*) *v* reduce; decrease, lessen

**Dinamarca** (dee-ner-*mahr*-ker) *f* Denmark

**dinamarquês** (dee-ner-mahr-*kaysh*) *adj* Danish; *m* Dane

**dínamo** (*dee*-ner-moo) *m* dynamo

**dinheiro** (dee-*ñay*-roo) *m* money; cash

**diploma** (dee-*ploa*-mer) *m* certificate, diploma

**diplomar-se** (dee-ploo-*mahr*-ser) *v* graduate

**diplomata** (dee-ploa-*mah*-ter) *m* diplomat

**direcção** (dee-reh-*serng*ᵂ) *f* (pl -ções) leadership, management, lead, direction; way; **em ~ a** towards

**directamente** (dee-reh-ter-*mayng*ter) *adv* straight; straight away

**directiva** (dee-reh-*tee*-ver) *f* directive

**directo** (dee-*reh*-too) *adj* direct

**director** (dee-reh-*toar*) *m* executive; manager, director; principal; **~ de escola** head teacher, headmaster

**direita** (dee-*ray*-ter) *f* right side; **à ~** on the right

**direito** (dee-*ray*-too) *adj* straight, right; upright, right-hand; level; *m* justice, law, right; **~ administrativo** administrative law; **~ civil** civil law; **~ comercial** commercial law; **~ de importação** duty; **~ de voto** franchise; **~ penal** criminal law; **direitos dues** *pl*; **direitos alfandegários** Customs duty; **direitos de importação** import duty; **isento de direitos** duty-free; **sempre a ~** straight ahead

**dirigente** (dee-ree-*zhayng*-ter) *m* leader

**dirigir** (dee-ree-*zheer*) *v* direct; conduct, head, *lead; **dirigir-se a** address

**disciplina** (dee-shee-*plee*-ner) *f* discipline

**disco** (*deesh*-koo) *m* disc; record; **~ de longa duração** long-playing record; **~ laser** compact disc; **toca-discos laser** CD player

**discordar** (deesh-koor-*dhahr*) *v* disagree

**discreto** (deesh-*kreh*-too) *adj* inconspicuous

**discurso** (deesh-*koor*-soo) *m* speech

**discussão** (deesh-koo-*serng*ᵂ) *f* (pl -sões) discussion; argument

**discutir** (deesh-koo-*teer*) *v* quarrel; discuss; argue, deliberate

**disenteria** (dee-zayngn-ter-*ree*-er) *f* dysentery

**disfarçar-se** (deesh-ferr-*sahr*-ser) *v* disguise

**disfarce** (deesh-*fahr*-ser) *m* disguise

**disforme** (deesh-*for*-mer) *adj* deformed

**disparar** (deesh-per-*rahr*) *v* fire, *shoot

**disparatado** (deesh-per-rer-*tah*-dhoo) *adj* silly

**disparate** (deesh-per-*rah*-ter) *m* nonsense; **disparates** rubbish; ***dizer disparates** talk rubbish

**dispensar** (deesh-payng-*sahr*) *v* exempt; spare; **~ de** discharge of

**dispersar** (deesh-perr-*sahr*) *v* scatter

**disponível** (deesh-poo-*nee*-vehl) *adj* (pl -eis) available

***dispor de** (deesh-*poar*) *have at one's disposal

**disposição** (deesh-poo-zee-*serng*ᵂ) *f* (pl -ções) disposal; mood

**dispositivo** (deesh-poo-zee-*tee*-voo) *m* apparatus

**disposto** (deesh-*poash*-too) *adj* willing; inclined; **bem ~** good-tempered

**disputa** (deesh-*poo*-ter) *f* dispute; argument

**disputar** (bree-*gahr*) *v* quarrel

**dissolver** (dee-soal-*vayr*) *v* dissolve

**dissuadir** (dee-swer-*dheer*) *v* dissuade from

**distância** (deesh-*terng*-sᵉer) *f* way, space, distance

**distante** (deesh-*terng*-ter) *adj* distant; remote, far-away; **o mais ~** furthest

**distensão** (deesh-tayng-*serng*ᵂ) *f* (pl -sões) sprain

**distinção** (deesh-teeng-*serng*ᵂ) *f* (pl

-ções) distinction; difference

**distinguir** (deesh-teeng-*geer*) *v* distinguish

**distinto** (deesh-*teengn*-too) *adj* distinct; separate; dignified, distinguished

**distracção** (deesh-trah-*serng*ʷ) *f* (pl -ções) amusement

**distribuidor** (deesh-tree-bhwee-*dhoar*) *m* distributor

*****distribuir** (deesh-tree-*bhweer*) *v* *deal, distribute; issue

**distrito** (deesh-*tree*-too) *m* district

**distúrbio** (deesh-*toor*-bʸoo) *m* disturbance

**ditado** (dee-*tah*-dhoo) *m* dictation

**ditador** (dee-ter-*dhoar*) *m* dictator

**ditafone** (dee-ter-*foa*-ner) *m* dictaphone

**ditar** (dee-*tahr*) *v* dictate

**divã** (dee-*verng*) *m* couch

**diversão** (dee-verr-*serng*ʷ) *f* (pl -sões) diversion; entertainment

**diversos** (dee-*vehr*-soosh) *adj* various

**divertido** (dee-verr-*tee*-dhoo) *adj* amusing; entertaining

**divertimento** (dee-verr-tee-*mayngn*-too) *m* entertainment, amusement; fun, pleasure

*****divertir** (dee-verr-*teer*) *v* amuse; entertain

**dívida** (*dee*-vee-dher) *f* debt

**dividir** (dee-vee-*dheer*) *v* divide; ~ **ao meio** halve

**divino** (der-*vee*-noo) *adj* divine

**divisa** (der-*vee*-zer) *f* motto

**divisão** (der-vee-*zerng*ʷ) *f* (pl -sões) division; section; room

**divorciar-se** (dee-voor-sʸ*ahr*-ser) *v* divorce

**divórcio** (dee-*vor*-sʸoo) *m* divorce

*****dizer** (dee-*zayr*) *v* *say; *tell; *que-rer dizer *mean

**doação** (dwer-*serng*ʷ) *f* (pl -ções) do-nation

**doador** (dwer-*dhoar*) *m* donor

**dobra** (*do*-bhrer) *f* fold, crease

**dobradiça** (doo-bhrer-*dhee*-ser) *f* hinge

**dobrar** (doo-*bhrahr*) *v* fold; *bend

**o dobro** (oo *doa*-bhroo) the double

**doca** (*do*-ker) *f* dock

**doce** (*doa*-ser) *adj* sweet; *m* sweet; ~ **de fruta** jam; ~ **de laranja** marmalade

**documento** (doo-koo-*mayngn*-too) *m* document

**doença** (*dwayng*-ser) *f* illness; sickness, disease; ~ **venérea** venereal disease

**doente** (*dwayngn*-ter) *adj* ill, sick; *m* patient

**doentio** (dwayngn-*tee*ᵒᵒ) *adj* unhealthy, unsound

*****doer** (dwayr) *v* ache

**doido** (*doi*-dhoo) *adj* crazy

**dois** (doish) *num* (f **duas**) two

**dólar** (*do*-lahr) *m* dollar

**doloroso** (doo-loo-*roa*-zoo) *adj* painful; sore

**dom** (dawng) *m* gift

**domesticado** (doo-*mehsh*-tee-kah-dhoo) *adj* tame

**domesticar** (doo-mɪsh-tee-*kahr*) *v* tame

**doméstico** (doo-*mehsh*-tee-koo) *adj* domestic

**domicílio** (doo-mee-*see*-lʸoo) *m* domicile

**dominação** (doo-mee-ner-*serng*ʷ) *f* (pl -ções) domination

**dominante** (doo-mee-*nerngn*-ter) *adj* leading

**dominar** (doo-mee-*nahr*) *v* master

**domingo** (doo-*meeng*-goo) *m* Sunday

**domínio** (doo-*mee*-nʸoo) *m* field; rule, dominion

**donativo** (doo-ner-*tee*-voo) *m* donation

**dono** (*doa*-noo) *m* master; owner

**dor** (doar) *f* ache, pain; sore; grief, sorrow; ~ **de barriga** stomach-ache; ~ **de cabeça** headache; ~ **de dentes** toothache; ~ **de estô-mago** stomach-ache; ~ **de gar-ganta** sore throat; ~ **de ouvidos** earache; **dores** labour; **dores nas costas** backache; **sem** ~ painless

*dormir (door-*meer*) *v* *sleep; ~ **de-mais** *oversleep

**dormitório** (door-mee-*to*-rʸoo) *m* dormitory

**dose** (*do*-zer) *f* dose

**dotado** (doo-*tah*-dhoo) *adj* talented, gifted

**dourado** (doa-*rah*-dhoo) *adj* gilt

**doutor** (doa-*toar*) *m* doctor

**doze** (*doa*-zer) *num* twelve

**dragão** (drer-*gerng*ʷ) *m* (pl -gões) dragon

**drama** (*drer*-mer) *m* drama

**dramático** (drer-*mah*-tee-koo) *adj* dramatic

**dramaturgo** (drer-mer-*toor*-goo) *m* dramatist; playwright

**drenar** (drer-*nahr*) *v* drain

**drogaria** (droo-ger-*ree*-er) *f* pharmacy, chemist's; drugstore *nAm*

**duche** (*doo*-sher) *m* shower

**duna** (*doo*-ner) *f* dune

**duplo** (*doo*-ploo) *adj* double

**duque** (*doo*-ker) *m* duke

**duquesa** (doo-*kay*-zer) *f* duchess

**duração** (doo-rer-*serng*ʷ) *f* (pl -ções) duration

**duradouro** (doo-rer-*dhoa*-roo) *adj* lasting; permanent

**durante** (doo-*rerngn*-ter) *prep* for, during

**durar** (doo-*rahr*) *v* last; continue

**duro** (*doo*-roo) *adj* hard; tough

**dúvida** (*doo*-vee-dher) *f* doubt; *pôr em* ~ query; **sem** ~ undoubtedly

**duvidar** (doo-vee-*dhahr*) *v* doubt

**duvidoso** (doo-vee-*dhoa*-zoo) *adj* doubtful

**dúzia** (*doo*-zʸer) *f* dozen

# E

**e** (ee) *conj* and

**ébano** (*eh*-bher-noo) *m* ebony

**eclipse** (er-*kleep*-ser) *m* eclipse

**eco** (*eh*-koo) *m* echo

**economia** (ee-koo-noo-*meeer*) *f* economy; **economias** savings *pl*

**económico** (ee-koo-*no*-mee-koo) *adj* economic; thrifty, economical; cheap

**economista** (ee-koo-noo-*meesh*-ter) *m* economist

**economizar** (ee-koo-noo-mee-*zahr*) *v* economize

**écran** (ehk-*rerng*) *m* screen

**eczema** (ehk-*zay*-mer) *m* eczema

**edição** (er-dhee-*serng*ʷ) *f* (pl -ções) edition; issue; ~ **da manhã** morning edition

**edificar** (ee-dher-fee-*kahr*) *v* erect; construct

**edifício** (ee-dher-*fee*-sʸoo) *m* construction, building

**editor** (er-dhee-*toar*) *m* publisher

**edredão** (ee-dhrer-*dherng*ʷ) *m* (pl -dões) eiderdown

**educação** (ee-dhoo-ker-*serng*ʷ) *f* (pl -ções) education

**educado** (ee-dhoo-*kah*-dhoo) *adj* polite, civil; **bem** ~ well brought-up; **mal** ~ badly brought-up

**educar** (ee-dhoo-*kahr*) *v* educate; raise, *bring up

**efectivamente** (ee-feh-tee-ver-*mayngn*-ter) *adv* indeed; as a matter of fact

**efectuar** (ee-feh-*twahr*) v effect

**efeito** (ee-*fay*-too) m effect; **com** ~ in fact, in effect

**efervescência** (ee-ferr-vɪsh-*sayng*-sʸer) f fizz

**eficaz** (er-fee-*kahsh*) adj effective

**eficiente** (er-fee-sʸ*ayngn*-ter) adj efficient

**efusivo** (ee-foo-zee-voo) adj hearty

**egípcio** (er-*zheep*-sʸoo) adj Egyptian; m Egyptian

**Egipto** (er-*zheep*-too) m Egypt

**egocêntrico** (ee-goo-*sayngn*-tree-koo) adj self-centred

**egoísmo** (ee-*gweezh*-moo) m selfishness

**egoísta** (ee-*gweesh*-ter) adj egoistic; selfish

**égua** (*eh*-gwer) f mare

**eixo** (*ay*-shoo) m axlc

**ela** (*eh*-ler) pron she; ~ **mesma** herself

**elaborar** (ee-ler-bhoo-*rahr*) v elaborate

**elas** (*eh*-lersh) pron they; ~ **mesmas** themselves

**elasticidade** (ee-lersh-ter-see-*dhah*-dher) f elasticity

**elástico** (ee-*lahsh*-tee-koo) adj elastic; m rubber band, elastic band

**ele** (*ay*-ler) pron he; ~ **mesmo** himself

**electricidade** (ee-lehk-trer-see-*dhah*-dher) f electricity

**electricista** (ee-lehk-trer-*seesh*-ter) m electrician

**eléctrico** (ee-*leh*-tree-koo) adj electric; m tram; streetcar nAm

**electrónico** (ee-leh-*troa*-nee-koo) adj electronic

**elefante** (ee-ler-*ferngn*-ter) m elephant

**elegância** (ee-ler-*gerng*-sʸer) f elegance

**elegante** (ee-ler-*gerngn*-ter) adj smart, elegant

**eleger** (ee-ler-*zhayr*) v elect

**eleição** (ee-lay-*serng*ʷ) f (pl -ções) election

**elementar** (ee-ler-*mayngn*-tahr) adj primary, elementary

**elemento** (ee-ler-*mayngn*-too) m element

**eles** (*ay*-lɪsh) pron they; ~ **mesmos** themselves

**elevação** (ee-ler-ver-*serng*ʷ) f (pl -ções) rise

**elevador** (ee-ler-ver-*dhoar*) m elevator nAm

**elfo** (*ehl*-foo) m elf

**eliminar** (ee-ler-mee-*nahr*) v eliminate

**elo** (*eh*-loo) m link

**elogio** (ee-loo-*zhee*ᵒᵒ) m praise

**elucidar** (ee loo-see-*dhahr*) v elucidate

**em** (erng ʸ) prep at; in, inside

**emagrecer** (ee-mer-grer-*sayr*) v slim

**emancipação** (ee-merng-see-per-*serng*ʷ) f emancipation

**embaixada** (ayngm-bigh-*shah*-dher) f embassy

**embaixador** (ayngm-bigh-shah-*dhoar*) m ambassador

**embalagem** (ayngm-ber-*lah*-zherngʸ) f packing

**embalar** (ayngm-ber-*lahr*) v pack up, pack

**embaraçado** (ayngm-ber-rer-*sah*-dhoo) adj embarrassed

**embaraçar** (ayngm-ber-rer-*sahr*) v embarrass

**embaraçoso** (ayngm-ber-rer-*soa*-zoo) adj awkward, embarrassing

**embarcação** (ayngm-berr-ker-*serng*ʷ) f (pl -ções) embarkation; vessel

**embarcar** (ayngm-berr-*kahr*) v embark

**embargo** (ayngm-*bahr*-goo) m embargo

**embeber** (ayngm-ber-*bhayr*) v soak

**emblema** (ayngm-*blay*-mer) m emblem

**embora** (ayŋgm-*bo*-rer) *conj* although, though; *adv* off

**emboscada** (ayŋgm-boosh-*kah*-dher) *f* ambush

**embotado** (ayŋgm-boo-*tah*-dhoo) *adj* dull

**embraiagem** (ayŋgm-brer-ᵞ*ah*-zherŋᵞ) *f* clutch

**embriagado** (ayŋgm-bree-er-*gah*-dhoo) *adj* intoxicated

**embrulhar** (ayŋgm-broo-*lᵞ*ahr) *v* wrap up, pack up; confuse

**embrulho** (ayŋgm-*broo*-lᵞoo) *m* parcel

**ementa** (ee-*mayng*-ter) *f* menu; ~ **fixa** set menu

**emergência** (ee-merr-*zhayng*-sᵞer) *f* emergency

**emigração** (er-mee-grer-*serng*ʷ) *f* (pl -ções) emigration

**emigrante** (er-mee-*grerng*n-ter) *m* emigrant

**emigrar** (er-mee-*grahr*) *v* emigrate

**eminente** (er-mee-*nayng*n-ter) *adj* outstanding

**emissão** (er-mee-*serng*ʷ) *f* (pl -sões) issue; broadcast

**emissário** (er-mee-*sah*-rᵞoo) *m* envoy

**emissor** (er-mee-*soar*) *m* transmitter

**emitir** (er-mee-*teer*) *v* utter; *broadcast

**emoção** (ee-moo-*serng*ʷ) *f* (pl -ções) emotion

**emocionante** (ee-moo-sᵞoo-*nerng*n-ter) *adj* exciting

**empatar** (ayŋgm-*pah*-terr) *v* hinder, disturb; tie

**empena** (ayŋgm-*pay*-ner) *f* gable

**empenhar** (ayŋgm-per-*ñahr*) *v* pawn

**empilhar** (ayŋgm-pee-*lᵞ*ahr) *v* pile

**empola** (ayŋgm-*poa*-ler) *f* blister

**empreender** (ayŋgm-prᵞayng-*dayr*) *v* *undertake

**empregada** (ayŋgm-prer-*gah*-dher) *f* maid; employee; ~ **de bar** bar-

maid; ~ **de mesa** waitress; ~ **doméstica** housemaid

**empregado** (ayŋgm-prer-*gah*-dhoo) *m* employee; ~ **de balcão** shop assistant; ~ **de bar** bartender; ~ **de escritório** clerk; ~ **de mesa** waiter; ~ **doméstico** domestic

**empregar** (ayŋgm-prer-*gahr*) *v* employ, engage; *spend

**emprego** (ayŋgm-*pray*-goo) *m* employment; job

**empreiteiro** (ayŋgm-pray-*tay*-roo) *m* contractor

**empresa** (ayŋgm-*pray*-zer) *f* undertaking, enterprise; business, concern

**emprestar** (ayŋgm-prɪsh-*tahr*) *v* *lend

**empréstimo** (ayŋgm-*prehsh*-tee-moo) *m* loan

**empurrão** (ayŋgm-poo-*rrerng*ʷ) *m* (pl -rões) push

**empurrar** (ayŋgm-poo-*rrahr*) *v* push

**encadernação** (ayŋgm-ker-dherr-ner-*serng*ʷ) *f* (pl -ções) binding

**encantado** (ayŋgng-kerng-*tah*-dhoo) *adj* delighted

**encantador** (ayŋgng-kerng-ter-*dhoar*) *adj* enchanting; sweet, lovely, charming, delightful

**encantamento** (ayŋgng-kerng-ter-*mayng*-too) *m* spell

**encantar** (ayŋgng-kerng-*tahr*) *v* bewitch; delight

**encanto** (ayŋgng-*kerng*-too) *m* charm; glamour

**encaracolado** (ayŋgng-ker-rer-koo-*lah*-dhoo) *adj* curly

**encaracolar** (ayŋgng-ker-rer-koo-*lahr*) *v* curl

**encarceramento** (ayŋgng-kerr-ser-rer-*mayng*-too) *m* imprisonment

**encarnado** (ayŋgng-kerr-*nah*-dhoo) *adj* red

**encarregar** (ayŋgng-ker-rrer-*gahr*) *v* charge; **encarregado de** in charge of; **encarregar-se de** *take charge of

**encenador** (ayнg-ser-ner-*dhoar*) *m* director

**encenar** (ayнg-ser-*nahr*) *v* direct

**encerrado** (ayнg-ser-*rrer*-dhoo) *adj* closed; shut

**encerrar** (ayнg-ser-*rrahr*) *v* lock up

**enchente** (ayнg-*shaynng*-ter) *f* flood

**encher** (ayнg-*shayr*) *v* fill; fill out *Am;* ~ **de ar** inflate

**enciclopédia** (ayнg-see-kloo-*peh*-dɪ<sup>y</sup>er) *f* encyclopaedia

**encoberto** (ayнgng-koo-*bhehr*-too) *adj* cloudy

**encolher** (ayнgng-koo-*l*<sup>y</sup>*ayr*) *v* *shrink; **não encolhe** shrinkproof

**encomenda** (ayнgng-koo-*maynng*-der) *f* parcel; order; **feito por** ~ made to order

**encomendar** (ayнgng-koo-maynng-*dahr*) *v* order

**encontrão** (ayнgng-kawнg-*trernng*<sup>w</sup>) *m* (pl -rões) bump

**encontrar** (ayнgng-kawнg-*trahr*) *v* *find; *come across; encounter, *meet

**encontro** (ayнgng-*kawнg*-troo) *m* encounter; date

**encorajar** (ayнgng-koo-rer-*zhahr*) *v* encourage

**encosta** (ayнgng-*kosh*-ter) *f* hillside

**encruzilhada** (ayнgng-kroo-zee-*l*<sup>y</sup>*ah*-dher) *f* crossing

**encurtar** (ayнgng-koor-*tahr*) *v* shorten

**endereçar** (ayнgn-der-rer-*sahr*) *v* address

**endereço** (ayнgn-der-*ray*-soo) *m* address

**endireitar** (ayнgn-dee-ray-*tahr*) *v* straighten

**endossar** (ayнgn-doo-*sahr*) *v* endorse

**energia** (ee-nerr-*zheeer*) *f* energy; power; ~ **nuclear** nuclear energy

**enérgico** (ee-*nehr*-zhee-koo) *adj* energetic

**enevoado** (ee-ner-*vwah*-dhoo) *adj* misty, hazy; foggy

**enfadonho** (ayнg-fer-*dhoa*-ñoo) *adj* dull

**ênfase** (*ayнg*-fer-zer) *f* stress

**enfeitiçar** (ayнg-fay-tee-*sahr*) *v* bewitch

**enfermaria** (ayнg-ferr-mer-*ree*-er) *f* infirmary

**enfermeira** (ayнg-ferr-*may*-rer) *f* nurse

**enfermeiro** (ayнg-ferr-*may*-roo) *m* male nurse

**enfiar** (ayнg-*f*<sup>y</sup>*ahr*) *v* thread; pierce

**enforcar** (ayнg-foor-*kahr*) *v* hang

**enfrentar** (ayнg-fraynng-*tahr*) *v* face

**enfurecer** (ayнg-foo-rer-*sayr*) *v* rage

**enganar** (ayнgng-ger-*nahr*) *v* deceive; cheat, fool; **enganar-se** *be mistaken

**engano** (ayнgng-*ger*-noo) *m* deceit; mistake

**engarrafamento** (ayнgng-ger-rer-fer-*maynng*-too) *m* bottling; obstruction; ~ **de trânsito** traffic jam

**engenheiro** (ayнg-zhɪ-*ñay*-roo) *m* engineer

**engenhoca** (ayнg-zhɪ-*ño*-ker) *f* gadget

*engolir (ayнgng-goo-*leer*) *v* swallow

**engomar** (ayнgng-goo-*mahr*) *v* starch; **engomado permanente** permanent press

**engordar** (ayнg-goor-*dahr*) *v* fatten; *grow fat

**engraçado** (ayнgng-grer-*sah*-dhoo) *adj* humorous, funny

**engrossar** (ayнgng-groo-*sahr*) *v* thicken

**enguia** (ayнgng-*gee*-er) *f* eel

**enigma** (ee-*neeg*-mer) *m* enigma, mystery; puzzle

**enjoado** (ayнg-*zhwah*-dhoo) *adj* sick; seasick

**enjoo** (ayng-*zhoa*-oo) *m* sickness, airsickness, seasickness

**enorme** (ee-*nor*-mer) *adj* enormous; huge, immense

**enquanto** (ayngng-*kwerngn*-too) *conj* whilst, while

**enredo** (ayng-*rray*-dhoo) *m* plot

**enrolar** (ayng-roo-*lahr*) *v* *wind

**enrugar** (ayng-roo-*gahr*) *v* crease

**ensaiar** (ayng-ser-*Yahr*) *v* rehearse

**ensaio** (ayng-*sigh*-oo) *m* rehearsal; essay

**enseada** (ayng-s*Yah*-dher) *f* inlet, creek

**ensinamentos** (ayng-see-ner-*mayngn*-toosh) *mpl* teachings *pl*

**ensinar** (ayng-see-*nahr*) *v* *teach

**ensopar** (ayng-soo-*pahr*) *v* soak

**entalhar** (ayngn-ter-*lYahr*) *v* carve

**no entanto** (noo ayng-*terngn*-too) though

**então** (ayngn-*terngᵂ*) *adv* then; **de ~** contemporary

**enteada** (ayngn-t*Yah*-dher) *f* stepdaughter

**enteado** (ayngn-t*Yah*-dhoo) *m* stepson, stepchild

**entender** (ayngn-tayngn-*dayr*) *v* *understand

**enterrar** (ayngn-ter-*rrahr*) *v* bury

**enterro** (ayngn-*tay*-rroo) *m* burial

**entornar** (ayngn-toor-*nahr*) *v* *spill

**entorpecido** (ayngn-toor-per-*see*-dhoo) *adj* numb

**entrada** (ayngn-*trah*-dher) *f* entry, way in, entrance; admittance; foyer; **~ proibida** no admittance

**entranhas** (ayngn-*trer*-ñersh) *fpl* insides

**entrar** (ayngn-*trahr*) *v* enter, *go in

**entravar** (ayngn-trer-*vahr*) *v* impede

**entre** (*ayngn*-trer) *prep* between; amid, among

**entrega** (ayngn-*treh*-ger) *f* delivery

**entregar** (ayngn-trer-*gahr*) *v* deliver; hand, *give; commit

**entretanto** (ayngn-trer-*terngn*-too) *adv* meanwhile, in the meantime

**entreter** (ayngn-trer-*tayr*) *v* entertain

**entrevista** (ayngn-trer-*veesh*-ter) *f* interview; appointment

**entusiasmo** (ayngn-too-z*Y*ahzh-moo) *m* enthusiasm

**entusiasta** (ayngn-too-z*Y*ahsh-ter) *adj* keen

**entusiástico** (ayngn-too-z*Y*ahsh-tee-koo) *adj* enthusiastic

**envelhecido** (ayng-veh-l*Y*er-*see*-dhoo) *adj* old, aged

**envenenar** (ayng-ver-ner-*nahr*) *v* poison

**envergonhado** (ayng-verr-goo-ñah-dhoo) *adj* embarrassed; ashamed

**envernizar** (ayng-verr-nee-*zahr*) *v* varnish

**enviar** (ayng-v*Y*ahr) *v* *send, dispatch

**envolver** (ayng-voal-*vayr*) *v* wrap

**envolvido** (ayng-voal-*vee*-dhoo) *adj* concerned; involved

**enxaguadela** (ayng-sher-gwer-*dhay*-ler) *f* rinse

**enxaguar** (ayng-sher-*gwahr*) *v* rinse

**enxaqueca** (ayng-sher-*keh*-ker) *f* migraine

**enxugar** (ayng-shoo-*gahr*) *v* dry

**épico** (*eh*-pee-koo) *adj* epic

**epidemia** (er-pee-dher-*mee*-er) *f* epidemic

**epilepsia** (er-pee-lehp-*see*-er) *f* epilepsy

**epílogo** (er-*pee*-loo-goo) *m* epilogue

**episódio** (er-pee-zo-dh*Y*oo) *m* episode

**época** (*eh*-poo-ker) *f* period; **fora da ~** off season

**epopeia** (ee-poo-*pay*-er) *f* epic

**Equador** (ee-kwer-*dhoar*) *m* Ecuador

**equador** (ee-kwer-*dhoar*) *m* equator

**equatoriano** (ı-kwer-too-r*Y*ah-noo) *m*

Ecuadorian

**equilíbrio** (ee-ker-*lee*-bhrYoo) *m* balance

**equipa** (ı-*kee*-per) *f* team; soccer team

**equipamento** (ı-kee-per-*mayngn*-too) *m* equipment; outfit, kit, gear; ~ **de pesca** fishing gear

**equipar** (ı-kee-*pahr*) *v* equip

**equitação** (ı-kee-ter-*serngw*) *f* riding; **escola de** ~ riding-school

**equitativo** (ı-kwee-ter-*tee*-voo) *adj* right

**equivalente** (ı-kee-ver-*layngn*-ter) *adj* equivalent

**equívoco** (ı-*kee*-voo-koo) *m* mistake; *adj* ambiguous

**erecto** (ee-*reh*-too) *adj* erect

**erguer** (eer-*gayr*) *v* lift; **erguer-se** *rise; *get up

**erigir** (ee-rer-*zheer*) *v* erect

**errado** (ee-*rrah*-dhoo) *adj* wrong; false, mistaken; *estar ~ *be wrong

**errar** (ee-*rrahr*) *v* err; wander

**erro** (*ay*-rroo) *m* mistake, error

**erudito** (ee-roo-*dhee*-too) *adj* learned; *m* scholar

**erupção** (ee-roop-*serngw*) *f* (pl -ções) rash

**erva** (*ehr*-ver) *f* herb; grass; ~ **daninha** weed; **folha de** ~ blade of grass

**ervilha** (ır-*vee*-lYer) *f* pea

**esbelto** (ızh-*bhehl*-too) *adj* slender

**esboçar** (ızh-bhoo-*sahr*) *v* sketch

**esboço** (ızh-*bhoa*-soo) *m* sketch

**escada** (ısh-*kah*-dher) *f* ladder; stairs *pl*; staircase; ~ **de incêndio** fire-escape; ~ **do portaló** gangway; ~ **rolante** escalator

**escala** (ısh-*kah*-ler) *f* scale

**escalar** (ısh-ker-*lahr*) *v* ascend

**escama** (ısh-*ker*-mer) *f* scale

**escândalo** (ısh-*kerngn*-der-loo) *m* scandal

**Escandinávia** (ısh-kerngn-dee-*ner*-vYer) *f* Scandinavia

**escandinavo** (ısh-kerngn-dee-*nah*-voo) *adj* Scandinavian; *m* Scandinavian

**escangalhado** (ısh-kerngn-ger-*lYah*-dhoo) *adj* broken

**escangalhar** (ısh-kerngn-ger-*lYahr*) *v* *break

**escapar** (ısh-ker-*pahr*) *v* slip, escape

**escape** (ısh-*kah*-per) *m* exhaust; **tubo de** ~ exhaust

**escaravelho** (ısh-ker-rer-*vay*-lYoo) *m* beetle; bug

**escarlate** (ısh-kerr-*lah*-ter) *adj* scarlet

**escárnio** (ısh-*kahr*-nYoo) *m* scorn

**escarpado** (ısh-kahr-*pah*-dhoo) *adj* steep

**escassez** (ısh-ker-*saysh*) *f* scarcity; shortage

**escasso** (ısh-*kah*-soo) *adj* scarce

**escavação** (ısh-ker-ver-*serngw*) *f* (pl -ções) excavation

**escavar** (ısh-ker-*vahr*) *v* *dig

**esclarecer** (ısh-kler-rer-*serr*) *v* clarify

**esclarecimento** (ısh-kler-rer-see-*mayngn*-too) *m* explanation

**escocês** (ısh-koo-*saysh*) *adj* Scottish, Scotch; *m* Scot

**Escócia** (ısh-ko-*s*Yer) *f* Scotland

**escola** (ısh-*ko*-ler) *f* school; ~ **secundária** secondary school

**escolar** (ısh-koo-*lahr*) *f* schoolgirl; *m* schoolboy; *adj* of or pertaining to school

**escolha** (ısh-*koa*-lYer) *f* choice, selection; pick

**escolher** (ısh-koo-*lYayr*) *v* *choose; pick; select; elect

**escolta** (ısh-*koal*-ter) *f* escort

**escoltar** (ısh-koal-*tahr*) *v* escort

**esconder** (ısh-kawngn-*dayr*) *v* *hide; conceal

**escorregadela** (ısh-koo-rrer-ger-*dheh-*

ler) f slip

**escorregadio** (ısh-koo-rrer-ger-*dhee*ᵒᵒ) *adj* slippery

**escorregadouro** (ısh-koo-rrer-ger-*dhoa*-roo) *m* slide

**escorregar** (ısh-koo-rrer-*gahr*) *v* glide, slip

**escova** (ısh-*koa*-ver) *f* brush; ~ **de cabelo** hairbrush; ~ **de dentes** toothbrush; ~ **de fato** clothesbrush; ~ **de unhas** nailbrush

**escovar** (ısh-koo-*vahr*) *v* brush

**escravo** (ısh-*krer*-voo) *m* slave

**escrevaninha** (ısh-kree-ver-*nee*-ñer) *f* bureau

**escrever** (ısh-krer-*vayr*) *v* *write; ~ à máquina type; por escrito written, in writing

**escrita** (ısh-*kree*-ter) *f* handwriting

**escritor** (ısh-kree-*toar*) *m* writer

**escritório** (ısh-kree-*to*-rʸoo) *m* office; study; **artigos de** ~ stationery

**escrivão** (ısh-kree-*verng*ʷ) *m* (pl -ães) clerk

**escultor** (ısh-kool-*toar*) *m* sculptor

**escultura** (ısh-kool-*too*-rer) *f* sculpture

**escuridão** (ısh-koo-ree-*dherng*ʷ) *f* darkness; gloom

**escuro** (ısh-*koo*-roo) *adj* dark; obscure

**escutar** (ısh-koo-*tahr*) *v* listen

**escuteira** (ısh-koo-*tay*-rer) *f* girl guide

**escuteiro** (ısh-koo-*tay*-roo) *m* boy scout, scout

**esfera** (ısh-*feh*-rer) *f* sphere

**esfomeado** (ısh-foo-*m*ʸah-dhoo) *adj* hungry; famished

**esforçar-se** (ısh-foor-*sahr*-ser) *v* try

**esforço** (ısh-*foar*-soo) *m* strain, effort

**esfregar** (ısh-frer-*gahr*) *v* rub, scrub

**esgalhos** (ızh-*gah*-lʸoosh) *mpl* antlers *pl*

**esgotado** (ısh-goo-*tah*-dhoo) *adj* sold out

**esgoto** (ısh-*goa*-too) *m* drain, sewer

**esgrimir** (ızh-gree-*meer*) *v* fence

**esguicho** (ızh-*gee*-shoo) *m* squirt

**esmagar** (ızh-mer-*gahr*) *v* mash

**esmaltado** (ızh-mahl-*tah*-dhoo) *adj* enamelled

**esmaltar** (ızh-mahl-*tahr*) *v* enamel

**esmalte** (ızh-*mahl*-ter) *m* enamel

**esmeralda** (ızh-mer-*rahl*-der) *f* emerald

**espaçar** (ısh-per-*sahr*) *v* space

**espaço** (ısh-*pah*-soo) *m* room, space

**espaçoso** (ısh-pah-*soa*-zoo) *adj* spacious; large, roomy

**espada** (ısh-*pah*-dher) *f* sword

**espalhafato** (ısh-per-lʸer-*fah*-too) *m* fuss

**espalhar** (ısh-per-*l*ʸahr) *v* *spread; *shed

**Espanha** (ısh-*per*-ñer) *f* Spain

**espanhol** (ısh-per-*ñol*) *adj* (pl -hóis) Spanish; *m* Spaniard

**espantar** (ısh-pern̄gn-*tahr*) *v* amaze, astonish

**espanto** (ısh-*pern̄gn*-too) *m* astonishment, amazement

**espantoso** (ısh-pern̄gn-*toa*-zoo) *adj* astonishing; dreadful

**esparadrapo** (ısh-per-rer-*dhrah*-poo) *mBr* adhesive tape, adhesive bandage, plaster

**espargo** (ısh-*pahr*-goo) *m* asparagus

**especial** (ısh-per-s*ʸahl*) *adj* (pl -aıs) special; particular, peculiar

**especialidade** (ısh-per-sʸer-lee-*dhah*-dher) *f* speciality

**especialista** (ısh-per-sʸer-*leesh*-ter) *m* specialist; expert

**especializado** (ısh-per-sʸer-lee-*zah*-dhoo) *adj* skilled

**especializar-se** (ısh-per-sʸer-lee-*zahr*-ser) *v* specialize

**especialmente** (ısh-per-s*ʸahl*-*mayngn*-ter) *adv* especially especiaria (ısh-per-s Yer-_ree_-er) f spice

espécie (ısh-_peh_-s Yer) f species; breed; **toda a ~ de** all sorts of

específico (ısh-per-_see_-fee-koo) adj specific

espectáculo (ısh-peh-_tah_-koo-loo) m sight; show, spectacle; **~ de variedades** variety show; floor show

espectador (ısh-peh-ter-_dhoar_) m spectator

especular (ısh-per-koo-_lahr_) v speculate

espelho (ısh-_pay_-lYoo) m looking-glass, mirror

espera (ısh-_peh_-rer) f waiting

esperado (ısh-per-_rer_-doo) adj due

esperança (ısh-per-_rerng_-ser) f hope

esperançado (ısh-per-rerng-_sah_-dhoo) adj hopeful

esperar (ısh-per-_rahr_) v expect; await, wait; hope

esperto (ısh-_pehr_-too) adj bright; smart, clever

espesso (ısh-_pay_-soo) adj thick

espeto (ısh-_peh_-too) m spit

espião (ısh-p Yerng ᵂ) m (pl -iões) spy

espinafres (ısh-pee-_nah_-frersh) mpl spinach

espingarda (ısh-peeng-_gahr_-dher) f rifle; gun

espinha (ısh-_pee_-ñer) f bone; **~ de peixe** fishbone; **~ dorsal** backbone, spine

espinho (ısh-_pee_-ñoo) m thorn

espírito (ısh-_pee_-ree-too) m spirit; soul; ghost

espiritual (ısh-per-ree-_twahl_) adj (pl -ais) spiritual

espirituoso (ısh-per-ree-_twoa_-zoo) adj humorous; witty

espirrar (ısh-pee-_rrahr_) v sneeze

esplanada (ısh-pler-_nah_-dher) f esplanade

esplêndido (ısh-_playngn_-dee-dhoo) adj splendid; glorious, enchanting, magnificent

esplendor (ısh-playngn-_doar_) m splendour; glare

esponja (ısh-_pawng_-zher) f sponge

esporte (ısh-_por_-ter) mBr sport

esposa (ısh-_poa_-zer) f wife

esposo (ısh-_poa_-zoo) m husband

espreitar (ısh-pray-_tahr_) v peep; watch for

espuma (ısh-_poo_-mer) f froth; foam, lather; **~ de borracha** foam-rubber

espumante (ısh-poo-_merngn_-ter) adj sparkling

espumar (ısh-poo-_mahr_) v foam

esquadrilha (ısh-kwer-_dhree_-lYer) f squadron

esquecer (ısh-keh-_sayr_) v *forget

esquecido (ısh-keh-_see_-dhoo) adj forgetful

esqueleto (ısh-ker-_lay_-too) m skeleton

esquema (ısh-_kay_-mer) m scheme, diagram

esquerdo (ısh-_kayr_-doo) adj left; left-hand

esqui (ısh-_kee_) m ski; skiing; **~ aquático** water ski; **varas de ~** ski sticks

esquiador (ısh-k Yer-_dhoar_) m skier

esquiar (ısh-k Y-_ahr_) v ski

esquilo (ısh-_kee_-loo) m squirrel

esquina (ısh-_kee_-ner) f corner

esquisito (ısh-ker-_zee_-too) adj queer

esquivo (ısh-_kee_-voo) adj shy

esse (_ay_-ser) adj that; **esses** those

essência (ee-_sayng_-s Yer) f essence

essencial (ee-sayng-s Yahl) adj (pl -ais) essential

essencialmente (ee-sayng-s Yahl-_mayngn_-ter) adv essentially

estabelecer (ısh-ter-bher-ler-_sayr_) v establish; found

estábulo (ısh-_tah_-bhoo-loo) m stable

**estação** (ish-ter-*serng*ᵂ) f (pl -ções) station; season; depot nAm; **alta ~** high season; **baixa ~** low season; **~ balnear** seaside resort; **~ central** central station; **~ de serviço** service station, filling station; **plena ~** peak season

**estacionamento** (ish-ter-sᵞoo-ner-*mayngn*-too) m parking; **~ proibido** no parking

**estacionar** (ish-ter-sᵞoo-*nahr*) v park

**estacionário** (ish-ter-sᵞoo-nah-rᵞoo) adj stationary

**estadia** (ish-*tah*-dhᵞer) f stay

**estádio** (ish-*tah*-dhᵞoo) m stadium

**estadista** (ish-ter-*dheesh*-ter.) m statesman

**estado** (ish-*tah*-dhoo) m state; condition; **do ~** national; **~ de emergência** emergency; **Estados Unidos** United States; the States

**estalagem** (ish-ter-*lah*-zherngᵞ) f inn, roadhouse

**estalajadeiro** (ish-ter-ler-zher-*dhay*-roo) m inn-keeper

**estalar** (ish-ter-*lahr*) v crack

**estaleiro** (ish-ter-*lay*-roo) m shipyard

**estalido** (ish-ter-*lee*-dhoo) m crack

**estampa** (ish-*terngm*-per) f engraving

**estandarte** (ish-terngn-*dahr*-ter) m banner

**estanho** (ish-*ter*-ñoo) m pewter, tin

**\*estar** (ish-*tahr*) v \*be

**estatística** (ish-ter-*teesh*-tee-ker) f statistics pl

**estátua** (ish-*tah*-twer) f statue

**estatura** (ish-*tah*-too-rer) f figure

**estável** (ish-*tah*-vehl) adj (pl -eis) stable; permanent

**este¹** (*aysh*-ter) adj this; pron this; **estes** these

**este²** (*ehsh*-ter) m east

**estenografia** (ish-ter-noo-grer-*fee*-er) f shorthand

**estenógrafo** (ish-ter-*no*-grer-foo) m stenographer

**esterco** (ish-*tayr*-koo) m dung

**estéril** (ish-*teh*-reel) adj (pl -eis) sterile

**esterilizar** (ish-ter-rer-lee-*zahr*) v sterilize

**estibordo** (ish-tee-*bhor*-doo) m starboard

**esticão** (ish-tee-*kerng*ᵂ) m (pl -ções) tug

**esticar** (ish-tee-*kahr*) v stretch

**estilo** (ish-*tee*-loo) m style

**estima** (ish-*tee*-mer) f respect, esteem

**estimar** (ish-tee-*mahr*) v esteem; estimate

**estimativa** (ish-tee-mer-*tee*-ver) f estimate; \*fazer a ~ estimate

**estimulante** (ish-tee-moo-*lerngn*-ter) m stimulant

**estimular** (ish-tee-moo-*lahr*) v stimulate

**estímulo** (ish-*tee*-moo-loo) m impulse

**estipulação** (ish-tee-poo-ler-*serng*ᵂ) f (pl -ções) stipulation

**estipular** (ish-tee-poo-*lahr*) v stipulate

**estivador** (ish-tee-ver-*dhoar*) m docker

**estofar** (ish-too-*fahr*) v upholster

**estojo** (ish-*toa*-zhoo) m case; **~ de toalete** toilet case

**estola** (ish-*to*-ler) f stole

**estômago** (ish-*toa*-mer-goo) m stomach

**estore** (ish-*to*-rer) m blind

**estorninho** (ish-toor-*nee*-ñoo) m starling

**estorvar** (ish-toor-*vahr*) v embarras, hinder; disturb

**estrábico** (ish-*trah*-bhee-koo) adj cross-eyed

**estrada** (ish-*trah*-dher) f road, drive; **~ com portagem** turnpike nAm; **~ de circunvalação** by-pass; **~ de ferro** Br railway, railroad nAm; **~**

**em obras** road works, road up; ~ **principal** main road; highway, thoroughfare

**estragar** (ish-trer-*gahr*) *v* \*spoil; mess up

**estrangeiro** (ish-trerng-*zhay*-roo) *m* alien, stranger, foreigner; *adj* alien, foreign; **no** ~ abroad; **para o** ~ abroad

**estrangular** (ish-trerng-goo-*lahr*) *v* choke, strangle

**estranho** (ish-*trer*-ño) *adj* funny; foreign, strange; queer, odd, quaint, peculiar; *m* alien

**estreitar** (ish-tray-*tahr*) *v* tighten

**estreito** (ish-*tray*-too) *adj* narrow; tight

**estrela** (ish-*tray*-ler) *f* star

**estremecimento** (ish-trer-mer-see-*mayngn*-too) *m* shudder

**estribo** (ish-*tree*-bhoo) *m* stirrup

**estrofe** (ish-*tro*-fer) *f* stanza

**estrume** (ish-*troo*-mer) *m* manure

**estrumeira** (ish-troo-*may*-rer) *f* dunghill

**estrutura** (ish-troo-*too*-rer) *f* structure; fabric

**estuário** (ish-*twah*-rʸoo) *m* estuary

**estudante** (ish-too-*dherngn*-ter) *m* student; *f* student

**estudar** (ish-too-*dhahr*) *v* study

**estudo** (ish-*too*-dhoo) *m* study

**estufa** (ish-*too*-fer) *f* greenhouse

**estupefaciente** (ish-too-per-fer-sʸ*ayngn*-ter) *m* drug

**estupendo** (ish-too-*payngn*-doo) *adj* wonderful

**estúpido** (ish-*too*-pee-dhoo) *adj* dumb, stupid

**estuque** (ish-*too*-ker) *m* plaster

**esvaziar** (izh-ver-zʸ*ahr*) *v* empty

**etapa** (ee-*tah*-per) *f* stage

**éter** (*eh*-tehr) *m* ether

**eternidade** (ee-terr-nee-*dhah*-der) *f* eternity

**eterno** (ee-*tehr*-noo) *adj* eternal

**etíope** (ɪ-*tee*ᵒᵒ-per) *adj* Ethiopian; *m* Ethiopian

**Etiópia** (ɪ-tʸoa-pʸer) *f* Ethiopia

**etiqueta** (er-tee-*kay*-ter) *f* tag, label

**etiquetar** (er-tee-ker-*tahr*) *v* label

**eu** (*ay*ᵒᵒ) *pron* I; ~ **mesmo** myself

**Europa** (ay**ᵒᵒ**-ro-per) *f* Europe

**europeu** (ay**ᵒᵒ**-roo-*pay*ᵒᵒ) *adj* European; *m* European

**evacuar** (ee-ver-*kwahr*) *v* evacuate

**evadir** (ee-ver-*dheer*) *v* escape

**evangelho** (ee-verng-*zheh*-lʸoo) *m* gospel

**evaporar** (ee-ver-poo-*rahr*) *v* evaporate

**evasão** (ee-ver-*zerng*ʷ) *f* (pl -sões) escape

**eventual** (ee-vayngn-*twahl*) *adj* (pl -ais) possible

**evidente** (er-vee-*dhayngn*-ter) *adj* evident

**evitar** (er-vee-*tahr*) *v* avoid; prevent

**evolução** (ee-voo-loo-*serng*ʷ) *f* (pl -ções) evolution

**exactamente** (ee-zah-ter-*mayngn*-ter) *adv* exactly

**exactidão** (ee-zah-tee-*dherng*ʷ) *f* correctness; precision

**exacto** (ee-*zah*-too) *adj* precise, exact; accurate

**exagerado** (ee-zer-zher-*rah*-dhoo) *adj* extravagant; excessive

**exagerar** (ee-zer-zher-*rahr*) *v* exaggerate

**exalar** (ee-zer-*lahr*) *v* exhale

**exame** (ee-*zer*-mer) *m* examination; ~ **médico** check-up

**examinar** (ee-zer-mee-*nahr*) *v* examine

**exausto** (ee-*zoush*-too) *adj* over-tired

**excedente** (ish-ser-*dhayngn*-ter) *m* remnant, surplus

**exceder** (ish-ser-*dhayr*) *v* exceed

**excelente** (ish-ser-*layngn*-ter) *adj* excellent; fine, first-rate

**excêntrico** (ish-*sayngn*-tree-koo) *adj* eccentric

**excepção** (ish-seh-*serng*ʷ) *f* (pl -ções) exception

**excepcional** (ish-seh-sʸoo-*nahl*) *adj* (pl -ais) exceptional

**excepto** (ish-*seh*-too) *prep* except

**excessivo** (ish-ser-*see*-voo) *adj* excessive

**excesso** (ish-*seh*-soo) *m* excess; ~ **de peso** overweight; ~ **de velocidade** speeding

**excitação** (ish-see-ter-*serng*ʷ) *f* (pl -ções) excitement

**excitar** (ish-see-*tahr*) *v* excite

**exclamação** (ish-kler-mer-*serng*ʷ) *f* (pl -ções) exclamation

**exclamar** (ish-kler-*mahr*) *v* exclaim

***excluir** (ish-*klweer*) *v* exclude

**exclusivamente** (ish-kloo-see-ver-*mayngn*-ter) *adv* exclusively; solely

**exclusivo** (ish-kloo-*zee*-voo) *adj* exclusive

**excursão** (ish-koor-*serng*ʷ) *f* (pl -sões) excursion; day trip

**execução** (ee-zer-koo-*serng*ʷ) *f* (pl -ções) execution

**executar** (ee-zer-koo-*tahr*) *v* execute, perform, carry out

**executivo** (ee-zer-koo-*tee*-voo) *adj* executive

**exemplar** (ee-zayngm-*plahr*) *m* specimen; copy

**exemplo** (ee-*zayngm*-ploo) *m* example; instance; **por** ~ for instance, for example

**exercer** (ee-zerr-*sayr*) *v* exercise

**exercício** (ee-zerr-*see*-sʸoo) *m* exercise

**exercitar** (ee-zerr-see-*tahr*) *v* exercise; **exercitar-se** practise

**exército** (ee-*zehr*-see-too) *m* army

**exibição** (ee-zer-bhee-*serng*ʷ) *f* (pl -ções) exhibition

**exibir** (ee-zer-*bheer*) *v* exhibit; display, *show

**exigência** (ee-zi-*zhayng*-sʸer) *f* demand

**exigente** (ee-zi-*zhayngn*-ter) *adj* particular, demanding

**exigir** (ee-zi-*zheer*) *v* demand; require

**exilado** (i-zee-*lah*-dhoo) *m* exile

**exílio** (i-*zee*-lʸoo) *m* exile

**existência** (i-zeesh-*tayng*-sʸer) *f* existence

**existir** (i-zeesh-*teer*) *v* exist

**êxito** (*ay*-zee-too) *m* success

**exótico** (ee-*zo*-tee-koo) *adj* exotic

**expandir** (ish-perngn-*deer*) *v* expand

**expectativa** (ish-peh-ter-*tee*-ver) *f* expectation

**expedição** (ish-per-dhee-*serng*ʷ) *f* (pl -ções) expedition

***expedir** (ish-per-*dheer*) *v* dispatch; ship, *send off

**experiência** (ish-per-rʸ*ayng*-sʸer) *f* experiment; trial, experience

**experiente** (ish-per-rʸ*ayngn*-ter) *adj* experienced

**experimentar** (ish-per-ree-mayngn-*tahr*) *v* try, experiment; test; experience

**expiração** (ish-pee-rer-*serng*ʷ) *f* (pl -ções) expiry

**expirar** (ish-pee-*rahr*) *v* expire

**explicação** (ish-plee-ker-*serng*ʷ) *f* (pl -ções) explanation

**explicar** (ish-plee-*kahr*) *v* explain

**explícito** (ish-*plee*-see-too) *adj* express, explicit

***explodir** (ish-ploo-*dheer*) *v* explode

**explorar** (ish-ploo-*rahr*) *v* explore; exploit

**explosão** (ish-ploo-*zerng*ʷ) *f* (pl -sões) blast, explosion; outbreak

**explosivo** (ish-ploo-*zee*-voo) *adj* explosive; *m* explosive

**\*expor** (ısh-*poar*) *v* exhibit, **\*show**, display

**exportação** (ısh-poor-ter-*serng*ʷ) *f* (pl -ções) export, exportation

**exportar** (ısh-poor-*tahr*) *v* export

**exposição** (ısh-poo-zee-*serng*ʷ) *f* (pl -ções) display; show, exhibition, exposition; exposure; ~ **de arte** art exhibition

**expressão** (ısh-prer-*serng*ʷ) *f* (pl -sões) expression; ~ **idiomática** idiom

**expressar** (ısh-prer-*sahr*) *v* express

**expresso** (ısh-*preh*-soo) *adj* express; **distribuição expressa** special delivery

**exprimir** (ısh-pree-*meer*) *v* express

**expulsar** (ısh-pool-*sahr*) *v* chase, expel

**êxtase** (*aysh*-ter-zer) *m* ecstasy

**extensão** (ısh-tayng-*serng*ʷ) *f* (pl -sões) extension

**extensivo** (ısh-tayng-see-voo) *adj* comprehensive

**extenso** (ısh-*tayng*-soo) *adj* extensive

**extenuar** (ısh-ter-*nwahr*) *v* exhaust

**exterior** (ısh-ter-*rʸoar*) *m* exterior, outside; *adj* exterior, external

**externo** (ısh-*tehr*-noo) *adj* outward

**extinguir** (ısh-teeng-*geer*) *v* extinguish

**extintor** (ısh-teengn-*toar*) *m* fire-extinguisher

**\*extorquir** (ısh-toor-*keer*) *v* extort

**extorsão** (ısh-toor-*serng*ʷ) *f* (pl -sões) extortion

**extraditar** (ısh-trah-dhee-*tahr*) *v* extradite

**\*extrair** (ısh-trer-*eer*) *v* extract

**extraordinário** (ısh-trer-oor-dhee-*nah*-rʸoo) *adj* extraordinary; exceptional

**extravagante** (ısh-trer-ver-*gerngn*-ter) *adj* extravagant

**extraviar** (ısh-trah-*vʸahr*) *v* \*mislay

**extremidade** (ısh-trer-mee-*dhah*-dher) *f* end

**extremo** (ısh-*tray*-moo) *adj* extreme; very; *m* extreme

**exuberante** (ee-zoo-bher-*rerngn*-ter) *adj* exuberant

# F

**fã** (ferng) *m Br* fan

**fábrica** (*fah*-bhree-ker) *f* factory; works *pl*, plant, mill

**fabricante** (fah-bhree-*kerngn*-ter) *m* manufacturer

**fabricar** (fah-bhree-*kahr*) *v* manufacture

**fábula** (*fah*-bhoo-ler) *f* fable

**faca** (*fah*-ker) *f* knife

**face** (*fah*-ser) *f* cheek

**fachada** (fer-*shah*-dher) *f* façade

**fácil** (*fah*-seel) *adj* (pl fáceis) easy

**facilidade** (fer-ser-lee-*dhah*-dher) *f* facility, ease

**facto** (*fahk*-too) *m* fact; **de** ~ as a matter of fact

**factor** (fah-*toar*) *m* factor

**factura** (fah-*too*-rer) *f* invoice

**facturar** (fah-too-*rahr*) *v* bill

**faculdade** (fer-kool-*dah*-dher) *f* faculty

**facultativo** (fer-kool-ter-*tee*-voo) *adj* optional

**fada** (*fah*-dher) *f* fairy

**faia** (*figh*-er) *f* beech

**faiança** (fer-*ʸerng*-ser) *f* faience; crockery

**faina** (*figh*-ner) *f* work

**faisão** (figh-*zerng*ʷ) *m* (pl -sões) pheasant

**faísca** (fer-*eesh*-ker) *f* spark

**faixa** (*figh*-sher) *f* strip; ~ **de roda-gem** carriageway

**fala** (*fah*-ler) *f* speech

**falador** (fer-ler-*dhoar*) *adj* talkative

**falar** (fer-*lahr*) *v* \*speak; talk

**falcão** (fahl-*kerng*ʷ) *m* (pl -cões) hawk

**falecer** (fer-ler-*sayr*) *v* depart, die

**falésia** (fer-*leh*-sᵞer) *f* cliff

**falha** (fah-lᵞer) *f* fault; shortcoming

**falhar** (fer-lᵞahr) *v* fail

**falido** (fer-*lee*-dhoo) *adj* bankrupt

**falsificação** (fahl-ser-fee-ker-*serng*ʷ) *f* (pl -cões) fake

**falsificar** (fahl-ser-fee-*kahr*) *v* counterfeit, forge

**falso** (*fahl*-soo) *adj* false; untrue; hypocritical

**falta** (*fahl*-ter) *f* want, lack; error; offence; **sem ~** without fail

**faltar** (fahl-*tahr*) *v* fail

**fama** (*fer*-mer) *f* fame

**família** (fer-mee-lᵞer) *f* family

**familiar** (fer-mee-lᵞahr) *adj* familiar

**famoso** (fer-*moa*-zoo) *adj* famous

**fanático** (fer-*nah*-tee-koo) *adj* fanatical

**fanfarra** (ferng-*fer*-rrer) *f* brass band

**fantasia** (ferng-ter-*zee*-er) *f* fantasy

**fantasma** (ferng-*tahzh*-mer) *m* spook, phantom, ghost

**fantástico** (ferng-*tahsh*-tee-koo) *adj* fantastic, terrific

**fardo** (*fahr*-doo) *m* burden, load

**farinha** (fer-*ree*-ñer) *f* flour

**farmacêutico** (ferr-mer-*say*ᵒᵒ-tee-koo) *m* chemist

**farmácia** (ferr-*mah*-sᵞer) *f* pharmacy, chemist's; drugstore *nAm*

**farmacologia** (fahr-mer-koo-loo-*zhee*-er) *f* pharmacology

**farol** (fer-*rol*) *m* (pl faróis) lighthouse; headlight, headlamp; **~ de nevoeiro** foglamp; **~ traseiro** tail-light

**farpa** (*fahr*-per) *f* splinter

**farsa** (*fahr*-ser) *f* farce

**farto de** (*fahr*-too der) tired of, fed up with

**fartura** (ferr-*too*-rer) *f* plenty

**fascinante** (fersh-see-*nerng*-ter) *adj* glamorous

**fascinar** (fersh-see-*nahr*) *v* fascinate

**fascismo** (fersh-*seesh*-moo) *m* fascism

**fascista** (fersh-*seesh*-ter) *m* fascist

**fase** (*fah*-zer) *f* phase; stage

**fastidioso** (fersh-tee-dhᵞoa-zoo) *adj* tedious

**fatal** (fer-*tahl*) *adj* (pl -ais) fatal, mortal

**fatia** (fer-*tee*-er) *f* slice

**fatigado** (fer-tee-*gah*-dhoo) *adj* tired

**fatigante** (fer-tee-*gerng*-ter) *adj* tiring

**fato** (*fah*-too) *m* suit; **~ de banho** swim-suit, bathing-suit

**fato-macaco** (fah-too-mer-*kah*-koo) *m* overalls *pl*

**favor** (fer-*voar*) *m* favour; **a ~ de** on behalf of; **por ~** please; **se faz ~** please

**favorável** (fer-voo-*rah*-vehl) *adj* (pl -eis) favourable

**favorecer** (fer-voo-rer-*sayr*) *v* favour

**favorito** (fer-voo-*ree*-too) *adj* pet; *m* favourite

**fax** (fahks) *m* fax; **mandar um ~** send a fax

**\*fazer** (fer-*zayr*) *v* \*do; \*make; **\*fazer-se** \*get; \*go, \*grow

**fé** (feh) *f* faith

**febre** (*feh*-bhrer) *f* fever, temperature; **~ dos fenos** hay fever

**febril** (feh-*breel*) *adj* (pl -is) feverish

**fechado** (fi-*shah*-dhoo) *adj* closed, shut

**fechadura** (fi-sher-*dhoo*-rer) *f* lock; **buraco da ~** keyhole

**fechar** (fi-*shahr*) *v* \*shut, close; lock up, \*shut in; fasten; turn off; **~ à chave** lock

**fecho** (*fay*-shoo) *m* fastener; ~ **éclair** zip; zipper

**federação** (fer-dher-rer-*serng*ᵂ) *f* (pl -ções) federation

**federal** (fer-dher-*rahl*) *adj* (pl -ais) federal

**feijão** (fay-*zherng*ᵂ) *m* (pl -jões) bean

**feio** (*fay*-oo) *adj* ugly

**feira** (*fay*-rer) *f* fair

**feito** (*fay*-too) *m* feat

**felicidade** (fer-ler-see-*dhah*-dher) *f* happiness

**felicitação** (fer-ler-see-ter-*serng*ᵂ) *f* (pl -ções) congratulation

**felicitar** (fer-ler-see-*tahr*) *v* compliment, congratulate

**feliz** (fer-*leesh*) *adj* happy

**feltro** (*fayl*-troo) *m* felt

**feminino** (fer-mer-*nee*-noo) *adj* feminine; female

**fenda** (*fayngn*-der) *f* crack; cleft, chasm; slot

**fender** (fayngn-*dayr*) *v* \*split

**feno** (*fay*-noo) *m* hay

**feriado** (fer-rᵞah-dhoo) *m* holiday

**férias** (*feh*-rᵞersh) *fpl* vacation, holiday; **em** ~ on holiday; **estância de** ~ holiday resort

**ferida** (fer-*ree*-dher) *f* wound; injury

**ferido** (fer-*ree*-dhoo) *adj* injured

**\*ferir** (fer-*reer*) *v* wound; \*hurt, injure

**fermentar** (ferr-mayngn-*tahr*) *v* ferment

**feroz** (fer-*rosh*) *adj* fierce; wild

**ferradura** (fer-rrer-*dhoo*-rer) *f* horseshoe

**ferragens** (fer-*rrah*-zherᵉᵉsh) *fpl* hardware

**ferramenta** (fer-rrer-*mayngn*-ter) *f* utensil, implement, tool

**ferreiro** (fer-*rray*-roo) *m* blacksmith, smith

**ferro** (*feh*-roo) *m* iron; **de** ~ iron; ~ **de engomar** iron; ~ **de frisar** curling-tongs *pl*; ~ **de soldar** soldering-iron; ~ **fundido** cast iron; **não passar a** ~ drip-dry

**ferrolho** (fer-*rroa*-lᵞoo) *m* bolt

**ferrugem** (fer-*rroo*-zhernᵞ) *f* rust

**ferrugento** (fer-rroo-*zhayngn*-too) *adj* rusty

**fértil** (*fehr*-teel) *adj* (pl -teis) fertile

**ferver** (ferr-*vayr*) *v* boil

**festa** (*fehsh*-ter) *f* feast; party

**festival** (fish-tee-*vahl*) *m* (pl -ais) festival

**festivo** (fish-*tee*-voo) *adj* festive

**feudal** (fayᵒᵒ-*dhahl*) *adj* (pl -ais) feudal

**Fevereiro** (fer-ver-*ray*-roo) February

**fiador** (fᵞer-*dhoar*) *m* guarantor

**fiança** (fᵞerng-ser) *f* security

**fiar** (fᵞahr) *v* \*spin

**fiasco** (fᵞahsh-koo) *m* failure

**fibra** (*fee*-bhrer) *f* fibre

**ficar** (fee-*kahr*) *v* stay, remain; ~ **bem** suit; \*become

**ficção** (feek-*serng*ᵂ) *f* (pl -ções) fiction

**ficha** (*fee*-sher) *f* token, chip; plug

**fiel** (fᵞehl) *adj* (pl fiéis) faithful; loyal

**fígado** (*fee*-ger-dhoo) *m* liver

**figo** (*fee*-goo) *m* fig

**figura** (fee-*goo*-rer) *f* figure

**fila** (*fee*-ler) *f* file; row, rank, line

**filha** (*fee*-lᵞer) *f* daughter

**filho** (*fee*-lᵞo) *m* son

**filiação** (fee-lᵞer-*serng*ᵂ) *f* membership

**filiado** (fee-lᵞah-dhoo) *adj* affiliated

**Filipinas** (fee-lee-*pee*-nersh) *fpl* Philippines *pl*

**filipino** (fee-lee-*pee*-noo) *adj* Philippine; *m* Filipino

**filmar** (feel-*mahr*) *v* film

**filme** (*feel*-mer) *m* film; movie; ~ **a cores** colour film

**filosofia** (fee-loo-zoo-*fee*-er) f philosophy

**filósofo** (fee-*lo*-zoo-foo) m philosopher

**filtrar** (feel-*trahr*) v strain

**filtro** (*feel*-troo) m filter; ~ **de ar** air-filter; ~ **de óleo** oil filter

**fim** (feeng) m ending, finish, end; issue, aim; **a** ~ **de** so that; **sem** ~ unlimited

**fim-de-semana** (feeng-der-ser-mer-*ner*) m weekend

**final** (fee-*nahl*) adj (pl -ais) final; eventual

**finalmente** (fee-nahl-*mayngn*-ter) adv at last

**finanças** (fee-*nerng*-sersh) fpl finances pl

**financeiro** (fee-nerng-*say*-roo) adj financial

**financiar** (fee-nerng-s*Yahr*) v finance

**fingir** (feeng-*zheer*) v pretend

**finlandês** (feeng-lerngn-*daysh*) adj Finnish; m Finn

**Finlândia** (feeng-*lerngn*-d*Y*er) f Finland

**fino** (*fee*-noo) adj fine; sheer, thin

**fio** (fee∞) m thread; yarn; wire; ~ **de extensão** extension cord; ~ **eléctrico** flex

**fiorde** (*feeor*-der) m fjord

**firma** (*feer*-mer) f firm; company

**firme** (*feer*-mer) adj firm; steady

**fiscalização** (feesh-ker-lee-zer-*serng*ʷ) f supervision

**fiscalizar** (feesh-ker-lee-*zahr*) v control

**física** (*fee*-zee-ker) f physics

**físico** (*fee*-zee-koo) adj physical; m physicist

**fisiologia** (fee-z*Y*oo-loo-*zhee*-er) f physiology

**fita** (*fee*-ter) f ribbon; tape; ~ **adesiva** adhesive tape; ~ **métrica** tape-measure

**fitar** (fee-*tahr*) v gaze, stare

**fivela** (fee-*veh*-ler) f buckle

**fixador de cabelos** (feek-ser-*dhoar* der ker-*bhay*-loosh) m hair gel

**fixar** (feek-*sahr*) v attach; **fixar-se** settle down

**fixo** (*feek*-soo) adj permanent, fixed

**flanela** (fler-*neh*-ler) f flannel

**flauta** (*flou*-ter) f flute

**flexível** (flehk-*see*-vehl) adj (pl -eis) flexible; supple, elastic

**flor** (floar) f flower

**floresta** (floo-*rehsh*-ter) f forest

**florista** (floo-*reesh*-ter) m florist

**fluente** (flwayngn-ter) adj fluent

**fluido** (*flwee*-dhoo) adj fluid

**flutuar** (floo-*twahr*) v float

**foca** (*fo*-ker) f seal

**focinho** (foo-*see*-ño) m snout; mouth

**foco** (*fo*-koo) m focus

**fogão** (foo-*gerng*ʷ) m (pl fogões) stove; cooker; ~ **a gás** gas stove; gas cooker

**fogo** (*foa*-goo) m fire; **à prova de** ~ fireproof

**foguete** (foo-*ger*-ter) m rocket

**folclore** (foalk-*lo*-rer) m folklore

**folha** (*foa*-l*Y*er) f leaf; sheet; ~ **de ouro** gold leaf

**folhetim** (foo-l*Y*er-*teeng*) m serial

**fome** (*fo*-mer) f hunger

**fonético** (foo-*neh*-tee-koo) adj phonetic

**fonte** (*fawngn*-ter) f fountain; source; temple

**fora** (*fo*-rer) adv out; prep apart from; **de** ~ outside; ~ **de** out of; outside; **para** ~ outwards

**forasteiro** (foo-rersh-*tay*-roo) m stranger, foreigner

**forca** (*foar*-ker) f gallows pl

**força** (*foar*-ser) f force, strength, energy; ~ **armada** military force; ~ **de vontade** will-power; ~ **motriz** driving force

**forçar** (foor-*sahr*) v force, strain

**forçosamente** (foor-soa-zer-*mayngn*-ter) *adv* by force

**forjar** (foor-*zhahr*) *v* forge; form; counterfeit

**forma** (*for*-mer) *f* form; shape

**formal** (foor-*mahl*) *adj* (pl -ais) formal

**formalidade** (foor-mer-lee-*dhah*-dher) *f* formality

**formar** (foor-*mahr*) *v* shape, form; educate, train

**formato** (foor-*mah*-too) *m* size

**formidável** (foor-mee-*dhah*-vehl) *adj* (pl -eis) swell; tremendous, huge

**formiga** (foor-*mee*-ger) *f* ant

**fórmula** (*for*-moo-ler) *f* formula

**formular** (foor-moo-*lahr*) *v* formulate

**formulário** (foor-moo-*lah*-rᵞoo) *m* form; ~ **de inscrição** registration form

**fornecer** (foor-ner-*sayr*) *v* supply, furnish, provide

**fornecimento** (foor-ner-see-*mayngn*-too) *m* supply

**forno** (*foar*-noo) *m* oven; furnace; **cozer no ~** bake; **de ir ao ~** fireproof; **~ de microonda** microwave oven

**forrar** (foo-*rrahr*) *v* upholster

**forro** (*foa*-rroo) *m* lining

**fortaleza** (foor-ter-*lay*-zer) *f* fortress

**forte** (*for*-ter) *adj* powerful, strong; loud; *m* fort

**fortemente** (foar-ter-*mayngn*-ter) *adv* strongly, firmly

**fortuna** (foor-*too*-ner) *f* fortune

**fósforo** (*fosh*-foo-roo) *m* match

**fosso** (*foa*-soo) *m* moat; ditch

**fotocópia** (fo-toa-*ko*-pᵞer) *f* photocopy

**fotografar** (foo-too-grer-*fahr*) *v* photograph

**fotografia** (foo-too-grer-*fee*-er) *f* photography; photo, photograph; ~ **de passe** passport photograph

**fotógrafo** (foo-*to*-grer-foo) *m* photographer

**fotómetro** (foo-*to*-mer-troo) *m* exposure meter

**foz** (fosh) *f* mouth

**fracassar** (frer-ker-*sahr*) *v* fail

**fracasso** (frer-*kah*-soo) *m* failure

**fracção** (frah-*serng*ᵂ) *f* (pl -ções) fraction

**fraco** (*frah*-koo) *adj* feeble, weak, faint; poor

**fractura** (frah-*too*-rer) *f* fracture; break

**fracturar** (frah-too-*rahr*) *v* fracture

**frágil** (*frah*-zheel) *adj* (pl -geis) fragile

**fragmento** (frerg-*mayngn*-too) *m* fragment; piece

**fralda** (*frahl*-der) *f* nappy; diaper *nAm*

**framboesa** (frerngm-*bway*-zer) *f* raspberry

**França** (*freng*-ser) *f* France

**francês** (freng-*saysh*) *adj* French; *m* Frenchman

**franco** (*freng*-koo) *adj* open

**franco-atirador** (frerng-koo-er-tee-rer-*dhoar*) *m* sniper

**frango** (*freng*-goo) *m* chicken

**franja** (*freng*-zher) *f* fringe

**franquia** (frerng-*kee*-er) *f* postage

**franquiar** (frerng-kᵞ*ahr*) *v* stamp

**fraqueza** (frer-*kay*-zer) *f* weakness

**frasco** (*frahsh*-koo) *m* flask

**frase** (*frah*-zer) *f* sentence; phrase

**fraternidade** (frer-terr-nee-*dhah*-dher) *f* fraternity

**fraude** (*frou*-dher) *f* fraud

*****frear** (fr*ᵞahr*) *v Br* slow down

**freguês** (freh-*gaysh*) *m* customer

**freira** (*fray*-rer) *f* nun

**frente** (*frayngn*-ter) *f* front; **em ~** forward; ahead; **em ~ de** opposite; **para a ~** onwards; **sempre em ~** straight ahead, straight on

**frequência** (frer-*kwayng*-s<sup>y</sup>er) *f* frequency

**frequentar** (frer-kwayngn-*tahr*) *v* mix with

**frequente** (frer-*kwayngn*-ter) *adj* frequent

**frequentemente** (frer-kwayngn-ter-*mayngn*-ter) *adv* often, frequently

**fresco** (*fraysh*-koo) *adj* fresh; chilly, cool

**fricção** (freek-*serng*<sup>w</sup>) *f* (pl -ções) friction

**frieira** (*fr*<sup>y</sup>*ay*-rer) *f* chilblain

**frigideira** (free-zher-*dhay*-rer) *f* frying-pan

**frigorífico** (free-goo-*ree*-fee-koo) *m* fridge, refrigerator

**frio** (*free*<sup>oo</sup>) *adj* cold; *m* cold

**frisar** (free-*zahr*) *v* emphasize

**fritar** (free-*tahr*) *v* fry

**fronha** (*froa*-nger) *f* pillow-case

**fronteira** (frawngn-*tay*-rer) *f* frontier; border; boundary

**frota** (*fro*-ter) *f* fleet

**frouxo** (*froa*-shoo) *adj* limp

**fruta** (*froo*-ter) *f* fruit

**fruto** (*froo*-too) *m* fruit

**fuga** (*foo*-ger) *f* leak; escape

**\*fugir** (foo-*zheer*) *v* escape

**fugitivo** (foo-zhee-*tee*-voo) *m* runaway

**fumador** (foo-mer-*dhoar*) *m* smoker

**fumar** (foo-*mahr*) *v* smoke

**fumo** (*foo*-moo) *m* smoke

**função** (foong-*serng*<sup>w</sup>) *f* (pl -ções) function

**funcionamento** (foong-s<sup>y</sup>oo-ner-*mayngn*-too) *m* operation; working

**funcionar** (foong-s<sup>y</sup>oo-*nahr*) *v* operate, work

**funcionário** (foong-s<sup>y</sup>oo-nah-r<sup>y</sup>oo) *m* civil servant; clerk; ~ **aduaneiro** Customs officer

**fundação** (foongn-der-*serng*<sup>w</sup>) *f* (pl -ções) foundation

**fundamentado** (foongn-der-mayngn-*tah*-dhoo) *adj* well-founded

**fundamental** (foongn-der-mayngn-*tahl*) *adj* (pl -ais) fundamental, basic

**fundamento** (foongn-der-*mayngn*-too) *m* basis

**fundar** (foongn-*dahr*) *v* found

**fundição** (foongn-dee-*serng*<sup>w</sup>) *f* (pl -ções) ironworks

**fundo** (*foongn*-doo) *m* bottom, ground; background; fund; *adj* deep

**funeral** (foo-ner-*rahl*) *m* (pl -ais) funeral

**funil** (foo-*neel*) *m* (pl -is) funnel

**furacão** (foo-rer-*kerng*<sup>w</sup>) *m* (pl -ções) hurricane

**furado** (foo-*rah*-dhoo) *adj* punctured

**furar** (foo-*rahr*) *v* pierce, drill

**furgão** (foor-*gerng*<sup>w</sup>) *m* (pl -gões) luggage van

**furgoneta** (foor-goo-*nay*-ter) *f* van; delivery van, pick-up van

**fúria** (*foo*-r<sup>y</sup>er) *f* passion

**furibundo** (foo-ree-*bhoongn*-doo) *adj* furious

**furioso** (foo-r<sup>y</sup>*oa*-zoo) *adj* furious

**furo** (*foo*-roo) *m* puncture; blow-out

**furor** (foo-*roar*) *m* anger; rage

**furúnculo** (foo-*roong*-koo-loo) *m* boil

**fusco** (*foosh*-koo) *adj* hazy

**fusível** (foo-zee-vehl) *m* (pl -eis) fuse

**futebol** (foo-ter-*bhol*) *m* soccer; **jogo de** ~ football match

**fútil** (*foo*-teel) *adj* (pl fúteis) petty; insignificant; idle

**futuro** (foo-*too*-roo) *adj* future; *m* future

# G

**gabardina** (ger-bherr-*dee*-ner) *f* mackintosh

**gabar-se** (ger-*bhahr*-ser) v boast

**gabinete** (ger-bhee-*nay*-ter) m cabinet; ~ **de provas** fitting room

**gado** (*gah*-dhoo) m cattle pl

**gafanhoto** (ger-fer-*ñoa*-too) m grasshopper

**gaiato** (ger-*Yah*-too) m boy

**gaivota** (gigh-*vo*-ter) f gull, seagull

**galeria** (ger-ler-*ree*-er) f gallery; ~ **de arte** art gallery

**galgo** (*gahl*-goo) m greyhound

**galinha** (ger-*lee*-ñer) f hen; **pele de** ~ goose-flesh

**galo** (*gah*-loo) m cock

**galope** (ger-*lo*-per) m gallop

**gamba** (*gerngm*-ber) f prawn

**ganancioso** (ger-nerng-*sYoa*-zoo) adj greedy

**gancho** (*gerng*-shoo) m hook; peg; ~ **de cabelo** hairpin; bobby pin Am

**gangorra** (gerng-*goa*-rrer) fBr seesaw

**ganhar** (loo-*krahr*) v gain; \*win; earn, \*make

**ganhos** (*ger*-ñoosh) mpl earnings pl

**ganso** (*gerng*-soo) m goose

**garagem** (ger-*rah*-zherng<sup>Y</sup>) f garage; \***pôr na** ~ garage

**garagista** (ger-rer-*zheesh*-ter) m garage man

**garantia** (ger-rerngn-*tee*-er) f guarantee

**garantir** (ger-rerngn-*teer*) v assure, guarantee

**garça** (*gahr*-ser) f heron

**garçom** (gahr-*sawng*) mBr waiter

**garçonete** (*gahr*-soo-*nay*-ter) fBr waitress

**garfo** (*gahr*-foo) m fork

**gargalhada** (gerr-ger-*lYah*-der) f burst of laughter

**garganta** (gerr-*gerngn*-ter) f throat; gorge

**gargarejar** (gerr-ger-rı-*zhahr*) v gargle

**garoto** (ger-*roa*-too) m kid

**garra** (*gah*-rrer) f claw

**garrafa** (ger-*rrah*-fer) f bottle; carafe; ~ **termos** vacuum flask

**garrido** (ger-*rree*-dhoo) adj gay

**gás** (gahsh) m gas; **gases de escape** exhaust gases

**gasolina** (ger-zoo-*lee*-ner) f petrol; gas nAm, gasoline nAm; ~ **sem chumbo** unleaded petrol; **posto de** ~ petrol station; gas station Am

**gastador** (gersh-ter-*dhoar*) adj wasteful

**gastar** (gersh-*tahr*) v \*spend; wear out

**gasto** (*gahsh*-too) adj worn; worn-out

**gástrico** (*gahsh*-tree-koo) adj gastric

**gastrónomo** (gahsh-tro-*noo*-moo) m gourmet

**gatilho** (ger-*tee*-lYoo) m trigger

**gato** (*gah*-too) m cat

**gaveta** (ger-*vay*-ter) f drawer

**gavião** (ger-v<sup>Y</sup>*erng*<sup>w</sup>) m (pl -iões) hawk

**gaze** (*gah*-zer) f gauze

**geada** (zh<sup>Y</sup>*ah*-dher) f frost

**geladeira** (zher-ler-*dhay*-rer) fBr fridge, refrigerator

**gelado** (zher-*lah*-dhoo) adj freezing; m ice-cream

**gelar** (zher-*lahr*) v \*freeze

**geleia** (zher-*lay*-er) f jelly; **geléia** Br jam

**gelo** (*zhay*-loo) m ice

**gema** (*zhay*-mer) f yolk

**gémeos** (*zheh*-m<sup>Y</sup>oosh) mpl twins pl

**gemer** (zher-*mayr*) v moan, groan

**general** (zher-ner-*rahl*) m (pl -ais) general

**género** (*zheh*-ner-roo) m gender; sort, kind; **géneros** victuals pl

**generosidade** (zher-ner-roo-zee-*dhah*-dher) f generosity

**generoso** (zher-ner-*roa*-zoo) adj generous; liberal

**gengibre** (zhayng-*zhee*-bhrer) *m* ginger

**gengiva** (zhayng-*zhee*-ver) *f* gum

**génio** (*zeh*-nʸoo) *m* genius

**genital** (zher-nee-*tahl*) *adj* (pl -ais) genital

**genro** (*zhayng*-rroo) *m* son-in-law

**gente** (*zhayngn*-ter) *f* people *pl*; **a ~** we; **toda a ~** everybody, everyone

**gentil** (zhayngn-*teel*) *adj* (pl -is) kind

**genuíno** (zher-*nwee*-noo) *adj* genuine

**geografia** (zhʸoo-grer-*fee*-er) *f* geography

**geologia** (zhʸoo-loo-*zhee*-er) *f* geology

**geometria** (zhʸoo-mer-*tree*-er) *f* geometry

**geração** (zher-rer-*serng*ʷ) *f* (pl -ções) generation

**gerador** (zher-rer-*dhoar*) *m* generator

**geral** (zher-*rahl*) *adj* (pl -ais) universal, general; public; **em ~** in general

**geralmente** (zher-rahl-*mayngn*-ter) *adv* as a rule

**germe** (*zhehr*-mer) *m* germ

**gesso** (*zhay*-soo) *m* plaster

**gestão** (zhish-*terng*ʷ) *f* (pl -tões) administration; management

**gesticular** (zhersh-tee-koo-*lahr*) *v* gesticulate

**gesto** (*zhehsh*-too) *m* sign

**gigante** (zhee-*gerngn*-ter) *m* giant

**gigantesco** (zhee-gerngn-*taysh*-koo) *adj* gigantic; enormous

**gilete** (zhee-*leh*-ter) *f* safety-razor

**ginásio** (zhee-*nah*-zʸoo) *m* gymnasium

**ginasta** (zhee-*nahsh*-ter) *m* gymnast

**ginástica** (zhee-*nahsh*-tee-ker) *f* gymnastics *pl*

**ginecologista** (zhee-ner-koo-loo-*zheesh*-ter) *m* gynaecologist

**gira-discos** (zhee-rer-*deesh*-koosh) *m* (pl ~) record-player

**girar** (zhee-*rahr*) *v* turn around

**giz** (zheesh) *m* chalk

**glaciar** (gler-sʸ*ahr*) *m* glacier

**glândula** (*glerngn*-doo-ler) *f* gland

**global** (gloo-*bhahl*) *adj* (pl -ais) broad; overall

**globo** (*gloa*-bhoo) *m* globe

**glória** (*glo*-rʸer) *f* glory

**gola** (*go*-ler) *f* collar

**goleiro** (goo-*lay*-roo) *m Br* goalkeeper

**golfe** (*goal*-fer) *m* golf; **campo de ~** golf-course, golf-links; **clube de ~** golf-club

**golfo** (*goal*-foo) *m* gulf

**golo** (*goa*-loo) *m* goal

**golpe** (*gol*-per) *m* cut; blow

**goma** (*goa*-mer) *f* gum; starch; **~ de mascar** *Br* chewing-gum

**gôndola** (*gawngn*-doo-ler) *f* gondola

**gordo** (*goar*-doo) *adj* fat; stout

**gordura** (goor-*doo*-rer) *f* fat, grease

**gordurento** (goor-doo-*rayngn*-too) *adj* greasy

**gorduroso** (goor-doo-*roa*-zoo) *adj* fatty

**gorjeta** (goor-*zhay*-ter) *f* tip, gratuity

**gostar de** (goosh-*tahr*) like, *be fond of; fancy, care for

**gosto** (*goash*-too) *m* taste; zest; **com muito ~** gladly

**gota** (*goa*-ter) *f* drop; gout

**governador** (goo-verr-ner-*dhoar*) *m* governor

**governanta** (goo-verr-*nerngn*-ter) *f* housekeeper, governess

**governante** (goo-verr-*nerngn*-ter) *m* ruler

**governar** (goo-verr-*nahr*) *v* govern, rule

**governo** (goo-*vayr*-noo) *m* government, rule; **~ de casa** housekeeping, household

**gozar** (goo-*zahr*) *v* enjoy; **~ com** kid

**gozo** (*goa*-zoo) *m* enjoyment

**Grã-Bretanha** (grerng-bhrer-*ter*-ñer) *f* Great Britain

**graça** (*grah*-ser) *f* grace; joke

**gracioso** (grer-s<sup>y</sup>oa-zoo) *adj* graceful

**grade** (*grah*-dher) *f* crate

**gradeamento** (grer-dh<sup>y</sup>er-*mayngn*-too) *m* railing

**gradual** (grer-*dhwahl*) *adj* (pl -ais) gradual

**gradualmente** (grer-dhwahl-*mayngn*-ter) *adv* gradually

**gráfico** (*grah*-fee-koo) *adj* graphic; *m* diagram, graph, chart

**gralha** (*grah*-l<sup>y</sup>er) *f* crow

**grama** (*grer*-mer) *m* gram

**gramática** (grer-*mah*-tee-ker) *f* grammar

**gramatical** (grer-mer-tee-*kahl*) *adj* (pl -ais) grammatical

**grampo** (*grerngm*-poo) *m* clamp; *mBr* staple

**grande** (*grerngn*-der) *adj* big; great, large, major

**grandioso** (grerngn-d<sup>y</sup>oa-zoo) *adj* magnificent; superb, grand

**granito** (grer-*nee*-too) *m* granite

**granizo** (grer-*nee*-zoo) *m* hail

**grão** (grerng<sup>w</sup>) *m* (pl ~s) corn, grain

**gratidão** (grer-tee-*dherng*<sup>w</sup>) *f* (pl -dões) gratitude

**grato** (*grah*-too) *adj* grateful

**gratuito** (grer-*tōō*<sup>ee</sup>-too) *adj* free of charge; gratis

**grau** (grou) *m* grade, degree; **~ de latitude** latitude; **~ centígrado** centigrade degree; **por graus** by degrees

**gravação** (grer-ver-*serng*<sup>w</sup>) *f* (pl -ções) engraving; recording

**gravador** (grer-ver-*dhoar*) *m* tape-recorder; engraver; recorder

**gravar** (grer-*vahr*) *v* engrave; record

**gravata** (grer-*vah*-ter) *f* tie, necktie

**grave** (*grah*-ver) *adj* grave; bad, severe; serious

**grávida** (*grah*-vee-dher) *adj* pregnant

**gravidade** (grer-vee-*dhah*-dher) *f* gravity

**gravura** (grer-*voo*-rer) *f* picture, print

**graxa** (*grah*-sher) *f* shoe polish

**Grécia** (*greh*-s<sup>y</sup>er) *f* Greece

**grego** (*gray*-goo) *adj* Greek; *m* Greek

**grelha** (*greh*-l<sup>y</sup>er) *f* grate

**grelhador** (grı-l<sup>y</sup>er-*dhoar*) *m* grill

**grelhar** (grı-*l<sup>y</sup>ahr*) *v* grill; roast

**greta** (*gray*-ter) *f* chink

**greve** (*greh*-ver) *f* strike; **\*fazer ~** \*strike

**grilo** (*gree*-loo) *m* cricket

**gripe** (*gree*-per) *f* influenza, flu

**gritar** (gree-*tahr*) *v* cry; shriek, scream, shout

**grito** (*gree*-too) *m* cry; shout, scream

**groom** (groongm) *m* bellboy

**grosa** (*gro*-zer) *f* gross

**groselha** (groo-zeh-l<sup>y</sup>er) *f* currant; **~ negra** black-currant; **~ verde** gooseberry

**grosseiro** (groo-*say*-roo) *adj* gross; coarse, impolite

**grosso** (*groa*-soo) *adj* big, thick

**grossura** (groa-*soo*-rer) *f* thickness

**grotesco** (groo-*taysh*-koo) *adj* ludicrous

**grua** (*groo*-er) *f* crane

**grumo** (*groo*-moo) *m* lump

**grumoso** (groo-*moa*-zoo) *adj* lumpy

**grupo** (*groo*-poo) *m* group; bunch, party, set

**gruta** (*groo*-ter) *f* cave, grotto

**guarda** (*gwahr*-dher) *m* policeman; custodian, attendant, caretaker, guard, warden

**guarda-chuva** (gwahr-dher-*shoo*-ver) *m* umbrella

**guarda-costas** (gwahr-dher-*kosh*-tersh) *m* (pl ~) bodyguard

**guarda-florestal** (gwahr-dher-floo-rısh-

*tahl*) *m* (pl -ais) forester

**guarda-lama** (gwahr-dher-*ler*-mer) *m* mud-guard

**guardanapo** (gwahr-dher-*nah*-poo) *m* serviette, napkin; ~ **de papel** paper napkin

**guardar** (gwerr-*dhahr*) *v* guard; \*keep, \*hold; \*put away

**guarda-redes** (gwahr-dher-*ray*-dhısh) *m* goalkeeper

**guarda-roupa** (gwahr-dher-*roa*-per) *m* cloakroom, wardrobe

**guelra** (*gehl*-rrer) *f* gill

**guerra** (*geh*-rer) *f* war

**guia** (*gee*-er) *m* guide; guidebook; ~ **linguístico** phrase-book

**guiar** (g<sup>y</sup>ahr) *v* guide; \*drive

**guincho** (*geeng*-shoo) *m* shriek

**guita** (*gee*-ter) *f* twine

**guloseimas** (goo-loo-*zay*-mersh) *fpl* candy *nAm*

**guloso** (goo-*loa*-zoo) *adj* greedy

# H

**há** (ah) ago; ~ **pouco tempo** recently

**hábil** (*ah*-bheel) *adj* (pl hábeis) skilled, skilful

**habilidade** (er-bher-lee-*dhah*-dher) *f* art, skill, ability

**habilidoso** (er-bher-lee-*dhoa*-zoo) *adj* skilful

**habilitação** (er-bher-lee-ter-*serng*<sup>w</sup>) *f* (pl -ções) qualification

**habitação** (er-bhee-ter-*serng*<sup>w</sup>) *f* (pl -ções) house

**habitante** (er-bhee-*terngn*-ter) *m* inhabitant

**habitar** (er-bhee-*tahr*) *v* inhabit

**habitável** (er-bhee-*tah*-vehl) *adj* (pl -eis) habitable, inhabitable

**hábito** (*ah*-bhee-too) *m* habit; custom

**habituado** (er-bhee-*twah*-dhoo) *adj* accustomed

**habitual** (er-bhee-*twahl*) *adj* (pl -ais) habitual; common, customary

**habitualmente** (er-bhee-twahl-*mayngn*-ter) *adv* usually

**harmonia** (err-moo-*nee*-er) *f* harmony

**harpa** (*ahr*-per) *f* harp

**haste** (*ahsh*-ter) *f* stem

**\*haver** (er-*vayr*) *v* \*have; exist; \*be

**hebreu** (ee-*bhray*<sup>oo</sup>) *m* Hebrew

**hélice** (*eh*-lee-ser) *f* propeller

**hemorragia** (eh-mo-rrer-*zhee*-er) *f* haemorrhage; ~ **nasal** nosebleed

**hemorróidas** (eh-mo-*rroi*-dhersh) *fpl* piles, haemorrhoids *pl*

**hera** (*eh*-rer) *f* ivy

**herança** (ee-*rerng*-ser) *f* inheritance

**herdar** (eer-*dahr*) *v* inherit

**hereditário** (ee-rer-dhee-*tah*-r<sup>y</sup>oo) *adj* hereditary

**hermético** (eer-*meh*-tee-koo) *adj* airtight

**hérnia** (*ehr*-n<sup>y</sup>er) *f* hernia; ~ **discal** slipped disc

**herói** (ee-*roi*) *m* hero

**hesitar** (er-zee-*tahr*) *v* hesitate

**heterossexual** (eh-ter-roo-sehk-*swahl*) *adj* (pl -ais) heterosexual

**hidrogénio** (ee-dhro-*zheh*-n<sup>y</sup>oo) *m* hydrogen

**hierarquia** (<sup>y</sup>eh-rerr-*kee*-er) *f* hierarchy

**hífen** (*ee*-fayn) *m* hyphen

**higiene** (ee-zh<sup>y</sup>eh-ner) *f* hygiene

**higiénico** (ee-zh<sup>y</sup>eh-nee-koo) *adj* hygienic

**hino** (*ee*-noo) *m* hymn; ~ **nacional** national anthem

**hipocrisia** (ee-poo-kree-*zee*-er) *f* hypocrisy

**hipócrita** (ee-*po*-kree-ter) *adj* hypocritical; *m* hypocrite

**hipódromo** (ee-*po*-dhroo-moo) *m* race-course

**hipoteca** (ee-poo-*teh*-ker) *f* mortgage

**histérico** (eesh-*teh*-ree-koo) *adj* hysterical

**história** (eesh-*to*-rᵞer) *f* history; story; ~ **da arte** art history; ~ **de amor** love-story; ~ **de fadas** fairytale

**historiador** (eesh-too-rᵞer-*dhoar*) *m* historian

**histórico** (eesh-*to*-ree-koo) *adj* historic; historical

**hoje** (*oa*-zher) *adv* today; ~ **em dia** nowadays

**Holanda** (oo-*lerngn*-der) *f* Holland

**holandês** (oo-lerngn-*daysh*) *adj* Dutch; *m* Dutchman

**holofote** (oa-loa-*fo*-ter) *m* searchlight

**homem** (*o*-merngᵞ) *m* man; ~ **de negócios** businessman

**homenagem** (oo-mer-*nah*-zherngᵞ) *f* homage; tribute; **prestar** ~ honour

**homicídio** (oo-mee-*see*-dhᵞoo) *m* murder

**homossexual** (o-mo-sayk-*swahl*) *adj* (pl -ais) homosexual

**honestidade** (oo-nehsh-tee-*dhah*-dher) *f* honesty

**honesto** (oo-*nehsh*-too) *adj* honest

**honorário** (oo-noo-rah-rᵞoo) *m* fee

**honra** (*awng*-rrer) *f* honour, glory

**honrado** (awng-*rrah*-dhoo) *adj* honourable

**honrar** (awng-*rrahr*) *v* honour

**honroso** (awng-*rroa*-zoo) *adj* honourable

**hóquei** (*oa*-kay) *m* hockey

**hora** (*o*-rer) *f* hour; time of day; ~ **a hora** hourly; ~ **de chegada** time of arrival; ~ **de partida** time of departure; ~ **de ponta** rush-hour, peak hour; **horas de abertura** business hours; **horas de**

**consulta** consultation hours; **horas de serviço** office hours, business hours; **horas de visita** visiting hours; **quarto de** ~ quarter of an hour; **vinte e quatro horas** twenty-four hours

**horário** (oo-*rah*-rᵞoo) *m* timetable; schedule; ~ **de Verão** summer time

**horizontal** (oo-ree-zawngn-*tahl*) *adj* (pl -ais) horizontal

**horizonte** (oo-ree-*zawngn*-ter) *m* horizon

**horripilante** (oo-rree-pee-*lerngn*-ter) *adj* creepy, horrible

**horrível** (oo-*rree*-vehl) *adj* (pl -eis) awful, horrible

**horror** (oo-*rroar*) *m* horror

**horroroso** (oo-rroo-roa-zoo) *adj* horrible, hideous

**horta** (*or*-ter) *f* kitchen garden

**hortaliça** (oorr-ter-*lee*-ser) *f* greens *pl*; **vendedor de** ~ greengrocer

**hortelã** (oorr-ter-*lerng*) *f* mint

**hortelã-pimenta** (oorr-ter-lerng-pee-mayngn-ter) λ *f* peppermint

**horticultura** (oorr-tee-kool-*too*-rer) *f* horticulture

**hospedar** (oosh-per-*dhahr*) *v* lodge; **hospedar-se** stay

**hóspede** (*osh*-per-dher) *m* guest; lodger

**hospedeira** (oosh-per-*dhay*-rer) *f* hostess; stewardess

**hospedeiro** (oosh-per-*dhay*-roo) *m* host; innkeeper

**hospital** (oosh-pee-*tahl*) *m* (pl -ais) hospital

**hospitaleiro** (oosh-pee-ter-*lay*-roo) *adj* hospitable

**hospitalidade** (oosh-pee-ter-lee-*dhah*-dher) *f* hospitality

**hostil** (oosh-*teel*) *adj* (pl -is) hostile

**hotel** (o-*tehl*) *m* (pl hotéis) hotel

**humanidade** (oo-mer-nee-*dhah*-dher) *f* humanity, mankind

**humano** (oo-*mer*-noo) *adj* human

**humedecer** (oo-mer-dher-*sayr*) *v* moisten, damp

**humidade** (oo-mee-*dhah*-dher) *f* moisture, humidity, damp

**húmido** (*oo*-mee-dhoo) *adj* wet, humid, moist, damp

**humilde** (oo-*meel*-der) *adj* humble

**humor** (oo-*moar*) *m* humour; mood; spirit; **bem humorado** good-humoured

**húngaro** (*oong*-ger-roo) *adj* Hungarian; *m* Hungarian

**Hungria** (oong-*gree*-er) *f* Hungary

# I

**iate** (*Yah*-ter) *m* yacht

**içar** (ee-*sahr*) *v* hoist

**ícone** (ee-*koo*-ner) *m* icon

**icterícia** (eek-ter-*ree*-sYer) *f* jaundice

**idade** (ee-*dhah*-dher) *f* age; **de ~** elderly; **Idade Média** Middle Ages

**ideal** (ee-*dhYahl*) *adj* (pl -ais) ideal; *m* ideal

**ideia** (ee-*dhay*-er) *f* idea; **~ luminosa** brain-wave

**idêntico** (ee-*dhayngn*-tee-koo) *adj* identical

**identidade** (ee-dhayngn-tee-*dhah*-dher) *f* identity; **bilhete de ~** identity card

**identificação** (ee-dhayngn-tee-fee-ker-*serngʷ*) *f* (pl -ções) identification

**identificar** (ee-dhayngn-ter-fee-*kahr*) *v* identify

**idiomático** (ee-dhYoo-*mah*-tee-koo) *adj* idiomatic

**idiota** (ee-*dhYo*-ter) *m* idiot; fool; *adj* idiotic

**ídolo** (ee-*dhoo*-loo) *m* idol

**ignição** (eeg-nee-*serngʷ*) *f* ignition

**ignorante** (eeg-noo-*rerngn*-ter) *adj* ignorant

**ignorar** (eeg-noo-*rahr*) *v* ignore

**igreja** (ee-*gray*-zher) *f* church

**igual** (ee-*gwahl*) *adj* (pl -ais) alike, equal; even, level

**igualar** (ee-gwer-*lahr*) *v* equalize; equal

**igualdade** (ee-gwahl-*dah*-dher) *f* equality

**igualmente** (ee-gwahl-*mayngn*-ter) *adv* equally; likewise, also, alike

**ilegal** (ee-ler-*gahl*) *adj* (pl -ais) illegal; unlawful

**ilegível** (ee-ler-*zhee*-vehl) *adj* (pl -eis) illegible

**ileso** (ee-*lay*-zoo) *adj* unhurt

**ilha** (ee-*lʲer*) *f* island

**ilícito** (ee-*lee*-ser-too) *adj* unauthorized

**ilimitado** (ee-ler-mee-*tah*-dhoo) *adj* unlimited

**iluminação** (ee-loo-mee-ner-*serngʷ*) *f* (pl -ções) lighting, illumination

**iluminar** (ee-loo-mee-*nahr*) *v* illuminate

**ilusão** (ee-loo-*zerngʷ*) *f* (pl -sões) illusion

**ilustração** (ee-loosh-trer-*serngʷ*) *f* (pl -ções) picture, illustration

**ilustrar** (ee-loosh-*trahr*) *v* illustrate

**ilustre** (ee-*loosh*-trer) *adj* noted; illustrious

**imaculado** (ee-mer-koo-*lah*-dhoo) *adj* stainless; immaculate

**imagem** (ee-*mah*-zherngʸ) *f* image; picture; **~ reflectida** reflection

**imaginação** (ee-mer-zhee-ner-*serngʷ*) *f* (pl -ções) fancy, imagination

**imaginar** (ee-mer-zhee-*nahr*) *v* imagine; fancy, conceive

**imaginário** (ee-mer-zhee-nah-*rʸoo*) *adj*

imaginary

**imediatamente** (ee-mer-dh<sup>y</sup>ah-ter-mayngn-ter) *adv* immediately; straight away, at once, instantly

**imediato** (ee-mer-dh<sup>y</sup>ah-too) *adj* immediate, prompt

**imenso** (ee-mayng-soo) *adj* immense; vast

**imerecido** (ee-mer-rer-see-dhoo) *adj* unearned

**imigração** (ee-mee-grer-serng<sup>w</sup>) *f* (pl -ções) immigration

**imigrante** (ee-mee-grerngn-ter) *m* immigrant

**imigrar** (ee-mee-grahr) *v* immigrate

**imitação** (ee-mee-ter-serng<sup>w</sup>) *f* (pl -ções) imitation

**imitar** (ee-mee-tahr) *v* imitate; copy

**imodesto** (ee-moo-dhehsh-too) *adj* immodest

**impaciente** (eengm-per-s<sup>y</sup>ayngn-ter) *adj* impatient; eager

**ímpar** (eengm-pahr) *adj* odd

**imparcial** (eengm-perr-s<sup>y</sup>ahl) *adj* (pl -ais) impartial

**impecável** (eengm-per-kah-vehl) *adj* (pl -eis) faultless

**impedimento** (eengm-per-dhee-mayngn-too) *m* impediment

**\*impedir** (eengm-per-dheer) *v* prevent; impede

**imperador** (eengm-per-rer-dhoar) *m* emperor

**imperatriz** (eengm-per-rer-treesh) *f* empress

**imperfeição** (eengm-perr-fay-serng<sup>w</sup>) *f* (pl -ções) fault, imperfection

**imperfeito** (eengm-perr-fay-too) *adj* imperfect; faulty

**imperial** (eengm-per-r<sup>y</sup>ahl) *adj* (pl -ais) imperial

**império** (eengm-peh-r<sup>y</sup>oo) *m* empire

**impermeável** (eengm-perr-m<sup>y</sup>ah-vehl) *adj* (pl -eis) waterproof; rainproof;

*m* raincoat

**impertinência** (eengm-perr-tee-nayngs<sup>y</sup>er) *f* impertinence

**impertinente** (eengm-perr-tee-nayngn-ter) *adj* impertinent

**impessoal** (eengm-per-swahl) *adj* (pl -ais) impersonal

**ímpeto** (eengm-per-too) *m* impetuosity

**impetuoso** (eengm-per-twoa-zoo) *adj* violent

**implicado** (eengm-plee-kah-dhoo) *adj* involved

**implicar** (eengm-plee-kahr) *v* imply; involve; ~ **com** tease

**imponente** (eengm-poo-nayngn-ter) *adj* imposing

**impopular** (eengm-poo-poo-lahr) *adj* unpopular

**importação** (eengm-poor-ter-serng<sup>w</sup>) *f* (pl -ções) import

**importador** (eengm-poor-ter-dhoar) *m* importer

**importância** (eengm-poor-terng-s<sup>y</sup>er) *f* importance; \*ter ~ matter

**importante** (eengm-poor-terngn-ter) *adj* important; considerable, capital, big

**importar** (eengm-poor-tahr) *v* import; ~ **em** amount to; **importar-se com** mind

**impossível** (eengm-poo-see-vehl) *adj* (pl -eis) impossible

**imposto** (eengm-poash-too) *m* tax; ~ **sobre a cifra de negócios** turnover tax; ~ **sobre os rendimentos** income-tax; **isento de** ~ tax-free; **lançar impostos** tax

**impotência** (eengm-poo-tayng-s<sup>y</sup>er) *f* impotence

**impotente** (eengm-poo-tayngn-ter) *adj* impotent; powerless

**impraticável** (eengm-prer-tee-kah-vehl) *adj* (pl -eis) impassable

**imprensa** (eengm-*prayng*-ser) *f* press

**impressão** (eengm-prer-*serng*ᵂ) *f* (pl -sões) impression; ~ **digital** fingerprint

**impressionante** (eengm-prer-sᵞoo-*nerngn*-ter) *adj* striking, impressive

**impressionar** (eengm-prer-sᵞoo-*nahr*) *v* impress; \*strike

**impresso** (eengm-*preh*-soo) *m* printed matter

**imprevisto** (eengm-prer-*veesh*-too) *adj* unexpected

**imprimir** (eengm-pree-*meer*) *v* print

**impróprio** (eengm-*pro*-prᵞoo) *adj* improper; wrong

**improvável** (eengm-proo-*vah*-vehl) *adj* (pl -eis) unlikely, improbable

**improvisar** (eengm-proo-vee-*zhahr*) *v* improvise

**imprudente** (eengm-proo-*dhayngn*-ter) *adj* unwise

**impulsionar** (eengm-pool-sᵞoo-*nahr*) *v* propel

**impulsivo** (eengm-pool-*see*-voo) *adj* impulsive

**impulso** (eengm-*pool*-soo) *m* urge, impulse

**imundo** (ee-*moongn*-doo) *adj* filthy

**imunidade** (ee-moo-nee-*dhah*-dher) *f* immunity

**imunizar** (ee-moo-nee-*zahr*) *v* immunize

**inabitável** (ee-ner-bhee-*tah*-vehl) *adj* (pl -eis) uninhabitable

**inaceitável** (ee-ner-say-*tah*-vehl) *adj* (pl -eis) unacceptable

**inacessível** (ee-ner-ser-*see*-vehl) *adj* (pl -eis) inaccessible

**inadequado** (ee-ner-dher-*kwah*-dhoo) *adj* inadequate; unfit, unsuitable

**inadvertência** (een-erdh-verr-*tayng*-sᵞer) *f* oversight

**inalar** (*ee*-ner-*lahr*) *v* inhale

**incapacitado** (eeng-ker-per-see-*tah*- dhoo) *adj* disabled

**incapaz** (eeng-ker-*pahsh*) *adj* unable, incapable

**incêndio** (eeng-*sayngn*-dᵞoo) *m* fire

**incenso** (eeng-*sayng*-soo) *m* incense

**incerto** (eeng-*sehr*-too) *adj* doubtful, uncertain

**inchaço** (eeng-*shah*-soo) *m* swelling

**inchar** (eeng-*shahr*) *v* \*swell; inflate

**incidental** (eeng-see-dhayngn-*tahl*) *adj* (pl -ais) incidental

**incidente** (eeng-see-*dhayngn*-ter) *m* incident

**incineração** (eeng-see-ner-rer-*serng*ᵂ) *f* (pl -ções) cremation

**incinerar** (eeng-see-ner-*rahr*) *v* cremate

**incitar** (eeng-see-*tahr*) *v* urge, incite

**inclinação** (eeng-klee-ner-*serng*ᵂ) *f* (pl -ções) gradient; tendency, inclination; ~ **de cabeça** nod

**inclinado** (eeng-klee-*nah*-dhoo) *adj* slanting; sloping

**inclinar** (eeng-klee-*nahr*) *v* bow; **inclinar-se** slant

**incluir** (eeng-*klweer*) *v* include; enclose; count; **tudo incluído** in all

**inclusive** (eeng-kloo-*zee*-vay) *adv* including

**inclusivo** (eeng-kloo-*see*-voo) *adj* inclusive

**incluso** (eeng-*kloo*-zoo) *adj* included

**incomestível** (eeng-koa-mersh-*tee*-vehl) *adj* (pl -eis) inedible

**incomodar** (eeng-koo-moo-*dhahr*) *v* disturb; bother, trouble; **incomodar-se** bother

**incómodo** (eeng-*ko*-moo-dhoo) *m* nuisance, inconvenience, trouble, bother

**incompetente** (eeng-kawngm-per-*tayngn*-ter) *adj* unqualified, incompetent

**incompleto** (eeng-kawngm-*pleh*-too)

*adj* incomplete

**incompreensível** (eeng-kawngm-prᵞayngn-*see*-vehl) *adj* (pl -eis) puzzling

**inconcebível** (eeng-kawng-ser-*bhee*-vehl) *adj* (pl -eis) inconceivable

**incondicional** (eeng-kawngn-dee-sᵞoo-*nahl*) *adj* (pl -ais) unconditional

**inconsciente** (eeng-kawngsh-sᵞayngn-ter) *adj* unconscious; unaware

**inconveniência** (eeng-kawng-ver-nᵞayng-sᵞer) *f* inconvenience

**inconveniente** (eeng-kawng-ver-nᵞayngn-ter) *adj* inconvenient

**incorrecto** (eeng-koo-*rreh*-too) *adj* incorrect; inaccurate

**incrível** (eeng-*kree*-vehl) *adj* (pl -eis) incredible

**inculto** (eeng-*kool*-too) *adj* waste, uncultivated; uneducated

**incurável** (eeng-koo-*rah*-vehl) *adj* (pl -eis) incurable

**incursão** (eeng-koor-*serng*ʷ) *f* (pl -sões) raid

**indagar** (eeng-der-*gahr*) *v* inquire, enquire; query

**indecente** (eeng-der-*sayngn*-ter) *adj* indecent

**indefinido** (eeng-der-fer-nee-dhoo) *adj* indefinite

**indemnização** (eeng-der-mnee-zer-*serng*ʷ) *f* (pl -ções) indemnity; compensation

**independência** (eeng-der-payngn-dayng-sᵞer) *f* independence

**independente** (eeng-der-payngn-dayngn-ter) *adj* independent; self-employed

**indesejável** (eeng-der-zɪ-*zhah*-vehl) *adj* (pl -eis) undesirable

**Índia** (*eeng*-dᵞer) *f* India

**indiano** (eeng-dᵞer-noo) *adj* Indian; *m* Indian

**indicação** (eeng-dee-ker-*serng*ʷ) *f* (pl -ções) indication

**indicado** (eeng-dee-*kah*-dhoo) *adj* proper

**indicador** (eeng-dee-ker-*dhoar*) *m* index finger; indicator; ~ **de direcção** trafficator

**indicar** (eeng-dee-*kahr*) *v* point out, indicate

**indicativo** (eeng-dee-ker-*tee*-voo) *m* area code

**índice** (*eeng*-dee-ser) *m* index; table of contents

**indiferente** (eeng-dee-fer-*rayngn*-ter) *adj* indifferent

**indígena** (eeng-*dee*-zher-ner) *m* native

**indigestão** (eeng-dee-zhersh-*terng*ʷ) *f* (pl -tões) indigestion

**indignação** (eeng-deeg-ner-*serng*ʷ) *f* (pl -ções) indignation

**índio** (*eeng*-dᵞoo) *adj* Indian; *m* Indian

**indirecto** (eeng-dee-*reh*-too) *adj* indirect

**indispensável** (eeng-deesh-payng-*sah*-vehl) *adj* (pl -eis) essential

**indisposto** (eeng-deesh-*poash*-too) *adj* unwell

**individual** (eeng-der-vee-*dhwahl*) *adj* (pl -ais) individual

**indivíduo** (eeng-der-*vee*-dhwoo) *m* individual

**Indonésia** (eeng-doo-*neh*-sᵞer) *f* Indonesia

**indonésio** (eeng-doo-*neh*-zᵞoo) *adj* Indonesian; *m* Indonesian

**indulto** (eeng-*dool*-too) *m* pardon

**indústria** (eeng-*doosh*-trᵞer) *f* industry

**industrial** (eeng-doosh-*tr*ᵞahl) *adj* (pl -ais) industrial

**ineficiente** (ee-ner-fee-sᵞayngn-ter) *adj* inefficient

**inesperado** (ee-nɪsh-per-*rah*-dhoo) *adj*

unexpected

**inestimável** (ee-nish-tee-*mah*-vehl) *adj* (pl -eis) priceless

**inevitável** (ee-ner-vee-*tah*-vehl) *adj* (pl -eis) inevitable; unavoidable

**inexacto** (ee-nee-*zah*-too) *adj* incorrect

**inexperiente** (ee-nish-per-rᵞaᵞngn-ter) *adj* inexperienced

**inexplicável** (ee-nish-plee-*kah*-vehl) *adj* (pl -eis) unaccountable

**infame** (eeng-*fer*-mer) *adj* foul

**infantaria** (ee-ferngn-ter-*ree*-er) *f* infantry

**infecção** (eeng-feh-*serngᵂ*) *f* (pl -ções) infection

**infeccioso** (eeng-feh-sᵞ*oa*-zoo) *adj* infectious

**infectar** (eeng-feh-*tahr*) *v* infect; *become septic

**infelicidade** (eeng-fer-ler-see-*dhah*-dher) *f* misery, misfortune

**infeliz** (eeng-fer-*leesh*) *adj* unhappy

**infelizmente** (eeng-fer-leezh-*mayngn*-ter) *adv* unfortunately

**inferior** (eeng-fer-rᵞ*oar*) *adj* bottom, inferior

**inferno** (eeng-*fehr*-noo) *m* hell

**infiel** (eeng-fᵞ*ehl*) *adj* (pl -iéis) unfaithful

**infinitivo** (eeng-fer-nee-*tee*-voo) *m* infinitive

**infinito** (eeng-fer-*nee*-too) *adj* endless, infinite

**inflação** (eeng-flah-*serngᵂ*) *f* (pl -ções) inflation

**inflamação** (eeng-fler-mer-*serngᵂ*) *f* (pl -ções) inflammation

**inflamável** (eeng-fler-*mah*-vehl) *adj* (pl -eis) inflammable

**influência** (eeng-flwayng-sᵞer) *f* influence

**influenciar** (eeng-flwayng-sᵞ*ahr*) *v* influence

**influente** (eeng-*flwayngn*-ter) *adj* influential

**informação** (eeng-foor-mer-*serngᵂ*) *f* (pl -ções) information; enquiry; **agência de informações** inquiry office

**informar** (eeng-foor-*mahr*) *v* inform; **informar-se** inquire

**infortunado** (eeng-foor-too-*nah*-dhoo) *adj* unlucky

**infortúnio** (eeng-foor-*too*-nᵞoo) *m* misfortune

**infra-vermelho** (eeng-frah-verr-*meh*-lᵞoo) *adj* infra-red

**infringir** (eeng-freeng-*zheer*) *v* trespass

**ingénuo** (eeng-*zheh*-nwoo) *adj* naïve, simple

**Inglaterra** (eeng-gler-*teh*-rrer) *f* England; Britain

**inglês** (eeng-*glaysh*) *adj* English; *m* Briton, Englishman

**ingrato** (eeng-*grah*-too) *adj* ungrateful

**ingrediente** (eeng-grer-dhᵞ*ayngn*-ter) *m* ingredient

**íngreme** (*eeng*-grer-mer) *adj* steep

**inicial** (ee-nee-sᵞ*ahl*) *adj* (pl -ais) initial; *f* initial

**iniciar** (ee-nee-sᵞ*ahr*) *v* *begin

**iniciativa** (ee-nee-sᵞer-*tee*-ver) *f* initiative

**início** (ee-*nee*-sᵞoo) *m* beginning

**inimigo** (ee-ner-*mee*-goo) *m* enemy

**ininterrupto** (ee-neengn-ter-*rroop*-too) *adj* continuous

**injecção** (eeng-zheh-*serngᵂ*) *f* (pl -ções) shot, injection

**injectar** (eeng-zheh-*tahr*) *v* inject

**injuriar** (eeng-zhoo-rᵞ*ahr*) *v* call names

**injustiça** (eeng-zhoosh-*tee*-ser) *f* injustice

**injusto** (eeng-*zhoosh*-too) *adj* unjust; unfair

**inocência** (ee-noo-*sayng*-sᵞer) *f* innocence

**inocente** (ee-noo-*sayngn*-ter) *adj* innocent

**inoculação** (ee-noo-koo-ler-*serng*ᵂ) *f* (pl -ções) inoculation

**inocular** (ee-noo-koo-*lahr*) *v* inoculate

**inofensivo** (ee-noo-fayng-*see*-voo) *adj* harmless

**inoportuno** (ee-noo-poor-*too*-noo) *adj* misplaced

**inquebrável** (eeng-ker-*bhrah*-vehl) *adj* (pl -eis) unbreakable

**inquérito** (eeng-*keh*-ree-too) *m* enquiry; inquiry

**inquieto** (eeng-*k*ᵛ*eh*-too) *adj* anxious; restless

**inquilino** (eeng-ker-*lee*-noo) *m* tenant

**inquirir** (eeng-ker-*reer*) *v* inquire

**insatisfatório** (cong-ser-teesh-fer-to-rᵛoo) *adj* unsatisfactory

**insatisfeito** (eeng-ser-teesh-*fay*-too) *adj* dissatisfied

**inscrever** (eengsh-krer-*vayr*) *v* enter; list, book; **inscrever-se** check in; register

**inscrição** (eengsh-kree-*serng*ᵂ) *f* (pl -ções) inscription

**insecticida** (eeng-seh-tee-*see*-dher) *m* insecticide

**insecto** (eeng-*seh*-too) *m* insect; bug *nAm*

**inseguro** (eeng-ser-*goo*-roo) *adj* unsafe

**insensato** (eeng-sayng-*sah*-too) *adj* mad

**insensível** (eeng-sayng-*see*-vehl) *adj* (pl -eis) insensitive; heartless

\***inserir** (eeng-ser-*reer*) *v* insert

**insignificante** (eeng-seeg-ner-fee-*kerngn*-ter) *adj* unimportant, petty, insignificant

**insípido** (eeng-*see*-pee-dhoo) *adj* tasteless; dull

**insistir** (eeng-seesh-*teer*) *v* insist

**insolação** (eeng-soo-ler-*serng*ᵂ) *f* (pl -ções) sunstroke

**insolência** (eeng-soo-*layng*-sᵛer) *f* insolence

**insolente** (eeng-soo-*layngn*-ter) *adj* impertinent, insolent

**insólito** (eeng-*so*-lee-too) *adj* uncommon; strange

**insónia** (eeng-*so*-nᵛer) *f* insomnia

**inspecção** (eengsh-peh-*serng*ᵂ) *f* (pl -ções) inspection

**inspeccionar** (eengsh-peh-sᵛoo-*nahr*) *v* inspect

**inspector** (eengsh-peh-*toar*) *m* inspector

**inspirar** (eengsh-pee-*rahr*) *v* inspire

**instalação** (eengsh-ter-ler-*serng*ᵂ) *f* (pl -ções) installation

**instalar** (eengsh-ter-*lahr*) *v* install

**instantaneamente** (congsh-terngn-ter-nᵛer-*mayngn*-ter) *adv* instantly

**instantâneo** (eengsh-tern-*ter*-nᵛoo) *m* snapshot

**instante** (eengsh-*terngn*-ter) *m* instant; second, moment

**instável** (eengsh-*tah*-vehl) *adj* (pl -eis) unsteady; unstable

**instinto** (eengsh-*teengn*-too) *m* instinct

**instituição** (eengsh-tee-twee-*serng*ᵂ) *f* (pl -ções) institution, institute

\***instituir** (eengsh-tee-*tweer*) *v* institute; found

**instituto** (eengsh-tee-*too*-too) *m* institute; ~ **de beleza** beauty parlour

**instrução** (eengsh-troo-*serng*ᵂ) *f* (pl -ções) tuition, instruction; direction

\***instruir** (eengsh-*trweer*) *v* instruct

**instrumento** (eengsh-troo-*mayngn*-too) *m* instrument; tool; ~ **musical** musical instrument

**instrutivo** (eengsh-troo-*tee*-voo) *adj* instructive

**instrutor** (eengsh-troo-*toar*) *m* instructor

**insuficiente** (eeng-soo-fee-s*Y*ayngn-ter) *adj* insufficient

**insultante** (eeng-sool-*terngn*-ter) *adj* offensive

**insultar** (eeng-sool-*tahr*) *v* insult

**insulto** (eeng-*sool*-too) *m* insult

**insuperável** (eeng-soo-per-*rah*-vehl) *adj* (pl -eis) unsurpassed

**insuportável** (eeng-soo-poor-*tah*-vehl) *adj* (pl -eis) unbearable

**insurreição** (eeng-soo-rray-*serng*ʷ) *f* (pl -ções) rising

**intacto** (eengn-*tah*-too) *adj* intact, whole

**inteiramente** (eengn-tay-rer-*mayngn*-ter) *adv* entirely; altogether, completely

**inteiro** (eengn-*tay*-roo) *adj* entire; unbroken, whole

**intelecto** (eengn-ter-*leh*-too) *m* intellect

**intelectual** (eengn-ter-leh-*twahl*) *adj* (pl -ais) intellectual

**inteligência** (eengn-ter-lee-*zhayng*-s*Y*er) *f* intelligence; brain

**inteligente** (eengn-ter-lee-*zhayngn*-ter) *adj* intelligent; clever; bright; smart

**intenção** (eengn-tayng-*serng*ʷ) *f* (pl -ções) intention, purpose

**intencional** (eengn-tayng-s*Y*oo-*nahl*) *adj* (pl -ais) intentional

**intenso** (eengn-*tayng*-soo) *adj* intense

**intento** (eengn-*tayngn*-too) *m* purpose

**interdição** (eengn-terr-dee-*serng*ʷ) *f* (pl -ções) prohibition

**interessado** (eengn-ter-rer-*sah*-dhoo) *adj* interested

**interessante** (eengn-ter-rer-*serngn*-ter) *adj* interesting

**interessar** (eengn-ter-rer-*sahr*) *v* interest

**interesse** (eengn-ter-*ray*-ser) *m* interest

**interferência** (eengn-terr-fer-*rayng*-s*Y*er) *f* interference

***interferir** (eengn-terr-fer-*reer*) *v* interfere

**interim** (eengn-ter-*reeng*) *m* interim

**interior** (eengn-ter-r*Y*oar) *adj* inner; inside; *m* interior, inside

**interlúdio** (eengn-terr-*loo*-dh*Y*oo) *m* interlude

**intermediário** (eengn-terr-mer-*dh*ʸahr*Y*oo) *m* mediator, intermediary; ***servir de ~** mediate

**internacional** (eengn-terr-nerng-s*Y*oo-*nahl*) *adj* (pl -ais) international

**interno** (eengn-*tehr*-noo) *adj* internal; indoor; domestic, resident

**interpretar** (eengn-terr-prer-*tahr*) *v* interpret

**intérprete** (eengn-*tehr*-prer-ter) *m* interpreter

**interrogar** (eengn-ter-rroo-*gahr*) *v* interrogate

**interrogativo** (eengn-ter-rroo-ger-*tee*-voo) *adj* interrogative

**interrogatório** (eengn-ter-rroo-ger-*to*-r*Y*oo) *m* examination; interrogation

**interromper** (eengn-ter-rrawngm-*payr*) *v* interrupt; ***cut off**

**interrupção** (eengn-ter-rroop-*serng*ʷ) *f* (pl -ções) interruption

**interruptor** (eengn-ter-rroop-*toar*) *m* switch

**intersecção** (eengn-terr-sehk-*serng*ʷ) *f* (pl -ções) intersection

**intervalo** (eengn-terr-*vah*-loo) *m* space; pause, interval, intermission; break; half-time

***intervir** (eengn-terr-*veer*) *v* intervene

**intestino** (eengn-tɪsh-*tee*-noo) *m* intestine; gut; **intestinos** bowels *pl*

**intimidade** (eengn-tee-mee-*dhah*-dher) *f* privacy

**íntimo** (*eengn*-tee-moo) *adj* intimate; cosy

**intolerável** (eengn-too-ler-*rah*-vehl) *adj* (pl -eis) intolerable

**intriga** (eengn-*tree*-ger) *f* intrigue

**introdução** (eengn-troo-dhoo-*serng*ʷ) *f* (pl -ções) introduction

**\*introduzir** (eengn-troo-dhoo-*zeer*) *v* introduce

**intrometer-se em** (eengn-troo-mer-*tayr*-ser) interfere with

**intruso** (eeengn-*troo*-zoo) *m* trespasser

**inundação** (ee-noongn-der-*serng*ʷ) *f* (pl -ções) flood

**inútil** (een-*oo*-teel) *adj* (pl -teis) useless

**inutilmente** (ee-noo-teel-*mayng*-ter) *adv* in vain

**invadir** (eeng-ver-*dheer*) *v* invade

**inválido** (eeng-*vah*-lee-dhoo) *adj* disabled, invalid; *m* invalid

**invasão** (eeng-ver-*zerng*ʷ) *f* (pl -sões) invasion

**inveja** (eeng-*veh*-zher) *f* envy

**invejar** (eeng-vi-*zhahr*) *v* envy; grudge

**invejoso** (eeng-vi-*zhoa*-zoo) *adj* envious

**invenção** (eeng-vayng-*serng*ʷ) *f* (pl -ções) invention

**inventar** (eeng-vayngn-*tahr*) *v* invent

**inventário** (eeng-vayngn-*tah*-rʸoo) *m* inventory

**inventivo** (eeng-vayngn-*tee*-voo) *adj* inventive

**inventor** (eeng-vayngn-*toar*) *m* inventor

**Inverno** (eeng-*vehr*-noo) *m* winter

**inverso** (eeng-*vehr*-soo) *adj* reverse

**inverter** (eeng-verr-*tayr*) *v* invert; turn over

**investigação** (eeng-vish-tee-ger-*serng*ʷ) *f* (pl -ções) enquiry; research, investigation

**investigar** (eeng-vish-tee-*gahr*) *v* enquire, investigate

**investimento** (eeng-vish-tee-*mayngn*-too) *m* investment

**\*investir** (eeng-vish-*teer*) *v* invest

**invisível** (eeng-ver-*zee*-vehl) *adj* (pl -eis) invisible

**involuntário** (eeng-voo-loongn-*tah*-rʸoo) *adj* unintentional

**invulgar** (eeng-vool-*gahr*) *adj* odd

**iodo** (ʸoa-dhoo) *m* iodine

**\*ir** (eer) *v* \*go; ~ **buscar** fetch; \*get; pick up; **\*ir-se** depart; **\*ir-se embora** \*go away

**ira** (*ee*-rer) *f* anger

**iraniano** (ee-rer-*n*ʸer-noo) *adj* Iranian; *m* Iranian

**Irão** (ee-*rerng*ʷ) *m* Iran

**Iraque** (ee-*rah*-ker) *m* Iraq

**iraquiano** (ee-rer-*k*ʸer-noo) *adj* Iraqi; *m* Iraqi

**irascível** (ee-rersh-*see*-vehl) *adj* (pl -eis) irascible; quick-tempered, hot-tempered

**Irlanda** (eer-*lern*-der) *f* Ireland

**irlandês** (eer-lern-*daysh*) *adj* Irish; *m* Irishman

**irmã** (eer-*merng*) *f* sister

**irmão** (eer-*merng*ʷ) *m* (pl ~s) brother

**ironia** (ee-roo-*nee*-er) *f* irony

**irónico** (ee-ro-nee-koo) *adj* ironical

**irreal** (ee-rrʸahl) *adj* (pl -ais) unreal

**irreflectido** (ee-rrer-fleh-*tee*-dhoo) *adj* rash

**irregular** (ee-rrer-goo-*lahr*) *adj* irregular; uneven

**irrelevante** (ee-rrer-ler-*verngn*-ter) *adj* insignificant

**irreparável** (ee-rrer-per-*rah*-vehl) *adj* (pl -eis) irreparable

**irrevogável** (ee-rrer-voo-*gah*-vehl) *adj* (pl -eis) irrevocable

**irritado** (ee-rree-*tah*-dhoo) *adj* cross

**irritante** (ee-rree-*terngn*-ter) *adj* an-

noying
**irritar** (ee-rree-*tahr*) *v* irritate; annoy
**irritável** (ee-rree-*tah*-vehl) *adj* (pl -eis) irritable
**isca** (*eesh*-ker) *f* bait
**isenção** (ee-zayng-*serng*ʷ) *f* (pl -ções) exemption
**isentar** (ee-zayng-*tahr*) *v* exempt
**isento** (ee-*zayng*-too) *adj* exempt
**islandês** (eezh-lerngn-*daysh*) *adj* Icelandic; *m* Icelander
**Islândia** (eezh-*lerngn*-dᵛah) *f* Iceland
**isolado** (ee-zoo-*lah*-dhoo) *adj* isolated
**isolador** (ee-zoo-ler-*dhoar*) *m* insulator
**isolamento** (ee-zoo-ler-*mayngn*-too) *m* isolation; insulation
**isolar** (ee-zoo-*lahr*) *v* isolate; insulate
**isqueiro** (eesh-*kay*-roo) *m* cigarette-lighter, lighter
**Israel** (eezh-rrer-*ehl*) *m* Israel
**israeliano** (eezh-rrer-ay-*lᵛer*-noo) *adj* Israeli; *m* Israeli
**isso** (*ee*-soo) *pron* that
**istmo** (*eesht*-moo) *m* isthmus
**Itália** (ee-*tah*-lᵛer) *f* Italy
**italiano** (ee-ter-*lᵛer*-noo) *adj* Italian; *m* Italian
**itálico** (ee-*tah*-lee-koo) *m* italics *pl*
**itinerante** (een-tee-ner-*rerngn*-ter) *adj* itinerant
**itinerário** (ee-tee-ner-*rah*-rᵛoo) *m* itinerary

# J

**já** (zhah) *adv* at once, immediately; already; ~ **não** any more; ~ **que** because
**jacto** (*zhahk*-too) *m* jet
**jade** (*zhah*-dher) *m* jade
**jamais** (zher-*mighsh*) *adv* ever
**Janeiro** (zher-*nay*-roo) January

**janela** (zher-*neh*-ler) *f* window; ~ **de madeira** shutter
**jantar** (zherngn-*tahr*) *m* dinner; *v* dine
**jante** (*zherngn*-ter) *f* rim
**Japão** (zher-*perng*ʷ) *m* Japan
**japonês** (zher-poo-*naysh*) *adj* Japanese; *m* Japanese
**jardim** (zherr-*deeng*) *m* garden; ~ **infantil** kindergarten; ~ **público** public garden; ~ **zoológico** zoological gardens
**jardineiro** (zherr-dee-*nay*-roo) *m* gardener
**jarra** (*zhah*-rrer) *f* jar
**jarro** (*zhah*-roo) *m* jug
**jaula** (*zhou*-ler) *f* cage
**jeitoso** (zhay-*too*-zoo) *adj* handy
**jersey** (*zherr*-seh) *m* jersey
**joalharia** (zhwer-lᵛer-*ree*-er) *f* jewellery
**joalheiro** (zhwer-*lᵛay*-roo) *m* jeweller
**joelho** (zhway-*lᵛoo*) *m* knee
**jogada** (zhoo-*gah*-dher) *f* move
**jogador** (zhoo-ger-*dhoar*) *m* player
**jogar** (zhoo-*gahr*) *v* play
**jogo** (*zhoa*-goo) *m* game, play; set; **campo de jogos** recreation ground; ~ **das damas** draughts; ~ **electrónico** electronic game
**jóia** (*zho*-ᵛer) *f* jewel; gem; **jóias** jewellery
**jóquei** (*zho*-kay) *m* jockey
**Jordânia** (zhoor-*der*-nᵛer) *f* Jordan
**jordaniano** (zhoor-der-*nᵛer*-noo) *adj* Jordanian; *m* Jordanian
**jornal** (zhoor-*nahl*) *m* (pl -ais) paper, newspaper; journal; ~ **da manhã** morning paper
**jornalismo** (zhoor-ner-*leezh*-moo) *m* journalism
**jornalista** (zhoor-ner-*leesh*-ter) *m* journalist
**jorro** (*zhoa*-rroo) *m* spout
**jovem** (*zho*-verngᵛ) *adj* young

**jovial** (zhoo-v<sup>y</sup>ahl) adj (pl -ais) jolly; cheerful

**jubileu** (zhoo-bhee-lay<sup>oo</sup>) m jubilee

**judaico** (zhoo-dhigh-koo) adj Jewish

**judeu** (zhoo-dhay<sup>oo</sup>) m Jew

**judicioso** (zhoo-dhee-syoa-zoo) adj judicious

**juiz** (zhweesh) m judge

**juízo** (zhwee-zoo) m sense; judgment

**julgamento** (zhool-ger-mayngn-too) m judgment; trial

**julgar** (zhool-gahr) v judge

**Julho** (zhoo-l<sup>y</sup>oo) July

**junção** (zhoong-serng<sup>w</sup>) f (pl -ções) junction

**junco** (zhoong-koo) m rush

**Junho** (zhoo-ño) June

**júnior** (zhoo-n<sup>y</sup>oar) adj junior

**junquilho** (zhoong-kee-l<sup>y</sup>oo) m daffodil

**juntar** (zhoong-tahr) v join; attach, enclose; add

**junto** (zhoong-too) adj joined; joint; ~ a next to; por~ wholesale

**juntos** (zhoong-toosh) adv together

**juramento** (zhoo-rer-mayngn-too) m oath, vow

**jurar** (zhoo-rahr) v *swear, vow

**júri** (zhoo-ree) m jury

**jurídico** (zhoo-ree-dhee-koo) adj legal

**jurisdição** (zhoo-reesh-dhee-serng<sup>w</sup>) n jurisdiction

**jurista** (zhoo-reesh-ter) m lawyer

**juro** (zhoo-roo) m interest

**justamente** (zhoosh-ter-mayngn-ter) adv just; rightly; exactly

**justiça** (zhoosh-tee-ser) f justice

**justificar** (zhoosh-tee-fee-kahr) v justify, prove

**justo** (zhoosh-too) adj righteous, just, right; proper, fair, appropriate

**juvenil** (zhoo-ver-neel) adj (pl -nis) juvenile

**juventude** (zhoo-vayngn-too-dher) f youth

# L

**lá** (lah) adv there

**lã** (lerng) f wool; de ~ woollen; ~ cardada worsted

**lábio** (lah-bh<sup>y</sup>oo) m lip

**labirinto** (ler-bher-reengn-too) m labyrinth, maze

**laboratório** (ler-bhoo-rer-to-r<sup>y</sup>oo) m laboratory; ~ de línguas language laboratory

**labutar** (ler-bhoo-tahr) v labour

**laca para o cabelo** (lah-ker per-rer oo ker-bhay-loo) hair-spray

**laço** (lah-soo) m link; bow tie

**lado** (lah-dhoo) m side; way; ao ~ next-door; ao ~ de beside; de ~ aside; sideways; do outro ~ de across; em qualquer ~ anywhere; em todo o ~ anywhere, everywhere; no outro ~ across; noutro ~ elsewhere

**ladrão** (ler-dhrerng<sup>w</sup>) m (pl -rões) thief; burglar, robber

**ladrar** (ler-dhrahr) v bark, bay

**lago** (lah-goo) m lake

**lagoa** (ler-goa-er) f small lake

**lagosta** (ler-goash-ter) f lobster

**lágrima** (lah-gree-mer) f tear

**laguna** (ler-goo-ner) f lagoon

**lama** (ler-mer) f mud

**lamacento** (ler-mer-sayngn-too) adj muddy

**lamber** (lerngm-bayr) v lick

**lambril** (lerngm-breel) m (pl -is) panelling

**lamechice** (ler-mer-shee-ser) f tear-jerker

**lamentar** (ler-mayngn-tahr) v regret

**lamentável** (ler-mayngn-tah-vehl) adj

(pl -eis) lamentable

**lâmina** (*ler*-mee-ner) *f* blade; ~ **de barbear** razor-blade

**lâmpada** (*lerngm*-per-dher) *f* light bulb; ~ **de flash** flash-bulb; ~ **de tempestade** hurricane lamp

**lança** (*lerng*-ser) *f* spear

**lançamento** (lerng-ser-*mayngn*-too) *m* launching; throw; entry

**lançar** (lerng-*sahr*) *v* *cast, *throw, toss; launch

**lance** (*lerng*-ser) *m* cast

**lanche** (*lerng*-sher) *m* tea, snack

**lanterna** (lerngn-*tehr*-ner) *f* lantern; ~ **de bolso** torch; ~ **de mão** flashlight

**lapela** (ler-*peh*-ler) *f* lapel

**lápide** (*lah*-pee-dher) *f* gravestone

**lápis** (*lah*-peesh) *m* (pl ~) pencil; ~ **para os olhos** eye-pencil

**lar** (lahr) *m* home

**laranja** (ler-*rerng*-zher) *f* orange

**lareira** (ler-ray-rer) *f* fireplace, hearth

**largo** (*lahr*-goo) *adj* broad, wide

**largura** (lerr-*goo*-rer) *f* breadth, width

**laringite** (ler-reeng-*zhee*-ter) *f* laryngitis

**lasca** (*lahsh*-ker) *f* chip

**lascar** (lersh-*kahr*) *v* chip

**lastimar** (lersh-tee-*mahr*) *v* deplore

**lata** (*lah*-ter) *f* tin, can; canister

**latão** (ler-*terng*ᵂ) *m* brass; **utensílios de** ~ brassware

**lavabos** (ler-*vah*-bhoosh) *mpl* washroom *nAm;* ~ **das senhoras** powder-room; ~ **dos homens** men's room

**lava-louça** (lah-ver-*loa*-ser) *m* (pl ~s) sink

**lavandaria** (ler-verngn-der-*ree*-er) *f* laundry; ~ **automática** launderette

**lavar** (ler-*vahr*) *v* wash; ~ **a loiça** wash up

**lavatório** (ler-ver-*to*-rᵞoo) *m* washstand; wash-basin

**lavável** (ler-*vah*-vehl) *adj* (pl -eis) washable

**lavrador** (ler-vrer-*dhoar*) *m* farmer

**lavrar** (ler-*vrahr*) *v* plough

**laxante** (ler-*shern*gn-ter) *m* laxative

**leal** (lᵞahl) *adj* (pl leais) loyal; true

**leão** (lᵞerng ᵂ) *m* (pl leões) lion

**lebre** (*leh*-bhrer) *f* hare

**legação** (ler-ger-*serng*ᵂ) *f* (pl -ções) legation

**legado** (ler-*gah*-doo) *m* legacy

**legal** (ler-*gahl*) *adj* (pl -ais) legal; lawful

**legalização** (ler-ger-lee-zer-*serng*ᵂ) *f* (pl -ções) legalization

**legenda** (lɪ-*zhayngn*-der) *f* subtitle

**legítimo** (lɪ-*zhee*-tee-moo) *adj* legitimate, legal

**legível** (lɪ-*zhee*-vehl) *adj* (pl -eis) legible

**legume** (ler-*goo*-mer) *m* vegetable

**lei** (lay) *f* law

**leigo** (*lay*-goo) *m* layman

**leilão** (lay-*lerng*ᵂ) *m* (pl -lões) auction

**leitão** (lay-*terng*ᵂ) *m* (pl -tões) piglet

**leitaria** (lay-ter-*ree*-er) *f* dairy

**leite** (*lay*-ter) *m* milk; **batido de** ~ milk-shake

**leiteiro** (lay-*tay*-roo) *m* milkman

**leitoso** (lay-*toa*-zoo) *adj* milky

**leitura** (lay-*too*-rer) *f* reading

**lema** (*lay*-mer) *m* slogan

**lembrança** (layngm-*brerng*-ser) *f* remembrance

**lembrar** (layngm-*brahr*) *v* remind; **lembrar-se** remember

**leme** (*leh*-mer) *m* rudder, helm

**lenço** (*layng*-soo) *m* handkerchief; ~ **da cabeça** scarf; ~ **de assoar** handkerchief; ~ **de papel** tissue; ~ **do pescoço** scarf

**lençol** (layng-*sol*) *m* (pl -çóis) sheet

**lente** (*layngn*-ter) *f* lens; **lentes de contacto** contact lenses; **~ zoom** zoom lens

**lento** (*layngn*-too) *adj* slow; slack

**lepra** (*leh*-prer) *f* leprosy

**leque** (*leh*-ker) *m* fan

**\*ler** (layr) *v* \*read

**lesão** (ler-*zerng* ʷ) *f* (pl lesões) injury

**lesar** (ler-*zahr*) *v* wrong

**letra** (*lay*-trer) *f* letter; draft

**levantar** (ler-verngn-*tahr*) *v* raise, lift; \*bring up; cash, \*draw; **levantar-se** \*rise; \*get up

**levar** (ler-*vahr*) *v* \*take; \*bear; \*take away; **~ a mal** resent

**leve** (*leh*-ver) *adj* light

**levedura** (ler-ver-*dhoo*-rer) *f* yeast

**lhe** (lʸer) *pron* him; her; **lhes** them

**libanês** (lee-bher-*naysh*) *adj* Lebanese; *m* Lebanese

**Líbano** (*lee*-bher-noo) *m* Lebanon

**liberal** (lee-bher-*rahl*) *adj* (pl -ais) liberal

**liberdade** (lee-bherr-*dhah*-dher) *f* freedom, liberty

**Libéria** (lee-*bheh*-rʸer) *f* Liberia

**liberiano** (lee-bher-*rʸer*-noo) *adj* Liberian; *m* Liberian

**libertação** (lee-bherr-ter-*serng* ʷ) *f* (pl -cões) liberation; delivery

**libra** (*lee*-bhrer) *f* pound

**lição** (lee-*serng* ʷ) *f* (pl lições) lesson

**licença** (lee-*sayng*-ser) *f* licence, permit, permission; leave

**licor** (lee-*koar*) *m* liqueur

**lida** (*lee*-dher) *f* work

**liga** (*lee*-ger) *f* league, union

**ligação** (lee-ger-*serng* ʷ) *f* (pl -cões) connection; affair

**ligadura** (lee-ger-*dhoo*-rer) *f* bandage; band

**ligar** (lee-*gahr*) *v* \*bind; connect, switch on, plug in, turn on; link

**ligeiro** (lee-*zhay*-roo) *adj* slight; gentle; swift; light

**lilás** (lee-*lahsh*) *adj* mauve

**lima** (*lee*-mer) *f* file; lime; **~ de unhas** nail-file

**limão** (lee-*merng* ʷ) *m* (pl limões) lemon

**limiar** (lee-*mʸahr*) *m* threshold

**limitar** (lee-mee-*tahr*) *v* limit

**limite** (lee-*mee*-ter) *m* limit; bound, boundary

**limonada** (lee-moo-*nah*-dher) *f* lemonade

**limpa-cachimbos** (leengm-per ker-*sheengm*-boosh) *m* (pl ~) pipe cleaner

**limpa-chaminés** (leengm-per-sher-mee-*nehsh*) *m* (pl ~) chimneysweep

**limpar** (leengm-*pahr*) *v* clean; wipe; **~ a seco** dry-clean

**limpeza** (leengm-*pay*-zer) *f* cleaning

**limpo** (*leengm*-poo) *adj* clean

**lindo** (*leengn*-doo) *adj* lovely

**língua** (*leeng*-gwer) *f* tongue; language; **~ materna** mother tongue, native language

**linguado** (leeng-*gwah*-dhoo) *m* sole

**linguagem** (leeng-*gwah*-zherng ʸ) *f* speech

**linha** (*lee*-ñer) *f* line; thread; **~ de passajar** darning wool; **~ principal** main line

**linho** (*lee*-ñoo) *m* linen

**liquidação** (lee-kee-dher-*serng* ʷ) *f* (pl -cões) clearance sale

**liquidar** (lee-kee-*dhahr*) *v* \*pay off; destroy

**líquido** (*lee*-kee-dhoo) *adj* liquid; net; *m* fluid; **~ dentifrico** mouthwash

**lírio** (*lee*-rʸoo) *m* lily

**liso** (*lee*-zoo) *adj* smooth; level; even

**lista** (*leesh*-ter) *f* list; **~ de espera** waiting-list; **~ de preços** price-list; ~ dos telefones telephone directory; telephone book *Am;* ~ dos vinhos wine-list; ~ telefónica telephone directory; telephone book *Am*

literário (lee-ter-*rah*-rʸoo) *adj* literary

literatura (lee-ter-rer-*too*-rer) *f* literature

litígio (lee-*tee*-zhʸoo) *m* dispute, quarrel

litoral (lee-too-*rahl*) *m* sea-coast

litro (*lee*-troo) *m* litre

livrar (lee-*vrahr*) *v* deliver

livraria (lee-vrer-*ree*-er) *f* bookstore

livre (*lee*-vrer) *adj* free

livreiro (lee-*vray*-roo) *m* bookseller

livro (*lee*-vroo) *m* book; ~ de bolso paperback; ~ de reclamações complaints book

lixa (*lee*-sher) *f* sandpaper

lixo (*lee*-shoo) *m* garbage; trash; refuse; litter, rubbish; caixote do ~ rubbish-bin, dustbin; lata de ~ *Br* rubbish-bin, dustbin

lobo (*loa*-bhoo) *m* wolf

local (loo-*kahl*) *adj* (pl -ais) local; *m* premises *pl;* spot

localidade (loo-ker-lee-*dhah*-dher) *f* locality

localização (loo-ker-lee-zer-*serng*ʷ) *f* (pl -ções) location

localizar (loo-ker-lee-*zahr*) *v* locate

loção (loo-*serng*ʷ) *f* (pl loções) lotion; ~ fixadora setting lotion; ~ para depois da barba aftershave lotion

locomotiva (loo-koo-moo-*tee*-ver) *f* engine, locomotive

lógica (*lo*-zhee-ker) *f* logic

lógico (*lo*-zhee-koo) *adj* logical

logo (*lo*-goo) *adv* immediately; soon; ~ que when

loiça (*loi*-ser) *f* crockery, pottery

loira (*loi*-rer) *f* blonde

loiro (*loi*-roo) *adj* fair

loja (*lo*-zher) *f* store, shop; ~ de artigos fotográficos camera shop; ~ de brinquedos toyshop; ~ de ferragens hardware store; ~ de vinhos off-licence

lojista (loo-*zheesh*-ter) *m* shopkeeper

lona (*loa*-ner) *f* canvas

longe (*lawng*-zher) *adv* far; de ~ by far

longínquo (lawng-*zheeng*-kwoo) *adj* far-off

longitude (lawng-zhee-*too*-dher) *f* longitude

longitudinalmente (lawng-zhee-too-dhee-nerl-*mayngn*-ter) *adv* lengthways

longo (*lawng*-goo) *adj* long; ao ~ de along

lotaria (loo-ter-*ree*-er) *f* lottery

lote (*lo*-ter) *m* batch

louco (*loa*-koo) *adj* crazy; insane, lunatic

loucura (loa-*koo*-rer) *f* lunacy

louro (*loa*-roo) *adj* blond

louvar (loa-*vahr*) *v* praise

louvor (loa-*voar*) *m* glory

lua (*loo*-er) *f* moon

lua-de-mel (*loo*-er-der-mehl) *f* honeymoon

luar (lwahr) *m* moonlight

lubrificação (loo-bhrer-fee-ker-*serng*ʷ) *f* (pl -ções) lubrication; sistema de lubrificação lubrication system

lubrificar (loo-bhrer-fee-*kahr*) *v* lubricate; grease

lúcio (*loo*-sʸoo) *m* pike

lucrativo (loo-krer-*tee*-voo) *adj* profitable

lucro (*loo*-kroo) *m* profit; gain, benefit; lucros winnings

lugar (loo-*gahr*) *m* place; room; seat; ~ de nascimento place of birth; *ter ~ *take place

lumbago (loongm-*bah*-goo) *m* lumbago

**luminoso** (loo-mee-*noa*-zoo) *adj* luminous

**lupa** (*loo*-per) *f* magnifying glass

**lúpulo** (*loo*-poo-loo) *m* hop

**lustro** (*loosh*-troo) *m* gloss

**lustroso** (loosh-*troa*-zoo) *adj* glossy

**luta** (*loo*-ter) *f* strife; combat, fight; contest, battle, struggle; ~ **de boxe** boxing match

**lutar** (loo-*tahr*) *v* \*fight; struggle

**luto** (*loo*-too) *m* mourning

**luva** (*loo*-ver) *f* glove; **luvas sem dedos** mittens *pl*

**luxo** (*loo*-shoo) *m* luxury

**luxuoso** (loo-*shwoa*-zoo) *adj* luxurious

**luz** (loosh) *f* light; ~ **da retaguarda** rear-light; ~ **de estacionamento** parking light; ~ **do dia** daylight; ~ **do sol** sunlight; **luzes de travão** brake lights; ~ **lateral** sidelight

# M

**maca** (*mah*-ker) *f* stretcher

**maçã** (mer-*serng*) *f* apple; ~ **do rosto** cheek-bone

**macacão** (mer-ker-*kerng*ᵂ) *mBr* (pl -cões) overalls *pl*

**macaco** (mer-*kah*-koo) *m* monkey; jack

**maçador** (mer-ser-*dhoar*) *adj* boring, annoying; troublesome, inconvenient; unpleasant; *m* bore

**maçaneta** (mer-ser-*nay*-ter) *f* handle, knob

**maçar** (mer-*sahr*) *v* bore; bother

**machado** (mer-*shah*-dhoo) *m* axe

**macho** (*mah*-shoo) *m* mule; male animal

**maciço** (mer-*see*-soo) *adj* massive; solid

**macio** (mer-*see*ᵒᵒ) *adj* mellow

**maço** (*mah*-soo) *m* mallet

**madeira** (mer-*dhay*-rer) *f* wood; **de** ~ wooden; ~ **de construção** timber

**madrasta** (mer-*dhrahsh*-ter) *f* stepmother

**madre-pérola** (mah-dhrer-*peh*-roo-ler) *f* mother-of-pearl

**madrugada** (mer-dhroo-*gah*-dher) *f* dawn

**maduro** (mer-*dhoo*-roo) *adj* ripe, mature

**mãe** (merngᵞ) *f* mother

**maestro** (mer-*ehsh*-troo) *m* conductor

**magia** (mer-*zhee*-er) *f* magic

**mágico** (*mah*-zhee-koo) *adj* magic

**magistrado** (mer-zheesh *trah*-dhoo) *m* magistrate

**magnânimo** (merg-*ner*-nee-moo) *adj* generous

**magnético** (merg-*neh*-tee-koo) *adj* magnetic

**magneto** (merg-*neh*-too) *m* magneto

**magnífico** (merg-*nee*-fee-koo) *adj* magnificent; gorgeous, splendid

**magoar** (mer-*gwahr*) *v* \*hurt; bruise

**magro** (*mah*-groo) *adj* lean, thin

**Maio** (*mah*-ᵞoo) May

**maior** (mer-ᵞor) *adj* major, superior; main; of age; ~ **parte** bulk

**maioria** (mer-ᵞoo-ree-er) *f* majority

**mais** (mighsh) *adj* more; most; *adv* plus; ~ **de** over; **não** ~ no longer

**maiúscula** (mer-ᵞoosh-koo-ler) *f* capital letter

**major** (mer-*zhor*) *m* major

**mal** (mahl) *m* (pl ~es) evil; wrong, harm; ailment; *adv* barely, hardly; \***fazer** ~ **a** harm; ~ **sucedido** unsuccessful

**mala** (*mah*-ler) *f* bag; case, suitcase; boot; trunk *nAm*; ~ **de mão** handbag

**malaio** (mer-*ligh*-oo) *adj* Malaysian; *m* Malay

**malandro** (mer-*lerngn*-droo) *m* rascal

**malária** (mer-*lah*-rᵞer) *f* malaria

**Malásia** (mer-*lah*-zᵞer) *f* Malaysia

**malcriado** (mahl-*krᵞah*-dhoo) *adj* impertinent

**maldade** (mahl-*dah*-dher) *f* mischief

***maldizer** (mahl-dee-*zayr*) *v* curse

**maleável** (merl-ᵞah-vehl) *adj* (pl -eis) supple; flexible

**mal-entendido** (mahl-eengn-tayngn-*dee*-dhoo) *m* misunderstanding

**malévolo** (mer-*leh*-voo-loo) *adj* spiteful

**malha** (*mah*-lᵞer) *f* mesh; ***fazer ~** knit; **malhas** hosiery

**malícia** (mer-*lee*-sᵞer) *f* mischief

**malicioso** (mer-lee-sᵞoa-zoo) *adj* malicious

**maligno** (mer-*leeg*-noo) *adj* malignant; ill

**maluco** (mer-*loo*-koo) *adj* foolish; mad

**mamífero** (mer-*mee*-fer-roo) *m* mammal

**mamute** (mer-*moo*-ter) *m* mammoth

**manada** (mer-*nah*-dher) *f* herd

**mancha** (*merng*-sher) *f* stain, spot; speck, blot; **sem ~** spotless

**manchar** (merng-*shahr*) *v* stain

**mandar** (merng*n*-*dahr*) *v* order, command; *send; *have; **~ vir** *send for

**mandato** (merngn-*dah*-too) *m* mandate

**maneira** (mer-*nay*-rer) *f* way, manner; fashion; **de qualquer ~** anyway; any way

**manejar** (mer-nı-*zhahr*) *v* handle

**manejável** (mer-nı-*zhah*-vehl) *adj* (pl -eis) manageable

**manequim** (mer-ner-*keeng*) *m* model, mannequin

**manga** (*merng*-ger) *f* sleeve

**manha** (*mer*-ñer) *f* trick

**manhã** (mer-*ñerng*) *f* morning; **esta ~** this morning

**manhoso** (mer-*ñoa*-zoo) *adj* cunning

**mania** (mer-*nee*-er) *f* craze

**manicura** (mer-nee-*koo*-rer) *f* manicure

**manifestação** (mer-nee-fısh-ter-*serng*ʷ) *f* (pl -ções) demonstration

**manifestar** (mer-nee-fısh-*tahr*) *v* demonstrate; express

**manjedoura** (merng-zher-*dhoa*-rer) *f* manger

**manso** (*merng*-soo) *adj* tame

**manteiga** (merngn-*tay*-ger) *f* butter

***manter** (merngn-*tayr*) *v* maintain; *keep

**manual** (mer-*nwahl*) *adj* (pl -ais) manual; *m* handbook

**manuscrito** (mer-noosh-*kree*-too) *m* manuscript

**manutenção** (mer-noo-tayng-*serng*ʷ) *f* maintenance, upkeep

**mão** (*merng*ʷ) *f* (pl ~s) hand; **em segunda ~** second-hand; **feito à ~** hand-made; **palma da ~** palm

**mapa** (*mah*-per) *m* map; **~ de estradas** road map; **~ marítimo** chart

**maquilhagem** (mer-kee-*lah*-zherng ᵞ) *f* make-up

**máquina** (*mah*-kee-ner) *f* machine, engine; **~ de barbear** shaver, electric razor; **~ de costura** sewing-machine; **~ de escrever** typewriter; **~ de filmar** camera; **~ de lavar** washing-machine; **~ fotográfica** camera

**maquinaria** (mer-kee-ner-*ree*-er) *f* machinery

**mar** (mahr) *m* sea

**maravilha** (mer-rer-*vee*-lᵞer) *f* marvel

**maravilhar-se** (mer-rer-vee-lᵞ*ahr*-ser) *v* marvel

**maravilhoso** (mer-rer-vee-lᵞ*oa*-zoo) *adj*

marvellous; fine, wonderful

**marca** (*mahr*-ker) f mark; sign; tick; brand; ~ **de fábrica** trademark

**marcar** (merr-*kahr*) v mark; tick off; score

**marceneiro** (merr-ser-*nay*-roo) m joiner

**marcha** (*mahr*-sher) f march; *fazer ~ à ré Br* reverse; *fazer ~ atrás* reverse; ~ **atrás** reverse

**marchar** (mahr-*shahr*) v march

**Março** (*mahr*-soo) March

**marco** (*mahr*-koo) m landmark; ~ **miliário** milestone

**maré** (mer-*reh*) f tide; ~ **baixa** low tide; ~ **cheia** high tide

**marfim** (merr-*feeng*) m ivory

**margarina** (merr-ger-*ree*-ner) f margarine

**margem** (*mahr*-zherng^y) f margin; river bank, shore

**marido** (mer-*ree*-dhoo) m husband

**marinha** (mer-*ree*-ñer) f navy

**marinheiro** (mer-ree-*ñay*-roo) m sailor, seaman

**mariposa** (mer-ree-*poa*-zer) f butterfly stroke

**marisco** (mer-*reesh*-koo) m shellfish

**marítimo** (mer-*ree*-tee-moo) adj maritime

**mármore** (*mahr*-moo-rer) m marble

**maroto** (mer-*roa*-too) adj naughty, mischievous

**Marrocos** (mer-*roa*-koosh) m Morocco

**marroquino** (mer-rroo-*kee*-noo) adj Moroccan; m Moroccan

**martelar** (merr-ter-*lahr*) v thump

**martelo** (merr-*teh*-loo) m hammer

**mártir** (*mahr*-teer) m martyr

**mas** (mersh) conj but; only, yet

**máscara** (*mahsh*-ker-rer) f mask; ~ **facial** face-pack

**masculino** (mersh-koo-*lee*-noo) adj

masculine, male

**massa** (*mah*-ser) f dough, batter; mass

**massagem** (mer-*sah*-zherng^y) f massage; ~ **facial** face massage

**massagista** (mer-ser-*zheesh*-ter) m masseur

**massajar** (mer-ser-*zhahr*) v massage

**mastigar** (mersh-tee-*gahr*) v chew

**mastro** (*mahsh*-troo) m mast

**mata** (*mah*-ter) f grove

**mata-borrão** (mah-ter-bhoo-*rrerng*^w) m (pl -rões) blotting paper

**matar** (mer-*tahr*) v kill

**mate** (*mah*-ter) adj dim, mat

**matemática** (mer-ter-*mah*-tee-ker) f mathematics

**matemático** (mer-ter-*mah*-tee-koo) adj mathematical; m mathematician

**matéria** (mer-*teh*-r^yer) f matter

**material** (mer-ter-r^y*ahl*) adj (pl -ais) substantial, material; m material

**matéria-prima** (mer-teh-r^yer-*pree*-mer) f raw material

**mato** (*mah*-too) m brush

**matrimonial** (mer-tree-moo-n^y*ahl*) adj (pl -ais) matrimonial

**matrimónio** (mer-tree-*mo*-n^yoo) m matrimony

**maturidade** (mer-too-ree-*dhah*-dher) f maturity

**mau** (mou) adj (f má) evil, bad; ill, wicked; ~ **génio** temper

**mausoléu** (mou-zoo-*leh*^oo) m mausoleum

**maxila** (mahk-*see*-ler) f jaw

**máximo** (*mah*-see-moo) adj utmost; **no ~** at most

**me** (mer) pron me; myself

**mecânico** (mer-*ker*-nee-koo) adj mechanical; m mechanic

**mecanismo** (mer-ker-*neezh*-moo) m mechanism; màchinery

**mecha** (*meh*-sher) f fuse

**medalha** (mer-*dhah*-l<sup>y</sup>er) *f* medal

**média** (*meh*-dh<sup>y</sup>er) *f* average, mean; **em ~** on the average

**mediano** (mer-dh<sup>y</sup>er-noo) *adj* medium

**medicamento** (mer-dhee-ker-*mayngn*-too) *m* drug, medicine

**medicina** (mer-dhee-*see*-ner) *f* medicine

**médico** (*meh*-dhee-koo) *m* physician, doctor; *adj* medical; **~ de clínica geral** general practitioner

**medida** (mer-*dhee*-dher) *f* measure; gauge, size; **feito à ~** tailor-made

**medidor** (mer-dee-*doar*) *m*Br meter

**medieval** (mer-dh<sup>y</sup>er-*vahl*) *adj* (pl -ais) mediaeval

**médio** (*meh*-dh<sup>y</sup>oo) *adj* average, medium; middle

**medíocre** (mer-*dhee*<sup>oo</sup>-krer) *adj* mediocre, second-rate

***medir** (mer-*dheer*) *v* measure

**meditar** (mer-dee-*tahr*) *v* meditate

**Mediterrâneo** (mer-dhee-ter-*rrer*-n<sup>y</sup>oo) *m* Mediterranean

**medo** (*may*-dhoo) *m* fear, fright; **com ~** afraid; **meter ~** frighten; ***ter ~** *be afraid

**medonho** (mer-*dhoa*-ño) *adj* frightful, terrible

**medula** (mer-*dhoo*-ler) *f* marrow

**medusa** (mer-*dhoo*-zer) *f*Br jelly-fish

**meia** (*may*-er) *f* stocking; **meias de descanso** support hose

**meia-calça** (may-er-*kahl*-ser) *f* pantyhose

**meia-noite** (may-er-*noi*-ter) *f* midnight

**meio** (*may*-oo) *adj* half; *m* midst, middle; means; *adv* half; **~ ambiente** environment, milieu; **no ~ de** amid; **por ~ de** by means of

**meio-dia** (may-oo-*dhee*-er) *m* noon, midday

**meio-fio** (may-<sup>y</sup>oo-*fee*<sup>oo</sup>) *m*Br curb

**mel** (mehl) *m* honey

**melancia** (mer-lerng-*see*-er) *f* watermelon

**melancolia** (mer-lerng-koo-*lee*-er) *f* melancholy

**melancólico** (mer-lerng-*ko*-lee-koo) *adj* sad

**melão** (mer-*lerng*<sup>w</sup>) *m* (pl melões) melon

**melhor** (mı-l<sup>y</sup>*oar*) *adj* better; superior; **o ~** best, the best

**melhoramento** (mı-l<sup>y</sup>oo-rer-*mayngn*-too) *m* improvement

**melhorar** (mı-l<sup>y</sup>oo-*rahr*) *v* improve

**melindrar-se por** (mer-leengn-*drahr*-ser) resent

**melodia** (mer-loo-*dhee*-er) *f* melody; tune

**melodioso** (mer-loo-dh<sup>y</sup>*oa*-zoo) *adj* tuneful

**melodrama** (mer-loo-*drer*-mer) *m* melodrama

**melro** (*mehl*-rroo) *m* blackbird

**membrana** (mayngm-*brer*-ner) *f* diaphragm

**membro** (*mayngm*-broo) *m* limb; associate, member

**memorando** (mer-moo-*rerngn*-doo) *m* memo

**memorável** (mer-moo-*rah*-vehl) *adj* (pl -eis) memorable

**memória** (mer-*mo*-r<sup>y</sup>er) *f* memory

**memorial** (mer-moo-r<sup>y</sup>*ahl*) *m* (pl -ais) memorial

**menção** (mayng-*serng*<sup>w</sup>) *f* (pl -ções) mention

**mencionar** (mayng-s<sup>y</sup>oo-*nahr*) *v* mention

**mendigar** (mayngn-dee-*gahr*) *v* beg

**mendigo** (mayngn-dee-goo) *m* beggar

**menina** (mer-*nee*-ner) *f* miss; small girl; **a ~** you

**menino** (mer-*nee*-noo) *m* small boy

**menor** (mer-*nor*) *adj* minor; inferior;

under age; *m* minor

**menos** (may-noosh) *adj* less, fewer; *adv* less; *prep* but; **pelo ~** at least

**menosprezar** (may-noosh-prer-*zahr*) *v* underestimate

**mensageiro** (mayꞑg-ser-*zhay*-roo) *m* messenger

**mensagem** (mayꞑg-*sah*-zherꞑgᵞ) *f* message

**mensal** (mayꞑg-*sahl*) *adj* (pl -ais) monthly

**menstruação** (mayꞑgsh-trwer-*serꞑg*ᵂ) *f* (pl -ções) menstruation

**mental** (mayꞑg-*tahl*) *adj* (pl -ais) mental

**mente** (*mayꞑgn*-ter) *f* mind

**\*mentir** (mayꞑgn-*teer*) *v* lie

**mentira** (mayꞑgn-*tee*-rer) *f* lie

**mercado** (merr-*kah*-dhoo) *m* market

**mercadoria** (merr-ker-dhoo-*ree*-er) *f* merchandise; **mercadorias** goods *pl*; wares *pl*

**mercearia** (merr-sᵞer-*ree*-er) *f* grocer's; **artigos de ~** groceries *pl*; **~ fina** delicatessen

**merceeiro** (merr-sᵞay-roo) *m* grocer

**mercúrio** (merr-*koo*-rᵞoo) *m* mercury

**merecer** (mer-rer-*sayr*) *v* deserve; merit

**mergulhar** (merr-goo-*lᵞahr*) *v* dive

**meridional** (mer-ree-dhᵞoo-*nahl*) *adj* (pl -ais) southerly

**mérito** (*meh*-ree-too) *m* merit

**mês** (maysh) *m* month

**mesa** (*may*-zer) *f* table

**mesmo** (*mayzh*-moo) *adj* same; *adv* even

**mesquinho** (mɪsh-*kee*-ñoo) *adj* stingy; mean

**mesquita** (mɪsh-*kee*-ter) *f* mosque

**mestre** (*mehsh*-trer) *m* master; teacher

**meta** (*meh*-ter) *f* finish

**metade** (mer-*tah*-dher) *f* half

**metal** (mer-*tahl*) *m* (pl -ais) metal

**metálico** (mer-*tah*-lee-koo) *adj* metal

**meter** (mer-*tayr*) *v* \*put

**meticuloso** (mer-tee-koo-*loa*-zoo) *adj* precise

**metódico** (mer-*to*-dhee-koo) *adj* methodical

**método** (*meh*-too-dhoo) *m* method

**métrico** (*meh*-tree-koo) *adj* metric

**metro** (*meh*-troo) *m* metre

**metropolitano** (mer-troo-poo-lee-*ter*-noo) *m* underground; subway *nAm*

**meu** (mayᵒᵒ) *adj* (f minha) my

**mexer** (mɪ-*shayr*) *v* stir; touch; **mexer-se** move

**mexericar** (mɪ-sher-ree-*kahr*) *v* gossip

**mexerico** (mɪ-sher-*ree*-koo) *m* gossip

**mexicano** (mɪ-shee-*ker*-noo) *adj* Mexican; *m* Mexican

**México** (*meh*-shee-koo) *m* Mexico

**mexilhão** (mɪ-shee-*lᵞerꞑg*ᵂ) *m* (pl -hões) mussel

**micróbio** (mee-*kro*-bhᵞoo) *m* germ

**microfone** (mee-kro-*fo*-ner) *m* microphone

**migalha** (mee-*gah*-lᵞer) *f* crumb

**mil** (meel) *num* thousand

**milagre** (mee-*lah*-grer) *m* wonder, miracle

**milagroso** (mee-ler-*groa*-zoo) *adj* miraculous

**milha** (*mee*-lᵞer) *f* mile

**milho** (*mee*-lᵞoo) *m* maize; **maçaroca de ~** corn on the cob

**milionário** (mee-lᵞoo-nah-rᵞoo) *m* millionaire

**militar** (mer-lee-*tahr*) *adj* military

**mim** (meeꞑg) *pron* me

**mina** (*mee*-ner) *f* mine; pit

**mineiro** (mee-*nay*-roo) *m* miner

**mineral** (mee-ner-*rahl*) *m* (pl -ais) mineral

**minério** (mee-*neh*-rᵞoo) *m* ore

**miniatura** (mee-nᵞer-*too*-rer) *f* miniature

**mínimo** (*mee*-nee-moo) *adj* least; *m* minimum; **no ~** at the very least

**ministério** (mer-neesh-*teh*-rYoo) *m* ministry

**ministro** (mer-*neesh*-troo) *m* minister

**minoria** (mee-noo-*ree*-er) *f* minority

**minucioso** (mee-noo-sYoa-zoo) *adj* thorough

**minúsculo** (mee-*noosh*-koo-loo) *adj* minute, tiny

**minuto** (mee-*noo*-too) *m* minute

**míope** (*mee⁰⁰*-per) *m* short-sighted

**miserável** (mee-zer-*rah*-vehl) *adj* (pl -eis) miserable

**miséria** (mee-*zeh*-rYer) *f* misery

**misericórdia** (mee-zer-ree-*kor*-dhYer) *f* mercy

**misericordioso** (mee-zer-ree-koor-dhYoa-zoo) *adj* merciful

**missa** (*mee*-ser) *f* Mass

**mistério** (meesh-*teh*-rYoo) *m* mystery

**misterioso** (meesh-ter-rYoa-zoo) *adj* mysterious

**mistura** (meesh-*too*-rer) *f* mixture

**misturado** (meesh-too-*rah*-dhoo) *adj* mixed; miscellaneous

**misturar** (meesh-too-*rahr*) *v* mix

**mito** (*mee*-too) *m* myth

**mobilar** (moo-bhee-*lahr*) *v* furnish

**mobília** (moo-*bhee*-lYer) *f* furniture

**moca** (*mo*-ker) *f* club

**moção** (moo-serngʷ) *f* (pl moções) motion

**mochila** (moo-*shee*-ler) *f* rucksack, knapsack

**mocho** (*moa*-shoo) *m* owl

**moço** (*moa*-soo) *m* boy; **~ de hotel** *Br* page-boy

**moda** (*mo*-dher) *f* fashion; **fora de ~** out of date; **na ~** fashionable

**modelar** (moo-dher-*lahr*) *v* model

**modelo** (moo-*dhay*-loo) *m* model

**moderado** (moo-dher-*rah*-dhoo) *adj*

moderate

**moderno** (moo-*dhehr*-noo) *adj* modern

**modéstia** (moo-*dhehsh*-tYer) *f* modesty

**modesto** (moo-*dhehsh*-too) *adj* modest

**modificação** (moo-dher-fee-ker-*serng*ʷ) *f* (pl -ções) change

**modificar** (moo-dher-fee-*kahr*) *v* modify; change

**modista** (moo-*dheesh*-ter) *f* dressmaker

**modo** (*mo*-dhoo) *m* way, manner; **de ~ nenhum** by no means; **de ~ que** so that; **de qualquer ~** at any rate, anyhow; **doutro ~** otherwise, else; **~ de emprego** directions for use

**moeda** (*mweh*-dher) *f* coin; currency; **~ estrangeira** foreign currency

***moer** (mwayr) *v* *grind

**mohair** (mo-*ehr*) *m* mohair

**moinho** (*mwee*-ño) *m* mill; **~ de vento** windmill

**moita** (*moi*-ter) *f* scrub

**mola** (*mo*-ler) *f* spring

**molar** (moo-*lahr*) *m* molar

**moldar** (moal-*dahr*) *v* model

**moldura** (moal-*doo*-rer) *f* frame

**mole** (*mo*-ler) *adj* soft

**moleiro** (moo-*lay*-roo) *m* miller

**molhado** (moo-lYah-dhoo) *adj* wet; damp, moist

**molhar** (moo-lYahr) *v* soak

**molhe** (*mo*-lYer) *m* pier, jetty

**molho¹** (*mo*-lYoo) *m* bundle

**molho²** (*moa*-lYoo) *m* gravy, sauce; **pôr de ~** soak

**momentâneo** (moo-mayngn-*ter*-nYoo) *adj* momentary

**momento** (moo-*mayngn*-too) *m* moment; while; **~ decisivo** turning-point

**monarca** (moo-*nahr*-ker) *m* ruler, monarch

**monarquia** (moo-nerr-*kee*-er) *f* monarchy

**monetário** (moo-ner-*tah*-rʸoo) *adj* monetary

**monge** (*mawng*-zher) *m* monk

**monólogo** (moo-*no*-loo-goo) *m* monologue

**monopólio** (moo-noo-*po*-lʸoo) *m* monopoly

**monótono** (moo-*no*-too-noo) *adj* monotonous

**montanha** (mawngn-*ter*-ñer) *f* mountain

**montanhoso** (mawngn-ter-*ñoa*-zoo) *adj* mountainous

**montão** (mawngn-*terng*ʷ) *m* (pl -tões) heap

**montar** (mawngn-*tahr*) *v* assemble; ~ a cavalo *ride

**monte** (*mawngn*-ter) *m* mount; heap; cume do ~ hilltop

**montículo** (mawngn-*tee*-koo-loo) *m* mound

**montra** (*mawngn*-trer) *f* shop-window

**monumento** (moo-noo-*mayngn*-too) *m* monument

**morada** (moo-*rah*-dher) *f* home

**morador** (moo-rer-*dhoar*) *m* occupant

**moral** (moo-*rahl*) *adj* (pl -ais) moral; *f* moral; *m* spirits

**moralidade** (moo-rer-lee-*dhah*-dher) *f* morality

**morango** (moo-*rerng*-goo) *m* strawberry

**morar** (moo-*rahr*) *v* live

**mordedura** (moor-der-*dhoo*-rer) *f* bite

**morder** (moor-*dayr*) *v* *bite

**morena** (moo-*ray*-ner) *f* brunette

**moreno** (moo-*ray*-noo) *adj* dark

**morfina** (moor-*fee*-ner) *f* morphia, morphine

**morno** (*moar*-noo) *adj* lukewarm

**morrer** (moo-*rrayr*) *v* die

**mortal** (moor-*tahl*) *adj* (pl -ais) mortal; fatal

**morte** (*mor*-ter) *f* death

**morto** (*moar*-too) *adj* dead

**mosaico** (moo-*zigh*-koo) *m* mosaic

**mosca** (*moash*-ker) *f* fly

**mosquiteiro** (moosh-kee-*tay*-roo) *m* mosquito-net

**mosquito** (moosh-*kee*-too) *m* mosquito

**mossa** (*mo*-ser) *f* dent

**mostarda** (moosh-*tahr*-der) *f* mustard

**mosteiro** (moosh-*tay*-roo) *m* monastery

**mostrar** (moosh-*trahr*) *v* *show; display

**motel** (mo-*tehl*) *m* (pl motéis) motel

**motim** (moo-*teeng*) *m* mutiny

**motivo** (moo-*tee*-voo) *m* motive; occasion, cause

**motocicleta** (mo-to-see-*klay*-ter) *f* motor-cycle

**motor** (moo-*toar*) *m* motor; engine; cobertura do ~ bonnet; hood *nAm;* ~ a jacto-propulsão turbojet; ~ de arranque starter motor

**motorista** (moo-too-*reesh*-ter) *m* chauffeur; ~ de táxi cab-driver, taxi-driver

**móvel** (*mo*-vehl) *adj* (pl -eis) mobile; movable

**mover** (moo-*vayr*) *v* move

**movimentado** (moo-vee-mayngn-*tah*-dhoo) *adj* busy

**movimento** (moo-vee-*mayngn*-too) *m* motion, movement

**mudança** (moo-*dherng*-ser) *f* variation, change; move

**mudar** (moo-*dhahr*) *v* vary; change, transform; ~ de roupa change clothes; ~ de velocidade change gear; mudar-se move

**mudo** (*moo*-dhoo) *adj* mute, dumb;

speechless

**muito** (*moong*Yn-too) *adv* very, quite; much; *adj* much; **muitos** many

**mulato** (moo-*lah*-too) *f* mulatto

**muleta** (moo-*lay*-ter) *f* crutch

**mulher** (moo-*l*Yayr) *f* woman, wife; ~ **a dias** cleaning woman

**mulo** (*moo*-loo) *m* mule

**multa** (*mool*-ter) *f* fine, ticket

**multidão** (mool-tee-*dherng*w) *f* (pl -dões) crowd

**multiplicação** (mool-tee-plee-ker-*serng*w) *f* (pl -ções) multiplication

**multiplicar** (mool-tee-plee-*kahr*) *v* multiply

**mundial** (moong-*d*Yahl) *adj* (pl -ais) global, world-wide

**mundo** (*moong*-doo) *m* world

**municipal** (moo-ner-see-*pahl*) *adj* (pl -ais) municipal

**municipalidade** (moo-ner-see-per-lee-*dhah*-dher) *f* municipality

**murmurar** (moor-moo-*rahr*) *v* whisper

**muro** (*moo*-roo) *m* wall

**músculo** (*moosh*-koo-loo) *m* muscle

**musculoso** (moosh-koo-*loa*-zoo) *adj* muscular

**museu** (moo-*zay*oo) *m* museum; ~ **das ceras** waxworks *pl*

**musgo** (*moozh*-goo) *m* moss

**música** (*moo*-zee-ker) *f* music; ~ **pop** pop music

**musical** (moo-zee-*kahl*) *adj* (pl -ais) musical; **comédia** ~ musical

**músico** (*moo*-zee-koo) *m* musician

**musselina** (moo-ser-*lee*-ner) *f* muslin

**mutuamente** (moo-twer-*mayngn*-ter) *adv* each other

**mútuo** (*moo*-twoo) *adj* mutual

# N

**nacional** (ner-s Yoo-*nahl*) *adj* (pl -ais) national

**nacionalidade** (ner-s Yoo-ner-lee-*dhah*-dher) *f* nationality

**nacionalizar** (ner-s Yoo-ner-lee-*zahr*) *v* nationalize

**nada** (*nah*-dher) *pron* nothing

**nadador** (ner-dher-*dhoar*) *m* swimmer

**nadar** (ner-*dhahr*) *v* *swim

**nádega** (*nah*-dher-ger) *f* buttock

**não** (nerng w) *adv* no; not; ~ **obstante** nevertheless

**narcose** (nerr-*ko*-zer) *f* narcosis

**narcótico** (nerr-*ko*-tee-koo) *m* narcotic

**narina** (ner-*ree*-ner) *f* nostril

**nariz** (ner-*reesh*) *m* nose

**narrativa** (ner-rrer-*tee*-ver) *f* tale

**nascente** (nersh-*sayngn*-ter) *f* spring

**nascer** (nersh-*sayr*) *v* *be born

**nascido** (nersh-*see*-dhoo) *adj* born

**nascimento** (nersh-see-*mayngn*-too) *m* birth

**nata** (*nah*-ter) *f* cream

**natação** (ner-ter-*serng*w) *f* swimming

**Natal** (ner-*tahl*) *m* (pl -ais) Xmas, Christmas

**nativo** (ner-*tee*-voo) *m* native

**nato** (*nah*-too) *adj* natural

**natural** (ner-too-*rahl*) *adj* (pl -ais) natural

**naturalmente** (ner-too-rahl-*mayngn*-ter) *adv* naturally; of course

**natureza** (ner-too-*ray*-zer) *f* nature; essence

**náusea** (nou-z Yer) *f* nausea

**naval** (ner-*vahl*) *adj* (pl -ais) naval

**navegação** (ner-ver-ger-*serng*w) *f* navigation

**navegar** (ner-ver-*gahr*) *v* sail, navigate

**navegável** (ner-ver-*gah*-vehl) *adj* (pl -eis) navigable navio (ner-*vee*-oo) *m* ship; vessel, boat

navio-cisterna (ner-vee<sup>oo</sup>-seesh-*tayr*-ner) *m* tanker

neblina (ner-*bhlee*-ner) *f* mist

necessário (ner-ser-*sah*-r<sup>Y</sup>oo) *adj* necessary; requisite

necessidade (ner-ser-see-*dhah*-dher) *f* necessity; requirement, want, need

necessitar (ner-ser-see-*tahr*) *v* need

negar (ner-*gahr*) *v* deny

negativo (ner-ger-*tee*-voo) *adj* negative; *m* negative

negligência (ner-glee-*zhayng*-s<sup>Y</sup>er) *f* neglect

negligente (ner-glee-*zhayngn*-ter) *adj* neglectful; careless

negociação (ner-goo-s<sup>Y</sup>er-*serng*<sup>w</sup>) *f* (pl -cões) negotiation

negociante (ner-goo-s<sup>Y</sup>e*rngn*-ter) *m* dealer; ~ de tecidos draper

*negociar (ner-goo-s<sup>Y</sup>*ahr*) *v* negotiate; trade

negócio (ner-*go*-s<sup>Y</sup>oo) *m* business; deal; *fazer negócios com *deal with; movimento de negócios turnover; para negócios on business; viagem de negócios business trip

negro (*nay*-groo) *m* Negro

nem ... nem (nern*g*<sup>Y</sup>) neither ... nor; nem um nem outro neither

nenhum (nɪ-*ñoong*) *adj* no; *pron* none

néon (*neh*-awng) *m* neon

nervo (*nayr*-voo) *m* nerve

nervoso (nerr-*voa*-zoo) *adj* nervous

neta (*neh*-ter) *f* granddaughter; grandchild

neto (*neh*-too) *m* grandson

neurose (nay<sup>oo</sup>-*ro*-zer) *f* neurosis

neutral (nay<sup>oo</sup>-*trahl*) *adj* (pl -ais) neutral

neutro (*nay*<sup>oo</sup>-troo) *adj* neuter; neutral

nevado (ner-*vah*-dhoo) *adj* snowy

nevar (ner-*vahr*) *v* snow

neve (*neh*-ver) *f* snow; tempestade de ~ blizzard, snowstorm

névoa (*nehv*-wer) *f* haze

nevoeiro (ner-*vway*-roo) *m* mist, fog

nevralgia (ner-vrahl-*zhee*-er) *f* neuralgia

nicotina (nee-koo-*tee*-ner) *f* nicotine

Nigéria (nee-*zheh*-r<sup>Y</sup>er) *f* Nigeria

nigeriano (nee-zher-r<sup>Y</sup>er-noo) *adj* Nigerian; *m* Nigerian

ninguém (neeng-*gerng*<sup>Y</sup>) *pron* no one, nobody

ninhada (nee-*ñah*-dher) *f* litter

ninho (*nee*-ñoo) *m* nest

níquel (*nee*-kehl) *m* nickel

nível (*nee*-vehl) *m* (pl -eis) level; ~ de vida standard of living

nivelar (nee-ver-*lahr*) *v* level

nó (no) *m* knot; lump; *dar um ~ tie; *fazer um ~ knot; ~ corredio loop; ~ dos dedos knuckle

nobre (*no*-bhrer) *adj* noble

nobreza (noo-*bhray*-zer) *f* nobility

noção (noo-*serng*<sup>w</sup>) *f* (pl noções) notion; idea

nocivo (noo-*see*-voo) *adj* harmful

nocturno (no-*toor*-noo) *adj* nightly

nódoa (*no*-dhwer) *f* spot, stain; ~ negra bruise

nogado (noo-*gah*-dhoo) *m* nougat

noite (*noi*-ter) *f* night; evening; de ~ by night; durante a ~ overnight; esta ~ tonight

noiva (*noi*-ver) *f* fiancée; bride

noivado (noi-vah-dhoo) *m* engagement

noivo (*noi*-voo) *adj* engaged; *m* fiancé; bridegroom

nojento (noo-*zhayngn*-too) *adj* revolting

nome (*noa*-mer) *m* name; denomination; em ~ de on behalf of, in the name of; ~ **de batismo** *Br* Christian name; ~ **próprio** first name, Christian name

**nomeação** (noo-mᵞer-*serng*ʷ) *f* (pl -ções) nomination; appointment

***nomear** (noo-mᵞahr) *v* name; mention; nominate, appoint

**nominal** (noo-mee-*nahl*) *adj* (pl -ais) nominal

**nono** (*noa*-noo) *num* ninth

**nordeste** (nor-*dehsh*-ter) *m* north-east

**nórdico** (*nor*-dhee-koo) *adj* northern

**norma** (*nor*-mer) *f* standard; rule

**normal** (nor-*mahl*) *adj* (pl -ais) regular, normal; standard

**noroeste** (no-*rwehsh*-ter) *m* northwest

**norte** (*nor*-ter) *m* north; **do** ~ northerly

**Noruega** (no-rweh-ger) *f* Norway

**norueguês** (no-rway-*gaysh*) *adj* Norwegian; *m* Norwegian

**nos** (noosh) *pron* us, to us, ourselves

**nós** (noosh) *pron* we; us; ~ **próprios** ourselves

**nosso** (*no*-soo) *adj* our

**nostalgia** (noosh-tahl-*zhee*-er) *f* homesickness

**nota** (*no*-ter) *f* note; mark; ~ **de banco** banknote; ~ **de encomenda** order-form

**notar** (noo-*tahr*) *v* notice

**notário** (noo-*tah*-rᵞoo) *m* notary

**notável** (noo-*tah*-vehl) *adj* (pl -eis) remarkable, striking, noticeable; considerable

**notícia** (noo-*tee*-sᵞer) *f* news; notice

**noticiário** (noo-tee-sᵞah-rᵞoo) *m* news

**notificar** (noo-ter-fee-*kahr*) *v* notify

**notório** (noo-*to*-rᵞoo) *adj* notorious

**Nova Zelândia** (*no*-ver zer-*lerngn*-dᵞer) New Zealand

**nove** (*no*-ver) *num* nine

**Novembro** (noo-*vayngm*-broo) No-

vember

**noventa** (noo-*vayngn*-ter) *num* ninety

**novo** (*noa*-voo) *adj* new; **de** ~ again

**noz** (nosh) *f* nut; walnut; ~ **moscada** nutmeg

**nu** (noo) *adj* nude; naked, bare; *m* nude

**nuance** (*nwerng*-ser) *f* nuance

**nublado** (noo-*bhlah*-dhoo) *adj* cloudy, overcast

**nuca** (*noo*-ker) *f* nape of the neck

**nuclear** (noo-klᵞahr) *adj* nuclear

**núcleo** (*noo*-klᵞoo) *m* core, nucleus

**nulo** (*noo*-loo) *adj* void

**numeral** (noo-mer-*rahl*) *m* (pl -ais) numeral

**número** (*noo*-mer-roo) *m* number; quantity; act; ~ **de matrícula** registration number

**numeroso** (noo-mer-*roa*-zoo) *adj* numerous

**nunca** (*noong*-ker) *adv* never

**nutritivo** (noo-tree-*tee*-voo) *adj* nutritious

**nuvem** (*noo*-verngᵞ) *f* cloud

**nylon** (*nigh*-lon) *m* nylon

# O

**o¹** (oo) *art* (f a) the *art*

**o²** (oo) *pron* it, him; ~ **que** what; ~ **quê** what

**oásis** (*wah*-zeesh) *m* oasis

**obedecer** (oo-bher-dher-*sayr*) *v* obey

**obediência** (oo-bher-*dhᵞayng*-sᵞer) *f* obedience

**obediente** (oo-bher-*dhᵞayngn*-ter) *adj* obedient

**obesidade** (oo-bher-zee-*dhah*-dher) *f* fatness

**obeso** (oo-*bheh*-zoo) *adj* corpulent

**objécção** (oobh-zheh-*serng*ʷ) *f* (pl

-ções) objection; *fazer ~ a mind

**objectar** (oobh-zhee-*tahr*) v object

**objectivo** (oobh-zheh-*tee*-voo) adj objective; m design, goal, objective; target

**objecto** (oobh-*zheh*-too) m object

**oblíquo** (oo-*bhlee*-kwoo) adj slanting

**oblongo** (oobh-*lawng*-goo) adj oblong

**obra** (o-bhrer) f work; ~ **de arte** work of art

**obra-prima** (obh-rer-*pree*-mer) f masterpiece

**obrigação** (oobh-ree-ger-*serng*ʷ) f (pl -ções) bond

**obrigado** (oobh-ree-*gah*-dhoo) adj obliged; **obrigado!** thank you!

**obrigar** (oobh-ree-*gahr*) v oblige; compel, force

**obrigatório** (oobh-ree-ger-*to*-rʸoo) adj compulsory, obligatory

**obsceno** (oobhsh-*say*-noo) adj obscene

**obscuro** (oobhsh-*koo*-roo) adj dim; obscure

**observação** (oobh-serr-ver-*serng*ʷ) f (pl -ções) observation; remark

**observar** (oobh-serr-*vahr*) v observe; view, note, watch; remark

**observatório** (oobh-serr-ver-*to*-rʸoo) m observatory

**obsessão** (oobh-ser-*serng*ʷ) f (pl -sões) obsession

**obstáculo** (oobhsh-*tah*-koo-loo) m obstacle

**obstinado** (oobhsh-tee-*nah*-dhoo) adj dogged, obstinate

***obstruir** (oobhsh-*trweer*) v block

***obter** (oobh-*tayr*) v obtain; *get

**obturação** (oobh-too-rer-*serng*ʷ) f (pl -ções) filling

**obtuso** (oobh-*too*-zoo) adj dumb

**óbvio** (*obh*-vʸoo) adj obvious; apparent

**ocasião** (oo-ker-zʸ*erng*ʷ) f (pl -iões)

occasion; chance

**ocasionalmente** (oo-ker-zʸoo-nahl-*mayng*-ter) adv occasionally

**oceano** (oo-sʸ*er*-noo) m ocean; **Oceano Pacífico** Pacific Ocean

**ocidental** (oo-see-dhayng-*tahl*) adj (pl -ais) western, westerly

**ocidente** (oo-see-*dhayng*-ter) m west

**ocioso** (oo-sʸ*oa*-zoo) adj idle

**oco** (*oa*-koo) adj hollow

**ocorrência** (oo-koo-*rrayng*-sʸer) f occurrence

**oculista** (o-koo-*leesh*-ter) m optician; oculist

**óculos** (*o*-koo-loosh) mpl glasses; spectacles; ~ **escuros** sun-glasses pl; ~ **para mergulhar** diving goggles

**ocultar** (oo-kool-*tahr*) v conceal

**ocupação** (oo-koo-per-*serng*ʷ) f (pl -ções) business, occupation

**ocupado** (oo-koo-*pah*-dhoo) adj occupied; engaged, busy

**ocupar** (oo-koo-*pahr*) v occupy; *take up; **ocupar-se de** attend to; look after

***odiar** (oo-dhʸ*ahr*) v hate

**ódio** (o-dhʸoo) m hatred, hate

**odor** (oo-*dhoar*) m odour

**oeste** (*wehsh*-ter) m west

**ofender** (oo-fayng-*dayr*) v offend; wound, injure; *hurt

**ofensa** (oo-*fayng*-ser) f offence

**ofensiva** (oo-fayng-*see*-ver) f offensive

**ofensivo** (oo-fayng-*see*-voo) adj offensive

**oferecer** (oo-fer-rer-*sayr*) v present, offer

**oferta** (oo-*fehr*-ter) f offer; supply; gift

**oficial** (oo-fee-sʸ*ahl*) adj (pl -ais) official; m officer; ~ **de diligências** bailiff

**oficina** (oo-fee-*see*-ner) f workshop

**ofício** (oo-*fee*-s<sup>y</sup>oo) *m* trade

**oficioso** (oo-fee-s<sup>y</sup>oa-zoo) *adj* unofficial

**oitavo** (oi-*tah*-voo) *num* eighth

**oitenta** (oi-*tayngn*-ter) *num* eighty

**oito** (*oi*-too) *num* eight

**olá!** (o-*lah*) hello!

**olaria** (oo-ler-*ree*-er) *f* earthenware

**\*olear** (oo-l<sup>y</sup>ahr) *v* lubricate

**óleo** (*ol*-Yoo) *m* oil; ~ **capilar** hair-oil; ~ **combustível** fuel oil; ~ **de bronzear** suntan oil; ~ **de lubrificação** lubrication oil; ~ **de mesa** salad-oil

**oleoso** (oo-l<sup>y</sup>oa-zoo) *adj* oily; greasy

**olhadela** (oo-l<sup>y</sup>er-*dheh*-ler) *f* look

**olhar** (oo-l<sup>y</sup>ahr) *v* look; *m* look; ~ **para** look at

**olho** (*oa*-l<sup>y</sup>oo) *m* eye

**ombro** (*awngm*-broo) *m* shoulder

**omeleta** (oa-mer-*lay*-ter) *f* omelette

**omitir** (oo-mee-*teer*) *v* omit; \*leave out, fail

**omnipotente** (om-nee-poo-*tayngn*-ter) *adj* omnipotent

**onda** (*awngn*-der) *f* wave

**onde** (*awngn*-der) *adv* where; ~ **quer que** wherever; ~ **quer que seja** anywhere

**\*ondear** (awngn-d<sup>y</sup>ahr) *v* wave

**ondulação** (awngn-doo-ler-*serng*<sup>w</sup>) *f* (pl -ções) wave

**ondulado** (awngn-doo-*lah*-dhoo) *adj* wavy

**ondulante** (awngn-doo-*lerngn*-ter) *adj* undulating

**ônibus** (*o*-nee-bhoosh) *mBr* (pl ~) coach; bus

**ónix** (*oa*-neeks) *m* onyx

**ontem** (*awngn*-terng<sup>y</sup>) *adv* yesterday

**onze** (*awng*-zer) *num* eleven

**opala** (oo-*pah*-ler) *f* opal

**ópera** (*o*-per-rer) *f* opera; opera house

**operação** (oo-per-rer-*serng*<sup>w</sup>) *f* (pl -ções) operation; surgery

**operar** (oo-per-*rahr*) *v* operate

**operário** (oo-per-rah-r<sup>y</sup>oo) *m* workman; labourer

**opereta** (oo-per-*ray*-ter) *f* operetta

**opinião** (oo-pee-n<sup>y</sup>erng<sup>w</sup>) *f* (pl -iões) opinion; view

**\*opor** (oo-*poar*) *v* object; **\*opor-se** oppose; **\*opor-se a** object to

**oportunidade** (oo-poor-too-nee-*dhah*-dher) *f* opportunity; chance

**oportuno** (oo-poor-*too*-noo) *adj* convenient

**oposição** (oo-poo-zee-*serng*<sup>w</sup>) *f* (pl -ções) opposition

**oposto** (oo-*poash*-too) *adj* opposite

**oprimir** (oo-pree-*meer*) *v* oppress; press

**optimismo** (op-tee-*meezh*-moo) *m* optimism

**optimista** (op-tee-*meesh*-ter) *adj* optimistic; *m* optimist

**óptimo** (o-tee-moo) *adj* excellent

**oração** (oo-rer-*serng*<sup>w</sup>) *f* (pl -ções) prayer

**oral** (oo-*rahl*) *adj* (pl orais) oral

**orçamento** (oor-ser-*mayngn*-too) *m* budget

**ordem** (*or*-derng<sup>y</sup>) *f* order; method; command; congregation; **em** ~ in order; ~ **postal** money order

**ordenado** (oor-der-*nah*-dhoo) *m* salary, pay

**ordenar** (oor-der-*nahr*) *v* sort, arrange; order

**ordinário** (oor-dee-nah-r<sup>y</sup>oo) *adj* vulgar; simple; common

**orelha** (oo-*ray*-l<sup>y</sup>er) *f* ear

**órfão** (*or*-ferng<sup>w</sup>) *m* (pl ~s) orphan

**orgânico** (oor-*ger*-nee-koo) *adj* organic

**organização** (oor-ger-nee-zer-*serng*<sup>w</sup>) *f* (pl -ções) organization

**organizar** (oor-ger-*nee*-zahr) *v* arrange, organize

**orgão** (*or*-ger**ng**ʷ) *m* (pl ~s) organ

**orgulho** (oor-*goo*-lʸoo) *m* pride

**orgulhoso** (oor-goo-*lʸoa*-zoo) *adj* proud

**oriental** (oo-rʸay**ng**-*tahl*) *adj* (pl -ais) easterly; oriental, eastern

**orientar-se** (oo-rʸay**ng**-*tahr*-ser) *v* orientate

**oriente** (oo-*rʸayng*-ter) *m* Orient

**origem** (oo-ree-zher**ng**ʸ) *f* origin; rise

**original** (oo-ree-zhee-*nahl*) *adj* (pl -ais) original

**originalmente** (oo-ree-zhee-nahl-*mayng*-ter) *adv* originally

**orla** (*or*-ler) *f* edge

**ornamental** (oor-ner-mayng-*tahl*) *adj* (pl -ais) ornamental

**ornamento** (oor-ner-*mayng*-too) *m* ornament

**orquestra** (or-*kehsh*-trer) *f* orchestra

**ortodoxo** (or-toa-*dhok*-soo) *adj* orthodox

**ortografia** (or-toa-grer-*fee*-er) *f* spelling

**orvalho** (oor-*vah*-lʸoo) *m* dew

**os** (oosh) *pron* them

**osso** (*oa*-soo) *m* bone

**ostra** (*oash*-trer) *f* oyster

**ou** (oa) *conj* or; **ou ... ou** either ... or

**ouriço** (oa-*ree*-soo) *m* hedgehog

**ouriço-do-mar** (oa-*ree*-soo-doo-mahr) *m* sea-urchin

**ourives** (oa-*ree*-vish) *m* goldsmith; silversmith

**ouro** (*oa*-roo) *m* gold; **de** ~ golden; **mina de** ~ goldmine

**ousar** (oa-*zahr*) *v* dare

**outeiro** (oa-*tay*-roo) *m* hillock

**Outono** (oa-*toa*-noo) *m* autumn; fall *nAm*

**outro** (*oa*-troo) *adj* different, other; **um** ~ another

**Outubro** (oa-*too*-bhroo) October

**ouvido** (oa-*vee*-dhoo) *m* hearing

**ouvinte** (oa-*veeng*-ter) *m* listener; auditor

*****ouvir** (oa-*veer*) *v* *hear

**ova** (*o*-ver) *f* roe

**oval** (oo-*vahl*) *adj* (pl ovais) oval

**ovelha** (oo-*vay*-lʸer) *f* sheep

**ovo** (*oa*-voo) *m* egg; **gema de** ~ eggyolk

**oxigénio** (ok-see-*zheh*-nʸoo) *m* oxygen


# P

**pá** (pah) *f* spade; shovel

**paciência** (per-s**ʸayng**-s**ʸ**er) *f* patience

**paciente** (per-s**ʸayng**-ter) *adj* patient

**pacífico** (per-*see*-fee-koo) *adj* pacifist

**pacifismo** (per-ser-*feezh*-moo) *m* pacifism

**pacifista** (per-ser-*feesh*-ter) *m* pacifist

**pacote** (per-*ko*-ter) *m* packet

**padaria** (per-dher-*ree*-er) *f* bakery

**padeiro** (pah-*day*-roo) *m* baker

**padrão** (per-*dhreng*ʷ) *m* (pl -rões) pattern; standard

**padrasto** (per-*dhrahsh*-too) *m* stepfather

**padre** (*pah*-dhrer) *m* priest; father

**padrinho** (per-*dhree*-ñoo) *m* godfather

**pagamento** (per-ger-*mayng*-too) *m* payment

**pagão** (per-*gerng*ʷ) *adj* (pl ~s) pagan, heathen; *m* pagan, heathen

**pagar** (per-*gahr*) *v* *pay; **pago adiantado** prepaid; **porte pago** post-paid

**página** (*pah*-zhee-ner) *f* page

**pai** (pigh) *m* father; dad; **pais** parents *pl*; **pais adoptivos** foster-parents *pl*

**painel** (pigh-*nehl*) *m* (pl -néis) panel; ~ **de instrumentos** dashboard

**país** (per-*eesh*) *m* country, land; ~ **natal** native country

**paisagem** (pigh-*zah*-zherngY) *f* landscape; scenery; ~ **marítima** seascape

**Os Países Baixos** (oosh per-*ee*-zızh *bhigh*-shoosh) the Netherlands

**paixão** (pigh-*sherng*W) *f* (pl -xões) passion

**paizinho** (pigh-*zee*-ñoo) *m* daddy

**palacete** (per-ler-*say*-ter) *m* mansion

**palácio** (per-*lah*-sYoo) *m* palace

**paladar** (per-ler-*dhahr*) *m* taste

**palavra** (per-*lah*-vrer) *f* word

**palco** (*pahl*-koo) *m* stage

**palerma** (per-*lehr*-mer) *adj* silly

**palestra** (per-*lehsh*-trer) *f* lecture

**paletó** (per-ler-*to*) *mBr* jacket

**palha** (*pah*-lYer) *f* straw

**palhaço** (per-*lYah*-soo) *m* clown

**pálido** (*pah*-lee-dhoo) *adj* pale

**palito** (per-*lee*-too) *m* toothpick

**palmada** (pahl-*mah*-dher) *f* smack

**palmeira** (pahl-*may*-rer) *f* palm

**palpável** (pahl-*pah*-vehl) *adj* (pl -eis) palpable

**pálpebra** (*pahl*-per-bhrer) *f* eyelid

**palpitação** (pahl-pee-ter-*serng*W) *f* (pl -cões) palpitation

**pancada** (perng-*kah*-dher) *f* knock; bump, blow

**pancadinha** (perng-kah-*dhee*-ñah) *f* tap

**panela** (per-*neh*-ler) *f* pan; ~ **de pressão** pressure-cooker

**pânico** (*per*-nee-koo) *m* panic

**pano** (*per*-noo) *m* cloth; curtain; ~ **da loiça** tea-cloth; ~ **turco** terry cloth

**pântano** (*perngn*-ter-noo) *m* marsh, swamp, bog

**pantanoso** (perngn-ter-*noa*-zoo) *adj* marshy

**pantufa** (perngn-*too*-fer) *f* slipper

**pão** (*perng*W) *m* (pl pães) bread; loaf; ~ **integral** wholemeal bread

**pãozinho** (perng W-*zee*-ñoo) *m* (pl pãe-zinhos) roll

**papa** (*pah*-per) *m* pope

**papagaio** (per-per-*gigh*-oo) *m* parrot

**papeira** (per-*pay*-rer) *f* mumps

**papel** (per-*pehl*) *m* (pl -éis) paper; **de** ~ paper; ~ **carbono** *Br* carbon paper; ~ **de carta** notepaper; ~ **de embrulho** wrapping paper; ~ **de máquina** typing paper; ~ **de parede** wallpaper; ~ **higiénico** toilet-paper; ~ **para escrever** writing-paper; notepaper; ~ **químico** carbon paper

**papelão** (per-per-*lerng*W) *mBr* cardboard

**papelaria** (per-per-ler-*ree*-er) *f* stationer's

**papoila** (per-*poi*-ler) *f* poppy

**papoula** (per-*poa*-ler) *f* poppy

**paquete** (per-*kay*-ter) *m* liner; pageboy

**paquistanês** (per-keesh-ter-*naysh*) *adj* Pakistani; *m* Pakistani

**Paquistão** (per-kee-*shterng*W) *m* Pakistan

**par** (pahr) *adj* even; *m* couple, pair

**para** (*per*-rer) *prep* for, to, at, in order to; ~ **com** towards; ~ **que** so that; ~ **quê** what for; ~ **trás** backwards

**parabéns** (per-rer-*bherng*Ysh) *mpl* congratulations *pl*

**pára-brisas** (pah-rer-*bhree*-zersh) *m* (pl ~) windscreen; windshield *nAm*; **limpa** ~ windscreen wiper

**pára-choques** (per-rer-*sho*-kersh) *m* (pl ~) bumper; fender

**parada** (per-*rah*-dher) *f* parade; *fBr* stop

**parafuso** (per-rer-*foo*-zoo) *m* screw

**paragem** (per-rer-*zherng*Y) *f* stop; ~ **de táxis** taxi stand *Am*

**parágrafo** (per-*rah*-grer-foo) *m* paragraph

**paralelo** (per-rer-*leh*-loo) *adj* parallel; *m* parallel

**paralisar** (per-rer-lee-*zahr*) *v* paralyse

**paralisia infantil** (per-rer-lee-*zee*-er eeng-fer*ngn*-teel) polio

**paralítico** (per-rer-*lee*-tee-koo) *adj* lame

**parar** (per-*rahr*) *v* stop; pull up, halt

**pára-sol** (pah-rer-*sol*) *m* (pl -sóis) sunshade

**parceiro** (perr-*say*-roo) *m* partner

**parcela** (pahr-*seh*-ler) *f* plot

**parcial** (pahr-s^yahl) *adj* (pl -ais) partial

**parcialmente** (pahr-s^yahl-*mayngn*-ter) *adv* partly

**parcómetro** (perr-*ko*-mer-troo) *m* parking meter

**pardal** (perr-*dahl*) *m* (pl -ais) sparrow

**parecer** (per-rer-*sayr*) *v* appear; look, seem; *m* opinion, view

**paredão** (per-rer-*dherng*^w) *m* (pl -dões) embankment

**parede** (per-*ray*-dher) *f* wall

**parente** (per-*rayngn*-ter) *m* relative, relation

**pargo** (*pahr*-goo) *m* bream

**parlamentar** (perr-ler-mayngn-*tahr*) *adj* parliamentary

**parlamento** (perr-ler-*mayngn*-too) *m* parliament

**paróquia** (per-*ro*-k^yer) *f* parish

**parque** (*pahr*-ker) *m* park; ~ **de campismo** camping site; ~ **de estacionamento** car park; parking lot *Am*; ~ **nacional** national park

**parte** (*pahr*-ter) *f* part; share; **à** ~ apart, separately; **em** ~ partly; **em** ~ **alguma** nowhere; **em qualquer** ~ somewhere; ~ **de cima** top; ~ **superior** top side; **por toda a** ~ everywhere; throughout

**parteira** (perr-*tay*-rer) *f* midwife

**participação** (pahr-ter-see-per-*serng*^w) *f* (pl -ções) announcement; participation

**participante** (pahr-ter-see-*perngn*-ter) *m* participant

**participar** (perr-ter-see-*pahr*) *v* notify; report; participate

**particular** (perr-*tee*-koo-*lahr*) *adj* private; individual; special; **em** ~ in particular

**particularidade** (perr-tee-koo-ler-ree-*dhah*-dher) *f* detail; peculiarity

**particularmente** (perr-tee-koo-lerr-*mayngn*-ter) *adv* specially

**partida** (perr-*tee*-dher) *f* departure; **ponto de** ~ starting-point

**partido** (perr-*tee*-dhoo) *adj* broken; *m* party; side

**partilhar** (perr-tee-*l^yahr*) *v* share

**partir** (perr-*teer*) *v* *break, crack; *leave, depart, pull out, *set out; check out; **a** ~ **de** from, as from

**parto** (*pahr*-too) *m* childbirth, delivery

**parvo** (*pahr*-voo) *adj* foolish

**Páscoa** (*persh*-kwer) *f* Easter

**passa** (*pah*-ser) *f* raisin; ~ **de Corinto** currant

**passado** (per-*sah*-dhoo) *adj* past; *m* past

**passageiro** (per-ser-*zhay*-roo) *m* passenger

**passagem** (per-*sah*-zherng^y) *f* passage; aisle; ~ **de nível** level crossing, crossing; ~ **de pedestres** *Br* pedestrian crossing; crosswalk *nAm*; ~ **de peões** pedestrian crossing; crosswalk *nAm*; ~ **estreita** bottleneck

**passajar** (per-ser-*zhahr*) *v* darn

**passaporte** (per-ser-*por*-ter) *m* passport; **inspecção de passaportes** passport control

**passar** (per-*sahr*) *v* pass; *spend; **deixar** ~ overlook; **não** ~ **a ferro**

drip-dry, wash and wear; ~ **a fer-ro** iron; press; ~ **por** pass by; *go through

**pássaro** (*pah*-ser-roo) *m* small bird

**passatempo** (pah-ser-*tayngm*-poo) *m* hobby

**passeante** (per-sᵞ*erngn*-ter) *m* walker

*****passear** (per-sᵞ*ahr*) *v* walk

**passeio** (per-*say*-oo) *m* stroll, walk; promenade; trip; pavement, footpath; sidewalk *nAm*; **beira do** ~ curb; ~ **de carro** drive

**passivo** (per-*see*-voo) *adj* passive

**passo** (*pah*-soo) *m* pace; move, step; gait

**pasta** (*pahsh*-ter) *f* paste; briefcase, attaché case; ~ **da escola** satchel; ~ **de dentes** toothpaste

**pastagem** (persh-*tah*-zherngᵞ) *f* pasture

**pastar** (persh-*tahr*) *v* graze

**pastelaria** (persh-ter-ler-*ree*-er) *f* pastry shop; pastry

**pastilha** (persh-*tee*-lᵞer) *f* tablet; ~ **elástica** chewing-gum

**pastor** (persh-*toar*) *m* shepherd; parson, minister, rector; clergyman

**pata** (*pah*-ter) *f* paw

**patente** (per-*tayngn*-ter) *f* patent; rank

**patife** (per-*tee*-fer) *m* villain, bastard, rascal

**patim** (per-*teeng*) *m* skate

**patinagem** (per-tee-*nah*-zherngᵞ) *f* roller-skating; skating

**patinar** (per-tee-*nahr*) *v* skate

**patinhar** (per-tee-*ñahr*) *v* wade

**pátio** (*pah*-tᵞoo) *m* yard

**pato** (*pah*-too) *m* duck

**patrão** (per-*trerng*ʷ) *m* (pl -rões) master; boss, employer

**pátria** (*pah*-trᵞer) *f* fatherland, native country

**patriota** (per-trᵞo-ter) *m* patriot

**patroa** (per-*troa*-er) *f* mistress

**patrulha** (per-*troo*-lᵞer) *f* patrol

**patrulhar** (per-troo-lᵞ*ahr*) *v* patrol

**pau** (pou) *m* stick

**pausa** (*pou*-zer) *f* pause

**pavão** (per-*verng*ʷ) *m* (pl pavões) peacock

**pavilhão** (per-vee-lᵞ*erng*ʷ) *m* (pl -hões) pavilion; ~ **de caça** lodge

**pavimentar** (per-vee-mayngn-*tahr*) *v* pave

**pavimento** (per-vee-*mayngn*-too) *m* pavement

**pavor** (per-*voar*) *m* horror

**paz** (pahsh) *f* peace

**pé** (peh) *m* foot; **a** ~ on foot, walking; **em** ~ upright, erect; *****estar de** ~ *stand

**peão** (pᵞ*erng*ʷ) *m* (pl peões) pedestrian; pawn; **interdito a peões** no pedestrians

**peça** (*peh*-ser) *f* piece; **de duas peças** two-piece; ~ **de teatro** play; ~ **num acto** one-act play; ~ **sobresselente** spare part

**pecado** (per-*kah*-dhoo) *m* sin

**pechincha** (pɪ-*sheeng*-sher) *f* bargain

**peculiar** (per-koo-lᵞ*ahr*) *adj* peculiar

**pedaço** (per-*dhah*-soo) *m* scrap, bit; ~ **grosso** chunk

**pedal** (per-*dhahl*) *m* (pl -ais) pedal

**pé-de-cabra** (peh-dher-*kahbh*-rer) *m* crowbar

**pedestre** (per-*dhehsh*-trer) *m*Br pedestrian

**pedicuro** (per-dhee-*koo*-roo) *m* pedicure

**pedido** (per-*dhee*-dhoo) *m* request; application; ~ **de socorro** distress signal

*****pedir** (per-*dheer*) *v* ask; beg; charge; ~ **boleia** hitchhike; ~ **carona** *Br* hitchhike; ~ **emprestado** borrow

**pedra** (*peh*-dhrer) *f* stone; **de** ~

stone; ~ **de isqueiro** flint; ~ **preciosa** gem; stone; ~ **tumular** tombstone

**pedra-pomes** (peh-dhrer-*poa*-mısh) f pumice stone

**pedregulho** (per-dhrer-*goo*-lYoo) m boulder

**pedreira** (per-*dhray*-rer) f quarry

**pedreiro** (per-*dhray*-roo) m bricklayer

**pega**¹ (*peh*-ger) f handle

**pega**² (*pay*-ger) f magpie

**pegajoso** (per-ger-*zhoa*-zoo) adj sticky

**pegar** (per-*gahr*) v *stick

**peito** (*pay*-too) m chest; breast, bosom

**peitoril** (pay-too-*reel*) m (pl -is) window-sill

**peixaria** (pay-sher-*ree*-er) f fish shop

**peixe** (*pay*-sher) m fish; ~ **miúdo** whitebait

**pele** (*peh*-ler) f skin; hide; fur; furs; **de** ~ leather

**peleiro** (per-*lay*-roo) m furrier

**pelica** (per-*lee*-ker) f kid

**pelicano** (per-lee-*ker*-noo) m pelican

**película** (per-*lee*-koo-ler) f film

**pêlo** (*pay*-loo) m hair

**pélvis** (*pehl*-veesh) f pelvis

**pena** (*pay*-ner) f regret; feather; ~ **de morte** death penalty; **que pena!** what a pity!; *ter ~ **de** pity

**penalidade** (per-ner-lee-*dhah*-dher) f penalty; **grande** ~ penalty kick

**pender** (payngn-*dayr*) v *hang

**pendurar** (payngn-doo-*rahr*) v *hang

**peneira** (per-*nay*-rer) f sieve

**peneirar** (per-nay-*rahr*) v sieve; sift

**penetrar** (per-ner-*trahr*) v penetrate

**penhorista** (pı-ñoo-*reesh*-ter) m pawnbroker

**penicilina** (per-nee-see-*lee*-ner) f penicillin

**península** (per-*neeng*-soo-ler) f peninsula

**pensador** (payng-ser-*dhoar*) m thinker

**pensamento** (payng-ser-*mayngn*-too) m thought; idea

**pensão** (payng-*serng*ᵂ) f (pl -sões) pension; board; boarding-house, guest-house; ~ **alimentícia** alimony; ~ **completa** full board, bed and board, board and lodging

**pensar** (payng-*sahr*) v *think; guess; dress; ~ **em** *think of

**pensativo** (payng-ser-*tee*-voo) adj thoughtful

**pensionista** (payng-sYoo-*neesh*-ter) m boarder

**penso** (*payng*-soo) m dressing; ~ **higiénico** sanitary towel; ~ **rápido** plaster

**pente** (*payngn*-ter) m comb; ~ **de bolso** pocket-comb

**penteado** (payngn-*tYah*-dhoo) m hairdo

*pentear (payngn-*tYahr*) v comb

**Pentecostes** (payngn-ter-*kosh*-tısh) m Whitsun

**penugem** (per-*noo*-zherngY) f down

**pepino** (per-*pee*-noo) m cucumber

**pequeno** (per-*kay*-noo) adj little, small; petty, minor

**pêra** (*pay*-rer) f pear

**perca** (*pehr*-ker) f perch

**perceber** (perr-ser-*bhayr*) v *understand; *take, *see; sense, realize; ~ **mal** *misunderstand

**percentagem** (perr-sayngn-*tah*-zherngY) f percentage

**percepção** (perr-seh-*serng*ᵂ) f (pl -ções) perception

**perceptível** (perr-seh-*tee*-vehl) adj (pl -eis) perceptible; noticeable

**percevejo** (perr-ser-*vay*-zhoo) m bug

**perda** (*payr*-dher) f loss

**perdão** (perr-*dherng*ᵂ) m (pl -dões) pardon; grace; **perdão!** sorry!

*perder (perr-*dhayr*) v *lose; miss

**perdido** (perr-*dhee*-dhoo) *adj* lost; missing

**perdiz** (perr-*dheesh*) *f* partridge

**perdoar** (perr-*dhwahr*) *v* \*forgive

**perecer** (per-rer-*sayr*) *v* perish

**peregrinação** (per-rer-gree-ner-*serng*w) *f* (pl -ções) pilgrimage

**peregrino** (per-rer-*gree*-noo) *m* pilgrim

**perfeição** (perr-fay-*serng*w) *f* (pl -ções) perfection

**perfeito** (perr-*fay*-too) *adj* perfect; faultless

**perfume** (perr-*foo*-mer) *m* perfume; scent

**perfurar** (perr-foo-*rahr*) *v* pierce

**pergunta** (perr-*goongn*-ter) *f* question; inquiry, query

**perguntar** (perr-goongn-*tahr*) *v* ask; enquire; ~ **a si próprio** wonder

**perícia** (per-ree-sᵞer) *f* skill

**perigo** (per-*ree*-goo) *m* peril, danger; risk; distress

**perigoso** (per-ree-*goa*-zoo) *adj* perilous, dangerous; risky

**periódico** (per-rᵞo-dhee-koo) *adj* periodical; *m* periodical

**período** (per-*ree*ᵒᵒ-dhoo) *m* period; term

**periquito** (pı-ree-*kee*-too) *m* parakeet

**perito** (per-*ree*-too) *adj* skilled; *m* expert

**perjúrio** (perr-*zhoo*-rᵞoo) *m* perjury

**permanecer** (perr-mer-ner-*sayr*) *v* stay

**permanente** (perr-mer-*nayngn*-ter) *adj* permanent; *f* permanent wave

**permitir** (perr-mee-*teer*) *v* permit; allow; **permitir-se** afford

**perna** (*pehr*-ner) *f* leg; **barriga da** ~ calf; **de pernas para o ar** upside-down

**pérola** (*peh*-roo-ler) *f* pearl

**perpendicular** (perr-*payngn*-dee-koo-*lahr*) *adj* perpendicular

**persa** (*pehr*-ser) *adj* Persian; *m* Persian

\***perseguir** (pehr-ser-*geer*) *v* chase

**perseverar** (perr-ser-ver-*rahr*) *v* \*keep up

**Pérsia** (*pehr*-sᵞer) *f* Persia

**persiana** (perr-sᵞer-ner) *f* blind; shutter

**persistir** (perr-seesh-*teer*) *v* insist

**personalidade** (perr-soo-ner-lee-*dhah*-dher) *f* personality

**perspectiva** (perrsh-peh-*tee*-ver) *f* prospect; perspective

**perspicaz** (perrsh-pee-*kahsh*) *adj* keen

**perspiração** (perrsh-pee-rer-*serng*w) *f* perspiration

**persuadir** (perr-swer-*dheer*) *v* persuade

**pertencer** (perr-tayng-*sayr*) *v* belong; ~ **a** belong to

**perto** (*pehr*-too) *adv* near; ~ **de** near; by

**perturbação** (perr-toor-bher-*serng*w) *f* (pl -ções) disturbance

**perturbar** (perr-toor-*bhahr*) *v* embarrass; disturb

**peru** (per-*roo*) *m* turkey

**peruca** (per-*roo*-ker) *f* wig

**pesado** (per-*zah*-dhoo) *adj* heavy

**pesar** (per-*zahr*) *v* weigh

**pesca** (*pehsh*-ker) *f* fishing industry; **aparelho de** ~ fishing tackle; **cana de** ~ fishing rod; **licença de** ~ fishing licence; **linha de** ~ fishing line

**pescada** (pısh-*kah*-dher) *f* whiting

**pescador** (pısh-ker-*dhoar*) *m* fisherman

**pescar** (pısh-*kahr*) *v* fish; ~ **à linha** angle

**pescoço** (pısh-*koa*-soo) *m* neck

**peso** (*pay*-zoo) *m* weight

**pesquisar** (pısh-kee-*zahr*) *v* search

**pêssego** (*pay*-ser-goo) *m* peach

**pessimismo** (per-see-*meezh*-moo) *m* pessimism

**pessimista** (per-see-*meesh*-ter) *adj* pessimistic; *m* pessimist

**pessoa** (per-*soa*-er) *f* person; **pessoas** people *pl*; **por** ~ per person; **qualquer** ~ anyone, anybody; **uma** ~ one

**pessoal**[1] (per-*swahl*) *m* personnel, staff

**pessoal**[2] (per-*swahl*) *adj* (pl -ais) personal; private

**pestana** (pish-*ter*-ner) *f* eyelash

**pétala** (*peh*-ter-ler) *f* petal

**petição** (per-tee-*serng*ʷ) *f* (pl -ções) petition

**petróleo** (per-*tro*-lʸoo) *m* petroleum; paraffin, oil; **poço de** ~ oil-well

**peúga** (pʸoo-ger) *f* sock

**pianista** (pʸer-*neesh*-ter) *f* pianist

**piano** (pʸer-noo) *m* piano; ~ **de cauda** grand piano

**picada** (pee-*kah*-dher) *f* sting; bite

**picadela** (pee-ker-*dheh*-ler) *f* sting

**picante** (pee-*kerng*-ter) *adj* spicy, savoury

**picar** (pee-*kahr*) *v* prick; *sting; chop, mince

**picareta** (pee-ker-*ray*-ter) *f* pick-axe

**piedade** (pʸay-*dhah*-dher) *f* pity

**pijama** (pee-*zher*-mer) *m* pyjamas *pl*

**pilar** (pee-*lahr*) *m* pillar; column

**pilha** (*pee*-lʸer) *f* stack, pile; ~ **eléctrica** battery

**piloto** (pee-*loa*-too) *m* pilot

**pílula** (*pee*-loo-ler) *f* pill

**pimenta** (pee-*mayngn*-ter) *f* pepper

**pinça** (*peeng*-ser) *f* tweezers *pl*

**pincel** (peeng-*sehl*) *m* (pl -céis) brush; paint-brush; ~ **da barba** shaving-brush

**pingente** (peeng-*zhayngn*-ter) *m* pendant

**pinguim** (peeng-*gweeng*) *m* penguin

**pinheiro** (pee-*ñay*-roo) *m* fir-tree

**pintar** (peeng-*tahr*) *v* paint; dye

**pintarroxo** (peengn-ter-*rroa*-shoo) *m* robin

**pintor** (peengn-*toar*) *m* painter

**pintura** (peengn-*too*-rer) *f* painting; ~ **a óleo** oil-painting

**pio** (*pee*ᵒᵒ) *adj* pious

**piolho** (pʸoa-lʸoo) *m* louse

**pioneiro** (pʸoo-*nay*-roo) *m* pioneer

**pionés** (pʸoo-*nehsh*) *m* drawing-pin; thumbtack *nAm*

**pior** (pʸor) *adj* worse; *adv* worse, worst; **o** ~ worst, the worst

**pipa** (*pee*-per) *f* barrel

**piquenicar** (pee-ker-nee-*kahr*) *v* picnic

**piquenique** (pee-ker-*nee*-ker) *m* picnic

**pirata** (pee-*rah*-ter) *m* pirate

**pires** (*pee*-rish) *m* saucer

**pisca-pisca** (peesh-ker-*peesh*-ker) *m* indicator

**piscina** (peesh-*see*-ner) *f* swimming pool

**piso** (*pee*-zoo) *m* floor

**pista** (*peesh*-ter) *f* trail; ring; track; ~ **de descolagem** runway

**pistão** (peesh-*terng*ʷ) *m* (pl -tões) piston; **segmento do** ~ piston ring

**pistola** (peesh-*to*-ler) *f* pistol

**pitoresco** (pee-too-*raysh*-koo) *adj* picturesque; scenic

**planador** (pler-ner-*dhoar*) *m* glider

**planalto** (pler-*nahl*-too) *m* plateau

***planear** (pler-nʸahr) *v* plan; devise

**planeta** (pler-*nay*-ter) *m* planet

**planetário** (pler-ner-*tah*-rʸoo) *m* planetarium

**planície** (pler-*nee*-sʸer) *f* plain

**plano** (*pler*-noo) *adj* flat, even, plane; smooth, level; *m* plan, scheme, project; **primeiro** ~ foreground

**planta** (*plerngn*-ter) *f* plant; map

**plantação** (plerngn-ter-*serng*ʷ) *f* (pl -ções) plantation

**plantar** (pler*ng*n-*tahr*) *v* plant

**plástico** (*plahsh*-tee-koo) *m* plastic; **de ~** plastic

**plataforma** (pler-ter-*for*-mer) *f* platform

**plateia** (pler-*tay*-er) *f* stall; orchestra seat *Am*

**platina** (pler-*tee*-ner) *f* platinum

**plural** (ploo-*rahl*) *m* (pl -ais) plural

**pneu** (pnay⁰⁰) *m* tire, tyre; **~ furado** flat tyre; **~ sobresselente** spare tyre

**pneumático** (pnay⁰⁰-*mah*-tee-koo) *adj* pneumatic; inflatable

**pneumonia** (pnay⁰⁰-moo-*nee*-er) *f* pneumonia

**pó** (po) *m* powder; **~ de talco** talc powder; **pós dentífricos** toothpowder

**pobre** (*po*-bhrer) *adj* poor

**pobreza** (poo-*bhray*-zer) *f* poverty

**poço** (*poa*-soo) *m* well; **~ de petróleo** oil-well

**pó-de-arroz** (po-der-er-*rroash*) *m* facepowder; **borla de ~** powder-puff; **caixa de ~** powder compact

**poder** (poo-*dhayr*) *m* power; might, authority; **~ executivo** executive

***poder** (poo-*dhayr*) *v* *may; *might, *be able to; *can

**poderoso** (poo-dher-*roa*-zoo) *adj* mighty, powerful

**podre** (*poa*-dhrer) *adj* rotten

**poeira** (*pway*-rer) *f* dust

**poeirento** (pway-ray*ng*n-too) *adj* dusty

**poema** (*pway*-mer) *m* poem

**poesia** (pwɪ-*zee*-er) *f* poetry

**poeta** (*pweh*-ter) *m* poet

**pois** (*poish*) *conj* because; **~ bem** granted, so be it

**polaco** (poo-*lah*-koo) *adj* Polish; *m* Pole

**polegar** (poo-ler-*gahr*) *m* thumb

**polícia** (poo-lee-sᵞer) *f* police *pl*; *m* policeman; **delegacia de ~** *Br* police-station; **posto da ~** police-station

**pólio** (*po*-lᵞoo) *f* polio

***polir** (poo-*leer*) *v* polish

**política** (poo-*lee*-tee-ker) *f* politics; policy

**político** (poo-*lee*-tee-koo) *adj* political; *m* politician

**polivalente** (poo-lee-ver-*lay*ng*n*-ter) *adj* all-round

**Polónia** (poo-*loa*-nᵞer) *f* Poland

**pólo norte** (*po*-loo *nor*-ter) North Pole

**pólo sul** (*po*-loo sool) South Pole

**poltrona** (poal-*troa*-ner) *f* armchair, easy chair

**poluição** (poo-lwee-*serng*ʷ) *f* (pl -ções) pollution

**polvo** (*poal*-voo) *m* octopus

**pólvora** (*pol*-voo-rer) *f* gunpowder

**pomar** (poo-*mahr*) *m* orchard

**pombo** (*pawng*n-boo) *m* pigeon

**ponderado** (paw*ng*n-der-*rah*-dhoo) *adj* sober

**ponderar** (paw*ng*n-der-*rahr*) *v* consider, *think over

**pónei** (*po*-nay) *m* pony

**ponta** (*pawng*n-ter) *f* tip

**pontada** (paw*ng*n-*tah*-dher) *f* stitch

**pontapé** (paw*ng*n-ter-*peh*) *m* kick; ***dar um ~** kick; **~ de saída** kick-off

**ponte** (*pawng*n-ter) *f* bridge; **~ levadiça** drawbridge; **~ pênsil** suspension bridge

**pontiagudo** (paw*ng*n-tᵞer-*goo*-dhoo) *adj* pointed

**ponto** (*pawng*n-too) *m* stitch; point; period; item, issue; **~ de congelação** freezing-point; **~ de encontro** meeting-place; **~ de interesse** sight; **~ de interrogação** question mark; **~ e vírgula** semi-colon; **~**

final full stop

**pontual** (pawngn-*twahl*) *adj* (pl -ais) punctual

**popelina** (po-per-*lee*-ner) *f* poplin

**população** (poo-poo-ler-*serng*ᵂ) *f* (pl -cões) population

**popular** (poo-poo-*lahr*) *adj* popular; vulgar

**populoso** (poo-poo-*loa*-zoo) *adj* populous

**por** (poor) *prep* by; for; past

***pôr** (poar) *v* *put; *set; *lay

**porão** (poo-*rerng*ᵂ) *m* (pl porões) hold; *mBr* basement; cellar

**porca** (*por*-ker) *f* nut

**porção** (poor-*serng*ᵂ) *f* (pl -cões) portion; helping

**porcaria** (poor-ker-*ree*-er) *f* muck

**porcelana** (poor-ser-*ler*-ner) *f* porcelain; china

**porcento** (poor-*sayngn*-too) *m* percent

**porco** (*poar*-koo) *m* pig; *adj* foul, dirty; **pele de ~** pigskin

**porco-espinho** (poar-koo-eesh-*pee*-ñoo) *m* porcupine

**porque** (*poor*-ker) *conj* because; as, for

**porquê** (poor-*kay*) *adv* why

**porquinho-da-índia** (poor-kee-ñoo-der-*eengn*-dᵛer) *m* guinea-pig

**porta** (*por*-ter) *f* door; gate; **~ corrediça** sliding door; **~ giratória** revolving door

**portador** (poor-ter-*dhoar*) *m* bearer

**portagem** (poor-*ter*-zherngᵛ) *f* toll

**porta-moedas** (por-ter-*mweh*-dhersh) *m* (pl ~) purse

**portanto** (poor-*terngn*-too) *conj* so; therefore

**portão** (poor-*terng*ᵂ) *m* (pl -tões) gate

**portar-se** (poor-*tahr*-ser) *v* behave; **~ mal** misbehave

**portátil** (poor-*tah*-teel) *adj* (pl -teis) portable

**porteiro** (poor-*tay*-roo) *m* doorman, porter, door-keeper; concierge, janitor

**porte pago** (*por*-ter pah-goo) postage paid

**porto** (*poar*-too) *m* harbour, port; **~ marítimo** seaport

**Portugal** (poor-too-*gahl*) *m* Portugal

**português** (poor-too-*gaysh*) *adj* Portuguese; *m* Portuguese

**posição** (poo-zee-*serng*ᵂ) *f* (pl -cões) position

**positivo** (poo-zee-*tee*-voo) *adj* positive; *m* positive

**possante** (poo-*serngn*-ter) *adj* strong

**posse** (*po*-ser) *f* possession

**possesso** (poo-*seh*-soo) *adj* possessed

**possibilidade** (poo-ser-bher-lee-*dhah*-dher) *f* possibility

**possibilitar** (poo-ser-bher-lee-*tahr*) *v* enable

**possível** (poo-*see*-vehl) *adj* (pl -eis) possible; attainable

***possuir** (poo-*sweer*) *v* possess; own

**postal** (poosh-*tahl*) *m* (pl -ais) card; **~ ilustrado** picture postcard, postcard

**posta-restante** (posh-ter-rish-*terngn*-ter) poste restante

**poste** (*posh*-ter) *m* pole, post; **~ de iluminação** lamp-post; **~ indicador** milepost, signpost

**posto** (*poash*-too) *m* post; station; **~ de socorros** first-aid post

**potável** (poo-*tah*-vehl) *adj* (pl -veis) for drinking

**potência** (poo-*tayng*-sᵛer) *f* power; capacity

**pouco** (*poa*-koo) *adj* little; **daqui a ~** shortly; **dentro em ~** presently; **poucos** few; **um ~ mais** some more

**poupado** (poa-*pah*-dhoo) *adj* economi-

cal
**poupar** (poa-*pahr*) v save
**pousada** (poa-*zah*-dher) f inn
**pousar** (poa-*zahr*) v *lay; place, *set, *put
**povo** (*poa*-voo) m people; nation, folk
**praça** (*prah*-ser) f square; ~ **de táxis** taxi rank; ~ **de touros** bullring; ~ **do mercado** market-place
**praça-forte** (prah-ser-*for*-ter) f stronghold
**prado** (*prah*-dhoo) m meadow
**praga** (*prah*-ger) f curse; plague
**praguejar** (prer-ger-*zhahr*) v curse
**praia** (*prigh*-er) f beach; ~ **para nudistas** nudist beach
**prancha** (*prerng*-sher) f plank; ~ **de surf** surf-board
**prata** (*prah*-ter) f silver; **de** ~ silver; **pratas** silverware
**prateleira** (prer-ter-*lay*-rer) f shelf
**prática** (*prah*-tee-ker) f practice
**praticamente** (prah-tee-ker-*mayngn*-ter) adv practically
**praticar** (prer-tee-*kahr*) v practise; commit
**prático** (*prah*-tee-koo) adj practical
**prato** (*prah*-too) m plate, dish; course; ~ **de sopa** soup-plate
**prazer** (prer-*zayr*) m pleasure; joy, fun
**precário** (prer-*kah*-rYoo) adj precarious, critical
**precaução** (prer-kou-*serng*ᵂ) f (pl -ções) precaution
***precaver-se** (prer-ker-*vayr*-ser) v beware
**precedente** (prer-ser-*dhayngn*-ter) adj last, previous, preceding
**preceder** (prer-ser-*dhayr*) v precede
**preceptor** (prer-seh-*toar*) m tutor
**precioso** (prer-sYoa-zoo) adj precious
**precipício** (prer-ser-*pee*-sYoo) m precipice

**precipitação** (prer-ser-pee-ter-*serng*ᵂ) f (pl -ções) precipitation
**precipitado** (prer-ser-pee-*tah*-dhoo) adj rash
**precipitar-se** (prer-ser-pee-*tahr*-ser) v dash
**precisão** (prer-see-*zherng*ᵂ) f (pl -sões) need; precision
**precisar** (prer-see-*zahr*) v need
**preciso** (prer-*see*-zoo) adj precise
**preço** (*pray*-soo) m price; cost, charge; rate; **baixa de preços** slump; **fixar o** ~ **de** price; ~ **da viagem** fare; ~ **de compra** purchase price; ~ **de entrada** entrance-fee; ~ **do bilhete** fare
**preconceito** (prer-kawng-*say*-too) m prejudice
**predecessor** (prer-dher-ser-*soar*) m predecessor
**prédio** (*preh*-dhYoo) m building; house; ~ **de andares** block of flats, apartment house Am; ~ **de apartamentos** Br apartment house Am
***predizer** (prer-dhee-*zayr*) v predict
**preencher** (prYayng-*shayr*) v fill in; fill out Am
**preferência** (prer-fer-*rayng*-sYer) f preference; *dar ~ a prefer
**preferido** (prer-fer-*ree*-dhoo) adj favourite
***preferir** (prer-fer-*reer*) v prefer
**preferível** (prer-fer-*ree*-vehl) adj (pl -eis) preferable
**prefixo** (prer-*feek*-soo) m prefix
**prega** (*preh*-ger) f crease
**pregar**¹ (preh-*gahr*) v preach
**pregar**² (prer-*gahr*) v nail
**prego** (*preh*-goo) m nail
**preguiçoso** (prer-gee-*soa*-zoo) adj lazy
**preia-mar** (*pray*-er-mahr) f high tide
**prejudicar** (prer-zhoo-dhee-*kahr*) v

harm

**prejudicial** (prer-zhoo-dhee-s<sup>y</sup>ahl) *adj* (pl -ais) hurtful, harmful

**prejuízo** (prer-zhwee-zoo) *m* harm

**preliminar** (prer-ler-mee-nahr) *adj* preliminary

**prematuro** (prer-mer-too-roo) *adj* premature

**prémio** (preh-m<sup>y</sup>oo) *m* prize; award

**prender** (prayngn-dayr) *v* attach, fasten; imprison, arrest

**prenome** (prer-noa-mer) *mBr* first name

**preocupação** (pr<sup>y</sup>oo-koo-per-serng<sup>w</sup>) *f* (pl -ções) trouble; concern, worry; care

**preocupado** (pr<sup>y</sup>oo-koo-pah-dhoo) *adj* worried; concerned

**preocupar-se com** (pr<sup>y</sup>oo-koo-pahr-ser) care about

**preparação** (prer-per-rer-serng<sup>w</sup>) *f* (pl -ções) preparation; background

**preparado** (prer-per-rah-dhoo) *adj* prepared; ready

**preparar** (prer-per-rahr) *v* prepare; cook

**preposição** (prer-poo-zee-serng<sup>w</sup>) *f* (pl -ções) preposition

**presbitério** (prizh-bhee-teh-r<sup>y</sup>oo) *m* parsonage, vicarage

**prescrever** (prish-krer-vayr) *v* prescribe

**presença** (prer-zayng-ser) *f* presence

**presente** (prer-zayngn-ter) *adj* present; *m* present; gift

**preservativo** (prer-serr-ver-tee-voo) *m* condom

**presidente** (prer-zee-dhayngn-ter) *m* chairman, president; ~ **da Câmara** mayor

**pressa** (preh-ser) *f* haste, hurry; speed; **com** ~ in haste

**pressão** (prer-serng<sup>w</sup>) *f* (pl -sões) pressure; ~ **atmosférica** atmos-

pheric pressure; ~ **do óleo** oil pressure; ~ **dos pneus** tyre pressure

**prestação** (prish-ter-serng<sup>w</sup>) *f* (pl -ções) instalment; **pagar a prestações** *pay on account

**prestar** (prish-tahr) *v* render; ~ **contas de** account for

**prestidigitador** (prish-tee-dher-zhee-ter-dhoar) *m* magician

**prestígio** (prish-tee-zh<sup>y</sup>oo) *m* prestige

**presumível** (prer-zoo-mee-vehl) *adj* (pl -eis) presumable

**presunçoso** (prer-zoong-soa-zoo) *adj* presumptuous

**presunto** (prer-zoongn-too) *m* ham

**pretender** (prer-tayngn-dayr) *v* pursue

**pretensão** (prer-tayngn-serng<sup>w</sup>) *f* (pl -sões) claim

**pretensioso** (prer-tayngn-s<sup>y</sup>oa-zoo) *adj* conceited

**pretenso** (prer-tayng-soo) *adj* so-called

**pretexto** (prer-taysh-too) *m* pretext, pretence

**preto** (pray-too) *adj* black

***prevenir** (prer-ver-neer) *v* anticipate; warn

**preventivo** (prer-vayngn-tee-voo) *adj* preventive

***prever** (prer-vayr) *v* anticipate; forecast

**prévio** (preh-v<sup>y</sup>oo) *adj* previous

**previsão** (prer-vee-zerng<sup>w</sup>) *f* (pl -sões) outlook; forecast

**prima** (pree-mer) *f* cousin

**primário** (pree-mah-r<sup>y</sup>oo) *adj* primary

**Primavera** (pree-mer-veh-rer) *f* spring; springtime

**primeiro** (pree-may-roo) *num* first; *adj* primary, foremost; *adv* at first; before

**primeiro-ministro** (pree-may-roo-mer-neesh-troo) *m* Prime Minister, premier

**primo** (*pree*-moo) *m* cousin

**primordial** (pree-moor-*dʸahl*) *adj* (pl -ais) primary

**princesa** (preeng-*say*-zer) *f* princess

**principal** (preeng-see-*pahl*) *adj* (pl -ais) principal; chief, leading, main; cardinal; **sector** ~ mains *pl*

**principalmente** (preeng-see-perl-*mayngn*-ter) *adv* especially, mainly; mostly

**príncipe** (*preeng*-see-per) *m* prince

**principiante** (preeng-see-pʸerngn-ter) *m* beginner; learner

**principiar** (preeng-see-pʸahr) *v* commence, *begin

**princípio** (preeng-*see*-pʸoo) *m* beginning; principle

**prioridade** (prʸoo-ree-*dhah*-dher) *f* priority; right of way

**prisão** (pree-*zerngʷ*) *f* (pl -sões) arrest; jail, prison; ~ **de ventre** constipation

**prisioneiro** (pree-zʸoo-*nay*-roo) *m* prisoner; ~ **de guerra** prisoner of war

**privado** (pree-*vah*-dhoo) *adj* private

**privar de** (pree-*vahr* der) deprive of

**privilégio** (prer-vee-*leh*-zhʸoo) *m* privilege

**problema** (proo-*bhlay*-mer) *m* problem; question

**proceder** (proo-ser-*dhayr*) *v* proceed

**procedimento** (proo-ser-dhee-*mayngn*-too) *m* process

**processo** (proo-*seh*-soo) *m* process; lawsuit; procedure

**procissão** (proo-see-*serngʷ*) *f* (pl -sões) procession

**proclamar** (proo-kler-*mahr*) *v* proclaim

**procura** (proo-*koo*-rer) *f* demand

**procurar** (proo-koo-*rahr*) *v* hunt for, look for, search, *seek; look up

**pródigo** (*pro*-dhee-goo) *adj* lavish

**produção** (proo-dhoo-*serngʷ*) *f* (pl -ções) production; output; ~ **em série** mass production

**produto** (proo-*dhoo*-too) *m* product; produce; ~ **de limpeza** cleaning fluid; **produtos alimentícios** foodstuffs *pl*

**produtor** (proo-dhoo-*toar*) *m* producer

*****produzir** (proo-dhoo-*zeer*) *v* produce; generate

**professar** (proo-fer-*sahr*) *v* confess

**professor** (proo-fer-*soar*) *m* teacher, schoolmaster, master; professor

**professora** (proo-fer-*soa*-rer) *f* teacher

**profeta** (proo-*feh*-ter) *m* prophet

**profissão** (proo-fee-*serngʷ*) *f* (pl -sões) profession

**profissional** (proo-fee-sʸoo-*nahl*) *adj* (pl -ais) professional

**profundidade** (proo-foongn-dee-*dhah*-dher) *f* depth

**profundo** (proo-*foongn*-doo) *adj* deep; profound

**programa** (proo-*grer*-mer) *m* programme

*****progredir** (proo-gray-*dheer*) *v* *get on; *make progress

**progressista** (proo-grer-*seesh*-ter) *adj* progressive

**progressivo** (proo-grer-*see*-voo) *adj* progressive

**progresso** (proo-*greh*-soo) *m* progress

**proibido** (prwee-*bhee*-dhoo) *adj* prohibited; ~ **entrar** no entry; ~ **fumar** no smoking

**proibir** (prwee-*bheer*) *v* *forbid; prohibit

**proibitivo** (prwee-bhee-*tee*-voo) *adj* prohibitive

**projecto** (proo-*zheh*-too) *m* project; design

**projector** (proo-zheh-*toar*) *m* spotlight

**prolongamento** (proo-*lawng*-ger-*mayngn*-too) *m* extension

**prolongar** (proo-lawng-*gahr*) *v* extend; renew

**promessa** (proo-*meh*-ser) *f* promise

**prometer** (proo-mer-*tayr*) *v* promise

**promoção** (proo-moo-*serng*ʷ) *f* (pl -ções) promotion

**promontório** (proo-mawngn-*to*-rʸoo) *m* headland

**promover** (proo-moo-*vayr*) *v* promote

**pronome** (proo-*noa*-mer) *m* pronoun

**pronto** (*prawngn*-too) *adj* prompt; ready

**pronúncia** (proo-*noong*-sʸer) *f* pronunciation

**pronunciar** (proo-noong-sʸ*ahr*) *v* pronounce

**propaganda** (proo-per-*gerngn* der) *f* propaganda

**propenso** (proo-*payng*-soo) *adj* inclined

*****propor** (proo-*poar*) *v* propose

**proporção** (proo-poor-*serng*ʷ) *f* (pl -ções) proportion

**proporcional** (proo-poor-sʸoo-*nahl*) *adj* (pl -ais) proportional

**proporcionar** (proo-poor-sʸoo-*nahr*) *v* furnish, provide

**propositado** (proo-poo-zee-*tah*-dhoo) *adj* on purpose

**propósito** (proo-*po*-zee-too) *m* purpose; **a** ~ by the way; **de** ~ on purpose

**proposta** (proo-*posh*-ter) *f* proposal, proposition

**propriedade** (proo-prʸ*ay*-*dhah*-dher) *f* property; estate

**proprietário** (proo-prʸay-*tah*-rʸoo) *m* owner, proprietor; landlord

**próprio** (*pro*-prʸoo) *adj* own

**propulsionar** (proo-pool-sʸoo-*nahr*) *v* propel

**prospecto** (proosh-*peh*-too) *m* prospectus

**prosperidade** (proosh-per-ree-*dhah*-dher) *f* prosperity

**próspero** (*prosh*-per-roo) *adj* prosperous

*****prosseguir** (proo-ser-*geer*) *v* carry on; continue, pursue, proceed

**prostituta** (proosh-tee-*too*-ter) *f* whore, prostitute

**protecção** (proo-teh-*serng*ʷ) *f* (pl -ções) protection

**proteger** (proo-tɪ-*zhayr*) *v* protect

**proteína** (proa-tay-*ee*-ner) *f* protein

**protelação** (proo-ter-ler-*serng*ʷ) *f* (pl -ções) respite

**protestante** (proo-tɪsh-*terngn*-ter) *adj* Protestant

**protestar** (proo-tɪsh-*tahr*) *v* protest

**protesto** (proo-*tehsh*-too) *m* protest

**prova** (*pro*-ver) *f* proof; token, evidence; experiment, test; print

**provar** (proo-*vahr*) *v* prove; try on; taste

**provável** (proo-*vah*-vehl) *adj* (pl -eis) probable; likely

**provavelmente** (proo-vah-vehl-*mayngn*-ter) *adv* probably

**proveniência** (proo-ver-nʸ*ayng*-sʸer) *f* origin

**provérbio** (proo-*vehr*-bhʸoo) *m* proverb

*****prover de** (proo-*vayr* der) furnish with

**província** (proo-*veeng*-sʸer) *f* province

**provincial** (proo-veeng-sʸ*ahl*) *adj* (pl -ais) provincial

**provisão** (proo-vee-*zérng*ʷ) *f* (pl -sões) supply; **provisões** provisions *pl*

**provisório** (proo-vee-zo-rʸoo) *adj* provisional; temporary

**provocar** (proo-voo-*kahr*) *v* cause

**proximidades** (pro-ser-mee-*dhah*-dhersh) *fpl* vicinity

**próximo** (*pro*-see-moo) *adj* nearby, close; next; oncoming

**prudente** (proo-*dhayngn*-ter) *adj* cautious; wary

**prurido** (proo-*ree*-dhoo) *m* itch

**psicanalista** (psee-ker-ner-*leesh*-ter) *m* psychoanalyst; analyst

**psicologia** (psee-koo-loo-*zhee*-er) *f* psychology

**psicológico** (psee-koo-*lo*-zhee-koo) *adj* psychological

**psicólogo** (psee-*ko*-loo-goo) *m* psychologist

**psiquiatra** (psee-k*Y*ah-trer) *m* psychiatrist

**psíquico** (*psee*-kee-koo) *adj* psychic

**publicação** (poo-bhlee-ker-*serng*ʷ) *f* (pl -ções) publication

**publicar** (poo-*bhlee*-kahr) *v* publish

**publicidade** (poo-bhlee-see-*dhah*-dher) *f* advertising, publicity

**público** (*poo*-bhlee-koo) *adj* public; *m* public

**pulmão** (pool-*merng*ʷ) *m* (pl -mões) lung

**pulo** (*poo*-loo) *m* hop

**pulóver** (poo-*loa*-vehr) *m* pullover

**púlpito** (*pool*-pee-too) *m* pulpit

**pulseira** (pool-*say*-rer) *f* bracelet, bangle

**pulso** (*pool*-soo) *m* wrist; pulse

**pulverizador** (pool-ver-ree-zer-*dhoar*) *m* atomizer

**punhado** (poo-*ñah*-dhoo) *m* handful

**punho** (*poo*-ñoo) *m* fist; cuff

**puro** (*poo*-roo) *adj* pure; sheer; neat, clean; ~ **sangue** thoroughbred

**purulento** (poo-roo-*layngn*-too) *adj* purulent

**pus** (poosh) *m* pus

**puxar** (poo-*shahr*) *v* *draw; pull; ~ **o lustro a** brush

**puzzle** (*per*-zler) *m* puzzle

## Q

**quadrado** (kwer-*dhrah*-dhoo) *adj* square; *m* square; check

**quadriculado** (kwer-dhree-koo-*lah*-dhoo) *adj* chequered

**quadrilha** (kwer-*dhree*-l*Y*er) *f* gang

**quadro** (*kwah*-dhroo) *m* picture; board; cadre; ~ **de distribuição** switchboard; ~ **preto** blackboard

**qual** (kwahl) *pron* (pl quais) which

**qualidade** (kwer-lee-*dhah*-dher) *f* quality; **de primeira** ~ first-class; first-rate

**qualificado** (kwer-ler-fee-*kah*-dhoo) *adj* qualified

**qualificar-se** (kwer-ler-fee-*kahr*-ser) *v* qualify

**qualquer** (kwahl-*kehr*) *adj* any; whichever

**quando** (*kwerngn*-doo) *adv* when; *conj* when; ~ **muito** at most; ~ **quer que** whenever

**quantia** (kwerngn-*tee*-er) *f* amount

**quantidade** (kwerngn-tee-*dhah*-dher) *f* number, quantity; lot, amount

**quanto** (*kwerngn*-too) *adv* how much; ~ **a** as regards; ~ **mais ... mais** the ... the; **quantos** how many

**quarenta** (kwer-*rayngn*-ter) *num* forty

**quarentena** (kwer-rayngn-*tay*-ner) *f* quarantine

**quarta-feira** (kwahr-ter-*fay*-rer) *f* Wednesday

**quartel** (kwahr-*tehl*) *m* (pl -téis) barracks *pl*

**quartel-general** (kwahr-tehl-zher-ner-*rahl*) *m* headquarters *pl*

**quarto** (*kwahr*-too) *num* fourth; *m* quarter; chamber, room; bedroom; ~ **das crianças** nursery; ~ **de banho** bathroom; ~ **de hóspedes** spare room, guest-room; ~ **de**

**vestir** dressing-room; ~ **e peque-no almoço** bed and breakfast; ~ **individual** single room

**quase** (kwah-zer) adv almost; nearly

**quatro** (kwah-troo) num four

**que** (ker) pron that; which, who; adv how; conj that; as, than

**quebra-cabeças** (keh-bhrer-ker-bhay-sersh) m (pl ~) jigsaw puzzle

**quebradiço** (ker-bhrer-dhee-soo) adj fragile

**quebra-nozes** (keh-bhrer-no-zersh) m (pl ~) nutcrackers pl

**quebrar** (ker-bhrahr) v crack; fracture, \*break

**queda** (keh-dher) f fall; ~ **de água** waterfall

**queijo** (kay-zhoo) m cheese

**queimadura** (kay-mer-dhoo-rer) f burn; ~ **do sol** sunburn

**queimar** (kay-mahr) v \*burn

**queixa** (kay-sher) f complaint

**queixar-se** (kay-shahr-ser) v complain

**queixo** (kay-shoo) m chin

**quem** (kerngᵛ) pron who; a ~ whom; ~ **quer que** whoever

**Quénia** (kayng-nᵛah) m Kenya

**quente** (kayngn-ter) adj warm, hot

**\*querer** (ker-rayr) v want

**querido** (ker-ree-dhoo) adj beloved, dear; m darling, sweetheart

**querosene** (kay-roa-zeh-ner) m kerosene

**quer ... quer** (kehr) whether ... or

**questão** (kɪsh-terngʷ) f (pl -tões) question; matter, issue

**quiçá** (kee-ser) adv perhaps

**quieto** (kᵛeh-too) adj quiet

**quilate** (kee-lah-ter) m carat

**quilha** (kee-lᵛer) f keel

**quilo** (kee-loo) m kilogram

**quilograma** (kee-loo-grer-mer) m kilogram

**quilometragem** (kee-loo-mer-trah-zherngᵛ) m distance in kilometres

**quilómetro** (kee-lo-mer-troo) m kilometre

**química** (kee-mee-ker) f chemistry

**químico** (kee-mee-koo) adj chemical

**quinina** (kee-nee-ner) f quinine

**quinta** (keengn-ter) f farm

**quinta-feira** (keengn-ter-fay-rer) f Thursday

**quinto** (keengn-too) num fifth

**quinze** (keeng-zer) num fifteen

**quinzena** (keeng-zay-ner) f fortnight

**quiosque** (kᵛosh-ker) m kiosk; ~ **de jornais** newsstand; ~ **de livros** bookstand

**quota** (kwo-ter) f quota

**quotidiano** (kwoo-tee-dhᵛer-noo) adj everyday, daily

# R

**rã** (rrerng) f frog

**rabanete** (rrer-bher-nay-ter) m radish

**rábano** (rrah-bher-noo) m turnip; ~ **silvestre** horseradish

**rabo** (rrah-bhoo) m bottom

**raça** (rrah-ser) f race, breed

**ração** (rrer-serngʷ) f (pl rações) ration

**racial** (rrer-sᵛahl) adj (pl -ais) racial

**raciocinar** (rrer-sᵛoo-see-nahr) v reason

**radiador** (rrer-dhᵛer-dhoar) m radiator

**radical** (rrer-dhee-kahl) adj (pl -ais) radical

**rádio** (rrah-dhᵛoo) m wireless, radio

**radiografar** (rrah-dhᵛoo-grer-fahr) v X-ray

**radiografia** (rrah-dhᵛoo-grer-fee-er) f X-ray

**rainha** (rrer-ee-ñer) f queen

**raio** (rrigh-oo) m ray, beam; radius;

spoke

**raiva** (rrigh-ver) f rabies; rage

**raivoso** (rrigh-voa-zoo) adj mad

**raiz** (rrer-eesh) f root

**rajada** (rrer-zhah-dher) f blow, gust

**ralador** (rrer-ler-dhoar) m grater

**ralhar** (rrer-lYahr) v scold

**raminho** (rrer-mee-ñoo) m twig

**ramo** (rrer-moo) m bough, branch; bunch, bouquet

**rampa** (rrerngm-per) f ramp

**rançoso** (rrerng-soa-zoo) adj rancid

**ranger** (rrerng-zhayr) v creak

**rapariga** (rrer-per-ree-ger) f girl

**rapaz** (rrer-pahsh) m boy; lad

**rapidamente** (rrer-pee-dher-mayngn-ter) adv soon; rapidly

**rapidez** (rrer-pee-dhaysh) f speed; haste

**rápido** (rrah-pee-dhoo) adj rapid; quick, fast, swift

**rápidos** (rrah-pee-dhoosh) mpl rapids pl

**raposa** (rrah-poa-zer) f fox

**raptor** (rrerp-toar) m hijacker

**raqueta** (rrer-kay-ter) f racquet

**raramente** (rrer-rer-mayngn-ter) adv rarely; scarcely, seldom

**raro** (rrah-roo) adj rare; infrequent, uncommon

**rasgão** (rrerzh-gerngw) m (pl -gões) tear

**rasgar** (rrerzh-gahr) v rip; *tear

**raso** (rrah-zoo) adj flat

**raspar** (rrersh-pahr) v grate, scrape

**rastejar** (rrersh-tı-zhahr) v crawl, *creep

**rasto** (rrahsh-too) m trace; *seguir o ~ de trace

**ratazana** (rrer-ter-zer-ner) f rat

**rato** (rrah-too) m mouse

**ravina** (rrer-vee-ner) f glen

**razão** (rrer-zerngw) f (pl razões) reason; wits pl, sense; *ter ~ * be

right

**razoável** (rrer-zwah-vehl) adj (pl -eis) reasonable

**razoavelmente** (rrer-zwah-vehl-mayngn-ter) adv fairly

**reabilitação** (ree-er-bher-lee-ter-serngw) f (pl -ções) rehabilitation

**reacção** (rreeah-serngw) f (pl -ções) reaction

**real** (rrYahl) adj (pl reais) true; factual, actual, substantial; royal

**realejo** (rrYer-lay-zhoo) m street-organ

**realidade** (rrYer-lee-dhah-dher) f reality; na ~ really

**realista** (rrYer-leesh-ter) adj matter-of-fact

**realização** (rrYer-lee-zer-serngw) f (pl -ções) achievement; direction

**realizar** (rrYer-lee-zahr) v realize, accomplish; implement, carry out; achieve

**realizável** (rrYer-lee-zah-vehl) adj (pl -eis) feasible, realizable

**realmente** (rrYahl-mayngn-ter) adv really; actually

**rebanho** (rrer-bher-ñoo) m flock

**rebelião** (rrer-bher-lYerngw) f (pl -iões) revolt; rebellion

**rebentar** (rrer-bhayngn-tahr) v *burst, crack

**rebocador** (rrer-bhoo-ker-dhoar) m tug

**rebocar** (rrer-bhoo-kahr) v tow, tug

**reboque** (rrer-bho-ker) m trailer

**rebuçado** (rrer-bhoo-sah-dhoo) m sweet; candy nAm; **rebuçados** sweets

**rebuscar** (rrer-bhoosh-kahr) v search

**recado** (rrer-kah-dhoo) m message, errand

**recarga** (rrer-kahr-ger) f refill

***recear** (rrer-sYahr) v fear

**receber** (rrer-ser-bhayr) v receive; entertain

**receio** (rrer-say-Yoo) m fear

**receita** (rrer-*say*-ter) *f* revenue;
  recipe; prescription
**receitar** (rrer-say-*tahr*) *v* prescribe
**recente** (rrer-*sayngn*-ter) *adj* recent
**recentemente** (rrer-sayngn-ter-
  *mayngn*-ter) *adv* lately, recently
**receoso** (rrer-s<sup>y</sup>-oa-zoo) *adj* frightened
**recepção** (rrer-seh-s*erng*<sup>w</sup>) *f* (pl
  -ções) reception; receipt, reception
  office
**recepcionista** (rrer-seh-s<sup>y</sup>oo-*neesh*-ter)
  *f* receptionist
**recessão** (rrer-seh-*serng*<sup>w</sup>) *f* recession
**recheado** (rrer-sh<sup>y</sup>ah-dhoo) *adj*
  stuffed
**recheio** (rrer-*shay*-oo) *m* filling, stuffing
**recibo** (rrer-*see*-bhoo) *m* receipt
**reciclar** (rrer-see-*klahr*) *v* recycle
**reciclável** (rrer-see-*klah*-vehl) *adj*
  (pl -eis) recyclable
**recipiente** (rrer-see-p<sup>y</sup>*ayngn*-ter) *m*
  container
**recíproco** (rrer-*see*-proo-koo) *adj* mutual
**recolha** (rrer-*koa*-l<sup>y</sup>er) *f* collection
**recomeçar** (rrer-koo-mer-*sahr*) *v* recommence; resume
**recomendação** (rrer-koo-mayngn-der-
  *serng*<sup>w</sup>) *f* (pl -ções) recommendation
**recomendar** (rrer-koo-mayngn-*dahr*) *v*
  recommend
**recompensa** (rrer-kawngm-*payng*-ser)
  *f* prize, reward
**recompensar** (rrer-kawngm-payng-
  *sahr*) *v* reward
**reconciliação** (rrer-kawng-see-l<sup>y</sup>er-
  *serng*<sup>w</sup>) *f* (pl -ções) reconciliation
**reconhecer** (rrer-koo-ñer-*sayr*) *v* recognize, acknowledge; confess, admit
**reconhecido** (rrer-koo-ñer-*see*-dhoo)

*adj* grateful
**reconhecimento** (rrer-koo-ñer-see-
  *mayngn*-too) *m* recognition; gratitude
**recordação** (rrer-koor-dher-*serng*<sup>w</sup>) *f*
  (pl -ções) memory, remembrance;
  souvenir
**recordar** (rrer-koor-*dhahr*) *v* remind;
  **recordar-se** recall, remember; recollect
**recorde** (rrer-*kor*-dher) *m* record
**recreação** (rer-kr<sup>y</sup>er-*serng*<sup>w</sup>) *f* (pl
  -ções) recreation
**recreio** (rrer-*kray*-oo) *m* playground
**recruta** (rrer-*kroo*-ter) *m* conscript, recruit
**rectangular** (rreh-terng-goo-*lahr*) *adj*
  rectangular
**rectângulo** (rreh-*terng*-goo-loo) *m* oblong, rectangle
**rectificação** (rreh-tee-fee-ker-*serng*<sup>w</sup>) *f*
  (pl -ções) correction
**recto** (*rreh*-too) *adj* right; straight; *m*
  rectum
**recuar** (rrer-*kwahr*) *v* pull back; reverse
**recuperação** (rrer-koo-per-rer-*serng*<sup>w</sup>)
  *f* (pl -ções) recuperation; recovery
**recuperar** (rrer-koo-per-*rahr*) *v* recover
**recusa** (rrer-*koo*-zer) *f* refusal
**recusar** (rrer-koo-*zahr*) *v* refuse; reject, deny
**redactor** (rrer-dhah-*toar*) *m* editor
**rede** (*rray*-dher) *f* net; network; hammock; ~ **da bagagem** luggage
  rack; ~ **de pesca** fishing net; ~
  **rodoviária** road system
**redigir** (rrer-dher-*zheer*) *v* *write
**redimir** (rrer-dher-*meer*) *v* redeem
**redondo** (rrer-*dhawngn*-doo) *adj*
  round
**em redor** (erng<sup>y</sup> rrer-*dhor*) surrounding
**redução** (rrer-dhoo-*serng*<sup>w</sup>) *f* (pl

-ções) reduction, discount, rebate

**\*reduzir** (rrer-dhoo-*zeer*) v reduce; \*cut

**reembolsar** (rrʸayngm-boal-*sahr*) v reimburse; refund, \*repay

**reembolso** (rrʸayngm-*boal*-soo) m refund, repayment

**refeição** (rrer-fay-*serng*ʷ) f (pl -ções) meal; ~ **ligeira** snack

**refém** (rrer-*ferng*ʸ) m hostage

**referência** (rrer-fer-*rayng*-sʸer) f reference; **ponto de** ~ landmark

**referente a** (rrer-fer-*rayngn*-ter) concerning; about

**\*referir a** (rrer-fer-*reer*) refer to

**refinaria** (rrer-fee-ner-*ree*-er) f refinery; ~ **de petróleo** oil-refinery

**\*reflectir** (rrer-fleh-*teer*) v reflect; \*think

**reflector** (rrer-fleh-*toar*) m reflector

**reflexão** (rrer-flehk-*serng*ʷ) f (pl -xões) reflection

**Reforma** (rrer-*for*-mer) f reformation

**reformado** (rrer-foor-*mah*-dhoo) adj retired

**\*refrear** (rrer-*fr*ʸ*ahr*) v curb

**refrescar** (rrer-frnsh-*kahr*) v refresh

**refresco** (rrer-*fraysh*-koo) m refreshment

**refúgio** (rrer-*foo*-zhʸoo) m shelter, cover

**regata** (rrer-*gah*-ter) f regatta

**\*regatear** (rrer-ger-tʸ*ahr*) v bargain

**região** (rrer-zhʸ*erng*ʷ) f (pl -iões) region; zone, country, district, area; ~ **arborizada** woodland

**regime** (rrer-*zhee*-mer) m régime; rule, government

**regional** (rrn-zhʸoo-*nahl*) adj (pl -ais) regional

**registar** (rrn-zheesh-*tahr*) v register; book, record; **registar-se** check in

**registo** (rrn-*zheesh*-too) m record; registration

**regra** (*rreh*-grer) f rule; **em** ~ as a rule

**regressar** (rrer-grer-*sahr*) v \*get back, \*go back

**regresso** (rrer-*greh*-soo) m return; **viagem de** ~ return journey

**régua** (*rreh*-gwer) f ruler

**regulamentação** (rrer-goo-ler-mayngn-ter-*serng*ʷ) f (pl -ções) regulation

**regulamento** (rrer-goo-ler-*mayngn*-too) m regulation; arrangement

**regular** (rrer-goo-*lahr*) v regulate; adj regular

**regularizar** (rrer-goo-ler-ree-*zahr*) v settle

**rei** (rray) m king

**reinado** (rray-*nah*-dhoo) m reign

**reinar** (rray-*nahr*) v reign

**reino** (*rray*-noo) m kingdom

**reitor** (rray-*toar*) m headmaster, principal; rector

**reitoria** (rray-too-*ree*-er) f rectory

**reivindicação** (rray-veengn-dee-ker-*serng*ʷ) f (pl -ções) claim

**reivindicar** (rray-veengn-dee-*kahr*) v claim

**rejeitar** (rri-zhay-*tahr*) v turn down, reject

**relação** (rrer-ler-*serng*ʷ) f (pl -ções) report; relation, connection, reference; **relações** intercourse

**relâmpago** (rrer-*lerngm*-per-goo) m lightning; flash

**relance** (rrer-*lerng*-ser) m glance

**\*relancear** (rrer-lerng-sʸ*ahr*) v glance

**relatar** (rrer-ler-*tahr*) v report

**relativamente** (rrer-ler-tee-ver-*mayngn*-ter) adv quite; ~ **a** regarding

**relativo** (rrer-ler-*tee*-voo) adj relative; comparative; ~ **a** regarding, with reference to

**relato** (rrer-*lah*-too) m account

**relatório** (rrer-ler-*to*-rʸoo) m report

**relevante** (rrer-ler-*verngn*-ter) *adj* important

**relevo** (rrer-*lay*-voo) *m* relief; importance

**religião** (rrer-lee-zh<sup>Y</sup>*erng*<sup>W</sup>) *f* (pl -iões) religion

**religioso** (rrer-lee-zh<sup>Y</sup>*oa*-zoo) *adj* religious

**relíquia** (rrer-*lee*-k<sup>Y</sup>er) *f* relic

**relógio** (rrer-*lo*-zh<sup>Y</sup>oo) *m* watch; clock; ~ **de bolso** pocket-watch; ~ **de pulso** wrist-watch

**relojoeiro** (rrer-loo-*zhway*-roo) *m* watch-maker

**reluzente** (rrer-loo-*zayngn*-ter) *adj* bright

**\*reluzir** (rrer-loo-*zeer*) *v* \*shine

**relva** (*rrehl*-ver) *f* lawn

**relvado** (rrehl-*vah*-dhoo) *m* lawn

**remanescente** (rrer-mer-nɪsh-*sayngn*-ter) *m* remnant; remainder

**remar** (rrer-*mahr*) *v* row

**remédio** (rrer-*meh*-dh<sup>Y</sup>oo) *m* remedy

**remendar** (rrer-mayngn-*dhahr*) *v* mend; patch

**remessa** (rrer-*meh*-ser) *f* consignment; remittance

**remeter** (rrer-mer-*tayr*) *v* remit

**remo** (*rray*-moo) *m* oar; paddle

**remoção** (rrer-moo-*serng*<sup>W</sup>) *f* (pl -ções) removal

**remoto** (rrer-*mo*-too) *adj* remote

**remover** (rrer-moo-*vayr*) *v* remove

**remuneração** (rrer-moo-ner-rer-*serng*<sup>W</sup>) *f* (pl -ções) remuneration

**remunerar** (rrer-moo-ner-*rahr*) *v* remunerate

**rena** (*rray*-ner) *f* reindeer

**renda** (*rrayngn*-der) *f* lace; rent; \***fazer** ~ crochet

**render** (rrayngn-*dayr*) *v* yield; **render-se** surrender

**rendição** (rrayngn-dee-*serng*<sup>W</sup>) *f* (pl -ções) surrender

**rendimento** (rrayngn-dee-*mayngn*-too) *m* income, revenue; **rendimentos** earnings *pl*

**renome** (rrer-*noa*-mer) *m* reputation

**renovar** (rrer-noo-*vahr*) *v* renew

**rentável** (*rrayngn*-tah-vehl) *adj* (pl -eis) paying

**renunciar** (rrer-noong-*s<sup>Y</sup>ahr*) *v* \*give up

**reparação** (rrer-per-rer-*serng*<sup>W</sup>) *f* (pl -ções) reparation

**reparar** (rrer-per-*rahr*) *v* repair; mend, fix; ~ **em** notice

**repartição** (rrer-perr-tee-*serng*<sup>W</sup>) *f* (pl -ções) agency

**repartir** (rrer-perr-*teer*) *v* divide

**repelente** (rrer-per-*layngn*-ter) *adj* repellent, repulsive

**de repente** (der rrer-*payngn*-tahr) suddenly

**repentinamente** (rrer-payngn-tee-ner-*mayngn*-ter) *adv* suddenly

**repentino** (rrer-payngn-*tee*-noo) *adj* sudden

**repertório** (rrer-perr-*to*-r<sup>Y</sup>oo) *m* repertory

**repetição** (rrer-per-tee-*serng*<sup>W</sup>) *f* (pl -ções) repetition

**repetidamente** (rrer-per-tee-dher-*mayngn*-ter) *adv* again and again

**\*repetir** (rrer-per-*teer*) *v* repeat

**repleto** (rrer-*pleh*-too) *adj* full up; chock-full

**repórter** (rrer-*por*-tehr) *m* reporter

**repousar** (rrer-poa-*zahr*) *v* rest

**repreender** (rrer-pr<sup>Y</sup>ayngn-*dayr*) *v* scold, reprimand

**representação** (rrer-prer-zayngn-ter-*serng*<sup>W</sup>) *f* (pl -ções) representation; performance, show

**representante** (rrer-prer-zayngn-*terngn*-ter) *m* agent

**representar** (rrer-prer-zayngn-*tahr*) *v* represent; act

**representativo** (rrer-prer-zay*ng*-ter-*tee*-voo) *adj* representative

**reprimir** (rrer-pree-*meer*) *v* suppress; curb

**reprodução** (rrer-proo-dhoo-*serng*ʷ) *f* (pl -ções) reproduction

***reproduzir** (rrer-proo-dhoo-*zeer*) *v* reproduce

**reprovar** (rrer-proo-*vahr*) *v* reject; fail

**réptil** (*rrehp*-teel) *m* (pl -teis) reptile

**república** (rreh-*poo*-bhlee-ker) *f* republic

**republicano** (rreh-poo-bhlee-*ker*-noo) *adj* republican

**repugnância** (rrer-poog-*nerng*-sʸer) *f* dislike

**repugnante** (rrer-poog-*nerng*n-ter) *adj* repellent; disgusting

**reputação** (rrer-poo-ter-*serng*ʷ) *f* (pl -ções) reputation, fame

***requerer** (rrer-ker-*rayr*) *v* request; demand

**requintado** (rrer-keeng*n*-*tah*-dhoo) *adj* exquisite, delicious

**rés-do-chão** (rrehzh-doo-*sherng*ʷ) *m* ground floor

**reserva** (rrer-*zehr*-ver) *f* store, reserve; booking, reservation; qualification; **de** ~ spare; ~ **natural** game reserve

**reservar** (rrer-zehr-*vahr*) *v* reserve; book

**reservatório** (rrer-zerr-ver-*to*-rʸoo) *m* reservoir

**resgate** (rrizh-*gah*-ter) *m* ransom

**residência** (rrer-zee-*dhayng*-sʸer) *f* residence

**residente** (rrer-zee-*dhayng*n-ter) *m* resident; *adj* resident

**residir** (rrer-zee-*dheer*) *v* reside

**resina** (rrer-*zee*-ner) *f* resin

**resistência** (rrer-zeesh-*tayng*-sʸer) *f* resistance; strength; stamina

**resistir** (rrer-zeesh-*teer*) *v* resist

**resmungar** (rrizh-moo*ng*-*gahr*) *v* grumble

**resoluto** (rrer-zoo-*loo*-too) *adj* resolute; determined

**resolver** (rrer-zoal-*vayr*) *v* solve; settle; decide

**respectivo** (rrish-peh-*tee*-voo) *adj* respective

**respeitante a** (rrish-pay-*terng*n-ter er) as regards

**respeitar** (rrish-pay-*tahr*) *v* respect

**respeitável** (rrish-pay-*tah*-vehl) *adj* (pl -eis) respectable

**respeito** (rrish-*pay*-too) *m* respect; regard; **a** ~ **de** about; **com** ~ **a** regarding; ***dizer** ~ **a** concern; touch; **no que diz** ~ **a** as regards

**respeitoso** (rrish-pay-*toa*-zoo) *adj* respectful

**respiração** (rrish-pee-rer-*serng*ʷ) *f* respiration; breath, breathing

**respirar** (rrish-pee-*rahr*) *v* breathe

**responder** (rrish-pawng*n*-*dayr*) *v* answer, reply; ~ **a** answer

**responsabilidade** (rrish-pawng-ser-bher-lee-*dhah*-dher) *f* responsibility; liability

**responsável** (rrish-pawng-*sah*-vehl) *adj* (pl -eis) responsible; liable

**resposta** (rrish-*posh*-ter) *f* answer, reply; **em** ~ in reply; **sem** ~ unanswered

**ressaca** (rrer-*sah*-ker) *f* undercurrent; *mBr* hangover

**ressonar** (rrer-soo-*nahr*) *v* snore

**restabelecer-se** (rrish-ter-bher-ler-*sayr*-ser) *v* recover

**restabelecimento** (rrish-ter-bher-ler-see-*mayng*n-too) *m* recovery

**restante** (rrish-*terng*n-ter) *adj* remaining; *m* remainder

**restaurante** (rrish-tou-rer*ng*n-ter) *m* restaurant

**resto** (*rrehsh*-too) *m* rest; remainder

**restrição** (rrɪsh-tree-*serng*ʷ) f (pl -ções) limitation, restriction

**resultado** (rrer-zool-*tah*-dhoo) m result; effect, outcome, issue; score

**resultar** (rrer-zool-*tahr*) v result; appear

**resumo** (rrer-*zoo*-moo) m summary, résumé, survey

**retaguarda** (rreh-ter-*gwahr*-dher) f rear

**retalhista** (rrer-ter-*lʸeesh*-ter) m retailer

***reter** (rrer *tayr*) v restrain

**retina** (rrer-*tee*-ner) f retina

**retirar** (rrer-tee-*rahr*) v *withdraw

**retrato** (rrer-*trah*-too) m portrait

**retretes** (rrcr-*tray*-tersh) fpl toilet

**reumatismo** (rrayᵒᵒ-mer-*teezh*-moo) m rheumatism

**reunião** (rrʸoo-n*ʸerng*ʷ) f (pl -ides) meeting; assembly, rally

**reunir** (rrʸoo-*neer*) v reunite; unite, join; gather, assemble

**revelação** (rrer-ver-ler-*serng*ʷ) f (pl -ções) revelation

**revelar** (rrer-ver-*lahr*) v reveal; *give away; develop; **revelar-se** prove

**revendedor** (rrer-vayngn-der-*dhoar*) m retailer

***rever** (rrer-*vayr*) v overhaul, revise

**reverso** (rrer-*vehr*-soo) m reverse

**revés** (rrer-*vehsh*) m reverse; **de ~** askew

**reviravolta** (rrer-vee-rer-*vol*-ter) f reverse

**revisor** (rrer-vee-*zoar*) m ticket collector

**revista** (rrer-*veesh*-ter) f review, magazine; revue; **~ mensal** monthly magazine

**revistar** (rrer-veesh-*tahr*) v search

**revogar** (rrer-voo-*gahr*) v cancel

**revolta** (rrer-*vol*-ter) f revolt, rebellion

**revoltante** (rrer-voal-*terngn*-ter) adj revolting

**revoltar-se** (rrer-voal-*tahr*-ser) v revolt

**revolução** (rrer-voo-loo-*serng*ʷ) f (pl -ções) revolution

**revolucionário** (rrer-voo-loo-sʸoo-*nah*-rʸoo) adj revolutionary

**revólver** (rrer-*vol*-vehr) m gun, revolver

**rezar** (rrer-*zahr*) v pray

**riacho** (rrʸah-shoo) m brook

**ribeiro** (rree-*bhay*-roo) m stream

**rico** (rree-koo) adj rich; wealthy

**ridicularizar** (rree-dhee-koo-ler-ree-*zahr*) v ridicule

**ridículo** (rree-*dhee*-koo-loo) adj ludicrous, ridiculous

**rigoroso** (rree-goo-*roa*-zoo) adj severe, strict; bleak

**rim** (rreeng) m kidney

**rima** (rree-mer) f rhyme

**rímel** (rree-mehl) m mascara

**rinoceronte** (rree-noo-ser-*rawngn*-ter) m rhinoceros

**rio** (rreeᵒᵒ) m river; **~ abaixo** downstream; **~ acima** upstream

**riqueza** (rree-*kay*-zer) f wealth, riches pl; pet

***rir** (rreer) v laugh

**risada** (rree-*zah*-dher) f laughter

**risca** (rreesh-ker) f stripe; parting; **às riscas** striped

**riscar** (rreesh-*kahr*) v scratch

**risco** (rreesh-koo) m line; scratch; risk, hazard, chance

**riso** (rree-zoo) m laugh

**ritmo** (rreet-moo) m rhythm; pace

**rival** (rree-*vahl*) m (pl -ais) rival

**rivalidade** (rree-ver-lee-*dhah*-dher) f rivalry

**rivalizar** (rree-ver-*lɪe*-*zahr*) v rival

**robalo** (rroo-*bhah*-loo) m roach; bass

**robusto** (rroo-*bhoosh*-too) adj solid, robust

**rocha** (rro-sher) f rock

**rochoso** (rroo-*shoa*-zoo) *adj* rocky
**roda** (*rro*-dher) *f* wheel; ∼ **sobresselente** spare wheel
**rodar** (rroo-*dhahr*) *v* turn
*****rodear** (rroo-*dh*ʸ*ahr*) *v* circle, encircle; surround
**rodovalho** (rroo-dhoo-*vah*-lʸoo) *m* brill
**rola** (*rroa*-ler) *f* turtle dove
**rolar** (rroo-*lahr*) *v* roll
**roldana** (rroal-*der*-ner) *f* pulley
**roleta** (rroo-*lay*-ter) *f* roulette
**rolha** (*rroa*-lʸer) *f* cork; stopper
**roliço** (rroo-*lee*-soo) *adj* plump
**rolo** (*rroa*-loo) *m* roll; curler
**romance** (rroo-*merng*-ser) *m* romance; novel; ∼ **policial** detective story
**romancista** (rroo-merng-*seesh*-ter) *m* novelist
**romântico** (rroo-*merng*-tee-koo) *adj* romantic
**rombo** (*rrawngm*-boo) *adj* blunt
**Roménia** (rroo-*meh*-nʸer) *f* Rumania
**romeno** (rroo-*may*-noo) *adj* Rumanian; *m* Rumanian
**romper** (rrawngm-*payr*) *v* *break; *tear
**rosa** (*rro*-zer) *f* rose
**rosado** (rroo-*zah*-dhoo) *adj* rose
**rosário** (rroo-*zah*-rʸoo) *m* rosary; beads
**rosnar** (rroozh-*nahr*) *v* growl
**rosto** (*rroash*-too) *m* face; **feição do** ∼ feature
**rota** (*rro*-ter) *f* route; course
**rotação** (rroo-ter-*serng*ʷ) *f* (pl -ções) revolution
**rotim** (rroo-*teeng*) *m* rattan
**rotina** (rroo-*tee*-ner) *f* routine
**rótula** (*rro*-too-ler) *f* kneecap
**rotunda** (rroo-*toongn*-der) *f* roundabout
**roubar** (rroa-*bhahr*) *v* *steal; rob
**roubo** (*rroa*-bhoo) *m* theft, robbery
**rouco** (*rroa*-koo) *adj* hoarse

**rouge** (roozh) *m* rouge
**roupa** (*rroa*-per) *f* clothes *pl;* **lavar a** ∼ washing; ∼ **branca** linen; ∼ **de cama** bedding; ∼ **interior** underwear, lingerie; ∼ **para lavar** laundry; washing
**roupão** (rroa-*perng*ʷ) *m* (pl -pões) dressing-gown; ∼ **de banho** bathrobe
**roupeiro** (rroa-*pay*-roo) *m* wardrobe; closet *nAm*
**rouxinol** (rroa-shee-*nol*) *m* (pl -nóis) nightingale
**rua** (*rroo*-er) *f* road, street; ∼ **principal** main street
**rubi** (rroo-*bhee*) *m* ruby
**rubrica** (rroo-*bhree*-ker) *f* column
**rubricar** (rroo-bhree-*kahr*) *v* initial
**rude** (*rroo*-dher) *adj* rude
**ruga** (*rroo*-ger) *f* wrinkle
**rugido** (rroo-*zhee*-dhoo) *m* roar
**rugir** (rroo-*zheer*) *v* roar
**rugoso** (rroo-*goa*-zoo) *adj* uneven
**ruibarbo** (rrwee-*bhahr*-bhoo) *m* rhubarb
**ruído** (rrwee-dhoo) *m* noise
**ruidoso** (rrwee-*dhoa*-zoo) *adj* noisy
**ruína** (rrwee-ner) *f* destruction, ruin, ruination; ruins
**rulote** (rroa-*lot*) *f* caravan
**rumor** (rroo-*moar*) *m* rumour; roar
**rural** (rroo-*rahl*) *adj* (pl -ais) rural
**Rússia** (*rroo*-sʸer) *f* Russia
**russo** (*rroo*-soo) *adj* Russian; *m* Russian
**rústico** (*rroosh*-tee-koo) *adj* rustic

# S

**sábado** (*sah*-bher-dhoo) *m* Saturday
**sabão** (ser-*bherng*ʷ) *m* (pl sabões) soap; ∼ **da barba** shaving-soap; ∼

em pó soap powder

**sabedoria** (ser-bher-dhoo-*ree*-er) f wisdom; knowledge

***saber** (ser-*bhayr*) v *know; *be able to; ~ **a saber** namely; ~ **a taste**

**sabonete** (ser-bhoo-*nay*-ter) m toilet soap

**sabor** (ser-*bhoar*) m flavour

***saborear** (ser-bhoo-rᵞ*ahr*) v appreciate

**saboroso** (ser-bhoo-*roa*-zoo) adj savoury; tasty, enjoyable

**saca** (*sah*-ker) f sack

**sacar** (ser-*kahr*) v *draw

**sacarina** (ser-ker-*ree*-ner) f saccharin

**saca-rolhas** (sah-ker-*rroa*-lᵞersh) m (pl ~) corkscrew

**saco** (*sah*-koo) m bag; ~ **das compras** shopping bag; ~ **de gelo** icebag; ~ **de mão** grip nAm; ~ **de papel** paper bag

**saco-cama** (*sah*-koo-ker-mer) m sleeping-bag

**sacrificar** (ser-krer-fee-*kahr*) v sacrifice

**sacrifício** (ser-krer-*fee*-sᵞoo) m sacrifice

**sacrilégio** (ser-kree-*leh*-zhᵞoo) m sacrilege

**sacristão** (ser-kreesh-*terng*ʷ) m (pl -stães) sexton

***sacudir** (ser-koo-*dheer*) v *shake

**safira** (ser-*fee*-rer) f sapphire

**sagrado** (ser-*grah*-dhoo) adj holy, sacred

**saia** (*sigh*-er) f skirt; ~ **de baixo** slip

**saibro** (*sigh*-bhroo) m grit

**saída** (ser-*ee*-dher) f exit, way out; issue; ~ **de emergência** emergency exit

***sair** (ser-*eer*) v *go out; check out

**sal** (sahl) m (pl sais) salt; **sais de banho** bath salts

**sala** (*sah*-ler) f drawing-room; hall;

~ **de aula** classroom; ~ **de concertos** concert hall; ~ **de espera** waiting-room; ~ **de estar** living-room, sitting-room; ~ **de exposições** showroom; ~ **de fumo** smoking-room; ~ **de jantar** dining-room; ~ **de leitura** reading-room

**salada** (ser-*lah*-dher) f salad

**salão** (ser-*lerng*ʷ) m (pl salões) salon; lounge; ~ **de baile** ballroom; ~ **de banquetes** banqueting-hall; ~ **de beleza** beauty salon

**salário** (ser-*lah*-rᵞoo) m salary; wages pl, pay

**saldo** (*sahl*-doo) m balance; **saldos** sales

**saleiro** (ser-*lay*-roo) m salt-cellar

**salgado** (sahl-*gah*-dhoo) adj salty

**saliva** (ser-*lee*-ver) f spit

**salpicar** (sahl-pee-*kahr*) v splash

**salsa** (*sahl*-ser) f parsley

**salsicha** (sahl-*see*-sher) f sausage

**saltar** (sahl-*tahr*) v jump; *leap; skip

**saltitar** (sahl-tee-*tahr*) v hop; skip

**salto** (*sahl*-too) m jump, leap; heel; ~ **de esqui** ski-jump

**salvação** (sahl-ver-*serng*ʷ) f rescue

**salvador** (sahl-ver-*dhoar*) m saviour

**salvar** (sahl-*vahr*) v rescue, save

**sanatório** (ser-ner-to-rᵞoo) m sanatorium

**sandália** (serng-*dah*-lᵞer) f sandal

**sanduíche** (serngn-*dwee*-sher) f sandwich

**sangrar** (serng-*grahr*) v *bleed

**sangue** (*serng*-ger) m blood

**sanitário** (ser-nee-*tah*-rᵞoo) adj sanitary; m lavatory

**santo** (*serng*-too) m saint

**santo-e-senha** (serngn-twee-*say*-ñer) m password

**santuário** (serngn-*twah*-rᵞoo) m shrine

**são** (serng<sup>w</sup>) *adj* (pl ~s) healthy

**sapataria** (ser-per-ter-*ree*-er) *f* shoe-shop

**sapateiro** (ser-per-*tay*-roo) *m* shoe-maker

**sapato** (ser-*pah*-too) *m* shoe; **sapatos de ginástica** gym shoes; plimsolls *pl*, sneakers *plAm*; **sapatos de ténis** tennis shoes

**sapo** (*sah*-poo) *m* toad

**sarampo** (ser-*rerngm*-poo) *m* measles

**sarapintado** (ser-rer-peengn-*tah*-dhoo) *adj* spotted

**sarar** (ser-*rahr*) *v* heal

**sardinha** (serr-*dhee*-ñer) *f* sardine

**satélite** (ser-*teh*-lee-ter) *m* satellite

**satisfação** (ser-teesh-fer-*serng*<sup>w</sup>) *f* (pl -ções) satisfaction

***satisfazer** (ser-teesh-fer-*zayr*) *v* satisfy

**satisfeito** (ser-teesh-*fay*-too) *adj* satisfied; pleased, content

**saudação** (sou-dher-*serng*<sup>w</sup>) *f* (pl -ções) greeting

**saudar** (sou-*dhahr*) *v* salute

**saudável** (sou-*dhah*-vehl) *adj* (pl -eis) wholesome

**saúde** (ser-*oo*-dher) *f* health

**saudita** (sou-*dhee*-ter) *adj* Saudi Arabian

**sauna** (*sou*-ner) *f* sauna

**se** (ser) *pron* himself, herself, itself, oneself, yourself; themselves; yourselves; *conj* if; whether; ~ **bem que** though

**seara** (s<sup>y</sup>ah-rer) *f* cornfield

**sebe** (*seh*-bher) *f* hedge

**seca** (*seh*-ker) *f* drought

**secador** (ser-ker-*dhoar*) *m* dryer; ~ **de cabelo** hair-dryer

**secar** (ser-*kahr*) *v* dry; drain

**secção** (sehk-*serng*<sup>w</sup>) *f* (pl -ções) section; division

**seco** (*say*-koo) *adj* dry

**secretária** (ser-krer-*tah*-r<sup>y</sup>er) *f* secretary; bureau, desk

**secretário** (ser-krer-*tah*-r<sup>y</sup>oo) *m* secretary; clerk

**secreto** (ser-*kreh*-too) *adj* secret

**século** (*seh*-koo-loo) *m* century

**secundário** (ser-koongn-*dah*-r<sup>y</sup>oo) *adj* secondary; subordinate

**seda** (*say*-dher) *f* silk; ~ **artificial** rayon

**sedativo** (ser-dher-*tee*-voo) *m* sedative

**sede**<sup>1</sup> (*seh*-dher) *f* seat

**sede**<sup>2</sup> (*say*-dher) *f* thirst

**sedento** (ser-*dhayngn*-too) *adj* thirsty

**sedimento** (ser-dhee-*merngn*-too) *m* deposit

**sedoso** (ser-*dhoa*-zoo) *adj* silken

***seduzir** (ser-dhoo-*zeer*) *v* seduce

**segredo** (ser-*gray*-dhoo) *m* secret

**em seguida** (erng<sup>y</sup> ser-*gee*-dher) afterwards, then

**seguinte** (ser-*geengn*-ter) *adj* next; following

***seguir** (ser-*geer*) *v* follow; **a seguir** presently; ***fazer seguir** forward; ~ **o rasto de** trace

**segunda-feira** (ser-goongn-der-*fay*-rer) *f* Monday

**segundo** (ser-*goongn*-doo) *num* second; *m* second; *prep* according to

**segurança** (ser-goo-*rerng*-ser) *f* security; safety

**segurar** (ser-goo-*rahr*) *v* *hold; grasp; insure

**seguro** (ser-*goo*-roo) *adj* secure; safe; sound; *m* insurance; **apólice de ~** insurance policy; ~ **de viagem** travel insurance; ~ **de vida** life insurance

**seio** (*say*-oo) *m* bosom

**seis** (saysh) *num* six

**seixo** (*say*-shoo) *m* pebble

**seja ... seja** (*say*-zher) either ... or

**sela** (*seh*-ler) *f* saddle

**selecção** (ser-leh-*ser*ᵒᵒ) f (pl -ções) choice, selection

**seleccionado** (ser-leh-sᵞoo-*ner*-dhoo) adj select

**seleccionar** (ser-leh-sᵞoo-*nahr*) v select

**selecto** (ser-*leh*-too) adj select

**selo** (*say*-loo) m seal; stamp; ~ **postal** postage stamp

**selva** (*sehl*-ver) f jungle

**selvagem** (sehl-*vah*-zherng ᵞ) adj wild, savage

**sem** (serng ᵞ) prep without

**semáforo** (ser-*mah*-foo-roo) m traffic light

**semana** (ser-*mer*-ner) f week

**semanal** (ser-mer-*nahl*) adj (pl -ais) weekly

**\*semear** (ser-*mᵞahr*) v \*sow

**semelhança** (ser-mı-*lᵞerng*-ser) f resemblance, similarity

**semelhante** (ser-mı-*lᵞerng*n-ter) adj like, alike; similar

**semente** (ser-*mayng*n-ter) f seed

**semi-** (*ser*-mee) semi-

**semi-círculo** (ser-mee-*seer*-koo-loo) m semicircle

**sempre** (*sayng*m-prer) adv always, ever; ~ **que** whenever

**senado** (ser-*nah*-dhoo) m senate

**senador** (ser-ner-*dhoar*) m senator

**senão** (ser-*nerng* ᵂ) conj otherwise

**senhor** (sı-*ñoar*) mister; sir; **o** ~ you; **os senhores** you

**senhora** (sı-*ñoa*-rer) f madam; **a** ~ you

**senhoria** (sı-ñoa-*ree*-er) f landlady

**senhorio** (sı-ñoo-*ree*-oo) m landlord

**senil** (ser-*neel*) adj (pl -is) senile

**sensação** (sayng-ser-*serng* ᵂ) f (pl -ções) feeling, sensation

**sensacional** (sayng-ser-sᵞoo-*nahl*) adj (pl -ais) sensational

**sensato** (sayng-*sah*-too) adj sensible; down-to-earth

**sensível** (sayng-*see*-vehl) adj (pl -eis) sensitive

**senso** (*sayng*-soo) m reason

**sentar-se** (sayng-*tahr*-ser) v \*sit down; \***estar sentado** \*sit

**sentença** (sayng-*tayng*-ser) f sentence, verdict

**sentido** (sayng-*tee*-dhoo) m sense; **sem** ~ meaningless; senseless; ~ **único** one-way traffic

**sentimental** (sayng-tee-mayng-*tahl*) adj (pl -ais) sentimental

**\*sentir** (sayng-*teer*) v \*feel; sense

**separação** (ser-per-rer-*serng* ᵂ) f (pl -ções) division

**separadamente** (ser-per-rah-dher-*mayng*n-ter) adv apart; separately

**separado** (ser-per-*rah*-dhoo) adj separate

**separar** (ser-per-*rahr*) v separate; divide, part, detach

**septicemia** (sehp-tee-*seh*-mᵞer) f blood-poisoning

**séptico** (*sehp*-tee-koo) adj septic

**sepultura** (ser-pool-*too*-rer) f grave

**sequência** (ser-*kwayng*-sᵞer) f sequence

**ser** (sayr) m being, creature; ~ **humano** human being

**\*ser** (sayr) v \*be; ~ **preciso** \*be necessary

**sereia** (ser-*ray*-er) f mermaid

**sereno** (ser-*ray*-noo) adj serene

**série** (*seh*-rᵞer) f series, sequence

**seriedade** (ser-rᵞay-*dhah*-dher) f seriousness; gravity

**seringa** (ser-*reeng*-ger) f syringe

**sério** (*seh*-rᵞoo) adj serious

**sermão** (serr-*merng* ᵂ) m (pl -mões) sermon

**serpente** (serr-*payng*-ter) f snake

**serpentear** (serr-payng-*tᵞahr*) v \*wind

serra (seh-rrer) f saw; mountain range

serração (ser-rrer-serng<sup>w</sup>) f (pl -ções) saw-mill

serradura (ser-rrer-dhoo-rer) f sawdust

serviço (serr-vee-soo) m service; prestar ~ render services; ~ de chá tea-set; ~ de jantar dinner-service; ~ de quarto room service

*servir (serr-veer) v serve; wait on; *be of use

sessão (ser-serng<sup>w</sup>) f (pl -sões) session

sessenta (ser-sayngn-ter) num sixty

sete (seh-ter) num seven

Setembro (ser-tayngm-broo) September

setenta (ser-tayngn-ter) num seventy

setentrional (ser-tayngn-tr<sup>y</sup>oo-nahl) adj (pl -ais) northern

sétimo (seh-tee-moo) num seventh

seu (say<sup>oo</sup>) adj (f sua) his; her; your

severo (ser-veh-roo) adj strict; harsh

sexo (sehk-soo) m sex

sexta-feira (saysh-ter-fay-rer) f Friday

sexto (saysh-too) num sixth

sexual (sehk-swahl) adj (pl -ais) sexual

sexualidade (sehk-swer-lee-dhah-dher) f sex, sexuality

siamês (s<sup>y</sup>er-maysh) adj Siamese

SIDA (see-dher) f AIDS

sifão (see-ferng<sup>w</sup>) m (pl sifões) siphon, syphon

significado (seeg-ner-fee-kah-dhoo) m meaning

significar (seeg-ner-fee-kahr) v *mean

significativo (seeg-ner-fee-ker-tee-voo) adj significant

sílaba (see-ler-bher) f syllable

silêncio (see-layng-s<sup>y</sup>oo) m silence; stillness, quiet

silencioso (see-layng-s<sup>y</sup>oa-zoo) adj silent; m silencer

sim (seeng) yes

símbolo (seengm-boo-loo) m symbol

simpatia (seengm-per-tee-er) f sympathy

simpático (seengm-pah-tee-koo) adj nice; friendly, pleasant

simples (seengm-plish) adj plain, simple

simplesmente (seengm-plizh-mayngn-ter) adv simply

simular (see-moo-lahr) v simulate

simultaneamente (see-mool-ter-nay-er-mayngn-ter) adv simultaneously

simultâneo (see-mool-ter-n<sup>y</sup>oo) adj simultaneous

sinagoga (see-ner-go-ger) f synagogue

sinal (see-nahl) m (pl -ais) signal; token, sign; indication; down payment; *fazer sinais signal; sinais pessoais description; ~ de trânsito road sign

sincero (seeng-seh-roo) adj honest, sincere

sindicato (seengn-dee-kah-too) m trade-union

sinfonia (seeng-foo-nee-er) f symphony

singular (seeng-goo-lahr) adj singular; m singular

sinistro (see-neesh-troo) adj ominous, sinister; m accident

sino (see-noo) m bell

sinónimo (see-no-nee-moo) m synonym

sintético (seengn-teh-tee-koo) adj synthetic

sintoma (seengn-toa-mer) m symptom

sintonizar (seengn-too-nee-zahr) v tune in

sinuoso (see-nwoa-zoo) adj winding

sirene (see-reh-ner) f siren

Síria (see-r<sup>y</sup>er) f Syria

**sírio** (*see*-rʸoo) *adj* Syrian; *m* Syrian

**sistema** (seesh-*tay*-mer) *m* system; ~ **de arrefecimento** cooling system; ~ **decimal** decimal system

**sistemático** (seesh-ter-*mah*-tee-koo) *adj* systematic

**sítio** (*see*-tʸoo) *m* site; seat; place, spot

**situação** (see-twer-*serng*ʷ) *f* (pl -ções) situation; position

**situado** (see-*twer*-dhoo) *adj* situated

**slide** (*sligh*-der) *m* slide

**smoking** (*smo*-keengg) *m* dinner-jacket; tuxedo *nAm*

**só** (so) *adv* only, alone; *adj* single, only

**soalheiro** (swer-lʸay-roo) *adj* sunny

**soalho** (*swah*-lʸoo) *m* parquet flooring

**soar** (swahr) *v* sound

**sob** (soabher) *prep* under

**sobejar** (soobhı-*zhahr*) *v* remain, \*be left over

**soberano** (soo-bher-*rer*-noo) *m* sovereign

**soberbo** (soo-*bhayr*-bhoo) *adj* superb

**sobrancelha** (soo-bhrerng-*say*-lʸer) *f* eyebrow

**sobre** (*soa*-bhrer) *prep* on, upon; over, above

**sobreexcitado** (soa-bhrer-ısh-see-*tah*-dhoo) *adj* overstrung

**sobreloja** (soa-bhrer-*lo*-zher) *f* mezzanine

**sobremesa** (soa-bhrer-*may*-zer) *f* dessert

**sobrenome** (soa-bhrer-*noa*-mer) *m* surname

**sobrescrito** (soa-bhrısh-*kree*-too) *m* envelope

**\*sobressair** (soa-bhrer-ser-*eer*) *v* excel; attract attention

**sobresselente** (soa-bhrer-ser-*layngn*-ter) *adj* spare

**sobretaxa** (soa-bhrer-*tah*-sher) *f* surcharge

**sobretudo** (soa-bhrer-*too*-dhoo) *adv* most of all; *m* topcoat, overcoat

**sobrevivência** (soa-bhrer-vee-*vayng*-sʸer) *f* survival

**sobreviver** (soa-bhrer-vee-*vayr*) *v* survive

**sobrinha** (soo-*bhree*-ñah) *f* niece

**sobrinho** (soo-*bhree*-ñah) *m* nephew

**sóbrio** (*so*-bhrʸoo) *adj* sober

**socar** (soo-*kahr*) *v* punch

**social** (soo sʸahl) *adj* (pl -ais) social

**socialismo** (soo-sʸer-*leezh*-moo) *m* socialism

**socialista** (soo-sʸer-*leesh*-ter) *adj* socialist; *m* socialist

**sociedade** (soo-sʸay-*dhah*-dher) *f* society; community; company

**sócio** (*so*-sʸoo) *m* associate; partner

**soco** (*soa*-koo) *m* punch

**socorrer** (soo-koo-*rrayr*) *v* help

**socorro** (soo-*koa*-rroo) *m* help; **primeiros socorros** first-aid

**soda** (*so*-dher) *f* soda-water

**sofá** (soo-*fah*) *m* sofa

**sofrer** (soo-*frayr*) *v* suffer

**sofrimento** (soo-free-*mayngn*-too) *m* suffering; affliction

**sogra** (*so*-grer) *f* mother-in-law

**sogro** (*soa*-groo) *m* father-in-law; **sogros** parents-in-law *pl*

**sol** (sol) *m* sun; sunshine; **nascer do** ~ sunrise; **pôr do** ~ sunset

**sola** (*so*-ler) *f* sole

**solar** (soo-*lahr*) *m* manor-house

**soldado** (soal-*dah*-dhoo) *m* soldier

**soldadura** (soal-der-*dhoo*-rer) *f* joint

**soldar** (soal-*dahr*) *v* solder; weld

**solene** (soo-*leh*-ner) *adj* solemn

**soletrar** (soo-ler-*trahr*) *v* \*spell

**solha** (*soa*-lʸer) *f* plaice

**solícito** (soo-*lee*-see-too) *adj* obliging

**sólido** (*so*-lee-dhoo) *adj* firm, solid; *m*

solid

**solitário** (soo-lee-*tah*-r<sup>y</sup>oo) *adj* lonely

**solo** (*so*-loo) *m* ground; earth, soil

**soltar** (soal-*tahr*) *v* unfasten

**solteirão** (soal-tay-r*rerng*<sup>w</sup>) *m* (pl -rões) elderly bachelor

**solteiro** (soal-*tay*-roo) *adj* single

**solteirona** (soal-tay-*roa*-ner) *f* spinster

**solto** (*soal*-too) *adj* loose

**solução** (soo-loo-*serng*<sup>w</sup>) *f* (pl -ções) solution

**soluço** (soo-*loo*-soo) *m* hiccup

**solúvel** (soo-*loo*-vehl) *adj* (pl -eis) soluble

**som** (sawng) *m* sound; **à prova de ~** soundproof

**soma** (*soa*-mer) *f* amount, sum; **~ global** lump sum

**somar** (soo-*mahr*) *v* add up

**sombra** (*sawngm*-brer) *f* shadow, shade; **~ para os olhos** eyeshadow

**sombrio** (*sawngm*-bree<sup>oo</sup>) *adj* sombre; gloomy, shady

**somente** (so-*mayngn*-ter) *adv* only; merely

**soneca** (soo-*neh*-ker) *f* nap

**sonhar** (soo-*ñahr*) *v* *dream

**sonho** (*soa*-ñoo) *m* dream

**sono** (*soa*-noo) *m* sleep

**sonolento** (soo-noo-*layngn*-too) *adj* sleepy

**sopa** (*soa*-per) *f* soup

**soprar** (soo-*prahr*) *v* *blow

**sopro** (*soa*-proo) *m* breath

**soro** (*soa*-roo) *m* serum

***sorrir** (soo-*rrer*) *v* smile; ***sorrir-se** grin

**sorriso** (soo-*rree*-zoo) *m* smile

**sorte** (*sor*-ter) *f* lot, destiny, fortune; chance; luck

**sorteio** (soor-*tay*-oo) *m* draw

**sortido** (soor-*tee*-dhoo) *m* assortment

**sortimento** (soor-tee-*mayngn*-too) *m* assortment

**sorvete** (soor-*vay*-ter) *mBr* ice-cream; sorbet

**sorvo** (*soar*-voo) *m* sip

**sossegado** (soo-ser-*gah*-dhoo) *adj* restful; quiet

**sossego** (soo-*say*-goo) *m* leisure; quiet, peace

**sótão** (*so*-terng<sup>w</sup>) *m* (pl ~s) attic

**sotaque** (soo-*tah*-ker) *m* accent

**soutien** (soo-t<sup>y</sup>ang) *m* brassiere, bra

**sozinho** (so-zee-ñoo) *adj* alone

**suado** (*swah*-dhoo) *adj* sweaty

**suaili** (swigh-*lee*) *m* Swahili

**suar** (swahr) *v* sweat; perspire

**suave** (*swah*-ver) *adj* mild, gentle, smooth

**suavizar** (swer-vee-*zahr*) *v* soften

**subalimentação** (soo-bher-lee-mayngn-ter-*serng*<sup>w</sup>) *f* malnutrition

**súbdito** (*soobh*-dhee-too) *m* subject

**subida** (soo-*bhee*-dher) *f* ascent; rise, climb

***subir** (soo-*bheer*) *v* ascend; mount, *rise; **~ para** *get on

**sublinhar** (soobh-lee-*ñahr*) *v* underline; stress

**submarino** (soobh-mer-*ree*-noo) *adj* underwater; *m* submarine

***submergir** (soobh-merr-*zheer*) *v* overwhelm; submerge

**submeter** (soobh-mer-*tayr*) *v* subject

**subordinado** (soo-bhoor-dhee-*nah*-dhoo) *adj* subordinate

**subornar** (soo-bhoor-*nahr*) *v* bribe

**suborno** (soo-*bhoar*-noo) *m* bribery

**subsequente** (soobh-ser-*kwayngn*-ter) *adj* subsequent

**subsídio** (soobh-*see*-dh<sup>y</sup>oo) *m* subsidy; grant, allowance

**subsistência** (soobh-seesh-*tayng*-s<sup>y</sup>er) *f* livelihood

**substância** (soo-bhish-*terng*-s<sup>y</sup>er) *f* substance

**substancial** (soo-bhish-terng-s<sup>y</sup>ahl) *adj* (pl -ais) substantial

**substantivo** (soo-bhish-terng-tee-voo) *m* noun

**\*substituir** (soo-bhish-tee-tweer) *v* replace, substitute

**substituto** (soo-bhish-tee-too-too) *m* substitute; deputy

**subterrâneo** (soobh-ter-rrer-n<sup>y</sup>oo) *adj* underground

**subtil** (soobh-teel) *adj* (pl -is) subtle

**\*subtrair** (soobh-trer-eer) *v* deduct, subtract

**suburbano** (soo-bhoor-bher-noo) *adj* suburban

**subúrbio** (soo-bhoor-bh<sup>y</sup>oo) *m* suburb

**subvenção** (soobh-vayng-serng<sup>w</sup>) *f* (pl -ções) grant

**sucata** (soo-kah-ter) *f* scrap-iron

**suceder** (soo-ser-dhayr) *v* succeed; happen, occur

**sucesso** (soo-seh-soo) *m* success; hit

**sucumbir** (soo-koongm-beer) *v* collapse, succumb

**sucursal** (soo-koor-sahl) *f* (pl -ais) branch

**sudoeste** (soo-dhwehsh-ter) *m* south-west

**Suécia** (sweh-s<sup>y</sup>er) *f* Sweden

**sueco** (sweh-koo) *adj* Swedish; *m* Swede

**sueste** (swehsh-ter) *m* south-east

**suéter** (sweh-tehr) *m* Br sweater

**suficiente** (soo-fee-s<sup>y</sup>ayng-ter) *adj* sufficient; enough; adequate

**sufocante** (soo-foo-kerng-ter) *adj* stuffy

**sufocar** (soo-foo-kahr) *v* choke

**sufrágio** (soo-frah-zh<sup>y</sup>oo) *m* suffrage

**\*sugerir** (soo-zher-reer) *v* suggest

**sugestão** (soo-zhish-terng<sup>w</sup>) *f* (pl -tões) suggestion

**Suíça** (swee-ser) *f* Switzerland

**suíças** (swee-sersh) *fpl* whiskers *pl*, sideburns *pl*

**suicídio** (swee-see-dh<sup>y</sup>oo) *m* suicide

**suíço** (swee-soo) *adj* Swiss; *m* Swiss

**sujar** (soo-zhahr) *v* dirty

**sujeito** (soo-zhay-too) *adj* subordinate; liable; *m* individual; subject; ~ **a** subject to; liable to; ~ **a taxas** dutiable

**sujidade** (soo-zhee-dhah-dher) *f* dirt

**sujo** (soo-zhoo) *adj* soiled, dirty; unclean

**sul** (sool) *m* south; **do** ~ southern

**sul-americano** (sool-er-mer-ree-ker-noo) *adj* Latin-American

**sulco** (sool-koo) *m* groove

**sumarento** (soo-mer-rayngn-too) *adj* juicy

**sumo** (soo-moo) *m* juice; squash

**suor** (swor) *m* perspiration, sweat

**superar** (soo-peh-rahr) *v* exceed, \*outdo

**superficial** (soo-pehr-fee-s<sup>y</sup>ahl) *adj* (pl -ais) superficial

**superfície** (soo-perr-fee-s<sup>y</sup>er) *f* surface

**supérfluo** (soo-pehr-flwoo) *adj* redundant, superfluous

**superintendente** (soo-perr-eengn-tayngn-dayngn-ter) *m* supervisor

**superintender** (soo-perr-eengn-tayngn-dayr) *v* supervise

**superior** (soo-per-r<sup>y</sup>oar) *adj* superior; upper; top

**superlativo** (soo-perr-ler-tee-voo) *adj* superlative; *m* superlative

**supermercado** (soo-pehr-merr-kah-dhoo) *m* supermarket

**superstição** (soo-perr-shtee-serng<sup>w</sup>) *f* (pl -ções) superstition

**supervisão** (soo-pehr-vee-zerng<sup>w</sup>) *f* supervision

**suplementar** (soo-pler-mayngn-tahr) *adj* extra, additional

**suplemento** (soo-pler-mayngn-too) *m* supplement

**suplicar** (soo-plee-*kahr*) v beg

**\*supor** (soo-*poar*) v assume, suppose; guess; **supondo que** supposing that

**suportar** (soo-poor-*tahr*) v support; endure, sustain, \*bear; suffer

**suporte** (soo-*por*-ter) m support

**supositório** (soo-poo-zee-*to*-r<sup>y</sup>oo) m suppository

**surdo** (soor-dhoo) adj deaf

**surgir** (soor-*zheer*) v \*arise

**surpreender** (soor-pr<sup>y</sup>ayngn-*dayr*) v surprise; amaze; \*catch

**surpresa** (soor-*pray*-zer) f surprise

**suspeita** (soosh-*pay*-ter) f suspicion

**suspeitar** (soosh-pay-*tahr*) v suspect

**suspeito** (soosh-*pay*-too) adj suspect; m suspect

**suspender** (soosh-payngn-*dayr*) v discontinue; suspend

**suspensão** (soosh-payng-*serng*<sup>w</sup>) f (pl -sões) suspension

**suspensórios** (soosh-payng-so-r<sup>y</sup>oosh) mpl braces pl; suspenders plAm

**sussurrar** (soo-soo-*rrahr*) v whisper

**sussurro** (soo-soo-rroo) m whisper

**\*suster** (soosh-*tayr*) v \*hold up

**susto** (*soosh*-too) m scare, fright

**sutura** (soo-*too*-rer) f stitch

**suturar** (soo-too-*rahr*) v \*sew up

# T

**tabacaria** (ter-bher-ker-*ree*-er) f cigar shop; tobacconist, tobacconist's

**tabaco** (ter-*bhah*-koo) m tobacco; **bolsa de ~** tobacco pouch; **~ para cachimbo** pipe tobacco; **~ para cigarro** cigarette tobacco

**tabela** (ter-*bheh*-ler) f table; chart; **~ de conversão** conversion chart

**taberna** (ter-*bhehr*-ner) f tavern; pub

**tabique** (ter-*bhee*-ker) m partition

**tabu** (ter-*bhoo*) m taboo

**tábua** (*tah*-bhwer) f board

**tabuleiro** (ter-bhoo-*lay*-roo) m tray; **~ de damas** draught-board; **~ de xadrez** checkerboard nAm

**taça** (*tah*-ser) f cup

**tacanho** (ter-*ker*-ñoo) adj narrow-minded

**táctica** (*tah*-tee-ker) f tactics pl

**tacto** (*tah*-too) m touch

**tagarela** (ter-ger-*reh*-ler) m chatterbox

**tailandês** (tigh-lerngn-*daysh*) adj Thai; m Thai

**Tailândia** (tigh-*lern*-d<sup>y</sup>er) f Thailand

**tainha** (ter-*ee*-ñer) f mullet

**tal** (tahl) adj (pl tais) such; **~ como** such as

**tala** (*tah*-ler) f splint

**talão** (ter-*lerng*<sup>w</sup>) m (pl talões) stub, counterfoil; coupon; heel

**talento** (ter-*layng*-too) m talent

**talha** (*tah*-l<sup>y</sup>er) f wood-carving; **obra de ~** carving

**talher** (ter-*l<sup>y</sup>ehr*) m cutlery; **preço do ~** cover charge

**talho** (*tah*-l<sup>y</sup>oo) m butcher

**talismã** (ter-leezh-*merng*) m lucky charm

**talvez** (tahl-*vaysh*) adv maybe, perhaps

**tamanco** (ter-*merng*-koo) m wooden shoe

**tamanho** (ter-*mer*-ñoo) m size; **~ extra-grande** outsize

**tâmara** (*ter*-mer-rer) f date

**também** (terngm-*berng*<sup>y</sup>) adv as well, also, too; **~ não** neither

**tampa** (*terngm*-per) f top; lid, cover

**tampão** (terngm-*perng*<sup>w</sup>) m (pl -pões) tampon

**tangerina** (terng-zher-*ree*-ner) f mandarin, tangerine

**tangível** (terng-*zhee*-vehl) adj (pl -eis) tangible

**tanque** (terng-ker) m pond; tank

**tanto** (terngn-too) adv as much; as; **tanto ... como** both ... and; **um ~** rather; pretty; somewhat

**tão** (terng^w) adv such, so; as

**tapar** (ter-pahr) v cover

**tapeçaria** (ter-per-ser-ree-er) f tapestry

**tapete** (ter-pay-ter) m mat; rug; carpet

**tarde** (tahr-dher) f afternoon; adv late; **esta ~** this afternoon

**tardio** (tahr-dhee°°) adj late

**tarefa** (tah-reh-fer) f duty, task

**tareia** (ter-ray-er) f spanking

**tarifa** (tah-ree-fer) f tariff; rate; **~ de estacionamento** parking fee; **~ nocturna** night rate

**tartaruga** (terr ter-roo-ger) f turtle

**taxa** (tah-sher) f Customs duty, charge; **~ de desconto** bank-rate; **~ de serviço** service charge; **~ do câmbio** rate of exchange

**táxi** (tahk-see) m taxi; cab; **ponto de táxis** Br taxi rank, taxi stand Am

**taxímetro** (terk-see-mer-troo) m taximeter

**te** (ter) pron you; yourself

**teatro** (t^yah-troo) m theatre; drama; **~ de fantoches** puppet-show; **~ de variedades** variety theatre

**tecelão** (ter-ser-lerng^w) m (pl ~s) weaver

**tecer** (ter-sayr) v *weave

**tecido** (ter-see-dhoo) m textile; material, tissue, fabric

**técnica** (tehk-nee-ker) f technique

**técnico** (tehk-nee-koo) adj technical; m technician

**tecnologia** (tehk-noo-loo-zhee-er) f technology

**tecto** (teh-too) m ceiling

**teimoso** (tay-moa-zoo) adj stubborn, obstinate; pig-headed

**tela** (teh-ler) f screen

**telefonar** (ter-ler-foo-nahr) v ring up, phone; call; call up Am

**telefone** (ter-ler-fo-ner) m phone, telephone

**telefonema** (ter-ler-foo-nay-mer) m telephone call

**telefonia** (ter-ler-foo-nee-er) f radio

**telefonista** (ter-ler-foo-neesh-ter) f telephonist; telephone operator

**telegrafar** (ter-ler-grer-fahr) v cable, telegraph

**telegrama** (ter-ler-grer-mer) m cable, telegram

**teleobjectiva** (teh-leh-oabh-zheh-tee-ver) f telephoto lens

**telepatia** (ter-ler-per-tee-er) f telepathy

**telesqui** (teh-leh-shkee) m ski-lift

**televisão** (ter-ler-vee-zerng^w) f (pl -sões) television; **aparelho de ~** television set; **~ a cabo** cable television; **~ a satélite** satellite television

**telha** (tay-l^yer) f tile

**telhado** (tɪ-l^yah-dhoo) m roof; **~ de colmo** thatched roof

**tema** (tay-mer) m theme

**temer** (ter-mayr) v dread

**temerário** (ter-mer-rah-r^yoo) adj daring

**temor** (ter-moar) m dread

**temperar** (tayngm-per-rahr) v flavour

**temperatura** (tayngm-per-rer-too-rer) f temperature; **~ ambiente** room temperature

**tempestade** (tayngm-pɪsh-tah-dher) f storm, tempest

**tempestuoso** (tayngm-pɪsh-twoa-zoo) adj stormy; thundery

**templo** (tayngm-ploo) m temple

**tempo** (tayngm-poo) m time; weather; **a ~** in time; **de tempos a tempos** now and then; **~ livre** spare time

**temporal** (tayngm-poo-*rahl*) *m* (pl -ais) gale

**temporário** (tayngm-poo-*rah*-rYoo) *adj* temporary

**tenaz** (ter-*nahsh*) *f* tongs *pl*; pincers *pl*

**tencionar** (tayng-sYoo-*nahr*) *v* intend

**tenda** (*tayngn*-der) *f* tent; stall

**tendão** (tayngn-*derng*ʷ) *m* (pl -dões) tendon, sinew

**tendência** (tayngn-*dayng*-sYer) *f* tendency; **\*ter ~** tend

**tender** (tayngn-*dayr*) *v* \*be inclined to; **~ para** tend to

**ténis** (*teh*-neesh) *m* tennis; **campo de ~** tennis-court; **~ de mesa** table tennis

**tenro** (*tayng*-rroo) *adj* tender

**tensão** (tayng-*serng*ʷ) *f* (pl -sões) tension; pressure, strain, stress; **~ arterial** blood pressure

**tenso** (*tayng*-soo) *adj* tense

**tentação** (tayngn-ter-*serng*ʷ) *f* (pl -ções) temptation

**tentar** (tayngn-*tahr*) *v* try, tempt; attempt

**tentativa** (tayngn-ter-*tee*-ver) *f* try, attempt

**tentilhão** (tayngn-tee-*lYerng*ʷ) *m* (pl -hões) finch

**teologia** (tʸoo-loo-*zhee*-er) *f* theology

**teoria** (tʸoo-*ree*-er) *f* theory

**teórico** (tʸo-ree-koo) *adj* theoretical

**tépido** (*teh*-pee-dhoo) *adj* tepid

**\*ter** (tayr) *v* \*have; **~ ares** look; **~ de** \*have to; \*be obliged to, \*must, \*be bound to, need to; **~ em stock** stock; **~ êxito** manage, succeed

**terapia** (ter-rer-*pee*-er) *f* therapy

**terça-feira** (tayr-ser-*fay*-rer) *f* Tuesday

**terceiro** (terr-*say*-roo) *num* third

**terebentina** (ter-rer-bhayngn-*tee*-ner) *f* turpentine

**termas** (*tehr*-mersh) *fpl* spa

**terminal** (terr-mee-*nahl*) *m* (pl -ais) terminal

**terminar** (terr-mee-*nahr*) *v* finish, end; expire; accomplish

**termo**[1] (*tayr*-moo) *m* term

**termo**[2] (*tehr*-moo) *m* thermos flask

**termómetro** (terr-*mo*-mer-troo) *m* thermometer

**termóstato** (terr-*mosh*-ter-too) *m* thermostat

**terno** (*tehr*-noo) *adj* tender; gentle; *mBr* suit

**terra** (*teh*-rrer) *f* earth; soil; land; **a ~** ashore; **em ~** ashore; **~ firme** mainland; **tremor de ~** earthquake

**terraço** (teh-*rrah*-soo) *m* terrace

**terreno** (ter-*rray*-noo) *m* terrain; grounds

**território** (ter-rree-*to*-rYoo) *m* territory

**terrível** (ter-*rree*-vehl) *adj* (pl -eis) terrible; awful, frightful, dreadful

**terror** (ter-*rroar*) *m* terror

**terrorismo** (ter-rroo-*reezh*-moo) *m* terrorism

**terrorista** (ter-rroo-*reesh*-ter) *m* terrorist

**tese** (*teh*-zer) *f* thesis

**teso** (*tay*-zoo) *adj* stiff; broke

**tesoura** (ter-*zoa*-rer) *f* scissors *pl*; **~ de unhas** nail-scissors *pl*

**tesoureiro** (ter-zoa-*ray*-roo) *m* treasurer

**tesouro** (ter-*zoa*-roo) *m* treasure; **~ público** treasury

**testa** (*tehsh*-ter) *f* forehead

**testamento** (tısh-ter-*mayngn*-too) *m* will

**teste** (*tehsh*-ter) *m* test

**testemunha** (tısh-ter-*moo*-ñer) *f* witness; **~ ocular** eye-witness

**testemunhar** (tısh-ter-moo-*ñahr*) *v* testify

**teu** (tay⁰⁰) *adj* (f **tua**) your; **teus** your

**têxteis** (*taysh*-taysh) *mpl* drapery

**texto** (*taysh*-too) *m* text

**tez** (taysh) *f* complexion

**tia** (*tee*-er) *f* aunt

**tifo** (*tee*-foo) *m* typhoid

**tigela** (tee-*zheh*-ler) *f* basin, bowl

**tigre** (*tee*-grer) *m* tiger

**tijolo** (tee-*zhoa*-loo) *m* brick

**tília** (*tee*-lᵞah) *f* lime; limetree

**timbre** (*teengm*-brer) *m* tone

**timidez** (tee-mee-*dhehsh*) *f* timidity; shyness

**tímido** (*tee*-mee-dhoo) *adj* timid; shy

**timoneiro** (tee-moo-*nay*-roo) *m* steersman, helmsman

**tímpano** (*teengm*-per-noo) *m* eardrum

**tingir** (teeng-*zheer*) *v* dye; **não tinge** fast-dyed

**tinta** (*teengn*-ter) *f* ink; dye, paint; ~ **de água** water-colour

**tinturaria** (teengn-too-rer-*ree*-er) *f* dry-cleaner's

**tio** (*tee*⁰⁰) *m* uncle

**típico** (*tee*-pee-koo) *adj* characteristic, typical

**tipo** (*tee*-poo) *m* type; fellow, guy, chap

**tiragem** (tee-rer-zher�) *f* issue

**tirano** (tee-*rer*-noo) *m* tyrant

**tira-nódoas** (tee-rer-*no*-dhwersh) *m* (pl ~) stain remover

**tirar** (tee-*rahr*) *v* *take out, *take away

**tiritar** (tee-ree-*tahr*) *v* tremble, shiver

**tiro** (*tee*-roo) *m* shot

**título** (*tee*-too-loo) *m* title; degree; heading

**toalha** (*twah*-lᵞer) *f* towel; ~ **de banho** bath towel; ~ **de mesa** tablecloth

**toca** (*to*-ker) *f* den

**toca-discos** (to-ker-*dheesh*-koosh) *mBr* (pl ~) record-player

**tocante** (too-*kerngn*-ter) *adj* touching

**tocar** (too-*kahr*) *v* touch; play; *ring; **não** ~ *keep off

**todavia** (toa-dher-*vee*-er) *conj* but; however; still

**todo** (*toa*-dhoo) *adj* entire, all; *m* whole; **de** ~ at all; ~ **o mundo** *Br* everyone, everybody

**toldo** (*toal*-doo) *m* awning; ~ **impermeável** tarpaulin

**tolerável** (too-ler-rah-*vehl*) *adj* (pl -eis) tolerable

**tolo** (*toa*-loo) *adj* foolish; *m* fool

**tom** (tawng) *m* tone; shade

**tomar** (too-*mahr*) *v* *catch, *take; ~ **conta de** *take over

**tomate** (too-*mah*-ter) *m* tomato

**tomilho** (too-mee-lᵞoo) *m* thyme

**tonelada** (too-ner-*lah*-dher) *f* ton

**tónico** (*to*-nee-koo) *m* tonic; ~ **capilar** hair tonic

**tontura** (tawngn-*too*-rer) *f* giddiness

**tópico** (*to*-pee-koo) *m* topic

**topo** (*toa*-poo) *m* height

**toque** (*to*-ker) *m* touch

**toranja** (too-*rerng*-zher) *f* grapefruit

**torção** (toor-*serng*ʷ) *f* (pl -ções) twist

**torcedor** (toor-ser-*dhoar*) *mBr* supporter

**torcedura** (toor-ser-*dhoo*-rer) *f* wrench

**torcer** (toor-*sayr*) *v* twist; sprain, wrench; **torcer-se** sprain; **torcido** crooked

**tordo** (*toar*-dhoo) *m* thrush

**tormento** (toor-*mayngn*-too) *m* torment

**tornar-se** (toor-*nahr*-ser) *v* *get; *become

**torneio** (toor-*nay*-oo) *m* tournament

**torneira** (toor-*nay*-rer) *f* tap; faucet *nAm*

**em torno de** (erng<sup>y</sup> *toar*-noo der) round

**tornozelo** (toor-noo-*zeh*-loo) *m* ankle

**toro** (*toa*-roo) *m* log

**torrada** (too-*rrah*-dher) *f* toast

**torre** (*toa*-rrer) *f* tower

**torto** (*toar*-too) *adj* crooked

**tortura** (toor-*too*-rer) *f* torture

**torturar** (toor-too-*rahr*) *v* torture

**tosse** (*to*-ser) *f* cough

*****tossir** (too-*seer*) *v* cough

**total** (too-*tahl*) *adj* (pl -ais) total; utter; *m* total

**totalitário** (too-ter-lee-*tah*-r<sup>y</sup>oo) *adj* totalitarian

**totalizador** (too-ter-lee-zer-*dhoar*) *m* totalizator

**totalmente** (too-terl-*mayngn*-ter) *adv* completely; altogether

**toucador** (toa-ker-*dhoar*) *m* dressing-table

**tourada** (toa-*rah*-dher) *f* bullfight

**touro** (*toa*-roo) *m* bull

**tóxico** (*tok*-see-koo) *adj* toxic

**trabalhador** (trer-bher-l<sup>y</sup>er-*dhoar*) *adj* industrious; *m* worker

**trabalhar** (trer-bher-*l<sup>y</sup>ahr*) *v* work; ~ **demais** overwork

**trabalho** (trer-*bhah*-l<sup>y</sup>oo) *m* work, labour; job; difficulty; ~ **manual** handwork; handicraft

**traça** (*trah*-ser) *f* moth

**traço** (*trah*-soo) *m* dash; trait; ~ **caracterial** characteristic

**tractor** (trer-*toar*) *m* tractor

**tradição** (trer-dhee-*serng<sup>w</sup>*) *f* (pl -ções) tradition

**tradicional** (trer-dhee-s<sup>y</sup>oo-*nahl*) *adj* (pl -ais) traditional

**tradução** (trer-dhoo-*serng<sup>w</sup>*) *f* (pl -ções) translation

**tradutor** (trer-dhoo-*toar*) *m* translator

*****traduzir** (trer-dhoo-*zeer*) *v* translate; interpret

**tragédia** (trer-*zheh*-dh<sup>y</sup>er) *f* tragedy; drama

**trágico** (*trer*-zhee-koo) *adj* tragic

**traição** (trigh-*serng<sup>w</sup>*) *f* (pl -ções) treason

**traidor** (trigh-*dhoar*) *m* traitor

*****trair** (trer-*eer*) *v* betray

**traje** (*trah*-zher) *m* dress; ~ **a rigor** evening dress; ~ **nacional** national dress

**tralha** (*trah*-l<sup>y</sup>er) *f* junk

**tranquilidade** (trerng-kwee-lee-*dhah*-dher) *f* quiet

**tranquilizar** (trerng-kwee-lee-*zahr*) *v* reassure

**tranquilo** (trerng-*kwee*-loo) *adj* tranquil; calm, peaceful, still, quiet

**transacção** (trerng-zah-*serng<sup>w</sup>*) *f* (pl -ções) transaction

**transatlântico** (trerng-zert-*lerngn*-tee-koo) *adj* transatlantic

*****fazer transbordo** (fer-*zayr* trerngz-*bhoar*-doo) change

**transeunte** (trerng-z<sup>y</sup>oongn-ter) *m* passer-by

*****transferir** (trerngsh-fer-*reer*) *v* transfer; postpone

**transformador** (trerngsh-foor-mer-*dhoar*) *m* transformer

**transformar** (trerngsh-foor-*mahr*) *v* transform; ~ **em** turn into

*****transgredir** (trerngzh-grer-*dheer*) *v* offend, violate

**transição** (trerng-zee-*serng<sup>w</sup>*) *f* (pl -ções) transition

**trânsito** (*trerng*-zee-too) *m* traffic

**translúcido** (trerngzh-*loo*-see-dhoo) *adj* sheer; translucent

**transmissão** (trerngzh-mee-*serng<sup>w</sup>*) *f* (pl -sões) transmission

**transmitir** (trerngzh-mee-*teer*) *v* transmit

**transparente** (trersh-per-*rerngn*-ter) *adj* transparent

**transpiração** (trerɐgsh-pee-rer-*serɐg*ᵂ) f perspiration

**transpirar** (trerɐgsh-pee-*rahr*) v perspire

**transportar** (trerɐgsh-poor-*tahr*) v transport; carry

**transporte** (trerɐgsh-*por*-ter) m transportation, transport

**transtornado** (trerɐgsh-toor-*nah*-dhoo) adj *upset

**transtornar** (trerɐgsh-toor-*nahr*) v *upset

**transversal** (trerɐgzh-verr-*sahl*) f (pl -ais) side-street

**trapalhada** (trer-per-*lᵞah*-dher) f mess; muddle; *fazer ~ muddle

**trapo** (*trah*-poo) m rag; cloth

**traquete** (trer-*kay*-ter) m foresail

**traseiro** (trer-*zay*-roo) m bottom

**tratado** (trer-*tah*-dhoo) m essay; treaty

**tratamento** (trer-ter-*mayɐgn*-too) m treatment; ~ de beleza beauty treatment

**tratar** (trer-*tahr*) v treat; handle; ~ com *deal with; ~ de nurse, *take care of; attend to, see to

*trautear (trou-t*ᵞahr*) v hum

**travão** (trer-*verɐg*ᵂ) m (pl -vões) brake; tambor do ~ brake drum; ~ de mão hand-brake; ~ de pé foot-brake

**travar** (trer-*vahr*) v slow down; break

**travessa** (trer-*veh*-ser) f dish

**travessão** (trer-ver-*serɐg*ᵂ) m (pl -sões) hair-grip

**travessia** (trer-verr-*see*-er) f crossing, passage

**travesso** (trer-*vay*-soo) adj naughty

*trazer (trer-*zayr*) v *bring

**trecho** (*tray*-shoo) m stretch; extract; excerpt; passage

**treinador** (tray-ner-*dhoar*) m coach

**treinar** (tray-*nahr*) v train

**treino** (*tray*-noo) m training

**trela** (*treh*-ler) f lead, leash

**trem** (trerɐgᵞ) mBr train

**tremendo** (trer-*mayɐgn*-doo) adj terrible

**tremer** (trer-*mayr*) v shiver, tremble

**trémulo** (*treh*-moo-loo) adj shivery

**trenó** (trer-*no*) m sleigh; sledge

**trepar** (trer-*pahr*) v climb

**três** (traysh) num three; ~ quartos three-quarter

**trevas** (*treh*-versh) fpl dark

**trevo** (*tray*-voo) m clover, shamrock

**treze** (*tray*-zer) num thirteen

**triangular** (tree-erɐg-goo-*lahr*) adj triangular

**triângulo** (tree-*erɐg*-goo-loo) m triangle

**tribo** (*tree*-bhoo) f tribe

**tribuna** (tree-*bhoo*-ner) f stand; pulpit

**tribunal** (tree-bhoo-*nahl*) m (pl -ais) law court; court

**tributar** (tree-bhoo-*tahr*) v raise

**tricotar** (tree-koo-*tahr*) v *knit

**trigésimo** (tree-*zheh*-zee-moo) num thirtieth

**trigo** (*tree*-goo) m wheat; corn

**trimestral** (tree-mɪsh-*trahl*) adj (pl -ais) quarterly

**trimestre** (tree-*mehsh*-trer) m quarter

**trinchar** (treeɐg-*shahr*) v carve

**trinta** (*treeɐgn*-ter) num thirty

**tripulação** (tree-poo-ler-*serɐg*ᵂ) f (pl -ções) crew

**triste** (*treesh*-ter) adj sad

**tristeza** (treesh-*tay*-zer) f sorrow, sadness

**triturar** (tree-too-*rahr*) v *grind

**triunfante** (trᵞoong-*ferɐgn*-ter) adj triumphant

**triunfar** (trᵞoong-*fahr*) v triumph

**triunfo** (trᵞoong-foo) m triumph

**troar** (trwahr) v thunder

**troca** (*tro*-ker) f exchange

troça (*tro*-ser) f mockery

trocar (troo-*kahr*) v change, exchange; switch; swap

troçar (tro-*sahr*) v mock, ridicule

troco (*troa*-koo) m change

troleicarro (tro-lay-*kah*-rroo) m trolley-bus

trombeta (trawngm-*bay*-ter) f trumpet

trompa (trawngm-per) f horn

tronco (trawng-koo) m trunk

trono (*troa*-noo) m throne

tropas (tro-persh) fpl troops pl

tropeçar (troo-per-*sahr*) v stumble

tropical (troo-pee-*kahl*) adj (pl -ais) tropical

trópicos (tro-pee-koosh) mpl tropics pl

trotineta (tro-tee-*neh*-ter) f scooter

trovão (troo-*verng*ʷ) m (pl -vões) thunder

trovoada (troo-*vwah*-dher) f thunderstorm

truque (*troo*-ker) m trick

truta (*troo*-ter) f trout

tu (too) pron you; ~ mesmo yourself

tubarão (too-bher-*rerng*ʷ) m (pl -rões) shark

tuberculose (too-bherr-koo-*lo*-zer) f tuberculosis

tubo (*too*-bhoo) m tube; ~ respirador snorkel

tudo (*too*-dhoo) pron everything; ~ o que whatever

tulipa (too-*lee*-per) f tulip

tumor (too-*moar*) m growth, tumour

túmulo (*too*-moo-loo) m tomb

túnel (*too*-nehl) m (pl -eis) tunnel

túnica (*too*-nee-ker) f tunic

Tunísia (too-nee-zee-er) f Tunisia

tunisino (too-nee-*see*-noo) adj Tunisian; m Tunisian

turba (*toor*-bher) f crowd

turbina (toor-*bhee*-ner) f turbine

turbulento (toor-bhoo-*layngn*-too) adj rowdy

turco (*toor*-koo) adj Turkish; m Turk

turismo (too-*reezh*-moo) m tourism

turista (too-*reesh*-ter) m tourist

turno (*toor*-noo) m gang, shift

Turquia (toor-*kee*-er) f Turkey

tutela (too-*teh*-ler) f custody

tutor (too-*toar*) m tutor, guardian

tweed (tweed) m tweed

# U

úlcera (*ool*-ser-rer) f ulcer; sore; ~ gástrica gastric ulcer

ulmeiro (ool-*may*-roo) m elm

ulterior (ool-ter-rʸoar) adj further; subsequent

ultimamente (ool-tee-mer-*mayngn*-ter) adv lately

último (*ool*-tee-moo) adj ultimate, last

ultraje (ool-*trah*-zher) m outrage; offence

ultramarino (ool-trer-mer-*ree*-noo) adj overseas

ultrapassar (ool-trer-per-*sahr*) v pass, *overtake; ultrapassagem proibida no overtaking

ultravioleta (ool-trer-vʸoo-*lay*-ter) adj ultraviolet

um (oong) num (f uma) one; art a art; mais ~ another; ~ ou outro either

umbigo (oongm-*bee*-goo) m navel

unânime (oo-*ner*-nee-mer) adj unanimous; like-minded

unguento (oong-*gwayngn*-too) m ointment, salve

unha (*oo*-ñer) f nail; arranjar as unhas manicure

união (oo-nʸ*erng*ʷ) f (pl uniões)

union; **União Européia** European Union

**unicamente** (oonee-ker-*mayngn*-ter) *adv* exclusively

**único** (*oo*-nee-koo) *adj* sole, unique

**unidade** (oo-nee-*dhah*-der) *f* unit; unity; ~ **monetária** monetary unit

**unido** (oo-*nee*-dhoo) *adj* joint

**uniforme** (oo-nee-*for*-mer) *adj* uniform; *m* uniform

**unilateral** (oo-nee-ler-ter-*rahl*) *adj* (pl -ais) one-sided

**unir** (oo-*neer*) *v* unite; join; connect

**universal** (oonee-verr-*sahl*) *adj* (pl -ais) universal

**universidade** (oo-nee-verr-see-*dhah*-der) *f* university

**universo** (oo-nee-*vehr*-soo) *m* universe

**uns** (oongsh) *pron* (*f* umas) some

**untar** (oongn-*tahr*) *v* lubricate

**urbano** (oor-*bher*-noo) *adj* urban

**urgência** (oor-*zhayng*-s*Y*er) *f* urgency

**urgente** (oor-*zhayng*-ter) *adj* urgent; pressing

**urina** (oo-*ree*-ner) *f* urine

**urso** (*oor*-soo) *m* bear

**Uruguai** (oo-roo-*gwer*ee) *m* Uruguay

**uruguaio** (oo-roo-*gwigh*-oo) *adj* Uruguayan; *m* Uruguayan

**urzal** (oor-*zahl*) *m* moor

**urze** (*oor*-zay) *f* heather

**usar** (oo-*zahr*) *v* use; employ; *wear

**uso** (*oo*-zoo) *m* use; usage

**usual** (oo-*zwahl*) *adj* (pl -ais) usual; customary, ordinary

**utensílio** (oo-tayng-*seel*-*Y*oo) *m* utensil

**utente** (oo-*tayng*-ter) *m* user

**útero** (*oo*-ter-roo) *m* womb

**útil** (*oo*-teel) *adj* (pl úteis) useful; helpful

**utilidade** (oo-tee-lee-*dhah*-dher) *f* utility; use

**utilizar** (oo-tee-lee-*zahr*) *v* utilize; employ

**utilizável** (oo-ter-lee-*zah*-vehl) *adj* (pl -eis) usable

**uvas** (*oo*-versh) *fpl* grapes *pl*

# V

**vaca** (*vah*-ker) *f* cow; **pele de** ~ cowhide

**vacilante** (ver-see-*lerngn*-ter) *adj* unsteady; shaky

**vacilar** (ver-see-*lahr*) *v* falter

**vacinação** (ver-see-ner-*serng*ʷ) *f* (pl -ções) vaccination

**vacinar** (ver-see-*nahr*) *v* vaccinate

**vácuo** (*vah*-kwoo) *m* vacuum

**vadiagem** (ver-dh*Y*ah-zherng*Y*) *f* vagrancy

**vadiar** (ver-dh*Y*ahr) *v* tramp

**vadio** (ver-*dhee*ᵒᵒ) *m* tramp

**vaga** (*vah*-ger) *f* vacancy

***vagabundear** (ver-ger-bhoongn-d*Y*ahr) *v* roam

**vagabundo** (ver-ger-*bhoongn*-doo) *m* tramp

**vagão** (ver-*gerng*ʷ) *m* (pl vagões) waggon

**vagar** (ver-*gahr*) *v* vacate; *m* leisure

**vago** (*vah*-goo) *adj* vacant; faint, vague; obscure, dim

***vaguear** (ver-*g*ʸ*ahr*) *v* wander

**vaidoso** (vigh-*dhoa*-zoo) *adj* vain; proud

**vale** (*vah*-ler) *m* valley; voucher; ~ **postal** postal order

**valente** (ver-*layngn*-ter) *adj* brave; plucky

**valentia** (ver-layngn-*tee*-er) *f* courage

***valer** (ver-*layr*) *v* *be worth; ~ **a pena** *be worth-while

**valeta** (ver-*lay*-ter) *f* gutter

**valete** (ver-*leh*-ter) *m* knave

**válido** (*vah*-lee-dhoo) *adj* valid

**valioso** (ver-*lYoa*-zoo) *adj* valuable

**valor** (ver-*loar*) *m* value; worth; **de ~** valuable; **sem ~** worthless; **valores** valuables

**valsa** (*vahl*-ser) *f* waltz

**válvula** (*vahl*-voo-ler) *f* valve

**vantagem** (verngn-*tah*-zherngY) *f* profit, advantage; benefit

**vantajoso** (verngn-ter-*zhoa*-zoo) *adj* advantageous

**vão** (verngW) *adj* (f vã; pl ~s) vain

**vapor** (ver-*poar*) *m* vapour, steam

**vaporizador** (ver-poo-ree-zer-*dhoar*) *m* atomizer

**vara** (*vah*-rer) *f* rod

**varanda** (ver-*rerngn*-der) *f* veranda; balcony

**varão** (ver-*rerng*W) *m* (pl varões) rod

**variação** (ver-rYer-*serng*W) *f* (pl -ções) variation

**variado** (ver-*rYah*-dhoo) *adj* varied

**variar** (ver-*rYahr*) *v* vary

**variável** (ver-*rYah*-vehl) *adj* (pl -eis) variable

**varicela** (ver-ree-*seh*-ler) *f* chickenpox

**variedade** (ver-rYay-*dhah*-dher) *f* variety; **teatro de variedades** music-hall

**varíola** (ver-*ree∘∘*-ler) *f* smallpox

**vários** (*vah*-rYoosh) *adj* several

**variz** (vah-*reesh*) *f* varicose vein

**varrer** (ver-*rrayr*) *v* \*sweep

**vasilha** (ver-*zee*-ger) *f* vessel

**vaso** (*vah*-zoo) *m* vase; pot; **~ sanguíneo** blood-vessel

**vassoura** (ver-*soa*-rer) *f* broom

**vasto** (*vahsh*-too) *adj* vast; extensive; wide, broad

**vau** (vou) *m* ford

**vazar** (ver-*zahr*) *v* \*shed, leak; empty

**vazio** (ver-*zee∘∘*) *adj* empty

**veadinho** (vVer-*dhee*-ñoo) *m* fawn

**veado** (vVah-dhoo) *m* deer

**vegetariano** (vI-zher-ter-rYer-noo) *m* vegetarian

**veia** (*vay*-Yer) *f* vein

**veículo** (vay-*ee*-koo-loo) *m* vehicle

**vela** (*veh*-ler) *f* sail; yachting; candle; **~ de ignição** sparking-plug

**veleidade** (ver-lay-*dhah*-dher) *f* whim

**velhice** (vI-*lYee*-ser) *f* old age

**velhíssimo** (vI-*lYee*-see-moo) *adj* ancient

**velho** (*veh*-lYoo) *adj* old; aged; ancient; stale; **mais ~** elder; **o mais ~** eldest

**velhote** (veh-*lYo*-ter) *adj* old

**velocidade** (ver-loo-see-*dhah*-dher) *f* speed, rate; gear; \***ir com ~** \*speed; **limitação de ~** speed limit; **~ de cruzeiro** cruising speed; **~ máxima** speed limit

**velocímetro** (ver-loo-*see*-mer-troo) *m* speedometer

**velocípede** (ver-loo-*see*-per-dher) *m* cycle

**veloz** (ver-*losh*) *adj* rapid

**veludo** (ver-*loo*-dhoo) *m* velvet

**vencedor** (vayng-ser-*dhoar*) *adj* winning; *m* winner

**vencer** (vayng-*sayr*) *v* \*win; \*overcome

**vencido** (vayng-*see*-dhoo) *adj* due

**vencimento** (vayng-see-*mayngn*-too) *m* expiry; salary

**venda** (*vayngn*-der) *f* sale; **à ~** for sale; **~ por grosso** wholesale

**vendável** (vayngn-*dah*-vehl) *adj* (pl -eis) saleable

**vendedor** (vayngn-der-*dhoar*) *m* salesman; **~ de aves de criação** poulterer; **~ de jornais** newsagent

**vendedora** (vayngn-der-*dhoa*-rer) *f* salesgirl

**vender** (vayngn-*dayr*) *v* \*sell; **~ a retalho** retail

**veneno** (ver-*nay*-noo) *m* poison

**venenoso** (ver-ner-*noa*-zoo) *adj* poisonous

**veneração** (ver-ner-rer-*serng*ᵂ) *f* respect

**venerável** (ver-ner-*rah*-vehl) *adj* (pl -eis) venerable

**Venezuela** (ver-ner-*zway*-ler) *f* Venezuela

**venezuelano** (ver-ner-zway-*ler*-noo) *adj* Venezuelan; *m* Venezuelan

**ventilação** (vayngn-tee-ler-*ser*ᵒᵒ) *f* (pl -ções) ventilation

**ventilador** (vayngn-tee-ler-*dhoar*) *m* fan, ventilator

**ventilar** (vayngn-tee-*lahr*) *v* ventilate

**vento** (*vayngn*-too) *m* wind

**ventoso** (vayngn-*toa*-zoo) *adj* gusty, windy

**ventre** (*vayngn*-trer) *m* belly; **prisão de** ~ constipation

*****ver** (vayr) *v* *see; notice

**Verão** (ver-*rerng*ᵂ) *m* (pl -rões) summer; **pleno** ~ (high) summer

**verbal** (verr-*bhahl*) *adj* (pl -ais) verbal

**verbo** (*vehr*-bhoo) *m* verb

**verdade** (verr-*dhah*-dher) *f* truth

**verdadeiramente** (verr-dher-dhay-rer-*mayngn*-ter) *adv* really

**verdadeiro** (verr-dher-*dhay*-roo) *adj* true; very, real; actual

**verde** (*vayr*-dher) *adj* green

**veredicto** (ver-rer-*dhee*-too) *m* verdict

**vergonha** (verr-*ewoa*-ñer) *f* shame; **que vergonha!** shame!; *****ter** ~ *be ashamed

**verídico** (ver-*ree*-dhee-koo) *adj* truthful

**verificar** (ver-rer-fee-*kahr*) *v* verify; check

**verme** (*vehr*-mer) *m* worm

**vermelho** (verr-*meh*-lᵞoo) *adj* crimson, red

**verniz** (verr-*neesh*) *m* varnish; lacquer; ~ **de unhas** nail-polish

**verosímil** (vay-roa-*see*-meel) *adj* (pl

-meis) credible

**versão** (verr-*serng*ᵂ) *f* (pl -sões) version

**verso** (*vehr*-soo) *m* verse

**vertente** (vehr-*tayngn*-ter) *f* slope

**verter** (verr-*tayr*) *v* pour; leak

**vertical** (verr-tee-*kahl*) *adj* (pl -cais) vertical

**vertigem** (verr-tee-zhergᵞ) *f* vertigo; dizziness

**vespa** (*vaysh*-per) *f* wasp

**veste** (*vehsh*-ter) *f* robe

**vestiário** (vish-tᵞah-rᵞoo) *m* checkroom *nAm*

**vestíbulo** (vish-*tee*-bhoo-loo) *m* hall; lobby

**vestido** (vish-*tee*-dhoo) *m* dress; gown, frock; *****trazer** ~ *wear; ~ **comprido** robe

*****vestir** (vish-*teer*) *v* dress; *put on; *****vestir-se** dress

**vestuário** (vish-*twah*-rᵞoo) *m* clothes *pl*; ~ **de desporto** sportswear

**veterinário** (ver-ter-ree-*nah*-rᵞoo) *m* veterinary surgeon

**véu** (veh ᵒᵒ) *m* veil

**vez** (vaysh) *f* time; turn; **alguma** ~ some time; **às vezes** sometimes; **de** ~ **em quando** occasionally; **duas vezes** twice; **em** ~ **de** instead of; **muitas vezes** often; **outra** ~ again; **uma** ~ once; **uma** ~ **mais** once more

**via** (*vee*-er) *prep* via; *f* track; lane; ~ **férrea** railway; railroad *nAm*; ~ **navegável** waterway

**viaduto** (vᵞer-*dhoo*-too) *m* viaduct

**viagem** (vᵞah-zhergᵞ) *f* voyage; trip, journey; passage; ~ **de regresso** return journey

**viajante** (vᵞer-*zhern*-ter) *m* traveller

**viajar** (vᵞer-*zhahr*) *v* travel; ~ **de automóvel** motor

**vibração** (vee-bhrer-*serng*ᵂ) *f* (pl

-ções) vibration

**vibrar** (vee-*bhrahr*) v vibrate; tremble

**vicioso** (vee-*sᵞoa*-zoo) adj vicious

**vida** (vee-dher) f life; lifetime; **cheio de** ~ lively; **com** ~ alive

**videira** (vee-*dhay*-rer) f vine

**vídeo câmera** (vee-dhay-oo ker-mer-er) f video camera

**videocassete** (vee-dhay-oo-kah-*seh*-ter) m video cassette; video recorder

**vidraça** (vee-*dhrah*-ser) f window-pane

**vidro** (vee-dhroo) m glass; pane; **de** ~ glass; ~ **colorido** stained glass

**viela** (vᵞeh-ler) f lane

**vigésimo** (vee-*zheh*-zee-moo) num twentieth

**vigiar** (vee-*zhᵞahr*) v patrol; watch

**vigilante** (vee-zhee-*lerngn*-ter) adj vigilant

**vila** (vee-ler) f borough; fBr villa

**vinagre** (vee-*nah*-grer) m vinegar

**vindima** (veengn-dee-mer) f vintage

**vingança** (veeng-*gerng*-serng) f revenge

**vinha** (vee-ñer) f vineyard

**vinho** (vee-ñoo) m wine; **negociante de vinhos** wine-merchant

**vinte** (veengn-ter) num twenty

**viola** (vee-ᵞo-ler) f guitar

**violação** (vᵞoo-ler-*serngʷ*) f (pl -ções) violation

**violar** (vᵞoo-*lahr*) v assault, rape

**violência** (vᵞoo-*layng*-sᵞer) f violence

**violento** (vᵞoo-*layngn*-too) adj violent; fierce, severe

**violeta** (vᵞoo-*lay*-ter) f violet

**violino** (vᵞoo-*lee*-noo) m violin

***vir** (veer) v *come; ~ **a ser** *become

**viragem** (vee-*rah*-zherngᵞ) f turn

**virar** (vee-*rahr*) v turn; **virar-se** turn round

**virgem** (veer-zherngᵞ) f virgin

**vírgula** (veer-goo-ler) f comma

**virilha** (ver-*ree*-lᵞer) f groin

**virtude** (veer-*too*-dher) f virtue

**visão** (vee-*zerngʷ*) f (pl visões) vision

**visar** (vee-*zahr*) v aim at

**visibilidade** (vee-zee-bher-lee-*dhah*-dher) f visibility

**visita** (vee-*zee*-ter) f visit; call; ***fazer uma** ~ a call on

**visitante** (vee-zee-*terngn*-ter) m visitor

**visitar** (vee-zee-*tahr*) v visit; call on

**visível** (vee-*zee*-vehl) adj (pl -eis) visible

**vislumbrar** (veezh-loongm-*brahr*) v glimpse

**vislumbre** (veezh-*loongm*-brer) m glimpse

**vison** (vee-*son*) m mink

**visor** (vee-*zoar*) m view-finder

**vista** (veesh-ter) f sight; view; **em** ~ **de** considering; **ponto de** ~ point of view; outlook

**visto** (veesh-too) m visa; ~ **que** since; as

**vital** (vee-*tahl*) adj (pl -ais) vital

**vitamina** (vee-ter-*mee*-ner) f vitamin

**vitela** (vee-*teh*-ler) f veal

**vitelo** (vee-*teh*-loo) m calf

**vítima** (vee-tee-mer) f victim; casualty

**vitória** (vee-to-rᵞer) f victory

**vitrina** (vee-*tree*-ner) f show-case

**viúva** (vᵞoo-ver) f widow

**viúvo** (vᵞoo-voo) m widower

**viveiro** (vee-*vay*-roo) m nursery

**vivenda** (vee-*vayngn*-der) f villa

**viver** (vee-*vayr*) v live; experience

**vivo** (vee-voo) adj alive, live; brisk, vivid

**vizinhança** (vee-zee-*ñerng*-ser) f neighbourhood; vicinity

**vizinho** (vee-zee-ñoo) adj near; neighbouring; m neighbour

**voar** (vwahr) v *fly

**vocabulário** (voo-ker-bhoo-*lah*-rᵞoo) m

vocabulary

**vocal** (voo-*kahl*) *adj* (pl -ais) vocal

**vocalista** (voo-ker-*leesh*-ter) *m* vocalist

**vocês** (vo-*saysh*) *pron* you; ~ **mesmos** yourselves

**vogal** (voo-*gahl*) *f* (pl -ais) vowel

**volante** (voo-*lerngn*-ter) *m* steering-wheel

**volt** (voalt) *m* volt

**volta** (*vol*-ter) *f* way back; turn, curve, bend; round, ride; à ~ about; round; à ~ **de** around; **em** ~ about; **em** ~ **de** about, around; **ida e** ~ round trip *Am*

**voltagem** (voal-*tah*-zherng^Y) *f* voltage

**voltar** (voal-*tahr*) *v* return; turn round; ~ **atrás** turn back

**volume** (voo-*loo*-mer) *m* volume; bulk; package

**volumoso** (voo-loo-*moa*-zoo) *adj* bulky; big

**voluntário** (voo-loongn-*tah*-r^Yoo) *adj* voluntary; *m* volunteer

**volúpia** (voo-*loo*-p^Yer) *f* lust

**vomitar** (voo-mee-*tahr*) *v* vomit

**vontade** (vawngn-*tah*-dher) *f* will; desire; à ~ casual; **boa** ~ goodwill; **de boa** ~ gladly, willingly; **de má** ~ unwilling; **pouco à** ~ uneasy; *ter ~ **de** fancy, *feel like

**voo** (*voa*-oo) *m* flight; ~ **charter** charter flight; ~ **de regresso** return flight; ~ **nocturno** night flight

**vosso** (*vo*-soo) *adj* your

**votação** (voo-ter-*serng*^w) *f* (pl -ções) vote

**votar** (voo-*tahr*) *v* vote

**voto** (*vo*-too) *m* vote; vow

**voz** (vosh) *f* voice; **em** ~ **alta** aloud

**vulcão** (vool-*kerng*^w) *m* (pl -cões) volcano

**vulgar** (vool-*gahr*) *adj* vulgar; ordinary

**vulnerável** (vool-ner-*rah*-vehl) *adj* (pl -eis) vulnerable

# X

**xadrez** (sher-*dhraysh*) *m* chess; **em** ~ chequered

**xaile** (*shigh*-ler) *m* shawl

**xale** (*shah*-ler) *m* shawl

**xarope** (sher-*ro*-per) *m* syrup

**xeque!** (*sheh*-ker) check!

**xícara** (*shee*-ker-rer) *f Br* cup

# Z

**zangado** (zerng-*gah*-dhoo) *adj* angry, cross

**zaragata** (zer-rer-*gah*-ter) *f* row

**zebra** (*zay*-bhrer) *f* zebra

**zelo** (*zay*-loo) *m* zeal; diligence

**zeloso** (zer-*loa*-zoo) *adj* zealous; diligent

**zénite** (*zeh*-nee-ter) *m* zenith

**zero** (*zeh*-roo) *m* nought, zero

**zinco** (*zeeng*-koo) *m* zinc

**zodíaco** (zoo-*dhee*-er-koo) *m* zodiac

**zona** (*zoa*-ner) *f* area, zone; ~ **de estacionamento** parking zone; ~ **industrial** industrial area

**zoologia** (zoo-oa-loo-*zhee*-er) *f* zoology

# Menu Reader

## Food

à, à moda de in the style of
abacate avocado pear
abacaxi pineapple
abóbora pumpkin (US winter squash)
açafrão saffron
acará, acarajé portion of fritters made of black-eyed bean purée, ground, dried shrimps and hot peppers
acelga swiss chard
acepipes hors d'œuvre
acompanhamento vegetables, side dish
açorda thick soup or side dish where bread is a principal ingredient
  ~ alentejana with poached eggs, garlic, coriander leaves and olive-oil
  ~ de bacalhau with dried cod, sliced and fried in garlic-flavoured olive-oil
  ~ à moda de Sesimbra with fish, garlic and coriander leaves
açúcar sugar
agrião watercress
aipim cassava root
aipo celeriac

alcachofra artichoke
  fundo de ~ bottom
alcaparra caper
alecrim rosemary
aletria 1) vermicelli, thin noodles 2) dessert made with vermicelli
alface lettuce
alheira garlic sausage made of breadcrumbs and different kinds of minced meat
  ~ à transmontana served with fried eggs, fried potatoes and cabbage
alho garlic
  ~ francês/-porro leek
almoço lunch
almôndega ball of fish or meat
alperce apricot
amargo bitter
amêijoas baby clams
  ~ à bulhão pato fried in olive-oil with garlic and coriander
  ~ à espanhola baked in the oven with onions, tomatoes, peppers, garlic and herbs
  ~ ao natural steamed with herbs and served with melted butter and lemon juice
ameixa plum
  ~ seca prune

**amêndoa** almond
**amendoim** peanut
**amora** blackberry
**ananás** pineapple
**anchova** anchovy
**angu** cassava-root flour or maize boiled in water and salt
**ao** in the style of
**arenque** herring
**arroz** rice
~ **de Cabidela** kind of risotto with giblets and chicken blood, flavoured with vinegar
~ **doce** pudding flavoured with cinnamon
~ **de frango** baked with chicken
~ **de manteiga** cooked in water and butter
~ **de pato no forno** duck cooked with bacon and *chouriço* then baked with rice
~ **tropeiro** with *carne de sol*
**asparago** asparagus
**assado** roast
**atum** tuna fish
**bife de** ~ cutlet (US steak) marinated in white wine and fried in olive-oil
**aveia** oats
**avelã** hazelnut
**aves** fowl
**azeda** sorrel
**azedo** sour
**azeite** olive-oil
~ **de dendê** palm-oil
**azeitona** olive
~ **preta** black
~ **verde (de Elvas)** green
**babá de moça** dessert made of egg yolks poached in coconut milk and syrup
**bacalhau** cod, usually dried and salted

~ **à Brás** fried with onions and potatoes, then baked with a topping of beaten eggs
~ **de caldeirada** braised with chopped onions, tomatoes, parsley, garlic and coriander (or saffron)
~ **cozido com todos** poached and served with boiled cabbage, onions, potatoes, chickpeas and eggs
~ **à Gomes de Sá** fried with onions, boiled potatoes, garlic and garnished with hard-boiled eggs and black olives
~ **com leite de coco** poached in coconut milk seasoned with coriander
~ **com natas no forno** boiled, then baked with potatoes in a white sauce with cream
~ **à provinciana** a gratin of poached cod, potatoes and *grelos* (or broccoli), topped with minced hard-boiled eggs, flour and port wine
~ **à transmontana** braised with cured pork or *chouriço,* white wine, parsley, garlic and tomatoes
**batata** potato
~ **doce** yam, sweet potato
~ **frita** chip (US french fry)
~ **palha** matchstick
**baunilha** vanilla
**berbigão** type of cockle
**beringela** aubergine (US eggplant)
**besugo** sunfish, type of sea-bream
**beterraba** beetroot
**bifana** slice of pork tenderloin usually served in a bun
**bife** steak, escalope

~ **a cavalo** of beef topped with a fried egg

~ **à cortador** of beef fried in garlic-flavoured butter

~ **de espadarte** swordfish cutlet (US steak) fried with onions and potatoes

~ **à milanesa** breaded escalope of veal

**bifinhos de vitela** slices of veal fillet served with a Madeira wine sauce

**biscoito** biscuit (US cookie)

**bobó** dish made of dried shrimps, onions, cassava root, fish stock, palm-oil, coconut milk and served with bananas and grated coconut

**boi** beef

**bola de Berlim** doughnut

**bolacha** biscuit (US cookie)

~ **de água e sal** cracker

**bolinho de bacalhau** deep-fried croquette of dried cod and mashed potatoes flavoured with eggs and parsley

**bolo** cake

~ **caseiro** home-made

~ **podre** flavoured with honey and cinnamon

**borracho** young pigeon

**borrego** lamb

**(na) brasa** charcoal-grilled

**brioche** yeast bun

**broa** 1) thick maize-(US corn-). meal cracker  2) type of ginger-bread

**brócolos** broccoli

**cabrito** kid

~-**montês** roebuck

~ **à ribatejana** marinated and roasted with herbs and paprika

**caça** game

**(à) caçador(a)** simmered in white wine with carrots, onions, herbs and sometimes tomatoes

**cachorro (quente)** hot-dog

**cachucho** small sea-bream

**café da manhã** breakfast

**caju** cashew nut

**calamar** (sliced) squid

**caldeirada** fish stewed with potatoes, onions, tomatoes, pimentos, spices, wine and olive-oil

~ **de enguias** eel simmered with potatoes, onions, garlic, bay leaf and parsley

~ **à fragateira** fish, shellfish and mussels simmered in a fish stock with tomatoes and herbs; served on toast

~ **à moda da Póvoa** hake, skate, sea-bass and eel simmered with tomatoes in olive-oil

**caldo** clear soup, consommé

~ **verde** thick soup made from shredded cabbage, potatoes and *chouriço*

**camarões** shrimps

~ **à baiana** served in a spicy tomato sauce with boiled rice

~ **grandes** Dublin Bay prawns (US jumbo shrimps)

**cambuquira** tender shoots of pumpkin (US squash) stewed with meat

**canapé** small open sandwich

**canela** cinnamon

**canja** chicken-and-rice soup

**canjica** dessert made of peanuts and sweet-corn cooked in milk with cloves and cinnamon and served in fresh coconut milk

**capão** capon

**caqui** persimmon

**caracóis** snails

**caracol** 1) snail  2) a spiral-shaped bun filled with currants

**caranguejo** crab

**carapau** horse mackerel

  **~ de escabeche** fried and dipped in a sauce made of vinegar, olive-oil, fried onions and garlic

**cardápio** menu

**caril** curry

**carne** meat

  **~ de porco à alentejana** cubes of marinated pork fried with clams

  **~ de sol** salted and dried in the sun

**carneiro** mutton

  **~ guisado** stewed with tomatoes, garlic, bay leaf, parsley and often potatoes

**carnes frias** cold meat (US cold cuts)

**caruru** 1) green amaranth 2) a dish of minced herbs stewed in oil and spices

**castanha** chestnut

  **~ de caju** cashew nut

**(na) cataplana** steamed in a copper pan shaped like a big nutshell

**cavala** mackerel

**cebola** onion

**cebolada** fried-onion garnish

**cenoura** carrot

**cereja** cherry

**cherne** black grouper

**chicória** endive (US chicory)

**chispalhada** pig's trotters (US feet) stewed with navy beans, cabbage, bacon and blood sausage

**chispe** pig's trotter (US foot)

**chocos com tinta** cuttlefish cooked in their own ink

**chouriça, chouriço** smoked pork

sausage flavoured with paprika

**chuchu** type of marrow (US summer squash)

**churrasco** charcoal-grilled meat served in Brazil with *farofa* and a hot-pepper sauce

**cocada** coconut macaroon

**coco** coconut

**codorniz** quail

**coelho** rabbit

**coentro** coriander

**cogumelo** (button) mushroom

**colorau** paprika (used for colouring)

**cominho** caraway seed

**compota** compote, stewed fruit

**congro** conger eel

**conta** bill (US check)

**coração** heart

**cordeiro** lamb

**corvina** croaker (fish)

**costeleta** chop, cutlet

**couve** cabbage

  **~-de-bruxelas** brussels sprouts

  **~-flor** cauliflower

  **~ galega** galician (with a long stem, big dark green leaves and a slightly bitter taste)

  **~ lombarda** savoy

  **~ portuguesa** portuguese (like the galician but smaller)

  **~ roxa** red

**cozido** 1) boiled stew 2) boiled 3) cooked

  **~ em lume brando** simmered

  **~ à portuguesa** beef and pork boiled with *chouriço,* carrots, turnips and cabbage *(couve portuguesa)*

**creme** cream

  **~ de leite** fresh

**criação** fowl

**croissant** crescent roll

**cru** raw

**curau** mashed sweet-corn cooked in coconut milk with sugar and cinnamon

**damasco** apricot

**dióspiro** persimmon

**dobrada, dobradinha** tripe

**doce** 1) sweet 2) jam
~ **de laranja** marmalade

**dourada** guilt-head (fish)

**eiró** eel

**eiroses fritas** fried eel

**ementa** 1) menu 2) set menu

**empada** small type of pie

**empadão** large type of pie
~ **de batata** shepherd's pie (with minced meat and mashed potato topping)

**enchidos** assorted pork products made into sausages

**endívia** chicory (US endive)

**enguia** eel

**ensopado** meat or fish casserole served on (or with) slices of bread

**entrecosto** sparerib

**ervilha** green pea

**escabeche** sauce of fried onions, garlic, olive-oil and vinegar

**escalfado** poached

**escalope de vitela** escalope of veal, thin, flattened breaded slice of veal

**espadarte** swordfish

**espargo** asparagus
**ponta de** ~ tip

**esparregado** purée of assorted greens in cream

**especiaria** spice

**espetada** kebab

**(no) espeto** spit-roasted

**espinafre** spinach

**estragão** tarragon

**estufado** braised

**esturjão** sturgeon

**farofa** cassava-root meal browned in oil or butter

**farófias** floating island

**fatias** slices
~ **da China** cold, baked egg yolks topped with syrup flavoured with lemon and cinnamon
~ **douradas** slices of bread dipped into milk and egg yolk, fried and sprinkled with sugar (US french toast)

**favas** broad beans
~ **guisadas com chouriço** stewed with *chouriço* and coriander leaves

**febras de porco à alentejana** pieces of pork fillet grilled with onions, *chouriço* and bacon

**feijão** bean
~ **branco** navy
~ **catarino** pink
~ **encarnado** red
~ **frade** black-eyed
~ **guisado** stewed with bacon in a tomato sauce
~ **preto** black
~ **tropeiro** black beans fried with chopped *carne de sol* and served with *farofa*
~ **verde** runner (US green)

**feijoada** dish of dried beans stewed with pig's head and trotters (US feet) bacon, sausages and sometimes vegetables; served in Brazil with *farofa*, rice, sliced oranges and a hot-pepper sauce

**fiambre** cooked (US boiled) ham

**fígado** liver
~ **de aves** chicken

**figo** fig

**filete** fillet of fish

**filhó** fritter
  ~ **de abóbora** of pumpkin
  purée
**fios de ovos** dessert of fine golden
  strands made from beaten egg
  yolk and melted sugar
**folhado** sweet puff-pastry
  delicacy
**(no) forno** baked
**framboesa** raspberry
**frango** chicken
  ~ **com farofa** served with
  *farofa* mixed with olives,
  hard-boiled eggs and giblets
  ~ **na púcara** chicken casserole
  flavoured with port wine,
  prepared in a special earthenware pot
**fresco** fresh
**fressura de porco guisada**
  casserole of pork offal (US
  variety meat), sometimes with
  navy beans
**fricassé** casserole, usually of
  lamb or veal in a cream sauce
**(na) frigideira** sautéed
**frio** cold
**fritada de peixe** deep-fried fish
**frito** 1) fried  2) fritter
**fruta** fruit
  ~ **em calda** in syrup
  ~ **do conde** variety of tropical
  fruit
  ~ **cristalizada** candied
**fubá** maizeflour (US cornflour)
**fumado** smoked
**galantina** pressed meat in gelatine
**galinha** boiling chicken
**galinhola** woodcock
**ganso** goose
**garoupa** large grouper (fish)
**gaspacho** chilled soup with diced
  tomatoes, sweet peppers,
  onions, cucumber and

croutons
**gelado** 1) ice-cream  2) chilled
**geleia** 1) jelly  2) jam (Brazil)
**gengibre** ginger
**ginja** morello cherry
**goiaba** guava
**goiabada** guava paste
**gombo** okra (GB lady's finger)
**grão(-de-bico)** chickpeas
  ~ **com bacalhau** stew made of
  chickpeas, potatoes and dried-
  cod fillets
**gratinado** oven-browned
**grelhado** grilled
**grelos** turnip greens
**groselha** red currant
**guaraná** very sweet tropical fruit
**guisado** 1) stew  2) stewed
**hortaliça** fresh vegetables
**hortelã** mint
**incluído** included
**inhame** yam, variety of sweet
  potato
**iscas** thinly sliced liver
  ~ **à portuguesa** marinated in
  white wine with herbs and
  garlic then fried
**jabuticaba** bing cherry
**jambu** variety of cress
**jantar** dinner
**jardineira** mixed vegetables
**javali** wild boar
**lagosta** spiny lobster
  ~ **americana** fried with onions
  and garlic, flambéed in brandy
  and served in a sauce flavoured
  with Madeira wine
  ~ **suada** with onions, garlic,
  tomatoes and flavoured with
  port wine
**lagostim** Norwegian lobster,
  langoustine
  ~**-do-rio** fresh-water crayfish
**lampreia** lamprey

~ **à moda do Minho** marinated in "green" wine, port wine, brandy, blood and spices then poached in the marinade and served with rice

**lanche** snack

**laranja** orange

**lavagante** lobster

**lebre** hare

**legumes** vegetables

~ **variados** mixed

**leitão** suck(l)ing pig

~ **à Bairrada** coated with spicy lard and roasted on a spit in a very hot bread-oven

~ **recheado** stuffed with a spicy, brandy-flavoured mince of bacon, *chouriço* and giblets and then roasted

**leite-creme** blancmange (US pudding) often sprinkled with caramelised sugar

**lentilha** lentil

**lima** lime

**limão** lemon

~ **verde** lime

**língua** tongue

**linguado** sole

~ **à meunière** sautéed in butter, served with parsley and lemon-juice

~ **com recheio de camarão** filled with shrimps in a white sauce

**linguíça** thin pork sausage flavoured with paprika

**lista dos vinhos** wine list

**lombo** loin

**louro** bay leaf

**lulas** squid

~ **de caldeirada** simmered with white wine, olive-oil, diced potatoes, tomatoes, onions and parsley

~ **recheadas** braised with a stuffing of eggs, onions and *chouriço*

**maçã** apple

~ **assada** baked

**maçapão, massapão** 1) marzipan 2) almond macaroon

**macarrão** macaroni

**macaxeira** cassava root

**maionese** mayonnaise

**malagueta** hot pepper

**mamão** papaya

**mandioca** cassava root

**manjar de coco** coconut blancmange (US pudding) topped with plum syrup

**manjericão** basil

**manteiga** butter

**mãozinhas de vitela guisadas** calves' trotters (US feet) braised with onions, parsley and vinegar, served with vegetables

**maracujá** passion fruit

**marinado** marinated

**(à) marinheira** with white wine, onions, parsley and sometimes tomatoes

**marisco** seafood

**marmelada** quince paste

**marmelo** quince

**massa** 1) dough, pastry 2) pasta, all types of noodle

**medalhão** medallion, small choice cut of meat

**medronho** arbutus berry

**meia desfeita** poached pieces of dried cod fried with chickpeas, onions and vinegar, topped with hard-boiled eggs and chopped garlic

**mel** honey

**melancia** watermelon

**melão** melon, usually a honeydew

melon
~ **com vinho do Porto** with
port wine
**merengue** meringue
**mero** red grouper (fish)
**mexilhão** mussel
**mexerica** tangerine
**migas** meat or fish fried in olive-
oil with onions and garlic and
thickened with bread
**mil-folhas** flaky pastry with
cream filling (US napoleon)
**milho doce** sweet-corn
**mioleira** brains
**miolos** brains
~ **mexidos com ovos** of
lamb fried and served with
scrambled eggs
**misto** mixed
**miúdos de galinha** chicken giblets
**mocotós** stewed calves' trotters
(US feet), usually served with
*farofa* and a hot-pepper sauce
**molho** sauce
~ **branco** white
~ **de manteiga** with butter and
lemon
~ **tártaro** mayonnaise with
chopped gherkins, chives,
capers, olives
~ **verde** olive-oil and vinegar
with chopped spinach, parsley
and coriander leaves
**com** ~ with
**sem** ~ without
**moqueca de peixe** fish cooked in
an earthenware casserole with
coconut milk, palm-oil,
coriander leaves, ginger and
ground shrimps
**morango** strawberry
~ **silvestre** wild
**morcela** black pudding, blood
sausage

**mortadela** mortadella
(US Bologna sausage)
**mostarda** mustard
**nabiça** turnip greens
**nabo** turnip
**nata(s)** fresh cream
~ **batida(s)** whipped
**(ao) natural** plain, without
dressing, sauce, stuffing etc.
**nêspera** medlar, a small apple-
like fruit eaten when over-ripe
**noz** nut, walnut
~ **moscada** nutmeg
**óleo** oil
~ **de amendoim** peanut oil
**omeleta** omelette
~ **simples** plain
**osso** bone
**ostras** oysters
~ **recheadas** oystershells
stuffed with oysters, onions,
garlic, breadcrumbs, egg yolk,
lemon juice, spice and then
oven-browned
**ouriço-do-mar** sea-urchin
**ovas** fish roe
**ovos** eggs
~ **cozidos** hard-boiled
~ **escalfados** poached
~ **estrelados** fried, sunny side
up
~ **mexidos** scrambled
~ **moles** beaten egg yolks
cooked in syrup
~ **quentes** soft-boiled
~ **verdes** stuffed with hard-
boiled yolks mixed with onions
flavoured with vinegar and
deep-fried in olive-oil
**paçoca** 1) roast *carne de sol*
ground with cassava root and
served with sliced bananas
2) dessert made with roast
peanuts crushed with

sweetened cassavaroot meal

**paio** spicy cured pork fillet presented in a casing

~ **com ervilhas** simmered with peas and chopped onions

**palmito** palm heart

**panado** breaded

**pão** bread

~ **de centeio** rye

~ **de forma** white, for toast

**pão-de-ló** tea bread (US coffee cake)

**pãozinho** roll

**papos de anjo** baked egg yolks topped with syrup

**pargo** red porgy (fish)

**passa (de uva)** raisin, sultana

**(bem) passado** well done

**(mal) passado** medium

**(muito mal) passado** rare

**pastel** usually a type of pie

~ **de bacalhau** deep-fried croquette of dried cod and mashed potatoes flavoured with eggs and parsley

~ **de Belém/de nata** custard pie

~ **folhado** flaky pastry

~ **de massa tenra** soft crust-pastry pie filled with minced meat

~ **de Santa Clara** tartlet with almond-paste filling

~ **de Tentúgal** flaky pastry filled with beaten eggs cooked in syrup

**pastelão de palmito e camarão** shrimp and palm-heart pie

**pato** duck

~ **estufado** braised in white wine with onions, parsley and bay leaf

~ **ao tucupi** roasted, braised with carrots and *jambu* in cassava-root juice and served

with fruit

**pé de moleque** peanut brittle

**pé de porco** pig's trotters (US feet)

**peito** breast

**peixe** fish

~~**-espada** cutlass fish, scabbard fish

~~**-galo** 1) moonfish 2) John Dory

~ **da horta** runner beans deep-fried in batter

**pepino** cucumber

**pequeno almoço** breakfast

**pêra** pear

**perca** perch

**perceve** barnacle

**perdiz** partridge

~ **à caçador(a)** simmered with carrots, onions, white wine, herbs and often tomatoes

~ **com molho de vilão** poached and served with a cold sauce of olive-oil, vinegar, onions, garlic and chopped parsley

**perna** leg

**pernil** ham

**pêro** variety of eating apple

**peru** turkey

**pescada** whiting

~ **cozida com todos** poached and served with boiled potatoes and runner beans

**pescadinhas de rabo na boca** plate of whitings fried whole

**pêssego** peach

**pevide** 1) pip (US seed) 2) salted pumpkin pip (US seed)

**picado de carne** minced meat

**picante** hot, spicy, highly seasoned

**pimenta** peppercorn

**piment(ã)o** sweet pepper

**pinhão** pine kernel

**pinhoada** pine-kernel brittle
**piripiri** tiny hot peppers
(preserved in olive-oil)
**polvo** octopus
**pombo** pigeon
~ **estufado** braised with bacon, onions and white wine, served with fried bread
**porco** pork
**posta** slice of fish or meat
**prato** 1) plate 2) dish
~ **do dia** speciality of the day
**preço** price
**prego** small steak often served in a roll
**presunto** 1) cured ham 2) cooked (US boiled) ham (Brazil)
~ **cru** dried ham
**pudim** pudding
~ **de bacalhau** dried-cod loaf, served with tomato sauce
~ **flan** caramel custard
~ **à portuguesa** custard flavoured with brandy and raisins
**puré** puree
~ **de batata** mashed potatoes
**queijada** small cottage-cheese tart
~ **de Sintra** flavoured with cinnamon
**queijinhos do céu** marzipan balls rolled in sugar
**queijo** cheese
~ **de Azeitão** soft or hard and made with ewe's milk
~ **cabreiro** made with goat's milk
~ **cardiga** made with goat's and ewe's milk
~ **catupiri** small, white cream cheese
~ **flamengo** Dutch type of cheese
~ **da ilha** made in the Azores

and not unlike Cheddar
~ **de Minas** plain
~ **Prata** mild and yellow
~ **rabaçal** made with goat's milk
~ **requeijão** type of cottage cheese
~ **São Jorge** not unlike Cheddar
~ **da Serra** made with ewe's milk
**quente** hot
~ **e frio** chocolate-nut (US hot-fudge) sundae
**quiabo** okra (GB lady's finger)
**quindim** sweet made with eggs and grated coconut
**rabanada** slice of bread dipped into egg batter and sprinkled with sugar (US french toast)
**rabanete** radish
**raia** skate
**rainha-cláudia** greengage plum
**recheado** stuffed
**recheio** stuffing, forcemeat
**refeição** meal
~ **ligeira** snack
**refogado** onions fried in olive-oil (base of a stew)
**repolho** green cabbage
**rins** kidneys
**rissol** fritter with minced meat or fish
**robalo** sea-bass
**rodela** round slice
**rojões à alentejana** pork cubes fried with baby clams, diced potatoes and onions
**rojões à moda do Minho** pork cubes marinated in dry white wine with garlic and paprika, fried and mixed with boiled blood cubes
**rolo de carne picada** meatloaf

**rolos de couve lombarda**
savoy-cabbage leaves stuffed
with minced or sausage
meat

**romã** pomegranate

**rosca** ring-shaped white bread

**ruivo** red gurnard (fish)

**sal** salt

**salada** salad

~ **de fruta** fruit

~ **mista** mixed

~ **de pimentos assados** made
with grilled sweet peppers

~ **russa** cooked, diced
vegetables in mayonnaise

**salgado** 1), salty 2) salted

**salmão** salmon

~ **fumado** smoked

**salmonete** surmullet

~ **grelhado com molho de
manteiga** grilled and served
with melted butter, chopped
parsley and lemon

**salsa** parsley

**salsicha** sausage

**salva** sage

**sande, sanduíche** sandwich

**santola** spider-crab

~ **ao natural** boiled in salted
water with lemon

~ **recheada** stuffed with its
own flesh, generally seasoned
with mustard, curry powder,
lemon and white wine

**sarda** mackerel

**sardinha** sardine

**sável** shad

**seco** 1) dry 2) dried

**sêmola** semolina

**sericá alentejano** cinnamon
soufflé

**serviço incluído** service
included

**siri** crab

**sobremesa** dessert

**solha** plaice

**sonho** type of doughnut

**sopa** soup

~ **de agriões** with watercress
and potatoes

~ **de coentros** with coriander
leaves, bread, poached eggs,
olive-oil and garlic

~ **do dia** of the day

~ **de feijão** with kidney beans,
cabbage, carrots and rice

~ **de hortaliça** with fresh
vegetables

~ **juliana** with shredded
vegetables

~ **de rabo de boi** oxtail

~ **de tomate à alentejana** with
tomatoes, onions and poached
eggs

~ **transmontana** with
vegetables, ham, bacon and
slices of bread

**sorvete** ice-cream

~ **com água** water-ice
(US sherbet)

**sururu** type of cockle

**suspiro** meringue

**tainha** grey mullet (fish)

**tâmara** date

**tangerina** tangerine

**tempero** seasoning

**tenro** tender

**tigelada** dessert of eggs beaten
with milk and cinnamon,
baked in an earthenware bowl

**toranja** grapefruit

**torrada** toast

**torrão de ovos** marzipan sweet

**torta** swiss roll

~ **de Viana** filled with lemon
curd

**tosta mista** toasted ham-and-
cheese sandwich

**toucinho** bacon
  ~ **do céu** kind of marzipan
  pudding
**tornedó** round cut of prime beef
**tremoço** salted lupine seed
**tripas** tripe (usually minced)
  ~ **à moda do Porto** cooked
  with assorted pork products,
  navy beans and pieces of
  chicken; served with rice
**trouxa de vitela** veal olive (US
  veal bird)
**trouxas de ovos** egg yolks
  poached in sweetened water
  and topped with syrup
**trufa** truffle
**truta** trout
**tutano** marrow
**tutu à mineira** puree of black
  beans mixed with cassava-root

meal and served with cabbage
and fried bacon
**uva** grape
  ~ **moscatel** muscat
**vaca** beef
**vagens** runner beans (US green
  beans)
**variado** assorted
**vatapá** fish and shrimp puree
  flavoured with coconut milk
  and palm-oil and served with a
  peanut-and-cashew sauce
**vieira** scallop
**vinagre** vinegar
**vitela** veal
**ximxim de galinha** chicken
  braised in palm-oil and served
  with a sauce of ground shrimp,
  sweet peppers, onions, peanuts
  and ginger

# Drinks

**adocicado** slightly sweet
**água** water
  ~ **de coco** coconut milk
  ~-**pé** weak wine, made from a
  base of watered-down wine
  draff
  ~ **tónica** tonic
**água mineral** mineral water
  ~ **com gás/gaseificada** fizzy
  (US carbonated)
  ~ **sem gás** still
**aguardente** spirit distilled from
  vegetable matter or fruit
  ~ **bagaceira** spirit distilled
  from grape husks
  ~ **de figo** spirit distilled from

figs
  ~ **de medronho** spirit distilled
  from arbutus berries
  ~ **velha** well-aged brandy
**Antiqua** Portuguese grape
  brandy, aged
**aperitivo** aperitif
**batida** long drink (US highball)
  of rum, sugar and fruit juice,
  usually lemon juice
**batido** milk-shake flavoured with
  a scoop of ice-cream
**bebida** drink
  ~ **sem álcool/não alcoólica**
  soft drink
  ~ **espirituosa** spirits

**bica** black coffee

**Borges** Portuguese grape brandy, aged

**branco** white

**Bucelas** region north of Lisbon which produces the famous dry, straw-coloured *Bucelas* wine

**cacau** cocoa

**cachaça** white rum

**café** coffee
  **~ sem cafeína** caffeine-free
  **~ duplo** large cup of coffee
  **~ frio** iced coffee
  **~ com leite** white coffee
  **~ puro** genuine coffee

**cafezinho** strong black coffee

**caipirinha** white rum served with lemon juice, ice cubes and a slice of lime or lemon

**caldo de cana** sugar-cane juice

**caneca** pint-size beer mug

**Carcavelos** region west of Lisbon producing good fortified wines

**carioca** small weak coffee

**(água de) Castelo** fizzy (US carbonated) mineral water

**cerveja** 1) beer 2) lager
  **~ em garrafa** bottled
  **~ imperial** draught (US draft)
  **~ preta** stout

**chá** tea
  **~ com leite** with milk
  **~ com limão** with lemon
  **~ de limão** made from an infusion of lemon peel
  **~ maté** made from an infusion of the maté-tree leaf and usually served chilled with a slice of lemon

**clarete** light red wine

**Colares** region to the north-west of Lisbon, producing good quality red and white wine; the reds have good colour and body and are rich in tanning; the whites have a strong aromatic flavour

**conhaque** cognac, French brandy
  **~ espanhol** Spanish brandy

**Constantino** Portuguese brandy, aged

**copo** glass

**Cuba livre** rum and Coke

**Dão** some of the best wines of Portugal, normally drunk quite young, come from this region, in the south-east of Oporto; the reds are strong and of good flavour, the whites dry and fruity

**doce** sweet
  **meio- ~** medium-sweet (usually in reference to sparkling wine)

**Douro** the upper part of this valley, east of Oporto produces the renowned port wine (see *Porto*) and pleasant table wines

**espumante** 1) sparkling 2) sparkling wine

**Favaios** dessert wine similar to muscatel

**fino** draught (US draft) beer

**fresco** fresh, chilled

**frio** cold

**galão** white coffee served in a big glass

**garoto** white coffee served in a small cup

**garrafa** bottle
  **meia-~** half bottle

**gasosa** fizzy (US carbonated) soft drink

**gelado** iced

**gelo** ice, ice cubes
  **com ~** with ice
  **sem ~** without ice

**genebra** Dutch gin, usually produced under licence

**gim** gin

**ginjinha** spirit distilled from morello cherries

**girafa** draught (US draft) beer served in a fluted glass

**guaraná** soft drink flavoured with *guaraná,* a very sweet tropical fruit

**jarro** carafe

**jeropiga** locally made fortified wine (see also *vinho abafado*)

**laranjada** orangeade

**leite** milk

~ **com chocolate** chocolate drink

**licor** liqueur

**limonada** type of lemon squash (US lemon drink)

**Madeira** excellent red and white aperitif and dessert wines are produced on this island; *Sercial* is the driest, and this, with *Verdelho* (medium-dry), can be drunk as an aperitif; *Boal* (or *Bual*) is smoky and less sweet than the rich dark-amber *Malmsey* (or *Malvásia*), which is best served for dessert at room temperature

**maduro** mature (wine produced from ripe grapes, as opposed to "green wine"; see *Minho*)

**(suco/sumo de) maracujá** passion-fruit (juice)

**Mateus rosé** famous rosé wine from the district of Trás-os-Montes

**mazagrã** chilled black coffee served on the rocks with sugar and a slice of lemon

**Minho** area in the north-west of Portugal where the famous young *vinho verde,* or "green wine", is produced; it is made from unripened grapes; faintly sparkling and acid in taste, very refreshing and with low alcohol content; the whites are more popular than the reds, both should be drunk young and chilled

**moscatel** 1) muscat grape 2) muscatel, a rich, aromatic dessert wine

**pinga** 1) wine 2) crude white rum (Brazil)

**(vinho do) Porto** this famous fortified wine from the upper Douro valley, east of Oporto, is classified by *vintage* and *blend;* the *vintage* ports, only made in exceptional years (indicated on the label), are bottled at least two years after harvesting and then stored to age for 10 to 20 years or more, while the *blended* ports, a subtle mixture of the harvests of different years, are kept in barrels for a minimum of 5 years; there are two types of *blended* ports: the younger *Ruby* variety is full-coloured, full-bodied, and the *Tawny* amber-coloured and delicate; moreover, less sweet, aromatic white ports are also available and are suitable as an aperitif

**quente** hot

**região demarcada** controlled and classified wine-producing area, e.g. *Bucelas, Colares, Dão, Douro, Minho,* etc.

**seco** dry

**extra-~** extra-dry

**meio-~** medium-dry

**Setubal** region south of Lisbon noted for its famous dessert wines *(moscatel)* and some good red and rosé table wines

**sidra** cider

**simples** neat (US straight)

**suco/sumo** fruit or vegetable juice

**taça** long-stemmed glass, cup

**tinto** red

**uísque** whisky

**vermute** vermouth

**vinho** wine

  ~ **abafado** locally made fortified wine (see also *jeropiga*)

  ~ **adamado** sweet wine

  ~ **da casa** house or carafe wine

  ~ **espumante natural** sparkling wine produced in a similar fashion to French champagne and available in extra-dry, dry and medium-dry blends

  ~ **generoso** well-aged and fortified wine, high in alcohol content

  ~ **licoroso** naturally sweet wine, high in alcohol content e.g. *Moscatel de Setúbal*

  ~ **da Madeira** Madeira wine (see *Madeira*)

  ~ **do Porto** port wine (see *Porto*)

  ~ **da região** local wine

  ~ **verde** "green wine" (see *Minho*)

**xerez** sherry

# Mini-Grammar

Here's the briefest possible outline of some essential features of Portuguese grammar.

## Articles

Articles agree with the noun in gender and number.
Definite article (the):

|  | masculine | feminine |
|---|---|---|
| singular | o | a |
| plural | os | as |

Indefinite article (a/an):

|  | masculine | feminine |
|---|---|---|
| singular | um | uma |
| plural | uns | umas |

*Note:* The plural corresponds to the English "some" or "a few".

To show possession, the preposition **de** (of) + the article is contracted to **do, da, dos** or **das.**

| o princípio do mês | the beginning of the month |
|---|---|
| o fim da semana | the end of the week |

## Nouns

All nouns in Portuguese are either masculine or feminine. Normally, those ending in **o** are masculine and those ending in **a** are feminine. Generally, nouns which end in a vowel add -s to form the plural:

| a menina | the little girl |
|---|---|
| as meninas | the little girls |
| o pato | the duck |
| os patos | the ducks |

Words ending in **r, s** or **z** form the plural by adding -es:

| a mulher | the woman |
|---|---|
| as mulheres | the women |
| o país | the country |
| os países | the countries |
| a luz | the light |
| as luzes | the lights |

Words ending in a nasal sound (**em, im, om, um**) change their endings to **ens, ins, ons, uns** in the plural.

## Adjectives

These agree with the nouns they modify in gender and number.

| | |
|---|---|
| **o belo livro** | the nice book |
| **a bela estátua** | the fine statue |
| **os homens altos** | the tall men |
| **as mulheres altas** | the tall women |

From these examples you can see that adjectives can come before or after the noun. This is a matter of sound and idiom.

## Demonstrative adjectives

| | |
|---|---|
| this | **este** (masc.)/**esta** (fem.) |
| that | **esse, aquele** (masc.)/ **essa, aquela** (fem.) |
| these | **estes** (masc.)/**estas** (fem.) |
| those | **esses, aqueles** (masc.)/ **essas, aquelas** (fem.) |

The difference between the three forms is that **este** means within reach, **esse** a bit farther and **aquele** means out of reach. There are also three invariable demonstrative adjectives in Portuguese: **isto, isso** and **aquilo.**

| | |
|---|---|
| **Tome isto.** | Take this. |
| **Deixe isso, por favor.** | Leave that, please. |
| **Dê-me aquilo, ali.** | Give me that, over there. |

## Possessive adjectives

These agree in number and gender with the noun they modify, i.e., with the thing possessed and not the possessor.

| | masculine | feminine |
|---|---|---|
| my | **meu** | **minha** |
| your | **teu** | **tua** |
| his/her/its | **seu** | **sua** |
| our | **nosso** | **nossa** |
| your | **vosso** | **vossa** |
| their | **seu** | **sua** |

All these forms add an s to form the plural.

*Note:* The form of the third person can be used instead of the second, as a form of politeness:

| | |
|---|---|
| **Meu amigo, o seu livro** | My friend, your book made |
| **deixou-me óptima impressão.** | a very good impression on me. |

## Personal pronouns

| | subject | direct object | indirect object |
|---|---|---|---|
| I | **eu** | **me** | **mim** |
| you | **tu** | **te** | **ti** |
| he/it | **ele** | **o** | **lhe** |

|         | subject | direct object | indirect object |
|---------|---------|---------------|-----------------|
| she/it  | **ela** | **a** | **lhe** |
| we      | **nós** | **nos** | **nos** |
| you     | **vós** | **vos** | **vos** |
| they (masc.) | **eles** | **os** | **lhes** |
| they (fem.)  | **elas** | **as** | **lhes** |

There are two forms for "you" (singular) in Portuguese: the intimate **tu** when talking to relatives, friends and children and **você**, which is used in all other cases between people who don't know each other very well. But when addressing someone you normally use the third person of the singular or of the plural:

**Como está (estão)?**          How are you?

## Verbs

There are four auxiliary verbs in Portuguese:

**ter/haver**          to have
**ser/estar**          to be

**Ter** indicates possession or a condition:

**Tenho uma casa.**          I have a house.
**Tenho febre.**          I have a fever.

**Haver** in the meaning of "to exist" is only used in the third person of the singular (there is/there are):

**Há muitas pessoas aqui.**          There are too many people here.

**Ser** indicates a permanent state:

**Sou inglês.**          I am English.

**Estar** indicates movement or a non-permanent state:

**Estou a passear**          I am walking.
  **[Estou passeando]**.
**Está doente.**          He is ill.

The **negative** is formed by placing **não** before the verb.

**Falo português.**          I speak Portuguese.
**Não falo português.**          I don't speak Portuguese.

In Portuguese, **questions** are often formed by changing the intonation of your voice.

**Está bem.**          It's all right.
**Está bem?**          Is it all right?
**Falo inglês.**          I speak English.
**Fala inglês?**          Do you speak English?

Three regular conjugations appear below, grouped by families according to their infinitive endings, *-ar*, *-er* and *-ir*. Verbs which do not follow the conjugations below are considered irregular (see irregular verb list). Note that there are some verbs which follow the regular conjugation of the category they belong to, but present some minor changes in spelling. Examples: *boiar, bóio; tocar, toque; almoçar, almoce; cegar, cegue; dirigir, dirijo; distinguir, distingo*. The personal pronoun is not generally expressed since the verb endings clearly indicate the person.

|  |  | 1st conj. | 2nd conj. | 3rd conj. |
|---|---|---|---|---|
| Infinitive |  | **am ar**<br>*(love)* | **tem er**<br>*(fear)* | **part ir**<br>*(leave for)* |
| Present | (eu) | am o | tem o | part o |
|  | (tu) | am as | tem es | part es |
|  | (ele) | am a | tem e | part e |
|  | (nós) | am amos | tem emos | part imos |
|  | (vós) | am ais | tem eis | part is |
|  | (eles) | am am | tem em | part em |
| Imperfect | (eu) | am ava | tem ia | part ia |
|  | (tu) | am avas | tem ias | part ias |
|  | (ele) | am ava | tem ia | part ia |
|  | (nós) | am ávamos | tem íamos | part íamos |
|  | (vós) | am áveis | tem íeis | part íeis |
|  | (eles) | am avam | tem iam | part iam |
| Past def. | (eu) | am ei | tem i | part i |
|  | (tu) | am aste | tem este | part iste |
|  | (ele) | am ou | tem eu | part iu |
|  | (nós) | am ámos | tem emos | part imos |
|  | (vós) | am astes | tem estes | part istes |
|  | (eles) | am aram | tem eram | part iram |
| Future | (eu) | am arei | tem erei | part irei |
|  | (tu) | am arás | tem erás | part irás |
|  | (ele) | am ará | tem erá | part irá |
|  | (nós) | am aremos | tem eremos | part iremos |
|  | (vós) | am areis | tem ereis | part ireis |
|  | (eles) | am arão | tem erão | part irão |
| Conditional | (eu) | am aria | tem eria | part iria |
|  | (tu) | am arias | tem erias | part irias |
|  | (ele) | am aria | tem eria | part iria |
|  | (nós) | am aríamos | tem eríamos | part iríamos |
|  | (vós) | am aríeis | tem eríeis | part iríeis |
|  | (eles) | am ariam | tem eriam | part iriam |

| Pres. subj. | (eu) | am **e** | tem **a** | part **a** |
|---|---|---|---|---|
| | (tu) | am **es** | tem **as** | part **as** |
| | (ele) | am **e** | tem **a** | part **a** |
| | (nós) | am **emos** | tem **amos** | part **amos** |
| | (vós) | am **eis** | tem **ais** | part **ais** |
| | (eles) | am **em** | tem **am** | part **am** |
| Imp. subj. | (eu) | am **asse** | tem **esse** | part **isse** |
| | (tu) | am **asses** | tem **esses** | part **isses** |
| | (ele) | am **asse** | tem **esse** | part **isse** |
| | (nós) | am **ássemos** | tem **êssemos** | part **íssemos** |
| | (vós) | am **ásseis** | tem **êsseis** | part **ísseis** |
| | (eles) | am **assem** | tem **essem** | part **issem** |
| Present part. | | am **ando** | tem **endo** | part **indo** |
| Past part. | | am **ado** | tem **ido** | part **ido** |

## Auxiliary Verbs

| | **ser** *(be)* | | **ter** *(have)* | |
|---|---|---|---|---|
| | *Present* | *Imperfect* | *Present* | *Imperfect* |
| (eu) | sou | era | tenho | tinha |
| (tu) | és | eras | tens | tinhas |
| (ele) | é | era | tem | tinha |
| (nós) | somos | éramos | temos | tínhamos |
| (vós) | sois | éreis | tendes | tínheis |
| (eles) | são | eram | têm | tinham |
| | *Past def.* | *Future* | *Past def.* | *Future* |
| (eu) | fui | serei | tive | terei |
| (tu) | foste | serás | tiveste | terás |
| (ele) | foi | será | teve | terá |
| (nós) | fomos | seremos | tivemos | teremos |
| (vós) | fostes | sereis | tivestes | tereis |
| (eles) | foram | serão | tiveram | terão |
| | *Pres. subj.* | *Imp. subj.* | *Pres. subj.* | *Imp. subj.* |
| (eu) | seja | fosse | tenha | tivesse |
| (tu) | sejas | fosses | tenhas | tivesses |
| (ele) | seja | fosse | tenha | tivesse |
| (nós) | sejamos | fôssemos | tenhamos | tivéssemos |
| (vós) | sejais | fôsseis | tenhais | tivésseis |
| (eles) | sejam | fossem | tenham | tivessem |
| | *Pres. part.* | *Past part.* | *Pres. part.* | *Past part.* |
| | sendo | sido | tendo | tido |

# Irregular Verbs

Below is a list of the irregular verbs with the tenses most commonly used in Portuguese. In the listing, a) stands for the present tense, b) for the imperfect, c) for the past definite, d) for the future, e) for the present subjunctive and f) for the past participle. All forms of the present tense are given plus the 1st person of the other tenses unless further irregularities occur in the conjugation of the particular tense.

Unless otherwise indicated, verbs with prefixes (*ab-, ad-, ante-, bem-, circum-, com-, contra-, de-, des-, dis-, em-, entre-, ex-, in-, inter-, intro-, mal-, ob-, per-, pre-, pro-, re-, retro-, sob-, sobre-, sub-, sus-, trans-, etc.*) are conjugated like the stem verb.

Although they are irregular, verbs ending in *-ear*, *-uzir* and *-uir* do not figure below. All those in *-ear* are conjugated as in *barbear*; those in *-uzir* as in *conduzir* and those in *-uir* as in *constituir*, with the exception of *destruir* and *construir* (see list).

**abolir**
*abrogate, abolish*
a) -, -, -, abolimos, abolis, -; b) abolia; c) aboli;
d) abolirei; e) -; f) abolido

**acudir**
*help, assist*
a) acudo, acodes, acode, acudimos, acudis, acodem;
b) acudia; c) acudi; d) acudirei; e) acuda; f) acudido

**aderir**
*join, agree*
a) adiro, aderes, adere, aderimos, aderis, aderem;
b) aderia; c) aderi; d) aderirei; e) adira; f) aderido

**advertir**
*warn, admonish*
→aderir

**agredir**
*attack*
a) agrido, agrides, agride, agredimos, agredis, agridem;
b) agredia; c) agredi; d) agredirei; e) agrida; f) agredido

**ansiar**
*crave for; worry*
a) anseio, anseias, anseia, ansiamos, ansiais, anseiam;
b) ansiava; c) ansiei; d) ansiarei; e) anseie, anseies,
anseie, ansiemos, ansieis, anseiem; f) ansiado

**aprazer**[1]
*please*
a) apraz; b) aprazia; c) aprouve; d) aprazerá; e) apraza;
f) aprazido

**barbear**
*shave*
a) barbeio, barbeias, barbeia, barbeamos, barbeais,
barbeiam; b) barbeava; c) barbeei; d) barbearei;
e) barbeie, barbeies, barbeie, barbeemos, barbeeis,
barbeiem; f) barbeado

**bulir**
*move, touch*
→acudir

**caber**
*fit*
a) caibo, cabes, cabe, cabemos, cabeis, cabem; b) cabia;
c) coube, coubeste, coube, coubemos, coubestes,
couberam; d) caberei; e) caiba; f) cabido

**cair**
*fall*
a) caio, cais, cai, caímos, caís, caiem; b) caía; c) caí;
d) cairei; e) caia; f) caído

**cobrir**
*cover*
a) cubro, cobres, cobre, cobrimos, cobris, cobrem;
b) cobria; c) cobri; d) cobrirei; e) cubra;
f) coberto/cobrido

---

[1] impersonal

| **colorir** | →abolir |
| *colour, paint* | |
| **compelir** | →aderir |
| *compel, force* | |
| **conduzir** | a) conduzo, conduzes, conduz, conduzimos, conduzis, |
| *lead, drive* | conduzem; b) conduzia; c) conduzi; d) conduzirei; |
| | e) conduza; f) conduzido |
| **constituir** | a) constituo, constituis, constitui, constituímos, |
| *constitute* | constituís, constituem; b) constituía; c) constituí; |
| | d) constituirei; e) constitua; f) constituído |
| **construir** | a) construo, constróis, constrói, construímos, |
| *build* | construís, constroem; b) construía; c) construí; |
| | d) construirei; e) construa; f) construído |
| **consumir** | →acudir |
| *consume* | |
| **convergir** | →emergir |
| *converge* | |
| **crer** | a) creio, crês, crê, cremos, credes, crêem; b) cria; c) cri; |
| *believe* | d) crerei; e) creia; f) crido |
| **cuspir** | →acudir |
| *spit* | |
| **dar** | a) dou, dás, dá, damos, dais, dão; b) dava; c) dei, deste, |
| *give* | deu, demos, destes, deram; d) darei; e) dê, dês, dê, |
| | demos, deis, dêem; f) dado |
| **demolir** | →abolir |
| *demolish* | |
| **despir** | →aderir |
| *undress* | |
| **destruir** | →construir |
| *destroy* | |
| **digerir** | →aderir |
| *digest* | |
| **discernir** | →aderir |
| *perceive, see* | |
| **divertir** | →aderir |
| *amuse* | |
| **dizer** | a) digo, dizes, diz, dizemos, dizeis, dizem; b) dizia; |
| *say* | c) disse, disseste, disse, dissemos, dissestes, disseram; |
| | d) direi; e) diga; f) dito |
| **doer** | →moer (only in 3rd person singular and plural) |
| *hurt* | |
| **dormir** | →cobrir; f) dormido |
| *sleep* | |

**emergir**
*emerge*
a) –, emerges, emerge, emergimos, emergis, emergem;
b) emergia; c) emergi; d) emergirei; e) –; f) emergido/
emerso

**engolir**
*swallow*
→cobrir; f) engolido

**estar**
*be*
a) estou, estás, está, estamos, estais, estão; b) estava;
c) estive, estiveste, esteve, estivemos, estivestes,
estiveram; d) estarei; e) esteja; f) estado

**explodir**
*explode, burst*
→abolir

**extorquir**
*extort*
→abolir

**fazer**
*do, make*
a) faço, fazes, faz, fazemos, fazeis, fazem; b) fazia;
c) fiz, fizeste, fez, fizemos, fizestes, fizeram; d) farei;
e) faça; f) feito

**ferir**
*wound, hurt*
→aderir

**fugir**
*run away, escape*
a) fujo, foges, foge, fugimos, fugis, fogem; b) fugia;
c) fugi; d) fugirei; e) fuja; f) fugido

**gerir**
*administer, organize*
→aderir

**haver**[1]
*have; be*
a) há; b) havia; c) houve; d) haverá; e) haja; f) havido

**haver de**
*have to*
a) hei-de, hás-de, há-de, havemos de, haveis de, hão-de;
b) havia de; c) –; d) –; e) –; f) –

**impelir**
*drive, force*
→aderir

**incendiar**
*set on fire*
→ansiar

**inserir**
*insert*
→aderir

**ir**
*go*
a) vou, vais, vai, vamos, ides, vão; b) ia; c) fui, foste,
foi, fomos, fostes, foram; d) irei; e) vá, vás, vá, vamos,
vades, vão; f) ido

**jazer**
*lie (here lies)*
a) jazo, jazes, jaz, jazemos, jazeis, jazem; b) jazia;
c) jazi; d) jazerei; e) jaza; f) jazido

**ler**
*read*
a) leio, lês, lê, lemos, ledes, lêem; b) lia; c) li; d) lerei;
e) leia; f) lido

**mediar**
*mediate*
→ansiar

**medir**
*measure*
a) meço, medes, mede, medimos, medis, medem;
b) media; c) medi; d) medirei; e) meça; f) medido

---

[1] impersonal

**mentir** →aderir
*lie (tell lies)*

**moer** a) moo, móis, mói, moemos, moeis, moem;
*grind* b) moía; c) moí; d) moerei; e) moa; f) moído

**negociar** →ansiar
*negociate*

**odiar** →ansiar
*hate*

**ouvir** a) ouço, ouves, ouve, ouvimos, ouvis, ouvem; b) ouvia;
*hear, listen* c) ouvi; d) ouvirei; e) ouça; f) ouvido

**pedir** →medir
*ask*

**perder** a) perco, perdes, perde, perdemos, perdeis, perdem;
*lose* b) perdia; c) perdi; d) perderei; e) perca; f) perdido

**poder** a) posso, podes, pode, podemos, podeis, podem;
*be able to* b) podia; c) pude, pudeste, pôde, pudemos, pudestes,
puderam; d) poderei; e) possa; f) podido

**polir** →abolir
*polish*

**por** a) ponho, pões, põe, pomos, pondes, põem; b) punha,
*put* punhas, punha, púnhamos, púnheis, punham; c) pus,
puseste, pôs, pusemos, pusestes, puseram; d) porei;
e) ponha; f) posto

**premiar** →ansiar
*award*

**prevenir** →agredir
*prevent; warn*

**prover** a) provejo, provês, provê, provemos, provedes,
*provide* provêem; b) provia; c) provi; d) proverei; e) proveja;
f) provido

**querer** a) quero, queres, quer, queremos, quereis, querem;
*want, wish* b) queria; c) quis, quiseste, quis, quisemos, quisestes,
quiseram; d) quererei; e) queira; f) querido

**reflectir** →aderir
*reflect; ponder*

**remediar** →ansiar
*put right, palliate*

**repetir** →aderir
*repeat*

**requerer** a) requeiro, requeres, requer, requeremos, requereis,
*request* requerem; b) requeria; c) requeri; d) requererei;
e) requeira; f) requerido

**rir** a) rio, ris, ri, rimos, rides, riem; b) ria; c) ri; d) rirei;
*laugh* e) ria; f) rido

| | |
|---|---|
| **saber**<br>*know* | a) sei, sabes, sabe, sabemos, sabeis, sabem; b) sabia;<br>c) soube, soubeste, soube, soubemos, soubestes,<br>souberam; d) saberei; e) saiba; f) sabido |
| **sair**<br>*go out* | a) saio, sais, sai, saímos, saís, saem; b) saía;<br>c) saí; d) sairei; e) saia; f) saído |
| **seguir**<br>*follow* | →aderir |
| **sentir**<br>*feel; be sorry* | →aderir |
| **servir**<br>*serve* | →aderir |
| **subir**<br>*go up, ascend* | →acudir |
| **sugerir**<br>*suggest* | →aderir |
| **tossir**<br>*cough* | →cobrir; f) tossido |
| **trair**<br>*betray* | →cair |
| **trazer**<br>*bring* | a) trago, trazes, traz, trazemos, trazeis, trazem;<br>b) trazia; c) trouxe, trouxeste, trouxe, trouxemos,<br>trouxestes, trouxeram; d) trarei; e) traga; f) trazido |
| **valer**<br>*be worth* | a) valho, vales, vale, valemos, valeis, valem; b) valia;<br>c) vali; d) valerei; e) valha; f) valido |
| **ver**<br>*see, watch* | a) vejo, vês, vê, vemos, vedes, vêem; b) via; c) vi, viste,<br>viu, vimos, vistes, viram; d) verei; e) veja; f) visto |
| **vestir**<br>*dress* | →aderir |
| **vir**<br>*come* | a) venho, vens, vem, vimos, vindes, vêm; b) vinha,<br>vinhas, vinha, vínhamos, vínheis, vinham; c) vim,<br>vieste, veio, viemos, viestes, vieram; d) virei; e) venha;<br>f) vindo |

# Portuguese abbreviations

| | | |
|---|---|---|
| (a) | *assinado* | signed |
| a/c | *ao cuidado de* | c/o |
| a.C., A.C. | *antes de Cristo* | B.C. |
| A.C.B. | *Automóvel Clube do Brasil* | Brazilian Automobile Association |
| A.C.P. | *Automóvel Clube de Portugal* | Portuguese Automobile Association |
| A.D. | *anno Domini* | A.D. |
| Al. | *alameda* | lane, alley |
| apart., ap. | *apartamento* | flat, apartment |
| Av. | *avenida* | avenue; alley |
| BB | *Banco do Brasil* | Bank of Brazil |
| B.º | *beco* | cul-de-sac, blind alley |
| c/ | *com; conta* | with; account |
| c/c | *conta corrente* | current account |
| c/v | *cave* | basement, cellar |
| C.ª, Cia, Cia | *companhia* | company |
| Calç. | *calçada* | paved street |
| CEE | *Comunidade Económica Europeia* | EEC, Common Market |
| C.M. | *Câmara Municipal* | Local council |
| CP | *Caminhos de Ferro Portugueses* | Portuguese Railways |
| C.P. | *caixa postal* | p.o. box |
| Cr$ | *cruzeiro* | Brazilian monetary unit |
| C.T.B. | *Companhia Telefônica Brasileira* | Brazilian Telephone Company |
| C.T.T. | *Correios, Telégrafos e Telefones* | Post Office, Telegraph, Telephone |
| Cv., ctv. | *centavo* | $\frac{1}{100}$ of an escudo (or a cruzeiro) |
| c.v. | *cavalo-vapor* | horsepower |
| D. | *Dona* | Miss, Mrs. (title of courtesy) |
| d., dto. | *direito* | on the right (part of an address) |
| d.C., D.C. | *depois de Cristo* | A.D. |
| D.F. | *Distrito Federal (Brasília)* | Federal District of Brasilia |
| Dr. | *Doutor* | Doctor |

| Dra. | *Doutora* | Doctor (fem) |
|---|---|---|
| e., esq. | *esquerdo* | left-hand (part of an address) |
| E.C.T. | *Empresa de Correios e Telégrafos* | Brazilian Post and Telegraph Company |
| E.F.C.B. | *Estrada de Ferro Central do Brasil* | Brazilian Railways |
| ENATUR | *Empresa Nacional de Turismo* | Portuguese National Tourist Office |
| End. | *endereço* | address |
| E.R. | *Espera resposta* | please reply |
| Esc. | *escudo* | Portuguese monetary unit |
| Ex.ᵃ, Excia. | *Excelência* | Excellency |
| Ex.ᵐᵃ (Sra.) | *Excelentíssima (Senhora)* | title of courtesy |
| Ex.ᵐᵒ (Sr.) | *Excelentíssimo (Senhor)* | (followed by Mrs. or Mr.) |
| G.B. | *Estado da Guanabara* | State of Guanabara |
| G.N.R. | *Guarda Nacional Republicana* | National Republican Guard (police) |
| h | *hora(s)* | o'clock |
| Ilma. (Sra.) | *Ilustríssima (Senhora)* | title of courtesy |
| Ilmo. (Sr.) | *Ilustríssimo (Senhor)* | (followed by Mrs. or Mr.) |
| L., L.ᵒ | *Largo* | square, plaza |
| Lda., Ltda. | *limitada* | Limited |
| Lx.ᵃ | *Lisboa* | Lisbon |
| méd. | *médico* | physician |
| Men.ᵃ | *Menina* | Miss |
| n/ | *nosso, nossa* | our |
| Obg., Obr.ᵒ | *obrigado* | thank you |
| P., Pr. | *praça* | square |
| pág., p. | *página* | page |
| R. | *rua* | street |
| r/c | *rés-do-chão* | ground floor |
| reg.ᵒ | *registado; regulamento* | registered; regulation |
| Rem., Rem.ᵗᵉ | *remetente* | sender |
| Revmo. | *Reverendíssimo* | Reverend Father |
| R.P. | *Rádio-Patrulha* | Police-Patrol |

| | | |
|---|---|---|
| **R.S.F.F.** | *responda se faz favor* | please reply, R.S.V.P. |
| **RTI** | *Rádio e Televisão* | Independent Portuguese |
| | *Independente* | Broadcasting Company |
| **RTP** | *Rádio e Televisão* | Portuguese Broadcasting |
| | *Portuguesa* | Company |
| s/ | *sem; seu, sua* | without; your |
| **S., Sto.** | *São, Santo* | saint |
| **S.A.** | *Sociedade Anónima* | Incorporated |
| **s.f.f.** | *se faz favor* | please |
| **S.P.** | *Estado de São Paulo* | State of São Paulo |
| **Sr., Sra.** | *Senhor, Senhora* | Mr., Mrs. |
| **Sta.** | *Santa* | saint (fem) |
| **Tr., Trav.** | *travessa* | by-lane, passageway |
| v/ | *vosso, vossa* | your |
| **v.** | *você* | you |
| **v.°** | *verso* | back, reverse |
| **V.S.F.F.** | *volte se faz favor* | please turn over |

# Numerals

| Cardinal numbers | | Ordinal numbers | |
|---|---|---|---|
| 0 | zero | 1. | primeiro |
| 1 | um | 2. | segundo |
| 2 | dois | 3. | terceiro |
| 3 | três | 4. | quarto |
| 4 | quatro | 5. | quinto |
| 5 | cinco | 6. | sexto |
| 6 | seis | 7. | sétimo |
| 7 | sete | 8. | oitavo |
| 8 | oito | 9. | nono |
| 9 | nove | 10. | décimo |
| 10 | dez | 11. | décimo primeiro |
| 11 | onze | 12. | décimo segundo |
| 12 | doze | 13. | décimo terceiro |
| 13 | treze | 14. | décimo quarto |
| 14 | catorze | 15. | décimo quinto |
| 15 | quinze | 16. | décimo sexto |
| 16 | dezasseis | 17. | décimo sétimo |
| 17 | dezassete | 20. | vigésimo |
| 18 | dezoito | 21. | vigésimo primeiro |
| 19 | dezanove | 22. | vigésimo segundo |
| 20 | vinte | 30. | trigésimo |
| 21 | vinte e um | 40. | quadragésimo |
| 22 | vinte e dois | 50. | quinquagésimo |
| 30 | trinta | 60. | sexagésimo |
| 31 | trinta e um | 70. | septuagésimo |
| 40 | quarenta | 80. | octogésimo |
| 50 | cinquenta | 90. | nonagésimo |
| 60 | sessenta | 100. | centésimo |
| 70 | setenta | 101. | centésimo primeiro |
| 80 | oitenta | 200. | ducentésimo |
| 90 | noventa | 300. | tricentésimo |
| 100 | cem | 400. | quadringentésimo |
| 101 | cento e um | 500. | quingentésimo |
| 200 | duzentos | 600. | seiscentésimo |
| 300 | trezentos | 700. | septingentésimo |
| 500 | quinhentos | 800. | octingentésimo |
| 1.000 | mil | 900. | nongentésimo |
| 1.107 | mil cento e sete | 1.000. | milésimo |
| 2.000 | dois mil | 1.107. | milésimo centésimo sétimo |
| 1.000.000 | um milhão | 2.000. | dois milésimo |

# Time

If you have to indicate that it is a.m. or p.m., add *da manhã, da tarde* or *da noite*.

Thus:

| | |
|---|---|
| *oito da manhã* | 8 a.m. |
| *duas da tarde* | 2 p.m. |
| *oito da noite* | 8 p.m. |

## Days of the week

| | | | |
|---|---|---|---|
| *domingo* | Sunday | *quinta-feira* | Thursday |
| *segunda-feira* | Monday | *sexta-feira* | Friday |
| *terça-feira* | Tuesday | *sábado* | Saturday |
| *quarta-feira* | Wednesday | | |

## Some Basic Phrases

## Algumas expressões de uso corrente

| | |
|---|---|
| Please. | Por favor. |
| Thank you very much. | Muito obrigado. |
| Don't mention it. | Não tem de quê. |
| Good morning. | Bom dia. |
| Good afternoon. | Boa tarde. |
| Good evening. | Boa noite. |
| Good night. | Boa noite. |
| Good-bye. | Adeus. |
| See you later. | Até logo. |
| Where is/Where are…? | Onde é/Onde são…? |
| What do you call this? | Como chama isto? |
| What does that mean? | O que quer dizer isso? |
| Do you speak English? | Fala inglês? |
| Do you speak German? | Fala alemão? |
| Do you speak French? | Fala francês? |
| Do you speak Spanish? | Fala espanhol? |
| Do you speak Italian? | Fala italiano? |
| Could you speak more slowly, please? | Não se importava de falar mais devagar, por favor? |
| I don't understand. | Não compreendo. |
| Can I have…? | Pode dar-me…? |
| Can you show me…? | Pode indicar-me…? |
| Can you tell me…? | Pode dizer-me…? |
| Can you help me, please? | Pode ajudar-me, por favor? |
| I'd like… | Gostava… |
| We'd like… | Gostávamos… |
| Please give me… | Por favor, dê-me… |
| Please bring me… | Por favor, traga-me… |
| I'm hungry. | Tenho fome. |
| I'm thirsty. | Tenho sede. |
| I'm lost. | Perdi-me. |
| Hurry up! | Despache-se! |

| There is/There are... | Há... |
| There isn't/There aren't... | Não há... |

## Arrival / Chegada

| Your passport, please. | O seu passaporte, por favor. |
| Have you anything to declare? | Tem alguma coisa a declarar? |
| No, nothing at all. | Não, nada. |
| Can you help me with my luggage, please? | Pode levar-me a bagagem, por favor? |
| Where's the bus to the centre of town, please? | Onde se apanha o autocarro (ônibus) para o centro da cidade, por favor? |
| This way, please. | Por aqui, por favor. |
| Where can I get a taxi? | Onde posso arranjar um táxi? |
| What's the fare to...? | Qual é o preço do percurso para...? |
| Take me to this address, please. | Leve-me a esta direcção, por favor. |
| I'm in a hurry. | Estou com pressa. |

## Hotel / Hotel

| My name is... | Chamo-me... |
| Have you a reservation? | Reservou? |
| I'd like a room with a bath. | Queria um quarto com casa de banho (banheiro). |
| What's the price per night? | Qual é o preço por noite? |
| May I see the room? | Posso ver o quarto? |
| What's my room number, please? | Qual é o número do meu quarto, por favor? |
| There's no hot water. | Não há água quente. |
| May I see the manager, please? | Posso ver o director, por favor? |
| Did anyone telephone me? | Não houve nenhum telefonema para mim? |
| Is there any mail for me? | Há correio para mim? |
| May I have my bill (check), please? | Pode dar-me a conta, por favor? |

## Eating out | Restaurante

| Eating out | Restaurante |
|---|---|
| Do you have a fixed-price menu? | Tem uma ementa (um cardápio)? |
| May I see the menu? | Posso ver a lista? |
| May we have an ashtray, please? | Pode trazer-nos um cinzeiro, por favor? |
| Where's the toilet, please? | Onde são os lavabos, por favor? |
| I'd like an hors d'œuvre (starter). | Queria um acepipe. |
| Have you any soup? | Tem sopa? |
| I'd like some fish. | Queria peixe. |
| What kind of fish do you have? | Que peixe tem? |
| I'd like a steak. | Queria um bife. |
| What vegetables have you got? | Que legumes tem? |
| Nothing more, thanks. | Mais nada, obrigado. |
| What would you like to drink? | Que desejava beber? |
| I'll have a beer, please. | Queria uma cerveja, por favor. |
| I'd like a bottle of wine. | Queria uma garrafa de vinho. |
| May I have the bill (check), please? | Pode trazer-me a conta, por favor? |
| Is service included? | O serviço está incluído? |
| Thank you, that was a very good meal. | Obrigado, a comida estava muito boa. |

## Travelling | Excursões

| Travelling | Excursões |
|---|---|
| Where's the railway station, please? | Onde é a estação, por favor? |
| Where's the ticket office, please? | Onde é a bilheteira (bilheteria), por favor? |
| I'd like a ticket to… | Queria um bilhete para… |
| First or second class? | Primeira ou segunda classe? |
| First class, please. | Primeira classe, por favor. |
| Single or return (one way or roundtrip)? | Ida ou ida e volta? |
| Do I have to change trains? | Devo mudar de comboio (trem)? |
| What platform does the train for… leave from? | De que cais parte o comboio (trem) para…? |

| Where's the nearest underground (subway) station? | Onde é a estação do metro mais próxima? |
| Where's the bus station, please? | Onde é a paragem dos autocarros (ônibus), por favor? |
| When's the first bus to…? | A que horas parte o primeiro autocarro (ônibus) para…? |
| Please let me off at the next stop. | Por favor, deixe-me na próxima paragem (parada). |

| **Relaxing** | **Distracções** |
| What's on at the cinema (movies)? | O que vai no cinema? |
| What time does the film begin? | A que horas começa o filme? |
| Are there any tickets for tonight? | Ainda há bilhetes para hoje à noite? |
| Where can we go dancing? | Onde podemos ir dançar? |

| **Meeting people** | **Encontros** |
| How do you do. | Bom dia. |
| How are you? | Como está? |
| Very well, thank you. And you? | Bem, obrigado. E você/a senhora/a menina/o senhor? |
| May I introduce…? | Posso apresentar-lhe…? |
| My name is… | Chamo-me… |
| I'm very pleased to meet you. | Muito prazer em conhecê-lo (la). |
| How long have you been here? | Há quanto tempo está aqui? |
| It was nice meeting you. | Tive muito gosto em conhecê-lo (la). |
| Do you mind if I smoke? | Não se importa que eu fume? |
| Do you have a light, please? | Tem lume (fogo), por favor? |
| May I get you a drink? | Posso oferecer-lhe uma bebida? |
| May I invite you for dinner tonight? | Posso convidá-la para jantar hoje à noite? |
| Where shall we meet? | Onde nos encontramos? |

## Shops, stores and services

Where's the nearest bank, please?

Where can I cash some travellers' cheques?

Can you give me some small change, please?

Where's the nearest chemist's (pharmacy)?

How do I get there?

Is it within walking distance?

Can you help me, please?

How much is this? And that?

It's not quite what I want.

I like it.

Can you recommend something for sunburn?

I'd like a haircut, please.

I'd like a manicure, please.

## Estabelecimentos

Onde é o banco mais próximo, por favor?

Onde posso trocar cheques de viagem?

Pode-me dar dinheiro trocado, por favor?

Onde é a farmácia mais próxima?

Como posso ir para lá?

Pode-se ir a pé?

Pode ajudar-me, por favor?

Quanto custa isto? E aquilo?

Não é bem o que quero.

Gosto.

Pode aconselhar-me qualquer coisa contra as queimaduras do sol?

Queria cortar o cabelo, por favor.

Queria arranjar as unhas, por favor.

## Street directions

Can you show me on the map where I am?

You are on the wrong road.

Go/Walk straight ahead.

It's on the left/on the right.

## Direcções

Pode mostrar-me no mapa onde estou?

Enganou-se na estrada.

Siga sempre em frente.

É à esquerda/à direita.

## Emergencies

Call a doctor quickly.

Call an ambulance.

Please call the police.

## Urgências

Chame depressa um médico.

Chame uma ambulância.

Chame a polícia, por favor.

# inglês-português

# english-portuguese

# Introdução

Este dicionário foi elaborado com um fim prático. A informação linguística é a estritamente necessária. As palavras encontram-se por ordem alfabética, quer sejam simples ou compostas, quer levem ou não traço de união. Única excepção à regra: os verbos reflexos e algumas expressões idiomáticas que foram ordenados em relação ao verbo simples ou à palavra principal.

Quando uma palavra é seguida de expressões correntes ou locuções, estas encontram-se igualmente dispostas por ordem alfabética na rubrica da palavra principal.

Todas as palavras principais trazem a respectiva transcrição fonética e a indicação da classe morfológica (substantivo, verbo, adjectivo, etc.). Quando uma palavra principal pertence a várias classes morfológicas, as respectivas traduções encontram-se a seguir a cada uma delas.

Damos todos os plurais irregulares dos substantivos, assim como certos plurais que possam suscitar dúvidas.

Para evitarmos repetições, usámos um til (~) em lugar da palavra principal.

No plural dos nomes compostos, o travessão (-) substitui o elemento que permanece invariável.

Um asterisco (*) assinala os verbos irregulares. Para mais pormenores, consulte a lista destes verbos.

Este dicionário toma em consideração a ortografia inglesa. As palavras e as definições dos termos tipicamente americanos são indicados como tais (veja a lista das abreviaturas usadas no texto).

## Abreviaturas

| | | | |
|---|---|---|---|
| *adj* | adjectivo | *n* | nome (substantivo) |
| *adv* | advérbio | *nAm* | nome (americano) |
| *Am* | americano | *num* | numeral |
| *art* | artigo | *p* | imperfeito |
| *Br* | brasileiro | *pl* | plural |
| *conj* | conjunção | *plAm* | plural (americano) |
| *f* | feminino | *pp* | particípio passado |
| *fBr* | feminino (brasileiro) | *pr* | presente do indicativo |
| *fpl* | feminino plural | *pref* | prefixo |
| *fplBr* | feminino plural | *prep* | preposição |
| | (brasileiro) | *pron* | pronome |
| *m* | masculino | *v* | verbo |
| *mBr* | masculino (brasileiro) | *vAm* | verbo |
| *mpl* | masculino plural | | (americano) |
| *mplBr* | masculino plural | *vBr* | verbo |
| | (brasileiro) | | (brasileiro) |

# Guia de pronúncia

Cada palavra principal desta parte do dicionário traz uma transcrição fonética que lhe indica a pronúncia. Deve lê-la como se cada letra ou grupo de letras tivesse o mesmo valor do que em português. A seguir figuram unicamente as letras e os símbolos ambíguos ou particularmente difíceis de compreender.

As sílabas estão separadas por traços de união e as tónicas estão impressas em *itálico*.

É evidente que os sons das duas línguas raras vezes coincidem exactamente, mas, se seguir cuidadosamente as nossas indicações, será capaz de pronunciar as palavras estrangeiras de maneira a fazer-se entender. Para facilitar o seu trabalho, as nossas transcrições simplificam, por vezes, ligeiramente, o sistema fonético da língua, sem deixar, por isso, de reflectir as diferenças de sons essenciais.

## Consoantes

| | |
|---|---|
| b | sempre como em boca |
| d | sempre como em dia |
| ð | parecido com o d de nada |
| gh | como o g de gato |
| h | pronuncia-se expirando rápida e fortemente |
| k | como o c de casa; mas, antes de uma vogal tónica, ouve-se um h aspirado depois do k |
| ng | como o n de branco |
| p | como em porto; mas, antes de uma vogal tónica, ouve-se um h aspirado depois do p |
| r | parecido com o r de cara, mas mais fraco |
| t | como em todo; mas, antes de uma vogal tónica, ouve-se um h aspirado depois do t |
| θ | como o s de saco, pronunciado com a língua entre os dentes |

## Vogais e ditongos

| | |
|---|---|
| a | como em saco |
| ă | como o a de porta |

| æ | entre o **a** de saco e o **é** de café |
| i | parecido com o **i** de fácil |

1) As vogais longas estão impressas em duplicado.

2) As letras impressas em caracteres pequenos e elevados (por ex.: <sup>i</sup>éç, ai<sup>a</sup>) devem pronunciar-se rapidamente e com menos intensidade.

## Pronúncia americana

A nossa transcrição corresponde à pronúncia da Grã-Bretanha. Embora existam variações regionais notáveis na língua americana, esta apresenta, em geral, algumas diferenças importantes em relação ao inglês da Grã-Bretanha.

Eis aqui alguns exemplos:

1) O **r**, diante de uma consoante ou no final de uma palavra, pronuncia-se sempre (ao contrário da pronúncia inglesa habitual).

2) Em muitas palavras (por ex.: *ask, castle, laugh,* etc.) o **aa** transforma-se em **æœ**.

3) O som inglês **o** pronuncia-se **a** ou também **óó**.

4) Em palavras como *duty, tune, new,* etc., **uu** transforma-se muitas vezes em <sup>i</sup>**uu**.

5) Por último, o acento tónico de algumas palavras pode variar consideravelmente.

# A

**a** (ei-ă) *art* (an) um, uma

**abbey** (æ-bi) *n* abadia *f*

**abbreviation** (ă-brii-vi-*ei*-chänn) *n* abreviatura *f*

**aberration** (æ-bä-*rei*-chänn) *n* aberra-cão *f*

**ability** (ă-*bi*-lä-ti) *n* capacidade *f*; habilidade *f*

**able** (*ei*-băl) *adj* capaz; *be ~ to *ser capaz de; *poder

**abnormal** (æb-*nóó*-măl) *adj* anormal

**aboard** (ă-*bóód*) *adv* a bordo

**abolish** (ă-*bó*-lich) *v* *abolir

**abortion** (ă-*bóó*-chänn) *n* aborto *m*

**about** (ă-*baut*) *prep* acerca de; a respeito de, referente a; em volta de; *adv* cerca de, aproximadamente; à volta, em volta

**above** (ă-*bav*) *prep* sobre; *adv* em cima

**abroad** (ă-*bróód*) *adv* no estrangeiro, para o estrangeiro

**abscess** (æb-*çéç*) *n* abcesso *m*

**absence** (æb-çännç) *n* ausência *f*

**absent** (æb-çännt) *adj* ausente

**absolutely** (æb-çă-luut-li) *adv* absolutamente

**abstain from** (äb-*çteinn*) *abster-se de

**abstract** (æb-çtrækt) *adj* abstracto

**absurd** (ăb-*çáád*) *adj* absurdo

**abundance** (ă-bann-dännç) *n* abundância *f*

**abundant** (ă-bann-dännt) *adj* abundante

**abuse** (ă-*b¹uuç*) *n* abuso *m*

**abyss** (ă-*biç*) *n* abismo *m*

**academy** (ă-kæ-dä-mi) *n* academia *f*

**accelerate** (ăk-*çé*-lă-reit) *v* acelerar

**accelerator** (ăk-çé-lă-rei-tä) *n* acelerador *m*

**accent** (æk-çännt) *n* sotaque *m*; acento *m*

**accept** (ăk-*çépt*) *v* aceitar

**access** (æk-çéç) *n* acesso *m*

**accessary** (ăk-çé-çă-ri) *n* cúmplice *m*

**accessible** (ăk-çé-çă-băl) *adj* acessível

**accessories** (ăk-çé-çă-riz) *pl* acessórios

**accident** (æk-çi-dännt) *n* acidente *m*, desastre *m*

**accidental** (æk-çi-*dénn*-täl) *adj* acidental

**accommodate** (ă-*kó*-mă-deit) *v* acomodar, alojar

**accommodation** (ă-kó-mă-*dei*-chänn) *n* acomodação *f*, alojamento *m*

**accompany** (ă-*kamm*-pă-ni) *v* acompanhar

**accomplish** (ă-*kamm*-plich) *v* terminar; realizar

**in accordance with** (inn ă-*kóó*-dănnç ᵘið) conforme

**according to** (ă-*kóó*-dinng tuu) conforme, segundo

**account** (ă-*kaunnt*) n conta f; relato m; ~ **for** explicar, justificar; **on** ~ **of** por causa de

**accountable** (ă-*kaunn*-tă-băl) adj explicável

**accurate** (æ-kⁱu-răt) adj exacto

**accuse** (ă-kⁱuuz) v acusar

**accused** (ă-kⁱuuzd) n acusado m

**accustom** (ă-ka-çtămm) v acostumar; **accustomed** costumado, habituado

**ache** (eik) v *doer; n dor f

**achieve** (ă-*tchiiv*) v alcançar; realizar, *concluir

**achievement** (ă-*tchiiv*-mănnt) n realização f

**acid** (æ-çid) n ácido m

**acknowledge** (ăk-*nó*-lidj) v reconhecer; admitir

**acne** (æk-ni) n acne f

**acorn** (*ei*-kóónn) n bolota f

**acquaintance** (ă-kᵘ*einn*-tănnç) n conhecido m, conhecimento m

**acquire** (ă-kᵘaiˢ) v adquirir

**acquisition** (æ-kᵘi-zi-chănn) n aquisição f

**acquittal** (ă-kᵘi-tăl) n absolvição f

**across** (ă-*króç*) prep através; do outro lado de; adv no outro lado

**act** (ækt) n acto m; número m; v agir; comportar-se; representar

**action** (æk-chănn) n acção f

**active** (æk-tiv) adj activo

**activity** (æk-*ti*-vă-ti) n actividade f

**actor** (æk-tă) n actor m

**actress** (æk-triç) n actriz f

**actual** (æk-tchu-ăl) adj verdadeiro, real, efectivo

**actually** (æk-tchu-ă-li) adv realmente

**acute** (ă-kⁱuut) adj agudo

**adapt** (ă-*dæpt*) v adaptar

**add** (æd) v adicionar; juntar

**adaptor** (ă-*dæp*-tă) n adaptador m

**addition** (ă-*di*-chănn) n adição f

**additional** (ă-*di*-chă-năl) adj adicional; suplementar; acessório

**address** (ă-*dréç*) n endereço m; v endereçar; dirigir-se a

**addressee** (æ-dré-çii) n destinatário m

**adequate** (æ-di-kᵘăt) adj adequado, apropriado

**adjective** (æ-djik-tiv) n adjectivo m

**adjourn** (ă-*djäänn*) v adiar

**adjust** (ă-*djaçt*) v ajustar

**administer** (ăd-*mi*-ni-çtă) v administrar

**administration** (ăd-mi-ni-*çtrei*-chănn) n administração f; gestão f

**administrative** (ăd-*mi*-ni-çtră-tiv) adj administrativo; ~ **law** direito administrativo

**admiral** (æd-mă-răl) n almirante m

**admiration** (æd-mă-*rei*-chănn) n admiração f

**admire** (ăd-*mai*ˢ) v admirar

**admission** (ăd-*mi*-chănn) n admissão f

**admit** (ăd-*mit*) v admitir; reconhecer

**admittance** (ăd-*mi*-tănnç) n entrada f; **no** ~ entrada proibida

**adopt** (ă-*dópt*) v adoptar

**adorable** (ă-*dóó*-ră-băl) adj adorável

**adult** (æ-dalt) n adulto m; adj adulto

**advance** (ăd-*vaannç*) n avanço m; adiantamento m; v avançar; adiantar; **in** ~ antecipadamente, adiantadamente

**advanced** (ăd-*vaannçt*) adj avançado

**advantage** (ăd-*vaann*-tidj) n vantagem f

**advantageous** (æd-vănn-*tei*-djăç) adj vantajoso

**adventure** (ăd-*vénn*-tchă) n aventura f

adverb (æd-vääb) n advérbio m

advertisement (ăd-vää-tiç-mănnt) n anúncio m

advertising (æd-vă-tai-zinng) n publicidade f

advice (ăd-vaiç) n conselho m

advise (ăd-vaiz) v aconselhar

advocate (æd-vă-kăt) n advogado m, defensor m

aerial (éá-ri-ăl) n antena f

aeroplane (éá-ră-pleinn) n avião m

affair (ă-féá) n assunto m; ligação f, aventura f

affect (ă-fékt) v afectar

affected (ă-fék-tid) adj afectado

affection (ă-fék-chănn) n afecção f; afeição f

affectionate (ă-fék-chă-nit) adj afectuoso

affiliated (ă-fi-li-ei-tid) adj filiado

affirmative (ă-fáá-mă-tiv) adj afirmativo

affliction (ă-flik-chănn) n sofrimento m

afford (ă-fóód) v permitir-se

afraid (ă-freid) adj assustado, com medo; *be ~ *ter medo

Africa (æ-fri-kă) África f

African (æ-fri-kănn) adj africano

after (aaf-tă) prep depois de; conj depois que

afternoon (aaf-tă-nuunn) n tarde f

afterwards (aaf-tă-ᵘădz) adv depois; em seguida

again (ă-ghénn) adv outra vez; de novo; again and again repetidamente

against (ă-ghénnçt) prep contra

age (eidj) n idade f; of ~ maior; under ~ menor

aged (ei-djid) adj velho

agency (ei-djănn-çi) n agência f; repartição f

agenda (ă-djénn-dă) n agenda f; ordem do dia

agent (ei-djännt) n agente m, representante m

aggressive (ă-ghré-çiv) adj agressivo

ago (ă-ghoᵘ) adv há; long ~ há muito tempo

agrarian (ă-ghréá-ri-ănn) adj agrário, agrícola

agree (ă-ghrii) v concordar; *consentir

agreeable (ă-ghrii-ă-băl) adj agradável

agreement (ă-ghrii-mănnt) n contrato m; acordo m

agriculture (æ-ghri-kal-tchă) n agricultura f

ahead (ă-héd) adv em frente; ~ of adiante de; *go ~ continuar; straight ~ sempre a direita

aid (eid) n ajuda f; v ajudar, auxiliar

AIDS (eidz) n SIDA f; AIDS Br

ailment (eil-mănnt) n mal m; achaque m

aim (eimm) n objectivo m; ~ at apontar para, visar; aspirar (a)

air (éá) n ar m; v arejar

air-conditioning (éá-kănn-di-chă-ninng) n ar condicionado; air-conditioned com ar condicionado

aircraft (éá-kraaft) n (pl ~) avião m

airfield (éá-fiild) n campo de aviação

air-filter (éá-fil-tă) n filtro de ar

airline (éá-lainn) n companhia de aviação

airmail (éá-meil) n correio aéreo

airplane (éá-pleinn) nAm avião m

airport (éá-póót) n aeroporto m

air-sickness (éá-çik-năç) n enjoo m

airtight (éá-tait) adj hermético

airy (éá-ri) adj arejado

aisle (ail) n nave lateral; passagem f

alarm (ă-laamm) n alarme m; v alarmar

alarm-clock (ă-laamm-klók) n despertador m

**album** (ǽl-bămm) *n* álbum *m*

**alcohol** (ǽl-kă-hól) *n* álcool *m*

**alcoholic** (ǽl-kă-hó-lik) *adj* alcoólico

**ale** (eil) *n* cerveja *f*

**algebra** (ǽl-dji-bră) *n* álgebra *f*

**Algeria** (ǽl-djiᵃ-ri-ă) Argélia *f*

**Algerian** (ǽl-djiᵃ-ri-ănn) *adj* argelino

**alien** (ei-li-ănn) *n* estrangeiro *m*; estranho *m; adj* estrangeiro

**alike** (ă-laik) *adj* igual, semelhante; *adv* igualmente

**alimony** (ǽ-li-mă-ni) *n* pensão alimentícia

**alive** (ă-laiv) *adj* vivo, com vida

**all** (óól) *adj* todo; tudo; ~ in tudo incluído; ~ right! está bem!; at ~ de todo

**alleged** (ă-lé-djăd) *adj* suposto

**allergy** (ǽ-lă-dji) *n* alergia *f*

**alley** (ǽ-li) *n* viela *f*, beco *m*

**alliance** (ă-lai-ănnç) *n* aliança *f*

**allot** (ă-lót) *v* \*atribuir

**allow** (ă-lau) *v* permitir, \*consentir; ~ to autorizar a; \*be allowed \*estar autorizado

**allowance** (ă-lau-ănnç) *n* subsídio *m*

**all-round** (óól-raunnd) *adj* polivalente

**almanac** (óól-mă-næk) *n* almanaque *m*

**almond** (aa-mănnd) *n* amêndoa *f*

**almost** (óól-mouçt) *adv* quase

**alone** (ă-lounn) *adv* só

**along** (ă-lónn) *prep* ao longo de

**aloud** (ă-laud) *adv* em voz alta

**alphabet** (ǽl-fă-bét) *n* alfabeto *m*

**already** (óól-ré-di) *adv* já

**also** (óól-çouᵘ) *adv* também, igualmente

**altar** (óól-tă) *n* altar *m*

**alter** (óól-tă) *v* alterar

**alteration** (óól-tă-rei-chănn) *n* alteração *f*

**alternate** (óól-tăă-năt) *adj* alternado

**alternative** (óól-tăă-nă-tiv) *n* alterna-

tiva *f*

**although** (óól-ðouᵘ) *conj* embora

**altitude** (ǽl-ti-tiuud) *n* altitude *f*

**alto** (ǽl-touᵘ) *n* (pl ~s) contralto *m*

**altogether** (óól-tă-ghé-ðă) *adv* inteiramente; totalmente; ao todo

**always** (óól-ᵘeiz) *adv* sempre

**am** (æmm) *v* (pr be)

**amaze** (ă-meiz) *v* espantar, surpreender

**amazement** (ă-meiz-mănnt) *n* espanto *m*

**ambassador** (æmm-bæ-çă-dă) *n* embaixador *m*

**amber** (æmm-bă) *n* âmbar *m*

**ambiguous** (æmm-bi-ghiᵘ-ăç) *adj* ambíguo; equívoco

**ambitious** (æmm-bi-chăç) *adj* ambicioso

**ambulance** (æmm-biᵘ-lănnç) *n* ambulância *f*

**ambush** (æmm-buch) *n* emboscada *f*

**America** (ă-mé-ri-kă) América *f*

**American** (ă-mé-ri-kănn) *adj* americano

**amethyst** (æ-mi-θiçt) *n* ametista *f*

**amid** (ă-mid) *prep* entre, no meio de

**ammonia** (ă-mouᵘ-ni-ă) *n* amoníaco *m*

**amnesty** (æmm-ni-çti) *n* amnistia *f*

**among** (ă-mánng) *prep* entre; ~ other things entre outras coisas

**amount** (ă-maunnt) *n* quantidade *f*; quantia *f*, soma *f*; ~ to importar em; \*equivaler a

**amuse** (ă-miᵘuuz) *v* \*divertir

**amusement** (ă-miᵘuuz-mănnt) *n* divertimento *m*, distracção *m*

**amusing** (ă-miᵘuu-zinng) *adj* divertido, engraçado

**anaemia** (ă-nii-mi-ă) *n* anemia *f*

**anaesthesia** (æ-niç-θii-zi-ă) *n* anestesia *f*

**anaesthetic** (æ-niç-θé-tik) *n* anestésico *m*

**analyse** (æ-nǎ-laiz) v analisar

**analysis** (ǎ-næ-lǎ-çiç) n (pl -ses) análise f

**analyst** (æ-nǎ-liçt) n analista m; psicanalista m

**anarchy** (æ-nǎ-ki) n anarquia f

**anatomy** (ǎ-næ-tǎ-mi) n anatomia f

**ancestor** (ænn-çé-çtǎ) n antepassado m

**anchor** (ænng-kǎ) n âncora f

**anchovy** (ænn-tchǎ-vi) n anchova f

**ancient** (einn-chǎnnt) adj antigo, velho; antiquado, envelhecido; velhíssimo

**and** (ænnd ǎnnd) conj e

**angel** (einn-djǎl) n anjo m

**anger** (æng-ghǎ) n cólera f, ira f; furor m

**angle** (æng-ghǎl) v pescar à linha; n ângulo m

**angry** (æng-ghri) adj zangado

**animal** (æ-ni-mǎl) n animal m

**ankle** (æng-kǎl) n tornozelo m

**annex**[1] (æ-nékç) n anexo m

**annex**[2] (ǎ-nékç) v anexar

**anniversary** (æ-ni-vǎǎ-çǎ-ri) n aniversário m

**announce** (ǎ-naunnç) v anunciar

**announcement** (ǎ-naunnç-mǎnnt) n anúncio m, participação f

**annoy** (ǎ-noi) v irritar; aborrecer

**annoyance** (ǎ-noi-ǎnnç) n aborrecimento m

**annoying** (ǎ-noi-inng) adj irritante, maçador

**annual** (æ-n¡u-ǎl) adj anual; n anuário m

**per annum** (pǎr æ-nǎmm) anualmente

**anonymous** (ǎ-nó-ni-mǎç) adj anónimo

**another** (ǎ-na-ðǎ) adj mais um; um outro

**answer** (aann-çǎ) v responder a; n resposta f

**ant** (ænnt) n formiga f

**anthology** (ænn-θó-lǎ-dji) n antologia f

**antibiotic** (ænn-ti-bai-ó-tik) n antibiótico m

**anticipate** (ænn-ti-çi-peit) v *prever; esperar, *prevenir

**antifreeze** (ænn-ti-friiz) n anticongelante m

**antipathy** (ænn-ti-pǎ-θi) n antipatia f

**antique** (ænn-tiik) adj antigo; n antiguidade f; ~ **dealer** antiquário m

**antiquity** (ænn-ti-kᵘǎ-ti) n antiguidade f

**antiseptic** (ænn-ti-çép-tik) n antisséptico m

**antlers** (ænnt-lǎz) pl esgalhos mpl

**anxiety** (ænng-zai-ǎ-ti) n ansiedade f

**anxious** (ænngk-chǎç) adj ansioso; inquieto

**any** (é-ni) adj qualquer

**anybody** (é-ni-bó-di) pron qualquer pessoa

**anyhow** (é-ni-hau) adv de qualquer modo

**anyone** (é-ni-ᵘann) pron qualquer pessoa

**anything** (é-ni-θinng) pron qualquer coisa

**anyway** (é-ni-ᵘei) adv de qualquer maneira

**anywhere** (é-ni-ᵘéᵃ) adv onde quer que seja; em qualquer lado

**apart** (ǎ-paat) adv à parte, separadamente; ~ **from** fora, à parte

**apartment** (ǎ-paat-mǎnnt) nAm apartamento m; andar m; ~ **house** Am prédio de andares; prédio de apartamentos Br

**ape** (eip) n macaco m

**aperitif** (ǎ-pé-rǎ-tiv) n aperitivo m

**apologize** (ǎ-pó-lǎ-djaiz) v pedir desculpa, desculpar-se

**apology** (ǎ-pó-lǎ-dji) n desculpa f

**apparatus** (æ-pă-*rei*-tăç) *n* dispositivo *m*, aparelho *m*

**apparent** (ă-*pæ*-rănnt) *adj* aparente; óbvio

**apparently** (ă-*pæ*-rănnt-li) *adv* aparentemente; evidentemente

**apparition** (æ-pă-*ri*-chänn) *n* aparição *f*

**appeal** (ă-*piil*) *n* apelo *m*

**appear** (ă-*pi*ă) *v* parecer; resultar; aparecer; apresentar-se

**appearance** (ă-*pi*ă-rănnç) *n* aparência *f*; aparecimento *m*

**appendicitis** (ă-pénn-di-*çai*-tiç) *n* apendicite *f*

**appendix** (ă-*pénn*-dikç) *n* (pl -dices, -dixes) apêndice *m*

**appetite** (æ-pă-tait) *n* apetite *m*

**appetizer** (æ-pă-tai-ză) *n* aperitivos *m*

**appetizing** (æ-pă-tai-zinng) *adj* apetitoso

**applause** (ă-*plóóz*) *n* aplausos *mpl*

**apple** (æ-păl) *n* maçã *f*

**appliance** (ă-*plai*-ănnç) *n* aparelho *m*

**application** (æ-pli-*kei*-chănn) *n* aplicação *f*; pedido *m*; candidatura *f*

**apply** (ă-*plai*) *v* aplicar; solicitar um emprego; aplicar-se a

**appoint** (ă-*poinnt*) *v* *nomear, designar

**appointment** (ă-*poinnt*-mănnt) *n* consulta *f*, entrevista *f*; nomeação *f*

**appreciate** (ă-*prii*-chi-eit) *v* avaliar; apreciar

**appreciation** (ă-prii-chi-*ei*-chănn) *n* avaliação *f*; apreciação *f*

**approach** (ă-*pro*utch) *v* aproximar-se; *n* maneira de proceder; acesso *m*

**appropriate** (ă-*pro*u-pri-ăt) *adj* apropriado, justo, adequado

**approval** (ă-*pruu*-văl) *n* aprovação *f*; on ~ à condição

**approve** (ă-*pruuv*) *v* aprovar; ~ of concordar com

**approximate** (ă-*prók*-çi-măt) *adj* aproximado

**approximately** (ă-*prók*-çi-măt-li) *adv* aproximadamente

**apricot** (*ei*-pri-kót) *n* alperche *m*

**April** (*ei*-prăl) Abril

**apron** (*ei*-pränn) *n* avental *m*

**Arab** (æ-răb) *adj* árabe

**arbitrary** (aa-bi-tră-ri) *adj* arbitrário

**arcade** (aa-*keid*) *n* arcada *f*

**arch** (aatch) *n* arco *m*; abóbada *f*

**archaeologist** (aa-ki-ó-lă-djiçt) *n* arqueólogo *m*

**archaeology** (aa-ki-ó-lă-dji) *n* arqueologia *f*

**archbishop** (aatch-*bi*-chăp) *n* arcebispo *m*

**arched** (aatcht) *adj* arqueado

**architect** (aa-ki-tékt) *n* arquitecto *m*

**architecture** (aa-ki-ték-tchă) *n* arquitectura *f*

**archives** (aa-kaivz) *pl* arquivo *m*

**are** (aa) *v* (pr be)

**area** (é*ă*-ri-ă) *n* região *f*; zona *f*; área *f*; ~ code indicativo *m*

**Argentina** (aa-djänn-*tii*-nă) Argentina *f*

**Argentinian** (aa-djänn-*ti*-ni-änn) *adj* argentino

**argue** (aa-gh*i*uu) *v* discutir, argumentar

**argument** (aa-gh*i*u-männt) *n* argumento *m*; discussão *f*; disputa *f*

**arid** (æ-rid) *adj* árido

**\*arise** (ă-*raiz*) *v* surgir

**arithmetic** (ă-*ri*β-mă-tik) *n* aritmética *f*

**arm** (aamm) *n* braço *m*; arma *f*; *v* armar

**armchair** (*aamm*-tché*ă*) *n* cadeira de braços, poltrona *f*

**armed** (aammd) *adj* armado; ~ forces forças armadas

**armour** (aa-mă) *n* armadura *f*

**army** (*aa-*mi) *n* exército *m*

**aroma** (ă-*ro*ᵘ-mă) *n* aroma *m*

**around** (ă-*raunnd*) *prep* em volta de, à volta de; *adv* à volta de

**arrange** (ă-*reinndj*) *v* ordenar, agrupar, arranjar, organizar

**arrangement** (ă-*reinndj*-mănnt) *n* regulamento *m;* acordo *m*

**arrest** (ă-*réçt*) *v* prender; *n* prisão *f*

**arrival** (ă-*rai*-văl) *n* chegada *f*

**arrive** (ă-*raiv*) *v* chegar

**arrow** (*æ*-roᵘ) *n* seta *f*

**art** (aat) *n* arte *f;* habilidade *f;* ~ **collection** colecção de obras de arte; ~ **exhibition** exposição de arte; ~ **gallery** galeria de arte; ~ **history** história da arte; **arts and crafts** artes e ofícios; ~ **school** academia das belas-artes

**artery** (*aa-*tă-ri) *n* artéria *f*

**artichoke** (*aa-*ti-tchoᵘk) *n* alcachofra *f*

**article** (*aa-*ti-kăl) *n* artigo *m*

**artifice** (*aa-*ti-fiç) *n* artifício *m*

**artificial** (aa-ti-*fi*-chăl) *adj* artificial

**artist** (*aa-*tiçt) *n* artista *m*

**artistic** (aa-*ti*-çtik) *adj* artístico

**as** (æz) *conj* como; tanto; que; porque, visto que; ~ **from** desde; a partir de; ~ **if** como se

**asbestos** (æz-*bé*-çtoç) *n* amianto *m*

**ascend** (ă-*çénnd*) *v* ascender; *subir; escalar

**ascent** (ă-*çénnt*) *n* ascensão *f;* subida *f*

**ascertain** (æ-çă-*teinn*) *v* constatar; certificar-se de

**ash** (æch) *n* cinza *f*

**ashamed** (ă-*cheimmd*) *adj* envergonhado; *be ~ *ter vergonha

**ashore** (ă-*chóó*) *adv* a terra, em terra

**ashtray** (*æch-*trei) *n* cinzeiro *m*

**Asia** (*ei-*chă) Ásia *f*

**Asian** (*ei-*chănn) *adj* asiático

**aside** (ă-*çaid*) *adv* de lado; à parte

**ask** (aaçk) *v* perguntar; *pedir; convidar

**asleep** (ă-*çliip*) *adj* adormecido

**asparagus** (ă-*çpæ*-ră-ghăç) *n* espargo *m*

**aspect** (*æ*-çpékt) *n* aspecto *m*

**asphalt** (*æç*-fælt) *n* asfalto *m*

**aspire** (ă-*çpai*ᵃ) *v* aspirar

**aspirin** (*æ*-çpă-rinn) *n* aspirina *f*

**ass** (æç) *n* burro *m*

**assassination** (ă-çæ-çi-*nei*-chănn) *n* assassínio *m*

**assault** (ă-*çóólt*) *v* atacar; violar

**assemble** (ă-*çémm*-băl) *v* reunir; montar

**assembly** (ă-*çémm*-bli) *n* reunião *f,* assembleia *f*

**assign to** (ă-*çainn*) *atribuir a

**assist** (ă-*çiçt*) *v* auxiliar, assistir; ~ **at** assistir a

**assistance** (ă-*çi*-çtănnç) *n* ajuda *f;* assistência *f*

**assistant**[1] (ă-*çi*-çtănnt) *n* assistente *m*

**associate**[1] (ă-*ço*ᵘ-chi-ăt) *n* sócio *m,* companheiro *m;* aliado *m;* membro *m*

**associate**[2] (ă-*ço*ᵘ-chi-eit) *v* associar; ~ **with** andar com, associar-se com

**association** (ă-ço*ᵘ*-çi-*ei*-chănn) *n* associação *f*

**assort** (ă-*çóót*) *v* classificar

**assortment** (ă-*çóót*-mănnt) *n* sortido *m,* sortimento *m*

**assume** (ă-*çiuumm*) *v* *supor

**assure** (ă-*chu*ᵃ) *v* assegurar, garantir

**asthma** (*æç*-mă) *n* asma *f*

**astonish** (ă-*çtó*-nich) *v* espantar

**astonishing** (ă-*çtó*-ni-chinng) *adj* espantoso

**astonishment** (ă-*çtó*-nich-mănnt) *n* espanto *m*

**astronomy** (ă-*çtró*-nă-mi) *n* astronomia *f*

**asylum** (ă-*çai*-lămm) *n* asilo *m*

**at** (æt) *prep* em, a; para

**ate** (ét) *v* (p eat)

**atheist** (*ei*-θi-içt) *n* ateu *m*

**athlete** (æθ-liit) *n* atleta *m*

**athletics** (æθ-\è-tikç) *pl* atletismo *m*

**Atlantic** (ăt-*lænn*-tik) Atlântico *m*

**atmosphere** (æt-măç-fiă) *n* atmosfera *f*: ambiente *m*

**atom** (æ-tămm) *n* átomo *m*

**atomic** (ă-*tó*-mik) *adj* atómico *m*

**atomizer** (æ-tă-mai-ză) *n* vaporizador *m*: pulverizador *m*

**attach** (ă-*tætch*) *v* atar, prender; fixar: juntar; **attached to** dedicado a

**attack** (ă-*tæk*) *v* atacar, *agredir; *n* ataque *m*

**attain** (ă-*teinn*) *v* atingir

**attainable** (ă-*tei*-nă-băl) *adj* possível; acessível

**attempt** (ă-*témmpt*) *v* tentar; *n* tentativa *f*

**attend** (ă-*ténnd*) *v* assistir a; ~ **on** atender; ~ **to** ocupar-se de, tratar de; prestar atenção a

**attendance** (ă-*ténn*-dănç) *n* assistência *f*

**attendant** (ă-*ténn*-dănnt) *n* guarda *m*

**attention** (ă-*ténn*-chănn) *n* atenção *f*; *pay ~ prestar atenção

**attentive** (ă-*ténn*-tiv) *adj* atento

**attic** (æ-tik) *n* sótão *m*

**attitude** (æ-ti-tʲuud) *n* atitude *f*

**attorney** (ă-*tăă*-ni) *n* advogado *m*

**attract** (ă-*trækt*) *v* *atrair

**attraction** (ă-*træk*-chănn) *n* atracção *f*: atractivo *m*

**attractive** (ă-*træk*-tiv) *adj* atraente

**auburn** (óó-bănn) *adj* castanho encarnicado

**auction** (óók-chănn) *n* leilão *m*

**audible** (óó-di-băl) *adj* audível

**audience** (óó-di-ănnç) *n* audiência *f*;

auditório *m*

**auditor** (óó-di-tă) *n* ouvinte *m*

**auditorium** (óó-di-*tóó*-ri-ămm) *n* auditório *m*

**August** (óó-ghăçt) Agosto

**aunt** (aannt) *n* tia *f*

**Australia** (ó-*çtrei*-li-ă) Austrália *f*

**Australian** (ó-*çtrei*-li-ănn) *adj* australiano

**Austria** (ó-çtri-ă) Áustria *f*

**Austrian** (ó-çtri-ănn) *adj* austríaco

**authentic** (óó-*θénn*-tik) *adj* autêntico

**author** (óó-θă) *n* autor *m*

**authoritarian** (óó-θó-ri-*téă*-ri-ănn) *adj* autoritário

**authority** (óó-*θó*-ră-ti) *n* autoridade *f*; poder *m*

**authorization** (óó-θă-rai-*zei*-chănn) *n* autorização *f*

**automatic** (óó-tă-*mæ*-tik) *adj* automático; ~ **teller** caixa automática

**automation** (óó-tă-*mei*-chănn) *n* automatização *f*

**automobile** (óó-tă-mă-biil) *n* automóvel *m*; ~ **club** automóvel clube

**autonomous** (óó-*tó*-nă-măç) *adj* autónomo

**autopsy** (óó-tó-pçi) *n* autópsia *f*

**autumn** (óó-tămm) *n* Outono *m*

**available** (ă-*vei*-lă-băl) *adj* disponível

**avalanche** (æ-vă-laannch) *n* avalanche *f*

**avaricious** (æ-vă-*ri*-chăç) *adj* avarento

**avenue** (æ-vă-nʲuu) *n* avenida *f*

**average** (æ-vă-ridj) *adj* médio; *n* média *f*; **on the** ~ em média

**averse** (ă-*văăç*) *adj* adverso

**aversion** (ă-*văă*-chănn) *n* aversão *f*

**avert** (ă-*văăt*) *v* desviar

**avoid** (ă-*void*) *v* evitar

**await** (ă-*ᵘeit*) *v* esperar

**awake** (ă-*ᵘeik*) *adj* acordado

***awake** (ă-*ᵘeik*) *v* despertar, acordar

**award** (ă-*ᵘóód*) *n* prémio *m*; *v* *atri-

buir
**aware** (ă-ᵘéᵃ) *adj* ciente
**away** (ă-ᵘei) *adv* ausente; **\*go ~**
**\*ir-se embora**
**awful** (óó-făl) *adj* terrível, horrível
**awkward** (óó-kᵘăd) *adj* embaraçoso;
desastrado
**awning** (óó-ninng) *n* toldo *m*
**axe** (ækç) *n* machado *m*
**axle** (æk-çăl) *n* eixo *m*

# B

**baby** (beɪ-bi) *n* bebé *m*; **~ carriage**
*Am* carrinho de bebé
**babysitter** (bei-bi-çi-tă) *n* babysitter
*m*
**bachelor** (bæ-tchă-lă) *n* celibatário *m*
**back** (bæk) *n* costas; *adv* atrás; **\*go**
**~ regressar**
**backache** (bæ-keik) *n* dores nas costas
**backbone** (bæk-boᵘnn) *n* espinha dorsal
**background** (bæk-ghraunnd) *n* fundo
*m*
**backwards** (bæk-ᵘădz) *adv* para trás
**bacon** (bei-kănn) *n* bacon *m*
**bacterium** (bæk-tii-ri-ămm) *n* (pl -ria)
bactéria *f*
**bad** (bæd) *adj* mau; grave
**bag** (bægh) *n* saco *m*; carteira *f*, bolsa *f*; mala *f*
**baggage** (bæ-ghidj) *n* bagagem *f*;
**hand ~** *Am* bagagem de mão
**bail** (beil) *n* caução *f*
**bailiff** (bei-lif) *n* oficial de diligências
**bait** (beit) *n* isca *f*
**bake** (beik) *v* cozinhar no forno, cozer no forno
**baker** (bei-kă) *n* padeiro *m*
**bakery** (bei-kă-ri) *n* padaria *f*

**balance** (bæ-lănnç) *n* equilíbrio *m*;
balanço *m*; saldo *m*
**balcony** (bæl-kă-ni) *n* varanda *f*
**bald** (bóóld) *adj* careca
**ball** (bóól) *n* bola *f*; baile *m*
**ballet** (bæ-lei) *n* bailado *m*
**balloon** (bă-luunn) *n* balão *m*
**ballpoint-pen** (bóól-poinnt-pénn) *n* caneta esferográfica
**ballroom** (bóól-ruumm) *n* salão de baile
**bamboo** (bæmm-buu) *n* (pl ~s) bambu *m*
**banana** (bă-naa-nă) *n* banana *f*
**band** (bænnd) *n* banda *f*; ligadura *f*
**bandage** (bænn-didj) *n* ligadura *f*
**bandit** (bænn-dit) *n* bandido *m*
**bangle** (bæng-ghăl) *n* pulseira *f*
**banisters** (bæ-ni-çtăz) *pl* corrimão *m*
**bank** (bænngk) *n* beira *f*; banco *m*; *v*
depositar; **~ account** conta bancária
**banknote** (bænngk-noᵘt) *n* nota de
banco
**bank-rate** (bænngk-reit) *n* taxa de
desconto
**bankrupt** (bænngk-rapt) *adj* falido
**banner** (bæ-nă) *n* estandarte *m*
**banquet** (bænng-kᵘit) *n* banquete *m*
**banqueting-hall** (bænng-kᵘi-tinng-
hóól) *n* salão de banquetes
**baptism** (bæp-ti-zămm) *n* baptismo *m*
**baptize** (bæp-taiz) *v* baptizar
**bar** (baa) *n* bar *m*; barra *f*
**barber** (baa-bă) *n* barbeiro *m*
**bare** (béᵃ) *adj* nu, despido; descoberto
**barely** (béᵃ-li) *adv* mal
**bargain** (baa-ghinn) *n* pechincha *f*; *v*
**\*regatear**
**baritone** (bæ-ri-toᵘnn) *n* barítono *m*
**bark** (baak) *n* casca *f*; *v* ladrar
**barley** (baa-li) *n* cevada *f*
**barmaid** (baa-meid) *n* empregada de

bar

**barman** (*baa*-mănn) *n* (pl -men) barman *m*

**barn** (baann) *n* celeiro *m*

**barometer** (bă-*ró*-mi-tă) *n* barómetro *m*

**baroque** (bă-*rók*) *adj* barroco

**barracks** (*bæ*-răkç) *pl* quartel *m*

**barrel** (*bæ*-răl) *n* barril *m*, pipa *f*

**barrier** (*bæ*-ri-ă) *n* barreira *f*; cancela *f*

**barrister** (*bæ*-ri-çtă) *n* advogado *m*

**bartender** (baa-*ténn*-dă) *n* empregado de bar

**base** (beiç) *n* base *f*; alicerce *m*; *v* *basear

**baseball** (*beiç*-bóól) *n* basebol *m*

**basement** (*beiç*-mănnt) *n* cave *f*; porão *mBr*

**basic** (*bei*-çik) *adj* fundamental; básico

**basilica** (bă-*zi*-li-kă) *n* basílica *f*

**basin** (*bei*-çănn) *n* bacia *f*, tigela *f*

**basis** (*bei*-çiç) *n* (pl bases) base *f*, fundamento *m*

**basket** (*baa*-çkit) *n* cesto *m*

**bass**[1] (beiç) *n* baixo *m*

**bass**[2] (bæç) *n* (pl ~) robalo *m*

**bastard** (*baa*-çtăd) *n* bastardo *m*; patife *m*

**batch** (bætch) *n* lote *m*

**bath** (baaθ) *n* banho *m*; ~ **salts** sais de banho; ~ **towel** toalha de banho

**bathe** (beið) *v* tomar banho, banhar-se

**bathing-cap** (*bei*-ðinng-kæp) *n* touca de banho

**bathing-suit** (*bei*-ðinng-çuut) *n* fato de banho; traje de banho *Br*

**bathrobe** (*baaθ*-roᵘb) *n* roupão de banho

**bathroom** (*baaθ*-ruumm) *n* quarto de banho; casa de banho; banheiro

*mBr*

**batter** (*bæ*-tă) *n* massa *f*

**battery** (*bæ*-tă-ri) *n* pilha eléctrica; bateria *f*

**battle** (*bæ*-tăl) *n* batalha *f*; combate *m*, luta *f*; *v* combater

**bay** (bei) *n* baía *f*; *v* ladrar

***be** (bii) *v* *ser, *estar

**beach** (biitch) *n* praia *f*; **nudist** ~ praia para nudistas

**bead** (biid) *n* conta *f*; **beads** colar *m*; rosário *m*

**beak** (biik) *n* bico *m*

**beam** (biimm) *n* raio *m*; viga *f*

**bean** (biinn) *n* feijão *m*

**bear** (béᵃ) *n* urso *m*

***bear** (béᵃ) *v* levar; suportar

**beard** (biᵃd) *n* barba *f*

**bearer** (*béᵃ*-ră) *n* portador *m*

**beast** (biiçt) *n* animal *m*; ~ **of prey** animal de rapina

***beat** (biit) *v* bater

**beautiful** (*bⁱuu*-ti-făl) *adj* belo

**beauty** (*bⁱuu*-ti) *n* beleza *f*; ~ **parlour** instituto de beleza; ~ **salon** salão de beleza; ~ **treatment** tratamento de beleza

**beaver** (*bii*-vă) *n* castor *m*

**because** (bi-*kóz*) *conj* porque; já que; ~ **of** por causa de

***become** (bi-*kamm*) *v* *vir a ser, tornar-se; ficar bem

**bed** (béd) *n* cama *f*; ~ **and board** pensão completa; ~ **and breakfast** quarto e pequeno almoço

**bedding** (*bé*-dinng) *n* roupa de cama

**bedroom** (*béd*-ruumm) *n* quarto de cama

**bee** (bii) *n* abelha *f*

**beech** (bii-tch) *n* faia *f*

**beef** (biif) *n* carne de vaca

**beehive** (*bii*-haiv) *n* colmeia *f*

**been** (biinn) *v* (pp be)

**beer** (biᵃ) *n* cerveja *f*

**beet** (biit) *n* beterraba *f*

**beetle** (*bii*-tål) *n* escaravelho *m*

**beetroot** (*biit*-ruut) *n* beterraba *f*

**before** (bi-fóó) *prep* antes de; *conj* antes que; *adv* antes; primeiro

**beg** (bégh) *v* mendigar, *\*pedir; suplicar

**beggar** (*bé*-ghå) *n* mendigo *m*

**\*begin** (bi-*ghinn*) *v* principiar, começar; iniciar

**beginner** (bi-*ghi*-nå) *n* principiante *m*

**beginning** (bi-*ghi*-ninng) *n* princípio *m*; início *m*

**on behalf of** (ónn bi-*haaf* óv) em nome de; a favor de

**behave** (bi-*heiv*) *v* portar-se

**behaviour** (bi-*hei*-v$^i$å) *n* comportamento *m*

**behind** (bi-*hainnd*) *prep* atrás de; *adv* atrás

**beige** (beij) *adj* bege

**being** (*bii*-inng) *n* ser *m*

**Belgian** (*bél*-djånn) *adj* belga

**Belgium** (*bél*-djåmm) Bélgica *f*

**belief** (bi-*liif*) *n* crença *f*

**believe** (bi-*liiv*) *v* acreditar

**bell** (bél) *n* sino *m*; campainha *f*

**bellboy** (*bél*-boi) *n* groom *m*

**belly** (*bé*-li) *n* ventre *m*

**belong** (bi-*lónn*) *v* pertencer

**belongings** (bi-*lónn*-inngz) *pl* bens *mpl*

**beloved** (bi-*lavd*) *adj* querido

**below** (bi-*lo*$^u$) *prep* debaixo de; *adv* em baixo, debaixo

**belt** (bélt) *n* cinto *m*

**bench** (bénntch) *n* banco *m*

**bend** (bénnd) *n* volta *f*, curva *f*; curvatura *f*

**\*bend** (bénnd) *v* dobrar, curvar; ~ **down** curvar-se

**beneath** (bi-*nii$\theta$*) *prep* debaixo de; *adv* debaixo

**benefit** (*bé*-ni-fit) *n* benefício *m*, lucro *m*; vantagem *f*; *v* beneficiar

**bent** (bénnt) *adj* (pp bend) curvo; curvado; torto

**beret** (*bé*-rei) *n* boina *f*

**berry** (*bé*-ri) *n* baga *f*

**berth** (bãã$\theta$) *n* beliche *m*

**beside** (bi-*çaid*) *prep* ao lado de

**besides** (bi-*çaidz*) *adv* além de; além disso; *prep* além de

**best** (béçt) *adj* o melhor

**bet** (bét) *n* aposta *f*

**\*bet** (bét) *v* apostar

**betray** (bi-*trei*) *v* \*trair

**better** (*bé*-tå) *adj* melhor

**between** (bi-t$^u$*iinn*) *prep* entre

**beverage** (*bé*-vå-ridj) *n* bebida *f*

**beware** (bi-$^u$*é*$^å$) *v* \*ter cuidado, \*precaver-se

**bewitch** (bi-$^u$*itch*) *v* enfeitiçar, encantar

**beyond** (bi-$^i$*ónnd*) *prep* além de; *adv* além

**bible** (*bai*-bål) *n* bíblia *f*

**bicycle** (*bai*-çi-kål) *n* bicicleta *f*

**big** (bigh) *adj* grande; volumoso; importante

**bile** (bail) *n* bílis *f*

**bilingual** (bai-*linng*-gh$^u$ål) *adj* bilíngue

**bill** (bil) *n* conta *f*; *v* facturar

**billiards** (*bil*-$^i$ådz) *pl* bilhar *m*

**\*bind** (bainnd) *v* atar, ligar

**binding** (*bainn*-dinng) *n* encadernação *f*

**binoculars** (bi-*nó*-k$^i$å-låz) *pl* binóculo *m*

**biology** (bai-*ó*-lå-dji) *n* biologia *f*

**birch** (bãã$t$ch) *n* bétula *f*

**bird** (bãåd) *n* ave *f*

**birth** (bãã$\theta$) *n* nascimento *m*

**birthday** (*bãã$\theta$*-dei) *n* dia dos anos *m*

**biscuit** (*biç*-kit) *n* biscoito *m*

**bishop** (*bi*-chåp) *n* bispo *m*

**bit** (bit) *n* pedaço *m*; bocadinho *m*

**bitch** (bitch) *n* cadela *f*

**bite** (bait) *n* bocado *m*; mordedura *f*;

picada f
*bite (bait) v morder
bitter (bi-tă) adj amargo
black (blæk) adj preto; ~ market mercado negro
blackberry (blæk-bă-ri) n amora silvestre
blackbird (blæk-bääd) n melro m
blackboard (blæk-bóód) n quadro preto
black-currant (blæk-ka-rănnt) n groselha negra
blackmail (blæk-meil) n chantagem f; v *fazer chantagem
blacksmith (blæk-çmiθ) n ferreiro m
bladder (blæ-dă) n bexiga f
blade (bleid) n lâmina f; ~ of grass folha de erva
blame (bleimm) n culpa f; censura f; v censurar, acusar, culpar
blank (blænngk) adj em branco
blanket (blænng-kit) n cobertor m
blast (blaaçt) n explosão f
blazer (blei-ză) n casaco desportivo
bleach (bliitch) v descolorir
bleak (bliik) adj rigoroso
*bleed (bliid) v sangrar
bless (bléç) v *bendizer, abençoar
blessing (blé-çinng) n bênção f
blind (blainnd) n persiana f, estore m; adj cego; v cegar
blister (bli-çtă) n empola f, bolha f
blizzard (bli-zăd) n tempestade de neve
block (blók) v *bloquear, *obstruir; n bloco m; ~ of flats prédio de andares
blonde (blónnd) n loira f
blood (blad) n sangue m; ~ pressure tensão arterial
blood-poisoning (blad-poi-ză-ninng) n septicemia f
blood-vessel (blad-vé-çăl) n vaso sanguíneo

blot (blót) n borrão m; mancha f; blotting paper mata-borrão m
blouse (blauz) n blusa f
blow (blou) n pancada f, golpe m; rajada f
*blow (blou) v assoprar; soprar
blow-out (blou-aut) n furo m
blue (bluu) adj azul; deprimido
blunt (blannt) adj rombo
blush (blach) v corar
board (bóód) n tábua f; quadro m; pensão f; conselho m; ~ and lodging pensão completa
boarder (bóó-dă) n pensionista m
boarding-house (bóó-dinng-hauç) n pensão f
boarding-school (bóó-dinng-çkuul) n colégio interno
boast (bouçt) v gabar-se
boat (bout) n barco m, navio m
body (bó-di) n corpo m
bodyguard (bó-di-ghaad) n guarda-costas m
body-work (bó-di-uăăk) n carroçaria f
bog (bógh) n pântano m
boil (boil) v ferver; n furúnculo m
bold (bould) adj arrojado; atrevido, descarado
Bolivia (bă-li-vi-ă) Bolívia f
Bolivian (bă-li-vi-ănn) adj boliviano
bolt (boult) n ferrolho m; cavilha f
bomb (bómm) n bomba f; v *bombardear
bond (bónnd) n obrigação f
bone (bounn) n osso m; espinha f; v desossar
bonnet (bó-nit) n cobertura do motor
book (buk) n livro m; v reservar; inscrever, registar
booking (bu-kinng) n reserva f
bookmaker (buk-mei-kă) n corretor de apostas
bookseller (buk-çé-lă) n livreiro m
bookstand (buk-çtænnd) n quiosque

de livros
**bookstore** (*buk-çtóó*) *n* livraria *f*
**boot** (buut) *n* bota *f*; porta-bagagem *m*
**booth** (buuð) *n* cabina *f*
**border** (*bóó-dã*) *n* fronteira *f*; borda *f*
**bore**[1] (*bóó*) *v* maçar; brocar; *n* maçador *m*
**bore**[2] (bóó) *v* (p bear)
**boring** (*bóór-inng*) *adj* maçador, aborrecido
**born** (bóónn) *adj* nascido
**borrow** (*bó-ro*u) *v* *pedir emprestado
**bosom** (*bu-zãmm*) *n* peito *m*; seio *m*
**boss** (bóç) *n* patrão *m*, chefe *m*
**botany** (*bó-tã-ni*) *n* botânica *f*
**both** (bo*u*þ) *adj* ambos; **both ... and** tanto ... como
**bother** (*bó-ðã*) *v* incomodar, maçar; incomodar-se; *n* incómodo *m*
**bottle** (*bó-tãl*) *n* garrafa *f*; ~ **opener** abre-garrafas *m*; **hot-water** ~ botija de água quente
**bottleneck** (*bó-tãl-nék*) *n* passagem estreita
**bottom** (*bó-tãmm*) *n* fundo *m*; traseiro *m*, rabo *m*; *adj* inferior
**bough** (bau) *n* ramo *m*
**bought** (bóót) *v* (p, pp buy)
**boulder** (*bo*u*l-dã*) *n* pedregulho *m*
**bound** (baunnd) *n* limite *m*; *be ~ to* *ter de; ~ **for** a caminho de
**boundary** (*baunn-dã-ri*) *n* limite *m*; fronteira *f*
**bouquet** (bu-*kei*) *n* ramo *m*
**bourgeois** (*bu*ã*-*juaa) *adj* burguês
**boutique** (bu-*tiik*) *n* boutique *f*
**bow**[1] (bau) *v* inclinar
**bow**[2] (bo*u*) *n* arco *m*; ~ **tie** laço *m*
**bowels** (bau*ã*lz) *pl* intestinos *mpl*
**bowl** (bo*u*l) *n* tigela *f*
**bowling** (*bo*u*-linng*) *n* jogo dos paulitos, bowling *m*; ~ **alley** pista de bowling

**box**[1] (bókç) *v* jogar o boxe; **boxing match** luta de boxe
**box**[2] (bókç) *n* caixa *f*
**box-office** (*bókç-ó-fiç*) *n* bilheteira de reservação, bilheteira *f*; bilheteria *fBr*
**boy** (boi) *n* rapaz *m*; moço *m*, gaiato *m*; criado *m*; ~ **scout** escuteiro *m*
**bra** (braa) *n* soutien *m*
**bracelet** (*breiç-lit*) *n* pulseira *f*
**braces** (*brei-çiz*) *pl* suspensórios *mpl*
**brain** (breinn) *n* cérebro *m*; inteligência *f*
**brain-wave** (*breinn-*u*eiv*) *n* ideia luminosa
**brake** (breik) *n* travão *m*; ~ **drum** tambor do travão; ~ **lights** luzes de travão
**branch** (braanntch) *n* ramo *m*; sucursal *f*
**brand** (brænnd) *n* marca *f*
**brand-new** (brænnd-n*i*uu) *adj* novinho em folha
**brass** (braaç) *n* latão *m*; ~ **band** fanfarra *f*
**brassiere** (*bræ-zi*ã) *n* soutien *m*
**brassware** (*braaç-*u*é*ã) *n* utensílios de latão
**brave** (breiv) *adj* corajoso, valente
**Brazil** (brã-*zil*) Brasil *m*
**Brazilian** (brã-*zil-*iänn) *adj* brasileiro
**breach** (briitch) *n* brecha *f*; ruptura *f*
**bread** (bréd) *n* pão *m*; **wholemeal** ~ pão integral
**breadth** (brédþ) *n* largura *f*
**break** (breik) *n* fractura *f*; intervalo *m*
*break** (breik) *v* quebrar, partir; ~ **down** avariar-se
**breakdown** (*breik-daunn*) *n* avaria *f*
**breakfast** (*brék-fãçt*) *n* pequeno almoço
**bream** (briimm) *n* (pl ~) pargo *m*
**breast** (bréçt) *n* peito *m*

breaststroke (bréçt-çtrou k) n bruços mpl

breath (bréθ) n respiração f; sopro m

breathe (briið) v respirar

breathing (brii-ðinŋ) n respiração f

breed (briid) n raça f; espécie f

*breed (briid) v criar

breeze (briiz) n brisa f

brew (bruu) v fabricar cerveja

brewery (bruu-ă-ri) n fábrica de cerveja f

bribe (braib) v subornar

bribery (brai-bă-ri) n suborno m

brick (brik) n tijolo m

bricklayer (brik-leiă) n pedreiro m

bride (braid) n noiva f

bridegroom (braid-ghruumm) n noivo m

bridge (bridj) n ponte f; bridge m

brief (briif) adj breve

briefcase (briif-keiç) n pasta f

briefs (briifç) pl calções mpl, cuecas fpl

bright (brait) adj claro; reluzente; esperto, inteligente

brill (bril) n rodovalho m

brilliant (bril-iănnt) adj brilhante

brim (brimm) n borda f

*bring (brinnɡ) v *trazer; ~ back devolver; ~ up criar, educar; levantar

brisk (briçk) adj vivo

Britain (bri-tănn) Inglaterra f

British (bri-tich) adj britânico

Briton (bri-tănn) n britânico m; inglês m

broad (bróód) adj largo; vasto, amplo; global

broadcast (bróód-kaaçt) n emissão f

*broadcast (bróód-kaaçt) v emitir

brochure (brou-chuă) n brochura f

broke[1] (brou k) v (p break)

broke[2] (brou k) adj teso

broken (brou-kǎnn) adj (pp break)

partido, escangalhado; avariado

broker (brou-kǎ) n corretor m

bronchitis (brónn-kai-tiç) n bronquite f

bronze (brónnz) n bronze m; adj de bronze

brooch (brou tch) n broche m

brook (bruk) n riacho m

broom (bruumm) n vassoura f

brothel (bró-θǎl) n bordel m

brother (bra-ðǎ) n irmão m

brother-in-law (bra-ðǎ-rinn-lóó) n (pl brothers-) cunhado m

brought (bróót) v (p, pp bring)

brown (braunn) adj castanho

bruise (bruuz) n contusão f, nódoa negra; v magoar

brunette (bruu-nét) n morena f

brush (brach) n escova f; pincel m; v puxar o lustro a, escovar

brutal (bruu-tǎl) adj brutal

bubble (ba-bǎl) n bolha f

bucket (ba-kit) n balde m

buckle (ba-kǎl) n fivela f

bud (bad) n botão m

budget (ba-djit) n orçamento m

buffet (bu-fei) n bufete m

bug (bagh) n percevejo m; escaravelho m; nAm insecto m

*build (bild) v *construir

building (bil-dinnɡ) n prédio m

bulb (balb) n bolbo m; cebola f; light ~ lâmpada f

Bulgaria (bal-ghéǎ-ri-ǎ) Bulgária f

Bulgarian (bal-ghéǎ-ri-ǎnn) adj búlgaro

bulk (balk) n volume m; maior parte f

bulky (bal-ki) adj volumoso

bull (bul) n touro m

bullet (bu-lit) n bala f

bullfight (bul-fait) n tourada f

bullring (bul-rinnɡ) n praça de touros f

bump (bammp) v bater; chocar; n encontrão m, pancada f

**bumper** (bamm-pă) n pára-choques m

**bumpy** (bamm-pi) adj acidentado

**bun** (bann) n brioche m

**bunch** (banntch) n ramo m; grupo m

**bundle** (bann-dăl) n molho m; v atar num molho, atar

**bunk** (banngk) n beliche m

**buoy** (boi) n bóia f

**burden** (băă-dănn) n fardo m

**bureau** (biu$^a$-ro$^u$) n (pl ~x, ~s) escrevaninha f, secretária f; nAm cómoda f

**bureaucracy** (bi$^u$$^a$-ró-kră-çi) n burocracia f

**burglar** (băă-ghlă) n ladrão m

**burgle** (băă-ghăl) v assaltar

**burial** (bé-ri-ăl) n enterro m

**burn** (băănn) n queimadura f

**\*burn** (băănn) v arder; queimar

**\*burst** (băăçt) v rebentar

**bury** (bé-ri) v enterrar

**bus** (baç) n autocarro m; ônibus mBr

**bush** (buch) n arbusto m; mato m

**business** (biz-năç) n negócios m, comércio m; negócio m, empresa f; ocupação f; assunto m; ~ **hours** horas de serviço, horas de abertura; ~ **trip** viagem de negócios; **on** ~ para negócios

**businessman** (biz-năç-mănn) n (pl -men) homem de negócios

**bust** (baçt) n busto m

**bustle** (ba-çăl) n azáfama f

**busy** (bi-zi) adj ocupado; movimentado, atarefado

**but** (bat) conj mas; todavia; prep menos

**butcher** (bu-tchă) n talho m

**butter** (ba-tă) n manteiga f

**butterfly** (ba-tă-flai) n borboleta f; ~ **stroke** mariposa f

**buttock** (ba-tăk) n nádega f

**button** (ba-tănn) n botão m; v abotoar

**buttonhole** (ba-tănn-ho$^u$l) n casa de botão

**\*buy** (bai) v comprar; adquirir

**buyer** (bai-ă) n comprador m

**by** (bai) prep por; com; perto de; por meio de

**by-pass** (bai-paaç) n estrada de circunvalação; v contornar

# C

**cab** (kæb) n táxi m

**cabaret** (kæ-bă-rei) n cabaré m; clube nocturno

**cabbage** (kæ-bidj) n couve f

**cab-driver** (kæb-drai-vă) n motorista de táxi

**cabin** (kæ-binn) n cabina f; cabana f

**cabinet** (kæ-bi-năt) n gabinete m

**cable** (kei-băl) n cabo m; telegrama m; v telegrafar

**café** (kæ-fei) n café m

**cafeteria** (kæ-fă-ti$^a$-ri-ă) n cafetaria f

**caffeine** (kæ-fiinn) n cafeína f

**cage** (keidj) n jaula f

**cake** (keik) n bolo m

**calamity** (kă-læ-mă-ti) n catástrofe f, calamidade f

**calcium** (kæl-çi-ămm) n cálcio m

**calculate** (kæl-k$^i$u-leit) v calcular

**calculation** (kæl-k$^i$u-lei-chănn) n cálculo m

**calculator** (kæl-k$^i$u-lei-tă) n calculadora f

**calendar** (kæ-lănn-dă) n calendário m

**calf** (kaaf) n (pl calves) vitelo m; barriga da perna; ~ **skin** calfe m

**call** (kóól) v chamar; telefonar; n chamada f; visita f; **\*be called** chamar-se; ~ **names** injuriar; ~ **on** visitar, \*fazer uma visita a; ~ **up** Am telefonar

**callus** (kæ-lăç) n calo m

**calm** (kaamm) *adj* calmo, tranquilo; ~ **down** acalmar

**calorie** (*kæ*-lã-ri) *n* caloria *f*

**Calvinism** (*kæl*-vi-ni-zãmm) *n* calvinismo *m*

**came** (keimm) *v* (p come)

**camel** (*kæ*-mãl) *n* camelo *m*

**cameo** (*kæ*-mi-oᵘ) *n* (pl ~s) camafeu *m*

**camera** (*kæ*-mã-rã) *n* máquina fotográfica; máquina de filmar; ~ **shop** loja de artigos fotográficos

**camp** (kæmmp) *n* acampamento *m*; *v* acampar

**campaign** (kæmm-*peinn*) *n* campanha *f*

**camp-bed** (kæmmp-*béd*) *n* maca *f*, cama de acampamento

**camper** (*kæmm*-pã) *n* campista *f*

**camping** (*kæmm*-pinng) *n* campismo *m*; ~ **site** parque de campismo

**camshaft** (*kæmm*-chaaft) *n* árvore de cames

**can** (kænn) *n* lata *f*; ~ **opener** abre-latas *m*

***can** (kænn) *v* *poder

**Canada** (*kæ*-nã-dã) Canadá *m*

**Canadian** (kã-*nei*-di-ãnn) *adj* canadiano

**canal** (kã-*næl*) *n* canal *m*

**canary** (kã-*né*ᵃ-ri) *n* canário *m*

**cancel** (*kænn*-çãl) *v* anular; cancelar

**cancellation** (kænn-çã-*lei*-chãnn) *n* cancelamento *m*

**cancer** (*kænn*-çã) *n* cancro *m*

**candelabrum** (kænn-dã-*laa*-brämm) *n* (pl -bra) candelabro *m*

**candidate** (*kænn*-di-dãt) *n* candidato *m*

**candle** (*kænn*-dãl) *n* vela *f*

**candy** (*kænn*-di) *nAm* rebuçado *m*; guloseimas *fpl*

**cane** (keinn) *n* cana *f*; bengala *f*

**canister** (*kæ*-ni-çtã) *n* lata *f*

**canoe** (kã-*nuu*) *n* canoa *f*

**canteen** (kænn-*tiinn*) *n* cantina *f*

**canvas** (*kænn*-väç) *n* lona *f*

**cap** (kæp) *n* boné *m*, barrete *m*

**capable** (*kei*-pã-bãl) *adj* capaz

**capacity** (kã-*pæ*-çã-ti) *n* capacidade *f*; potência *f*; competência *f*

**cape** (keip) *n* capa *f*; cabo *m*

**capital** (*kæ*-pi-tãl) *n* capital *f*; capital *m*; *adj* importante, capital; ~ **letter** maiúscula *f*

**capitalism** (*kæ*-pi-tã-li-zãmm) *n* capitalismo *m*

**capitulation** (kã-pi-tⁱu-*lei*-chãnn) *n* capitulação *f*

**capsule** (*kæp*-çⁱuul) *n* cápsula *f*

**captain** (*kæp*-tinn) *n* capitão *m*; comandante *m*

**capture** (*kæp*-tchã) *v* capturar; *n* captura *f*

**car** (kaa) *n* carro *m*; ~ **hire** aluguer de carros; ~ **park** parque de estacionamento

**carafe** (kã-*ræf*) *n* garrafa *f*

**caramel** (*kæ*-rã-mãl) *n* caramelo *m*

**carat** (*kæ*-rãt) *n* quilate *m*

**caravan** (*kæ*-rã-vænn) *n* caravana *f*; rulote *f*

**carburettor** (kaa-bⁱu-*ré*-tã) *n* carburador *m*

**card** (kaad) *n* cartão *m*; postal *m*

**cardboard** (*kaad*-bóód) *n* cartão *m*; papelão *mBr*; *adj* de cartão

**cardigan** (*kaa*-di-ghänn) *n* casaco de malha

**cardinal** (*kaa*-di-nãl) *n* cardeal *m*; *adj* principal, cardeal

**care** (kéᵃ) *n* cuidado *m*; preocupação *f*; ~ **about** preocupar-se com; ~ **for** gostar de; *take ~ of** tratar de, cuidar de

**career** (kã-*ri*ᵃ) *n* carreira *f*

**carefree** (*ké*ᵃ-frii) *adj* despreocupado

**careful** (*ké*ᵃ-fãl) *adj* cuidadoso

**careless** (kéᵃ-lǎç) adj negligente, descuidado

**caretaker** (kéᵃ-tei-kǎ) n guarda m

**cargo** (kaa-ghoᵘ) n (pl ~es) carregamento m, carga f

**carnival** (kaa-ni-vǎl) n Carnaval m

**carpenter** (kaa-pinn-tǎ) n carpinteiro m

**carpet** (kaa-pit) n tapete m

**carriage** (kæ-ridj) n carruagem f; coche m

**carriageway** (kæ-ridj-ᵘei) n faixa de rodagem

**carrot** (kæ-rǎt) n cenoura f

**carry** (kæ-ri) v transportar; *conduzir; ~ on continuar; *prosseguir; ~ out executar, realizar

**carry-cot** (kæ-ri-kót) n alcofa de bébé

**cart** (kaat) n carroça f

**cartilage** (kaa-ti-lidj) n cartilagem f

**carton** (kaa-tǎnn) n caixa de cartão; caixa m; caixa de papelão Br

**cartoon** (kaa-tuunn) n desenho animado

**cartridge** (kaa-tridj) n cartucho m

**carve** (kaav) v trinchar; entalhar

**carving** (kaa-vinng) n obra de talha

**case** (keiç) n caso m; causa f; mala f; estojo m; **attaché ~ pasta** f; **in any ~ seja como for; in ~ no caso de; in ~ of em caso de**

**cash** (kæch) n dinheiro m; v descontar, levantar; *pay ~ pagar à vista; ~ dispenser caixa automática

**cashier** (kæ-chiᵃ) n caixa f

**cashmere** (kæch-miᵃ) n caxemira f

**casino** (kǎ-çii-noᵘ) n (pl ~s) casino m; cassino mBr

**cask** (kaaçk) n barril m

**cast** (kaaçt) n lance m

**cast** (kaaçt) v lançar, atirar; **cast iron ferro fundido**

**castle** (kaa-çǎl) n castelo m

**casual** (kæ-ju-ǎl) adj à vontade; casual

**casualty** (kæ-ju-ǎl-ti) n vítima f

**cat** (kæt) n gato m

**catacomb** (kæ-tǎ-koᵘmm) n catacumba f

**catalogue** (kæ-tǎ-lógh) n catálogo m

**catarrh** (kǎ-taa) n catarro m

**catastrophe** (kǎ-tæ-çtrǎ-fi) n catástrofe f

**catch** (kætch) v apanhar; agarrar; surpreender; tomar

**category** (kæ-ti-ghǎ-ri) n categoria f

**cathedral** (kǎ-θii-drǎl) n catedral f

**catholic** (kæ-θǎ-lik) adj católico

**cattle** (kæ-tǎl) pl gado m

**caught** (kóót) v (p, pp catch)

**cauliflower** (kó-li-flauᵃ) n couve-flor f

**cause** (kóóz) v causar; provocar; n causa f; motivo m

**caution** (kóó-chǎnn) n cautela f; v avisar, *advertir

**cautious** (kóó-chǎç) adj prudente

**cave** (keiv) n gruta f; caverna f

**cavern** (kæ-vǎnn) n caverna f

**caviar** (kæ-vi-aa) n caviar m

**cavity** (kæ-vǎ-ti) n cavidade f

**cease** (çiiç) v cessar

**ceiling** (çii-linng) n tecto m

**celebrate** (çé-li-breit) v celebrar

**celebration** (çé-li-brei-chǎnn) n celebração f

**celebrity** (çi-lé-brǎ-ti) n celebridade f

**celery** (çé-lǎ-ri) n aipo m

**celibacy** (çé-li-bǎ-çi) n celibato m

**cell** (çél) n célula f

**cellar** (çé-lǎ) n cave f; porão mBr

**cellophane** (çé-lǎ-feinn) n celofane m

**cement** (çi-ménnt) n cimento m

**cemetery** (çé-mi-tri) n cemitério m

**censorship** (çénn-çǎ-chip) n censura f

**centimetre** (çénn-ti-mii-tǎ) n centímetro m

**central** (çénn-trǎl) adj central; ~ heating aquecimento central; ~

station estação central
**centralize** (*cénn*-tră-laiz) *v* centralizar
**centre** (*cénn*-tă) *n* centro *m*
**century** (*cénn*-tchă-ri) *n* século *m*
**ceramics** (çi-*ræ*-mikç) *n* cerâmica *f*
**ceremony** (*cé*-ră-mă-ni) *n* cerimónia *f*
**certain** (*çăă*-tănn) *adj* certo
**certificate** (çă-*ti*-fi-kăt) *n* certificado *m*, atestado *m*, diploma *m*, certidão *f*
**chain** (tcheinn) *n* cadeia *f*
**chair** (tché<sup>ă</sup>) *n* cadeira *f*; assento *m*
**chairman** (*tché*<sup>ă</sup>-männ) *n* (pl -men) presidente *m*
**chalet** (*chæ*-lei) *n* chalé *m*
**chalk** (tchóók) *n* giz *m*
**challenge** (*tchæ*-lănndj) *v* desafiar; *n* desafio *m*
**chamber** (*tcheimm*-bă) *n* quarto *m*
**chambermaid** (*tcheimm*-bă-meid) *n* criada de quarto
**champagne** (chæmm-*peinn*) *n* champanhe *m*
**champion** (*tchæmm*-pi<sup>ă</sup>nn) *n* campeão *m*; defensor *m*
**chance** (tchaannç) *n* sorte *f*; ocasião *f*, oportunidade *f*; risco *m*; azar *m*; **by ~** por acaso
**change** (tcheinndj) *v* mudar, modificar; trocar; mudar de roupa; *fazer transbordo; *n* modificação *f*, mudança *f*; troco *m*
**channel** (*tchæ*-năl) *n* canal *m*; **English Channel** Canal da Mancha
**chaos** (*kei*-óç) *n* caos *m*
**chaotic** (kei-*ó*-tik) *adj* caótico
**chap** (tchæp) *n* tipo *m*
**chapel** (*tchæ*-păl) *n* capela *f*
**chaplain** (*tchæ*-plinn) *n* capelão *m*
**character** (*kæ*-răk-tă) *n* carácter *m*
**characteristic** (kæ-răk-tă-*ri*-çtik) *adj* típico, característico; *n* característica *f*; traço caracterial
**characterize** (*kæ*-răk-tă-raiz) *v* carac-

terizar
**charcoal** (*tchaa*-ko<sup>u</sup>l) *n* carvão de lenha
**charge** (tchaadj) *v* *pedir; encarregar; acusar; carregar; *n* preço *m*; carregamento *m*, carga *f*, taxa *f*; acusação *f*; **~ plate** *Am* cartão de crédito; **free of ~** gratuito; **in ~ of** encarregado de; ***take ~ of** encarregar-se de
**charity** (*tchæ*-ră-ti) *n* caridade *f*
**charm** (tchaamm) *n* encanto *m*; amuleto *m*
**charming** (*tchaa*-minng) *adj* encantador
**chart** (tchaat) *n* tabela *f*; gráfico *m*; mapa marítimo; **conversion ~** tabela de conversão
**chase** (tcheiç) *v* *perseguir; expulsar, afugentar; *n* caça *f*
**chasm** (kæ-zămm) *n* fenda *f*
**chassis** (*chæ*-çi) *n* (pl ~) chassi *m*
**chaste** (tcheiçt) *adj* casto
**chat** (tchæt) *v* conversar, *cavaquear; *n* conversa *f*, cavaco *m*
**chatterbox** (*tchæ*-tă-bókç) *n* tagarela *m*
**chauffeur** (cho<sup>u</sup>-fă) *n* motorista *m*
**cheap** (tchiip) *adj* barato; económico
**cheat** (tchiit) *v* enganar; defraudar
**check** (tchék) *v* *conferir, verificar; *n* quadrado *m*; *Am* conta *f*; cheque *m*; **check!** xeque!; **~ in** inscrever-se, registar-se; **~ out** partir, *sair
**check-book** (*tchék*-buk) *nAm* livro de cheques
**checkerboard** (*tché*-kă-bóód) *nAm* tabuleiro de xadrez
**checkroom** (*tchék*-ruumm) *nAm* vestiário *m*
**check-up** (*tché*-kap) *n* exame médico
**cheek** (tchiik) *n* face *f*
**cheek-bone** (*tchiik*-bo<sup>u</sup>nn) *n* maçã do

rosto

**cheer** (tchi[a]) v aplaudir, aclamar; ~ **up** animar, alegrar

**cheerful** (tchi[a]-fál) adj jovial, alegre

**cheese** (tchiiz) n queijo m

**chef** (chéf) n cozinheiro-chefe m

**chemical** (ké-mi-kǎl) adj químico

**chemist** (ké-miçt) n farmacêutico m; **chemist's** farmácia f; drogaria f

**chemistry** (ké-mi-çtri) n química f

**cheque** (tchék) n cheque m

**cheque-book** (tchék-buk) n livro de cheques

**chequered** (tché kǎd) adj em xadrez, quadriculado

**cherry** (tché-ri) n cereja f

**chess** (tchéç) n xadrez m

**chest** (tchéçt) n peito m; arca f; ~ **of drawers** cómoda f

**chestnut** (tchéç-nat) n castanha f

**chew** (tchuu) v mastigar

**chewing-gum** (tchuu-inng-ghamm) n goma de mascar Br, pastilha elástica

**chicken** (tchi-kinn) n frango m

**chickenpox** (tchi-kinn-pókç) n varicela f

**chief** (tchiif) n chefe m; adj principal

**chieftain** (tchiif-tǎnn) n chefe m

**chilblain** (tchil-bleinn) n frieira f

**child** (tchaild) n (pl children) criança f

**childbirth** (tchaild-bǎǎθ) n parto m

**childhood** (tchaild-hud) n infância f

**Chile** (tchi-li) Chile m

**Chilean** (tchi-li-ǎnn) adj chileno

**chill** (tchil) n calafrio m

**chilly** (tchi-li) adj fresco

**chimes** (tchaimmz) pl carrilhão m

**chimney** (tchimm-ni) n chaminé f

**chin** (tchinn) n queixo m

**China** (tchai-nǎ) China f

**china** (tchai-nǎ) n porcelana f

**Chinese** (tchai-niiz) adj chinês

**chink** (tchinngk) n greta f

**chip** (tchip) n lasca f; ficha f; v lascar, cortar; **chips** batatas fritas

**chiropodist** (ki-ró-pǎ-diçt) n calista m

**chisel** (tchi-zǎl) n cinzel m

**chivalrous** (chi-vǎl-rǎç) adj cavalheiroso

**chives** (tchaivz) pl cebolinho m

**chlorine** (klóó-riinn) n cloro m

**chocolate** (tchó-klát) n chocolate m; bombom m

**choice** (tchoiç) n escolha f; selecção f

**choir** (k[u]ai[a]) n coro m

**choke** (tcho[u]k) v sufocar; estrangular; n choke m; afogador mBr

**\*choose** (tchuuz) v escolher

**chop** (tchóp) n costeleta f; v picar

**Christ** (kraiçt) Cristo

**christen** (kri-çǎnn) v baptizar

**christening** (kri-çǎ-ninng) n baptismo m

**Christian** (kriç-tchǎnn) adj cristão; ~ **name** nome próprio; nome de batismo Br

**Christmas** (kriç-mǎç) Natal m

**chromium** (kro[u]-mi-ǎmm) n crómio m

**chronic** (kró-nik) adj crónico

**chronological** (kró-nǎ-ló-dji-kǎl) adj cronológico

**chuckle** (tcha-kǎl) v \*rir entre dentes

**chunk** (tchanngk) n pedaço grosso

**church** (tchǎǎtch) n igreja f

**churchyard** (tchǎǎtch-[i]aad) n cemitério m

**cigar** (çi-ghaa) n charuto m; ~ **shop** tabacaria f

**cigarette** (çi-ghǎ-rét) n cigarro m

**cigarette-case** (çi-ghǎ-rét-keiç) n cigarreira f

**cigarette-holder** (çi-ghǎ-rét-ho[u]l-dǎ) n boquilha f

**cigarette-lighter** (çi-ghǎ-rét-lai-tǎ) n isqueiro m

**cinema** (çi-nǎ-mǎ) n cinema m

cinnamon (*çi*-nă-mănn) *n* canela *f*

circle (*çăă*-kăl) *n* círculo *m;* balcão *m; v* circundar, \*rodear

circulation (çăă-k<sup>i</sup>u-*lei*-chănn) *n* circulação *f*

circumstance (*çăă*-kămm-çtænnç) *n* circunstância *f*

circus (*çăă*-kăç) *n* circo *m*

citizen (*çi*-ti-zănn) *n* cidadão *m*

citizenship (*çi*-ti-zănn-chip) *n* cidadania *f*

city (*çi*-ti) *n* cidade *f*

civic (*çi*-vik) *adj* cívico

civil (*çi*-văl) *adj* civil; educado; ~ **law** direito civil; ~ **servant** funcionário público

civilian (çi-*vil*-<sup>i</sup>ănn) *adj* civil; *n* civil *m*

civilization (çi-vă-lai-*zei*-chănn) *n* civilização *f*

civilized (*çi*-vă-laizd) *adj* civilizado

claim (kleimm) *v* reivindicar; afirmar; *n* pretensão *f*, reivindicação *f*

clamp (klæmmp) *n* grampo *m*

clap (klæp) *v* aplaudir, bater as palmas

clarify (klæ-ri-fai) *v* esclarecer, aclarar

class (klaaç) *n* classe *f*

classical (klæ-çi-kăl) *adj* clássico

classify (klæ-çi-fai) *v* classificar

class-mate (klaaç-meit) *n* colega de turma; colega de classe *Br*

classroom (klaaç-ruumm) *n* sala de aula

clause (klóóz) *n* cláusula *f*

claw (klóó) *n* garra *f*

clay (klei) *n* argila *f*

clean (kliinn) *adj* puro, limpo; *v* limpar

cleaning (klii-ninng) *n* limpeza *f;* ~ **fluid** produto de limpeza

clear (kli<sup>ă</sup>) *adj* claro; *v* limpar

clearing (kli<sup>ă</sup>-rinng) *n* clareira *f*

cleft (kléft) *n* fenda *f*

clergyman (klăă-dji-mănn) *n* (pl -men) pastor *m;* clérigo *m*

clerk (klaak) *n* empregado de escritório, funcionário *m;* escrivão *m;* secretário *m*

clever (klé-vă) *adj* inteligente; esperto, astuto

client (klai-ănnt) *n* cliente *m*

cliff (klif) *n* falésia *f*

climate (klai-mit) *n* clima *m*

climb (klaimm) *v* trepar; *n* subida *f*

clinic (klii-nik) *n* clínica *f*

cloak (klo<sup>u</sup>k) *n* casacão *m*

cloakroom (klo<sup>u</sup>k-ruumm) *n* guarda-roupa *m*

clock (klók) *n* relógio *m;* **at ... o'clock** às ... horas

cloister (kloi-çtă) *n* convento *m*

close¹ (klo<sup>u</sup>z) *v* fechar; **closed** fechado, encerrado

close² (klo<sup>u</sup>ç) *adj* próximo

closet (kló-zit) *n* armário *m; nAm* roupeiro *m*

cloth (kló<sup>θ</sup>) *n* trapo *m;* pano *m*

clothes (klo<sup>u</sup>ðz) *pl* vestuário *m,* roupa *f*

clothes-brush (klo<sup>u</sup>ðz-brach) *n* escova de fato

clothing (klo<sup>u</sup>-ðinng) *n* vestuário *m*

cloud (klaud) *n* nuvem *f*

cloud-burst (klaud-băăçt) *n* chuvada *f*

cloudy (klau-di) *adj* nublado, encoberto

clover (klo<sup>u</sup>-vă) *n* trevo *m*

clown (klaunn) *n* palhaço *m*

club (klab) *n* clube *m;* associação *f,* círculo *m;* moca *f,* cacete *m*

clumsy (klamm-zi) *adj* desajeitado

clutch (klatch) *n* embraiagem *f;* aperto *m*

coach (ko<sup>u</sup>tch) *n* autocarro *m;* carruagem *f;* coche *m;* treinador *m;* ônibus *mBr*

coagulate (ko<sup>u</sup>-æ-gh<sup>i</sup>u-leit) *v* coagular

coal (koᵘl) n carvão m
coarse (kóóç) adj grosseiro
coast (koᵘçt) n costa f
coat (koᵘt) n casacão m, casaco m
coat-hanger (koᵘt-hænng-ä) n cabide m
cobweb (kób-ᵘéb) n teia de aranha
cocaine (koᵘ-keinn) n cocaína f
cock (kók) n galo m
cocktail (kók-teil) n beberete m; coquetel mBr
coconut (koᵘ-kä-nat) n coco m
cod (kód) n (pl ~) bacalhau m
code (koᵘd) n código m
coffee (kó-fi) n café m
cognac (kó-niæk) n conhaque m
coherence (koᵘ-hiã-rännç) n coerência f
coin (koinn) n moeda f
coincide (koᵘ-inn-çaid) v coincidir
cold (koᵘld) adj frio; n frio m; constipação f; *catch a ~ constipar-se
collapse (kä-læpç) v sucumbir, desmoronar-se
collar (kó-lä) n coleira f; colarinho m, gola f; ~ stud botão de colarinho
collarbone (kó-lä-boᵘnn) n clavícula f
colleague (kó-liigh) n colega m
collect (kä-lékt) v coleccionar; *ir buscar; *fazer um pediţório
collection (kä-lék-chänn) n colecção f; recolha f
collective (kä-lék-tiv) adj colectivo
collector (kä-lék-tä) n coleccionador m; colector m
college (kó-lidj) n escola universitária; colégio m
collide (kä-laid) v colidir, chocar
collision (kä-li-jänn) n colisão f, choque m; abalroamento m
Colombia (kä-lómm-bi-ä) Colômbia f
Colombian (kä-lómm-bi-änn) adj colombiano
colonel (kää-näl) n coronel m

colony (kó-lä-ni) n colónia f
colour (ka-lä) n cor f; v *colorir; ~ film filme a cores
colourant (ka-lä-rännt) n corante m
colour-blind (ka-lä-blainnd) adj daltónico
coloured (ka-läd) adj de cor
colourful (ka-lä-fäl) adj colorido
column (kó-lämm) n coluna f, pilar m; rubrica f
coma (koᵘ-mä) n coma m
comb (koᵘmm) v *pentear; n pente m
combat (kómm-bæt) n combate m, luta f; v combater
combination (kómm-bi-nei-chänn) n combinação f
combine (kämm-bainn) v combinar
*come (kamm) v *vir; ~ across encontrar
comedian (kä-mii-di-änn) n comediante m; cómico m
comedy (kó-mä-di) n comédia f; musical ~ comédia musical
comfort (kamm-fät) n conforto m, bem-estar m, comodidade f; consolação f; v consolar, confortar
comfortable (kamm-fä-tä-bäl) adj confortável
comic (kó-mik) adj cómico
comics (kó-mikç) pl banda desenhada
coming (ka-minng) n chegada f
comma (kó-mä) n vírgula f
command (kä-maand) v comandar, mandar; n ordem f
commander (kä-maann-dä) n comandante m
commemoration (kä-mé-mä-rei-chänn) n comemoração f
commence (kä-ménnç) v começar, principiar
comment (kó-ménnt) n comentário m; v comentar
commerce (kó-määç) n comércio m
commercial (kä-mää-chäl) adj comer-

cial; *n* anúncio *m;* ~ **law** direito comercial

**commission** (kă-*mi*-chănn) *n* comissão *f*

**commit** (kă-*mit*) *v* confiar, entregar; cometer, praticar

**committee** (kă-*mi*-ti) *n* comité *m*, comissão *f*

**common** (*kó*-mănn) *adj* comum; habitual; ordinário

**communicate** (kă-*m*ᶦ*uu*-ni-keit) *v* comunicar

**communication** (kă-mᶦuu-ni-*kei*-chănn) *n* comunicação *f*

**communiqué** (kă-*m*ᶦ*uu*-ni-kei) *n* comunicado *m*

**communism** (*kó*-mᶦu-ni-zămm) *n* comunismo *m*

**community** (kă-*m*ᶦ*uu*-nă-ti) *n* comunidade *f*, sociedade *f*

**compact** (*kómm*-pækt) *adj* compacto

**compact disc** (*kómm*-pækt diçk) *n* disco laser *m;* ~ **player** tocadiscos laser

**companion** (kămm-*pæ*-nᶦănn) *n* companheiro *m*

**company** (*kamm*-pă-ni) *n* companhia *f;* firma *f*, sociedade *f*

**comparative** (kămm-*pæ*-ră-tiv) *adj* relativo; comparativo

**compare** (kămm-*pé*ᵈ) *v* comparar

**comparison** (kămm-*pæ*-ri-çănn) *n* comparação *f*

**compartment** (kămm-*paat*-mănnt) *n* compartimento *m*

**compass** (*kamm*-păç) *n* bússola *f*

**compel** (kămm-*pél*) *v* obrigar

**compensate** (*kómm*-pănn-çeit) *v* compensar

**compensation** (kómm-pănn-*çei*-chănn) *n* compensação *f;* indemnização *f*

**compete** (kămm-*piit*) *v* *competir

**competition** (kómm-pă-*ti*-chănn) *n* competição *f;* concorrência *f*

**competitor** (kămm-*pé*-ti-tăr) *n* concorrente *m*

**compile** (kămm-*pail*) *v* compilar

**complain** (kămm-*pleinn*) *v* queixar-se

**complaint** (kămm-*pleinnt*) *n* queixa *f*

**complete** (kămm-*pliit*) *adj* completo; *v* completar

**completely** (kămm-*pliit*-li) *adv* totalmente, completamente, inteiramente

**complex** (*kómm*-plékç) *n* complexo *m; adj* complexo

**complexion** (kămm-*plék*-chănn) *n* tez *f;* aspecto *m*

**complicated** (*kómm*-pli-kei-tid) *adj* complicado

**compliment** (*kómm*-pli-mănnt) *n* cumprimento *m; v* felicitar, cumprimentar

**compose** (kămm-*po*ᵘ*z*) *v* *compor

**composer** (kămm-*po*ᵘ-ză) *n* compositor *m*

**composition** (kómm-pă-*zi*-chănn) *n* composição *f*

**comprehensive** (kómm-pri-*hénn*-çiv) *adj* extensivo

**comprise** (kămm-*praiz*) *v* compreender, *conter

**compromise** (*kómm*-pră-maiz) *n* compromisso *m*

**compulsory** (kămm-*pal*-çă-ri) *adj* obrigatório

**computer** (kămm-*p*ᶦ*u*-tă) *n* computador *m*

**comrade** (*kómm*-reid) *n* camarada *m*

**conceal** (kănn-*çiil*) *v* ocultar, esconder

**conceited** (kănn-*çii*-tid) *adj* pretensioso

**conceive** (kănn-*çiiv*) *v* compreender, conceber; imaginar

**concentrate** (*kónn*-çănn-treit) *v* concentrar

**concentration** (kónn-çănn-*trei*-chănn) *n* concentração *f*

**conception** (kănn-çép-chănn) *n* concepção *f*

**concern** (kănn-çăănn) *v* *dizer respeito a; *n* preocupação *f*; assunto *m*; empresa *f*

**concerned** (kănn-çăănnd) *adj* preocupado; envolvido

**concerning** (kănn-çăă-ninng) *prep* referente a

**concert** (kónn-çăt) *n* concerto *m*; ~ **hall** sala de concertos

**concession** (kănn-çé-chănn) *n* concessão *f*

**concise** (kănn-çaiç) *adj* conciso

**conclusion** (kănng-kluu-jănn) *n* conclusão *f*

**concrete** (kónn-kriit) *adj* concreto; *n* betão *m*: concreto *mBr*

**concussion** (kănng-ka-chănn) *n* comoção cerebral

**condition** (kănn-di-chănn) *n* condição *f*, estado *m*; circunstância *f*

**conditional** (kănn-di-chă-năl) *adj* condicional

**conditioner** (kănn-di-chă-nă) *n* condicionador de cabelos *m*

**condom** (kónn-dóm) *n* preservativo *m*

**conduct**[1] (kónn-dakt) *n* conduta *f*

**conduct**[2] (kănn-dakt) *v* *conduzir; acompanhar; dirigir

**conductor** (kănn-dak-tă) *n* cobrador *m*: maestro *m*

**confectioner** (kănn-fék-chă-nă) *n* confeiteiro *m*

**conference** (kónn-fă-rănnç) *n* conferência *f*

**confess** (kănn-féç) *v* reconhecer; confessar-se; professar

**confession** (kănn-fé-chănn) *n* confissão *f*

**confidence** (kónn-fi-dănnç) *n* confiança *f*

**confident** (kónn-fi-dănnt) *adj* confiante

**confidential** (kónn-fi-dénn-chăl) *adj* confidencial

**confirm** (kănn-făămm) *v* confirmar

**confirmation** (kónn-fă-mei-chănn) *n* confirmação *f*

**confiscate** (kónn-fi-çkeit) *v* confiscar

**conflict** (kónn-flikt) *n* conflito *m*

**confuse** (kănn-fᵘuuz) *v* confundir; **confused** confuso

**confusion** (kănn-fᵘuu-jănn) *n* confusão *f*

**congratulate** (kănng-ghræ-tchu-leit) *v* felicitar, congratular

**congratulation** (kănng-ghræ-tchu-lei-chănn) *n* felicitação *f*

**congregation** (kónn-ghri-ghei-chănn) *n* congregação *f*, comunidade *f*, ordem *f*

**congress** (kónn-ghréç) *n* congresso *m*

**connect** (kă-nékt) *v* unir, ligar

**connection** (kă-nék-chănn) *n* relação *f*; ligação *f*, correspondência *f*

**connoisseur** (kó-nă-çăă) *n* conhecedor *m*

**conquer** (kónn-kă) *v* conquistar; vencer

**conqueror** (kónn-kă-ră) *n* conquistador *m*

**conquest** (kónn-kᵘéçt) *n* conquista *f*

**conscience** (kónn-chănnç) *n* consciência *f*

**conscious** (kónn-chăç) *adj* consciente

**consciousness** (kónn-chăç-năç) *n* consciência *f*

**conscript** (kónn-çkript) *n* recruta *m*

**consent** (kănn-çénnt) *v* *consentir; aprovar; *n* consentimento *m*

**consequence** (kónn-çi-kᵘănnç) *n* consequência *f*

**consequently** (kónn-çi-kᵘănnt-li) *adv* consequentemente

**conservative** (kănn-çăă-vă-tiv) *adj* conservador

**consider** (kănn-çi-dă) *v* considerar;

ponderar; achar

**considerable** (kănn-çi-dă-rā-băl) *adj* considerável; notável, importante

**considerate** (kănn-çi-dă-răt) *adj* atencioso

**consideration** (kănn-çi-dă-*rei*-chănn) *n* consideração *f*; atenção *f*

**considering** (kănn-çi-dă-rinng) *prep* em vista de

**consignment** (kănn-*çainn*-mănnt) *n* remessa *f*

**consist of** (kănn-*çiçt*) consistir em

**conspire** (kănn-*çpai³*) *v* conspirar

**constant** (*kónn*-çtănnt) *adj* constante

**constipated** (*kónn*-çti-pei-tid) *adj* com prisão de ventre

**constipation** (kónn-çti-*pei*-chănn) *n* prisão de ventre

**constituency** (kănn-*çti*-tchu-ănn-çi) *n* círculo eleitoral

**constitution** (kónn-çti-t'*uu*-chănn) *n* constituição *f*

**construct** (kănn-*çtrakt*) *v* \*construir; edificar

**construction** (kănn-*çtrak*-chănn) *n* construção *f*, edifício *m*

**consul** (*kónn*-çăl) *n* cônsul *m*

**consulate** (*kónn*-ç'u-lăt) *n* consulado *m*

**consult** (kănn-*çalt*) *v* consultar

**consultation** (kónn-çăl-*tei*-chănn) *n* consulta *f*; ~ **hours** horas de consulta

**consumer** (kănn-ç'*uu*-mă) *n* consumidor *m*

**contact** (*kónn*-tăkt) *n* contacto *m*; *v* contactar com; ~ **lenses** lentes de contacto

**contagious** (kănn-*tei*-djăç) *adj* contagioso

**contain** (kănn-*teinn*) *v* \*conter

**container** (kănn-*tei*-nă) *n* recipiente *m*

**contemporary** (kănn-*témm*-pă-ră-ri) *adj* contemporâneo; de então; *n*

contemporâneo *m*

**contempt** (kănn-*témmpt*) *n* desdém *m*, desprezo *m*

**content** (kănn-*ténnt*) *adj* satisfeito

**contents** (*kónn*-ténntç) *pl* conteúdo *m*

**contest** (*kónn*-téçt) *n* luta *f*; concurso *m*

**continent** (*kónn*-ti-nănnt) *n* continente *m*

**continental** (kónn-ti-*nénn*-tăl) *adj* continental

**continual** (kănn-*ti*-n'u-ăl) *adj* contínuo

**continue** (kănn-*ti*-n'uu) *v* continuar; durar, \*prosseguir

**continuous** (kănn-*ti*-n'u-ăç) *adj* contínuo, ininterrupto

**contour** (*kónn*-tu³) *n* contorno *m*

**contraceptive** (kónn-tră-*çép*-tiv) *n* contraceptivo *m*

**contract¹** (*kónn*-trækt) *n* contrato *m*

**contract²** (kănn-*trækt*) *v* \*contrair

**contractor** (kănn-*træk*-tă) *n* empreiteiro *m*

**contradict** (kónn-tră-*dikt*) *v* \*contradizer

**contradictory** (kónn-tră-*dik*-tă-ri) *adj* contraditório

**contrary** (*kónn*-tră-ri) *n* contrário *m*; *adj* contrário; **on the** ~ pelo contrário

**contrast** (*kónn*-traaçt) *n* contraste *m*; diferença *f*

**contribution** (kónn-tri-b'*uu*-chănn) *n* contribuição *f*

**control** (kănn-*tro*ᵘl) *n* controle *m*; *v* fiscalizar, controlar

**controversial** (kónn-tră-*vää*-chăl) *adj* controverso

**convenience** (kănn-*vii*-n'ănnç) *n* comodidade *f*

**convenient** (kănn-*vii*-n'ănnt) *adj* cómodo; oportuno, apropriado, conveniente

**convent** (*kónn*-vănnt) *n* convento *m*

**conversation** (kónn-vă-*çei*-chănn) *n* conversação *f*, conversa *f*

**convert** (kănn-*văăt*) *v* converter

**convict**[1] (kănn-*vikt*) *v* declarar culpado

**convict**[2] (*kónn*-vikt) *n* condenado *m*

**conviction** (kănn-*vik*-chănn) *n* convicção *f*; condenação *f*

**convince** (kănn-*vinnç*) *v* convencer

**convulsion** (kănn-*val*-chănn) *n* convulsão *f*

**cook** (kuk) *n* cozinheiro *m*; *v* cozinhar; preparar

**cooker** (*ku*-kă) *n* fogão *m*; **gas ~** fogão a gás

**cookery-book** (*ku*-kă-ri-buk) *n* livro de cozinha

**cookie** (*ku*-ki) *n*Am biscoito *m*

**cool** (kuul) *adj* fresco; **cooling system** sistema de arrefecimento

**co-operation** (kou-ó-pă-*rei*-chănn) *n* cooperação *f*

**co-operative** (kou-ó-pă-ră-tiv) *adj* cooperativo; cooperador, colaborador; *n* cooperativa *f*

**co-ordinate** (kou-óó-di-neit) *v* coordenar

**co-ordination** (kou-óó-di-*nei*-chănn) *n* coordenação *f*

**copper** (*kó*-pă) *n* cobre *m*

**copy** (*kó*-pi) *n* cópia *f*; exemplar *m*; *v* copiar; imitar; **carbon ~** cópia *f*

**coral** (*kó*-răl) *n* coral *m*

**cord** (kóód) *n* corda *f*; cordão *m*

**cordial** (*kóó*-di-ăl) *adj* cordial

**corduroy** (*kóó*-dă-roi) *n* bombazina *f*

**core** (kóó) *n* núcleo *m*; coração *m*

**cork** (kóók) *n* rolha *f*

**corkscrew** (*kóók*-çkruu) *n* saca-rolhas *m*

**corn** (kóónn) *n* grão *m*; trigo *m*, cereais; calo *m*; **~ on the cob** maçaroca de milho

**corner** (*kóó*-nă) *n* esquina *f*; canto *m*

**cornfield** (*kóónn*-fiild) *n* seara *f*

**corpse** (kóópç) *n* cadáver *m*

**corpulent** (*kóó*-pⁱu-lănt) *adj* corpulento; obeso, balofo

**correct** (kă-*rékt*) *adj* certo, correcto; *v* corrigir

**correction** (kă-*rék*-chănn) *n* correcção *f*; rectificação *f*

**correctness** (kă-*rékt*-năç) *n* exactidão *f*

**correspond** (kó-ri-*çpónnd*) *v* corresponder

**correspondence** (kó-ri-*çpónn*-dănnç) *n* correspondência *f*

**correspondent** (kó-ri-*çpónn*-dănnt) *n* correspondente *m*

**corridor** (*kó*-ri-dóó) *n* corredor *m*

**corrupt** (kă-*rapt*) *adj* corrupto; *v* corromper

**corruption** (kă-*rap*-chănn) *n* corrupção *f*

**corset** (*kóó*-çit) *n* corpete *m*

**cosmetics** (kóz-*mé*-tikç) *pl* cosméticos *mpl*

**cost** (kóçt) *n* custo *m*; preço *m*

*****cost** (kóçt) *v* custar

**cosy** (kou-zi) *adj* íntimo, aconchegado

**cot** (kót) *n*Am cama de acampamento

**cottage** (*kó*-tidj) *n* casa de campo

**cotton** (*kó*-tănn) *n* algodão *m*; de algodão

**cotton-wool** (*kó*-tănn-ul) *n* algodão *m*

**couch** (kautch) *n* divã *m*

**cough** (kóf) *n* tosse *f*; *v* *****tossir

**could** (kud) *v* (p can)

**council** (*kaunn*-çăl) *n* conselho *m*

**councillor** (*kaunn*-çă-lă) *n* conselheiro *m*

**counsel** (*kaunn*-çăl) *n* conselho *m*

**counsellor** (*kaunn*-çă-lă) *n* conselheiro *m*

**count** (kaunnt) *v* contar; incluir; considerar; *n* conde *m*

**counter** (*kaunn*-tă) *n* balcão *m*

**counterfeit** (*kaunn*-tă-fiit) *v* falsificar

**counterfoil** (*kaunn*-tă-foil) *n* talão *m*

**counterpane** (*kaunn*-tă-peinn) *n* colcha *f*

**countess** (*kaunn*-tiç) *n* condessa *f*

**country** (*kann*-tri) *n* país *m*; campo *m*; região *f*; ~ **house** casa de campo

**countryman** (*kann*-tri-mănn) *n* (pl -men) compatriota *m*

**countryside** (*kann*-tri-çaid) *n* campo *m*

**county** (*kaunn*-ti) *n* condado *m*

**couple** (*ka*-păl) *n* par *m*; casal *m*

**coupon** (*kuu*-pónn) *n* cupão *m*, talão *m*

**courage** (*ka*-ridj) *n* valentia *f*, coragem *f*

**courageous** (kă-*rei*-djăç) *adj* corajoso

**course** (kóóç) *n* rota *f*; prato *m*; curso *m*; **intensive** ~ curso intensivo; **of** ~ com certeza, naturalmente

**court** (kóót) *n* tribunal *m*; corte *f*

**courteous** (*kăă*-ti-ăç) *adj* cortês

**cousin** (*ka*-zănn) *n* prima *f*, primo *m*

**cover** (*ka*-vă) *v* \*cobrir, tapar; *n* abrigo *m*, refúgio *m*; tampa *f*; capa *f*; ~ **charge** preço do talher

**cow** (kau) *n* vaca *f*

**coward** (*kau*-ăd) *n* cobarde *m*

**cowardly** (*kau*-ăd-li) *adj* cobarde

**cow-hide** (*kau*-haid) *n* pele de vaca

**crab** (kræb) *n* caranguejo *m*

**crack** (kræk) *n* estalido *m*; fenda *f*; *v* estalar; rebentar, quebrar, partir

**cradle** (*krei*-dăl) *n* berço *m*

**cramp** (kræmmp) *n* cãibra *f*

**crane** (kreinn) *n* grua *f*

**crankcase** (*krænngk*-keiç) *n* cárter *m*

**crankshaft** (*krænngk*-chaaft) *n* cambota *f*

**crash** (kræch) *n* choque *m*; *v* colidir; despenhar-se; ~ **barrier** barreira de protecção

**crate** (kreit) *n* grade *f*

**crater** (*krei*-tă) *n* cratera *f*

**crawl** (króól) *v* rastejar

**craze** (kreiz) *n* mania *f*

**crazy** (*krei*-zi) *adj* louco, doido

**creak** (kriik) *v* ranger

**cream** (kriimm) *n* creme *m*; nata *f*; *adj* creme

**creamy** (*krii*-mi) *adj* cremoso

**crease** (kriiç) *v* enrugar, amarrotar; *n* dobra *f*; prega *f*

**create** (kri-*eit*) *v* criar

**creature** (*krii*-tchă) *n* criatura *f*; ser *m*

**credible** (*kré*-di-băl) *adj* verosímil

**credit** (*kré*-dit) *n* crédito *m*; *v* creditar; ~ **card** cartão de crédito

**creditor** (*kré*-di-tă) *n* credor *m*

**credulous** (*kré*-di^u-lăç) *adj* crédulo

**creek** (kriik) *n* enseada *f*

\***creep** (kriip) *v* rastejar

**creepy** (*krii*-pi) *adj* horripilante, assustador

**cremate** (kri-*meit*) *v* incinerar

**cremation** (kri-*mei*-chănn) *n* incineração *f*

**crew** (kruu) *n* tripulação *f*

**cricket** (*kri*-kit) *n* críquete *m*; grilo *m*

**crime** (kraimm) *n* crime *m*

**criminal** (*kri*-mi-năl) *n* criminoso *m*, delinquente *m*; *adj* criminal, criminoso; ~ **law** direito penal

**criminality** (kri-mi-*næ*-lă-ti) *n* criminalidade *f*

**crimson** (*krimm*-zănn) *adj* vermelho

**crippled** (*kri*-păld) *adj* aleijado

**crisis** (*krai*-çiç) *n* (pl crises) crise *f*

**crisp** (kriçp) *adj* quebradiço

**critic** (*kri*-tik) *n* crítico *m*

**critical** (*kri*-ti-kăl) *adj* crítico; precário

**criticism** (*kri*-ti-çi-zămm) *n* crítica *f*

**criticize** (*kri*-ti-çaiz) *v* criticar

**crochet** (kro<sup>u</sup>-chei) v *fazer renda
**crockery** (kró-kǎ-ri) n faiança f, loiça f
**crocodile** (kró-kǎ-dail) n crocodilo m
**crooked** (kru-kid) adj torto, torcido; desonesto
**crop** (króp) n colheita f
**cross** (króc) v atravessar; adj irritado, zangado; n cruz f
**cross-eyed** (króc-aid) adj estrábico
**crossing** (kró-çinng) n travessia f; encruzilhada f
**crossroads** (króc-ro<sup>u</sup>dz) n cruzamento m
**crosswalk** (króc-<sup>u</sup>óók) nAm passagem de peões; passagem de pedestres Br
**crow** (kro<sup>u</sup>) n gralha f
**crowbar** (kro<sup>u</sup>-baa) n pé-de-cabra m
**crowd** (kraud) n turba f, multidão f
**crowded** (krau-did) adj animado; apinhado
**crown** (kraunn) n coroa f; v coroar
**crucifix** (kruu-çi-fikç) n crucifixo m
**crucifixion** (kruu-çi-fik-chǎnn) n crucificação f
**crucify** (kruu-çi-fai) v crucificar
**cruel** (kru<sup>ǎ</sup>l) adj cruel
**cruise** (kruuz) n cruzeiro m
**crumb** (kramm) n migalha f
**crusade** (kruu-çeid) n cruzada f
**crust** (kraçt) n côdea f
**crutch** (kratch) n muleta f
**cry** (krai) v chorar; gritar; chamar; n grito m; brado m
**crystal** (kri-çtǎl) n cristal m; adj de cristal
**Cuba** (k<sup>i</sup>uu-bǎ) Cuba f
**Cuban** (k<sup>i</sup>uu-bǎnn) adj cubano
**cube** (k<sup>i</sup>uub) n cubo m
**cuckoo** (ku-kuu) n cuco m
**cucumber** (k<sup>i</sup>uu-kǎmm-bǎ) n pepino m
**cuddle** (ka-dǎl) v acarinhar
**cudgel** (ka-djǎl) n cacete m

**cuff** (kaf) n punho m
**cuff-links** (kaf-linngkç) pl botões de punho; abotoaduras fplBr
**cul-de-sac** (kal-dǎ-çæk) n beco sem saída
**cultivate** (kal-ti-veit) v cultivar
**culture** (kal-tchǎ) n cultura f
**cultured** (kal-tchǎd) adj culto
**cunning** (ka-ninng) adj manhoso
**cup** (kap) n chávena f; taça f; xícara fBr
**cupboard** (ka-bǎd) n armário m
**curb** (kǎǎb) n beira do passeio; meio-fio mBr; v reprimir, *refrear
**cure** (k<sup>i</sup>u<sup>ǎ</sup>) v curar; n cura f
**curio** (k<sup>i</sup>u<sup>ǎ</sup>-ri-o<sup>u</sup>) n (pl ~s) curiosidade f
**curiosity** (k<sup>i</sup>u<sup>ǎ</sup>-ri-ó-çǎ-ti) n curiosidade f
**curious** (k<sup>i</sup>u<sup>ǎ</sup>-ri-ǎç) adj curioso
**curl** (kǎǎl) v encaracolar; n caracol m
**curler** (kǎǎ-lǎ) n rolo m
**curling-tongs** (kǎǎ-linng-tónnz) pl ferro de frisar
**curly** (kǎǎ-li) adj encaracolado
**currant** (ka-rǎnnt) n passa de Corinto; groselha f
**currency** (ka-rǎnn-çi) n moeda f; **foreign** ~ moeda estrangeira
**current** (ka-rǎnnt) n corrente f; adj corrente; **alternating** ~ corrente alterna; **direct** ~ corrente contínua
**curry** (ka-ri) n caril m
**curse** (kǎǎç) v praguejar; amaldiçoar, *maldizer; n praga f
**curtain** (kǎǎ-tǎnn) n cortina f; pano m
**curve** (kǎǎv) n curva f; volta f
**curved** (kǎǎvd) adj curvado, curvo
**cushion** (ku-chǎnn) n almofada f
**custodian** (ka-çto<sup>u</sup>-di-ǎnn) n guarda m
**custody** (ka-çtǎ-di) n detenção f; custódia f; tutela f

custom (ka-çtămm) n costume m; hábito m

customary (ka-çtă-mă-ri) adj usual, costumado, habitual

customer (ka-çtă-mă) n freguês m; cliente m

Customs (ka-çtămmz) pl alfândega f; ~ duty taxa f; ~ officer funcionário aduaneiro

cut (kat) n corte m; golpe m

*cut (kat) v cortar; *reduzir; ~ off cortar; interromper

cutlery (kat-lă-ri) n talher m

cutlet (kat-lăt) n costeleta f

cycle (çai-kăl) n velocípede m; bicicleta f; ciclo m

cyclist (çai-kliçt) n ciclista f

cyclone (çai-klo"nn) n ciclone m

cylinder (çi-linn-dă) n cilindro m; ~ head cabeça do motor

Cyprus (çai-prăç) Chipre m

cystitis (çi-çtai-tiç) n cistite f

Czech (tchék) adj checo

# D

dad (dæd) n pai m

daddy (dæ-di) n paizinho m

daffodil (dæ-fă-dil) n junquilho m

daily (dei-li) adj diário; n diário m

dairy (déª-ri) n leitaria f

dam (dæmm) n barragem f; dique m

damage (dæ-midj) n dano m; v danificar

damp (dæmmp) adj húmido; molhado; n humidade f; v humedecer

dance (daannç) v dançar; n dança f

dandelion (dænn-di-lai-ănn) n dente-de-leão m

dandruff (dænn-drăf) n caspa f

Dane (deinn) n dinamarquês m

danger (deinn-djă) n perigo m

dangerous (deinn-djă-răç) adj perigoso

Danish (dei-nich) adj dinamarquês

dare (déª) v ousar; desafiar

daring (déª-rinng) adj temerário

dark (daak) adj escuro; n escuridão f, trevas fpl

darling (daa-linng) n querido m, amor m

darn (daann) v passajar

dash (dæch) v precipitar-se; n traço m

dashboard (dæch-bóód) n painel de instrumentos

data (dei-tă) pl dados mpl

date¹ (deit) n data f; encontro m; v datar; out of ~ fora de moda

date² (deit) n tâmara f

daughter (dóó-tă) n filha f

dawn (dóónn) n madrugada f; aurora f

day (dei) n dia m; by ~ de dia; ~ trip excursão f; per ~ por dia; the ~ before yesterday anteontem

daybreak (dei-breik) n amanhecer m

daylight (dei-lait) n luz do dia

dead (déd) adj morto

deaf (déf) adj surdo

deal (diil) n negócio m

*deal (diil) v *distribuir; ~ with tratar com; *fazer negócios com

dealer (dii-lă) n negociante m

dear (diª) adj querido; caro

death (déθ) n morte f; ~ penalty pena de morte

debate (di-beit) n debate m

debit (dé-bit) n débito m

debt (dét) n dívida f

decaffeinated (dii-kæ-fi-nei-tid) adj descafeinado

deceit (di-çiit) n engano m

deceive (di-çiiv) v enganar

December (di-çémm-bă) Dezembro

decency (dii-çănn-çi) n decência f

decent (dii-çännt) adj decente

decide (di-çaid) v decidir, resolver

decision (di-çi-jänn) n decisão f

deck (dék) n convés m; ~ cabin camarote de convés; ~ chair cadeira de lona

declaration (dé-klä-rei-chänn) n declaração f

declare (di-kléaᵈ) v declarar

decoration (dé-kä-rei-chänn) n decoração f

decrease (dii-kriiç) v *diminuir; n diminuição f

dedicate (dé-di keit) v dedicar

deduce (di-dᶦuuç) v *deduzir

deduct (di-dakt) v *deduzir, *subtrair

deed (diid) n acção f

deep (diip) adj profundo

deep-freeze (diip-friiz) n congelador m

deer (diaᵈ) n (pl ~) veado m

defeat (di-fiit) v derrotar; n derrota f

defective (di-fék-tiv) adj defeituoso

defence (di-fénnç) n defesa f

defend (di-fénnd) v defender

deficiency (di-fi-chänn-çi) n deficiência f

deficit (dé-fi-çit) n défice m

define (di-fainn) v definir, determinar

definite (dé-fi-nit) adj determinado; definido

definition (dé-fi-ni-chänn) n definição f

deformed (di-fóómmd) adj deformado, disforme

degree (di-ghrii) n grau m; título m

delay (di-lei) v atrasar; adiar; n atraso m, demora f; adiamento m

delegate (dé-li-ghät) n delegado m

delegation (dé-li-ghei-chänn) n delegação f

deliberate¹ (di-li-bä-reit) v deliberar, discutir

deliberate² (di-li-bä-rät) adj deliberado

deliberation (di-li-bä-rei-chänn) n deliberação f

delicacy (dé-li-kä-çi) n acepipe m

delicate (dé-li-kät) adj delicado

delicatessen (dé-li-kä-té-çänn) n manjar fino; mercearia fina

delicious (di-li-châç) adj delicioso

delight (di-lait) n delícia f, deleite m; v deliciar; delighted encantado

delightful (di-lait-fäl) adj encantador, delicioso

deliver (di-li-vä) v entregar; livrar

delivery (di-li-vä-ri) n entrega f; parto m; libertação f; ~ van furgoneta f

demand (di-maannd) v exigir, *requerer; n exigência f; procura f

democracy (di-mó-krä-çi) n democracia f

democratic (dé-mä-kræ-tik) adj democrático

demolish (di-mó-lich) v *demolir

demolition (dé-mä-li-chänn) n demolição f

demonstrate (dé-männ-çtreit) v demonstrar; manifestar

demonstration (dé-männ-çtrei-chänn) n demonstração f; manifestação f

den (dénn) n toca f

Denmark (dénn-maak) Dinamarca f

denomination (di-nó-mi-nei-chänn) n designação f

dense (dénnç) adj denso

dent (dénnt) n mossa f

dentist (dénn-tiçt) n dentista m

denture (dénn-tchä) n dentadura f

deny (di-nai) v negar, recusar, denegar

deodorant (dii-oᵘ-dä-rännt) n desodorizante m; desodorante mBr

depart (di-paat) v partir, *ir-se; falecer

department (di-paat-männt) n departamento *m*; ~ **store** armazém *m*

**departure** (di-*paa*-tchă) *n* partida *f*,
despedida *f*

**dependant** (di-*pénn*-dănnt) *adj* dependente

**depend on** (di-*pénnd*) depender de

**deposit** (di-*pó*-zit) *n* depósito *m*; sedimento *m*; *v* depositar

**depository** (di-*pó*-zi-tă-ri) *n* armazém
*m*

**depot** (*dé*-po^u) *n* armazém *m*; *nAm*
estação *f*

**depress** (di-*préç*) *v* deprimir

**depression** (di-*pré*-chănn) *n* depressão
*f*; recessão *f*

**deprive of** (di-*praiv*) privar de

**depth** (dépθ) *n* profundidade *f*

**deputy** (*dé*-p^iu-ti) *n* deputado *m*;
substituto *m*

**descend** (di-*cénnd*) *v* descer

**descendant** (di-*cénn*-dănnt) *n* descendente *m*

**descent** (di-*cénnt*) *n* descida *f*

**describe** (di-*ckraib*) *v* descrever

**description** (di-*ckrip*-chănn) *n* descrição *f*; sinais pessoais

**desert**[1] (*dé*-zăt) *n* deserto *m*; *adj* selvagem, deserto

**desert**[2] (di-*zăăt*) *v* desertar; abandonar

**deserve** (di-*zăăv*) *v* merecer

**design** (di-*zainn*) *v* desenhar; *n* projecto *m*; objectivo *m*

**designate** (*dé*-zigh-neit) *v* designar

**desirable** (di-*zai*ă-ră-băl) *adj* desejável

**desire** (di-*zai*ă) *n* desejo *m*; vontade *f*;
*v* desejar, cobiçar

**desk** (déck) *n* secretária *f*; carteira *f*;
carteira de escola

**despair** (di-*cpé*ă) *n* desespero *m*; *v*
desesperar

**despatch** (di-*cpætch*) *v* despachar

**desperate** (*dé*-cpă-răt) *adj* desesperado

**despise** (di-*cpaiz*) *v* desprezar

**despite** (di-*cpait*) *prep* apesar de

**dessert** (di-*zăăt*) *n* sobremesa *f*

**destination** (dé-çti-*nei*-chănn) *n* destino *m*

**destine** (*dé*-çtinn) *v* destinar

**destiny** (*dé*-çti-ni) *n* sorte *f*, destino *m*

**destroy** (di-*çtroi*) *v* *destruir

**destruction** (di-*çtrak*-chănn) *n* destruição *f*; ruína *f*

**detach** (di-*tætch*) *v* separar

**detail** (*dii*-teil) *n* particularidade *f*,
detalhe *m*

**detailed** (*dii*-teild) *adj* detalhado

**detect** (di-*tékt*) *v* *descobrir

**detective** (di-*ték*-tiv) *n* detective *m*;
~ **story** romance policial

**detergent** (di-*tăă*-djănnt) *n* detergente
*m*

**determine** (di-*tăă*-minn) *v* definir, determinar

**determined** (di-*tăă*-minnd) *adj* resoluto

**detour** (*dii*-tuă) *n* desvio *m*

**devaluation** (dii-væl-^iu-ei-chănn) *n* desvalorização *f*

**devalue** (dii-*væl*-^iuu) *v* desvalorizar

**develop** (di-*vé*-lăp) *v* desenvolver; revelar

**development** (di-*vé*-lăp-mănnt) *n* desenvolvimento *m*

**deviate** (*dii*-vi-eit) *v* desviar-se

**devil** (*dé*-văl) *n* diabo *m*

**devise** (di-*vaiz*) *v* *planear

**devote** (di-*vo*^ut) *v* dedicar

**dew** (d^iuu) *n* orvalho *m*

**diabetes** (dai-ă-*bii*-tiiz) *n* diabetes *f*

**diabetic** (dai-ă-*bé*-tik) *n* diabético *m*

**diagnose** (dai-ăgh-*no*^uz) *v* diagnosticar; constatar

**diagnosis** (dai-ăgh-*no*^u-çiç) *n* (pl -ses)
diagnóstico *m*

**diagonal** (dai-æ-*ghă*-năl) *n* diagonal *f*;
*adj* diagonal

diagram 221 discard

**diagram** (dai-ă-ghræmm) n diagrama m; gráfico m, esquema m

**dialect** (dai-ă-lékt) n dialecto m

**diamond** (dai-ă-mănnd) n diamante m

**diaper** (dai-ă-pă) nAm fralda f

**diaphragm** (dai-ă-fræmm) n membrana f; diafragma m

**diarrhoea** (dai-ă-ri-ă) n diarreia f

**diary** (dai-ă-ri) n agenda f; diário m

**Dictaphone®** (dik-tă-foᵘnn) n ditafone m

**dictate** (dik-teit) v ditar

**dictation** (dik-tei-chănn) n ditado m

**dictator** (dik-tei-tă) n ditador m

**dictionary** (dik-chă-nă-ri) n dicionário m

**did** (did) v (p do)

**die** (dai) v morrer

**diet** (dai-ăt) n dieta f

**differ** (di fă) v *diferir

**difference** (di-fă-rănnç) n diferença f; distinção f

**different** (di-fă-rănnt) adj diferente; outro

**difficult** (di-fi-kălt) adj difícil

**difficulty** (di-fi-kăl-ti) n dificuldade f; obstáculo m

**\*dig** (digh) v cavar; escavar

**digest** (di-djéçt) v *digerir

**digestible** (di-djé-çtă-băl) adj digestivo

**digestion** (di-djéç-tchănn) n digestão f

**digit** (di-djit) n algarismo m

**digital** (di-dji-tăl) adj digital

**dignified** (digh-ni-faid) adj distinto

**dilapidated** (di-læ-pi-dei-tid) adj delapidado

**diligence** (di-li-djănnç) n aplicação f, zelo m

**diligent** (di-li-djănnt) adj aplicado, zeloso

**dilute** (dai-lⁱuut) v *diluir

**dim** (dimm) adj mate, baço; obscuro, vago

**dine** (dainn) v jantar

**dinghy** (dinng-ghi) n barquinho m

**dining-car** (dai-ninng-kaa) n carruagem-restaurante f

**dining-room** (dai-ninng-ruumm) n sala de jantar

**dinner** (di-nă) n jantar m; almoço m

**dinner-jacket** (di-nă-djæ-kit) n smoking m

**dinner-service** (di-nă-çăă-viç) n serviço de jantar

**diphtheria** (dif-θiⁱă-ri-ă) n difteria f

**diploma** (di-ploᵘ-mă) n diploma m

**diplomat** (di-plă-mæt) n diplomata m

**direct** (di-rékt) adj directo; v dirigir; encenar

**direction** (di-rék-chănn) n direcção f; instrução f; realização f; administração **directions for use** modo de emprego

**directive** (di-rék-tiv) n directiva f

**director** (di-rék-tă) n director m; encenador m

**dirt** (dăăt) n sujidade f

**dirty** (dăă-ti) adj porco, sujo

**disabled** (di-çei-băld) adj incapacitado, inválido

**disadvantage** (di-çăd-vaann-tidj) n desvantagem f

**disagree** (di-çă-ghrii) v discordar

**disagreeable** (di-çă-ghrii-ă-băl) adj desagradável

**disappear** (di-çă-piⁱă) v desaparecer

**disappoint** (di-çă-poinnt) v desapontar

**disappointment** (di-çă-poinnt-mănnt) n desilusão f

**disapprove** (di-çă-pruuv) v desaprovar

**disaster** (di-zaa-çtă) n desastre m; desgraça f, catástrofe f

**disastrous** (di-zaa-çtrăç) adj desastroso

**disc** (diçk) n disco m; **slipped ~** hérnia discal

**discard** (di-çkaad) v *desfazer-se de

discharge (diç-*tchaadj*) v descarregar;
~ **of** dispensar de

discipline (*di*-çi-plinn) n disciplina f

discolour (di-*çka*-lä) v descolorir

disconnect (di-çkä-*nékt*) v desligar

discontented (di-çkänn-*ténn*-tid) adj
descontente

discontinue (di-çkänn-*ti*-n[i]uu) v cessar,
suspender

discount (*di*-çkaunnt) n redução f,
desconto m

discover (di-*çka*-vä) v *descobrir

discovery (di-*çka*-vä-ri) n descoberta f

discuss (di-*çkaç*) v discutir; debater

discussion (di-*çka*-chänn) n discussão
f; conversa f, debate m

disease (di-*ziiz*) n doença f

disembark (di-çimm-*baak*) v desembarcar

disgrace (diç-*ghreiç*) n desonra f; desgraça f

disguise (diç-*ghaiz*) v disfarçar-se; n
disfarce m

disgusting (diç-*gha*-çtinng) adj repugnante

dish (dich) n prato m, travessa f

dishonest (di-ç-niçt) adj desonesto

disinfect (di-çinn-*fékt*) v desinfectar

disinfectant (di-çinn-*fék*-tännt) n desinfectante m

dislike (di-*çlaik*) v não gostar, detestar; n antipatia f, aversão f, repugnância f

dislocated (*di*-çlä-kei-tid) adj deslocado

dismiss (diç-*miç*) v *despedir

disorder (di-*çóó*-dä) n desordem f

dispatch (di-*çpætch*) v enviar, *expedir

display (di-*çplei*) v *expor, exibir;
mostrar; n exposição f

displease (di-*pliiz*) v desagradar, desgostar

disposable (di-*çpo*[u]-zä-bäl) adj para
deitar fora

disposal (di-*çpo*[u]-zäl) n disposição f

dispose of (di-*çpo*[u]z) desembara-
çar-se de

dispute (di-*çp*[i]uut) n disputa f; briga
f, litígio m; v altercar, contestar

dissatisfied (di-cæ-tiç-faid) adj insatisfeito

dissolve (di-*zólv*) v *diluir, dissolver

dissuade from (di-ç[u]*eid*) dissuadir

distance (*di*-çtännç) n distância f; ~
**in kilometres** quilometragem m

distant (*di*-çtännt) adj distante

distinct (di-*çtinngkt*) adj distinto

distinction (di-*çtinngk*-chänn) n distinção f, diferença f

distinguish (di-*çtinng*-gh[u]ich) v distinguir

distinguished (di-*çtinng*-gh[u]icht) adj
distinto

distress (di-*tréç*) n perigo m; ~ **signal** pedido de socorro

distribute (di-*çtri*-b[i]uut) v *distribuir

distributor (di-*çtri*-b[i]u-tä) n distribuidor m

district (*di*-çtrikt) n distrito m; região
f; bairro m

disturb (di-*çtääb*) v incomodar

disturbance (di-*çtää*-bännç) n perturbação f; distúrbio m

ditch (ditch) n fosso m

dive (daiv) v mergulhar

diversion (dai-*vää*-chänn) n desvio m;
diversão f

divide (di-*vaid*) v dividir; repartir; separar

divine (di-*vainn*) adj divino

division (di-*vi*-jänn) n divisão f; separação f; secção f

divorce (di-*vóóç*) n divórcio m; v divorciar-se

dizziness (*di*-zi-näç) n vertigem f

dizzy (*di*-zi) adj atordoado

*do (duu) v *fazer; bastar

**dock** (dók) n doca f; v entrar em doca

**docker** (dó-kă) n estivador m

**doctor** (dók-tă) n médico m; doutor m

**document** (dó-kʲu-mănnt) n documento m

**dog** (dógh) n cão m

**dogged** (dó-ghid) adj obstinado

**doll** (dól) n boneca f

**dome** (doᵘmm) n cúpula f

**domestic** (dă-mé-çtik) adj doméstico; interno; n empregado doméstico

**domicile** (dó-mi-çail) n domicílio m

**domination** (dó-mi-nei-chănn) n dominação f

**dominion** (dă-mi-nⁱänn) n domínio m

**donate** (doᵘ neit) v *dar

**donation** (doᵘ-nei-chănn) n donativo m, doação f

**done** (dann) v (pp do)

**donkey** (dónn-ki) n burro m

**donor** (doᵘ-nă) n doador m

**door** (dóó) n porta f; **revolving ~** porta giratória; **sliding ~** porta corrediça

**doorbell** (dóó-bél) n campainha da porta

**door-keeper** (dóó-kii-pă) n porteiro m

**doorman** (dóó-mănn) n (pl -men) porteiro m

**dormitory** (dóó-mi-tri) n dormitório m

**dose** (doᵘç) n dose f

**dot** (dot) n ponto m

**double** (da-băl) adj duplo

**doubt** (daut) v duvidar; n dúvida f; **without ~** sem dúvida

**doubtful** (daut-făl) adj duvidoso; incerto

**dough** (doᵘ) n massa f

**down¹** (daunn) adv abaixo, para baixo; adj abatido; prep ao longo de, para baixo; **~ payment** sinal m

**down²** (daunn) n penugem f

**downpour** (daunn-póó) n aguaceiro m

**downstairs** (daunn-çté⁴z) adv em baixo, para baixo

**downstream** (daunn-çtriimm) adv rio abaixo

**down-to-earth** (daunn-tu-ăăθ) adj sensato

**downwards** (daunn-ᵘădz) adv para baixo

**dozen** (da-zănn) n (pl ~, ~s) dúzia f

**draft** (draaft) n letra f

**drag** (drægh) v arrastar

**dragon** (dræ-ghănn) n dragão m

**drain** (dreinn) v secar; drenar; n esgoto m

**drama** (draa-mă) n drama m; tragédia f; teatro m

**dramatic** (dră-mæ-tik) adj dramático

**dramatist** (dræ-mă-tiçt) n dramaturgo m

**drank** (drænngk) v (p drink)

**draper** (drei-pă) n negociante de tecidos

**drapery** (drei-pă-ri) n têxteis mpl

**draught** (draaft) n corrente de ar; **draughts** jogo das damas

**draught-board** (draaft-bóód) n tabuleiro de damas

**draw** (dróó) n sorteio m

**\*draw** (dróó) v desenhar; puxar; levantar, sacar; **~ up** redigir

**drawbridge** (dróó-bridj) n ponte levadiça

**drawer** (dróó-ă) n gaveta f; **drawers** cuecas fpl

**drawing** (dróó-inng) n desenho m

**drawing-pin** (dróó-inng-pinn) n pionés m

**drawing-room** (dróó-inng-ruumm) n sala f

**dread** (dréd) v temer; n temor m

**dreadful** (dréd-făl) adj espantoso, terrível

**dream** (driimm) n sonho m

**\*dream** (driimm) v sonhar

**dress** (dréç) v *vestir; *vestir-se; pensar; n vestido m

**dressing-gown** (dré-çinng-ghaunn) n roupão m

**dressing-room** (dré-çinng-ruumm) n quarto de vestir

**dressing-table** (dré-çinng-tei-băl) n toucador m

**dressmaker** (dréç-mei-kă) n modista f

**drill** (dril) v brocar; adestrar; n broca f

**drink** (drinngk) n bebida f

***drink** (drinngk) v beber

**drinking-water** (drinng-kinng-ᵁóó-tă) n água potável

**drip-dry** (drip-drai) adj não passar a ferro

**drive** (draiv) n estrada f; passeio de carro

***drive** (draiv) v guiar; *conduzir

**driver** (drai-vă) n condutor m

**drizzle** (dri-zăl) n chuva miudinha

**drop** (dróp) v deixar *cair; n gota f

**drought** (draut) n seca f

**drown** (draunn) v afogar; *be drowned afogar-se

**drug** (dragh) n estupefaciente m; medicamento m

**drugstore** (dragh-çtóó) nAm farmácia f; drogaria f

**drunk** (dranngk) adj (pp drink) bêbado

**dry** (drai) adj seco; v secar; enxugar

**dry-clean** (drai-kliinn) v limpar a seco

**dry-cleaner's** (drai-klii-năz) n tinturaria f

**dryer** (drai-ă) n secador m

**duchess** (da-tchiç) n duquesa f

**duck** (dak) n pato m

**due** (dᶦuu) adj esperado; devido; vencido

**dues** (dᶦuuz) pl direitos mpl

**dug** (dagh) v (p, pp dig)

**duke** (dᶦuuk) n duque m

**dull** (dal) adj enfadonho, insípido; apagado, baço; embotado

**dumb** (damm) adj mudo; obtuso, estúpido

**dune** (dᶦuunn) n duna f

**dung** (danng) n esterco m

**dunghill** (danng-hil) n estrumeira f

**duration** (dᶦu-rei-chänn) n duração f

**during** (dᶦuᵃ-rinng) prep durante

**dusk** (daçk) n anoitecer m

**dust** (daçt) n poeira f

**dustbin** (daçt-binn) n caixote do lixo; lata de lixo Br

**dusty** (da-çti) adj poeirento

**Dutch** (datch) adj holandês

**Dutchman** (datch-mănn) n (pl -men) holandês m

**dutiable** (dᶦuu-ti-ă-băl) adj sujeito a taxas

**duty** (dᶦuu-ti) n dever m; tarefa f; direito de importação; Customs ~ direitos alfandegários

**duty-free** (dᶦuu-ti-frii) adj isento de direitos

**dwarf** (dᵁóóf) n anão m

**dye** (dai) v pintar, tingir; n tinta f

**dynamo** (dai-nă-moᵁ) n (pl ~s) dínamo m

**dysentery** (di-çänn-tri) n disenteria f

# E

**each** (iitch) adj cada; ~ other mutuamente

**eager** (ii-ghă) adj impaciente, desejoso

**eagle** (ii-ghăl) n águia f

**ear** (iᵃ) n orelha f

**earache** (iᵃ-reik) n dor de ouvidos

**ear-drum** (iᵃ-dramm) n tímpano m

**earl** (ăăl) n conde m

**early** (ăă-li) adj cedo

**earn** (äänn) *v* ganhar
**earnest** (ää-niçt) *n* seriedade *f*
**earnings** (ää-ninngz) *pl* ganhos *mpl*, rendimentos *mpl*
**earring** (i<sup>ä</sup>-rinng) *n* brinco *m*
**earth** (ää<sup>θ</sup>) *n* terra *f*; solo *m*
**earthenware** (ää-θänn-<sup>u</sup>é<sup>ä</sup>) *n* olaria *f*
**earthquake** (ääθ-k<sup>u</sup>eik) *n* tremor de terra
**ease** (iiz) *n* facilidade *f*, à-vontade *m*
**east** (iiçt) *n* este *m*
**Easter** (ii-çtä) Páscoa *f*
**easterly** (ii-çtä-li) *adj* oriental
**eastern** (ii-çtänn) *adj* oriental
**easy** (ii-zi) *adj* fácil; cómodo; ~ **chair** poltrona *f*
**easy-going** (ii-zi-gho<sup>u</sup>-inng) *adj* descontraído
**\*eat** (iit) *v* comer
**eavesdrop** (iivz-dróp) *v* escutar indiscretamente
**ebony** (é-bä-ni) *n* ébano *m*
**eccentric** (ik-çénn-trik) *adj* excêntrico
**echo** (é-ko<sup>u</sup>) *n* (pl ~es) eco *m*
**eclipse** (i-klipç) *n* eclipse *m*
**economic** (ii-kä-nó-mik) *adj* económico
**economical** (ii-kä-nó-mi-käl) *adj* económico, poupado
**economist** (i-kó-nä-miçt) *n* economista *m*
**economize** (i-kó-nä-maiz) *v* economizar
**economy** (i-kó-nä-mi) *n* economia *f*
**ecstasy** (ék-çtä-zi) *n* êxtase *m*
**Ecuador** (é-k<sup>u</sup>ä-dóó) Equador *m*
**Ecuadorian** (é-k<sup>u</sup>ä-dóó-ri-änn) *n* equatoriano *m*
**eczema** (ék-çi-mä) *n* eczema *m*
**edge** (édj) *n* orla *f*, borda *f*
**edible** (é-di-bäl) *adj* comestível
**edition** (i-di-chänn) *n* edição *f*; **morning** ~ edição da manhã
**editor** (é-di-tä) *n* redactor *m*

**educate** (é-dju-keit) *v* educar, formar
**education** (é-dju-kei-chänn) *n* educação *f*
**eel** (iil) *n* enguia *f*
**effect** (i-fékt) *n* efeito *m*, resultado *m*; *v* efectuar; in ~ com efeito
**effective** (i-fék-tiv) *adj* eficaz
**efficient** (i-fi-chännt) *adj* eficiente
**effort** (é-fät) *n* esforço *m*
**egg** (égh) *n* ovo *m*
**egg-cup** (égh-kap) *n* copinho para os ovos
**eggplant** (égh-plaannt) *n* beringela *f*
**egg-yolk** (égh-<sup>i</sup>o<sup>u</sup>k) *n* gema de ovo
**egoistic** (é-gho<sup>u</sup>-i-çtik) *adj* egoísta
**Egypt** (ii-djipt) Egipto *m*
**Egyptian** (i-djip-chänn) *adj* egípcio
**eiderdown** (ai-dä-daunn) *n* edredão *m*
**eight** (eit) *num* oito
**eighteen** (ei-tiinn) *num* dezoito
**eighteenth** (ei-tiinnθ) *num* décimo oitavo
**eighth** (eitθ) *num* oitavo
**eighty** (ei-ti) *num* oitenta
**either** (ai-ðä) *pron* um ou outro; **either ... or** seja ... seja, ou ... ou
**elaborate** (i-læ-bä-reit) *v* elaborar
**elastic** (i-læ-çtik) *adj* elástico; flexível; ~ **band** elástico *m*
**elasticity** (é-læ-çti-çä-ti) *n* elasticidade *f*
**elbow** (él-bo<sup>u</sup>) *n* cotovelo *m*
**elder** (él-dä) *adj* mais velho
**elderly** (él-dä-li) *adj* de idade
**eldest** (él-diçt) *adj* o mais velho
**elect** (i-lékt) *v* escolher, eleger
**election** (i-lék-chänn) *n* eleição *f*
**electric** (i-lék-trik) *adj* eléctrico; ~ **razor** máquina de barbear; barbeador eléctrico *Br*
**electrician** (i-lék-tri-chänn) *n* electricista *m*
**electricity** (i-lék-tri-çä-ti) *n* electricidade *f*

**electronic** (i-lék-*tró*-nik) *adj* electrónico; ~ **game** jogo electrónico

**elegance** (é-li-ghánç) *n* elegância *f*

**elegant** (é-li-ghánnt) *adj* elegante

**element** (é-li-männt) *n* elemento *m*

**elephant** (é-li-fännt) *n* elefante *m*

**elevator** (é-li-vei-tä) *nAm* elevador *m*

**eleven** (i-*lé*-vänn) *num* onze

**eleventh** (i-*lé*-vännθ) *num* décimo primeiro

**elf** (élf) *n* (pl elves) elfo *m*

**eliminate** (i-*li*-mi-neit) *v* eliminar

**elm** (élm) *n* ulmeiro *m*

**else** (élç) *adv* doutro modo

**elsewhere** (él-ç*ué*ª) *adv* noutro lado

**elucidate** (i-*luu*-çi-deit) *v* elucidar

**emancipation** (i-männ-çi-*pei*-chänn) *n* emancipação *f*

**embankment** (imm-*bänngk*-männt) *n* paredão *m*

**embargo** (émm-*baa*-ghoᵘ) *n* (pl ~es) embargo *m*

**embark** (imm-*baak*) *v* embarcar

**embarkation** (émm-baa-*kei*-chänn) *n* embarcação *f*

**embarrass** (imm-*bæ*-räç) *v* perturbar, embaraçar; estorvar

**embassy** (émm-bä-çi) *n* embaixada *f*

**emblem** (émm-blämm) *n* emblema *m*

**embrace** (imm-*breiç*) *v* abraçar; *n* abraço *m*

**embroider** (imm-*broi*-dä) *v* bordar

**embroidery** (imm-*broi*-dä-ri) *n* bordado *m*

**emerald** (é-mä-räld) *n* esmeralda *f*

**emergency** (i-*mää*-djänn-çi) *n* emergência *f*; estado de emergência; ~ **exit** saída de emergência

**emigrant** (é-mi-ghrännt) *n* emigrante *m*

**emigrate** (é-mi-ghreit) *v* emigrar

**emigration** (é-mi-*ghrei*-chänn) *n* emigração *f*

**emotion** (i-*moᵘ*-chänn) *n* emoção *f*

**emperor** (émm-pä-rä) *n* imperador *m*

**emphasize** (émm-fä-çaiz) *v* acentuar, frisar

**empire** (émm-paiª) *n* império *m*

**employ** (imm-*ploi*) *v* empregar; utilizar, usar

**employee** (émm-ploi-*ii*) *n* empregado *m*

**employer** (imm-*ploi*-ä) *n* patrão *m*

**employment** (imm-*ploi*-männt) *n* emprego *m*; ~ **exchange** agência de colocação

**empress** (émm-priç) *n* imperatriz *f*

**empty** (émmp-ti) *adj* vazio; *v* esvaziar

**enable** (i-*nei*-bäl) *v* possibilitar

**enamel** (i-*næ*-mäl) *n* esmalte *m*

**enamelled** (i-*næ*-mäld) *adj* esmaltado

**enchanting** (inn-*tchaann*-tinng) *adj* encantador, esplêndido

**encircle** (inn-ç*áä*-käl) *v* cercar; *rodear

**enclose** (inng-*kloᵘz*) *v* incluir, juntar

**enclosure** (inng-*kloᵘ*-jä) *n* anexo *m*

**encounter** (inng-*kaunn*-tä) *v* encontrar; *n* encontro *m*

**encourage** (inng-ka-ridj) *v* encorajar

**encyclopaedia** (énn-çai-klä-*pii*-di-ä) *n* enciclopédia *f*

**end** (énnd) *n* extremidade *f*, fim *m*; conclusão *f*; *v* acabar, terminar

**ending** (énn-dinng) *n* fim *m*

**endless** (énnd-läç) *adj* infinito

**endorse** (inn-*dóóç*) *v* endossar

**endure** (inn-*dⁱuª*) *v* suportar

**enemy** (é-nä-mi) *n* inimigo *m*

**energetic** (é-nä-*djé*-tik) *adj* enérgico

**energy** (é-nä-dji) *n* energia *f*; força *f*

**engage** (inng-*gheidj*) *v* empregar; contratar; comprometer-se; **engaged** noivo; ocupado

**engagement** (inng-*gheidj*-männt) *n* noivado *m*; compromisso *m*; ~ **ring** anel de noivado

**engine** (énn-djinn) *n* motor *m*, máquina f; locomotiva f

**engineer** (énn-dji-*ni*ə) n engenheiro m

**England** (inng-ghlännd) Inglaterra f

**English** (inng-ghlich) adj inglês

**Englishman** (inng-ghlich-männ) n (pl -men) inglês m

**engrave** (inng-*ghreiv*) v gravar

**engraver** (inng-*ghrei*-vă) n gravador m

**engraving** (inng-*ghrei*-vinng) n estampa f; gravação f

**enigma** (i-*nigh*-mă) n enigma m

**enjoy** (inn-*djoi*) v desfrutar, gozar

**enjoyable** (inn-*djoi*-ă-băl) adj agradável

**enjoyment** (inn-*djoi*-mănnt) n gozo m

**enlarge** (inn-*laadj*) v ampliar

**enlargement** (inn-*laadj*-mănnt) n ampliação f

**enormous** (i-*nóó*-măç) adj gigantesco, enorme

**enough** (i-*naf*) adv bastante; adj suficiente

**enquire** (inng-k*u*ai*ə*) v indagar, perguntar; investigar

**enquiry** (inng-k*u*ai*ə*-ri) n informação f; investigação f; inquérito m

**enter** (*énn*-tă) v entrar; inscrever

**enterprise** (*énn*-tă-praiz) n empresa f

**entertain** (énn-tă-*teinn*) v *divertir, *entreter; receber

**entertaining** (énn-tă-*tei*-ninng) adj divertido

**entertainment** (énn-tă-*teinn*-mănnt) n diversão f, divertimento m

**enthusiasm** (inn-*θ*iuu-zi-æ-zămm) n entusiasmo m

**enthusiastic** (inn-θ iuu-zi-æ-çtik) adj entusiástico

**entire** (inn-*tai*ə) adj todo, inteiro

**entirely** (inn-*tai*ə-li) adv inteiramente

**entrance** (*énn*-trănnç) n entrada f; acesso m

**entrance-fee** (*énn*-trănnç-fii) n preço de entrada

**entry** (*énn*-tri) n entrada f; lançamento m; no ~ proibido entrar

**envelope** (*énn*-vă-lo*u*p) n sobrescrito m, envelope m

**envious** (*énn*-vi-ăç) adj invejoso

**environment** (inn-*vai*ə-rănn-mănnt) n meio ambiente; arredores mpl

**envoy** (*énn*-voi) n emissário m

**envy** (*énn*-vi) n inveja f; v invejar

**epic** (*é*-pik) n epopeia f; adj épico

**epidemic** (é-pi-*dé*-mik) n epidemia f

**epilepsy** (*é*-pi-lép-çi) n epilepsia f

**epilogue** (*ó* pi lógh) n epílogo m

**episode** (*é*-pi-ço*u*d) n episódio m

**equal** (*ii*-k*u*ăl) adj igual; v igualar

**equality** (i-k*u*ó-lă-ti) n igualdade f

**equalize** (*ii*-k*u*ă-laiz) v igualar

**equally** (*ii*-k*u*ă-li) adv igualmente

**equator** (i-k*u*ei-tă) n equador m

**equip** (i-k*u*ip) v equipar

**equipment** (i-k*u*ip-mănnt) n equipamento m

**equivalent** (i-k*u*i-vă-lănnt) adj equivalente

**eraser** (i-*rei*-ză) n borracha f

**erect** (i-*rékt*) v erigir, edificar; adj erecto, em pé

**err** (ăă) v errar

**errand** (*é*-rănnd) n recado m

**error** (*é*-ră) n erro m, falta f

**escalator** (*é*-çkă-lei-tă) n escada rolante

**escape** (i-*çkeip*) v escapar; *fugir, evadir; n evasão f

**escort**[1] (*é*-çkóót) n escolta f

**escort**[2] (i-çkóót) v escoltar

**especially** (i-*çpé*-chă-li) adv principalmente, especialmente

**esplanade** (é-çplă-*neid*) n esplanada f

**essay** (*é*-çei) n ensaio m; composição f, tratado m

**essence** (*é*-çănnç) n essência f; natureza f

**essential** (i-*çénn*-chăl) adj indispensável; essencial

**essentially** (i-çénn-chă-li) *adv* essencialmente

**establish** (i-çtǽ-blich) *v* estabelecer

**estate** (i-çteit) *n* propriedade *f*; fazenda *f*

**esteem** (i-çtiimm) *n* estima *f*; *v* estimar

**estimate**[1] (é-çti-meit) *v* estimar, *fazer a estimativa

**estimate**[2] (é-çti-măt) *n* estimativa *f*

**eternal** (i-tǽ-năl) *adj* eterno

**eternity** (i-tǽ-nă-ti) *n* eternidade *f*

**ether** (ii-θǽ) *n* éter *m*

**Ethiopia** (i-θi-o-u-pi-ă) Etiópia *f*

**Ethiopian** (i-θi-o-u-pi-ănn) *adj* etíope

**Europe** ('u-ǽ-răp) Europa *f*

**European** ('u-ǎ-rǎ-pii-ănn) *adj* europeu; **European Union** União Européia

**evacuate** (i-vǽ-k-u-eit) *v* evacuar

**evaluate** (i-vǽl-u-eit) *v* avaliar

**evaporate** (i-vǽ-pǎ-reit) *v* evaporar

**even** (ii-vănn) *adj* liso, igual, plano, constante; par; *adv* mesmo

**evening** (iiv-ninng) *n* noite *f*; ~ **dress** traje a rigor

**event** (i-vénnt) *n* acontecimento *m*; caso *m*

**eventual** (i-vénn-tchu-ăl) *adj* final

**ever** (é-vă) *adv* jamais; sempre

**every** (év-ri) *adj* cada

**everybody** (év-ri-bó-di) *pron* toda a gente; todo o mundo *Br*

**everyday** (év-ri-dei) *adj* quotidiano

**everyone** (év-ri-u-ann) *pron* cada um, toda a gente; todo o mundo *Br*

**everything** (év-ri-θinng) *pron* tudo

**everywhere** (év-ri-u-é-ǎ) *adv* por toda a parte

**evidence** (é-vi-dănnç) *n* prova *f*

**evident** (é-vi-dănnt) *adj* evidente

**evil** (ii-văl) *n* mal *m*; *adj* mau

**evolution** (ii-vǎ-luu-chǎnn) *n* evolucão *f*

**exact** (igh-zǽkt) *adj* exacto

**exactly** (igh-zǽkt-li) *adv* exactamente

**exaggerate** (igh-zǽ-djǎ-reit) *v* exagerar

**examination** (igh-zǽ-mi-nei-chǎnn) *n* exame *m*; interrogatório *m*

**examine** (igh-zǽ-minn) *v* examinar

**example** (igh-zaamm-pǎl) *n* exemplo *m*; **for** ~ por exemplo

**excavation** (ékç-kǎ-vei-chǎnn) *n* escavação *f*

**exceed** (ik-çiid) *v* exceder; superar

**excel** (ik-çél) *v* *sobressair

**excellent** (ék-çǎ-lǎnnt) *adj* excelente, óptimo

**except** (ik-çépt) *prep* excepto

**exception** (ik-çép-chǎnn) *n* excepção *f*

**exceptional** (ik-çép-chǎ-nǎl) *adj* excepcional, extraordinário

**excerpt** (ék-çǎǎpt) *n* trecho *m*

**excess** (ik-çéç) *n* excesso *m*

**excessive** (ik-çé-çiv) *adj* excessivo

**exchange** (ikç-tcheinndj) *v* trocar; *n* troca *f*; bolsa *f*; ~ **office** casa de câmbio; ~ **rate** câmbio *m*

**excite** (ik-çait) *v* excitar

**excitement** (ik-çait-mǎnnt) *n* excitação *f*

**exciting** (ik-çai-tinng) *adj* emocionante

**exclaim** (ik-çkleimm) *v* exclamar

**exclamation** (ék-çklǎ-mei-chǎnn) *n* exclamação *f*

**exclude** (ik-çkluud) *v* *excluir

**exclusive** (ik-çkluu-çiv) *adj* exclusivo

**exclusively** (ik-çkluu-çiv-li) *adv* unicamente, exclusivamente

**excursion** (ik-çkǎǎ-chǎnn) *n* excursão *f*

**excuse**[1] (ik-çk-u-uç) *n* desculpa *f*

**excuse**[2] (ik-çk-u-uz) *v* desculpar

**execute** (ék-çi-k-u-uut) *v* desempenhar, executar

**execution** (ék-çi-k-u-uu-chǎnn) *n* execução f

**executioner** (ék-çi-k'uu-chă-nă) n carrasco m

**executive** (igh-zé-k'u-tiv) adj executivo; n poder executivo; director m

**exempt** (igh-zémmpt) v isentar, dispensar; adj isento

**exemption** (igh-zémmp-chănn) n isenção f

**exercise** (ék-çă-çaiz) n exercício m; v exercitar; exercer

**exhale** (ékç-heil) v exalar

**exhaust** (igh-zóóçt) n tubo de escape, escape m; v extenuar; ~ **gases** gases de escape

**exhibit** (igh-zi-bit) v *expor, exibir

**exhibition** (ék-çi-bi-chănn) n exibição f, exposição f

**exile** (ék-çail) n exílio m; exilado m

**exist** (igh-ziçt) v existir

**existence** (igh-zi-çtănnç) n existência f

**exit** (ék-çit) n saída f

**exotic** (igh-zó-tik) adj exótico

**expand** (ik-çpænnd) v expandir; desenvolver

**expect** (ik-çpékt) v esperar

**expectation** (ék-çpék-tei-chănn) n expectativa f

**expedition** (ék-çpă-di-chănn) n expedição f

**expel** (ik-çpél) v expulsar

**expenditure** (ik-çpénn-di-tchă) n despesa f

**expense** (ik-çpénnç) n despesa f

**expensive** (ik-çpénn-çiv) adj caro

**experience** (ik-çpiă-ri-ănnç) n experiência f; v experimentar, viver; **experienced** experiente

**experiment** (ik-çpé-ri-mănnt) n experiência f, prova f; v experimentar

**expert** (ik-çpăăt) n especialista m, perito m; adj competente

**expire** (ik-çpaiă) v expirar, terminar;

**expired** expirado

**expiry** (ik-çpaiă-ri) n expiração f, vencimento m

**explain** (ik-çpleinn) v explicar

**explanation** (ék-çplă-nei-chănn) n explicação f, esclarecimento m

**explicit** (ik-çpli-çit) adj explícito, categórico

**explode** (ik-çploud) v *explodir

**exploit** (ik-çploit) v explorar

**explore** (ik-çplóó) v explorar

**explosion** (ik-çplou-jänn) n explosão f

**explosive** (ik-çplou-çiv) adj explosivo; n explosivo m

**export**[1] (ik-çpóót) v exportar

**export**[2] (ék-çpóót) n exportação f

**exportation** (ék-çpóó-tei-chănn) n exportação f

**exports** (ék-çpóótç) pl exportações fpl

**exposition** (ék-çpă-zi-chănn) n exposição f

**exposure** (ik-çpou-jă) n exposição f; ~ **meter** fotómetro m

**express** (ik-çpréç) v expressar, exprimir; manifestar; adj expresso; explícito; ~ **train** comboio rápido

**expression** (ik-çpré-chănn) n expressão f

**exquisite** (ik-çkui-zit) adj requintado

**extend** (ik-çténnd) v prolongar; ampliar; conceder

**extension** (ik-çténn-chănn) n prolongamento m; ampliação f; extensão f; ~ **cord** fio de extensão

**extensive** (ik-çténn-çiv) adj amplo; extenso, vasto

**extent** (ik-çténnt) n dimensão f

**exterior** (ék-çtiă-ri-ă) adj exterior; n exterior m

**external** (ék-çtăă-năl) adj exterior

**extinguish** (ik-çtinng-ghuich) v apagar, extinguir

**extort** (ik-çtóót) v *extorquir

**extortion** (ik-çtóó-chänn) *n* extorsão *f*

**extra** (ék-çtră) *adj* suplementar

**extract¹** (ik-çtrǽkt) *v* *extrair, arrancar

**extract²** (ék-çtrǽkt) *n* trecho *m*

**extradite** (ék-çtră-dait) *v* extraditar

**extraordinary** (ik-çtróó-dänn-ri) *adj* extraordinário

**extravagant** (ik-çtrǽ-vă-ghännt) *adj* extravagante, exagerado

**extreme** (ik-çtriimm) *adj* extremo; *n* extremo *m*

**exuberant** (igh-z'uu-bă-rännt) *adj* exuberante

**eye** (ai) *n* olho *m*

**eyebrow** (ai-brau) *n* sobrancelha *f*

**eyelash** (ai-læch) *n* pestana *f*

**eyelid** (ai-lid) *n* pálpebra *f*

**eye-pencil** (ai-pénn-çăl) *n* lápis para os olhos

**eye-shadow** (ai-chæ-doᵘ) *n* sombra para os olhos

**eye-witness** (ai-ᵘit-nǎç) *n* testemunha ocular

# F

**fable** (fei-băl) *n* fábula *f*

**fabric** (fæ-brik) *n* tecido *m*; estrutura *f*

**façade** (fă-çaad) *n* fachada *f*

**face** (feiç) *n* rosto *m*; *v* enfrentar; ~ **massage** massagem facial; **facing** defronte de

**face-cream** (feiç-kriimm) *n* creme de beleza

**face-pack** (feiç-pæk) *n* máscara facial

**face-powder** (feiç-pau-dă) *n* pó-de-arroz *m*

**facility** (fă-çi-lă-ti) *n* facilidade *f*

**fact** (fækt) *n* facto *m*; **in** ~ com efeito

**factor** (fæk-tă) *n* factor *m*

**factory** (fæk-tă-ri) *n* fábrica *f*

**factual** (fæk-tchu-ăl) *adj* real

**faculty** (fæ-kăl-ti) *n* faculdade *f*; aptidão *f*, capacidade *f*

**fad** (fæd) *n* capricho *m*

**fade** (feid) *v* desbotar, desvanecer

**faience** (fai-ăç) *n* faiança *f*

**fail** (feil) *v* fracassar; falhar; faltar; omitir; reprovar; **without** ~ sem falta

**failure** (feil-ⁱă) *n* fracasso *m*; fiasco *m*

**faint** (feinnt) *v* desmaiar; *adj* vago, desfalecido, fraco

**fair** (féᵃ) *n* feira *f*; *adj* justo; loiro; bonito

**fairly** (féᵃ-li) *adv* bastante, razoavelmente

**fairy** (féᵃ-ri) *n* fada *f*

**fairytale** (féᵃ-ri-teil) *n* história de fadas

**faith** (feiθ) *n* fé *f*; confiança *f*

**faithful** (feiθ-ful) *adj* fiel

**fake** (feik) *n* falsificação *f*

**fall** (fóól) *n* queda *f*; *nAm* Outono *m*

***fall** (fóól) *v* *cair

**false** (fóólç) *adj* falso, errado; ~ **teeth** dentadura *f*

**falter** (fóól-tă) *v* vacilar; balbuciar

**fame** (feimm) *n* fama *f*; reputação *f*

**familiar** (fă-mil-ⁱă) *adj* familiar

**family** (fæ-mă-li) *n* família *f*; ~ **name** apelido *m*

**famous** (fei-măç) *adj* famoso

**fan** (fænn) *n* ventilador *m*; leque *m*; admirador *m*; fã *mBr*; ~ **belt** correia de ventoinha

**fanatical** (fă-næ-ti-kăl) *adj* fanático

**fancy** (fænn-çi) *v* *ter vontade de, gostar de; imaginar; *n* capricho *m*; imaginação *f*

**fantastic** (fænn-tæ-çtik) *adj* fantástico

**fantasy** (fænn-tă-zi) *n* fantasia *f*

**far** (faa) *adj* longe; *adv* muito; **by** ~

de longe; **so** ~ até agora
**far-away** (faa-ră-ᵘei) adj distante
**farce** (faac) n farsa f
**fare** (féᵃ) n preço da viagem, preço do bilhete; comida f, alimentação f
**farm** (faamm) n quinta f; fazenda f
**farmer** (faa-mă) n lavrador m; **farmer's wife** mulher do lavrador
**farmhouse** (faamm-hauç) n casal m
**far-off** (faa-róf) adj longínquo
**fascinate** (fæ-çi-neit) v fascinar
**fascism** (fæ-chi-zămm) n fascismo m
**fascist** (fæ-chiçt) adj fascista
**fashion** (fæ-chănn) n moda f; maneira f
**fashionable** (fæ-chă-nă-băl) adj na moda
**fast** (faaçt) adj rápido; firme
**fast-dyed** (faaçt-daid) adj de cor fixa, não tinge
**fasten** (faa-çănn) v prender, atar; fechar
**fastener** (faa-çă-nă) n fecho m
**fat** (fæt) adj gordo; n gordura f
**fatal** (fei-tăl) adj fatal, mortal
**fate** (feit) n destino m
**father** (faa-ðă) n pai m; padre m
**father-in-law** (faa-ðă-rinn-lóó) n (pl fathers-) sogro m
**fatherland** (faa-ðă-lännd) n pátria f
**fatness** (fæt-năç) n obesidade f
**fatty** (fæ-ti) adj gorduroso
**faucet** (fóó-çit) nAm torneira f
**fault** (fóólt) n culpa f; defeito m, imperfeição f, falha f
**faultless** (fóólt-lăç) adj impecável; perfeito
**faulty** (fóól-ti) adj defeituoso, imperfeito
**favour** (fei-vă) n favor m; v favorecer
**favourable** (fei-vă-ră-băl) adj favorável
**favourite** (fei-vă-rit) n favorito m; adj preferido

**fax** (faakç) n fax m; **send a** ~ mandar um fax
**fear** (fiᵃ) n receio m, medo m; v *recear
**feasible** (fii-ză-băl) adj realizável
**feast** (fiiçt) n festa f
**feat** (fiit) n feito m
**feather** (fé-ðă) n pena f
**feature** (fii-tchă) n característica f; feição do rosto
**February** (fé-bru-ă-ri) Fevereiro
**federal** (fé-dă-răl) adj federal
**federation** (fé-dă-rei-chănn) n federação f
**fee** (fii) n honorário m
**feeble** (fii-băl) adj fraco
***feed** (fiid) v alimentar; **fed up with** farto de
***feel** (fiil) v *sentir; apalpar; ~ **like** apetecer
**feeling** (fii-linng) n sensação f
**fell** (fél) v (p fall)
**fellow** (fé-loᵘ) n tipo m
**felt¹** (félt) n feltro m
**felt²** (félt) v (p, pp feel)
**female** (fii-meil) adj feminino
**feminine** (fé-mi-ninn) adj feminino
**fence** (fénnç) n cerca f; v esgrimir
**fender** (fénn-dă) n pára-choques m
**ferment** (făă-ménnt) v fermentar
**ferry-boat** (fé-ri-boᵘt) n ferry-boat m
**fertile** (făă-tail) adj fértil
**festival** (fé-çti-văl) n festival m
**festive** (fé-çtiv) adj festivo
**fetch** (fétch) v *ir buscar
**feudal** (fᵘuu-dăl) adj feudal
**fever** (fii-vă) n febre f
**feverish** (fii-vă-rich) adj febril
**few** (fᶦuu) adj poucos
**fiancé** (fi-ă-çei) n noivo m
**fiancée** (fi-ă-çei) n noiva f
**fibre** (fai-bă) n fibra f
**fiction** (fik-chănn) n ficção f
**field** (fiild) n campo m; domínio m; ~

**glasses** binóculo *m*

**fierce** (fiᵃç) *adj* feroz, violento

**fifteen** (fif-*tiinn*) *num* quinze

**fifteenth** (fif-*tiinnθ*) *num* décimo quinto

**fifth** (fifθ) *num* quinto

**fifty** (*fif*-ti) *num* cinquenta

**fig** (figh) *n* figo *m*

**fight** (fait) *n* luta *f*

***fight** (fait) *v* combater, lutar

**figure** (*fi*-ghă) *n* estatura *f*, figura *f*; algarismo *m*

**file** (fail) *n* lima *f*; arquivo *m*; fila *f*

**Filipino** (fi-li-*pii*-noᵘ) *n* filipino *m*

**fill** (fil) *v* encher; ~ **in** preencher; **filling station** estação de serviço; ~ **out** *Am* encher, preencher; ~ **up** atestar

**filling** (*fi*-linng) *n* obturação *f*; recheio *m*

**film** (film) *n* filme *m*; película *f*; *v* filmar

**filter** (*fil*-tă) *n* filtro *m*

**filthy** (*fil*-θi) *adj* imundo

**final** (*fai*-năl) *adj* final

**finance** (fai-*nænnç*) *v* financiar

**finances** (fai-*nænn*-çiz) *pl* finanças *fpl*

**financial** (fai-*nænn*-chăl) *adj* financeiro

**finch** (finntch) *n* tentilhão *m*

***find** (fainnd) *v* achar, encontrar

**fine** (fainn) *n* multa *f*; *adj* fino; belo; maravilhoso, excelente; ~ **arts** belas-artes *fpl*

**finger** (*finng*-ghă) *n* dedo *m*; **little ~** dedo mínimo

**fingerprint** (*finng*-ghă-prinnt) *n* impressão digital

**finish** (*fi*-nich) *v* terminar, acabar; *n* fim *m*; meta *f*; **finished** acabado

**Finland** (*finn*-lănnd) Finlândia *f*

**Finn** (finn) *n* finlandês *m*

**Finnish** (*fi*-nich) *adj* finlandês

**fire** (faiᵃ) *n* fogo *m*; incêndio *m*; *v* disparar; *despedir

**fire-alarm** (*faiᵃ*-ră-laamm) *n* alarme de incêndio

**fire-brigade** (*faiᵃ*-bri-gheid) *n* bombeiros *mpl*

**fire-escape** (*faiᵃ*-ri-çkeip) *n* escada de incêndio

**fire-extinguisher** (*faiᵃ*-rik-çtinng-ghᵘi-chă) *n* extintor *m*

**fireplace** (*faiᵃ*-pleiç) *n* lareira *f*

**fireproof** (*faiᵃ*-pruuf) *adj* à prova de fogo; de ir ao forno

**firm** (făămm) *adj* firme; sólido; *n* firma *f*

**first** (făăçt) *num* primeiro; **at ~** primeiro; ~ **name** nome próprio; prenome *mBr*

**first-aid** (făăçt-*eid*) *n* primeiros socorros; ~ **kit** caixa de primeiros socorros; ~ **post** posto de socorros

**first-class** (făăçt-*klaaç*) *adj* de primeira qualidade

**first-rate** (făăçt-*reit*) *adj* excelente, de primeira qualidade

**fir-tree** (*făă*-trii) *n* pinheiro *m*, abeto *m*

**fish¹** (fich) *n* (pl ~, ~es) peixe *m*; ~ **shop** peixaria *f*

**fish²** (fich) *v* pescar; **fishing gear** equipamento de pesca; **fishing hook** anzol *m*; **fishing industry** pesca *f*; **fishing licence** licença de pesca; **fishing line** linha de pesca; **fishing net** rede de pesca; **fishing rod** cana de pesca; **fishing tackle** aparelho de pesca

**fishbone** (*fich*-boᵘnn) *n* espinha de peixe

**fisherman** (*fi*-chă-mănn) *n* (pl -men) pescador *m*

**fist** (fiçt) *n* punho *m*

**fit** (fit) *adj* apropriado; *n* ataque *m*; *v* *condizer; **fitting room** gabinete de provas five (faiv) *num* cinco

fix (fikç) *v* reparar

fixed (fikçt) *adj* fixo

fizz (fiz) *n* efervescência *f*

fjord (fióód) *n* fiorde *m*

flag (flægh) *n* bandeira *f*

flame (fleimm) *n* chama *f*

flamingo (flã-*minng*-gho^u) *n* (pl ~s, ~es) flamingo *m*

flannel (*flæ*-năl) *n* flanela *f*

flash (flæch) *n* relâmpago *m*

flash-bulb (*flæch*-balb) *n* lâmpada de flash

flash-light (*flæch*-lait) *n* lanterna de mão

flask (flaaçk) *n* frasco *m*; thermos ~ termo *m*

flat (flæt) *adj* raso, plano; *n* apartamento *m*; ~ tyre pneu furado

flavour (*flei*-vă) *n* sabor *m*; *v* temperar

fleet (fliit) *n* frota *f*

flesh (fléch) *n* carne *f*

flew (fluu) *v* (p fly)

flex (flékç) *n* fio eléctrico

flexible (*flék*-çi-băl) *adj* flexível; maleável

flight (flait) *n* voo *m*; charter ~ voo charter

flint (flinnt) *n* pedra de isqueiro

float (flo^ut) *v* flutuar; *n* flutuador *m*

flock (flók) *n* rebanho *m*

flood (flad) *n* inundação *f*; enchente *f*

floor (flóó) *n* chão *m*; andar *m*, piso *m*; ~ show espectáculo de variedades

florist (*fló*-riçt) *n* florista *m*

flour (flau^ă) *n* farinha *f*

flow (flo^u) *v* correr

flower (flau^ă) *n* flor *f*

flowerbed (*flau^ă*-béd) *n* canteiro *m*

flown (flo^unn) *v* (pp fly)

flu (fluu) *n* gripe *f*

fluent (fluu-ănnt) *adj* fluente

fluid (fluu-id) *adj* fluido; *n* líquido *m*

flute (fluut) *n* flauta *f*

fly (flai) *n* mosca *f*; braguilha *f*

*fly (flai) *v* voar

foam (fo^umm) *n* espuma *f*; *v* espumar

foam-rubber (*fo^umm*-ra-bă) *n* espuma de borracha

focus (*fo^u*-kăç) *n* foco *m*

fog (fógh) *n* nevoeiro *m*

foggy (*fó*-ghi) *adj* enevoado

foglamp (*fógh*-læmmp) *n* farol de nevoeiro

fold (fo^uld) *v* dobrar; *n* dobra *f*

folk (fo^uk) *n* povo *m*; ~ song canção popular

folk-dance (*fo^uk*-daannç) *n* dança folclórica

folklore (*fo^uk*-lóó) *n* folclore *m*

follow (*fó*-lo^u) *v* *seguir; following *adj* seguinte

*be fond of (bii fónnd óv) gostar de

food (fuud) *n* alimento *m*; comida *f*; ~ poisoning intoxicação alimentar

foodstuffs (*fuud*-çtafç) *pl* produtos alimentícios

fool (fuul) *n* idiota *m*, tolo *m*; *v* enganar

foolish (*fuu*-lich) *adj* tolo, maluco; absurdo

foot (fut) *n* (pl feet) pé *m*; ~ powder pó para os pés; on ~ a pé

football (*fut*-bóól) *n* bola de futebol; ~ match jogo de futebol

foot-brake (*fut*-breik) *n* travão de pé

footpath (*fut*-paaθ) *n* passeio *m*; atalho *m*

footwear (*fut*-ʉé^ă) *n* calçado *m*

for (fóó) *prep* para; durante; por causa de, por, em consequência de; *conj* porque

*forbid (fă-*bid*) *v* proibir

force (fóóç) *v* forçar, obrigar; *n* força *f*; by ~ forçosamente; driving ~

força motriz
**ford** (fóód) n vau m
**forecast** (fóó-kaaçt) n previsão f; v
*prever
**foreground** (fóó-ghraunnd) n primeiro
plano
**forehead** (fó-réd) n testa f
**foreign** (fó-rinn) adj estrangeiro; estranho
**foreigner** (fó-ri-nă) n estrangeiro m;
forasteiro m
**foreman** (fóó-männ) n (pl -men) capataz m
**foremost** (fóó-moᵘçt) adj primeiro
**foresail** (fóó-çeil) n traquete m
**forest** (fó-riçt) n floresta f
**forester** (fó-ri-çtă) n guarda-florestal
m
**forge** (fóódj) v falsificar
*forget** (fă-ghét) v esquecer
**forgetful** (fă-ghét-făl) adj esquecido
*forgive** (fă-ghiv) v perdoar
**fork** (fóók) n garfo m; bifurcação f; v
bifurcar
**form** (fóómm) n forma f; formulário
m; classe f; v formar
**formal** (fóó-măl) adj formal
**formality** (fóó-mæ-lă-ti) n formalidade f
**former** (fóó-mă) adj antigo; antecedente; **formerly** anteriormente, antigamente
**formula** (fóó-mⁱu-lă) n (pl ~e, ~s)
fórmula f
**fort** (fóót) n forte m
**fortnight** (fóót-nait) n quinzena f
**fortress** (fóó-triç) n fortaleza f
**fortunate** (fóó-tchă-năt) adj afortunado
**fortune** (fóó-tchuunn) n fortuna f; sorte f
**forty** (fóó-ti) num quarenta
**forward** (fóó-ᵘăd) adv em frente,
avante; v *fazer seguir

**foster-parents** (fó-çtă-péᵃ-rănntç) pl
pais adoptivos
**fought** (fóót) v (p, pp fight)
**foul** (faul) adj porco; infame
**found**¹ (faunnd) v (p, pp find)
**found**² (faunnd) v fundar, estabelecer, *instituir
**foundation** (faunn-dei-chănn) n fundação f; ~ **cream** creme de base
**fountain** (faunn-tinn) n fonte f
**fountain-pen** (faunn-tinn-pénn) n caneta de tinta permanente
**four** (fóó) num quatro
**fourteen** (fóó-tiinn) num catorze
**fourteenth** (fóó-tiinnθ) num décimo
quarto
**fourth** (fóóθ) num quarto
**fowl** (faul) n (pl ~s, ~) aves de criação
**fox** (fókç) n raposa f
**foyer** (foi-ei) n entrada f
**fraction** (fræk-chănn) n fracção f
**fracture** (fræk-tchă) v quebrar, fracturar; n fractura f
**fragile** (fræ-djail) adj frágil
**fragment** (frægh-männt) n fragmento
m; bocado m
**frame** (freimm) n moldura f; armação
f
**France** (fraannç) França f
**franchise** (frænn-tchaiz) n direito de
voto
**fraternity** (fră-tă-nă-ti) n fraternidade f
**fraud** (fróód) n fraude f
**fray** (frei) v desfiar
**free** (frii) adj livre; ~ **of charge** gratuito; ~ **ticket** bilhete gratuito
**freedom** (frii-dămm) n liberdade f
*freeze** (friiz) v gelar; congelar
**freezing** (frii-zinng) adj gelado
**freezing-point** (frii-zinng-poinnt) n
ponto de congelação
**freight** (freit) n carga f

**French** (frénntch) *adj* francês

**Frenchman** (frénntch-männ) *n* (pl -men) francês *m*

**frequency** (frii-kᵘänn-çi) *n* frequência *f*

**frequent** (frii-kᵘännt) *adj* frequente

**fresh** (fréch) *adj* fresco; ~ **water** água doce

**friction** (frik-chänn) *n* fricção *f*

**Friday** (frai-di) sexta-feira *f*

**fridge** (fridj) *n* frigorífico *m*; geladeira *fBr*

**friend** (frénnd) *n* amigo *m*; amiga *f*

**friendly** (frénnd-li) *adj* afável; simpático, amistoso

**friendship** (frénnd-chip) *n* amizade *f*

**fright** (frait) *n* susto *m*, medo *m*

**frighten** (frai-tänn) *v* assustar

**frightened** (frai-tännd) *adj* assustado; *be* ~ assustar-se

**frightful** (frait-fäl) *adj* terrível, medonho

**fringe** (frinndj) *n* franja *f*

**frock** (frók) *n* vestido *m*

**frog** (frógh) *n* rã *f*

**from** (frómm) *prep* de; a partir de

**front** (frannt) *n* frente *f*; **in** ~ **of** diante de

**frontier** (frann-tiᵃ) *n* fronteira *f*

**frost** (fróçt) *n* geada *f*

**froth** (fróθ) *n* espuma *f*

**frozen** (froᵘ-zänn) *adj* congelado; ~ **food** comida congelada

**fruit** (fruut) *n* fruta *f*; fruto *m*

**fry** (frai) *v* fritar

**frying-pan** (frai inng-pænn) *n* frigideira *f*

**fuel** (fⁱuu-äl) *n* combustível *m*; ~ **pump** *Am* bomba de gasolina

**full** (ful) *adj* cheio; ~ **board** pensão completa; ~ **stop** ponto final; ~ **up** repleto

**fun** (fann) *n* divertimento *m*; prazer *m*

**function** (fanngk-chänn) *n* função *f*

**fund** (fannd) *n* fundo *m*

**fundamental** (fann-dä-ménn-täl) *adj* fundamental

**funeral** (fⁱuu-nä-räl) *n* funeral *m*

**funnel** (fa-näl) *n* funil *m*

**funny** (fa-ni) *adj* engraçado; estranho

**fur** (fää) *n* pele *f*; ~ **coat** casaco de peles; **furs** pele *f*

**furious** (fⁱuᵃ-ri-äç) *adj* furioso, furibundo

**furnace** (fää-niç) *n* forno *m*

**furnish** (fää-nich) *v* fornecer, proporcionar; mobilar; ~ **with** *prover de

**furniture** (fää-ni-tchä) *n* mobília *f*

**furrier** (fa-ri-ä) *n* peleiro *m*

**further** (fää-ðä) *adj* mais além; ulterior

**furthermore** (fää-ðä-móó) *adv* além disso

**furthest** (fää-ðiçt) *adj* o mais distante

**fuse** (fⁱuuz) *n* fusível *m*; mecha *f*

**fuss** (faç) *n* espalhafato *m*

**future** (fⁱuu-tchä) *n* futuro *m*; *adj* futuro

## G

**gable** (ghei-bäl) *n* empena *f*

**gadget** (ghæ-djit) *n* engenhoca *f*

**gaiety** (ghei-ä-ti) *n* alegria *f*

**gain** (gheinn) *v* ganhar; *n* lucro *m*

**gait** (gheit) *n* passo *m*, andar *m*

**gale** (gheil) *n* temporal *m*

**gall** (ghóól) *n* bílis *f*; ~ **bladder** vesícula biliar

**gallery** (ghæ-lä-ri) *n* galeria *f*

**gallop** (ghæ-läp) *n* galope *m*

**gallows** (ghæ-loᵘz) *pl* forca *f*

**gallstone** (ghóól-çtoᵘnn) *n* cálculo biliar

**game** (gheimm) n jogo m; caça f; ~ **reserve** reserva natural

**gang** (ghænng) n quadrilha f; turno m

**gangway** (ghænng-ᵘei) n escada do portaló

**gaol** (djeil) n cadeia f

**gap** (ghæp) n brecha f

**garage** (ghæ-raaj) n garagem f; v *pôr na garagem

**garbage** (ghaa-bidj) n lixo m

**garden** (ghaa-dänn) n jardim m; **public** ~ jardim público; **zoological gardens** jardim zoológico

**gardener** (ghaa-dä-nä) n jardineiro m

**gargle** (ghaa-ghäl) v gargarejar

**garlic** (ghaa-lik) n alho m

**gas** (ghæc) n gás m; nAm gasolina f; ~ **cooker** fogão a gás; ~ **station** Am posto de gasolina; ~ **stove** fogão a gás

**gasoline** (ghæ-çä-liinn) nAm gasolina f

**gastric** (ghæ-çtrik) adj gástrico; ~ **ulcer** úlcera gástrica

**gasworks** (ghæc-ᵘääkç) n depósito de gás

**gate** (gheit) n porta f; portão m

**gather** (ghæ-ðä) v coleccionar; reunir; colher

**gauge** (gheidj) n medida f

**gauze** (ghóóz) n gaze f

**gave** (gheiv) v (p give)

**gay** (ghei) adj alegre; garrido

**gaze** (gheiz) v fitar

**gazetteer** (ghæ-zä-*ti*ᵃ) n dicionário geográfico

**gear** (ghi ᵃ) n velocidade f; equipamento m; **change** ~ mudar de velocidade; ~ **lever** alavanca das mudanças

**gear-box** (ghi ᵃ-bókç) n caixa de velocidades

**gem** (djémm) n jóia f, pedra preciosa

**gender** (djénn-dä) n género m

**general** (djé-nä-räl) adj geral; in general m; ~ **practitioner** médico de clínica geral; **in** ~ em geral

**generate** (djé-nä-reit) v *produzir

**generation** (djé-nä-*rei*-chänn) n geração f

**generator** (djé-nä-rei-tär) n gerador m

**generosity** (djé-nä-ró-çä-ti) n generosidade f

**generous** (djé-nä-räç) adj magnânimo, generoso

**genital** (djé-ni-täl) adj genital

**genius** (djii-ni-äç) n génio m

**gentle** (djénn-täl) adj suave; ligeiro, terno; delicado

**gentleman** (djénn-täl-männ) n (pl -men) cavalheiro m

**genuine** (djé-nᶦu-inn) adj genuíno

**geography** (dji-ó-ghrä-fi) n geografia f

**geology** (dji-ó-lä-dji) n geologia f

**geometry** (dji-ó-mä-tri) n geometria f

**germ** (djäämm) n micróbio m; germe m

**German** (djää-männ) adj alemão

**Germany** (djää-mä-ni) Alemanha f

**gesticulate** (dji-çti-kᶦu-leit) v gesticular

*****get** (ghét) v *obter; *ir buscar; *fazer-se, tornar-se; ~ **back** regressar; ~ **off** descer, *apear-se; ~ **on** *subir para; avançar, *progredir; ~ **up** levantar-se, erguer-se

**ghost** (ghoᵘçt) n fantasma m; espírito m

**giant** (djai-ännt) n gigante m

**giddiness** (ghi-di-näç) n tontura f

**giddy** (ghi-di) adj atordoado

**gift** (ghift) n oferta f, presente m; dom m

**gifted** (ghif-tid) adj dotado

**gigantic** (djai-*ghænn*-tik) adj gigantesco

**giggle** (ghi-ghäl) v *dar risadinhas

gill (ghil) *n* guelra *f*

gilt (ghilt) *adj* dourado

ginger (*djinn*-djä) *n* gengibre *m*

gipsy (*djip*-çi) *n* cigano *m*

girdle (*ghää*-däl) *n* cinta *f*

girl (ghääl) *n* rapariga *f*; ~ **guide** escuteira *f*

*give (ghiv) *v* *dar; entregar; ~ **away** revelar; ~ **in** ceder; ~ **up** desistir, renunciar

glacier (*ghlæ*-çi-ä) *n* glaciar *m*

glad (ghlæd) *adj* contente; **gladly** com muito gosto, de boa vontade

gladness (*ghlæd*-näç) *n* alegria *f*

glamorous (*ghlæ*-mä-räç) *adj* fascinante

glamour (*ghlæ*-mä) *n* encanto *m*

glance (ghlaannç) *n* relance *m*; *v* *relancear

gland (ghlænnd) *n* glândula *f*

glare (ghléª) *n* brilho *m*; esplendor *m*

glaring (ghléª-rinng) *adj* deslumbrante

glass (ghlaaç) *n* copo *m*; vidro *m*; de vidro; **glasses** óculos *mpl*; **magnifying** ~ lupa *f*

glaze (ghleiz) *v* vidrar

glen (ghlénn) *n* ravina *f*

glide (ghlaid) *v* planar; deslizar

glider (*ghlai*-dä) *n* planador *m*

glimpse (ghlimmpç) *n* vislumbre *m*; *v* vislumbrar

g!obal (*ghlo*ᵁ-bäl) *adj* mundial

globe (ghloᵁb) *n* globo *m*

gloom (ghluumm) *n* obscuridade *f*; melancolia *f*

gloomy (*ghluu*-mi) *adj* sombrio

glorious (*ghlóó*-ri-äç) *adj* esplêndido

glory (*ghlóó*-ri) *n* glória *f*; louvor *m*, honra *f*

gloss (ghlóç) *n* lustro *m*

glossy (*ghló*-çi) *adj* lustroso

glove (ghlav) *n* luva *f*

glow (ghloᵁ) *v* brilhar; *n* brilho *m*

glue (ghluu) *n* cola *f*

*go (ghoᵁ) *v* *ir; andar; *fazer-se; ~ **ahead** avançar; ~ **away** *ir-se embora; ~ **back** regressar; ~ **home** *ir para casa; ~ **in** entrar; ~ **on** continuar, avançar; ~ **out** *sair; ~ **through** atravessar, passar por

goal (ghoᵁl) *n* objectivo *m*, baliza *f*; golo *m*

goalkeeper (*ghoᵁl*-kii-pä) *n* guarda-redes *m*; goleiro *mBr*

goat (ghoᵁt) *n* bode *m*, cabra *f*

god (ghód) *n* deus *m*

goddess (*ghó*-diç) *n* deusa *f*

godfather (*ghód*-faa-ðä) *n* padrinho *m*

goggles (*ghó*-ghälz) *pl* óculos de protecção

gold (ghoᵁld) *n* ouro *m*; ~ **leaf** folha de ouro

golden (*ghoᵁl*-dänn) *adj* de ouro

goldmine (*ghoᵁld*-mainn) *n* mina de ouro

goldsmith (*ghoᵁld*-çmiθ) *n* ourives *m*

golf (ghólf) *n* golfe *m*

golf-club (*ghólf*-klab) *n* clube de golfe

golf-course (*ghólf*-kóóç) *n* campo de golfe

golf-links (*ghólf*-linngkç) *n* campo de golfe

gondola (*ghónn*-dä-lä) *n* gôndola *f*

good (ghud) *adj* bom

good-bye! (ghud-*bai*) adeus!

good-humoured (ghud-*h'uu*-mäd) *adj* bem humorado

good-looking (ghud-*lu*-kinng) *adj* bonito

good-natured (ghud-*nei*-tchäd) *adj* bondoso

goods (ghudz) *pl* mercadorias *fpl*, bens *mpl*; ~ **train** comboio de mercadorias

good-tempered (ghud-*témm*-päd) *adj* bem disposto

goodwill (ghud-ᵁil) *n* boa vontade

**goose** (ghuuç) *n* (pl geese) ganso *m*

**gooseberry** (ghuz-bă-ri) *n* groselha verde

**goose-flesh** (ghuuç-fléch) *n* pele de galinha

**gorge** (ghóódj) *n* garganta *f*

**gorgeous** (ghóó-djăç) *adj* magnífico

**gospel** (ghó-çpăl) *n* evangelho *m*

**gossip** (ghó-çip) *n* mexerico *m; v* mexericar

**got** (ghót) *v* (p, pp get)

**gourmet** (ghuᵃ-mei) *n* gastrónomo *m*

**gout** (ghaut) *n* gota *f*

**govern** (gha-vănn) *v* governar

**governess** (gha-vă-niç) *n* governanta *f*

**government** (gha-vănn-mănnt) *n* regime *m*, governo *m*

**governor** (gha-vă-nă) *n* governador *m*

**gown** (ghaunn) *n* vestido *m*

**grace** (ghreiç) *n* graça *f*; perdão *m*

**graceful** (ghreiç-făl) *adj* gracioso

**grab** (ghræb) *v* agarrar, arrebatar; prender

**grade** (ghreid) *n* grau *m; v* classificar

**gradient** (ghrei-di-ănnt) *n* inclinação *f*

**gradual** (ghræ-dju-ăl) *adj* gradual

**graduate** (ghræ-dju-eit) *v* diplomar-se

**grain** (ghreinn) *n* cereal *m*, grão *m*

**gram** (ghræmm) *n* grama *m*

**grammar** (ghræ-mă) *n* gramática *f*

**grammatical** (ghră-mæ-ti-kăl) *adj* gramatical

**grand** (ghrænnd) *adj* grandioso

**granddad** (ghrænn-dæd) *n* avô *m*

**granddaughter** (ghrænn-dóó-tă) *n* neta *f*

**grandfather** (ghrænn-faa-ðă) *n* avô *m*, avozinho

**grandmother** (ghrænn-ma-ðă) *n* avó *f*, avozinha

**grandparents** (ghrænn-péᵃ-rănntç) *pl* avós *mpl*

**grandson** (ghrænn-çann) *n* neto *m*

**granite** (ghræ-nit) *n* granito *m*

**grant** (ghraannt) *v* conceder, aceder; *n* subsídio *m*, subvenção *f*

**grapefruit** (ghreip-fruut) *n* toranja *f*

**grapes** (ghreipç) *pl* uvas *fpl*

**graph** (ghræf) *n* gráfico *m*

**graphic** (ghræ-fik) *adj* gráfico

**grasp** (ghraaçp) *v* agarrar, segurar; *n* aperto *m*

**grass** (ghraaç) *n* erva *f*

**grasshopper** (ghraaç-hó-pă) *n* gafanhoto *m*

**grate** (ghreit) *n* grelha *f; v* raspar

**grateful** (ghreit-făl) *adj* grato, reconhecido

**grater** (ghrei-tă) *n* ralador *m*

**gratis** (ghræ-tiç) *adj* gratuito

**gratitude** (ghræ-ti-tⁱuud) *n* gratidão *f*

**gratuity** (ghră-tⁱuu-ă-ti) *n* gorjeta *f*

**grave** (ghreiv) *n* sepultura *f; adj* grave

**gravel** (ghræ-văl) *n* cascalho *m*

**gravestone** (ghreiv-çtoᵘnn) *n* lápide *f*

**graveyard** (ghreiv-ⁱaad) *n* cemitério *m*

**gravity** (ghræ-vă-ti) *n* gravidade *f*; seriedade *f*

**gravy** (ghrei-vi) *n* molho de carne

**graze** (ghreiz) *v* pastar; *n* arranhão *m*

**grease** (ghriiç) *n* gordura *f; v* lubrificar

**greasy** (ghrii-çi) *adj* gordurento, oleoso

**great** (ghreit) *adj* grande; **Great Britain** Grã-Bretanha *f*

**Greece** (ghriiç) Grécia *f*

**greed** (ghriid) *n* cupidez *f*

**greedy** (ghrii-di) *adj* ganancioso; guloso

**Greek** (ghriik) *adj* grego

**green** (ghriinn) *adj* verde; ~ **card** carta verde

**greengrocer** (ghriinn-ghroᵘ-çă) *n* vendedor de hortaliça

**greenhouse** (ghriinn-hauç) *n* estufa *f*

**greens** (ghriinnz) *pl* hortaliça *f*
**greet** (ghriit) *v* cumprimentar
**greeting** (*ghrii*-tinng) *n* saudação *f*
**grey** (ghrei) *adj* cinzento
**greyhound** (*ghrei*-haunnd) *n* galgo *m*
**grief** (ghriif) *n* desgosto *m*; aflição *f*, dor *f*
**grieve** (ghriiv) *v* *ter desgosto; afligir
**grill** (ghril) *n* grelhador *m*; *v* grelhar
**grill-room** (*ghril*-ruumm) *n* churrasqueira *f*
**grin** (ghrinn) *v* *sorrir-se; *n* careta *f*
**\*grind** (ghrainnd) *v* *moer; triturar
**grip** (ghrip) *v* agarrar; *n* abraço *m*, acção de agarrar; *nAm* saco de mão
**grit** (ghrt) *n* saibro *m*
**groan** (ghro**u**nn) *v* gemer
**grocer** (*ghro**u***-çà) *n* merceeiro *m*; **grocer's** mercearia *f*
**groceries** (*ghro**u***-çà-riz) *pl* artigos de mercearia
**groin** (ghroinn) *n* virilha *f*
**groove** (ghruuv) *n* sulco *m*
**gross**[1] (ghro**u**ç) *n* (pl ~) grosa *f*
**gross**[2] (ghro**u**ç) *adj* grosseiro; bruto
**grotto** (*ghró*-to**u**) *n* (pl ~es, ~s) gruta *f*
**ground**[1] (ghraunnd) *n* solo *m*, fundo *m*; ~ **floor** rés-do-chão *m*; andar térreo *Br*; **grounds** terreno *m*
**ground**[2] (ghraunnd) *v* (p, pp grind)
**group** (ghruup) *n* grupo *m*
**grove** (ghro**u**v) *n* mata *f*
**\*grow** (ghro**u**) *v* crescer; cultivar; *fazer-se
**growl** (ghraul) *v* rosnar
**grown-up** (*ghro**u**nn*-ap) *adj* adulto; *n* adulto *m*
**growth** (ghro**u**þ) *n* crescimento *m*; tumor *m*
**grudge** (ghradj) *v* invejar
**grumble** (*ghramm*-bàl) *v* resmungar
**guarantee** (ghæ-rànn-*tii*) *n* garantia *f*; caução *f*; *v* garantir
**guarantor** (ghæ-rànn-*tóó*) *n* fiador *m*
**guard** (ghaad) *n* guarda *m*; *v* guardar
**guardian** (*ghaa*-di- änn) *n* tutor *m*
**guess** (ghéç) *v* adivinhar; pensar, *supor; *n* conjectura *f*
**guest** (ghéçt) *n* hóspede *m*, convidado *m*
**guest-house** (*ghéçt*-hauç) *n* pensão *f*
**guest-room** (*ghéçt*-ruumm) *n* quarto de hóspedes
**guide** (ghaid) *n* guia *m*; *v* guiar
**guidebook** (*ghaid*-buk) *n* guia *m*
**guide-dog** (*ghaid*-dógh) *n* cão de cego
**guilt** (ghilt) *n* culpa *f*
**guilty** (*ghil*-ti) *adj* culpado
**guinea-pig** (*ghi*-ni-pigh) *n* porquinho-da-índia *m*
**guitar** (ghi-*taa*) *n* viola *f*
**gulf** (ghalf) *n* golfo *m*
**gull** (ghal) *n* gaivota *f*
**gum** (ghamm) *n* gengiva *f*; goma *f*; cola *f*
**gun** (ghann) *n* revólver *m*, espingarda *f*; canhão *m*
**gunpowder** (*ghann*-pau-dà) *n* pólvora *f*
**gust** (ghaçt) *n* rajada *f*
**gusty** (*gha*-çti) *adj* ventoso
**gut** (ghat) *n* intestino *m*; **guts** coragem *f*
**gutter** (*gha*-tà) *n* valeta *f*
**guy** (ghai) *n* tipo *m*
**gymnasium** (djimm-*nei*-zi-ämm) *n* (pl ~s, -sia) ginásio *m*
**gymnast** (*djimm*-næçt) *n* ginasta *m*
**gymnastics** (djimm-*næ*-çtikç) *pl* ginástica *f*
**gynaecologist** (ghai-nà-*kó*-là-djiçt) *n* ginecologista *m*

# H

**haberdashery** (hæ-bă-dæ-chă-ri) *n* capelista *m*; armarinho *mBr*

**habit** (hæ-bit) *n* hábito *m*

**habitable** (hæ-bi-tă-băl) *adj* habitável

**habitual** (hă-*bi*-tchu-ăl) *adj* habitual

**had** (hæd) *v* (p, pp have)

**haddock** (hæ-dăk) *n* (pl ~) arinca *f*

**haemorrhage** (hé-mă-ridj) *n* hemorragia *f*

**haemorrhoids** (hé-mă-roidz) *pl* hemorróidas *fpl*

**hail** (heil) *n* granizo *m*

**hair** (hé<sup>ă</sup>) *n* cabelo *m*: ~ **cream** creme para o cabelo; ~ **gel** fixador de cabelos; ~ **piece** cabelo postiço; ~ **rollers** rolos de cabelo; ~ **tonic** tónico capilar

**hairbrush** (hé<sup>ă</sup>-brach) *n* escova de cabelo

**haircut** (hé<sup>ă</sup>-kat) *n* corte de cabelo

**hair-do** (hé<sup>ă</sup>-duu) *n* penteado *m*

**hairdresser** (hé<sup>ă</sup>-dré-çă) *n* cabeleireiro *m*

**hair-dryer** (hé<sup>ă</sup>-drai-ă) *n* secador de cabelo

**hair-grip** (hé<sup>ă</sup>-ghrip) *n* travessão *m*

**hair-net** (hé<sup>ă</sup>-nét) *n* rede para o cabelo

**hairpin** (hé<sup>ă</sup>-pinn) *n* gancho de cabelo

**hair-spray** (hé<sup>ă</sup>-çprei) *n* laca para o cabelo

**hairy** (hé<sup>ă</sup>-ri) *adj* cabeludo

**half[1]** (haaf) *adj* meio; *adv* meio

**half[2]** (haaf) *n* (pl halves) metade *f*

**half-time** (haaf-*taimm*) *n* intervalo *m*

**halfway** (haaf-*uei*) *adv* a meio caminho

**halibut** (hæ-li-băt) *n* (pl ~) alabote *m*

**hall** (hóól) *n* vestíbulo *m*; sala *f*

**halt** (hóólt) *v* parar

**halve** (haav) *v* dividir ao meio

**ham** (hæmm) *n* fiambre *m*, presunto *m*

**hamlet** (hæmm-lăt) *n* aldeola *f*

**hammer** (hæ-mă) *n* martelo *m*

**hammock** (hæ-măk) *n* rede *f*

**hamper** (hæmm-pă) *n* cesta *f*

**hand** (hænnd) *n* mão *f*; *v* entregar; ~ **cream** creme para as mãos

**handbag** (hænnd-bægh) *n* mala de mão

**handbook** (hænnd-buk) *n* manual *m*

**hand-brake** (hænnd-breik) *n* travão de mão

**handcuffs** (hænnd-kafç) *pl* algemas *fpl*

**handful** (hænnd-ful) *n* punhado *m*

**handicraft** (hænn-di-kraaft) *n* trabalho manual; artesanato *m*

**handkerchief** (hænng-kă-tchif) *n* lenço de assoar

**handle** (hænn-dăl) *n* cabo *m*, pega *f*; *v* manejar; tratar

**hand-made** (hænnd-*meid*) *adj* feito à mão

**handshake** (hænnd-cheik) *n* aperto de mão

**handsome** (hænn-çămm) *adj* belo

**handwork** (hænnd-<sup>u</sup>ăăk) *n* trabalho manual

**handwriting** (hænnd-rai-tinng) *n* escrita *f*

**handy** (hænn-di) *adj* jeitoso; à mão, conveniente

***hang** (hænng) *v* pendurar; pender

**hanger** (hænng-ă) *n* cabide *m*

**hangover** (hænng-o<sup>u</sup>-vă) *n* ressaca *mBr*

**happen** (hæ-pănn) *v* suceder, acontecer

**happening** (hæ-pă-ninng) *n* acontecimento *m*

**happiness** (hæ-pi-năç) *n* felicidade *f*

**happy** (hæ-pi) *adj* contente, feliz

**harbour** (haa-bă) *n* porto *m*

hard (haad) *adj* duro; difícil; **hardly** mal

hardware (haad-ᵘéᵃ) *n* ferragens *fpl*; ~ **store** loja de ferragens

hare (héᵃ) *n* lebre *f*

harm (haamm) *n* prejuízo *m;* mal *m*, dano *m; v* prejudicar, \*fazer mal a

harmful (haamm-fål) *adj* prejudicial, nocivo

harmless (haamm-låç) *adj* inofensivo

harmony (haa-må-ni) *n* harmonia *f*

harp (haap) *n* harpa *f*

harpsichord (haap-çi-kóód) *n* cravo *m*

harsh (haach) *adj* áspero; severo; cruel

harvest (haa-viçt) *n* colheita *f*

has (hæz) *v* (pr have)

haste (heiçt) *n* rapidez *f*, pressa *f*

hasten (hei-çånn) *v* apressar-se

hasty (hei-çti) *adj* apressado

hat (hæt) *n* chapéu *m;* ~ **rack** bengaleiro *m*

hatch (hætch) *n* alçapão *m*

hate (heit) *v* detestar; \*odiar; *n* ódio *m*

hatred (hei-trid) *n* ódio *m*

haughty (hóó-ti) *adj* altivo

haul (hóól) *v* arrastar

\*have (hæv) *v* \*ter; mandar; ~ **to** \*ter de

hawk (hóók) *n* gavião *m;* falcão *m*

hay (hei) *n* feno *m;* ~ **fever** febre dos fenos

hazard (hæ-zåd) *n* risco *m*

haze (heiz) *n* bruma *f;* névoa *f*

hazelnut (hei-zål-nat) *n* avelã *f*

hazy (hei-zi) *adj* fusco; enevoado

he (hii) *pron* ele

head (héd) *n* cabeça *f; v* dirigir; ~ **of state** chefe de estado; ~ **teacher** director de escola

headache (hé-deik) *n* dor de cabeça

heading (hé-dinng) *n* título *m*

headlamp (héd-læmmp) *n* farol *m*

headland (héd-lånnd) *n* promontório *m*

headlight (héd-lait) *n* farol *m*

headline (héd-lainn) *n* cabeçalho *m*

headmaster (héd-maa-çtå) *n* director de escola; reitor *m*

headquarters (héd-kᵘóó-tåz) *pl* quartel-general *m*

head-strong (héd-çtrónn) *adj* obstinado

head-waiter (héd-ᵘei-tå) *n* chefe de mesa

heal (hiil) *v* sarar, curar

health (hélθ) *n* saúde *f;* ~ **centre** centro de saúde; ~ **certificate** atestado de saúde

healthy (hél-θi) *adj* são

heap (hiip) *n* monte *m*, montão *m*

\*hear (hiᵃ) *v* \*ouvir

hearing (hiᵃ-rinng) *n* ouvido *m*

heart (haat) *n* coração *m;* âmago *m;* **by** ~ de cor; ~ **attack** ataque de coração

heartburn (haat-båånn) *n* azia *f*

hearth (haaθ) *n* lareira *f*

heartless (haat-låç) *adj* insensível

hearty (haa-ti) *adj* efusivo

heat (hiit) *n* calor *m; v* aquecer; **heating pad** almofada eléctrica

heater (hii-tå) *n* aquecedor *m;* **immersion** ~ aquecedor de imersão

heath (hiiθ) *n* charneca *f*

heathen (hii-ðånn) *n* pagão *m*

heather (hé-ðå) *n* urze *f*

heating (hii-tinng) *n* aquecimento *m*

heaven (hé-vånn) *n* céu *m*

heavy (hé-vi) *adj* pesado

Hebrew (hii-bruu) *n* hebreu *m*

hedge (hédj) *n* sebe *f*

hedgehog (hédj-hógh) *n* ouriço *m*

heel (hiil) *n* calcanhar *m;* salto *m*

height (hait) *n* altura *f;* topo *m*, apogeu *m*

hell (hél) *n* inferno *m*

hello! (hé-*lo*u) olá!; bom dia!

helm (hélm) n leme m

helmet (hél-mit) n capacete m

helmsman (hélmz-männ) n timoneiro m

help (hélp) v ajudar, socorrer; n socorro m

helper (hél-pä) n ajudante m

helpful (hélp-fäl) adj útil

helping (hél-pinng) n porção f

hem (hémm) n bainha f

hemp (hémmp) n cânhamo m

hen (hénn) n galinha f

henceforth (hénnç-*fóóθ*) adv de agora em diante

her (hää) pron lhe, a; adj seu

herb (hääb) n erva f

herd (hääd) n manada f

here (hi*a*) adv aqui; ~ you are aqui está

hereditary (hi-ré-di-tä-ri) adj hereditário

hernia (hää-ni-ä) n hérnia f

hero (hi*a*-rou) n (pl ~es) herói m

heron (hé-ränn) n garça f

herring (hé-rinng) n (pl ~, ~s) arenque m

herself (hää-çélf) pron se; ela mesma

hesitate (hé-zi-teit) v hesitar

heterosexual (hé-tä-rä-çék-chu-äl) adj heterossexual

hiccup (hi-kap) n soluço m

hide (haid) n pele f

*hide (haid) v esconder

hideous (hi-di-äç) adj horroroso

hierarchy (hai*a*-raa-ki) n hierarquia f

high (hai) adj alto

highway (hai-uei) n estrada principal; nAm auto-estrada f

hijack (hai-djæk) v *saltear

hijacker (hai-djæ-kä) n salteador m, raptor m

hike (haik) v viajar a pé

hill (hil) n colina f

hillside (hil-çaid) n encosta f

hilltop (hil-tóp) n cume do monte

hilly (hi-li) adj acidentado

him (himm) pron o, lhe

himself (himm-çélf) pron se; ele mesmo

hinder (hinn-dä) v estorvar

hinge (hinndj) n dobradiça f

hip (hip) n anca f

hire (hai*a*) v alugar; for ~ para alugar

hire-purchase (hai*a*-*pää*-tchäç) n compra a prestações

his (hiz) adj seu

historian (hi-çtóó-ri-änn) n historiador m

historic (hi-çtó-rik) adj histórico

historical (hi-çtó-ri-käl) adj histórico

history (hi-çtä-ri) n história f

hit (hit) n sucesso m

*hit (hit) v bater; acertar, atingir

hitchhike (hitch-haik) v *pedir boleia; *pedir carona Br

hitchhiker (hitch-hai-kä) n pessoa que pede boleia

hoarse (hóóç) adj rouco

hobby (hó-bi) n passatempo m

hobby-horse (hó-bi-hóóç) n cavalo-de-pau m

hockey (hó-ki) n hóquei m

hoist (hoiçt) v içar

hold (hould) n porão m

*hold (hould) v segurar; guardar; ~ on agarrar-se; ~ up *suster

hold-up (hou*l*-dap) n assalto à mão armada

hole (houl) n buraco m

holiday (hó-lä-di) n férias fpl; feriado m; ~ camp colónia de férias; ~ resort estância de férias; on ~ em férias

Holland (hó-lännd) Holanda f

hollow (hó-lou) adj oco

holy (hou-li) adj sagrado

**homage** (*hó*-midj) *n* homenagem *f*

**home** (ho*u*mm) *n* lar *m*; morada *f*; *adv* para casa; **at** ~ em casa

**home-made** (ho*u*mm-*meid*) *adj* caseiro

**homesickness** (ho*u*mm-çik-năç) *n* nostalgia *f*

**homosexual** (ho*u*-mă-*çék*-chu-ăl) *adj* homossexual

**honest** (*ó*-niçt) *adj* honesto; sincero

**honesty** (*ó*-ni-çti) *n* honestidade *f*

**honey** (*ha*-ni) *n* mel *m*

**honeymoon** (*ha*-ni-muunn) *n* lua-de-mel *f*

**honour** (*ó*-nă) *n* honra *f*; *v* prestar homenagem, honrar

**honourable** (*ó*-nă-ră-băl) *adj* honroso; honrado

**hood** (hud) *n* capuz *m*; *nAm* cobertura do motor

**hoof** (huuf) *n* casco *m*

**hook** (huk) *n* gancho *m*

**hoot** (huut) *v* buzinar

**hooter** (*huu*-tă) *n* buzina *f*

**hoover** (*huu*-vă) *v* aspirar

**hop**[1] (hóp) *v* saltitar; *n* pulo *m*

**hop**[2] (hóp) *n* lúpulo *m*

**hope** (ho*u*p) *n* esperança *f*; *v* esperar

**hopeful** (*ho*u*p*-fál) *adj* esperançado

**hopeless** (*ho*u*p*-lăç) *adj* desesperado

**horizon** (hă-*rai*-zănn) *n* horizonte *m*

**horizontal** (hó-ri-*zónn*-tăl) *adj* horizontal

**horn** (hóónn) *n* chifre *m*; trompa *f*; buzina *f*

**horrible** (*hó*-ri-băl) *adj* horrível; atroz, horripilante, horroroso

**horror** (*hó*-ră) *n* horror *m*, pavor *m*

**hors-d'œuvre** (óó-*dăă*vr) *n* acepipes *mpl*

**horse** (hóóç) *n* cavalo *m*

**horseman** (*hóóç*-mănn) *n* (pl -men) cavaleiro *m*

**horsepower** (*hóóç*-pau*ă*) *n* cavalo-va-

**horserace** (*hóóç*-reiç) *n* corrida de cavalos

**horseradish** (*hóóç*-ræ-dich) *n* rábano silvestre

**horseshoe** (*hóóç*-chuu) *n* ferradura *f*

**horticulture** (*hóó*-ti-kal-tchă) *n* horticultura *f*

**hosiery** (*ho*u*-jă-ri) *n* malhas

**hospitable** (*hó*-çpi-tă-băl) *adj* hospitaleiro

**hospital** (*hó*-çpi-tăl) *n* hospital *m*

**hospitality** (hó-çpi-*tæ*-lă-ti) *n* hospitalidade *f*

**host** (ho*u*çt) *n* hospedeiro *m*

**hostage** (*hó*-çtidj) *n* refém *m*

**hostel** (*hó*-çtăl) *n* albergue *m*

**hostess** (*ho*u*-çtiç) *n* hospedeira *f*

**hostile** (*hó*-çtail) *adj* hostil

**hot** (hót) *adj* quente

**hotel** (ho*u*-*tél*) *n* hotel *m*

**hot-tempered** (hót-*témm*-păd) *adj* irascível

**hour** (au*ă*) *n* hora *f*

**hourly** (au*ă*-li) *adj* hora a hora

**house** (hauç) *n* casa *f*; habitação *f*; prédio *m*; ~ **agent** agente imobiliário; ~ **block** *Am* bloco habitacional; **public** ~ bar *m*

**houseboat** (*hauç*-bo*u*t) *n* casa flutuante

**household** (*hauç*-ho*u*ld) *n* lar *m*; família *f*

**housekeeper** (*hauç*-kii-pă) *n* governanta *f*

**housekeeping** (*hauç*-kii-pinng) *n* governo de casa, lida da casa

**housemaid** (*hauç*-meid) *n* empregada doméstica

**housewife** (*hauç*-*u*aif) *n* dona de casa

**housework** (*hauç*-*u*ăăk) *n* lida da casa

**how** (hau) *adv* como; que; ~ **many** quantos; ~ **much** quanto

**however** (hau-*é*-vă) *conj* todavia, contudo

**hug** (hagh) *v* abraçar; *n* abraço *m*

**huge** (h*i*uudj) *adj* enorme, formidável

**hum** (hamm) *v* *trautear

**human** (*h*iuu-männ) *adj* humano; ~ **being** ser humano

**humanity** (h*i*u-*mæ*-nă-ti) *n* humanidade *f*

**humble** (hamm-băl) *adj* humilde

**humid** (*h*iuu-mid) *adj* húmido

**humidity** (h*i*u-*mi*-dă-ti) *n* humidade *f*

**humorous** (*h*iuu-mă-răç) *adj* espirituoso, engraçado

**humour** (*h*iuu-mă) *n* humor *m*

**hundred** (hann-drăd) *n* cem

**Hungarian** (hanng-*ghé*ă-ri-ănn) *adj* húngaro

**Hungary** (*hanng*-ghă-ri) Hungria *f*

**hunger** (*hanng*-ghă) *n* fome *f*

**hungry** (*hanng*-ghri) *adj* esfomeado

**hunt** (hannt) *v* caçar; *n* caça *f*; ~ **for** procurar

**hunter** (*hann*-tă) *n* caçador *m*

**hurricane** (*ha*-ri-kănn) *n* furacão *m*; ~ **lamp** lâmpada de tempestade

**hurry** (*ha*-ri) *v* apressar-se, despachar-se; *n* pressa *f*; **in a** ~ apressadamente

*****hurt** (hăăt) *v* magoar, *ferir; ofender

**hurtful** (*hăăt*-făl) *adj* prejudicial

**husband** (*haz*-bănnd) *n* marido *m*, esposo *m*

**hut** (hat) *n* cabana *f*

**hydrogen** (*hai*-dră-djänn) *n* hidrogénio *m*

**hygiene** (*hai*-djiinn) *n* higiene *f*

**hygienic** (hai-*djii*-nik) *adj* higiénico

**hymn** (himm) *n* hino *m*

**hyphen** (*hai*-fănn) *n* hífen *m*

**hypocrisy** (hi-*pó*-kră-çi) *n* hipocrisia *f*

**hypocrite** (*hi*-pă-krit) *n* hipócrita *m*

**hypocritical** (hi-pă-*kri*-ti-kăl) *adj* falso, hipócrita

**hysterical** (hi-çté-ri-kăl) *adj* histérico

# I

**I** (ai) *pron* eu

**ice** (aiç) *n* gelo *m*

**ice-bag** (*aiç*-bægh) *n* saco de gelo

**ice-cream** (*aiç*-kriimm) *n* gelado *m*; sorvete *mBr*

**Iceland** (*aiç*-lănnd) Islândia *f*

**Icelander** (*aiç*-lănn-dă) *n* islandês *m*

**Icelandic** (aiç-*lænn*-dik) *adj* islandês

**icon** (*ai*-kónn) *n* ícone *m*

**idea** (ai-*di*ă) *n* ideia *f*; pensamento *m*; noção *f*, conceito *m*

**ideal** (ai-*di*ăl) *adj* ideal; *n* ideal *m*

**identical** (ai-*dénn*-ti-kăl) *adj* idêntico

**identification** (ai-dénn-ti-fi-*kei*-chănn) *n* identificação *f*

**identify** (ai-*dénn*-ti-fai) *v* identificar

**identity** (ai-*dénn*-tă-ti) *n* identidade *f*; ~ **card** bilhete de identidade

**idiom** (*i*-di-ămm) *n* expressão idiomática

**idiomatic** (i-di-ă-*mæ*-tik) *adj* idiomático

**idiot** (*i*-di-ăt) *n* idiota *m*

**idiotic** (i-di-*ó*-tik) *adj* idiota

**idle** (*ai*-dăl) *adj* ocioso; fútil

**idol** (*ai*-dăl) *n* ídolo *m*

**if** (if) *conj* se

**ignition** (igh-*ni*-chănn) *n* ignição *f*; ~ **coil** bobina de ignição

**ignorant** (*igh*-nă-rănnt) *adj* ignorante

**ignore** (igh-*nóó*) *v* ignorar

**ill** (il) *adj* doente; mau; maligno

**illegal** (i-*lii*-ghăl) *adj* ilegal

**illegible** (i-*lé*-djă-băl) *adj* ilegível

**illiterate** (i-*li*-tă-răt) *n* analfabeto *m*

**illness** (*il*-năç) *n* doença *f*

**illuminate** (i-*luu*-mi-neit) *v* iluminar,

alumiar

**illumination** (i-luu-mi-*nei*-chänn) *n* iluminação *f*

**illusion** (i-*luu*-jänn) *n* ilusão *f*

**illustrate** (*i*-lä-çtreit) *v* ilustrar

**illustration** (i-lä-*çtrei*-chänn) *n* ilustração *f*

**image** (*i*-midj) *n* imagem *f*

**imaginary** (i-*mæ*-dji-nä-ri) *adj* imaginário

**imagination** (i-*mæ*-dji-*nei*-chänn) *n* imaginação *f*

**imagine** (i-*mæ*-djinn) *v* imaginar

**imitate** (*i*-mi-teit) *v* imitar

**imitation** (i-mi-*tei*-chänn) *n* imitação *f*

**immediate** (i-*mii*-d¹ät) *adj* imediato

**immediately** (i-*mii*-d¹ät-li) *adv* já, imediatamente

**immense** (i-*ménnç*) *adj* enorme, imenso

**immigrant** (*i*-mi-ghränt) *n* imigrante *m*

**immigrate** (*i*-mi-ghreit) *v* imigrar

**immigration** (i-mi-*ghrei*-chänn) *n* imigração *f*

**immodest** (i-*mó*-diçt) *adj* imodesto

**immunity** (i-*m¹uu*-nä-ti) *n* imunidade *f*

**immunize** (*i*-m¹u-naiz) *v* imunizar

**impartial** (imm-*paa*-chäl) *adj* imparcial

**impassable** (imm-*paa*-çä-bäl) *adj* impraticável

**impatient** (imm-*pei*-chännt) *adj* impaciente

**impede** (imm-*piid*) *v* entravar, *impedir

**impediment** (imm-*pé*-di-männt) *n* impedimento *m*

**imperfect** (imm-*pää*-fikt) *adj* imperfeito

**imperial** (imm-*pi*ª-ri-äl) *adj* imperial

**impersonal** (imm-*pää*-çä-näl) *adj* impessoal

**impertinence** (imm-*pää*-ti-nännç) *n*

impertinência *f*

**impertinent** (imm-*pää*-ti-nännt) *adj* impertinente, insolente, malcriado

**implement¹** (*imm*-pli-männt) *n* ferramenta *f*

**implement²** (*imm*-pli-ménnt) *v* realizar

**imply** (imm-*plai*) *v* implicar

**impolite** (imm-pä-*lait*) *adj* grosseiro

**import¹** (imm-*póót*) *v* importar

**import²** (*imm*-póót) *n* importações *fpl*, importação *f*; ~ **duty** direitos de importação

**importance** (imm-*póó*-tännç) *n* importância *f*, relevo *m*

**important** (imm-*póó*-tännt) *adj* importante, relevante

**importer** (imm-*póó*-tä) *n* importador *m*

**imposing** (imm-*po*ᵘ-zinng) *adj* imponente

**impossible** (imm-*pó*-çä-bäl) *adj* impossível

**impotence** (*imm*-pä-tännç) *n* impotência *f*

**impotent** (*imm*-pä-tännt) *adj* impotente

**impound** (imm-*paunnd*) *v* apreender

**impress** (imm-*préç*) *v* impressionar

**impression** (imm-*pré*-chänn) *n* impressão *f*

**impressive** (imm-*pré*-çiv) *adj* impressionante

**imprison** (imm-*pri*-zänn) *v* prender

**imprisonment** (imm-*pri*-zänn-männt) *n* encarceramento *m*

**improbable** (imm-*pró*-bä-bäl) *adj* improvável

**improper** (imm-*pró*-pä) *adj* impróprio

**improve** (imm-*pruuv*) *v* melhorar

**improvement** (imm-*pruuv*-männt) *n* melhoramento *m*

**improvise** (*imm*-prä-vaiz) *v* improvisar

**impudent** (*imm*-p¹u-dännt) *adj* desavergonhado

**impulse** (*imm*-palç) *n* impulso *m*; estímulo *m*

**impulsive** (imm-*pal*-çiv) *adj* impulsivo

**in** (inn) *prep* em; dentro de; *adv* dentro

**inaccessible** (i-næk-*cé*-çă-băl) *adj* inacessível

**inaccurate** (i-*næ*-kⁱu-răt) *adj* incorrecto

**inadequate** (i-*næ*-di-kᵘăt) *adj* inadequado

**incapable** (inng-*kei*-pă-băl) *adj* incapaz

**incense** (*inn*-çénnç) *n* incenso *m*

**incident** (*inn*-çi-dănnt) *n* incidente *m*

**incidental** (inn-çi-*dénn*-tăl) *adj* incidental

**incite** (inn-*çait*) *v* incitar

**inclination** (inng-kli-*nei*-chănn) *n* inclinação *f*

**incline** (inng-*klainn*) *n* declive *m*

**inclined** (inng-*klainnd*) *adj* propenso, disposto; \*be ~ to tender

**include** (inng-*kluud*) *v* incluir

**inclusive** (inng-*kluu*-çiv) *adj* inclusivo

**income** (*inng*-kămm) *n* rendimento *m*

**income-tax** (*inng*-kămm-tækç) *n* imposto sobre os rendimentos

**incompetent** (inng-*kómm*-pă-tănnt) *adj* incompetente

**incomplete** (inn-kămm-*pliit*) *adj* incompleto

**inconceivable** (inng-kănn-*çii*-vă-băl) *adj* inconcebível

**inconspicuous** (inng-kănn-*çpi*-kⁱu-ăç) *adj* discreto

**inconvenience** (inng-kănn-*vii*-nⁱănnç) *n* inconveniência *f*, incómodo *m*

**inconvenient** (inng-kănn-*vii*-nⁱănnt) *adj* inconveniente; maçador

**incorrect** (inng-kă-*rékt*) *adj* inexacto, incorrecto

**increase¹** (inng-*kriiç*) *v* aumentar, crescer

**increase²** (*inng*-kriiç) *n* aumento *m*

**incredible** (inng-*kré*-dă-băl) *adj* incrível

**incurable** (inng-kⁱuᵃ-ră-băl) *adj* incurável

**indecent** (inn-*dii*-çănnt) *adj* indecente

**indeed** (inn-*diid*) *adv* efectivamente

**indefinite** (inn-*dé*-fi-nit) *adj* indefinido

**indemnity** (inn-*démm*-nă-ti) *n* indemnização *f*, compensação *f*

**independence** (inn-di-*pénn*-dănnç) *n* independência *f*

**independent** (inn-di-*pénn*-dănnt) *adj* independente; autónomo

**index** (*inn*-dékç) *n* índice *m*; ~ **finger** indicador *m*

**India** (*inn*-di-ă) Índia *f*

**Indian** (*inn*-di-ănn) *adj* indiano; índio; *n* indiano *m*; índio *m*

**indicate** (*inn*-di-keit) *v* indicar, assinalar

**indication** (inn-di-*kei*-chănn) *n* indicação *f*, sinal *m*

**indicator** (*inn*-di-kei-tă) *n* pisca-pisca *m*

**indifferent** (inn-*di*-fă-rănnt) *adj* indiferente

**indigestion** (inn-di-*djéc*-tchănn) *n* indigestão *f*

**indignation** (inn-digh-*nei*-chănn) *n* indignação *f*

**indirect** (inn-di-*rékt*) *adj* indirecto

**individual** (inn-di-*vi*-dju-ăl) *adj* particular, individual; *n* indivíduo *m*

**Indonesia** (inn-dă-*nii*-zi-ă) Indonésia *f*

**Indonesian** (inn-dă-*nii*-zi-ănn) *adj* indonésio

**indoor** (*inn*-dóó) *adj* interno

**indoors** (inn-*dóóz*) *adv* dentro de casa

**indulge** (inn-*daldj*) *v* ceder

**industrial** (inn-*da*-çtri-ăl) *adj* industrial; ~ **area** zona industrial

**industrious** (inn-*da*-çtri-ăç) *adj* traba-

lhador
**industry** (*inn*-dă-çtri) *n* indústria *f*
**inedible** (i-*né*-di-băl) *adj* incomestível
**inefficient** (i-ni-*fi*-chănnt) *adj* ineficiente
**inevitable** (i-*né*-vi-tă-băl) *adj* inevitável
**inexpensive** (i-nik-*çpénn*-çiv) *adj* barato
**inexperienced** (i-nik-*çpiª*-ri-ănnçt) *adj* inexperiente
**infant** (*inn*-fănnt) *n* criança de peito
**infantry** (*inn*-fănn-tri) *n* infantaria *f*
**infect** (inn-*fékt*) *v* infectar
**infection** (inn-*fék* chănn) *n* infecção *f*
**infectious** (inn-*fék*-chăç) *adj* infeccioso
**infer** (inn-*făă*) *v* *deduzir
**inferior** (inn-*fiª*-ri-ă) *adj* inferior, menor
**infinite** (*inn*-fi-năt) *adj* infinito
**infinitive** (inn-*fi*-ni-tiv) *n* infinitivo *m*
**infirmary** (inn-*făă*-mă-ri) *n* enfermaria *f*
**inflammable** (inn-*flæ*-mă-băl) *adj* inflamável
**inflammation** (inn-flă-*mei*-chănn) *n* inflamação *f*
**inflatable** (inn-*flei*-tă-băl) *adj* pneumático
**inflate** (inn-*fleit*) *v* inchar, encher de ar
**inflation** (inn-*flei*-chănn) *n* inflação *f*
**influence** (*inn*-flu-ănnç) *n* influência *f*; *v* influenciar
**influential** (inn-flu-*énn*-chăl) *adj* influente
**influenza** (inn-flu-*énn*-ză) *n* gripe *f*
**inform** (inn-*fóómm*) *v* informar; comunicar, *pôr ao corrente
**informal** (inn-*fóó*-măl) *adj* sem cerimónia
**information** (inn-fă-*mei*-chănn) *n* informação *f*, comunicação *f*; ~

**bureau** agência de informações
**infra-red** (inn-fră-*réd*) *adj* infra-vermelho
**infrequent** (inn-*frii*-kᵘănnt) *adj* raro
**ingredient** (inng-*ghrii*-di-ănnt) *n* ingrediente *m*
**inhabit** (inn-*hæ*-bit) *v* habitar
**inhabitable** (inn-*hæ*-bi-tă-băl) *adj* habitável
**inhabitant** (inn-*hæ*-bi-tănnt) *n* habitante *m*
**inhale** (inn-*heil*) *v* inalar
**inherit** (inn *hé*-rlt) *v* herdar
**inheritance** (inn-*hé*-ri-tănnç) *n* herança *f*
**initial** (i-*ni*-chăl) *adj* inicial; *n* inicial *f*; *v* rubricar
**initiative** (i-*ni*-chă-tiv) *n* iniciativa *f*
**inject** (inn-*djékt*) *v* injectar
**injection** (inn-*djék*-chănn) *n* injecção *f*
**injure** (*inn*-djă) *v* *ferir; ofender
**injury** (*inn*-djă-ri) *n* ferida *f*, lesão *f*
**injustice** (inn-*dja*-çtiç) *n* injustiça *f*
**ink** (inngk) *n* tinta *f*
**inlet** (*inn*-lét) *n* enseada *f*; entrada *f*, passagem *f*
**inn** (inn) *n* pousada *f*
**inner** (*i*-nă) *adj* interior; ~ **tube** câmara-de-ar *f*
**inn-keeper** (*inn*-kii-pă) *n* estalajadeiro *m*
**innocence** (*i*-nă-çănnç) *n* inocência *f*
**innocent** (*i*-nă-çănnt) *adj* inocente
**inoculate** (i-*nó*-kⁱu-leit) *v* inocular
**inoculation** (i-nó-kⁱu-*lei*-chănn) *n* inoculação *f*
**inquire** (inng-kᵘ*aiª*) *v* informar-se, indagar, inquirir
**inquiry** (inng-kᵘ*aiª*-ri) *n* pergunta *f*, inquérito *m*; ~ **office** agência de informações
**inquisitive** (inng-kᵘ*i*-ză-tiv) *adj* curioso
**insane** (inn-*çeinn*) *adj* louco
**inscription** (inn-*çkrip*-chănn) *n* inscri-

ção *f*
**insect** (*inn*-çékt) *n* insecto *m*
**insecticide** (inn-çék-ti-çaid) *n* insecticida *m*
**insensitive** (inn-çénn-çă-tiv) *adj* insensível
**insert** (inn-çăăt) *v* *inserir
**inside** (inn-çaid) *n* interior *m; adj* interior; *adv* dentro; por dentro; *prep* em, dentro de; ~ **out** do avesso; **insides** entranhas *fpl*
**insight** (*inn*-çait) *n* compreensão *f*
**insignificant** (inn-çigh-*ni*-fi-kánnt) *adj* insignificante; irrelevante; fútil
**insist** (inn-çiçt) *v* insistir; persistir
**insolence** (inn-çă-lănnç) *n* insolência *f*
**insolent** (*inn*-çă-lănnt) *adj* insolente
**insomnia** (inn-çómm-ni-ă) *n* insónia *f*
**inspect** (inn-çpékt) *v* inspeccionar
**inspection** (inn-çpék-chănn) *n* inspecção *f*
**inspector** (inn-çpék-tă) *n* inspector *m*
**inspire** (inn-çpaiᵃ) *v* inspirar
**install** (inn-çtóól) *v* instalar
**installation** (inn-çtă-*lei*-chănn) *n* instalação *f*
**instalment** (inn-çtóól-mănnt) *n* prestação *f*
**instance** (*inn*-çtănnç) *n* exemplo *m; caso m; for* ~ por exemplo
**instant** (*inn*-çtănnt) *n* instante *m*
**instantly** (*inn*-çtănnt-li) *adv* instantaneamente, imediatamente
**instead of** (inn-*çtéd* óv) em vez de
**instinct** (*inn*-çtingngkt) *n* instinto *m*
**institute** (*inn*-çti-t*i*uut) *n* instituto *m;* instituição *f; v* *instituir
**institution** (inn-çti-t*i*uu-chănn) *n* instituição *f*
**instruct** (inn-çtrakt) *v* *instruir
**instruction** (inn-çtrak-chănn) *n* instrução *f*
**instructive** (inn-çtrak-tiv) *adj* instrutivo

**instructor** (inn-çtrak-tă) *n* instrutor *m*
**instrument** (*inn*-çtru-mănnt) *n* instrumento *m;* **musical** ~ instrumento musical
**insufficient** (inn-çă-*fi*-chănnt) *adj* insuficiente
**insulate** (*inn*-ç*i*u-leit) *v* isolar
**insulation** (inn-ç*i*u-*lei*-chănn) *n* isolamento *m*
**insulator** (*inn*-ç*i*u-lei-tă) *n* isolador *m*
**insult**¹ (inn-çalt) *v* insultar
**insult**² (*inn*-çalt) *n* insulto *m*
**insurance** (inn-chu*ᵃ*-rănnç) *n* seguro *m;* ~ **policy** apólice de seguro
**insure** (inn-chu*ᵃ*) *v* segurar; garantir
**intact** (inn-tækt) *adj* intacto
**intellect** (*inn*-tă-lékt) *n* intelecto *m*
**intellectual** (inn-tă-*lék*-tchu-ăl) *adj* intelectual
**intelligence** (inn-*té*-li-djănnç) *n* inteligência *f*
**intelligent** (inn-*té*-li-djănnt) *adj* inteligente
**intend** (inn-ténnd) *v* tencionar
**intense** (inn-ténnç) *adj* intenso
**intention** (inn-*ténn*-chănn) *n* intenção *f*
**intentional** (inn-*ténn*-chă-năl) *adj* intencional
**intercourse** (*inn*-tă-kóóç) *n* relações *fpl*
**interest** (*inn*-trăçt) *n* interesse *m;* juro *m; v* interessar
**interesting** (*inn*-tră-çtinng) *adj* interessante
**interfere** (inn-tă-fi*ᵃ*) *v* *interferir; ~ **with** intrometer-se em
**interference** (inn-tă-fi*ᵃ*-rănnç) *n* interferência *f*
**interim** (*inn*-tă-rimm) *n* interim *m*
**interior** (inn-ti*ᵃ*-ri-ă) *n* interior *m*
**interlude** (*inn*-tă-luud) *n* interlúdio *m*
**intermediary** (inn-tă-*mii*-d*i*ă-ri) *n* in-

termediário m

**intermission** (inn-tă-*mi*-chănn) n intervalo m

**internal** (inn-*tăă*-năl) adj interno

**international** (inn-tă-*næ*-chă-năl) adj internacional

**interpret** (inn-*tăă*-prit) v interpretar, *traduzir

**interpreter** (inn-*tăă*-pri-tă) n intérprete m

**interrogate** (inn-*té*-ră-gheit) v interrogar

**interrogation** (inn-té-ră-*ghei*-chănn) n interrogatório m

**interrogative** (inn-tă-*ró*-ghă-tiv) adj interrogativo

**interrupt** (inn-tă-*rapt*) v interromper

**interruption** (inn-tă-*rap*-chănn) n interrupção f

**intersection** (inn-tă-*cék*-chănn) n intersecção f

**interval** (*inn*-tă-văl) n intervalo m

**intervene** (inn-tă-*viinn*) v *intervir

**interview** (*inn*-tă-v¹uu) n entrevista f

**intestine** (inn-*té*-çtinn) n intestino m

**intimate** (*inn*-ti-măt) adj íntimo

**into** (*inn*-tu) prep dentro de; para dentro

**intolerable** (inn-*tó*-lă-ră-băl) adj intolerável

**intoxicated** (inn-*tók*-çi-kei-tid) adj embriagado

**intrigue** (inn-*triigh*) n intriga f

**introduce** (inn-tră-*d*¹uuç) v apresentar; *introduzir

**introduction** (inn-tră-*dak*-chănn) n apresentação f; introdução f

**invade** (inn-*veid*) v invadir

**invalid¹** (*inn*-vă-liid) n inválido m; adj inválido

**invalid²** (inn-*vă*-lid) adj sem validade

**invasion** (inn-*vei*-jănn) n invasão f

**invent** (inn-*vénnt*) v inventar

**invention** (inn-*vénn*-chănn) n invenção

f

**inventive** (inn-*vénn*-tiv) adj inventivo

**inventor** (inn-*vénn*-tă) n inventor m

**inventory** (*inn*-vănn-tri) n inventário m

**invert** (inn-*văăt*) v inverter

**invest** (inn-*véçt*) v *investir

**investigate** (inn-vé-çti-gheit) v investigar

**investigation** (inn-vé-çti-*ghei*-chănn) n investigação f

**investment** (inn-*véçt*-mănnt) n investimento m

**investor** (inn-*vé*-çtă) n aquele que faz investimento

**invisible** (inn-*vi*-ză-băl) adj invisível

**invitation** (inn-vi-*tei*-chănn) n convite m

**invite** (inn-*vait*) v convidar

**invoice** (*inn*-voiç) n factura f

**involve** (inn-*vólv*) v implicar

**inwards** (*inn*-ᵘădz) adv para dentro

**iodine** (*ai*-ă-diinn) n iodo m

**Iran** (i-*raann*) Irão m

**Iranian** (i-*rei*-ni-ănn) adj iraniano

**Iraq** (i-*raak*) Iraque m

**Iraqi** (i-*raa*-ki) adj iraquiano

**irascible** (i-*ræ*-çi-băl) adj irascível

**Ireland** (*aiᵃ*-lănnd) Irlanda f

**Irish** (*aiᵃ*-rich) adj irlandês

**Irishman** (*aiᵃ*-rich-mănn) n (pl -men) irlandês m

**iron** (*ai*-ănn) n ferro m; ferro de engomar; de ferro; v passar a ferro

**ironical** (ai-*ró*-ni-kăl) adj irónico

**ironworks** (*ai*-ănn-ᵘăăkç) n fundição f

**irony** (*aiᵃ*-ră-ni) n ironia f

**irregular** (i-*ré*-ghᶦu-lă) adj irregular

**irreparable** (i-*ré*-pă-ră-băl) adj irreparável

**irrevocable** (i-*ré*-vă-kă-băl) adj irrevogável

**irritable** (*i*-ri-tă-băl) adj irritável

**irritate** (*i*-ri-teit) v irritar

**is** (iz) v (pr be)
**island** (ai-lănnd) n ilha f
**isolate** (ai-çă-leit) v isolar
**isolation** (ai-çă-lei-chănn) n isolamento m
**Israel** (iz-reil) Israel m
**Israeli** (iz-rei-li) adj israeliano
**issue** (i-chuu) v *distribuir; n edição f, emissão f, tiragem f; questão f, ponto m; consequência f, resultado m, fim m, conclusão f; saída f
**isthmus** (iç-măç) n istmo m
**Italian** (i-tæl-iănn) adj italiano
**italics** (i-tæ-likç) pl itálico m
**Italy** (i-tă-li) Itália f
**itch** (itch) n comichão f; prurido m; v *ter comichão
**item** (ai-tămm) n artigo m; ponto m
**itinerant** (ai-ti-nă-rănnt) adj itinerante
**itinerary** (ai-ti-nă-ră-ri) n itinerário m
**ivory** (ai-vă-ri) n marfim m
**ivy** (ai-vi) n hera f

# J

**jack** (djæk) n macaco m
**jacket** (djæ-kit) n casaco m; paletó mBr; capa f
**jade** (djeid) n jade m
**jail** (djeil) n prisão f
**jailer** (djei-lă) n carcereiro m
**jam** (djæmm) n doce de fruta; geléia fBr; engarrafamento m
**janitor** (djæ-ni-tă) n porteiro m
**January** (djæ-niu-ă-ri) Janeiro
**Japan** (djă-pænn) Japão m
**Japanese** (djæ-pă-niiz) adj japonês
**jar** (djaa) n jarra f
**jaundice** (djóónn-diç) n icterícia f
**jaw** (djóó) n maxila f
**jealous** (djé-lăç) adj ciumento
**jealousy** (djé-lă-çi) n ciúme m

**jeans** (djiinnz) pl calças de ganga
**jelly** (djé-li) n geleia f
**jelly-fish** (djé-li-fich) n alforreca f; medusa fBr
**jeopardy** (djé-pă-di) n perigo m, risco m
**jersey** (djăă-zi) n jersey m; camisola de malha
**jet** (djét) n jacto m; avião a jacto
**jetty** (djé-ti) n molhe m
**Jew** (djuu) n judeu m
**jewel** (djuu-ăl) n jóia f
**jeweller** (djuu-ă-lă) n joalheiro m
**jewellery** (djuu-ăl-ri) n jóias fpl; joalharia f
**Jewish** (djuu-ich) adj judaico
**job** (djób) n trabalho m; emprego m
**jockey** (djó-ki) n jóquei m
**join** (djoinn) v unir, juntar; associar-se a, *aderir a; reunir
**joint** (djoinnt) n articulação f; soldadura f; adj unido, conjunto
**jointly** (djoinnt-li) adv conjuntamente
**joke** (djouk) n anedota f, graça f
**jolly** (djó-li) adj jovial
**Jordan** (djóó-dănn) Jordânia f
**Jordanian** (djóó-dei-ni-ănn) adj jordaniano
**journal** (djăă-năl) n jornal m
**journalism** (djăă-nă-li-zămm) n jornalismo m
**journalist** (djăă-nă-liçt) n jornalista m
**journey** (djăă-ni) n viagem f
**joy** (djoi) n prazer m, alegria f
**joyful** (djoi-făl) adj contente, alegre
**jubilee** (djuu-bi-lii) n jubileu m
**judge** (djadj) n juiz m; v julgar
**judgment** (djadj-mănnt) n juízo m; julgamento m
**jug** (djagh) n jarro m, cântaro m, moringa fBr
**juice** (djuuç) n sumo m
**juicy** (djuu-çi) adj sumarento
**July** (dju-lai) Julho

**jump** (djammp) *v* saltar; *n* salto *m*

**jumper** (*djamm*-pă) *n* camisola *f*

**junction** (*djanngk*-chänn) *n* cruzamento *m*; junção *f*

**June** (djuunn) Junho

**jungle** (*djanng*-ghăl) *n* selva *f*

**junior** (*djuu*-n[i]ă) *adj* júnior

**junk** (djanngk) *n* tralha *f*

**jury** (*dju*[u̯]-ri) *n* júri *m*

**just** (djaçt) *adj* justo; *adv* acabado de; justamente

**justice** (*dja*-çtiç) *n* direito *m*; justiça *f*

**juvenile** (*djuu*-vă-nail) *adj* juvenil

# K

**kangaroo** (kænng-ghă-*ruu*) *n* canguru *m*

**keel** (kiil) *n* quilha *f*

**keen** (kiinn) *adj* entusiasta; perspicaz

***keep** (kiip) *v* *manter; guardar; não cessar de; ~ **away from** *manter-se à distância; ~ **off** não tocar; ~ **on** continuar a, continuar; ~ **quiet** calar-se; ~ **up** perseverar; ~ **up with** não lhe ficar atrás

**keg** (kégh) *n* barrica *f*

**kennel** (*ké*-năl) *n* casota do cão; canil *m*

**Kenya** (*ké*-n[i]ă) Quénia *m*

**kerosene** (*ké*-ră-çiinn) *n* querosene *m*

**kettle** (*ké*-tăl) *n* chaleira *f*

**key** (kii) *n* chave *f*

**keyhole** (*kii*-ho[u]l) *n* buraco da fechadura *f*

**khaki** (*kaa*-ki) *n* caqui *m*

**kick** (kik) *v* *dar um pontapé; *n* pontapé *m*

**kick-off** (ki-*kóf*) *n* pontapé de saída

**kid** (kid) *n* criança *f*, garoto *m*; pelica *f*; *v* gozar com

**kidney** (*kid*-ni) *n* rim *m*

**kill** (kil) *v* matar

**kilogram** (*ki*-lă-ghræmm) *n* quilograma *m*

**kilometre** (*ki*-lă-mii-tă) *n* quilómetro *m*

**kind** (kainnd) *adj* gentil, bondoso; bom; *n* género *m*

**kindergarten** (*kinn*-dă-ghaa-tänn) *n* jardim infantil

**king** (kinng) *n* rei *m*

**kingdom** (*kinng*-dămm) *n* reino *m*

**kiosk** (*kii*-óçk) *n* quiosque *m*

**kiss** (kiç) *n* beijo *m*; *v* beijar

**kit** (kit) *n* equipamento *m*

**kitchen** (*ki*-tchinn) *n* cozinha *f*; ~ **garden** horta *f*

**knapsack** (*næp*-çæk) *n* mochila *f*

**knave** (neiv) *n* valete *m*

**knee** (nii) *n* joelho *m*

**kneecap** (*nii*-kæp) *n* rótula *f*

***kneel** (niil) *v* ajoelhar

**knew** (n[i]uu) *v* (p know)

**knickers** (*ni*-kăz) *pl* calcinhas *fpl*

**knife** (naif) *n* (pl knives) faca *f*

**knight** (nait) *n* cavaleiro *m*

***knit** (nit) *v* tricotar

**knob** (nób) *n* maçaneta *f*

**knock** (nók) *v* bater; *n* pancada *f*; ~ **against** chocar com; ~ **down** derrubar

**knot** (nót) *n* nó *m*; *v* *fazer um nó

***know** (no[u]) *v* *saber, conhecer

**knowledge** (*nó*-lidj) *n* conhecimento *m*

**knuckle** (*na*-kăl) *n* nó dos dedos; jarrete *m*

# L

**label** (*lei*-băl) *n* etiqueta *f*; *v* etiquetar

**laboratory** (lă-*bó*-ră-tă-ri) *n* laboratório *m*

**labour** (*lei*-bă) *n* trabalho *m*; dores; *v* trabalhar arduamente, labutar; **labor permit** *Am* autorização de trabalho

**labourer** (*lei*-bă-ră) *n* operário *m*

**labour-saving** (*lei*-bă-çei-vinng) *adj* economisador de trabalho

**labyrinth** (*læ*-bă-rinnθ) *n* labirinto *m*

**lace** (leiç) *n* renda *f*; atacador *m*

**lack** (læk) *n* falta *f*, carência *f*; *v* carecer de

**lacquer** (*læ*-kă) *n* verniz *m*

**lad** (læd) *n* rapaz *m*

**ladder** (*læ*-dă) *n* escada *f*

**lagoon** (lă-*ghuunn*) *n* laguna *f*

**lake** (leik) *n* lago *m*

**lamb** (læmm) *n* cordeiro *m*; borrego *m*

**lame** (leimm) *adj* coxo, paralítico

**lamentable** (*læ*-mănn-tă-băl) *adj* lamentável

**lamp** (læmmp) *n* candeeiro *m*

**lamp-post** (*læmmp*-pouçt) *n* poste de iluminação

**lampshade** (*læmmp*-cheid) *n* abajur *m*

**land** (lænnd) *n* terra *f*, país *m*; *v* aterrar; desembarcar

**landlady** (*lænnd*-lei-di) *n* senhoria *f*

**landlord** (*lænnd*-lóód) *n* senhorio *m*, proprietário *m*

**landmark** (*lænnd*-maak) *n* ponto de referência; marco *m*

**landscape** (*lænnd*-çkeip) *n* paisagem *f*

**lane** (leinn) *n* azinhaga *f*, viela *f*; via *f*

**language** (*lænng*-ghuidj) *n* língua *f*; ~ **laboratory** laboratório de línguas

**lantern** (*lænn*-tănn) *n* lanterna *f*

**lapel** (lă-*pél*) *n* lapela *f*

**larder** (*laa*-dă) *n* despensa *f*

**large** (laadj) *adj* grande; espaçoso

**lark** (laak) *n* cotovia *f*

**laryngitis** (*læ*-rinn-djai-tiç) *n* laringite *f*

**last** (laaçt) *adj* último; precedente; *v* durar; **at** ~ finalmente

**lasting** (*laa*-çtinng) *adj* duradouro

**latchkey** (*lætch*-kii) *n* chave de trinco

**late** (leit) *adj* tardio; atrasado

**lately** (*leit*-li) *adv* ultimamente, recentemente

**lather** (*laa*-ðă) *n* espuma *f*

**Latin America** (*læ*-tinn ă-*mé*-ri-kă) América Latina

**Latin-American** (*læ*-tinn-ă-*mé*-ri-kănn) *adj* sul-americano

**latitude** (*læ*-ti-t'uud) *n* grau de latitude

**laugh** (laaf) *v* *rir; *n* riso *m*

**laughter** (*laaf*-tă) *n* risada *f*

**launch** (lóónntch) *v* lançar; *n* barco a motor

**launching** (*lóónn*-tchinng) *n* lançamento *m*

**launderette** (lóónn-dă-*rét*) *n* lavandaria automática

**laundry** (*lóónn*-dri) *n* lavandaria *f*; roupa para lavar

**lavatory** (*læ*-vă-tă-ri) *n* sanitário *m*

**lavish** (*læ*-vich) *adj* pródigo

**law** (lóó) *n* lei *f*; direito *m*; ~ **court** tribunal *m*

**lawful** (*lóó*-făl) *adj* legal

**lawn** (lóónn) *n* relvado *m*

**lawsuit** (*lóó*-çuut) *n* causa judicial, processo *m*

**lawyer** (*lóó*-iă) *n* advogado *m*; jurista *m*

**laxative** (*læk*-çă-tiv) *n* laxante *m*

***lay** (lei) *v* pousar, colocar, *pôr; ~ **bricks** *fazer trabalho de pedreiro

**layer** (*lei*ă) *n* camada *f*

**layman** (*lei*-mănn) *n* leigo *m*

**lazy** (*lei*-zi) *adj* preguiçoso

***lead** (liid) *v* dirigir

**lead¹** (liid) *n* avanço *m*; direcção *f*; trela *f*

**lead²** (léd) *n* chumbo *m*

**leader** (*lii*-dă) *n* chefe *m*, dirigente *m*

**leadership** (*lii*-dă-chip) *n* direcção *f*

leading (*lii*-dinng) *adj* principal, dominante

leaf (liif) *n* (pl leaves) folha *f*

league (liigh) *n* liga *f*

leak (liik) *v* verter, vazar; *n* fuga *f*

leaky (*lii*-ki) *adj* com fuga

lean (liinn) *adj* magro

*lean (liinn) *v* apoiar-se

leap (liip) *n* salto *m*

*leap (liip) *v* saltar

leap-year (*liip*-i<sup>i</sup>ä) *n* ano bissexto

*learn (lǎǎnn) *v* aprender

learner (*lǎǎ*-nǎ) *n* principiante *m*

lease (liiç) *n* contrato de arrendamento; arrendamento *m*; *v* alugar, arrendar

leash (liich) *n* trela *f*

least (liiçt) *adj* mínimo, menos; at ~ pelo menos

leather (*lé*-ðǎ) *n* couro *m*; de pele, de cabedal

leave (liiv) *n* licença *f*

*leave (liiv) *v* deixar, partir, abandonar; ~ out omitir

Lebanese (lé-bǎ-*niiz*) *adj* libanês

Lebanon (*lé*-bǎ-nǎnn) Líbano *m*

lecture (*lék*-tchǎ) *n* palestra *f*, conferência *f*

left¹ (léft) *adj* esquerdo

left² (léft) *v* (p, pp leave)

left-hand (*léft*-hænnd) *adj* esquerdo

left-handed (léft-*hænn*-did) *adj* canhoto

leg (légh) *n* perna *f*

legacy (*lé*-ghǎ-çi) *n* legado *m*

legal (*lii*-ghǎl) *adj* legal, legítimo; jurídico

legalization (lii-ghǎ-lai-*zei*-chǎnn) *n* legalização *f*

legation (li-*ghei*-chǎnn) *n* legação *f*

legible (*lé*-dji-bǎl) *adj* legível

legitimate (li-*dji*-ti-mǎt) *adj* legítimo

leisure (*lé*-jǎ) *n* vagar *m*; sossego *m*

lemon (*lé*-mǎnn) *n* limão *m*

lemonade (lé-mǎ-*neid*) *n* limonada *f*

*lend (lénnd) *v* emprestar

length (lénngθ) *n* comprimento *m*

lengthen (*lénng*-θǎnn) *v* alongar

lengthways (*lénng*θ-<sup>u</sup>eiz) *adv* longitudinalmente

lens (lénnz) *n* lente *f*; telephoto ~ teleobjectiva *f*; zoom ~ lente zoom

leprosy (*lé*-prǎ-çi) *n* lepra *f*

less (léç) *adv* menos

lessen (*lé*-çǎnn) *v* *diminuir

lesson (*lé*-çǎnn) *n* lição *f*, aula *f*

*let (lét) *v* deixar; alugar; ~ down desiludir

letter (*lé*-tǎ) *n* carta *f*; letra *f*; ~ of credit carta de crédito; ~ of recommendation carta de recomendação

letter-box (*lé*-tǎ-bókç) *n* caixa do correio

lettuce (*lé*-tiç) *n* alface *f*

level (*lé*-vǎl) *adj* igual; liso, plano, direito; *n* nível *m*; *v* aplanar, nivelar; ~ crossing passagem de nível

lever (*lii*-vǎ) *n* alavanca *f*

liability (lai-ǎ-*bi*-lǎ-ti) *n* responsabilidade *f*

liable (*lai*-ǎ-bǎl) *adj* responsável; ~ to sujeito a

liberal (*li*-bǎ-rǎl) *adj* liberal; generoso

liberation (li-bǎ-*rei*-chǎnn) *n* libertação *f*

Liberia (lai-*bi*<sup>ǎ</sup>-ri-ǎ) Libéria *f*

Liberian (lai-*bi*<sup>ǎ</sup>-ri-ǎnn) *adj* liberiano

liberty (*li*-bǎ-ti) *n* liberdade *f*

library (*lai*-brǎ-ri) *n* biblioteca *f*

licence (*lai*-çǎnnç) *n* licença *f*; driving ~ carta de condução; carteira de motorista *Br*

license (*lai*-çǎnnç) *v* autorizar

lick (lik) *v* lamber

lid (lid) *n* tampa *f*

lie (lai) *v* *mentir; *n* mentira *f*

**\*lie** (lai) *v* **\*estar deitado; ~ down** deitar-se

**life** (laif) *n* (pl **lives**) vida *f*; **~ insurance** seguro de vida

**lifebelt** (*laif*-bélt) *n* colete salva-vidas

**lifetime** (*laif*-taimm) *n* vida *f*

**lift** (lift) *v* levantar, erguer; *n* ascensor *m*; boleia *f*; carona *fBr*

**light** (lait) *n* luz *f*; *adj* leve; claro; **~ bulb** lâmpada *f*

**\*light** (lait) *v* acender

**lighter** (*lai*-tã) *n* isqueiro *m*

**lighthouse** (*lait*-hauç) *n* farol *m*

**lighting** (*lai*-tinng) *n* iluminação *f*

**lightning** (*lait*-ninng) *n* relâmpago *m*

**like** (laik) *v* gostar de; *adj* semelhante; *conj* como

**likely** (*lai*-kli) *adj* provável

**like-minded** (laik-*mainn*-did) *adj* unânime

**likewise** (*laik*-ᵘaiz) *adv* igualmente

**lily** (*li*-li) *n* lírio *m*

**limb** (limm) *n* membro *m*

**lime** (laimm) *n* cal *f*; tília *f*; lima *f*

**limetree** (*laimm*-trii) *n* tília *f*

**limit** (*li*-mit) *n* limite *m*; *v* limitar

**limp** (limmp) *v* \*coxear; *adj* frouxo

**line** (lainn) *n* linha *f*; risco *m*; cordão *m*; fila *f*

**linen** (*li*-ninn) *n* linho *m*; roupa branca

**liner** (*lai*-nã) *n* paquete *m*

**lingerie** (*lón*-jã-rii) *n* roupa interior

**lining** (*lai*-ninng) *n* forro *m*

**link** (linngk) *v* ligar; *n* laço *m*; elo *m*

**lion** (*lai*-ãnn) *n* leão *m*

**lip** (lip) *n* lábio *m*

**lipsalve** (*lip*-çaav) *n* pomada para os lábios

**lipstick** (*lip*-çtik) *n* baton *m*

**liqueur** (li-kⁱuᵃ) *n* licor *m*

**liquid** (*li*-kᵘid) *adj* líquido; *n* líquido *m*

**liquor** (*li*-kã) *n* bebidas alcoólicas

**list** (liçt) *n* lista *f*; *v* inscrever

**listen** (*li*-çãnn) *v* escutar

**listener** (*liç*-nã) *n* ouvinte *m*

**literary** (*li*-trã-ri) *adj* literário

**literature** (*li*-trã-tchã) *n* literatura *f*

**litre** (*lii*-tã) *n* litro *m*

**litter** (*li*-tã) *n* lixo *m*; ninhada *f*

**little** (*li*-tãl) *adj* pequeno; pouco

**live¹** (liv) *v* viver; morar

**live²** (laiv) *adj* vivo

**livelihood** (*laiv*-li-hud) *n* subsistência *f*

**lively** (*laiv*-li) *adj* cheio de vida, animado

**liver** (*li*-vã) *n* fígado *m*

**living-room** (*li*-vinng-ruumm) *n* sala de estar

**load** (loᵘd) *n* carregamento *m*; fardo *m*; *v* carregar

**loaf** (loᵘf) *n* (pl **loaves**) pão *m*

**loan** (loᵘnn) *n* empréstimo *m*

**lobby** (*ló*-bi) *n* átrio *m*; vestíbulo *m*

**lobster** (*lób*-çtã) *n* lagosta *f*

**local** (*loᵘ*-kãl) *adj* local; **~ call** chamada local; **~ train** comboio suburbano

**locality** (loᵘ-*kæ*-lã-ti) *n* localidade *f*

**locate** (loᵘ-*keit*) *v* localizar

**location** (loᵘ-*kei*-chãnn) *n* localização *f*

**lock** (lók) *v* fechar à chave; *n* fechadura *f*; comporta *f*; **~ up** fechar, encerrar

**locomotive** (loᵘ-kã-*moᵘ*-tiv) *n* locomotiva *f*

**lodge** (lódj) *v* hospedar; *n* pavilhão de caça

**lodger** (*ló*-djã) *n* hóspede *m*

**lodgings** (*ló*-djinngz) *pl* alojamento *m*

**log** (lógh) *n* toro *m*

**logic** (*ló*-djik) *n* lógica *f*

**logical** (*ló*-dji-kãl) *adj* lógico

**lonely** (*loᵘnn*-li) *adj* solitário

**long** (lónn) *adj* longo; **~ for** desejar; **no longer** não mais

**longing** (*lónn*-inng) *n* desejo *m*

**longitude** (*lónn*-dji-t¹uud) *n* longitude *f*

**look** (luk) *v* olhar; parecer, *ter ares; *n* olhar *m*, olhadela *f*; aparência *f*, aspecto *m*; ~ **after** ocupar-se de, cuidar de; ~ **at** olhar para; ~ **for** procurar; ~ **out** *ter cuidado, prestar atenção; ~ **up** procurar

**looking-glass** (*lu*-kinng-ghlaaç) *n* espelho *m*

**loop** (luup) *n* nó corrediço

**loose** (luuç) *adj* solto

**loosen** (*luu*-çánn) *v* desprender, desapertar

**lord** (lóód) *n* lorde *m*

**lorry** (*ló*-ri) *n* camião *m*

***lose** (luuz) *v* *perder

**loss** (lóç) *n* perda *f*

**lost** (lóçt) *adj* perdido; desaparecido; ~ **and found** achados e perdidos; ~ **property office** depósito de objectos perdidos

**lot** (lót) *n* sorte *f*, destino *m*; quantidade *f*

**lotion** (*loᵘ*-chánn) *n* loção *f*; **after-shave** ~ loção para depois da barba

**lottery** (*ló*-tã-ri) *n* lotaria *f*

**loud** (laud) *adj* forte, alto

**loud-speaker** (laud-*çpii*-kã) *n* altifalante *m*

**lounge** (launndj) *n* salão *m*

**louse** (lauç) *n* (pl lice) piolho *m*

**love** (lav) *v* amar; *n* amor *m*; **in** ~ apaixonado

**lovely** (*lav*-li) *adj* lindo, encantador, delicioso

**lover** (*la*-vã) *n* amante *m*

**love-story** (*lav*-çtóó-ri) *n* história de amor

**low** (loᵘ) *adj* baixo; deprimido; ~ **tide** baixa-mar *f*

**lower** (*loᵘ*-ã) *v* abaixar; baixar; *adj* inferior

**lowlands** (*loᵘ*-lãnndz) *pl* terras baixas

**loyal** (loi-ãl) *adj* leal

**lubricate** (*luu*-bri-keit) *v* *olear, untar, lubrificar

**lubrication** (luu-bri-*kei*-chánn) *n* lubrificação *f*; ~ **oil** óleo de lubrificação; ~ **system** sistema de lubrificação

**luck** (lak) *n* sorte *f*; acaso *m*; **bad** ~ azar *m*

**lucky** (*la*-ki) *adj* afortunado; ~ **charm** talismã *m*

**ludicrous** (*luu*-di-krãç) *adj* ridículo, grotesco

**luggage** (*la*-ghidj) *n* bagagem *f*; **hand** ~ bagagem de mão; **left** ~ **office** depósito de bagagens; ~ **rack** rede da bagagem, bagageira *f*; ~ **van** furgão *m*

**lukewarm** (*luuk*-ᵘóómm) *adj* morno

**lumbago** (lamm-*bei*-ghoᵘ) *n* lumbago *m*

**luminous** (*luu*-mi-nãç) *adj* luminoso

**lump** (lammp) *n* bocado *m*, nó *m*, grumo *m*; alto *m*; ~ **of sugar** torrão de açúcar; ~ **sum** soma global

**lumpy** (*lamm*-pi) *adj* grumoso

**lunacy** (*luu*-nã-çi) *n* loucura *f*

**lunatic** (*luu*-nã-tik) *adj* louco

**lunch** (lanntch) *n* almoço *m*

**luncheon** (*lann*-tchánn) *n* almoço *m*

**lung** (lanng) *n* pulmão *m*

**lust** (laçt) *n* volúpia *f*

**luxurious** (lagh-*juᵈ*-ri-ãç) *adj* luxuoso

**luxury** (*lak*-chã-ri) *n* luxo *m*

# M

**machine** (mã-*chiinn*) *n* máquina *f*

**machinery** (mã-*chii*-nã-ri) *n* maquinaria *f*; mecanismo *m*

**mackerel** (*mæ*-krãl) *n* (pl ~) cavala *f*

**mackintosh** (*mæ*-kinn-tóch) *n* gabardina f; capa de chuva Br

**mad** (mæd) adj insensato, maluco, demente; raivoso

**madam** (mæ-dămm) n senhora f

**madness** (mæd-năç) n demência f

**magazine** (mæ-ghă-ziinn) n revista f

**magic** (mæ-djik) n magia f; adj mágico

**magician** (mă-dji-chănn) n prestidigitador m

**magistrate** (mæ-dji-çtreit) n magistrado m

**magnetic** (mægh-né-tik) adj magnético

**magneto** (mægh-nii-to[u]) n (pl ~s) magneto m

**magnificent** (mægh-ni-fi-cănnt) adj magnífico; grandioso, esplêndido

**magpie** (mægh-pai) n pega f

**maid** (meid) n empregada f

**maiden name** (mei-dănn neimm) apelido de solteira

**mail** (meil) n correio m; v *pôr no correio

**mailbox** (meil-bókç) nAm caixa do correio

**main** (meinn) adj principal; maior; ~ deck convés principal; ~ line linha principal; ~ road estrada principal; ~ street rua principal

**mainland** (meinn-lănnd) n terra firme

**mainly** (meinn-li) adv principalmente

**mains** (meinnz) pl sector principal

**maintain** (meinn-teinn) v *manter, conservar

**maintenance** (meinn-tă-nănnç) n manutenção f

**maize** (meiz) n milho m

**major** (mei-djă) adj grande; maior; n major m

**majority** (mă-djó-ră-ti) n maioria f; maioridade f

*****make** (meik) v *fazer; ganhar; *conseguir; ~ do with arranjar-se

com; ~ **good** compensar; ~ **up** *compor

**make-up** (mei-kap) n maquilhagem f

**malaria** (mă-lé[ă]-ri-ă) n malária f

**Malay** (mă-lei) n malaio m

**Malaysia** (mă-lei-zi-ă) Malásia f

**Malaysian** (mă-lei-zi-ănn) adj malaio

**male** (meil) adj masculino

**malicious** (mă-li-chăç) adj malicioso

**malignant** (mă-ligh-nănnt) adj maligno

**mallet** (mæ-lit) n maço m

**malnutrition** (mæl-n[i]u-tri-chănn) n subalimentação f

**mammal** (mæ-măl) n mamífero m

**mammoth** (mæ-măθ) n mamute m

**man** (mænn) n (pl men) homem m; **men's room** lavabos dos homens

**manage** (mæ-nidj) v administrar; *ter êxito, *conseguir

**manageable** (mæ-ni-djă-băl) adj manejável

**management** (mæ-nidj-mănnt) n direcção f; gestão f

**manager** (mæ-ni-djă) n gerente m, chefe m, director m

**mandarin** (mænn-dă-rinn) n tangerina f

**mandate** (mænn-deit) n mandato m

**manger** (meinn-djă) n manjedoura f

**manicure** (mæ-ni-k[i]u[ă]) n manicura f; v arranjar as unhas

**mankind** (mænn-kainnd) n humanidade f

**mannequin** (mæ-nă-kinn) n manequim m

**manner** (mæ-nă) n maneira f, modo m; **manners** maneiras fpl

**man-of-war** (mæ-năv-[u]óó) n navio de guerra

**manor-house** (mæ-nă-hauç) n solar m

**mansion** (mænn-chănn) n palacete m

**manual** (mæ-n[i]u-ăl) adj manual

**manufacture** (mæ-n[i]u-fæk-tchă) v fabricar

**manufacturer** (mæ-n<sup>i</sup>u-fæk-tchă-ră) *n* fabricante *m*

**manure** (mă-n<sup>i</sup>u<sup>ă</sup>) *n* estrume *m*

**manuscript** (mæ-n<sup>i</sup>u-çkript) *n* manuscrito *m*

**many** (mé-ni) *adj* muitos

**map** (mæp) *n* mapa *m*; planta *f*

**maple** (mei-păl) *n* ácer *m*

**marble** (maa-băl) *n* mármore *m*; berlinde *m*

**March** (maatch) Março

**march** (maatch) *v* marchar; *n* marcha *f*

**mare** (mé<sup>ă</sup>) *n* égua *f*

**margarine** (maa-djă-riinn) *n* margarina *f*

**margin** (maa-djinn) *n* margem *f*

**maritime** (mæ-ri-taimm) *adj* marítimo

**mark** (maak) *v* marcar; caracterizar; *n* marca *f*; nota *f*; alvo *m*

**market** (maa-kit) *n* mercado *m*

**market-place** (maa-kit-pleiç) *n* praça do mercado

**marmalade** (maa-mă-leid) *n* doce de laranja

**marriage** (mæ-ridj) *n* casamento *m*

**marrow** (mæ-ro<sup>u</sup>) *n* medula *f*

**marry** (mæ-ri) *v* casar-se, desposar; **married couple** casal *m*

**marsh** (maach) *n* pântano *m*

**marshy** (maa-chi) *adj* pantanoso

**martyr** (maa-tă) *n* mártir *m*

**marvel** (maa-văl) *n* maravilha *f*; *v* maravilhar-se

**marvellous** (maa-vă-lăç) *adj* maravilhoso

**mascara** (mæ-çkaa-ră) *n* rímel *m*

**masculine** (mæ-çk<sup>i</sup>u-linn) *adj* masculino

**mash** (mæch) *v* esmagar

**mask** (maaçk) *n* máscara *f*

**Mass** (mæç) *n* missa *f*

**mass** (mæç) *n* massa *f*; ~ **produc-**

**tion** produção em série

**massage** (mæ-çaaj) *n* massagem *f*; *v* massajar

**masseur** (mæ-çăă) *n* massagista *m*

**massive** (mæ-çiv) *adj* maciço

**mast** (maaçt) *n* mastro *m*

**master** (maa-çtă) *n* mestre *m*; patrão *m*; professor *m*; *v* dominar

**masterpiece** (maa-çtă-piiç) *n* obra-prima *f*

**mat** (mæt) *n* tapete *m*; *adj* baço, mate

**match** (mætch) *n* fósforo *m*; desafio *m*; *v* \*condizer com

**match-box** (mætch-bókç) *n* caixa de fósforos

**material** (mă-ti<sup>ă</sup>-ri-ăl) *n* material *m*; tecido *m*; *adj* material

**mathematical** (mæ-θă-mæ-ti kăl) *adj* matemático

**mathematics** (mæ-θă-mæ-tikç) *n* matemática *f*

**matrimonial** (mæ-tri-mo<sup>u</sup>-ni-ăl) *adj* matrimonial

**matrimony** (mæ-tri-mă-ni) *n* matrimónio *m*

**matter** (mæ-tă) *n* matéria *f*; assunto *m*, questão *f*; *v* \*ter importância; **as a** ~ **of fact** de facto, efectivamente

**matter-of-fact** (mæ-tă-răv-fækt) *adj* realista

**mattress** (mæ-trăç) *n* colchão *m*

**mature** (mă-t<sup>i</sup>u<sup>ă</sup>) *adj* maduro

**maturity** (mă-t<sup>i</sup>u<sup>ă</sup>-ră-ti) *n* maturidade *f*

**mausoleum** (móó-çă-lii-ămm) *n* mausoléu *m*

**mauve** (mo<sup>u</sup>v) *adj* lilás

**May** (mei) Maio

**\*may** (mei) *v* \*poder

**maybe** (mei-bii) *adv* talvez

**mayor** (mé<sup>ă</sup>) *n* presidente da Câmara

**maze** (meiz) n labirinto m

**me** (mii) pron me; mim

**meadow** (mé-do<sup>u</sup>) n prado m

**meal** (miil) n refeição f

**mean** (miinn) adj mesquinho; n média f

***mean** (miinn) v significar; *querer dizer

**meaning** (mii-ninng) n significado m

**meaningless** (mii-ninng-lăç) adj sem sentido

**means** (miinnz) n meio m; **by no ~** em caso algum, de modo nenhum

**in the meantime** (inn ðă miinn-taimm) entretanto

**meanwhile** (miinn-<sup>u</sup>ail) adv entretanto

**measles** (mii-zălz) n sarampo m

**measure** (mé-jă) v *medir; n medida f

**meat** (miit) n carne f

**mechanic** (mi-kæ-nik) n mecânico m

**mechanical** (mi-kæ-ni-kăl) adj mecânico

**mechanism** (mé-kă-ni-zămm) n mecanismo m

**medal** (mé-dăl) n medalha f

**mediaeval** (mé-di-ii-văl) adj medieval

**mediate** (mii-di-eit) v *servir de intermediário

**mediator** (mii-di-ei-tă) n intermediário m

**medical** (mé-di-kăl) adj médico

**medicine** (méd-çinn) n medicamento m; medicina f

**meditate** (mé-di-teit) v meditar

**Mediterranean** (mé-di-tă-rei-ni-ănn) Mediterrâneo m

**medium** (mii-di-ămm) adj médio, mediano

***meet** (miit) v encontrar

**meeting** (mii-tinng) n reunião f, assembleia f

**meeting-place** (mii-tinng-pleiç) n ponto de encontro

**melancholy** (mé-lănng-kă-li) n melancolia f

**mellow** (mé-lo<sup>u</sup>) adj macio

**melodrama** (mé-lă-draa-mă) n melodrama m

**melody** (mé-lă-di) n melodia f

**melon** (mé-lănn) n melão m

**melt** (mélt) v derreter

**member** (mémm-bă) n membro m; **Member of Parliament** deputado m

**membership** (mémm-bă-chip) n filiação f

**memo** (mé-mo<sup>u</sup>) n (pl ~s) memorando m

**memorable** (mé-mă-ră-băl) adj memorável

**memorial** (mă-móó-ri-ăl) n memorial m

**memorize** (mé-mă-raiz) v decorar

**memory** (mé-mă-ri) n memória f, recordação f

**mend** (ménnd) v remendar, reparar

**menstruation** (ménn-çtru-ei-chănn) n menstruação f

**mental** (ménn-tăl) adj mental

**mention** (ménn-chănn) v mencionar, *nomear; n menção f

**menu** (mé-n<sup>i</sup>uu) n ementa f; cardápio mBr

**merchandise** (măă-tchănn-daiz) n mercadoria f

**merchant** (măă-tchănnt) n comerciante m

**merciful** (măă-çi-făl) adj misericordioso

**mercury** (măă-k<sup>i</sup>u-ri) n mercúrio m

**mercy** (măă-çi) n clemência f, misericórdia f

**mere** (mi<sup>ă</sup>) adj simples

**merely** (mi<sup>ă</sup>-li) adv somente

**merit** (mé-rit) v merecer; n mérito m

**mermaid** (măă-meid) n sereia f

**merry** (*mé*-ri) *adj* alegre

**merry-go-round** (*mé*-ri-gho<sup>u</sup>-raunnd) *n* carrossel *m*

**mesh** (méch) *n* malha *f*

**mess** (méç) *n* trapalhada *f*, desordem *f*; ~ **up** estragar

**message** (*mé*-çidj) *n* mensagem *f*, recado *m*

**messenger** (*mé*-çinn-djä) *n* mensageiro *m*

**metal** (*mé*-tăl) *n* metal *m*; metálico

**meter** (*mii*-tă) *n* contador *m*; medidor *mBr*

**method** (*mé*-θăd) *n* método *m*; ordem *f*

**methodical** (mă-θó-di-kăl) *adj* metódico

**methylated spirits** (*mé*-θă-lei-tid çpiritç) álcool desnaturado

**metre** (*mii*-tă) *n* metro *m*

**metric** (*mé*-trik) *adj* métrico

**Mexican** (*mék*-çi-kănn) *adj* mexicano

**Mexico** (*mék*-çi-ko<sup>u</sup>) México *m*

**mezzanine** (*mé*-ză-niinn) *n* sobreloja *f*

**microphone** (*mai*-kră-fo<sup>u</sup>nn) *n* microfone *m*

**midday** (*mid*-dei) *n* meio-dia *m*

**middle** (*mi*-dăl) *n* meio *m*; *adj* médio; **Middle Ages** Idade Média; ~ **class** classe média; **middle-class** *adj* burguês

**midnight** (*mid*-nait) *n* meia-noite *f*

**midst** (midçt) *n* meio *m*

**midsummer** (*mid*-ça-mă) *n* pleno Verão

**midwife** (*mid*-<sup>u</sup>aif) *n* (pl -wives) parteira *f*

**might** (mait) *n* poder *m*

***might** (mait) *v* *poder

**mighty** (*mai*-ti) *adj* poderoso

**migraine** (*mi*-ghreinn) *n* enxaqueca *f*

**mild** (maild) *adj* suave

**mildew** (*mil*-d<sup>i</sup>u) *n* bolor *m*

**mile** (mail) *n* milha *f*

**milestone** (*mail*-çto<sup>u</sup>nn) *n* marco miliário

**milieu** (*mii*-l<sup>i</sup>ăă) *n* meio ambiente

**military** (*mi*-li-tă-ri) *adj* militar; ~ **force** força armada

**milk** (milk) *n* leite *m*

**milkman** (*milk*-mănn) *n* (pl -men) leiteiro *m*

**milk-shake** (*milk*-cheik) *n* batido de leite

**milky** (*mil*-ki) *adj* leitoso

**mill** (mil) *n* moinho *m*; fábrica *f*

**miller** (*mi*-lă) *n* moleiro *m*

**milliner** (*mi*-li-nă) *n* chapeleira de senhoras

**millionaire** (mil-<sup>i</sup>ă-né<sup>ă</sup>) *n* milionário *m*

**mince** (minnç) *v* picar

**mind** (mainnd) *n* mente *f*; *v* *fazer objecção a; prestar atenção a, importar-se com, prestar atenção

**mine** (mainn) *n* mina *f*

**miner** (*mai*-nă) *n* mineiro *m*

**mineral** (*mi*-nă-răl) *n* mineral *m*; ~ **water** água mineral

**miniature** (*minn*-<sup>i</sup>ă-tchă) *n* miniatura *f*

**minimum** (*mi*-ni-mămm) *n* mínimo *m*

**mining** (*mai*-ninng) *n* exploração mineira

**minister** (*mi*-ni-çtă) *n* ministro *m*; pastor *m*; **Prime Minister** primeiro-ministro *m*

**ministry** (*mi*-ni-çtri) *n* ministério *m*

**mink** (minngk) *n* vison *m*

**minor** (*mai*-nă) *adj* menor, pequeno; *n* menor *m*

**minority** (mai-nó-ră-ti) *n* minoria *f*; menoridade *f*

**mint** (minnt) *n* hortelã *f*

**minus** (*mai*-năç) *prep* menos

**minute**[1] (*mi*-nit) *n* minuto *m*; **minutes** acta *f*

**minute**[2] (mai-n<sup>i</sup>uut) *adj* minúsculo

**miracle** (*mi*-ră-kăl) *n* milagre *m*

**miraculous** (mi-ræ-k'u-lăç) *adj* milagroso

**mirror** (*mi*-ră) *n* espelho *m*

**misbehave** (miç-bi-*heiv*) *v* portar-se mal

**miscarriage** (miç-*kæ*-ridj) *n* aborto *m*

**miscellaneous** (mi-că-*lei*-ni-ăç) *adj* misturado

**mischief** (*miç*-tchif) *n* diabrura *f*; maldade *f*, malícia *f*, dano *m*

**mischievous** (*miç*-tchi-văç) *adj* maroto

**miserable** (*mi*-ză-ră-băl) *adj* miserável; triste

**misery** (*mi*-ză-ri) *n* miséria *f*, infelicidade *f*

**misfortune** (miç-*fóó*-tchénn) *n* infortúnio *m*, infelicidade *f*

**\*mislay** (miç-*lei*) *v* desencaminhar, extraviar

**misplaced** (miç-*pleict*) *adj* inoportuno; despropositado

**mispronounce** (miç-pră-*naunnç*) *v* pronunciar mal

**miss**[1] (miç) menina

**miss**[2] (miç) *v* \*perder

**missing** (*mi*-çinng) *adj* perdido; ~ **person** desaparecido *m*

**mist** (miçt) *n* neblina *f*, nevoeiro *m*

**mistake** (mi-*çteik*) *n* engano *m*, erro *m*, equívoco *m*

**\*mistake** (mi-*çteik*) *v* confundir

**mistaken** (mi-*çtei*-kănn) *adj* errado; **\*be** ~ enganar-se

**mister** (*mi*-çtă) senhor

**mistress** (*mi*-çtrăç) *n* dona de casa; patroa *f*; amante *f*

**mistrust** (miç-*traçt*) *v* desconfiar

**misty** (*mi*-çti) *adj* enevoado

**\*misunderstand** (mi-çann-dă-*çtænnd*) *v* perceber mal, compreender mal

**misunderstanding** (mi-çann-dă-*çtænn*-dinng) *n* mal-entendido *m*

**misuse** (miç-*'uuç*) *n* abuso *m*

**mittens** (*mi*-tănnz) *pl* luvas sem dedos

**mix** (mikç) *v* misturar; ~ **with** frequentar

**mixed** (mikçt) *adj* misturado

**mixer** (*mik*-çă) *n* batedeira *f*

**mixture** (*mikç*-tchă) *n* mistura *f*

**moan** (mou<sup>u</sup>nn) *v* gemer; queixar-se

**moat** (mou<sup>u</sup>t) *n* fosso *m*

**mobile** (mou<sup>u</sup>-bail) *adj* móvel

**mock** (mók) *v* troçar

**mockery** (*mó*-kă-ri) *n* troça *f*

**model** (*mó*-dăl) *n* modelo *m*; manequim *m*; *v* modelar, moldar

**moderate** (*mó*-dă-răt) *adj* moderado; medíocre

**modern** (*mó*-dănn) *adj* moderno

**modest** (*mó*-diçt) *adj* modesto

**modesty** (*mó*-di-çti) *n* modéstia *f*

**modify** (*mó*-di-fai) *v* modificar

**mohair** (mou<sup>u</sup>-hé<sup>ă</sup>) *n* mohair *m*

**moist** (moiçt) *adj* húmido, molhado

**moisten** (*moi*-çănn) *v* humedecer

**moisture** (*moiç*-tchă) *n* humidade *f*; **moisturizing cream** creme hidratante

**molar** (mou<sup>u</sup>-lă) *n* molar *m*

**moment** (mou<sup>u</sup>-mănnt) *n* momento *m*, instante *m*

**momentary** (mou<sup>u</sup>-mănn-tă-ri) *adj* momentâneo

**monarch** (*mó*-năk) *n* monarca *m*

**monarchy** (*mó*-nă-ki) *n* monarquia *f*

**monastery** (*mó*-nă-çtri) *n* mosteiro *m*

**Monday** (*mann*-di) segunda-feira *f*

**monetary** (*ma*-ni-tă-ri) *adj* monetário; ~ **unit** unidade monetária

**money** (*ma*-ni) *n* dinheiro *m*; ~ **exchange** casa de câmbio; ~ **order** ordem postal

**monk** (manngk) *n* monge *m*

**monkey** (*manng*-ki) *n* macaco *m*

**monologue** (*mó*-nó-lógh) *n* monólogo *m*

monopoly (mǎ-nó-pǎ-li) n monopólio m

monotonous (mǎ-nó-tǎ-nǎç) adj monótono

month (mannθ) n mês m

monthly (mannθ-li) adj mensal; ~ magazine revista mensal

monument (mó-n¹u-mǎnnt) n monumento m

mood (muud) n humor m, disposição f

moon (muunn) n lua f

moonlight (muunn-lait) n luar m

moor (muǎ) n charneca f, urzal m

moose (muuç) n (pl ~, ~s) alce m

moped (moᵘ-péd) n bicicleta a motor

moral (mó-rǎl) n moral f; adj moral; morals costumes mpl

morality (mǎ-ræ-lǎ-ti) n moralidade f

more (móó) adj mais; once ~ uma vez mais

moreover (móó-roᵘ-vǎ) adv demais a mais, além disso

morning (móó-ninng) n manhã f; ~ paper jornal da manhã

Moroccan (mǎ-ró-kǎnn) adj marroquino

Morocco (mǎ-ró-koᵘ) Marrocos m

morphia (móó-fi-ǎ) n morfina f

morphine (móó-fiinn) n morfina f

morsel (móó-çǎl) n bocado m

mortal (móó-tǎl) adj mortal, fatal

mortgage (móó-ghidj) n hipoteca f

mosaic (mǎ-zei-ik) n mosaico m

mosque (móçk) n mesquita f

mosquito (mǎ-çkii-toᵘ) n (pl ~es) mosquito m

mosquito-net (mǎ-çkii-toᵘ-nét) n mosquiteiro m

moss (móç) n musgo m

most (moᵘçt) adj mais; at ~ no máximo, quando muito; ~ of all sobretudo

mostly (moᵘçt-li) adv principalmente

motel (moᵘ-tél) n motel m

moth (móθ) n traça f

mother (ma-ðǎ) n mãe f; ~ tongue língua materna

mother-in-law (ma-ðǎ-rinn-lóó) n (pl mothers-) sogra f

mother-of-pearl (ma-ðǎ-rǎv-pǎǎl) n madre-pérola f

motion (moᵘ-chǎnn) n movimento m; moção f

motive (moᵘ-tiv) n motivo m

motor (moᵘ-tǎ) n motor m; v viajar de automóvel; starter ~ motor de arranque

motorbike (moᵘ-tǎ-baik) nAm bicicleta a motor

motor-boat (moᵘ-tǎ-boᵘt) n barco a motor

motor-car (moᵘ-tǎ-kaa) n automóvel m

motor-cycle (moᵘ-tǎ-çai-kǎl) n motocicleta f

motoring (moᵘ-tǎ-rinng) n automobilismo m

motorist (moᵘ-tǎ-riçt) n automobilista m

motorway (moᵘ-tǎ-ᵘei) n auto-estrada f

motto (mó-toᵘ) n (pl ~es, ~s) divisa f

mouldy (moᵘl-di) adj bolorento

mound (maunnd) n montículo m

mount (maunnt) v *subir; n monte m

mountain (maunn-tinn) n montanha f; ~ pass desfiladeiro m; ~ range cordilheira f

mountaineering (maunn-ti-niǎ-rinng) n alpinismo m

mountainous (maunn-ti-nǎç) adj montanhoso

mourning (móó-ninng) n luto m

mouse (mauç) n (pl mice) rato m

moustache (mǎ-çtaach) n bigode m

mouth (mauθ) n boca f, focinho m;

foz f

**mouthwash** (*mauθ-*ᵘ*óch*) *n* líquido dentífrico

**movable** (*muu-vă-băl*) *adj* móvel

**move** (muuv) *v* mover; deslocar; mexer-se; mudar-se; comover; *n* jogada *f*, passo *m*; mudança *f*

**movement** (*muuv-mănnt*) *n* movimento *m*

**movie** (*muu-vi*) *n* filme *m*

**much** (match) *adj* muito; **as ~** tanto

**muck** (mak) *n* porcaria *f*

**mud** (mad) *n* lama *f*

**muddle** (*ma-dăl*) *n* confusão *f*, trapalhada *f*; *v* *fazer trapalhada

**muddy** (*ma-di*) *adj* lamacento

**mud-guard** (*mad*-ghaad) *n* guarda-lama *m*

**mug** (magh) *n* caneca *f*

**mulberry** (*mal-bă-ri*) *n* amora *f*

**mule** (m*ⁱ*uul) *n* macho *m*, mulo *m*

**mullet** (*ma-lit*) *n* tainha *f*

**multiplication** (mal-ti-pli-*kei-*chănn) *n* multiplicação *f*

**multiply** (*mal*-ti-plai) *v* multiplicar

**mumps** (mammpç) *n* papeira *f*

**municipal** (m*ⁱ*uu-*ni-*çi-păl) *adj* municipal

**municipality** (m*ⁱ*uu-ni-çi-*pæ-*lă-ti) *n* municipalidade *f*

**murder** (*mă̆-dă̆*) *n* homicídio *m*; *v* assassinar

**murderer** (*mă̆ă̆-dă̆-ră̆*) *n* assassino *m*

**muscle** (*ma-çăl*) *n* músculo *m*

**muscular** (*ma-çk*ⁱ*u-lă*) *adj* musculoso

**museum** (m*ⁱ*uu-*zii-ă̆*mm) *n* museu *m*

**mushroom** (*mach-*ruumm) *n* cogumelo *m*

**music** (m*ⁱ*uu-zik) *n* música *f*; **~ academy** conservatório *m*

**musical** (m*ⁱ*uu-zi-kăl) *adj* musical; *n* comédia musical

**music-hall** (m*ⁱ*uu-zik-hóól) *n* teatro de variedades

**musician** (m*ⁱ*uu-*zi-*chănn) *n* músico *m*

**muslin** (*maz-*linn) *n* musselina *f*

**mussel** (*ma-çăl*) *n* mexilhão *m*

***must** (maçt) *v* *ter de, dever

**mustard** (*ma-*çtăd) *n* mostarda *f*

**mute** (m*ⁱ*uut) *adj* mudo

**mutiny** (*m*ⁱ*uu-*ti-ni) *n* motim *m*

**mutton** (*ma-*tănn) *n* carne de carneiro

**mutual** (m*ⁱ*uu-tchu-ăl) *adj* mútuo, recíproco

**my** (mai) *adj* meu

**myself** (mai-*çélf*) *pron* me; eu mesmo

**mysterious** (mi-*çtiă̆*-ri-ăç) *adj* misterioso

**mystery** (*mi-*çtă-ri) *n* mistério *m*, enigma *m*

**myth** (miθ) *n* mito *m*

# N

**nail** (neil) *n* unha *f*; prego *m*

**nailbrush** (*neil-*brach) *n* escova de unhas

**nail-file** (*neil-*fail) *n* lima de unhas

**nail-polish** (*neil-*pó-lich) *n* verniz de unhas

**nail-scissors** (*neil-*çi-zăz) *pl* tesoura de unhas

**naïve** (naa-*iiv*) *adj* ingénuo

**naked** (*nei-*kid) *adj* nu, despido

**name** (neimm) *n* nome *m*; *v* chamar, *nomear; **in the ~ of** em nome de

**namely** (*neimm-*li) *adv* a saber

**nap** (næp) *n* soneca *f*

**napkin** (*næp-*kinn) *n* guardanapo *m*

**nappy** (*næ-*pi) *n* fralda *f*

**narcosis** (naa-*koᵘ-*çiç) *n* (pl -ses) narcose *f*

**narcotic** (naa-*kó-*tik) *n* narcótico *m*

**narrow** (*næ-*roᵘ) *adj* apertado, estreito

**narrow-minded** (næ-roᵘ-*mainn-*did)

*adj* tacanho

**nasty** (*naa*-çti) *adj* antipático, desagradável

**nation** (*nei*-chänn) *n* povo *m*

**national** (*næ*-chă-năl) *adj* nacional; do estado; ~ **anthem** hino nacional; ~ **dress** traje nacional; ~ **park** parque nacional

**nationality** (*næ*-chă-*næ*-lă-ti) *n* nacionalidade *f*

**nationalize** (*næ*-chă-nă-laiz) *v* nacionalizar

**native** (*nei*-tiv) *n* indígena *m*; *adj* nativo *m*; ~ **country** pátria *f*, país natal; ~ **language** língua materna

**natural** (*næ*-tchă-răl) *adj* natural; nato

**naturally** (*næ*-tchă-ră-li) *adv* naturalmente, certamente

**nature** (*nei*-tchă) *n* natureza *f*

**naughty** (*nóó*-ti) *adj* travesso, maroto

**nausea** (*nóó*-çi-ă) *n* náusea *f*

**naval** (*nei*-văl) *adj* naval

**navel** (*nei*-văl) *n* umbigo *m*

**navigable** (*næ*-vi-ghă-băl) *adj* navegável

**navigate** (*næ*-vi-gheit) *v* navegar

**navigation** (*næ*-vi-*ghei*-chänn) *n* navegação *f*

**navy** (*nei*-vi) *n* marinha *f*

**near** (niᵃ) *prep* perto de; *adj* vizinho, chegado

**nearby** (*niᵃ*-bai) *adj* próximo

**nearly** (*niᵃ*-li) *adv* quase

**neat** (niit) *adj* asseado; puro

**necessary** (*né*-çă-çă-ri) *adj* necessário

**necessity** (nă-*çé*-çă-ti) *n* necessidade *f*

**neck** (nék) *n* pescoço *m*; **nape of the** ~ nuca *f*

**necklace** (*nék*-lăç) *n* colar *m*

**necktie** (*nék*-tai) *n* gravata *f*

**need** (niid) *v* necessitar, precisar; *n* necessidade *f*, precisão *f*; ~ **to** *ter

de

**needle** (*nii*-dăl) *n* agulha *f*

**needlework** (*nii*-dăl-ᵘăăk) *n* costura *f*

**negative** (*né*-ghă-tiv) *adj* negativo; *n* negativo *m*

**neglect** (ni-*ghlékt*) *v* descuidar; *n* negligência *f*

**neglectful** (ni-*ghlékt*-făl) *adj* negligente

**negotiate** (ni-*ghoᵘ*-chi-eit) *v* *negociar

**negotiation** (ni-ghoᵘ-chi-*ei*-chänn) *n* negociação *f*

**Negro** (*nii*-ghroᵘ) *n* (pl ~es) negro *m*

**neighbour** (*nei*-bă) *n* vizinho *m*

**neighbourhood** (*nei*-bă-hud) *n* vizinhança *f*

**neighbouring** (*nei*-bă-rinng) *adj* contíguo, vizinho

**neither** (*nai*-ðă) *pron* nem um nem outro; **neither ... nor** nem ... nem

**neon** (*nii*-ónn) *n* néon *m*

**nephew** (*né*-fᵘuu) *n* sobrinho *m*

**nerve** (nääv) *n* nervo *m*; audácia *f*

**nervous** (*nää*-văç) *adj* nervoso

**nest** (néçt) *n* ninho *m*

**net** (nét) *n* rede *f*; *adj* líquido

**the Netherlands** (*né*-ðă-lănndz) Os Países Baixos

**network** (*nét*-ᵘăăk) *n* rede *f*

**neuralgia** (nⁱuᵃ-*ræl*-djă) *n* nevralgia *f*

**neurosis** (nⁱuᵃ-*roᵘ*-çiç) *n* neurose *f*

**neuter** (*nⁱuu*-tă) *adj* neutro

**neutral** (*nⁱuu*-trăl) *adj* neutral

**never** (*né*-vă) *adv* nunca

**nevertheless** (né-vă-ðă-*léç*) *adv* não obstante

**new** (nⁱuu) *adj* novo; **New Year** Ano Novo

**news** (nⁱuuz) *n* notícias, notícia *f*; noticiário *m*

**newsagent** (*nⁱuu*-zei-djănnt) *n* vendedor de jornais

**newspaper** (*nⁱuuz*-pei-pă) *n* jornal *m*

**newsstand** (*nⁱuuz*-çtænnd) *n* quiosque

de jornais

**New Zealand** (n<sup>i</sup>uu *zii*-lǎnnd) Nova
Zelândia

**next** (nékçt) *adj* próximo, seguinte;
~ **to** junto a

**next-door** (nékçt-dóó) *adv* ao lado

**nice** (naiç) *adj* bonito, agradável;
bom; simpático

**nickel** (*ni*-kǎl) *n* níquel *m*

**nickname** (*nik*-neimm) *n* alcunha *f*;
apelido *mBr*

**nicotine** (*ni*-kǎ-tiinn) *n* nicotina *f*

**niece** (niiç) *n* sobrinha *f*

**Nigeria** (nai-*dji*ᵃ-ri-ǎ) Nigéria *f*

**Nigerian** (nai-*dji*ᵃ-ri-ǎnn) *adj* nigeriano

**night** (nait) *n* noite *f*; **by** ~ de noite;
~ **flight** voo nocturno; ~ **rate** tarifa nocturna; ~ **train** comboio
nocturno

**nightclub** (*nait*-klab) *n* boate *f*

**night-cream** (*nait*-kriimm) *n* creme de
noite

**nightdress** (*nait*-dréç) *n* camisa de
dormir; camisola *fBr*

**nightingale** (*nai*-tinng-gheil) *n* rouxinol
*m*

**nightly** (*nait*-li) *adj* nocturno

**nil** (nil) *n* nada

**nine** (nainn) *num* nove

**nineteen** (nainn-*tiinn*) *num* dezanove

**nineteenth** (nainn-*tiinn*θ) *num* décimo
nono

**ninety** (*nainn*-ti) *num* noventa

**ninth** (nainnθ) *num* nono

**nitrogen** (*nai*-trǎ-djǎnn) *n* azoto *m*

**no** (no<sup>u</sup>) não; *adj* nenhum; ~ **one**
ninguém

**nobility** (no<sup>u</sup>-*bi*-lǎ-ti) *n* nobreza *f*

**noble** (*no*<sup>u</sup>-bǎl) *adj* nobre

**nobody** (*no*<sup>u</sup>-bó-di) *pron* ninguém

**nod** (nód) *n* inclinação de cabeça; *v*
inclinar a cabeça

**noise** (noiz) *n* ruído *m*, barulho *m*

**noisy** (*noi*-zi) *adj* ruidoso

**nominal** (*nó*-mi-nǎl) *adj* nominal

**nominate** (*nó*-mi-neit) *v* \*nomear

**nomination** (nó-mi-*nei*-chǎnn) *n* nomeação *f*

**none** (nann) *pron* nenhum

**nonsense** (*nónn*-çǎnnç) *n* disparate *m*

**noon** (nuunn) *n* meio-dia *m*

**normal** (*nóó*-mǎl) *adj* normal

**north** (nóóθ) *n* norte *m*; *adj* setentrional; **North Pole** pólo norte

**north-east** (nóóθ-*üçt*) *n* nordeste *m*

**northerly** (*nóó*-ðǎ-li) *adj* do norte

**northern** (*nóó*-ðǎnn) *adj* nórdico

**north-west** (nóóθ-*ü*eçt) *n* noroeste *m*

**Norway** (*nóó*-<sup>u</sup>ei) Noruega *f*

**Norwegian** (nóó-<sup>u</sup>*ii*-djǎnn) *adj* norueguês

**nose** (no<sup>u</sup>z) *n* nariz *m*

**nosebleed** (*no*<sup>u</sup>z-bliid) *n* hemorragia
nasal

**nostril** (*nó*-çtril) *n* narina *f*

**not** (nót) *adv* não

**notary** (*no*<sup>u</sup>-tǎ-ri) *n* notário *m*

**note** (no<sup>u</sup>t) *n* nota *f*, apontamento *m*;
*v* anotar; constatar, observar

**notebook** (*no*<sup>u</sup>t-buk) *n* agenda *f*

**noted** (*no*<sup>u</sup>-tid) *adj* ilustre

**notepaper** (*no*<sup>u</sup>t-pei-pǎ) *n* papel para
escrever, papel de carta

**nothing** (*na*-θinng) *n* nada *m*

**notice** (*no*<sup>u</sup>-tiç) *v* notar, reparar em;
\*ver; *n* notícia *f*, aviso *m*; atenção *f*

**noticeable** (*no*<sup>u</sup>-ti-çǎ-bǎl) *adj* perceptível; notável

**notify** (*no*<sup>u</sup>-ti-fai) *v* notificar, participar; avisar

**notion** (*no*<sup>u</sup>-chǎnn) *n* noção *f*

**notorious** (no<sup>u</sup>-*tóó*-ri-ǎç) *adj* notório

**nougat** (*nuu*-ghaa) *n* nogado *m*

**nought** (nóót) *n* zero *m*

**noun** (naunn) *n* substantivo *m*

**nourishing** (*na*-ri-chinng) *adj* alimentício

**novel** (*nó*-vǎl) *n* romance *m*

**novelist** (nó-vă-lişt) n romancista m

**November** (noᵘ-vémm-bă) Novembro

**now** (nau) adv agora; actualmente; ~ **and then** de tempos a tempos

**nowadays** (nau-ă-deiz) adv hoje em dia

**nowhere** (noᵘ-ᵘé̆ă) adv em parte alguma

**nozzle** (nó-zăl) n bocal m

**nuance** (nʲuu-ăç) n cambiante m; nuance f

**nuclear** (nʲuu-kli-ă) adj nuclear; ~ **energy** energia nuclear

**nucleus** (nʲuu-kli-ăç) n núcleo m

**nude** (nʲuud) adj nu; n nu m

**nuisance** (nʲuu-çănnç) n incómodo m

**numb** (namm) adj entorpecido

**number** (namm-bă) n número m, algarismo m; quantidade f

**numeral** (nʲuu-mă-răl) n numeral m

**numerous** (nʲuu-mă-răç) adj numeroso

**nun** (nann) n freira f

**nunnery** (na-nă-ri) n convento m

**nurse** (năăç) n enfermeira f; ama-seca f; v tratar de; amamentar

**nursery** (năă-çă-ri) n quarto das crianças; creche f; viveiro m

**nut** (nat) n noz f; porca f

**nutcrackers** (nat-kræ-kăz) pl quebra-nozes m

**nutmeg** (nat-mégh) n noz moscada

**nutritious** (nʲuu-tri-chăç) adj nutritivo

**nutshell** (nat-chél) n casca de noz

**nylon** (nai-lónn) n nylon m

# O

**oak** (oᵘk) n carvalho m

**oar** (óó) n remo m

**oasis** (oᵘ-ei-çiç) n (pl oases) oásis m

**oath** (oᵘθ) n juramento m

**oats** (oᵘtç) pl aveia f

**obedience** (ă-bii-di-ănnç) n obediência f

**obedient** (ă-bii-di-ănnt) adj obediente

**obey** (ă-bei) v obedecer

**object¹** (ób-djikt) n objecto m

**object²** (ăb-djékt) v objectar, *opor; ~ **to** *opor-se a

**objection** (ăb-djék-chănn) n objecção f

**objective** (ăb-djék-tiv) adj objectivo; n objectivo m

**obligatory** (ă-bli-ghă-tă-ri) adj obrigatório

**oblige** (ă-blaidj) v obrigar; *be obliged to *ser obrigado a; *ter de

**obliging** (ă-blai-djinng) adj solícito

**oblong** (ób-lónn) adj oblongo; n rectângulo m

**obscene** (ăb-çiinn) adj obsceno

**obscure** (ăb-çkʲuă) adj obscuro, confuso, vago, escuro

**observation** (ób-ză-vei-chănn) n observação f

**observatory** (ăb-zăă-vă-tri) n observatório m

**observe** (ăb-zăăv) v observar

**obsession** (ăb-çé-chănn) n obsessão f

**obstacle** (ób-çtă-kăl) n obstáculo m

**obstinate** (ób-çti-năt) adj obstinado; teimoso

**obtain** (ăb-teinn) v *conseguir, *obter

**obvious** (ób-vi-ăç) adj óbvio

**occasion** (ă-kei-jănn) n ocasião f; motivo m

**occasionally** (ă-kei-jă-nă-li) adv de vez em quando, ocasionalmente

**occupant** (ó-kʲu-pănnt) n morador m

**occupation** (ó-kʲu-pei-chănn) n ocupação f

**occupy** (ó-kʲu-pai) v ocupar

**occur** (ă-kăă) v suceder, acontecer

**occurrence** (ă-ka-rănnç) n ocorrência f

**ocean** (oᵘ-chănn) n oceano m

**October** (ók-to<sup>u</sup>-bă) Outubro

**octopus** (ók-tă-pằç) n polvo m

**oculist** (ó-k<sup>i</sup>u-liçt) n oculista m

**odd** (ód) adj invulgar, estranho; ímpar

**odour** (o<sup>u</sup>-dă) n odor m

**of** (óv ăv) prep de

**off** (óf) adv embora; prep de

**offence** (ă-fénnç) n falta f; ofensa f, ultraje m

**offend** (ă-fénnd) v ofender; *transgredir

**offensive** (ă-fénn-çiv) adj ofensivo, insultante; n ofensiva f

**offer** (ó-fă) v oferecer; n oferta f

**office** (ó-fiç) n escritório m; cargo m; ~ **hours** horas de serviço

**officer** (ó-fi-çă) n oficial m

**official** (ă-fi-chăl) adj oficial

**off-licence** (óf-lai-çănnç) n loja de vinhos

**often** (ó-fănn) adv muitas vezes, frequentemente

**oil** (oil) n óleo m; petróleo m; **fuel** ~ óleo combustível; ~ **filter** filtro de óleo; ~ **pressure** pressão do óleo

**oil-painting** (oil-peinn-tinng) n pintura a óleo

**oil-refinery** (oil-ri-fai-nă-ri) n refinaria de petróleo

**oil-well** (oil-<sup>u</sup>él) n poço de petróleo

**oily** (oi-li) adj oleoso

**ointment** (oinnt-mănnt) n unguento m

**okay!** (o<sup>u</sup>-kei) de acordo!

**old** (o<sup>u</sup>ld) adj velho; ~ **age** velhice f

**old-fashioned** (o<sup>u</sup>ld-fæ-chănnd) adj antiquado

**olive** (ó-liv) n azeitona f; ~ **oil** azeite m

**omelette** (ómm-lăt) n omeleta f

**ominous** (ó-mi-năç) adj sinistro

**omit** (ă-mit) v omitir

**omnipotent** (ómm-ni-pă-tănnt) adj omnipotente

**on** (ónn) prep sobre; a

**once** (<sup>u</sup>annç) adv uma vez; **at** ~ já, imediatamente; ~ **more** uma vez mais

**oncoming** (ónn-ka-minng) adj próximo

**one** (<sup>u</sup>ann) num um; pron uma pessoa

**oneself** (<sup>u</sup>ann-çélf) pron si mesmo

**onion** (a-n<sup>i</sup>ănn) n cebola f

**only** (o<sup>u</sup>nn-li) adj só; adv somente, só; conj mas

**onwards** (ónn-<sup>u</sup>ădz) adv para a frente

**onyx** (ó-nikç) n ónix m

**opal** (o<sup>u</sup>-păl) n opala f

**open** (o<sup>u</sup>-pănn) v abrir; adj aberto; franco

**opening** (o<sup>u</sup>-pă-ninng) n abertura f

**opera** (ó-pă-ră) n ópera f

**operate** (ó-pă-reit) v funcionar, actuar; operar

**operation** (ó-pă-rei-chănn) n funcionamento m; operação f

**operator** (ó-pă-rei-tă) n telefonista f

**operetta** (ó-pă-ré-tă) n opereta f

**opinion** (ă-pi-n<sup>i</sup>ănn) n opinião f, parecer m

**opponent** (ă-po<sup>u</sup>-nănnt) n adversário m

**opportunity** (ó-pă-t<sup>i</sup>uu-nă-ti) n oportunidade f

**oppose** (ă-po<sup>u</sup>z) v *opor-se

**opposite** (ó-pă-zit) prep em frente de; adj oposto, contrário

**opposition** (ó-pă-zi-chănn) n oposição f

**oppress** (ă-préç) v oprimir

**optician** (óp-ti-chănn) n oculista m

**optimism** (óp-ti-mi-zămm) n optimismo m

**optimist** (óp-ti-miçt) n optimista m

**optimistic** (óp-ti-mi-çtik) adj optimista

**optional** (óp-chă-năl) adj facultativo

or (óó) *conj* ou
oral (óó-rãl) *adj* oral
orange (ó-rinndj) *n* laranja *f; adj* cor-de-laranja
orchard (óó-tchäd) *n* pomar *m*
orchestra (óó-ki-çträ) *n* orquestra *f;* ~ seat *Am* plateia *f*
order (óó-dä) *v* mandar, ordenar; encomendar; *n* ordem *f;* comando *m;* encomenda *f;* in ~ em ordem; in ~ to para; made to ~ feito por encomenda; out of ~ avariado; postal ~ vale postal
order-form (óó-dä-fóómm) *n* nota de encomenda
ordinary (óó-dänn-ri) *adj* usual, vulgar
ore (óó) *n* minério *m*
organ (óó-ghänn) *n* orgão *m*
organic (óó-*ghæ*-nik) *adj* orgânico
organization (óó-ghä-nai-*zei*-chänn) *n* organização *f*
organize (óó-ghä-naiz) *v* organizar
Orient (óó-ri-ännt) *n* oriente *m*
oriental (óó-ri-*énn*-tãl) *adj* oriental
orientate (óó-ri-änn-teit) *v* orientar-se
origin (ó-ri-djinn) *n* origem *f;* ascendência *f,* proveniência *f*
original (ä-*ri*-dji-nãl) *adj* autêntico, original
originally (ä-*ri*-dji-nä-li) *adv* originalmente
ornament (óó-nä-männt) *n* ornamento *m*
ornamental (óó-nä-*ménn*-tãl) *adj* ornamental
orphan (óó-fänn) *n* órfão *m*
orthodox (óó-θä-dókç) *adj* ortodoxo
ostrich (ó-çtritch) *n* avestruz *f*
other (a-ðä) *adj* outro
otherwise (a-ðä-ᵘaiz) *conj* senão; *adv* doutro modo
*ought to (óót) dever
our (auᵃ) *adj* nosso

ourselves (auᵃ-*çélvz*) *pron* nos; nós próprios
out (aut) *adv* fora; ~ of fora de, de
outbreak (aut-breik) *n* explosão *f*
outcome (aut-kamm) *n* resultado *m*
*outdo (aut-*duu*) *v* superar
outdoors (aut-*dóóz*) *adv* ao ar livre
outfit (aut-fit) *n* equipamento *m*
outline (aut-lainn) *n* contorno *m; v* esboçar
outlook (aut-luk) *n* previsão *f;* ponto de vista
output (aut-put) *n* produção *f*
outrage (aut-reidj) *n* ultraje *m*
outside (aut-çaid) *adv* de fora; *prep* fora de; *n* exterior *m*
outsize (aut-çaiz) *n* tamanho extra-grande
outskirts (aut-çkäätç) *pl* arredores *mpl*
outstanding (aut-*çtænn*-dinng) *adj* eminente
outward (aut-ᵘäd) *adj* externo
outwards (aut-ᵘädz) *adv* para fora
oval (oᵘ-vãl) *adj* oval
oven (a-vänn) *n* forno *m;* microwave ~ forno de microonda
over (oᵘ-vä) *prep* sobre, por cima de; mais de; *adv* por cima; abaixo; *adj* acabado; ~ there ali
overall (oᵘ-vä-róól) *adj* global
overalls (oᵘ-vä-róólz) *pl* fato-macaco *m;* macacão *mBr*
overcast (oᵘ-vä-kaaçt) *adj* nublado
overcoat (oᵘ-vä-koᵘt) *n* sobretudo *m*
*overcome (oᵘ-vä-kamm) *v* vencer
overdue (oᵘ-vä-d'uu) *adj* atrasado
overgrown (oᵘ-vä-ghroᵘnn) *adj* coberto de vegetação
overhaul (oᵘ-vä-hóól) *v* *rever
overhead (oᵘ-vä-héd) *adv* em cima
overlook (oᵘ-vä-luk) *v* deixar passar
overnight (oᵘ-vä-nait) *adv* durante a noite

overseas (oᵘ-vă-çiiz) *adj* ultramarino
oversight (oᵘ-vă-çait) *n* inadvertência *f*
*oversleep (oᵘ-vă-çliip) *v* *dormir demais
overstrung (oᵘ-vă-çtranng) *adj* sobreexcitado
*overtake (oᵘ-vă-teik) *v* ultrapassar; no overtaking ultrapassagem proibida
over-tired (oᵘ-vă-taiᵃd) *adj* exausto
overture (oᵘ-vă-tchă) *n* abertura *f*
overweight (oᵘ-vă-ᵘeit) *n* excesso de peso
overwhelm (oᵘ-vă-ᵘélm) *v* *submergir, desconcertar
overwork (oᵘ-vă-ᵘăăk) *v* trabalhar demais
owe (oᵘ) *v* dever; owing to devido a
owl (aul) *n* mocho *m*
own (oᵘnn) *v* *possuir; *adj* próprio
owner (oᵘ-nă) *n* proprietário *m*
ox (ókç) *n* (pl oxen) boi *m*
oxygen (ók-çi-djănn) *n* oxigénio *m*
oyster (oi-çtă) *n* ostra *f*

# P

pace (peiç) *n* andar *m*; passo *m*; ritmo *m*
Pacific Ocean (pă-çi-fik oᵘ-chănn) Oceano Pacífico
pacifism (pæ-çi-fi-zămm) *n* pacifismo *m*
pacifist (pæ-çi-fiçt) *n* pacifista *m*
pack (pæk) *v* embalar; ~ up embalar
package (pæ-kidj) *n* volume *m*
packet (pæ-kit) *n* pacote *m*
packing (pæ-kinng) *n* embalagem *f*
pad (pæd) *n* almofadinha *f*; bloco de notas

paddle (pæ-dăl) *n* remo *m*
padlock (pæd-lók) *n* cadeado *m*
pagan (pei-ghănn) *adj* pagão; *n* pagão *m*
page (peidj) *n* página *f*
page-boy (peidj-boi) *n* paquete *m*; moço de hotel *Br*
pail (peil) *n* balde *m*
pain (peinn) *n* dor *f*; pains dificuldade *f*
painful (peinn-făl) *adj* doloroso
painless (peinn-lăç) *adj* sem dor
paint (peinnt) *n* tinta *f*; *v* pintar
paint-box (peinnt-bókç) *n* caixa de tintas
paint-brush (peinnt-brach) *n* pincel *m*
painter (peinn-tă) *n* pintor *m*
painting (peinn-tinng) *n* pintura *f*
pair (péᵃ) *n* par *m*
Pakistan (paa-ki-çtaann) Paquistão *m*
Pakistani (paa-ki-çtaa-ni) *adj* paquistanês
palace (pæ-lăç) *n* palácio *m*
pale (peil) *adj* pálido
palm (paamm) *n* palmeira *f*; palma da mão
palpable (pæl-pă-băl) *adj* palpável
palpitation (pæl-pi-tei-chănn) *n* palpitação *f*
pan (pænn) *n* panela *f*
pane (peinn) *n* vidro *m*
panel (pæ-năl) *n* painel *m*
panelling (pæ-nă-linng) *n* lambril *m*
panic (pæ-nik) *n* pânico *m*
pant (pænnt) *v* arquejar
panties (pænn-tiz) *pl* calcinhas *fpl*
pants (pænntç) *pl* cuecas *fpl*; *plAm* calças *fpl*
pant-suit (pænnt-çuut) *n* fato calça e casaco
panty-hose (pænn-ti-hoᵘz) *n* meia-calça *f*
paper (pei-pă) *n* papel *m*; jornal *m*; de papel; carbon ~ papel químico;

papel carbono *Br;* ~ **bag** saco de papel; ~ **napkin** guardanapo de papel; **typing** ~ papel de máquina; **wrapping** ~ papel de embrulho

**paperback** (*pei*-pă-bæk) *n* livro de bolso

**paper-knife** (*pei*-pă-naif) *n* corta-papel *m*

**parade** (pă-*reid*) *n* parada *f*, desfile *m*

**paraffin** (*pæ*-ră-finn) *n* petróleo *m*

**paragraph** (*pæ*-ră-ghraaf) *n* parágrafo *m*, alínea *f*

**parakeet** (*pæ*-ră-kiit) *n* periquito *m*

**parallel** (*pæ*-ră-lél) *adj* paralelo; *n* paralelo *m*

**paralyse** (*pæ*-ră-laiz) *v* paralisar

**parcel** (*paa*-căl) *n* embrulho *m*, encomenda *f*

**pardon** (*paa*-dănn) *n* perdão *m*; indulto *m*

**parents** (*péᵃ*-rănntç) *pl* pais *mpl*

**parents-in-law** (*péᵃ*-rănntç-inn-lóó) *pl* sogros *mpl*

**parish** (*pæ*-rich) *n* paróquia *f*

**park** (paak) *n* parque *m*; *v* estacionar

**parking** (*paa*-kinng) *n* estacionamento *m*; **no** ~ estacionamento proibido; ~ **fee** tarifa de estacionamento; ~ **light** luz de estacionamento; ~ **lot** *Am* parque de estacionamento; ~ **meter** parcómetro *m*; ~ **zone** zona de estacionamento

**parliament** (*paa*-lă-mănnt) *n* parlamento *m*

**parliamentary** (paa-lă-*ménn*-tă-ri) *adj* parlamentar

**parrot** (*pæ*-răt) *n* papagaio *m*

**parsley** (*paa*-çli) *n* salsa *f*

**parson** (*paa*-çănn) *n* vigário *m*, pároco *m*

**parsonage** (*paa*-çă-nidj) *n* presbitério *m*

**part** (paat) *n* parte *f*; bocado *m*; *v* separar; **spare** ~ peça sobresselente

**partial** (*paa*-chăl) *adj* parcial

**participant** (paa-*ti*-çi-pănnt) *n* participante *m*

**participate** (paa-*ti*-çi-peit) *v* participar

**particular** (pă-*ti*-kʲu-lă) *adj* especial; exigente; **in** ~ em particular

**parting** (*paa*-tinng) *n* despedida *f*; risca *f*

**partition** (paa-*ti*-chănn) *n* tabique *m*

**partly** (*paat*-li) *adv* parcialmente, em parte

**partner** (*paat*-nă) *n* parceiro *m*; sócio *m*

**partridge** (*paa*-tridj) *n* perdiz *f*

**party** (*paa*-ti) *n* partido *m*; festa *f*; grupo *m*

**pass** (paaç) *v* passar, ultrapassar; ~ **by** passar por; ~ **through** atravessar

**passage** (*pæ*-çidj) *n* passagem *f*; travessia *f*; trecho *m*; viagem *f*

**passenger** (*pæ*-çănn-djă) *n* passageiro *m*; ~ **train** comboio de passageiros

**passer-by** (paa-çă-*bai*) *n* transeunte *m*

**passion** (*pæ*-chănn) *n* paixão *f*; fúria *f*

**passionate** (*pæ*-chă-năt) *adj* apaixonado

**passive** (*pæ*-çiv) *adj* passivo

**passport** (*paaç*-póót) *n* passaporte *m*; ~ **control** inspecção de passaportes; ~ **photograph** fotografia de passe

**password** (*paaç*-ᵘăăd) *n* santo-e-senha *m*

**past** (paaçt) *n* passado *m*; *adj* passado; *prep* por, além de

**paste** (peiçt) *n* pasta *f*; *v* colar

**pastry** (*pei*-çtri) *n* pastelaria *f*; ~ **shop** pastelaria *f*

**pasture** (*paaç*-tchă) *n* pastagem *f*

**patch** (pætch) *v* remendar; *n* remendo *m*

**patent** (*pei*-tănnt) *n* patente *f*, alvará

*m*

**path** (paaθ) *n* carreiro *m*

**patience** (*pei*-chǎnnç) *n* paciência *f*

**patient** (*pei*-chǎnnt) *adj* paciente; *n* doente *m*

**patriot** (*pei*-tri-ǎt) *n* patriota *m*

**patrol** (pǎ-*tro*ul) *n* patrulha *f*; *v* patrulhar; vigiar

**pattern** (*pæ*-tǎnn) *n* desenho *m*, padrão *m*

**pause** (póóz) *n* intervalo *m*; *v* \*fazer uma pausa

**pave** (peiv) *v* pavimentar

**pavement** (*peiv*-mǎnnt) *n* passeio *m*; pavimento *m*

**pavilion** (pǎ-*vil*-iǎnn) *n* pavilhão *m*

**paw** (póó) *n* pata *f*

**pawn** (póónn) *v* empenhar; *n* peão *m*

**pawnbroker** (*póónn*-brou-kǎ) *n* penhorista *m*

**pay** (pei) *n* ordenado *m*, salário *m*

**\*pay** (pei) *v* pagar; compensar; ~ **attention to** prestar atenção a; **paying** rentável; ~ **off** liquidar; ~ **on account** pagar a prestações

**pay-desk** (*pei*-déçk) *n* caixa *f*

**payee** (pei-*ii*) *n* beneficiário *m*

**payment** (*pei*-mǎnnt) *n* pagamento *m*

**pea** (pii) *n* ervilha *f*

**peace** (piiç) *n* paz *f*

**peaceful** (*piiç*-fǎl) *adj* tranquilo

**peach** (piitch) *n* pêssego *m*

**peacock** (*pii*-kók) *n* pavão *m*

**peak** (piik) *n* cume *m*; apogeu *m*; ~ **hour** hora de ponta; ~ **season** plena estação

**peanut** (*pii*-nat) *n* amendoim *m*

**pear** (péǎ) *n* pêra *f*

**pearl** (pǎǎl) *n* pérola *f*

**peasant** (*pé*-zǎnnt) *n* camponês *m*

**pebble** (*pé*-bǎl) *n* seixo *m*

**peculiar** (pi-*ki*uul-iǎ) *adj* estranho; especial, peculiar

**peculiarity** (pi-kiuu-li-æ-rǎ-ti) *n* particularidade *f*

**pedal** (*pé*-dǎl) *n* pedal *m*

**pedestrian** (pi-*dé*-çtri-ǎnn) *n* peão *m*; pedestre *mBr*; **no pedestrians** interdito a peões; ~ **crossing** passagem de peões; passagem de pedestres *Br*

**pedicure** (*pé*-di-kiuǎ) *n* pedicuro *m*

**peel** (piil) *v* descascar; *n* casca *f*

**peep** (piip) *v* espreitar

**peg** (pégh) *n* gancho *m*

**pelican** (*pé*-li-kǎnn) *n* pelicano *m*

**pelvis** (*pél*-viç) *n* pélvis *f*

**pen** (pénn) *n* caneta *f*

**penalty** (*pé*-nǎl-ti) *n* penalidade *f*; castigo *m*; ~ **kick** grande penalidade

**pencil** (*pénn*-çǎl) *n* lápis *m*

**pencil-sharpener** (*pénn*-çǎl-chaap-nǎ) *n* apara-lápis *m*; apontador *mBr*

**pendant** (*pénn*-dǎnnt) *n* pingente *m*

**penetrate** (*pé*-ni-treit) *v* penetrar

**penguin** (*pénng*-ghuinn) *n* pinguim *m*

**penicillin** (pé-ni-çi-linn) *n* penicilina *f*

**peninsula** (pǎ-*ninn*-çiu-lǎ) *n* península *f*

**penknife** (*pénn*-naif) *n* (pl -knives) canivete *m*

**pension**¹ (pǎ-çi-ón) *n* pensão *f*

**pension**² (*pénn*-chǎnn) *n* pensão *f*

**people** (*pii*-pǎl) *pl* pessoas, gente *f*; gente *f*, povo *m*

**pepper** (*pé*-pǎ) *n* pimenta *f*

**peppermint** (*pé*-pǎ-minnt) *n* hortelã-pimenta *f*

**perceive** (pǎ-*çiiv*) *v* aperceber

**percent** (pǎ-*çénnt*) *n* porcento *m*

**percentage** (pǎ-*çénn*-tidj) *n* percentagem *f*

**perceptible** (pǎ-*çép*-ti-bǎl) *adj* perceptível

**perception** (pǎ-*çép*-chǎnn) *n* percepção *f*

**perch** (pǎǎtch) (pl ~) perca *f*

**percolator** (pää-kă-lei-tă) *n* cafeteira de filtro

**perfect** (*pää*-fikt) *adj* perfeito

**perfection** (pă-*fék*-chănn) *n* perfeição *f*

**perform** (pă-*fóómm*) *v* desempenhar, executar, cumprir

**performance** (pă-*fóó*-mănnç) *n* representação *f*

**perfume** (*pää*-f¹uumm) *n* perfume *m*

**perhaps** (pă-*hæpç*) *adv* talvez; quiçá

**peril** (*pé*-ril) *n* perigo *m*

**perilous** (*pé*-ri-lăç) *adj* perigoso

**period** (*pi*ă-ri-ăd) *n* período *m*, época *f*; ponto *m*

**periodical** (pi*ă*-ri-ó-di-kăl) *n* periódico *m*; *adj* periódico

**perish** (*pé*-rich) *v* perecer

**perishable** (*pé* ri-chă-băl) *adj* deteriorável

**perjury** (*pää*-djă-ri) *n* perjúrio *m*

**permanent** (*pää*-mă-nănnt) *adj* duradouro, permanente; estável, fixo; ~ **press** engomado permanente; ~ **wave** permanente *f*

**permission** (pă-*mi*-chănn) *n* autorização *f*; licença *f*

**permit¹** (pă-*mit*) *v* permitir

**permit²** (*pää*-mit) *n* autorização *f*, licença *f*

**peroxide** (pă-*rók*-çaid) *n* água oxigenada

**perpendicular** (păă-pănn-*di*-k¹u-lă) *adj* perpendicular

**Persia** (*pää*-chă) Pérsia *f*

**Persian** (*pää*-chănn) *adj* persa

**person** (*pää*-çănn) *n* pessoa *f*; **per** ~ por pessoa

**personal** (*pää*-çă-năl) *adj* pessoal

**personality** (pää-çă-*næ*-lă-ti) *n* personalidade *f*

**personnel** (pää-çă-*nél*) *n* pessoal *m*

**perspective** (pă-*çpék*-tiv) *n* perspectiva *f*

**perspiration** (pää-çpă-*rei*-chănn) *n* suor *m*, transpiração *f*, perspiração *f*

**perspire** (pă-*çpai*ă) *v* transpirar, suar

**persuade** (pă-*ç*ᵘ*eid*) *v* persuadir, convencer

**persuasion** (pă-ç*ᵘei*-jănn) *n* convicção *f*

**pessimism** (*pé*-çi-mi-zămm) *n* pessimismo *m*

**pessimistic** (pé-çi-*mi*-çtik) *adj* pessimista

**pet** (pét) *n* animal de estimação; riqueza *f*; favorito

**petal** (*pé*-tăl) *n* pétala *f*

**petition** (pi-*ti*-chănn) *n* petição *f*

**petrol** (*pé*-trăl) *n* gasolina *f*; ~ **pump** bomba de gasolina; ~ **station** posto de gasolina; ~ **tank** depósito da gasolina; **unleaded** ~ gasolina sem chumbo

**petroleum** (pi-*tro*ᵘ-li-ămm) *n* petróleo *m*

**petty** (*pé*-ti) *adj* insignificante, fútil, pequeno; ~ **cash** fundo de maneio

**pewter** (*p*ⁱ*uu*-tă) *n* peltre *m*

**phantom** (*fænn*-tămm) *n* fantasma *m*

**pharmacology** (faa-mă-*kó*-lă-dji) *n* farmacologia *f*

**pharmacy** (*faa*-mă-çi) *n* farmácia *f*; drogaria *f*

**phase** (feiz) *n* fase *f*

**pheasant** (*fé*-zănnt) *n* faisão *m*

**Philippine** (*fi*-li-painn) *adj* filipino

**Philippines** (*fi*-li-piinnz) *pl* Filipinas *fpl*

**philosopher** (fi-*ló*-çă-fă) *n* filósofo *m*

**philosophy** (fi-*ló*-çă-fi) *n* filosofia *f*

**phone** (fouⁿn) *n* telefone *m*; *v* telefonar

**phonetic** (fă-*né*-tik) *adj* fonético

**photo** (*fo*ᵘ-toᵘ) *n* (pl ~s) fotografia *f*

**photocopy** (*fo*ᵘ-tă-kó-pi) *n* fotocópia *f*

**photograph** (*fo*ᵘ-tă-ghraaf) *n* fotografia f; v fotografar

**photographer** (fă-*tó*-ghră-fă) n fotógrafo m

**photography** (fă-*tó*-ghră-fi) n fotografia f

**phrase** (freiz) n frase f

**phrase-book** (*freiz*-buk) n guia linguístico

**physical** (*fi*-zi-kăl) adj físico

**physician** (fi-*zi*-chănn) n médico m

**physicist** (*fi*-zi-çiçt) n físico m

**physics** (*fi*-zikç) n ciências naturais, física f

**physiology** (fi-zi-*ó*-lă-dji) n fisiologia f

**pianist** (*pii*-ă-niçt) n pianista m

**piano** (pi-*æ*-no<sup>u</sup>) n piano m; **grand ~** piano de cauda

**pick** (pik) v colher; escolher; n escolha f; **~ up** apanhar; *ir buscar; **pick-up van** furgoneta f

**pick-axe** (*pi*-kækç) n picareta f

**pickles** (*pi*-kălz) pl pickles mpl, conservas em vinagre

**picnic** (*pik*-nik) n piquenique m; v piquenicar

**picture** (*pik*-tchă) n quadro m; gravura f, ilustração f; imagem f; **~ postcard** postal ilustrado; **pictures** cinema m

**picturesque** (pik-tchă-*réçk*) adj pitoresco

**piece** (piiç) n fragmento m, peça f

**pier** (pi<sup>ă</sup>) n molhe m

**pierce** (pi<sup>ă</sup>ç) v perfurar

**pig** (pigh) n porco m

**pigeon** (*pi*-djănn) n pombo m

**pig-headed** (pigh-*hé*-did) adj teimoso

**piglet** (*pigh*-lăt) n leitão m

**pigskin** (*pigh*-çkinn) n pele de porco

**pike** (paik) n (pl ~) lúcio m

**pile** (pail) n pilha f; v empilhar, amontoar; **piles** hemorróidas fpl

**pilgrim** (*pil*-ghrimm) n peregrino m

**pilgrimage** (*pil*-ghri-midj) n peregrinação f

**pill** (pil) n pílula f

**pillar** (*pi*-lă) n coluna f, pilar m

**pillar-box** (*pi*-lă-bókç) n caixa do correio

**pillow** (*pi*-lo<sup>u</sup>) n almofada f, almofadão m

**pillow-case** (*pi*-lo<sup>u</sup>-keiç) n fronha f

**pilot** (*pai*-lăt) n piloto m

**pimple** (*pimm*-păl) n borbulha f

**pin** (pinn) n alfinete m; v prender com alfinetes; **bobby ~** Am gancho de cabelo

**pincers** (*pinn*-căz) pl tenaz f

**pinch** (pinntch) v beliscar

**pineapple** (*pai*-næ-păl) n ananás m; abacaxi mBr

**pink** (pinngk) adj cor-de-rosa

**pioneer** (pai-ă-*ni*<sup>ă</sup>) n pioneiro m

**pious** (*pai*-ăç) adj pio

**pip** (pip) n caroço m

**pipe** (paip) n cachimbo m; cano m; **~ cleaner** limpa-cachimbos m; **~ tobacco** tabaco para cachimbo

**pirate** (*pai*<sup>ă</sup>-răt) n pirata m

**pistol** (*pi*-çtăl) n pistola f

**piston** (*pi*-çtănn) n pistão m; **~ ring** segmento do pistão

**piston-rod** (*pi*-çtănn-ród) n biela f

**pit** (pit) n cova f; mina f

**pitcher** (*pi*-tchă) n bilha f

**pity** (*pi*-ti) n piedade f; v *condoer-se de, *ter pena de; **what a pity!** que pena!

**placard** (*plæ*-kaad) n cartaz m

**place** (pleiç) n lugar m; v colocar, pousar; **~ of birth** lugar de nascimento; *take **~** *ter lugar, acontecer

**plague** (pleigh) n praga f

**plaice** (pleiç) (pl ~) solha f

**plain** (pleinn) adj claro; comum, simples; n planície f

plan (plænn) n plano m; v *planear

plane (pleinn) adj plano; n avião m; ~ crash desastre de aviação

planet (plæ-nit) n planeta m

planetarium (plæ-ni-té-ri-ămm) n planetário m

plank (plænngk) n prancha f

plant (plaannt) n planta f; fábrica f; v plantar

plantation (plænn-tei-chänn) n plantação f

plaster (plaa-çtă) n estuque m, gesso m; penso rápido; esparadrapo mBr

plastic (plæ-çtik) adj de plástico; n plástico m

plate (pleit) n prato m; chapa f

plateau (plæ-to-u) n (pl ~x, ~s) planalto m

platform (plæt-fóómm) n plataforma f; ~ ticket bilhete de gare

platinum (plæ-ti-nämm) n platina f

play (plei) v jogar; tocar; n jogo m; peça de teatro; one-act ~ peça num acto; ~ truant *fazer gazeta

player (plei-ă) n jogador m

playground (plei-ghraunnd) n recreio m

playing-card (plei-inng-kaad) n carta de jogar

playwright (plei-rait) n dramaturgo m

plea (plii) n defesa f

plead (pliid) v advogar

pleasant (plé-zännt) adj simpático, agradável

please (pliiz) se faz favor; v agradar; pleased satisfeito; pleasing agradável

pleasure (plé-jă) n prazer m, divertimento m

plentiful (plénn-ti-făl) adj abundante

plenty (plénn-ti) n abundância f; fartura f

pliers (plai-ăz) pl alicate m

plimsolls (plimm-çălz) pl sapatos de ginástica

plot (plót) n conspiração f, conjura f; enredo m; parcela f

plough (plau) n arado m; v lavrar

plucky (pla-ki) adj valente

plug (plagh) n ficha f; ~ in ligar

plum (plamm) n ameixa f

plumber (pla-mă) n canalizador m

plump (plammp) adj roliço

plural (plu-răl) n plural m

plus (plaç) prep mais

pneumatic (n'uu-mæ-tik) adj pneumático

pneumonia (n'uu-mo-u-ni-ă) n pneumonia f

poach (po-utch) v caçar furtivamente

pocket (pó-kit) n bolso m

pocket-book (pó-kit-buk) n carteira f

pocket-comb (pó-kit-ko-umm) n pente de bolso

pocket-knife (pó-kit-naif) n (pl -knives) canivete m

pocket-watch (pó-kit-uótch) n relógio de bolso

poem (po-u-imm) n poema m

poet (po-u-it) n poeta m

poetry (po-u-i-tri) n poesia f

point (poinnt) n ponto m; bico m; v apontar; ~ of view ponto de vista; ~ out indicar, apontar

pointed (poinn-tid) adj pontiagudo

poison (poi-zănn) n veneno m; v envenenar

poisonous (poi-ză-năç) adj venenoso

Poland (po-u-lännd) Polónia f

Pole (po-ul) n polaco m

pole (po-ul) n poste m

police (pă-liiç) pl polícia f

policeman (pă-liiç-männ) n (pl -men) polícia m, guarda m

police-station (pă-liiç-çtei-chänn) n posto da polícia; delegacia de polícia Br

policy (pó-li-çi) n política f; apólice f

**polio** (*po*ᵘ-li-o*ᵘ*) *n* pólio *f*, paralisia infantil

**Polish** (*po*ᵘ-lich) *adj* polaco

**polish** (*pó*-lich) *v* *polir

**polite** (pă-*lait*) *adj* educado

**political** (pă-*li*-ti-kăl) *adj* político

**politician** (pó-li-*ti*-chănn) *n* político *m*

**politics** (*pó*-li-tikç) *n* política *f*

**pollution** (pă-*luu*-chănn) *n* poluição *f*

**pond** (pónnd) *n* tanque *m*

**pony** (*po*ᵘ-ni) *n* pónei *m*

**poor** (puᵃ) *adj* pobre; fraco

**pope** (poᵘp) *n* papa *m*

**poplin** (*pó*-plinn) *n* popelina *f*

**pop music** (póp *m*ʲ*uu*-zik) música pop

**poppy** (*pó*-pi) *n* papoila *f*; papoula *f*

**popular** (*pó*-pʲu-lă) *adj* popular

**population** (pó-pʲu-*lei*-chănn) *n* população *f*

**populous** (*pó*-pʲu-lăç) *adj* populoso

**porcelain** (*póó*-çă-linn) *n* porcelana *f*

**porcupine** (*póó*-kʲu-painn) *n* porco-espinho *m*

**pork** (póók) *n* carne de porco

**port** (póót) *n* porto *m*; bombordo *m*

**portable** (*póó*-tă-băl) *adj* portátil

**porter** (*póó*-tă) *n* carregador *m*; porteiro *m*

**porthole** (*póót*-hoᵘl) *n* vigia *f*

**portion** (*póó*-chănn) *n* porção *f*

**portrait** (*póó*-trit) *n* retrato *m*

**Portugal** (*póó*-tʲu-ghăl) Portugal *m*

**Portuguese** (póó-tʲu-*ghiiz*) *adj* português

**position** (pă-*zi*-chănn) *n* posição *f*; atitude *f*; situação *f*

**positive** (*pó*-ză-tiv) *adj* positivo; *n* positivo *m*

**possess** (pă-*zéç*) *v* *possuir; possessed possesso

**possession** (pă-*zé*-chănn) *n* posse *f*; possessions bens *mpl*

**possibility** (pó-çă-*bi*-lă-ti) *n* possibilidade *f*

**possible** (*pó*-çă-băl) *adj* possível; eventual

**post** (poᵘçt) *n* poste *m*; posto *m*; correio *m*; *v* deitar no correio; **post-office** correios

**postage** (*po*ᵘ-çtidj) *n* franquia *f*; ~ **paid** porte pago; ~ **stamp** selo postal

**postcard** (*po*ᵘçt-kaad) *n* bilhete postal; postal ilustrado

**poster** (*po*ᵘ-çtă) *n* cartaz *m*

**poste restante** (poᵘçt ré-*çtãt*) posta-restante

**postman** (*po*ᵘçt-mănn) *n* (pl -men) carteiro *m*

**post-paid** (poᵘçt-*peid*) *adj* porte pago

**postpone** (pă-*çpo*ᵘnn) *v* adiar, *transferir

**pot** (pót) *n* vaso *m*

**potato** (pă-*tei*-toᵘ) *n* (pl ~es) batata *f*

**pottery** (*pó*-tă-ri) *n* cerâmica *f*; loiça *f*

**pouch** (pautch) *n* bolsa *f*

**poulterer** (*po*ᵘl-tă-ră) *n* vendedor de aves de criação

**poultry** (*po*ᵘl-tri) *n* aves de criação

**pound** (paunnd) *n* libra *f*

**pour** (póó) *v* deitar, verter

**poverty** (*pó*-vă-ti) *n* pobreza *f*

**powder** (pau-dă) *n* pó *m*; ~ **compact** caixa de pó-de-arroz; **talc** ~ pó de talco

**powder-puff** (pau-dă-paf) *n* borla de pó-de-arroz

**powder-room** (pau-dă-ruumm) *n* lavabos das senhoras

**power** (pauᵃ) *n* energia *f*, potência *f*; poder *m*

**powerful** (pauᵃ-făl) *adj* poderoso; forte

**powerless** (pauᵃ-lăç) *adj* impotente

**power-station** (pauᵃ-çtei-chănn) *n* central eléctrica

**practical** (*præk*-ti-kăl) *adj* prático

**practically** (præk-ti-kli) *adv* praticamente

**practice** (præk-tiç) *n* prática *f*

**practise** (præk-tiç) *v* praticar; exercitar-se

**praise** (preiz) *v* louvar; *n* elogio *m*

**pram** (præmm) *n* carrinho de bebé

**prawn** (próónn) *n* gamba *f*, camarão grande

**pray** (prei) *v* rezar

**prayer** (pré$^{å}$) *n* oração *f*

**preach** (priitch) *v* pregar

**precarious** (pri-ké$^{å}$-ri-áç) *adj* precário

**precaution** (pri-kóó-chänn) *n* precaução *f*

**precede** (pri-çiid) *v* preceder

**preceding** (pri-çii-dinng) *adj* precedente

**precious** (pré-chäç) *adj* precioso; caro

**precipice** (pré-çi-piç) *n* precipício *m*

**precipitation** (pri-çi-pi-tei-chänn) *n* precipitação *f*

**precise** (pri-çaiç) *adj* exacto, preciso; meticuloso

**predecessor** (prii-di-çé-çä) *n* predecessor *m*

**predict** (pri-dikt) *v* *predizer

**prefer** (pri-fää) *v* *preferir, *dar preferência a

**preferable** (pré-fä-rä-bäl) *adj* preferível

**preference** (pré-fä-rännç) *n* preferência *f*

**prefix** (prii-fikç) *n* prefixo *m*

**pregnant** (prégh-nännt) *adj* grávida

**prejudice** (pré-djä-diç) *n* preconceito *m*

**preliminary** (pri-li-mi-nä-ri) *adj* preliminar

**premature** (pré-mä-tchu$^{å}$) *adj* prematuro

**premier** (prémm-i$^{å}$) *n* primeiro-ministro *m*

**premises** (pré-mi-çiz) *pl* local *m*

**premium** (prii-mi-ämm) *n* prémio *m*

**prepaid** (prii-peid) *adj* pago adiantado

**preparation** (pré-pä-rei-chänn) *n* preparação *f*

**prepare** (pri-pé$^{å}$) *v* preparar

**preposition** (pré-pä-zi-chänn) *n* preposição *f*

**prescribe** (pri-çkraib) *v* prescrever, receitar

**prescription** (pri-çkrip-chänn) *n* receita *f*

**presence** (pré-zännç) *n* presença *f*

**present**[1] (pré-zännt) *n* presente *m; adj* actual, presente

**present**[2] (pri-zénnt) *v* apresentar; oferecer

**presently** (pré-zännt-li) *adv* a seguir, dentro em pouco

**preservation** (pré-zä-vei-chänn) *n* conservação *f*

**preserve** (pri-zääv) *v* conservar; *pôr em conserva

**president** (pré-zi-dännt) *n* presidente *m*

**press** (préç) *n* imprensa *f; v* carregar em, carregar, oprimir; passar a ferro; ~ **conference** conferência de imprensa

**pressing** (pré-çinng) *adj* urgente

**pressure** (pré-chä) *n* pressão *f;* tensão *f;* **atmospheric** ~ pressão atmosférica

**pressure-cooker** (pré-chä-ku-kä) *n* panela de pressão

**prestige** (pré-çtiij) *n* prestígio *m*

**presumable** (pri-z$^{i}$uu-mä-bäl) *adj* presumível

**presumptuous** (pri-zammp-chäç) *adj* presunçoso

**pretence** (pri-ténnç) *n* pretexto *m*

**pretend** (pri-ténnd) *v* fingir

**pretext** (prii-tékçt) *n* pretexto *m*

**pretty** (pri-ti) *adj* bonito; *adv* assaz, bastante, um tanto

**prevent** (pri-*vénnt*) v *impedir; evitar

**preventive** (pri-*vénn*-tiv) adj preventivo

**previous** (*prii*-vi-ăç) adj anterior, precedente, prévio

**pre-war** (prii-*ᵘóó*) adj do anteguerra

**price** (praiç) n preço m; v fixar o preço de

**priceless** (*praiç*-lăç) adj inestimável

**price-list** (*praiç*-liçt) n lista de preços

**prick** (prik) v picar

**pride** (praid) n orgulho m

**priest** (priiçt) n padre m

**primary** (*prai*-mă-ri) adj primário; primeiro, primordial; elementar

**prince** (prinnç) n príncipe m

**princess** (prinn-*çéç*) n princesa f

**principal** (*prinn*-çă-păl) adj principal; n reitor m, director m

**principle** (*prinn*-çă-păl) n princípio m

**print** (prinnt) v imprimir; n prova f; gravura f; **printed matter** impresso m

**prior** (praiᵃ) adj anterior

**priority** (prai-ó-ră-ti) n prioridade f

**prison** (*pri*-zănn) n prisão f

**prisoner** (*pri*-ză-nă) n prisioneiro m, detido m; ~ **of war** prisioneiro de guerra

**privacy** (*prai*-vă-çi) n intimidade f

**private** (*prai*-vit) adj privado, particular; pessoal

**privilege** (*pri*-vi-lidj) n privilégio m

**prize** (praiz) n prémio m; recompensa f

**probable** (*pró*-bă-băl) adj provável

**probably** (*pró*-bă-bli) adv provavelmente

**problem** (*pró*-blămm) n problema m

**procedure** (pră-*çii*-djă) n processo m

**proceed** (pră-*çiid*) v *prosseguir; proceder

**process** (*proᵘ*-çéç) n processo m, procedimento m

**procession** (pră-*çé*-chănn) n procissão f, cortejo m

**proclaim** (pră-*kleimm*) v proclamar

**produce**[1] (pră-*dᶦuuç*) v *produzir

**produce**[2] (*pród*-ᶦuuç) n produto m

**producer** (pră-*dᶦuu*-çă) n produtor m

**product** (*pró*-dakt) n produto m

**production** (pră-*dak*-chănn) n produção f

**profession** (pră-*fé*-chănn) n profissão f

**professional** (pră-*fé*-chă-năl) adj profissional

**professor** (pră-*fé*-çă) n professor m

**profit** (*pró*-fit) n benefício m, lucro m; vantagem f; v aproveitar-se

**profitable** (*pró*-fi-tă-băl) adj lucrativo

**profound** (pră-*faunnd*) adj profundo

**programme** (*proᵘ*-ghræmm) n programa m

**progress**[1] (*proᵘ*-ghréç) n progresso m

**progress**[2] (pră-*ghréç*) v progredir

**progressive** (pră-*ghré*-çiv) adj progressista; progressivo

**prohibit** (pră-*hi*-bit) v proibir

**prohibition** (proᵘ-i-*bi*-chănn) n interdição f

**prohibitive** (pră-*hi*-bi-tiv) adj proibitivo

**project** (*pró*-djékt) n plano m, projecto m

**promenade** (pró-mă-*naad*) n passeio m

**promise** (*pró*-miç) n promessa f; v prometer

**promote** (pră-*moᵘt*) v promover

**promotion** (pră-*moᵘ*-chănn) n promoção f

**prompt** (*prómmpt*) adj imediato, pronto

**pronoun** (*proᵘ*-naunn) n pronome m

**pronounce** (pră-*naunnç*) v pronunciar

**pronunciation** (pră-nann-çi-*ei*-chănn) n pronúncia f

**proof** (pruuf) *n* prova *f*

**propaganda** (pró-pă-*ghænn*-dă) *n* propaganda *f*

**propel** (pră-*pél*) *v* impulsionar, propulsionar

**propeller** (pră-*pé*-lă) *n* hélice *f*

**proper** (*pró*-pă) *adj* justo; apropriado, devido, indicado

**property** (*pró*-pă-ti) *n* propriedade *f*

**prophet** (*pró*-fit) *n* profeta *m*

**proportion** (pră-*póó*-chănn) *n* proporção *f*

**proportional** (pră-*póó*-chă-năl) *adj* proporcional

**proposal** (pră-*po*u-zăl) *n* proposta *f*

**propose** (pră-*po*uz) *v* *propor

**proposition** (pro-pă-*zi*-chănn) *n* proposta *f*

**proprietor** (pră-*prai*-ă-tă) *n* proprietário *m*

**prospect** (*pró*-cpékt) *n* perspectiva *f*

**prospectus** (pră-*cpék*-tăc) *n* prospecto *m*

**prosperity** (pró-*cpé*-ră-ti) *n* prosperidade *f*

**prosperous** (*pró*-cpă-răc) *adj* próspero

**prostitute** (*pró*-cti-ti'uut) *n* prostituta *f*

**protect** (pră-*tékt*) *v* proteger

**protection** (pră-*ték*-chănn) *n* protecção *f*

**protein** (*pro*u-tiinn) *n* proteína *f*

**protest**[1] (*pro*u-téct) *n* protesto *m*

**protest**[2] (pră-*téct*) *v* protestar

**Protestant** (*pró*-ti-ctănnt) *adj* protestante

**proud** (praud) *adj* vaidoso; orgulhoso

**prove** (pruuv) *v* provar, demonstrar; revelar-se

**proverb** (*pró*-văăb) *n* provérbio *m*

**provide** (pră-*vaid*) *v* fornecer; **provided that** contando que

**province** (*pró*-vinnç) *n* província *f*

**provincial** (pră-*vinn*-chăl) *adj* provincial

**provisional** (pră-*vi*-jă-năl) *adj* provisório

**provisions** (pră-*vi*-jănnz) *pl* provisões *fpl*

**prune** (pruunn) *n* ameixa passada

**psychiatrist** (çai-*kai*-ă-triçt) *n* psiquiatra *m*

**psychic** (*çai*-kik) *adj* psíquico

**psychoanalyst** (çai-ko u-æ-nă-liçt) *n* psicanalista *m*

**psychological** (çai-kó-*ló*-dji-kăl) *adj* psicológico

**psychologist** (çai-*kó*-lă-djiçt) *n* psicólogo *m*

**psychology** (çai-*kó*-lă-dji) *n* psicologia *f*

**pub** (pab) *n* taberna *f*; cervejaria *f*

**public** (*pa*-blik) *adj* público; geral; *n* público *m*; ~ **garden** jardim público; ~ **house** bar *m*

**publication** (pa-bli-*kei*-chănn) *n* publicação *f*

**publicity** (pa-*bli*-çă-ti) *n* publicidade *f*

**publish** (*pa*-blich) *v* publicar

**publisher** (*pa*-bli-chă) *n* editor *m*

**puddle** (*pa*-dăl) *n* charco *m*

**pull** (pul) *v* puxar; ~ **out** partir; ~ **up** parar

**pulley** (*pu*-li) *n* (pl ~s) roldana *f*

**Pullman** (*pul*-mănn) *n* carruagem-cama *f*

**pullover** (*pu*-lo u-vă) *n* pulóver *m*

**pulpit** (*pul*-pit) *n* púlpito *m*, tribuna *f*

**pulse** (palç) *n* pulso *m*

**pump** (pammp) *n* bomba *f*; *v* *dar à bomba; *bombear *vBr*

**punch** (panntch) *v* socar; *n* soco *m*

**punctual** (*panngk*-tchu-ăl) *adj* pontual

**puncture** (*panngk*-tchă) *n* furo *m*

**punctured** (*panngk*-tchăd) *adj* furado

**punish** (*pa*-nich) *v* castigar

**punishment** (*pa*-nich-mănnt) *n* castigo *m*

**pupil** (p'uu-păl) n aluno m

**puppet-show** (pa-pit-cho<sup>u</sup>) n teatro de fantoches

**purchase** (păă-tchăç) v comprar; n compra f; ~ **price** preço de compra; ~ **tax** imposto de consumo

**purchaser** (păă-tchă-çă) n comprador m

**pure** (p<sup>i</sup>u<sup>ă</sup>) adj puro

**purple** (păă-păl) adj purpúreo

**purpose** (păă-păç) n intento m, intenção f, propósito m; **on** ~ propositado

**purse** (păăç) n porta-moedas m

**pursue** (pă-ç'uu) v *prosseguir; pretender

**pus** (paç) n pus m

**push** (puch) n empurrão m; v empurrar

**push-button** (puch-ba-tănn) n botão m

***put** (put) v pousar, colocar, *pôr; meter; formular; ~ **away** guardar; ~ **off** adiar; ~ **on** *vestir; ~ **out** apagar

**puzzle** (pa-zăl) n puzzle m; enigma m; v embaraçar; **jigsaw** ~ quebra-cabeças m

**puzzling** (paz-linng) adj incompreensível

**pyjamas** (pă-djaa-măz) pl pijama m

# Q

**quack** (k<sup>u</sup>æk) n curandeiro m, charlatão m

**quail** (k<sup>u</sup>eil) n (pl ~, ~s) codorniz f

**quaint** (k<sup>u</sup>einnt) adj estranho; antiquado

**qualification** (k<sup>u</sup>ó-li-fi-kei-chănn) n habilitação f; restrição f, reserva f

**qualified** (k<sup>u</sup>ó-li-faid) adj qualificado; competente

**qualify** (k<sup>u</sup>ó-li-fai) v qualificar-se

**quality** (k<sup>u</sup>ó-lă-ti) n qualidade f; característica f

**quantity** (k<sup>u</sup>ónn-tă-ti) n quantidade f; número m

**quarantine** (k<sup>u</sup>ó-rănn-tiinn) n quarentena f

**quarrel** (k<sup>u</sup>ó-răl) v disputar, discutir; n briga f, litígio m

**quarry** (k<sup>u</sup>ó-ri) n pedreira f

**quarter** (k<sup>u</sup>ó-tă) n quarto m; trimestre m; bairro m; ~ **of an hour** quarto de hora

**quarterly** (k<sup>u</sup>óó-tă-li) adj trimestral

**quay** (kii) n cais m

**queen** (k<sup>u</sup>iinn) n rainha f

**queer** (k<sup>u</sup>i<sup>ă</sup>) adj estranho, esquisito

**query** (k<sup>u</sup>i<sup>ă</sup>-ri) n pergunta f; v indagar; *pôr em dúvida

**question** (k<sup>u</sup>éç-tchănn) n pergunta f; questão f, problema m; v interrogar; pôr em dúvida; ~ **mark** ponto de interrogação

**queue** (k<sup>u</sup>uu) n bicha f; v *fazer bicha

**quick** (k<sup>u</sup>ik) adj rápido

**quick-tempered** (k<sup>u</sup>ik-témm-păd) adj irascível

**quiet** (k<sup>u</sup>ai-ăt) adj calmo, tranquilo, sossegado; n silêncio m, tranquilidade f

**quilt** (k<sup>u</sup>ilt) n colcha f

**quinine** (k<sup>u</sup>i-niinn) n quinina f

**quit** (k<sup>u</sup>it) v cessar

**quite** (k<sup>u</sup>ait) adv completamente; bastante, relativamente; muito

**quiz** (k<sup>u</sup>iz) n (pl ~zes) concurso m

**quota** (k<sup>u</sup>o<sup>u</sup>-tă) n quota f

**quotation** (k<sup>u</sup>o<sup>u</sup>-tei-chănn) n citação f; ~ **marks** aspas fpl

**quote** (k<sup>u</sup>o<sup>u</sup>t) v citar

# R

**rabbit** (ræ-bit) n coelho m

**rabies** (rei-biz) n raiva f

**race** (reiç) n corrida f; raça f

**race-course** (reiç-kóóç) n pista de corridas, hipódromo m

**race-horse** (reiç-hóóç) n cavalo de corridas

**race-track** (reiç-træk) n pista de corridas

**racial** (rei-chäl) adj racial

**racket** (ræ-kit) n alarido m

**racquet** (ræ-kit) n raqueta f

**radiator** (rei-di-ei-tä) n radiador m

**radical** (ræ-di-käl) adj radical

**radio** (rei-di-o$^u$) n rádio m

**radish** (ræ-dich) n rabanete m

**radius** (rei-di-äç) n (pl radii) raio m

**raft** (raaft) n jangada f

**rag** (rægh) n trapo m

**rage** (reidj) n raiva f, furor m; v enfurecer

**raid** (reid) n incursão f

**rail** (reil) n barra f, balaustrada f

**railing** (rei-linng) n gradeamento m

**railroad** (reil-ro$^u$d) nAm caminho-de-ferro; via férrea; estrada de ferro Br

**railway** (reil-$^u$ei) n via férrea, caminho-de-ferro; estrada de ferro Br

**rain** (reinn) n chuva f; v chover

**rainbow** (reinn-bo$^u$) n arco-íris m

**raincoat** (reinn-ko$^u$t) n impermeável m; capa de chuva Br

**rainproof** (reinn-pruuf) adj impermeável

**rainy** (rei-ni) adj chuvoso

**raise** (reiz) v levantar; aumentar; criar, educar, cultivar; v tributar; nAm aumento de salário

**raisin** (rei-zänn) n passa f

**rake** (reik) n ancinho m

**rally** (ræ-li) n reunião f

**ramp** (ræmmp) n rampa f

**ramshackle** (ræmm-chæ-käl) adj desmantelado

**rancid** (rænn-çid) adj rançoso

**rang** (rænng) v (p ring)

**range** (reinndj) n alcance m

**range-finder** (reinndj-fainn-dä) n telémetro m

**rank** (rænngk) n patente f; fila f

**ransom** (rænn-çämm) n resgate m

**rape** (reip) v violar

**rapid** (ræ-pid) adj rápido, veloz

**rapids** (ræ-pidz) pl rápidos mpl

**rare** (ré$^ä$) adj raro

**rarely** (ré$^ä$-li) adv raramente

**rascal** (raa-çkäl) n patife m, malandro m

**rash** (ræch) n erupção f; adj irreflectido, precipitado

**raspberry** (raaz-bä-ri) n framboesa f

**rat** (ræt) n ratazana f

**rate** (reit) n preço m, tarifa f; velocidade f; at any ~ de qualquer modo, seja como for; ~ of exchange taxa do câmbio

**rather** (raa-ðä) adv bastante, um tanto; antes

**ration** (ræ-chänn) n ração f

**rattan** (ræ-tænn) n rotim m

**raven** (rei-vänn) n corvo m

**raw** (róó) adj cru; ~ material matéria-prima f

**ray** (rei) n raio m

**rayon** (rei-ónn) n seda artificial

**razor** (rei-zä) n aparelho para barbear; navalha f

**razor-blade** (rei-zä-bleid) n lâmina de barbear

**reach** (riitch) v alcançar; n alcance m

**reaction** (ri-æk-chänn) n reacção f

**\*read** (riid) v \*ler

**reading** (rii-dinng) n leitura f

**reading-lamp** (*rii*-dinng-læmmp) *n* candeeiro de mesa

**reading-room** (*rii*-dinng-ruumm) *n* sala de leitura

**ready** (ré-di) *adj* pronto, preparado

**ready-made** (ré-di-*meid*) *adj* de confecção

**real** (ri³l) *adj* verdadeiro

**reality** (ri-æ-lã-ti) *n* realidade *f*

**realizable** (*ri³*-lai-zã-bãl) *adj* realizável

**realize** (*ri³*-laiz) *v* perceber; realizar

**really** (*ri³*-li) *adv* verdadeiramente, realmente; na realidade

**rear** (ri³) *n* retaguarda *f*; *v* criar

**rear-light** (ri³-*lait*) *n* luz da retaguarda

**reason** (*rii*-zänn) *n* razão *f*, causa *f*; senso *m*; *v* raciocinar

**reasonable** (*rii*-zã-nã-bãl) *adj* razoável

**reassure** (rii-ã-*chu³*) *v* tranquilizar

**rebate** (*rii*-beit) *n* redução *f*, desconto *m*

**rebellion** (ri-*bél*-¹änn) *n* revolta *f*, rebelião *f*

**recall** (ri-*kóól*) *v* recordar-se; chamar; revogar

**receipt** (ri-*çiit*) *n* recibo *m*; recepção *f*

**receive** (ri-*çiiv*) *v* receber

**receiver** (ri-*çii*-vã) *n* auscultador *m*

**recent** (*rii*-çãnnt) *adj* recente

**recently** (*rii*-çãnnt-li) *adv* recentemente. há pouco tempo

**reception** (ri-*çép*-chänn) *n* recepção *f*; acolhimento *m*; ~ **office** recepção *f*

**receptionist** (ri-*çép*-chã-niçt) *n* recepcionista *f*

**recession** (ri-*çé*-chänn) *n* recessão *f*

**recipe** (ré-çi-pi) *n* receita *f*

**recital** (ri-*çai*-tãl) *n* recital *m*

**reckon** (*ré*-känn) *v* calcular; considerar; *crer

**recognition** (ré-kãgh-*ni*-chänn) *n* reconhecimento *m*

**recognize** (ré-kãgh-naiz) *v* reconhecer

**recollect** (ré-kã-*lékt*) *v* recordar-se

**recommence** (rii-kã-*ménnç*) *v* recomeçar

**recommend** (ré-kã-*ménnd*) *v* recomendar; aconselhar

**recommendation** (ré-kã-ménn-*dei*-chänn) *n* recomendação *f*

**reconciliation** (ré-kãnn-çi-li-ei-chänn) *n* reconciliação *f*

**record**¹ (ré-*kóód*) *n* disco *m*; recorde *m*; registo *m*; **long-playing** ~ disco de longa duração

**record**² (ri-*kóód*) *v* registar

**recorder** (ri-*kóó*-dã) *n* gravador *m*

**recording** (ri-*kóó*-dinng) *n* gravação *f*

**record-player** (ré-*kóód*-plei³) *n* gira-discos *m*; toca-discos *mBr*

**recover** (ri-ka-vã) *v* recuperar; curar-se, restabelecer-se

**recovery** (ri-*ka*-vã-ri) *n* cura *f*, restabelecimento *m*

**recreation** (ré-kri-*ei*-chänn) *n* recreação *f*; ~ **centre** centro recreativo; ~ **ground** campo de jogos

**recruit** (ri-*kruut*) *n* recruta *m*

**rectangle** (*rék*-tænng-ghãl) *n* rectângulo *m*

**rector** (*rék*-tã) *n* pastor *m*, reitor *m*

**rectory** (*rék*-tã-ri) *n* reitoria *f*

**rectum** (*rék*-tãmm) *n* recto *m*

**recycle** (ri-*çai*-kãl) *v* reciclar

**recyclable** (ri-*çai*-klã-bãl) *adj* reciclável

**red** (réd) *adj* encarnado

**redeem** (ri-*diimm*) *v* redimir

**reduce** (ri-d¹*uuç*) *v* *reduzir, *diminuir

**reduction** (ri-*dak*-chänn) *n* redução *f*, desconto *m*

**redundant** (ri-*dann*-dännt) *adj* supérfluo

**reed** (riid) *n* cana *f*

**reef** (riif) *n* recife *m*

**reference** (*réf*-rännç) *n* referência *f*;

relação f; **with ~ to** relativo a

**refer to** (ri-*fáá*) \**referir a

**refill** (*rii*-fil) n recarga f

**refinery** (ri-*fai*-nă-ri) n refinaria f

**reflect** (ri-*flékt*) v \**reflectir

**reflection** (ri-*flék*-chänn) n reflexão f; imagem reflectida

**reflector** (ri-*flék*-tă) n reflector m

**reformation** (ré-fă-*mei*-chänn) n Reforma f

**refresh** (ri-*fréch*) v refrescar

**refreshment** (ri-*fréch*-männt) n refresco m

**refrigerator** (ri-*fri*-djă-rei-tă) n frigorífico m

**refund**[1] (ri-*fannd*) v reembolsar

**refund**[2] (*rii*-fannd) n reembolso m

**refusal** (ri-*f'uu*-zăl) n recusa f

**refuse**[1] (ri-*f'uuz*) v recusar

**refuse**[2] (ré-*f'uuç*) n lixo m

**regard** (ri-*ghaad*) v considerar; n respeito m; **as regards** quanto a, respeitante a, no que diz respeito a

**regarding** (ri-*ghaa*-dinng) prep relativamente a, relativo a; com respeito a

**regatta** (ri-*ghæ*-tă) n regata f

**régime** (rei-*jiimm*) n regime m

**region** (*rii*-djänn) n região f

**regional** (*rii*-djă-năl) adj regional

**register** (ré-dji-çtă) v inscrever-se, registar-se; registar; **registered letter** carta registada

**registration** (ré-dji-*çtrei*-chänn) n registo m; **~ form** formulário de inscrição; **~ number** número de matrícula; **~ plate** chapa da matrícula

**regret** (ri-*ghrét*) v lamentar; n pena f

**regular** (ré-gh'u-lă) adj regular; normal, corrente

**regulate** (ré-gh'u-leit) v regular

**regulation** (ré-gh'u-*lei*-chänn) n regulamento m; regulamentação f

**rehabilitation** (rii-hă-bi-li-*tei*-chänn) n reabilitação f

**rehearsal** (ri-*hăă*-çăl) n ensaio m

**rehearse** (ri-*hăăç*) v ensaiar

**reign** (reinn) n reinado m; v reinar

**reimburse** (rii-imm-*băăç*) v reembolsar

**reindeer** (*reinn*-di[ă]) n (pl ~) rena f

**reject** (ri-*djékt*) v recusar, rejeitar; reprovar

**relate** (ri-*leit*) v contar, relatar

**related** (ri-*lei*-tid) adj aparentado

**relation** (ri-*lei*-chänn) n relação f; parente m

**relative** (ré-lă-tiv) n parente m; adj relativo

**relax** (ri-*lækç*) v \**descontrair-se

**relaxation** (ri-læk-*çei*-chänn) n descontracção f

**reliable** (ri-*lai*-ă-băl) adj de confiança

**relic** (ré-lik) n relíquia f

**relief** (ri-*liif*) n alívio m; assistência f; relevo m

**relieve** (ri-*liiv*) v aliviar; render

**religion** (ri-*li*-djänn) n religião f

**religious** (ri-*li*-djăç) adj religioso

**rely on** (ri-*lai*) contar com

**remain** (ri-*meinn*) v ficar; sobejar

**remainder** (ri-*meinn*-dă) n remanescente m, restante m, resto m

**remaining** (ri-*mei*-ninng) adj restante

**remark** (ri-*maak*) n observação f; v observar

**remarkable** (ri-*maa*-kă-băl) adj notável

**remedy** (ré-mă-di) n remédio m

**remember** (ri-*mémm*-bă) v recordar-se, lembrar-se

**remembrance** (ri-*mémm*-brännç) n lembrança f, recordação f

**remind** (ri-*mainnd*) v recordar, lembrar

**remit** (ri-*mit*) v remeter

**remittance** (ri-*mi*-tănnç) n remessa f

**remnant** (*rémm*-nǎnnt) *n* excedente *m*, remanescente *m*

**remote** (ri-*mo*ᵘt) *adj* distante, remoto

**removal** (ri-*muu*-vǎl) *n* remoção *f*

**remove** (ri-*muuv*) *v* remover

**remunerate** (ri-*m*ʲ*uu*-nǎ-reit) *v* remunerar

**remuneration** (ri-*m*ʲ*uu*-nǎ-*rei*-chǎnn) *n* remuneração *f*

**renew** (ri-*n*ʲ*uu*) *v* renovar, prolongar

**rent** (rénnt) *v* arrendar, alugar; *n* renda *f*

**repair** (ri-*pé*ᵃ) *v* reparar; *n* conserto *m*

**reparation** (ré-pǎ-*rei*-chǎnn) *n* reparação *f*

***repay** (ri-*pei*) *v* reembolsar

**repayment** (ri-*pei*-mǎnnt) *n* reembolso *m*

**repeat** (ri-*piit*) *v* *repetir

**repellent** (ri-*pé*-lǎnnt) *adj* repugnante, repelente

**repentance** (ri-*pénn*-tǎnnç) *n* arrependimento *m*

**repertory** (ré-pǎ-tǎ-ri) *n* repertório *m*

**repetition** (ré-pǎ-*ti*-chǎnn) *n* repetição *f*

**replace** (ri-*pleiç*) *v* *substituir

**reply** (ri-*plai*) *v* responder; *n* resposta *f*; in ~ em resposta

**report** (ri-*póót*) *v* relatar; participar; apresentar-se; *n* relatório *m*, relação *f*

**reporter** (ri-*póó*-tǎ) *n* repórter *m*

**represent** (ré-pri-*zénnt*) *v* representar

**representation** (ré-pri-zénn-*tei*-chǎnn) *n* representação *f*

**representative** (ré-pri-*zénn*-tǎ-tiv) *adj* representativo

**reprimand** (ré-pri-maannd) *v* repreender

**reproach** (ri-*pro*ᵘtch) *n* censura *f*; *v* censurar

**reproduce** (rii-prǎ-*d*ʲ*uuç*) *v* *reproduzir

**reproduction** (rii-prǎ-*dak*-chǎnn) *n* reprodução *f*

**reptile** (*rép*-tail) *n* réptil *m*

**republic** (ri-*pa*-blik) *n* república *f*

**republican** (ri-*pa*-bli-kǎnn) *adj* republicano

**repulsive** (ri-*pal*-çiv) *adj* repelente

**reputation** (ré-pʲu-*tei*-chǎnn) *n* reputação *f*; renome *m*

**request** (ri-*k*ᵘ*éçt*) *n* pedido *m*; *v* *requerer

**require** (ri-k*ᵘai*ᵃ) *v* exigir

**requirement** (ri-k*ᵘai*ᵃ-mǎnnt) *n* necessidade *f*

**requisite** (*ré*-kᵘi-zit) *adj* necessário

**rescue** (*ré*-çkʲuu) *v* salvar; *n* salvação *f*

**research** (ri-*çǎǎtch*) *n* investigação *f*

**resemblance** (ri-*zémm*-blǎnnç) *n* semelhança *f*

**resemble** (ri-*zémm*-bǎl) *v* assemelhar-se

**resent** (ri-*zénnt*) *v* levar a mal, melindrar-se por

**reservation** (ré-zǎ-*vei*-chǎnn) *n* reserva *f*

**reserve** (ri-*zǎǎv*) *v* reservar; *n* reserva *f*

**reserved** (ri-*zǎǎvd*) *adj* reservado

**reservoir** (*ré*-zǎ-vᵘaa) *n* reservatório *m*

**reside** (ri-*zaid*) *v* residir

**residence** (*ré*-zi-dǎnnç) *n* residência *f*; ~ **permit** autorização de residência

**resident** (*ré*-zi-dǎnnt) *n* residente *m*; *adj* residente; interno

**resign** (ri-*zainn*) *v* demitir-se

**resignation** (ré-zigh-*nei*-chǎnn) *n* demissão *f*

**resin** (*ré*-zinn) *n* resina *f*

**resist** (ri-*ziçt*) *v* resistir

**resistance** (ri-*zi*-çtǎnnç) *n* resistência

*f*

**resolute** (ré-ză-luut) *adj* decidido, resoluto

**respect** (ri-çpékt) *n* respeito *m*; veneração *f*, estima *f*; *v* respeitar

**respectable** (ri-çpék-tă-băl) *adj* respeitável

**respectful** (ri-çpékt-făl) *adj* respeitoso

**respective** (ri-çpék-tiv) *adj* respectivo

**respiration** (ré-çpă-rei-chănn) *n* respiração *f*

**respite** (ré-çpait) *n* protelação *f*

**responsibility** (ri-çpónn-çă-bi-lă-ti) *n* responsabilidade *f*

**responsible** (ri-çpónn-çă-băl) *adj* responsável

**rest** (réçt) *n* descanso *m*; resto *m*; *v* repousar, descansar

**restaurant** (ré-çtă-rón) *n* restaurante *m*

**restful** (réçt-făl) *adj* sossegado

**rest-home** (réçt-ho**u**mm) *n* casa de repouso

**restless** (réçt-lăç) *adj* inquieto

**restrain** (ri-çtreinn) *v* \*conter, \*reter

**restriction** (ri-çtrik-chănn) *n* restrição *f*

**result** (ri-zalt) *n* resultado *m*; consequência *f*; *v* resultar

**resume** (ri-z**i**uumm) *v* recomeçar

**résumé** (ré-z**i**u-mei) *n* resumo *m*

**retail** (rii-teil) *v* vender a retalho; ~ **trade** comércio a retalho

**retailer** (rii-tei-lă) *n* retalhista *m*; revendedor *m*

**retina** (ré-ti-nă) *n* retina *f*

**retired** (ri-tai**ă**d) *adj* reformado

**return** (ri-tăănn) *v* voltar; *n* regresso *m*; ~ **flight** voo de regresso; ~ **journey** viagem de regresso

**reunite** (rii-**i**uu-nait) *v* reunir

**reveal** (ri-viil) *v* revelar

**revelation** (ré-vă-lei-chănn) *n* revelação *f*

**revenge** (ri-vénndj) *n* vingança *f*

**revenue** (ré-vă-n**i**uu) *n* receita *f*, rendimento *m*

**reverse** (ri-vǎăç) *n* contrário *m*; reverso *m*; marcha atrás; revés *m*, reviravolta *f*; *adj* inverso; *v* \*fazer marcha atrás; \*fazer marcha à ré *Br*

**review** (ri-v**i**uu) *n* crítica *f*; revista *f*

**revise** (ri-vaiz) *v* \*rever

**revolt** (ri-vo**u**lt) *v* revoltar-se; *n* rebelião *f*, revolta *f*

**revolting** (ri-vo**u**l-tinng) *adj* chocante, nojento, revoltante

**revolution** (ré-vă-luu-chănn) *n* revolução *f*; rotação *f*

**revolutionary** (ré-vă-luu-chă-nă-ri) *adj* revolucionário

**revolver** (ri-vól-vă) *n* revólver *m*

**revue** (ri-v**i**uu) *n* revista *f*

**reward** (ri-**u**óód) *n* recompensa *f*; *v* recompensar

**rheumatism** (ruu-mă-ti-zămm) *n* reumatismo *m*

**rhinoceros** (rai-nó-çă-răç) *n* (pl ~, ~es) rinoceronte *m*

**rhubarb** (ruu-baab) *n* ruibarbo *m*

**rhyme** (raimm) *n* rima *f*

**rhythm** (ri-ðămm) *n* ritmo *m*

**rib** (rib) *n* costela *f*

**ribbon** (ri-bănn) *n* fita *f*

**rice** (raiç) *n* arroz *m*

**rich** (ritch) *adj* rico

**riches** (ri-tchiz) *pl* riqueza *f*

**riddle** (ri-dăl) *n* adivinha *f*

**ride** (raid) *n* passeio *m*, volta *f*

\***ride** (raid) *v* andar de automóvel; montar a cavalo

**rider** (rai-dă) *n* cavaleiro *m*

**ridge** (ridj) *n* cumeada *f*

**ridicule** (ri-di-k**i**uul) *v* troçar, ridicularizar

**ridiculous** (ri-di-k**i**u-lăç) *adj* ridículo

**riding** (rai-dinng) *n* equitação *f*

**riding-school** (*rai*-dinng-çkuul) *n* escola de equitação

**rifle** (*rai*-fål) *v* espingarda *f*

**right** (rait) *n* direito *m; adj* correcto; recto; direito; equitativo, justo; **all right!** de acordo!; * **be** ~ *ter razão; ~ **of way** prioridade *f*

**righteous** (*rai*-tchåç) *adj* justo

**right-hand** (*rait*-hænnd) *adj* à direita, direito

**rightly** (*rait*-li) *adv* justamente

**rim** (rimm) *n* jante *f*; borda *f*

**ring** (rinng) *n* anel *m*; círculo *m*; pista *f*

* **ring** (rinng) *v* tocar; ~ **up** telefonar

**rinse** (rinnç) *v* enxaguar; *n* enxaguadela *f*

**riot** (*rai*-ăt) *n* motim *m*, desordem *f*

**rip** (rip) *v* rasgar

**ripe** (raip) *adj* maduro

**rise** (raiz) *n* aumento *m*; elevação *f*; subida *f*; origem *f*

* **rise** (raiz) *v* erguer-se, levantar-se; *subir

**rising** (*rai*-zinng) *n* insurreição *f*

**risk** (riçk) *n* risco *m*; perigo *m; v* arriscar

**risky** (*ri*-çki) *adj* perigoso, arriscado

**rival** (*rai*-vål) *n* rival *m; v* rivalizar

**rivalry** (*rai*-vål-ri) *n* rivalidade *f*; concorrência *f*

**river** (*ri*-vă) *n* rio *m; ~ **bank** margem *f*

**riverside** (*ri*-vă-çaid) *n* beira-rio *f*

**roach** (ro*u*tch) *n* (pl ~) robalo *m*

**road** (ro*u*d) *n* estrada *f; ~ **fork** bifurcação *f; ~ **map** mapa de estradas; ~ **system** rede rodoviária; ~ **up** estrada em obras

**roadhouse** (*ro*u*d*-hauç) *n* estalagem *f*

**roadside** (*ro*u*d*-çaid) *n* berma *f*

**roam** (ro*u*mm) *v* *vagabundear

**roar** (róó) *v* rugir, bramir; *n* rugido *m*, rumor *m*

**roast** (ro*u*çt) *v* grelhar, assar

**rob** (rób) *v* roubar

**robber** (*ró*-bă) *n* ladrão *m*

**robbery** (*ró*-bă-ri) *n* roubo *m*

**robe** (ro*u*b) *n* vestido comprido; veste *f*

**robin** (*ró*-binn) *n* pintarroxo *m*

**robust** (ro*u*-*baçt*) *adj* robusto

**rock** (rók) *n* rocha *f; v* baloiçar

**rocket** (*ró*-kit) *n* foguete *m*

**rocky** (*ró*-ki) *adj* rochoso

**rod** (ród) *n* vara *f*, varão *m*

**roe** (ro*u*) *n* ova *f*

**roll** (ro*u*l) *v* rolar; *n* rolo *m*; pãozinho *m*

**roller-skating** (*ro*u*-lă-çkei-tinng) *n* patinagem *f*

**Roman Catholic** (*ro*u*-männ kæ-θă-lik) católico

**romance** (ră-*mænnç*) *n* romance *m*

**romantic** (ră-*mænn*-tik) *adj* romântico

**roof** (ruuf) *n* telhado *m*; **thatched** ~ telhado de colmo

**room** (ruumm) *n* quarto *m*; espaço *m*, lugar *m; ~ **and board** cama e mesa; ~ **service** serviço de quarto; ~ **temperature** temperatura ambiente

**roomy** (*ruu*-mi) *adj* espaçoso

**root** (ruut) *n* raiz *f*

**rope** (ro*u*p) *n* corda *f*

**rosary** (*ro*u*-ză-ri) *n* rosário *m*

**rose** (ro*u*z) *n* rosa *f; adj* rosado

**rotten** (*ró*-tănn) *adj* podre

**rouge** (ruuj) *n* rouge *m*

**rough** (raf) *adj* áspero; brusco

**roulette** (ruu-*lét*) *n* roleta *f*

**round** (raunnd) *adj* redondo; *prep* em torno de, à volta; *n* volta *f; ~ **trip** *Am* ida e volta

**roundabout** (*raunn*-dă-baut) *n* rotunda *f*

**rounded** (*raunn*-did) *adj* arredondado

**route** (ruut) *n* rota *f*

**routine** (ruu-*tiinn*) n rotina f
**row¹** (roᵘ) n fila f; v remar
**row²** (rau) n zaragata f
**rowdy** (*rau*-di) adj turbulento
**rowing-boat** (*roᵘ*-inng-boᵘt) n barco a remos
**royal** (*roi*-ăl) adj real
**rub** (rab) v esfregar
**rubber** (*ra*-bă) n borracha f; ~ **band** elástico m
**rubbish** (*ra*-bich) n lixo m; disparates, asneira f; bobagem fBr; **talk** ~ *dizer disparates
**rubbish-bin** (*ra*-bich-binn) n caixote do lixo; lata de lixo Br
**ruby** (*ruu*-bi) n rubi m
**rucksack** (*rak*-çæk) n mochila f
**rudder** (*ra*-dă) n leme m
**rude** (ruud) adj rude
**rug** (ragh) n tapete m
**ruin** (*ruu*-inn) v arruinar; n ruína f
**ruination** (ruu-i-*nei*-chănn) n ruína f
**rule** (ruul) n regra f; governo m, regime m, domínio m; v governar; **as a** ~ em regra, geralmente
**ruler** (*ruu*-lă) n governante m, monarca m; régua f
**Rumania** (ruu-*mei*-ni-ă) Roménia f
**Rumanian** (ruu-*mei*-ni-ănn) adj romeno
**rumour** (*ruu*-mă) n rumor m
*run (rann) v correr; ~ **into** deparar com
**runaway** (*ra*-nă-ᵁei) n fugitivo m
**rung** (rann) v (pp ring)
**runway** (*rann*-ᵁei) n pista de descolagem
**rural** (*ruᵃ*-răl) adj rural
**ruse** (ruuz) n ardil m
**rush** (rach) v apressar-se; n junco m
**rush-hour** (*rach*-auᵃ) n hora de ponta
**Russia** (*ra*-chă) Rússia f
**Russian** (*ra*-chănn) adj russo
**rust** (raçt) n ferrugem f

**rustic** (*ra*-çtik) adj rústico
**rusty** (*ra*-çti) adj ferrugento

# S

**saccharin** (*çæ*-kă-rinn) n sacarina f
**sack** (çæk) n saca f
**sacred** (*cei*-krid) adj sagrado
**sacrifice** (*çæ*-kri-faiç) n sacrifício m; v sacrificar
**sacrilege** (*çæ*-kri-lidj) n sacrilégio m
**sad** (çæd) adj triste; desgostoso, melancólico
**saddle** (*çæ*-dăl) n sela f
**sadness** (*çæd*-năç) n tristeza f
**safe** (çeif) adj seguro; n cofre-forte m
**safety** (*çeif*-ti) n segurança f
**safety-belt** (*çeif*-ti-bélt) n cinto de segurança
**safety-pin** (*çeif*-ti-pinn) n alfinete de segurança
**safety-razor** (*çeif*-ti-rei-ză) n gilete f
**sail** (çeil) v navegar; n vela f
**sailing-boat** (*çei*-linng-boᵘt) n barco à vela
**sailor** (*çei*-lă) n marinheiro m
**saint** (çeinnt) n santo m
**salad** (*çæ*-lăd) n salada f
**salad-oil** (*çæ*-lăd-oil) n óleo para salada, azeite m
**salary** (*çæ*-lă-ri) n ordenado m, salário m
**sale** (çeil) n venda f; **clearance** ~ liquidação f; **for** ~ à venda; **sales** saldos mpl
**saleable** (*çei*-lă-băl) adj vendável
**salesgirl** (*çeilz*-ghăăl) n vendedora f
**salesman** (*çeilz*-mănn) n (pl -men) vendedor m
**salon** (*çæ*-lón) n salão m
**saloon** (çă-*luunn*) n bar m
**salt** (çóólt) n sal m

salt-cellar (çóólt-çé-lã) n saleiro m
salty (çóól-ti) adj salgado
salute (çã-luut) v saudar
salve (çaav) n unguento m
same (ceimm) adj mesmo
sample (çaamm-pãl) n amostra f
sanatorium (çæ-nã-tóó-ri-ãmm) n (pl
~s, -ria) sanatório m
sand (çænnd) n areia f
sandal (çænn-dãl) n sandália f
sandpaper (çænnd-pei-pã) n lixa f
sandwich (çænn-ⁿidj) n sanduíche f
sandy (çænn-di) adj arenoso
sanitary (çæ-ni-tã-ri) adj sanitário; ~
towel penso higiénico
sapphire (çæ-faiᵃ) n safira f
sardine (çaa-diinn) n sardinha f
satchel (çæ-tchãl) n pasta da escola
satellite (çæ-tã-lait) n satélite m
satin (çæ-tinn) n cetim m
satisfaction (çæ-tiç-fæk-chãnn) n satisfação f
satisfy (çæ-tiç-fai) v *satisfazer
Saturday (çæ-tã-di) sábado m
sauce (çóóç) n molho m
saucepan (çóóç-pãnn) n caçarola f
saucer (çóó-çã) n pires m
Saudi Arabia (çau-di-ã-rei-bi-ã) Arábia Saudita
Saudi Arabian (çau-di-ã-rei-bi-ãnn) adj
saudita
sauna (çóó-nã) n sauna f
sausage (çó-çidj) n salsicha f
savage (çæ-vidj) adj selvagem
save (çeiv) v salvar; poupar
savings (çei-vinngz) pl economias fpl;
~ bank caixa económica
saviour (çei-vⁱã) n salvador m
savoury (çei-vã-ri) adj saboroso; picante
saw¹ (çóó) v (p see)
saw² (çóó) n serra f
sawdust (çóó-daçt) n serradura f
saw-mill (çóó-mil) n serração f

*say (çei) v *dizer
scaffolding (çkæ-fãl-dinng) n andaime
m
scale (çkeil) n escala f; escama f;
scales balança f
scandal (çkænn-dãl) n escândalo m
Scandinavia (çkænn-di-nei-vi-ã)
Escandinávia f
Scandinavian (çkænn-di-nei-vi-ãnn) adj
escandinavo
scapegoat (çkeip-ghoᵘt) n bode expiatório
scar (çkaa) n cicatriz f
scarce (çkéᵃç) adj escasso
scarcely (çkéᵃ-çli) adv raramente
scarcity (çkéᵃ-çã-ti) n escassez f
scare (çkéᵃ) v assustar; n susto m
scarf (çkaaf) n (pl ~s, scarves) lenço
do pescoço, lenço da cabeça
scarlet (çkaa-lãt) adj escarlate
scary (çkéᵃ-ri) adj assustador
scatter (çkæ-tã) v dispersar
scene (çiinn) n cena f
scenery (çii-nã-ri) n paisagem f
scenic (çii-nik) adj pitoresco
scent (çénnt) n perfume m
schedule (ché-dⁱuul) n horário m
scheme (çkiimm) n esquema m; plano
m
scholar (çkó-lã) n erudito m; aluno m
scholarship (çkó-lã-chip) n bolsa de
estudos
school (çkuul) n escola f
schoolboy (çkuul-boi) n escolar m
schoolgirl (çkuul-ghããl) n escolar f
schoolmaster (çkuul-maa-çtã) n professor de escola
schoolteacher (çkuul-tii-tchã) n professor de escola
science (çai-ãnnç) n ciência f
scientific (çai-ãnn-ti-fik) adj científico
scientist (çai-ãnn-tiçt) n cientista m
scissors (çi-zãz) pl tesoura f
scold (çkoᵘld) v repreender; ralhar

scooter (çkuu-tă) n scooter f; trotineta f

score (çkóó) n resultado m; v marcar

scorn (çkóónn) n escárnio m, desprezo m; v desprezar

Scot (çkót) n escocês m

Scotch (çkótch) adj escocês

Scotland (çkót-lănnd) Escócia f

Scottish (çkó-tich) adj escocês

scout (çkaut) n escuteiro m

scrap (çkræp) n pedaço m

scrap-book (çkræp-buk) n álbum de recortes

scrape (çkreip) v raspar

scrap-iron (çkræ-paiănn) n sucata f

scratch (çkrætch) v arranhar, riscar; n risco m, arranhão m

scream (çkriimm) v gritar; n grito m

screen (çkriinn) n biombo m; tela f, é-cran m

screw (çkruu) n parafuso m; v aparafusar

screw-driver (çkruu-drai-vă) n chave de parafusos

scrub (çkrab) v esfregar; n moita f

sculptor (çkalp-tă) n escultor m

sculpture (çkalp-tchă) n escultura f

sea (çii) n mar m

sea-bird (çii-băăd) n ave marinha

sea-coast (çii-koᵘçt) n litoral m

seagull (çii-ghal) n gaivota f

seal (çiil) n selo m; foca f

seam (çiimm) n costura f

seaman (çii-mănn) n (pl -men) marinheiro m

seamless (çiimm-lăç) adj sem costura

seaport (çii-póót) n porto marítimo

search (çăătch) v procurar; revistar, rebuscar, pesquisar; n busca f

searchlight (çăătch-lait) n holofote m

seascape (çii-çkeip) n paisagem marítima

sea-shell (çii-chél) n concha f

seashore (çii-chóó) n beira-mar f

seasick (çii-çik) adj enjoado

seasickness (çii-çik-năç) n enjoo m

seaside resort estação balnear

season (çii-zănn) n estação f; high ~ alta estação; low ~ baixa estação; off ~ fora da época

season-ticket (çii-zănn-ti-kit) n assinatura de temporada

seat (çiit) n assento m; sítio m, lugar m; sede f

seat-belt (çiit-bélt) n cinto de segurança

sea-urchin (çii-ăă-tchinn) n ouriço-do-mar m

sea-water (çii-ᵘóó-tă) n água do mar

second (çé-kănnd) num segundo; n segundo m; instante m

secondary (çé-kănn-dă-ri) adj secundário; ~ school escola secundária

second-hand (çé-kănnd-hænnd) adj em segunda mão

secret (çii-krăt) n segredo m; adj secreto

secretary (çé-kră-tri) n secretária f; secretário m

section (çék-chănn) n secção f; divisão f

secure (çi-kⁱuᵃ) adj seguro

security (çi-kⁱuᵃ-ră-ti) n segurança f; fiança f

sedate (çi-deit) adj calmo

sedative (çé-dă-tiv) n sedativo m

seduce (çi-dⁱuuç) v *seduzir

*see (çii) v *ver; perceber, compreender; ~ to tratar de

seed (çiid) n semente f

*seek (çiik) v procurar

seem (çiimm) v parecer

seen (çiinn) v (pp see)

seesaw (çii-çóó) n balancé m; gangorra fBr

seize (çiiz) v agarrar

seldom (çél-dămm) adv raramente

select (çi-lékt) v escolher, seleccionar; *adj* seleccionado, selecto

**selection** (çi-*lék*-chänn) *n* selecção *f*, escolha *f*

**self-centred** (çélf-*çénn*-täd) *adj* egocêntrico

**self-employed** (çél-fimm-*ploid*) *adj* independente

**self-government** (çélf-*gha*-vă-mănnt) *n* autonomia *f*

**selfish** (çél-fich) *adj* egoísta

**selfishness** (çél-fich-năç) *n* egoísmo *m*

***sell** (çél) *v* vender

**semblance** (çémm-blănnç) *n* aparência *f*

**semi-** (çé-mi) semi-

**semicircle** (çé-mi-çăă-kăl) *n* semi-círculo *m*

**semi-colon** (çé-mi-*ko*u-lănn) *n* ponto e vírgula

**senate** (çé-năt) *n* senado *m*

**senator** (çé-nă-tă) *n* senador *m*

***send** (çénnd) *v* enviar, mandar; ~ **back** devolver; ~ **for** mandar vir; ~ **off** *expedir

**senile** (çii-nail) *adj* senil

**sensation** (çénn-*çei*-chänn) *n* sensação *f*

**sensational** (çénn-çei-chä-năl) *adj* sensacional

**sense** (çénnç) *n* sentido *m*; juízo *m*, razão *f*; *v* perceber, *sentir; ~ **of honour** sentimento de honra

**senseless** (çénnç-lăç) *adj* sem sentido

**sensible** (çénn-çă-băl) *adj* sensato

**sensitive** (çénn-çi-tiv) *adj* sensível

**sentence** (çénn-tännç) *n* frase *f*; sentença *f*; *v* condenar

**sentimental** (çénn-ti-*ménn*-tăl) *adj* sentimental

**separate**[1] (çé-pă-reit) *v* separar

**separate**[2] (çé-pă-răt) *adj* distinto, separado

**separately** (çé-pă-răt-li) *adv* à parte

**September** (çép-*témm*-bă) Setembro

**septic** (çép-tik) *adj* séptico; *become ~ infectar

**sequel** (çii-kuăl) *n* continuação *f*

**sequence** (çii-kuännç) *n* sequência *f*; série *f*

**serene** (çă-riinn) *adj* sereno

**serial** (çiă-ri-ăl) *n* folhetim *m*

**series** (çiă-riiz) *n* (pl ~) série *f*

**serious** (çiă-ri-ăç) *adj* sério

**seriousness** (çiă-ri-ăç-năç) *n* seriedade *f*

**sermon** (çăă-mănn) *n* sermão *m*

**serum** (çiă-rămm) *n* soro *m*

**servant** (çăă-vănnt) *n* criado *m*

**serve** (çăăv) *v* *servir

**service** (çăă-viç) *n* serviço *m*; ~ **charge** taxa de serviço; ~ **station** estação de serviço

**serviette** (çăă-vi-ét) *n* guardanapo *m*

**session** (çé-chänn) *n* sessão *f*

**set** (çét) *n* grupo *m*; jogo *m*

***set** (çét) *v* pousar, *pôr; ~ **menu** ementa fixa; ~ **out** partir

**setting** (çé-tinng) *n* cenário *m*; ~ **lotion** loção fixadora

**settle** (çé-tăl) *v* regularizar, resolver; ~ **down** fixar-se

**settlement** (çé-tăl-mănnt) *n* ajuste *m*, acordo *m*

**seven** (çé-vănn) *num* sete

**seventeen** (çé-vănn-tiinn) *num* dezassete

**seventeenth** (çé-vănn-tiinnθ) *num* décimo sétimo

**seventh** (çé-vănnθ) *num* sétimo

**seventy** (çé-vănn-ti) *num* setenta

**several** (çé-vă-răl) *adj* vários

**severe** (çi-viă) *adj* violento, grave, rigoroso

***sew** (çou) *v* coser; ~ **up** suturar

**sewer** (çuu-ă) *n* esgoto *m*

**sewing-machine** (çou-inng-mă-chiinn) *n* máquina de costura

**sex** (çékç) *n* sexo *m*; sexualidade *f*

**sexton** (çék-çtănn) *n* sacristão *m*

**sexual** (çék-chu-ăl) *adj* sexual

**sexuality** (çék-chu-æ-lă-ti) *n* sexualidade *f*

**shade** (cheid) *n* sombra *f*; tom *m*

**shadow** (chæ-do^u) *n* sombra *f*

**shady** (chei-di) *adj* sombrio

\***shake** (cheik) *v* \*sacudir, abanar

**shaky** (chei-ki) *adj* vacilante

\***shall** (chæl) *v* dever

**shallow** (chæ-lo^u) *adj* pouco profundo

**shame** (cheimm) *n* vergonha *f*; desonra *f*; **shame!** que vergonha!

**shampoo** (chæmm-*puu*) *n* champô *m*

**shamrock** (chæmm-rók) *n* trevo *m*

**shape** (cheip) *n* forma *f*; *v* formar

**share** (ché^ă) *v* partilhar; *n* parte *f*; acção *f*

**shark** (chaak) *n* tubarão *m*

**sharp** (chaap) *adj* afiado

**sharpen** (chaa-pănn) *v* afiar

**shave** (cheiv) *v* \*fazer a barba, \*barbear-se

**shaver** (chei-vă) *n* máquina de barbear; barbeador eléctrico *Br*

**shaving-brush** (chei-vinng-brach) *n* pincel da barba

**shaving-cream** (chei-vinng-kriimm) *n* creme para a barba

**shaving-soap** (chei-vinng-ço^u p) *n* sabão da barba

**shawl** (chóól) *n* xaile *m*, xale *m*

**she** (chii) *pron* ela

**shed** (chéd) *n* arrecadação *f*

\***shed** (chéd) *v* derramar, vazar; espalhar

**sheep** (chiip) *n* (pl ~) ovelha *f*

**sheer** (chi^ă) *adj* puro, absoluto; delicado, translúcido, fino

**sheet** (chiit) *n* lençol *m*; folha *f*; chapa *f*

**shelf** (chélf) *n* (pl shelves) prateleira *f*

**shell** (chél) *n* concha *f*; casca *f*

**shellfish** (chél-fich) *n* marisco *m*

**shelter** (chél-tă) *n* refúgio *m*, abrigo *m*; *v* abrigar

**shepherd** (ché-păd) *n* pastor *m*

**shift** (chift) *n* turno *m*

\***shine** (chainn) *v* brilhar; \*reluzir

**ship** (chip) *n* navio *m*; *v* \*expedir; **shipping line** companhia de navegação

**shipowner** (chi-po^u-nă) *n* armador *m*

**shipyard** (chip-¹aad) *n* estaleiro *m*

**shirt** (chăăt) *n* camisa *f*

**shiver** (chi-vă) *v* tremer, tiritar; *n* arrepio *m*

**shivery** (chi-vă-ri) *adj* trémulo

**shock** (chók) *n* choque *m*; *v* chocar; ~ **absorber** amortecedor *m*

**shocking** (chó-kinng) *adj* chocante

**shoe** (chuu) *n* sapato *m*; **gym shoes** sapatos de ginástica; ~ **polish** graxa *f*

**shoe-lace** (chuu-leiç) *n* atacador *m*

**shoemaker** (chuu-mei-kă) *n* sapateiro *m*

**shoe-shop** (chuu-chóp) *n* sapataria *f*

**shook** (chuk) *v* (p shake)

\***shoot** (chuut) *v* disparar

**shop** (chóp) *n* loja *f*; *v* \*fazer compras; ~ **assistant** empregado de balcão; **shopping bag** saco das compras; **shopping centre** centro comercial

**shopkeeper** (chóp-kii-pă) *n* lojista *m*

**shop-window** (chóp-^uinn-do^u) *n* montra *f*

**shore** (chóó) *n* margem *f*, beira-mar *f*

**short** (chóót) *adj* curto; baixo; ~ **circuit** curto-circuito *m*

**shortage** (chóó-tidj) *n* escassez *f*, carência *f*

**shortcoming** (chóót-ka-minng) *n* falha *f*

shorten (*chóó*-tànn) v encurtar

shorthand (*chóót*-hænnd) n estenografia f

shortly (*chóót*-li) adv dentro em breve, brevemente, daqui a pouco

shorts (*chóótç*) pl calções mpl; plAm cuecas fpl

short-sighted (*chóót-çai*-tid) adj míope m

shot (chót) n tiro m; injecção f

*should (chud) v dever

shoulder (*choᵘl*-dä) n ombro m

shout (chaut) v gritar; n grito m

shovel (*cha*-väl) n pá f

show (choᵘ) n representação f, espectáculo m; exposição f

*show (choᵘ) v mostrar; exibir, *expor; demonstrar

show-case (*choᵘ*-keiç) n vitrina f

shower (chauᵃ) n duche m; aguaceiro m

showroom (*choᵘ*-ruumm) n sala de exposições

shriek (chriik) v gritar; n guincho m

shrimp (chrimmp) n camarão m

shrine (chrainn) n santuário m

*shrink (chrinngk) v encolher

shrinkproof (*chrinngk*-pruuf) adj não encolhe

shrub (chrab) n arbusto m

shudder (*cha*-dä) n estremecimento m

shuffle (*cha*-fäl) v baralhar

*shut (chat) v fechar; shut fechado, encerrado; ~ in fechar

shutter (*cha*-tä) n janela de madeira, persiana f

shy (chai) adj tímido

shyness (*chai*-naç) n timidez f

Siamese (çai-ä-*miiz*) adj siamês

sick (çik) adj doente; enjoado

sickness (*çik*-näç) n doença f; enjoo m

side (çaid) n lado m; partido m;

one-sided unilateral

sideburns (çaid-*bäännz*) pl suíças fpl

sidelight (*çaid*-lait) n luz lateral

side-street (*çaid*-çtriit) n transversal f

sidewalk (*çaid*-ᵘóók) nAm passeio m

sideways (*çaid*-ᵘeiz) adv de lado

siege (ciidj) n cerco m

sieve (çiv) n peneira m; v peneirar

sift (çift) v peneirar

sight (çait) n vista f, espectáculo m; ponto de interesse

sign (çainn) n sinal m, marca f, gesto m; v assinar

signal (*çigh*-näl) n sinal m; v *fazer sinais

signature (*çigh*-nä-tchä) n assinatura f

significant (çigh-*ni*-fi-kännt) adj significativo

signpost (*çainn*-poᵘçt) n poste indicador

silence (*çai*-lännç) n silêncio m; v calar

silencer (*çai*-länn-çä) n silencioso m

silent (*çai*-lännt) adj calado, silencioso

silk (çilk) n seda f

silken (*çil*-känn) adj sedoso

silly (*çi*-li) adj palerma, disparatado

silver (*çil*-vä) n prata f; de prata

silversmith (*çil*-vä-çmiθ) n ourives m

silverware (*çil*-vä-ᵘéᵃ) n pratas fpl

similar (*çi*-mi-lä) adj semelhante, análogo

similarity (çi-mi-*læ*-rä-ti) n semelhança f

simple (*çimm*-päl) adj ingénuo; simples; ordinário

simply (*çimm*-pli) adv simplesmente

simulate (*çi*-mᵘu-leit) v simular

simultaneous (çi-mäl-*tei*-ni-äç) adj simultâneo

sin (çinn) n pecado m

since (çinnç) prep desde; adv desde

então; *conj* desde que; visto que

**sincere** (çinn-*çi*ᵃ) *adj* sincero

**sinew** (*çi*-n¹uu) *n* tendão *m*

*****sing** (çinng) *v* cantar

**singer** (çinng-ä) *n* cantor *m*; cantora *f*

**single** (ghäl) *adj* só; solteiro; ~ **room** quarto individual

**singular** (çinng-gh¹u-lä) *n* singular *m*; *adj* singular

**sinister** (*çi*-ni-çtä) *adj* sinistro

**sink** (çinngk) *n* lava-louça *m*

*****sink** (çinngk) *v* afundar-se

**sip** (çip) *n* sorvo *m*

**siphon** (*çai*-fänn) *n* sifão *m*

**sir** (çää) *senhor*

**siren** (*çai*ᵃ-zänn) *n* sirene *f*

**sister** (*çi*-çtä) *n* irmã *f*

**sister-in-law** (*çi*-çtä-rinn-lóó) *n* (pl sisters-) cunhada *f*

*****sit** (çit) *v* *estar sentado; ~ **down** sentar-se

**site** (çait) *n* sítio *m*

**sitting-room** (*çi*-tinng-ruumm) *n* sala de estar

**situated** (*çi*-tchu-ei-tid) *adj* situado

**situation** (çi-tchu-*ei*-chänn) *n* situação *f*

**six** (çikç) *num* seis

**sixteen** (çikç-*tiinn*) *num* dezasseis

**sixteenth** (çikç-*tiinn*θ) *num* décimo sexto

**sixth** (çikçθ) *num* sexto

**sixty** (*çikç*-ti) *num* sessenta

**size** (çaiz) *n* medida *f*, tamanho *m*, dimensão *f*; formato *m*

**skate** (çkeit) *v* patinar; *n* patim *m*

**skating** (*çkei*-tinng) *n* patinagem *f*

**skating-rink** (*çkei*-tinng-rinngk) *n* ringue de patinagem no gelo

**skeleton** (*çké*-li-tänn) *n* esqueleto *m*

**sketch** (çkétch) *n* esboço *m*, desenho *m*: *v* desenhar, esboçar

**sketch-book** (*çkétch*-buk) *n* caderno de desenho

**ski**¹ (çkii) *v* esquiar

**ski**² (çkii) *n* (pl ~, ~s) esqui *m*; ~ **boots** botas de esqui; ~ **pants** calças de esqui; ~ **sticks** varas de esqui

**skid** (çkid) *v* derrapar

**skier** (*çkii*-ä) *n* esquiador *m*

**skiing** (*çkii*-inng) *n* esqui *m*

**ski-jump** (*çkii*-djammp) *n* salto de esqui

**skilful** (*çkil*-fäl) *adj* hábil, destro

**ski-lift** (*çkii*-lift) *n* telesqui *m*

**skill** (çkil) *n* perícia *f*

**skilled** (çkild) *adj* perito, hábil; especializado

**skin** (çkinn) *n* pele *f*; casca *f*; ~ **cream** creme para a pele

**skip** (çkip) *v* saltitar; saltar

**skirt** (çkäät) *n* saia *f*

**skull** (çkal) *n* crânio *m*

**sky** (çkai) *n* céu *m*; ar *m*

**skyscraper** (*çkai*-çkrei-pä) *n* arranha-céus *m*

**slack** (çlæk) *adj* lento

**slacks** (çlækç) *pl* calças *fpl*

**slam** (çlæmm) *v* fechar violentamente

**slander** (*çlaann*-dä) *n* calúnia *f*

**slant** (çlaannt) *v* inclinar-se

**slanting** (*çlaann*-tinng) *adj* oblíquo, inclinado

**slap** (çlæp) *v* bater; *n* bofetada *f*

**slate** (çleit) *n* ardósia *f*

**slave** (çleiv) *n* escravo *m*

**sledge** (çlédj) *n* trenó *m*

**sleep** (çliip) *n* sono *m*

*****sleep** (çliip) *v* *dormir

**sleeping-bag** (*çlii*-pinng-bægh) *n* saco-cama *m*

**sleeping-car** (*çlii*-pinng-kaa) *n* carruagem-cama *f*

**sleeping-pill** (*çlii*-pinng-pil) *n* comprimido para dormir

**sleepless** (*çliip*-läç) *adj* sem dormir

**sleepy** (*çlii*-pi) *adj* sonolento

**sleeve** (çliiv) *n* manga *f*; capa *f*

**sleigh** (çlei) *n* trenó *m*

**slender** (çlénn-dä) *adj* esbelto

**slice** (çlaiç) *n* fatia *f*

**slide** (çlaid) *n* deslize *m*; escorrega-douro *m*; slide *m*

*****slide** (çlaid) *v* deslizar

**slight** (çlait) *adj* ligeiro

**slim** (çlimm) *adj* delgado; *v* emagre-cer

**slip** (çlip) *v* escorregar, deslizar; esca-par; *n* escorregadela *f*; saia de bai-xo

**slipper** (çli-pä) *n* pantufa *f*

**slippery** (çli-pä-ri) *adj* escorregadio

**slogan** (çlou-ghänn) *n* slogan *m*, lema *m*

**slope** (çloup) *n* vertente *f*; *v* inclinar, *****ter declive

**sloping** (çlou-pinng) *adj* inclinado

**slot** (çlót) *n* fenda *f*

**slot-machine** (çlót-mä-chiinn) *n* slot-machine *f*

**slovenly** (çla-vänn-li) *adj* descuidado

**slow** (çlou) *adj* lento; ~ **down** abrandar, afrouxar; travar; *****frear *vBr*

**sluice** (çluuç) *n* comporta *f*

**slum** (çlamm) *n* bairro pobre

**slump** (çlammp) *n* baixa de preços

**slush** (çlach) *n* neve meio derretida

**sly** (çlai) *adj* astuto

**smack** (çmæk) *v* bater; *n* palmada *f*

**small** (çmóól) *adj* pequeno

**smallpox** (çmóól-pókç) *n* varíola *f*

**smart** (çmaat) *adj* elegante; esperto, inteligente

**smell** (çmél) *n* cheiro *m*

*****smell** (çmél) *v* cheirar; cheirar mal

**smelly** (çmé-li) *adj* mal cheiroso

**smile** (çmail) *v* *****sorrir; *n* sorriso *m*

**smith** (çmiθ) *n* ferreiro *m*

**smoke** (çmouk) *v* fumar; *n* fumo *m*; **no smoking** proibido fumar

**smoker** (çmou-kä) *n* fumador *m*; compartimento para fumadores

**smoking-compartment** (çmou-kinng-kämm-paat-männt) *n* compartimento para fumadores

**smoking-room** (çmou-kinng-ruumm) *n* sala de fumo

**smooth** (çmuuð) *adj* plano, liso; sua-ve

**smuggle** (çma-ghäl) *v* *****contraban-dear

**snack** (çnæk) *n* refeição ligeira

**snail** (çneil) *n* caracol *m*

**snake** (çneik) *n* serpente *f*

**snapshot** (çnæp-chót) *n* instantâneo *m*

**sneakers** (çnii-käz) *plAm* sapatos de ginástica

**sneeze** (çniiz) *v* espirrar

**sniper** (çnai-pä) *n* franco-atirador *m*

**snooty** (çnuu-ti) *adj* arrogante

**snore** (çnóó) *v* ressonar

**snorkel** (çnóó-käl) *n* tubo respirador

**snout** (çnaut) *n* focinho *m*

**snow** (çnou) *n* neve *f*; *v* nevar

**snowy** (çnou-i) *adj* nevado

**so** (çou) *conj* portanto; *adv* assim; tão; **and** ~ **on** assim por diante; ~ **far** até agora; ~ **that** para que, de modo que, a fim de

**soak** (çouk) *v* embeber, ensopar, mo-lhar; pôr de molho

**soap** (çoup) *n* sabão *m*; ~ **powder** sabão em pó

**sober** (çou-bä) *adj* sóbrio; ponderado

**so-called** (çou-kóóld) *adj* pretenso

**soccer** (çó-kä) *n* futebol *m*; ~ **team** equipa *f*

**social** (çou-chäl) *adj* social

**socialism** (çou-chä-li-zämm) *n* socialis-mo *m*

**socialist** (çou-chä-liçt) *adj* socialista; *n* socialista *m*

**society** (çä-çai-ä-ti) *n* sociedade *f*, associação f; companhia f

**sock** (çók) n peúga f

**socket** (çó-kit) n casquilho m

**soda-water** (çoᵘ-dä-ᵘóó-tä) n soda f, água gasificada

**sofa** (çoᵘ-fä) n sofá m

**soft** (çóft) adj mole; ~ **drink** bebida não alcoólica

**soften** (çó-fänn) v suavizar

**soil** (çoil) n solo m; terra f

**soiled** (çoild) adj sujo

**sold** (çoᵘld) v (p, pp sell) ; ~ **out** esgotado

**solder** (çól-dä) v soldar

**soldering-iron** (çól-dä-rinng-aiänn) n ferro de soldar

**soldier** (çoᵘl-djä) n soldado m

**sole¹** (çoᵘl) adj único

**sole²** (çoᵘl) n sola f; linguado m

**solely** (çoᵘl-li) adv exclusivamente

**solemn** (çó-lämm) adj solene

**solicitor** (çä-li-çi-tä) n advogado m

**solid** (çó-lid) adj robusto, sólido; maciço; n sólido m

**soluble** (çó-lᵘu-bäl) adj solúvel

**solution** (çä-luu-chänn) n solução f

**solve** (çólv) v resolver

**sombre** (çómm-bä) adj sombrio

**some** (çamm) adj alguns; pron certos, uns; ~ **day** qualquer dia; ~ **more** um pouco mais; ~ **time** alguma vez

**somebody** (çamm-bä-di) pron alguém

**somehow** (çamm-hau) adv duma maneira au doutra

**someone** (çamm-ᵘann) pron alguém

**something** (çamm-θinng) pron alguma coisa

**sometimes** (çamm-taimmz) adv às vezes

**somewhat** (çamm-ᵘót) adv um tanto

**somewhere** (çamm-ᵘéᵃ) adv em qualquer parte

**son** (çann) n filho m

**song** (çónn) n canção f

**son-in-law** (ça-ninn-lóó) n (pl sons-) genro m

**soon** (çuunn) adv brevemente, rapidamente, em breve; **as** ~ **as** assim que

**soothe** (çuuð) v confortar; aliviar

**sooner** (çuu-nä) adv antes

**sore** (çóó) adj doloroso; n dor f; úlcera f; ~ **throat** dor de garganta

**sorrow** (çó-roᵘ) n desgosto m, tristeza f, dor f

**sorry** (çó-ri) adj desolado; **sorry!** desculpe!, perdão!

**sort** (çóót) v ordenar, classificar; n género m, categoria f; **all sorts of** toda a espécie de

**soul** (çoᵘl) n alma f; espírito m

**sound** (çaunnd) n som m; v parecer, soar; adj seguro; **safe and** ~ são e salvo

**soundproof** (çaunnd-pruuf) adj à prova de som

**soup** (çuup) n sopa f

**soup-plate** (çuup-pleit) n prato de sopa

**soup-spoon** (çuup-çpuunn) n colher de sopa

**sour** (çauᵃ) adj azedo

**source** (çóóç) n fonte f

**south** (çauθ) n sul m; **South Pole** pólo sul

**South Africa** (çauθ æ-fri-kä) África do Sul

**south-east** (çauθ-iiçt) n sueste m

**southerly** (ça-ðä-li) adj meridional

**southern** (ça-ðänn) adj do sul

**south-west** (çauθ-ᵘéçt) n sudoeste m

**souvenir** (çuu-vä-niᵃ) n recordação f

**sovereign** (çóv-rinn) n soberano m

*****sow** (çoᵘ) v *semear

**spa** (çpaa) n termas fpl

**space** (çpeiç) n espaço m; distância f, intervalo m; v espaçar

spacious (ςpei-chậç) *adj* espaçoso
spade (ςpeid) *n* pá *f*
Spain (ςpeinn) Espanha *f*
Spaniard (ςpæ-niåd) *n* espanhol *m*
Spanish (ςpæ-nich) *adj* espanhol
spanking (ςpænng-kinng) *n* tareia *f*
spanner (ςpæ-nä) *n* chave de porcas
spare (ςpéå) *adj* de reserva, sobresselente; *v* dispensar; ~ **part** peça sobresselente; ~ **room** quarto de hóspedes; ~ **time** tempo livre; ~ **tyre** pneu sobresselente; ~ **wheel** roda sobresselente
spark (ςpaak) *n* faísca *f*
sparking-plug (ςpaa-kinng-plagh) *n* vela de ignição
sparkling (ςpaa-klinng) *adj* cintilante; espumante
sparrow (ςpæ-roᵘ) *n* pardal *m*
*speak (ςpiik) *v* falar
spear (ςpiå) *n* lança *f*
special (ςpé-chäl) *adj* particular, especial; ~ **delivery** distribuição expressa
specialist (ςpé-chä-liçt) *n* especialista *m*
speciality (ςpé-chi-æ-lä-ti) *n* especialidade *f*
specialize (ςpé-chä-laiz) *v* especializar-se
specially (ςpé-chä-li) *adv* particularmente
species (ςpii-chiiz) *n* (pl ~) espécie *f*
specific (ςpä-çi-fik) *adj* específico
specimen (ςpé-çi-männ) *n* amostra *f*, exemplar *m*
speck (ςpék) *n* mancha *f*
spectacle (ςpék-tä-käl) *n* espectáculo *m*: **spectacles** óculos *mpl*
spectator (ςpék-tei-tä) *n* espectador *m*
speculate (ςpé-kⁱu-leit) *v* especular
speech (ςpiitch) *n* fala *f*; discurso *m*, alocução *f*; linguagem *f*

speechless (ςpiitch-läç) *adj* mudo
speed (ςpiid) *n* velocidade *f*; pressa *f*, rapidez *f*; **cruising** ~ velocidade de cruzeiro; ~ **limit** limitação de velocidade, velocidade máxima
*speed (ςpiid) *v* guiar com excesso de velocidade
speeding (ςpii-dinng) *n* excesso de velocidade
speedometer (ςpii-dó-mi-tä) *n* velocímetro *m*
spell (ςpél) *n* encantamento *m*
*spell (ςpél) *v* soletrar
spelling (ςpé-linng) *n* ortografia *f*
*spend (ςpénnd) *v* gastar; passar, empregar
sphere (çfiå) *n* esfera *f*
spice (ςpaiç) *n* especiaria *f*
spiced (ςpaiçt) *adj* condimentado
spicy (ςpai-çi) *adj* picante
spider (ςpai-dä) *n* aranha *f*; **spider's web** teia de aranha
*spill (ςpil) *v* entornar
*spin (ςpinn) *v* fiar; *fazer girar
spinach (ςpi-nidj) *n* espinafres *mpl*
spine (ςpainn) *n* espinha dorsal
spinster (ςpinn-çtä) *n* solteirona *f*
spire (ςpaiå) *n* agulha *f*
spirit (ςpi-rit) *n* espírito *m*; humor *m*; **spirits** bebidas alcoólicas; moral *m*; ~ **stove** lamparina de álcool
spiritual (ςpi-ri-tchu-äl) *adj* espiritual
spit (ςpit) *n* cuspo *m*, saliva *f*; espeto *m*
*spit (ςpit) *v* *cuspir
in spite of (inn ςpait óv) apesar de
spiteful (ςpait-fål) *adj* malévolo
splash (ςplæch) *v* salpicar
splendid (ςplénn-did) *adj* esplêndido, magnífico
splendour (ςplénn-dä) *n* esplendor *m*
splint (ςplinnt) *n* tala *f*
splinter (ςplinn-tä) *n* farpa *f*
*split (ςplit) *v* fender

**\*spoil** (çpoil) v estragar; amimar

**spoke¹** (çpoᵘk) v (p speak)

**spoke²** (çpoᵘk) n raio m

**sponge** (çpanndj) n esponja f

**spook** (çpuuk) n fantasma m

**spool** (çpuul) n bobina f

**spoon** (çpuunn) n colher f

**spoonful** (çpuunn-ful) n colherada f

**sport** (çpóót) n desporto m; esporte mBr; divertimento m; brincadeira f; v brincar, passar o tempo; adj desportivo

**sports-car** (çpóótç-kaa) n carro de desporto

**sports-jacket** (çpóótç-djæ-kit) n casaco desportivo

**sportsman** (çpóótç-männ) n (pl -men) desportista m

**sportswear** (çpóótç-ᵘéª) n vestuário de desporto

**spot** (çpót) n mancha f, nódoa f; local m

**spotless** (çpót-läç) adj sem mancha; impecável

**spotlight** (çpót-lait) n projector m

**spotted** (çpó-tid) adj sarapintado

**spout** (çpaut) n jorro m

**sprain** (çpreinn) v torcer, deslocar; n distensão f

**\*spread** (çpréd) v espalhar

**spring** (çprinng) n Primavera f; mola f; nascente f

**springtime** (çprinng-taimm) n Primavera f

**sprouts** (çprautç) pl couve-de-bruxelas

**spy** (çpai) n espião m

**squadron** (çkᵘó-dränn) n esquadrilha f

**square** (çkᵘéª) adj quadrado; n quadrado m; praça f

**squash** (çkᵘóch) n sumo m

**squirrel** (çkᵘi-räl) n esquilo m

**squirt** (çkᵘäät) n esguicho m

**stable** (çtei-bäl) adj estável; n estábulo m

**stack** (çtæk) n pilha f

**stadium** (çtei-di-ämm) n estádio m

**staff** (çtaaf) n pessoal m

**stage** (çteidj) n palco m; fase f; etapa f

**stain** (çteinn) v manchar; n nódoa f, mancha f; **stained glass** vidro colorido; ~ **remover** tira-nódoas m

**stainless** (çteinn-läç) adj imaculado; ~ **steel** aço inoxidável

**staircase** (çtéª-keiç) n escada f

**stairs** (çtéªz) pl escada f

**stale** (çteil) adj velho, estragado

**stall** (çtóól) n tenda f; plateia f

**stamina** (çtæ-mi-nä) n resistência f

**stamp** (çtæmmp) n selo m; v franquiar; calcar; ~ **machine** distribuidor automático de selos

**stand** (çtænnd) n stand m; tribuna f

**\*stand** (çtænnd) v \*estar de pé

**standard** (çtænn-däd) n padrão m, norma f; normal; ~ **of living** nível de vida

**stanza** (çtænn-zä) n estrofe f

**staple** (çtei-päl) n agrafo m; grampo mBr

**star** (çtaa) n estrela f

**starboard** (çtaa-bäd) n estibordo m

**starch** (çtaatch) n goma f; v engomar

**stare** (çtéª) v fitar

**starling** (çtaa-linng) n estorninho m

**start** (çtaat) v começar; n começo m; **starter motor** motor de arranque

**starting-point** (çtaa-tinng-poinnt) n ponto de partida

**state** (çteit) n estado m; v declarar

**the States** (ðä çteitç) Estados Unidos

**statement** (çteit-männt) n declaração f

**statesman** (çteitç-männ) n (pl -men) estadista m

**station** (çtei-chänn) n estação f; posto

*m*

**stationary** (çtei-chă-nă-ri) *adj* estacionário

**stationer's** (çtei-chă-năz) *n* papelaria *f*

**stationery** (çtei-chă-nă-ri) *n* artigos de escritório

**station-master** (çtei-chănn-maa-çtă) *n* chefe de estação

**statistics** (çtă-ti-çtikç) *pl* estatística *f*

**statue** (çtæ-tchuu) *n* estátua *f*

**stay** (çtei) *v* ficar; permanecer, hospedar-se; *n* estadia *f*

**steadfast** (çtéd-faaçt) *adj* constante

**steady** (çté-di) *adj* firme

**steak** (çteik) *n* bife *m*

*****steal** (çtiil) *v* roubar

**steam** (çtiimm) *n* vapor *m*

**steamer** (çtii-mă) *n* barco a vapor

**steel** (çtiil) *n* aço *m*

**steep** (çtiip) *adj* íngreme, escarpado

**steeple** (çtii-păl) *n* campanário *m*

**steering-column** (çti$^{ă}$-rinng-kó-lămm) *n* coluna de direcção

**steering-wheel** (çti$^{ă}$-rinng-$^{u}$iil) *n* volante *m*

**steersman** (çti$^{ă}$z-mănn) *n* (pl -men) timoneiro *m*

**stem** (çtémm) *n* haste *f*

**stenographer** (çté-nó-ghră-fă) *n* estenógrafo *m*

**step** (çtép) *n* passo *m*; degrau *m*; *v* caminhar, andar

**stepchild** (çtép-tchaild) *n* (pl -children) enteado *m*; enteada *f*

**stepfather** (çtép-faa-ðă) *n* padrasto *m*

**stepmother** (çtép-ma-ðă) *n* madrasta *f*

**sterile** (çté-rail) *adj* estéril

**sterilize** (çté-ri-laiz) *v* esterilizar

**steward** (çti$^{i}$uu-ăd) *n* comissário de bordo

**stewardess** (çti$^{i}$uu-ă-déç) *n* hospedeira *f*

**stick** (çtik) *n* pau *m*

*****stick** (çtik) *v* colar, pegar

**sticky** (çti-ki) *adj* pegajoso

**stiff** (çtif) *adj* teso

**still** (çtil) *adv* ainda; todavia; *adj* tranquilo

**stillness** (çtil-năç) *n* silêncio *m*

**stimulant** (çti-m$^{i}$u-lănnt) *n* estimulante *m*

**stimulate** (çti-m$^{i}$u-leit) *v* estimular

**sting** (çtinng) *n* picadela *f*, picada *f*

*****sting** (çtinng) *v* picar

**stingy** (çtinn-dji) *adj* mesquinho

*****stink** (çtinngk) *v* cheirar mal

**stipulate** (çti-p$^{i}$u-leit) *v* estipular

**stipulation** (çti-p$^{i}$u-lei-chănn) *n* estipulação *f*

**stir** (çtăă) *v* mexer

**stirrup** (çti-răp) *n* estribo *m*

**stitch** (çtitch) *n* ponto *m*, pontada *f*; sutura *f*

**stock** (çtók) *n* stock *m*; *v* *ter em stock; ~ **exchange** bolsa de valores, bolsa *f*; ~ **market** bolsa *f*; **stocks and shares** accões *fpl*

**stocking** (çtó-kinng) *n* meia *f*

**stole**[1] (çto$^{u}$l) *v* (p steal)

**stole**[2] (çto$^{u}$l) *n* estola *f*

**stomach** (çta-măk) *n* estômago *m*

**stomach-ache** (çta-mă-keik) *n* dor de barriga, dor de estômago

**stone** (çto$^{u}$nn) *n* pedra *f*; pedra preciosa; caroço *m*; de pedra; **pumice** ~ pedra-pomes *f*

**stood** (çtud) *v* (p, pp stand)

**stop** (çtóp) *v* acabar, parar; cessar; *n* paragem *f*; parada *fBr*; **stop!** alto!

**stopper** (çtó-pă) *n* rolha *f*

**storage** (çtóó-ridj) *n* armazenagem *f*

**store** (çtóó) *n* reserva *f*; loja *f*; *v* armazenar

**store-house** (çtóó-hauç) *n* armazém *m*

**storey** (çtóó-ri) *n* andar *m*

**stork** (ҫtóók) *n* cegonha *f*
**storm** (ҫtóómm) *n* tempestade *f*
**stormy** (ҫtóó-mi) *adj* tempestuoso
**story** (ҫtóó-ri) *n* história *f*
**stout** (ҫtaut) *adj* obeso, corpulento, gordo
**stove** (ҫtouᵛv) *n* fogão *m*
**straight** (ҫtreit) *adj* direito; recto; *adv* directamente; ~ **ahead** sempre em frente; ~ **away** imediatamente, directamente; ~ **on** sempre em frente
**strain** (ҫtreinn) *n* esforço *m*; tensão *f*; *v* forçar; filtrar
**strainer** (ҫtrei-nä) *n* coador *m*
**strange** (ҫtreinndj) *adj* estranho; insólito
**stranger** (ҫtreinn-djä) *n* estrangeiro *m*; forasteiro *m*
**strangle** (ҫtrænng-ghäl) *v* estrangular
**strap** (ҫtræp) *n* correia *f*
**straw** (ҫtróó) *n* palha *f*
**strawberry** (ҫtróó-bä-ri) *n* morango *m*
**stream** (ҫtriimm) *n* ribeiro *m*; corrente *f*; *v* correr
**street** (ҫtriit) *n* rua *f*
**streetcar** (ҫtriit-kaa) *nAm* eléctrico *m*; bonde *mBr*
**street-organ** (ҫtrii-tóó-ghänn) *n* realejo *m*
**strength** (ҫtrénngθ) *n* força *f*, resistência *f*
**stress** (ҫtréҫ) *n* tensão *f*; ênfase *f*; *v* acentuar, sublinhar
**stretch** (ҫtrétch) *v* esticar; *n* trecho *m*
**strict** (ҫtrikt) *adj* severo; rigoroso
***stride** *dar passadas
**strife** (ҫtraif) *n* luta *f*
**strike** (ҫtraik) *n* greve *f*
***strike** (ҫtraik) *v* bater; atacar; impressionar; *fazer greve
**striking** (ҫtrai-kinng) *adj* impressionante, notável
**string** (ҫtrinng) *n* cordel *m*; fio *m*,

cordão *m*
**strip** (ҫtrip) *n* faixa *f*
**stripe** (ҫtraip) *n* risca *f*
**striped** (ҫtraipt) *adj* às riscas
**stroke** (ҫtrouᵏk) *n* ataque *m*
**stroll** (ҫtrouᵘl) *n* passeio *m*
**strong** (ҫtrónn) *adj* forte; possante
**stronghold** (ҫtrónn-houᵘld) *n* praça-forte *f*
**structure** (ҫtrak-tchä) *n* estrutura *f*
**struggle** (ҫtra-ghäl) *n* combate *m*, luta *f*; *v* lutar
**stub** (ҫtab) *n* talão *m*
**stubborn** (ҫta-bänn) *adj* teimoso
**student** (ҫtⁱuu-dännt) *n* estudante *m*; estudante *f*
**study** (ҫta-dı) *v* estudar; *n* estudo *m*; escritório *m*
**stuff** (ҫtaf) *n* substância *f*; coisa *f*
**stuffed** (ҫtaft) *adj* recheado
**stuffing** (ҫta-finng) *n* recheio *m*
**stuffy** (ҫta-fi) *adj* sufocante
**stumble** (ҫtamm-bäl) *v* tropeçar
**stung** (ҫtanng) *v* (p, pp sting)
**stupid** (ҫtⁱuu-pid) *adj* estúpido
**style** (ҫtail) *n* estilo *m*
**subject¹** (ҫab-djikt) *n* assunto *m*; súbdito *m*; ~ **to** sujeito a
**subject²** (ҫäb-djékt) *v* submeter
**submit** (ҫäb-mit) *v* submeter-se
**subordinate** (ҫä-bóó-di-nät) *adj* subordinado; secundário
**subscriber** (ҫäb-ҫkrai-bä) *n* assinante *m*
**subscription** (ҫäb-ҫkrip-chänn) *n* assinatura *f*
**subsequent** (ҫab-çi-kᵘännt) *adj* subsequente
**subsidy** (ҫab-çi-di) *n* subsídio *m*
**substance** (ҫab-ҫtännҫ) *n* substância *f*
**substantial** (ҫäb-ҫtænn-chäl) *adj* material; real; substancial
**substitute** (ҫab-ҫti-tⁱuut) *v* *substituir; *n* substituto *m*

subtitle (*cab*-tai-tăl) *n* legenda *f*
subtle (*ca*-tăl) *adj* subtil
subtract (căb-*trækt*) *v* \*deduzir, \*subtrair
suburb (*ca*-băăb) *n* subúrbio *m*
suburban (că-*băă*-bănn) *adj* suburbano
subway (*cab*-ᵘei) *nAm* metropolitano *m*
succeed (căk-*ciid*) *v* \*ter êxito; suceder
success (căk-*céc*) *n* sucesso *m*
successful (căk-*céc*-făl) *adj* bem sucedido
succumb (că-*kamm*) *v* sucumbir
such (catch) *adj* tal; *adv* tão; ~ as tal como
suck (cak) *v* chupar
sudden (*ca*-dănn) *adj* repentino
suddenly (*ca*-dănn-li) *adv* repentinamente
suede (cᵘeid) *n* camurça *f*
suffer (*ca*-fă) *v* sofrer; suportar
suffering (*ca*-fă-rinng) *n* sofrimento *m*
suffice (că-*faiç*) *v* bastar
sufficient (că-*fi*-chănnt) *adj* bastante, suficiente
suffrage (*ca*-fridj) *n* sufrágio *m*
sugar (*chu*-ghă) *n* açúcar *m*
suggest (că-*djéçt*) *v* \*sugerir
suggestion (că-*djéç*-tchănn) *n* sugestão *f*
suicide (*cuu*-i-çaid) *n* suicídio *m*
suit (cuut) *v* \*convir; adaptar a; ficar bem; *n* fato *m*; terno *mBr*
suitable (*cuu*-tă-băl) *adj* apropriado
suitcase (*çuut*-keiç) *n* mala *f*
suite (cᵘiit) *n* apartamento *m*
sum (camm) *n* soma *f*
summary (*ca*-mă-ri) *n* resumo *m*
summer (*ca*-mă) *n* Verão *m*; ~ time horário de Verão
summit (*ca*-mit) *n* cima *m*
summons (*ca*-mănnz) *n* (pl ~es) convocação *f*

sun (cann) *n* sol *m*
sunbathe (*cann*-beið) *v* tomar um banho de sol
sunburn (*çann*-băănn) *n* queimadura do sol
Sunday (*çann*-di) domingo *m*
sun-glasses (*çann*-ghlaa-çiz) *pl* óculos escuros
sunlight (*çann*-lait) *n* luz do sol
sunny (*ça*-ni) *adj* soalheiro
sunrise (*çann*-raiz) *n* nascer do sol
sunset (*çann*-cét) *n* pôr do sol
sunshade (*çann*-cheid) *n* pára-sol *m*
sunshine (*çann*-chainn) *n* sol *m*
sunstroke (*çann*-çtroᵘk) *n* insolação *f*
suntan oil (*çann*-tænn-oil) óleo de bronzear
superb (çu-*păăb*) *adj* grandioso, soberbo
superficial (çuu-pă-*fi*-chăl) *adj* superficial
superfluous (çu-*păă*-flu-ăç) *adj* supérfluo
superior (çu-*piᵃ*-ri-ă) *adj* superior, melhor, maior
superlative (çu-*păă*-lă-tiv) *adj* superlativo; *n* superlativo *m*
supermarket (*çuu*-pă-maa-kit) *n* supermercado *m*
superstition (çuu-pă-*çti*-chănn) *n* superstição *f*
supervise (*çuu*-pă-vaiz) *v* superintender
supervision (çuu-pă-*vi*-jănn) *n* supervisão *f*, fiscalização *f*
supervisor (*çuu*-pă-vai-ză) *n* superintendente *m*
supper (*ca*-pă) *n* ceia *f*
supple (*ça*-păl) *adj* flexível, ágil, maleável
supplement (*ça*-pli-mănnt) *n* suplemento *m*
supply (çă-*plai*) *n* abastecimento *m*,

fornecimento *m*; provisão *f*; oferta
*f*; *v* fornecer

**support** (çã-*póót*) *v* suportar; *n* suporte *m*; ~ **hose** meias de descanso

**supporter** (çã-*póó*-tã) *n* adepto *m*;
torcedor *mBr*

**suppose** (çã-*pou*z) *v* \*supor; **supposing that** supondo que

**suppository** (çã-*pó*-zi-tã-ri) *n* supositório *m*

**suppress** (çã-*préç*) *v* reprimir; suprimir

**surcharge** (*çãã*-tchaadj) *n* sobretaxa *f*

**sure** (chu*ã*) *adj* certo

**surely** (*chu*ã-li) *adv* certamente

**surface** (*çãã*-fiç) *n* superfície *f*

**surf-board** (*çãã*f-*bóód*) *n* prancha de
surf

**surgeon** (*çãã*-djänn) *n* cirurgião *m*;
**veterinary** ~ veterinário *m*

**surgery** (*çãã*-djä-ri) *n* operação *f*; consultório *m*

**surname** (*çãã*-neimm) *n* apelido *m*;
sobrenome *m*

**surplus** (*çãã*-plãç) *n* excedente *m*

**surprise** (çã-*praiz*) *n* surpresa *f*; *v* surpreender

**surrender** (çã-*rénn*-dã) *v* render-se; *n*
rendição *f*

**surround** (çã-*raunnd*) *v* cercar, \*rodear

**surrounding** (çã-*raunn*-dinng) *adj* em
redor

**surroundings** (çã-*raunn*-dinngz) *pl* arredores *mpl*

**survey** (*çãã*-vei) *n* resumo *m*

**survival** (çã-*vai*-väl) *n* sobrevivência *f*

**survive** (çã-*vaiv*) *v* sobreviver

**suspect**[1] (çã-*çpékt*) *v* suspeitar

**suspect**[2] (ca-*çpékt*) *n* suspeito *m*

**suspend** (çã-*çpénnd*) *v* suspender

**suspenders** (çã-*çpénn*-däz) *plAm* suspensórios *mpl*; **suspender belt** cin-

to de ligas

**suspension** (çã-*çpénn*-chänn) *n* suspensão *f*; ~ **bridge** ponte pênsil

**suspicion** (çã-*çpi*-chänn) *n* suspeita *f*;
desconfiança *f*

**suspicious** (çã-*çpi*-chãç) *adj* suspeito;
desconfiado

**sustain** (çã-*çteinn*) *v* suportar

**Swahili** (ç*u*ã-*hii*-li) *n* suaíli *m*

**swallow** (ç*u*ó-lo*u*) *v* \*engolir; *n* andorinha *f*

**swam** (ç*u*æmm) *v* (p swim)

**swamp** (ç*u*ómmp) *n* pântano *m*

**swan** (ç*u*ónn) *n* cisne *m*

**swap** (ç*u*óp) *v* trocar

\***swear** (ç*u*é*ã*) *v* jurar; praguejar

**sweat** (ç*u*ét) *n* suor *m*; *v* suar

**sweater** (ç*u*é-tã) *n* camisola *f*; suéter
*mBr*

**Swede** (ç*u*iid) *n* sueco *m*

**Sweden** (ç*u*ii-dänn) Suécia *f*

**Swedish** (ç*u*ii-dich) *adj* sueco

\***sweep** (ç*u*iip) *v* varrer

**sweet** (ç*u*iit) *adj* doce; encantador; *n*
rebuçado *m*; doce *m*; **sweets** doces
*mpl*, rebuçados *mpl*; balas *fplBr*

**sweeten** (ç*u*ii-tänn) *v* adoçar

**sweetheart** (ç*u*iit-haat) *n* querido *m*,
meu amor

**sweetshop** (ç*u*iit-chóp) *n* confeitaria *f*

**swell** (ç*u*él) *adj* formidável

\***swell** (ç*u*él) *v* inchar

**swelling** (ç*u*é-linng) *n* inchaço *m*

**swift** (ç*u*ift) *adj* rápido

\***swim** (ç*u*imm) *v* nadar

**swimmer** (ç*u*i-mã) *n* nadador *m*

**swimming** (ç*u*i-minng) *n* natação *f*; ~
**pool** piscina *f*

**swimming-trunks** (ç*u*i-minng-tranngkç) *pl* calções de banho

**swim-suit** (ç*u*imm-çuut) *n* fato de banho

**swindle** (ç*u*inn-däl) *v* burlar; *n* burla *f*

**swindler** (ç*u*inn-dlã) *n* burlão *m*

**swing** (çᵘinng) n baloiço m; balanço mBr

*swing (çᵘinng) v balançar

**Swiss** (çᵘiç) adj suíço

**switch** (çᵘitch) n interruptor m; v trocar; ~ off desligar; ~ on ligar

**switchboard** (çᵘitch-bóód) n quadro de distribuição

**Switzerland** (çᵘit-çã-lãnnd) Suíça f

**sword** (çóód) n espada f

**swum** (çᵘamm) v (pp swim)

**syllable** (çi-lã-bãl) n sílaba f

**symbol** (çimm-bãl) n símbolo m

**sympathetic** (çimm-pã-θé-tik) adj cordial, compreensivo

**sympathy** (çimm-pã-θi) n simpatia f; compaixão f

**symphony** (çimm-fã-ni) n sinfonia f

**symptom** (çimm-tãmm) n sintoma m

**synagogue** (çi-nã-ghógh) n sinagoga f

**synonym** (çi-nã-nimm) n sinónimo m

**synthetic** (çinn-θé-tik) adj sintético

**syphon** (çai-fãnn) n sifão m

**Syria** (çi-ri-ã) Síria f

**Syrian** (çi-ri-ãnn) adj sírio

**syringe** (çi-rinndj) n seringa f

**syrup** (çi-rãp) n xarope m

**system** (çi-çtãmm) n sistema m; **decimal** ~ sistema decimal

**systematic** (çi-çtã-mæ-tik) adj sistemático

# T

**table** (tei-bãl) n mesa f; tabela f; ~ **of contents** índice m; ~ **tennis** ténis de mesa

**table-cloth** (tei-bãl-klóθ) n toalha de mesa

**tablespoon** (tei-bãl-çpuunn) n colher de sopa

**tablet** (tæ-blit) n pastilha f

**taboo** (tã-buu) n tabu m

**tactics** (tæk-tikç) pl táctica f

**tag** (tægh) n etiqueta f

**tail** (teil) n cauda f

**tail-light** (teil-lait) n farol traseiro

**tailor** (tei-lã) n alfaiate m

**tailor-made** (tei-lã-meid) adj feito à medida

*take (teik) v tomar; agarrar; levar; perceber, entender, compreender; ~ **away** levar, tirar; ~ **off** descolar; ~ **out** tirar; ~ **over** tomar conta de; ~ **place** acontecer

**take-off** (tei-kóf) n descolagem f

**tale** (teil) n narrativa f, conto m

**talent** (tæ-lãnnt) n talento m

**talented** (tæ-lãnn-tid) adj dotado

**talk** (tóók) v falar; n conversa f

**talkative** (tóó-kã-tiv) adj falador

**tall** (tóól) adj alto

**tame** (teimm) adj domesticado, manso; v domesticar

**tampon** (tæmm-pãnn) n tampão m

**tangerine** (tænn-djã-riinn) n tangerina f

**tangible** (tænn-dji-bãl) adj tangível

**tank** (tænngk) n tanque m

**tanker** (tænng-kã) n navio-cisterna m

**tanned** (tænnd) adj bronzeado

**tap** (tæp) n torneira f; pancadinha f; v bater

**tape** (teip) n fita f; **adhesive** ~ fita adesiva; adesivo m; esparadrapo mBr

**tape-measure** (teip-mé-jã) n fita métrica

**tape-recorder** (teip-ri-kóó-dã) n gravador m

**tapestry** (tæ-pi-çtri) n tapeçaria f

**tar** (taa) n alcatrão m

**target** (taa-ghit) n alvo m, objectivo m

**tariff** (tæ-rif) n tarifa f

**tarpaulin** (taa-póó-linn) n toldo impermeável

task (taaçk) n tarefa f

taste (teiçt) n gosto m, paladar m; v *saber a; provar

tasteless (teiçt-lăç) adj insípido

tasty (tei-çti) adj saboroso

taught (tóót) v (p, pp teach)

tavern (tæ-vănn) n taberna f

tax (tækç) n imposto m; v lançar impostos

taxation (tæk-çei-chănn) n impostos mpl

tax-free (tœkç frii) adj isento de imposto

taxi (tæk-çi) n táxi m; ~ rank praça de táxis; ponto de táxis Br; ~ stand Am paragem de táxis

taxi-driver (tæk-çi-drai-vă) n motorista de táxi

taxi-meter (tæk-çi-mii-tă) n taxímetro m

taxiplane (tæk-çi-pleinn) n táxi aéreo

tea (tii) n chá m

*teach (tiitch) v ensinar

teacher (tii-tchă) n professor m; professora f, mestre m

teachings (tii-tchinngz) pl ensinamentos mpl

tea-cloth (tii-klóθ) n pano da loiça

teacup (tii-kap) n chávena de chá

team (tiimm) n equipa f

teapot (tii-pót) n bule m

*tear (té³) v rasgar

tear[1] (ti³) n lágrima f

tear[2] (té³) n rasgão m

tear-jerker (ti³-djää-kă) n lamechice f

tease (tiiz) v arreliar

tea-set (tii-çét) n serviço de chá

tea-shop (tii-chóp) n salão de chá

teaspoon (tii-çpuunn) n colher de chá

technical (ték-ni-kăl) adj técnico

technician (ték-ni-chănn) n técnico m

technique (ték-niik) n técnica f

technology (ték-nó-lă-dji) n tecnologia

f

teenager (tii-nei-djă) n adolescente m

teetotaller (tii-to^u-tă-lă) n abstémio m

telegram (té-li-ghræmm) n telegrama m

telegraph (té-li-ghraaf) v telegrafar; ~ pole poste telegráfico

telepathy (ti-lé-pă-θi) n telepatia f

telephone (té-li-fo^unn) n telefone m; ~ book Am lista telefónica, lista dos telefones; ~ booth cabina telefónica; ~ call chamada telefónica, telefonema m; ~ directory lista telefónica, lista dos telefones; ~ operator telefonista f

television (té-li-vi-jănn) n televisão f; ~ set aparelho de televisão; cable ~ televisão a cabo; satellite ~ televisão a satélite

*tell (tél) v *dizer; contar

temper (témm-pă) n mau génio

temperature (témm-pră-tchă) n temperatura f

tempest (témm-piçt) n tempestade f

temple (témm-păl) n templo m; fonte f

temporary (témm-pă-ră-ri) adj temporário, provisório

tempt (témmpt) v tentar

temptation (témmp-tei-chănn) n tentação f

ten (ténn) num dez

tenant (té-nănnt) n inquilino m

tend (ténnd) v *ter tendência; cuidar; ~ to tender para

tendency (ténn-dănn-çi) n tendência f, inclinação f

tender (ténn-dă) adj terno, delicado; tenro

tendon (ténn-dănn) n tendão m

tennis (té-niç) n ténis m; ~ shoes sapatos de ténis

tennis-court (té-niç-kóót) n campo de

ténis
**tense** (ténnç) *adj* tenso
**tension** (ténn-chänn) *n* tensão *f*
**tent** (ténnt) *n* tenda *f*
**tenth** (ténnθ) *num* décimo
**tepid** (té-pid) *adj* tépido
**term** (tããmm) *n* termo *m*; período *m*; condição *f*
**terminal** (tãã-mi-näl) *n* terminal *m*
**terrace** (té-räç) *n* terraço *m*
**terrain** (té-*reinn*) *n* terreno *m*
**terrible** (té-ri-bäl) *adj* medonho, terrível, tremendo
**terrific** (tä-*ri*-fik) *adj* fantástico
**terrify** (té-ri-fai) *v* aterrorizar; **terrifying** aterrador
**territory** (té-ri-tä-ri) *n* território *m*
**terror** (té-rä) *n* terror *m*
**terrorism** (té-rä-ri-zämm) *n* terror *m*, terrorismo *m*
**terrorist** (té-rä-riçt) *n* terrorista *m*
**test** (téçt) *n* prova *f*, teste *m*; *v* experimentar
**testify** (té-çti-fai) *v* testemunhar
**text** (tékçt) *n* texto *m*
**textbook** (tékç-buk) *n* compêndio *m*
**textile** (ték-çtail) *n* tecido *m*; *adj* têxtil
**texture** (tékç-tchä) *n* contextura *f*
**Thai** (tai) *adj* tailandês
**Thailand** (*tai*-lænnd) Tailândia *f*
**than** (ðænn) *conj* que
**thank** (θænngk) *v* agradecer; ~ **you** obrigado
**thankful** (θænngk-fäl) *adj* agradecido
**that** (ðæt) *adj* esse, aquele; *pron* aquele, isso; que; *conj* que
**thaw** (θóó) *v* degelar, descongelar; *n* degelo *m*
**the** (ðä-ði) *art o art*; **the ... the** quanto mais ... mais
**theatre** (θi-ä-tä) *n* teatro *m*
**theft** (θéft) *n* roubo *m*
**their** (ðé-ä) *adj* deles

**them** (ðémm) *pron* os; lhes
**theme** (θiimm) *n* tema *m*, assunto *m*
**themselves** (ðämm-çélvz) *pron* se; eles mesmos
**then** (ðénn) *adv* então; em seguida, depois
**theology** (θi-ó-lä-dji) *n* teologia *f*
**theoretical** (θi-ä-ré-ti-käl) *adj* teórico
**theory** (θiä-ri) *n* teoria *f*
**therapy** (θé-rä-pi) *n* terapia *f*
**there** (ðéä) *adv* lá; para ali
**therefore** (ðéä-fóó) *conj* portanto
**thermometer** (θä-mó-mi-tä) *n* termómetro *m*
**thermostat** (θää-mä-çtæt) *n* termóstato *m*
**these** (ðiiz) *adj* estes
**thesis** (θii-çiç) *n* (pl theses) tese *f*
**they** (ðei) *pron* eles
**thick** (θik) *adj* grosso; espesso
**thicken** (θi-känn) *v* engrossar
**thickness** (θik-näç) *n* grossura *f*
**thief** (θiif) *n* (pl thieves) ladrão *m*
**thigh** (θai) *n* coxa *f*
**thimble** (θimm-bäl) *n* dedal *m*
**thin** (θinn) *adj* fino; magro
**thing** (θinng) *n* coisa *f*
**\*think** (θinngk) *v* pensar; \*reflectir; ~ **of** pensar em; ~ **over** ponderar
**thinker** (θinng-kä) *n* pensador *m*
**third** (θääd) *num* terceiro
**thirst** (θääçt) *n* sede *f*
**thirsty** (θää-çti) *adj* sedento
**thirteen** (θää-tiinn) *num* treze
**thirteenth** (θää-tiinnθ) *num* décimo terceiro
**thirtieth** (θää-ti-äθ) *num* trigésimo
**thirty** (θää-ti) *num* trinta
**this** (ðiç) *adj* este; *pron* este
**thistle** (θi-çäl) *n* cardo *m*
**thorn** (θóónn) *n* espinho *m*
**thorough** (θa-rä) *adj* minucioso
**thoroughbred** (θa-rä-bréd) *adj* puro sangue

**thoroughfare** (*θa-rä-fé*ª) *n* artéria principal, estrada principal

**those** (ðoᵘz) *adj* esses; *pron* aqueles

**though** (ðoᵘ) *conj* ainda que, se bem que, embora; *adv* no entanto

**thought**¹ (θóót) *v* (p, pp think)

**thought**² (θóót) *n* pensamento *m*

**thoughtful** (θóót-fäl) *adj* pensativo; atencioso

**thousand** (*θau*-zännd) *num* mil

**thread** (θréd) *n* fio *m*; linha *f*; *v* enfiar

**threadbare** (*θréd*-bé*ª) *adj* coçado

**threat** (θrét) *n* ameaça *f*

**threaten** (*θré*-tänn) *v* ameaçar; **threatening** ameaçador

**three** (θrii) *num* três

**three-quarter** (θrii-k*ᵘóó-tä) *adj* três quartos

**threshold** (*θré*-choᵘld) *n* limiar *m*

**threw** (θruu) *v* (p throw)

**thrifty** (*θrif*-ti) *adj* económico

**throat** (θroᵘt) *n* garganta *f*

**throne** (θroᵘnn) *n* trono *m*

**through** (θruu) *prep* através

**throughout** (θruu-*aut*) *adv* por toda a parte

**throw** (θroᵘ) *n* lançamento *m*

***throw** (θroᵘ) *v* atirar, lançar, deitar

**thrush** (θrach) *n* tordo *m*

**thumb** (θamm) *n* polegar *m*

**thumbtack** (*θamm*-tæk) *nAm* pionés *m*

**thump** (θammp) *v* martelar

**thunder** (*θann*-dä) *n* trovão *m*; *v* troar

**thunderstorm** (*θann*-dä-çtóómm) *n* trovoada *f*

**thundery** (*θann*-dä-ri) *adj* tempestuoso

**Thursday** (*θääz*-di) quinta-feira *f*

**thus** (ðaç) *adv* assim

**thyme** (taimm) *n* tomilho *m*

**tick** (tik) *n* marca *f*; ~ **off** marcar

**ticket** (*ti*-kit) *n* bilhete *m*; multa *f*; ~

**collector** revisor *m*; ~ **machine** bilheteira automática

**tickle** (*ti*-käl) *v* *fazer cócegas

**tide** (taid) *n* maré *f*; **high** ~ maré cheia; **low** ~ maré baixa

**tidings** (*tai*-dinngz) *pl* notícias *fpl*

**tidy** (*tai*-di) *adj* asseado; ~ **up** arrumar

**tie** (tai) *v* atar, *dar um nó; *n* gravata *f*

**tiger** (*tai*-ghä) *n* tigre *m*

**tight** (tait) *adj* apertado; estreito; *adv* fortemente

**tighten** (*tai*-tänn) *v* apertar, estreitar; apertar-se

**tights** (taitç) *pl* collants *mpl*

**tile** (tail) *n* azulejo *m*; telha *f*

**till** (til) *prep* até; *conj* até que

**timber** (*timm*-bä) *n* madeira de construção

**time** (taimm) *n* tempo *m*; vez *f*; **all the** ~ continuamente; **in** ~ a tempo; ~ **of arrival** hora de chegada; ~ **of departure** hora de partida

**time-saving** (*taimm*-çei-vinng) *adj* economizador de tempo

**timetable** (*taimm*-tei-bäl) *n* horário *m*

**timid** (*ti*-mid) *adj* tímido

**timidity** (ti-*mi*-dä-ti) *n* timidez *f*

**tin** (tinn) *n* estanho *m*; lata *f*; **tinned food** conservas *fpl*

**tin-opener** (*ti*-noᵘ-pä-nä) *n* abre-latas *m*

**tiny** (*tai*-ni) *adj* minúsculo

**tip** (tip) *n* ponta *f*; gorjeta *f*

**tire**¹ (tai*ª) *n* pneu *m*

**tire**² (tai*ª) *v* cansar

**tired** (tai*ªd) *adj* fatigado, cansado; ~ **of** farto de

**tiring** (*tai*ª-rinng) *adj* fatigante

**tissue** (*ti*-chuu) *n* tecido *m*; lenço de papel

**title** (*tai*-täl) *n* título *m*

**to** (tuu) *prep* até; a, para

**toad** (touᵈ) *n* sapo *m*

**toadstool** (touᵈ-çtuul) *n* cogumelo *m*

**toast** (touçt) *n* torrada *f*; brinde *m*

**tobacco** (tă-*bæ*-kouᵘ) *n* (pl ~s) tabaco *m*; ~ **pouch** bolsa de tabaco

**tobacconist** (tă-*bæ*-kă-niçt) *n* tabacaria *f*; **tobacconist's** tabacaria *f*

**today** (tă-*dei*) *adv* hoje

**toddler** (*tód*-lă) *n* criança pequenina

**toe** (touᵘ) *n* dedo do pé

**toffee** (*tó*-fi) *n* caramelo *m*

**together** (tă-*ghé*-ðă) *adv* juntos

**toilet** (*toi*-lăt) *n* retretes *fpl*; ~ **case** estojo de toalete

**toilet-paper** (*toi*-lăt-pei-pă) *n* papel higiénico

**toiletry** (*toi*-lă-tri) *n* artigos de toalete

**token** (*touᵘ*-kănn) *n* sinal *m*; prova *f*; ficha *f*

**told** (touᵘld) *v* (p, pp tell)

**tolerable** (*tó*-lă-ră-băl) *adj* tolerável

**toll** (touᵘl) *n* portagem *f*

**tomato** (tă-*maa*-touᵘ) *n* (pl ~es) tomate *m*

**tomb** (tuumm) *n* túmulo *m*

**tombstone** (*tuumm*-çtouᵘnn) *n* pedra tumular

**tomorrow** (tă-*mó*-rouᵘ) *adv* amanhã

**ton** (tann) *n* tonelada *f*

**tone** (touᵘnn) *n* tom *m*; timbre *m*

**tongs** (tónnz) *pl* tenaz *f*

**tongue** (tanng) *n* língua *f*

**tonic** (*tó*-nik) *n* tónico *m*

**tonight** (tă-*nait*) *adv* esta noite

**tonsilitis** (tónn-çă-*lai*-tiç) *n* amigdalite *f*

**tonsils** (tónn-çălz) *pl* amígdalas *fpl*

**too** (tuu) *adv* demasiado; também

**took** (tuk) *v* (p take)

**tool** (tuul) *n* ferramenta *f*, instrumento *m*; ~ **kit** caixa de ferramenta

**tooth** (tuuθ) *n* (pl teeth) dente *m*

**toothache** (*tuu*-θeik) *n* dor de dentes

**toothbrush** (*tuu*θ-brach) *n* escova de dentes

**toothpaste** (*tuu*θ-peiçt) *n* pasta de dentes

**toothpick** (*tuu*θ-pik) *n* palito *m*

**toothpowder** (*tuu*θ-pau-dă) *n* pós dentífricos

**top** (tóp) *n* cimo *m*; parte de cima; tampa *f*; superior; **on** ~ **of** em cima de; ~ **side** parte superior

**topcoat** (*tóp*-kouᵘt) *n* sobretudo *m*

**topic** (*tó*-pik) *n* tópico *m*

**topical** (*tó*-pi-kăl) *adj* actual

**torch** (tóótch) *n* archote *m*; lanterna de bolso

**torment**[1] (tóó-*ménnt*) *v* atormentar

**torment**[2] (*tóó*-ménnt) *n* tormento *m*

**torture** (*tóó*-tchă) *n* tortura *f*; *v* torturar

**toss** (tóç) *v* lançar, arremessar

**tot** (tót) *n* criança pequena

**total** (*touᵘ*-tăl) *adj* total; completo, absoluto; *n* total *m*

**totalitarian** (touᵘ-tæ-li-*té*ă-ri-ănn) *adj* totalitário

**totalizator** (*touᵘ*-tă-lai-zei-tă) *n* totalizador *m*

**touch** (tatch) *v* tocar; *dizer respeito a; *n* contacto *m*, toque *m*; tacto *m*

**touching** (*ta*-tchinng) *adj* tocante

**tough** (taf) *adj* duro

**tour** (tuă) *n* circuito turístico

**tourism** (*tu*ă-ri-zămm) *n* turismo *m*

**tourist** (*tu*ă-riçt) *n* turista *m*; ~ **class** classe turística; ~ **office** agência de turismo

**tournament** (*tu*ă-nă-mănnt) *n* torneio *m*

**tow** (touᵘ) *v* rebocar

**towards** (tă-*ᵘóódz*) *prep* em direcção a; para com

**towel** (tauăl) *n* toalha *f*

**towelling** (*tau*ă-linng) *n* pano para toalhas

**tower** (tauă) *n* torre *f*

**town** (taunn) *n* cidade *f;* ~ **centre** centro da cidade; ~ **hall** câmara municipal

**townspeople** (taunnz-pii-pǎl) *pl* citadinos *mpl*

**toxic** (tók-çik) *adj* tóxico

**toy** (toi) *n* brinquedo *m*

**toyshop** (toi-chóp) *n* loja de brinquedos

**trace** (treiç) *n* rasto *m; v* *seguir o rasto de

**track** (træk) *n* via *f;* pista *f*

**tractor** (træk-tǎ) *n* tractor *m*

**trade** (treid) *n* comércio *m;* ofício *m; v* comerciar, *negociar

**trademark** (treid-maak) *n* marca de fábrica

**trader** (trei-dǎ) *n* comerciante *m*

**tradesman** (treidz-mǎnn) *n* (pl -men) comerciante *m*

**trade-union** (treid-¹uu-n¹ǎnn) *n* sindicato *m*

**tradition** (trǎ-di-chǎnn) *n* tradição *f*

**traditional** (trǎ-di-chǎ-nǎl) *adj* tradicional

**traffic** (træ-fik) *n* trânsito *m;* ~ **jam** engarrafamento de trânsito; ~ **light** semáforo *m*

**trafficator** (træ-fi-kei-tǎ) *n* indicador de direcção

**tragedy** (træ-djǎ-di) *n* tragédia *f*

**tragic** (træ-djik) *adj* trágico

**trail** (treil) *n* pista *f,* atalho *m*

**trailer** (trei-lǎ) *n* reboque *m; nAm* caravana *f*

**train** (treinn) *n* comboio *m;* trem *mBr; v* treinar, adestrar; **stopping** ~ comboio correio; **through** ~ comboio directo; ~ **ferry** ferry-boat *m*

**training** (trei-ninng) *n* treino *m*

**trait** (treit) *n* traço *m*

**traitor** (trei-tǎ) *n* traidor *m*

**tram** (træmm) *n* eléctrico *m;* bonde *mBr*

**tramp** (træmmp) *n* vagabundo *m,* vadio *m; v* vadiar

**tranquil** (trænng-kⁱil) *adj* tranquilo

**tranquillizer** (trænng-kⁱi-lai-zǎ) *n* calmante *m*

**transaction** (trænn-zæk-chǎnn) *n* transacção *f*

**transatlantic** (trænn-zǎt-lænn-tik) *adj* transatlântico

**transfer** (trænnç-fǎǎ) *v* *transferir

**transform** (trænnç-fóómm) *v* transformar, mudar

**transformer** (trænnç-fóó-mǎ) *n* transformador *m*

**transition** (trænn-çi-chǎnn) *n* transição *f*

**translate** (trænnç-leit) *v* *traduzir

**translation** (trænnç-lei-chǎnn) *n* tradução *f*

**translator** (trænnç-lei-tǎ) *n* tradutor *m*

**transmission** (trænnz-mi-chǎnn) *n* transmissão *f*

**transmit** (trænnz-mit) *v* transmitir

**transmitter** (trænnz-mi-tǎ) *n* emissor *m*

**transparent** (trænn-çpéǎ-rǎnnt) *adj* transparente

**transport**¹ (trænn-çpóót) *n* transporte *m*

**transport**² (trænn-çpóót) *v* transportar

**transportation** (trænn-çpóó-tei-chǎnn) *n* transporte *m*

**trap** (træp) *n* armadilha *f*

**trash** (træch) *n* lixo *m*

**travel** (træ-vǎl) *v* viajar; ~ **agency** agência de viagens; ~ **agent** agente de viagens; ~ **insurance** seguro de viagem; **travelling expenses** despesas de viagem

**traveller** (træ-vǎ-lǎ) *n* viajante *m;* **traveller's cheque** cheque de viagem

**tray** (trei) *n* tabuleiro *m*

**treason** (*trii*-zänn) *n* traição *f*

**treasure** (tré-jä) *n* tesouro *m*

**treasurer** (tré-jä-rä) *n* tesoureiro *m*

**treasury** (tré-jä-ri) *n* tesouro público; caixa *f*

**treat** (triit) *v* tratar

**treatment** (*triit*-männt) *n* tratamento *m*

**treaty** (*trii*-ti) *n* tratado *m*

**tree** (trii) *n* árvore *f*

**tremble** (*trémm*-bäl) *v* tremer, tiritar; vibrar

**tremendous** (tri-*ménn*-däç) *adj* formidável

**trespass** (tréç-päç) *v* infringir

**trespasser** (tréç-pä-çä) *n* intruso *m*

**trial** (trai<sup>ä</sup>l) *n* julgamento *m*; experiência *f*

**triangle** (*trai*-ænng-ghäl) *n* triângulo *m*

**triangular** (trai-*ænng*-gh<sup>i</sup>u-lä) *adj* triangular

**tribe** (traib) *n* tribo *f*

**tributary** (*tri*-b<sup>i</sup>u-tä-ri) *n* afluente *m*

**tribute** (*tri*-b<sup>i</sup>uut) *n* homenagem *f*

**trick** (trik) *n* manha *f*; truque *m*

**trigger** (*tri*-ghä) *n* gatilho *m*

**trim** (trimm) *v* aparar

**trip** (trip) *n* viagem *f*, passeio *m*

**triumph** (*trai*-ämmf) *n* triunfo *m*; *v* triunfar

**triumphant** (trai-*amm*-fännt) *adj* triunfante

**trolley-bus** (*tró*-li-baç) *n* troleicarro *m*

**troops** (truupç) *pl* tropas *fpl*

**tropical** (*tró*-pi-käl) *adj* tropical

**tropics** (*tró*-pikç) *pl* trópicos *mpl*

**trouble** (*tra*-bäl) *n* incómodo *m*, preocupação *f*; *v* incomodar

**troublesome** (*tra*-bäl-çämm) *adj* macador

**trousers** (*trau*-zäz) *pl* calças *fpl*

**trout** (traut) *n* (pl ~) truta *f*

**truck** (trak) *nAm* camião *m*

**true** (truu) *adj* verdadeiro, real; fiel, leal

**trumpet** (*tramm*-pit) *n* trombeta *f*

**trunk** (tranngk) *n* baú *m*; tronco *m*; *nAm* mala *f*; **trunks** calções de ginástica

**trunk-call** (*tranngk*-kóól) *n* chamada interurbana

**trust** (traçt) *v* confiar em; *n* confiança *f*

**trustworthy** (traçt-<sup>u</sup>ää-ði) *adj* digno de confiança

**truth** (truuθ) *n* verdade *f*

**truthful** (*truuθ*-fäl) *adj* verídico

**try** (trai) *v* experimentar, tentar, esforçar-se; *n* tentativa *f*; ~ **on** provar

**tube** (t<sup>i</sup>uub) *n* cano *m*, tubo *m*

**tuberculosis** (t<sup>i</sup>uu-bää-k<sup>i</sup>u-*lo*<sup>u</sup>-çiç) *n* tuberculose *f*

**Tuesday** (*t<sup>i</sup>uuz*-di) terça-feira *f*

**tug** (tagh) *v* rebocar; *n* rebocador *m*; esticão *m*

**tuition** (t<sup>i</sup>uu-*i*-chänn) *n* instrução *f*

**tulip** (*t<sup>i</sup>uu*-lip) *n* tulipa *f*

**tumbler** (*tamm*-blä) *n* copo *m*

**tumour** (*t<sup>i</sup>uu*-mä) *n* tumor *m*

**tuna** (*t<sup>i</sup>uu*-nä) *n* (pl ~, ~s) atum *m*

**tune** (t<sup>i</sup>uunn) *n* melodia *f*; ~ **in** sintonizar

**tuneful** (*t<sup>i</sup>uunn*-fäl) *adj* melodioso

**tunic** (*t<sup>i</sup>uu*-nik) *n* túnica *f*

**Tunisia** (t<sup>i</sup>uu-*ni*-zi-ä) Tunísia *f*

**Tunisian** (t<sup>i</sup>uu-*ni*-zi-änn) *adj* tunisino

**tunnel** (*ta*-näl) *n* túnel *m*

**turbine** (*tää*-bainn) *n* turbina *f*

**turbojet** (tää-bo<sup>u</sup>-*djét*) *n* motor a jacto-propulsão

**Turk** (tääk) *n* turco *m*

**Turkey** (*tää*-ki) Turquia *f*

**turkey** (*tää*-ki) *n* peru *m*

**Turkish** (*tää*-kich) *adj* turco; ~ **bath**

banho turco

**turn** (tăănn) v virar; rodar; n viragem f, volta f; curva f; vez f; ~ **back** voltar atrás; ~ **down** rejeitar; ~ **into** transformar em; ~ **off** fechar; ~ **on** ligar, acender; abrir; ~ **over** inverter; ~ **round** voltar; virar-se

**turning** (tăă-ninng) n curva f

**turning-point** (tăă-ninng-poinnt) n momento decisivo

**turnover** (tăă-no⁰-vă) n movimento de negócios; ~ **tax** imposto sobre a cifra de negócios

**turnpike** (tăănn-paik) nAm estrada com portagem

**turpentine** (tăă-pănn-tainn) n terebentina f

**turtle** (tăă-tăl) n tartaruga f

**tutor** (tⁱuu-tă) n preceptor m; tutor m

**tuxedo** (tak-çii-do⁰) nAm (pl ~s, ~es) smoking m

**tweed** (tⁱuiid) n tweed m

**tweezers** (tⁱuii-zăz) pl pinça f

**twelfth** (tⁱuélfθ) num décimo segundo

**twelve** (tⁱuélv) num doze

**twentieth** (tⁱuénn-ti-ăθ) num vigésimo

**twenty** (tⁱuénn-ti) num vinte

**twice** (tⁱuaiç) adv duas vezes

**twig** (tⁱuigh) n raminho m

**twilight** (tⁱuai-lait) n crepúsculo m

**twine** (tⁱuainn) n guita f

**twins** (tⁱuinnz) pl gémeos mpl; **twin beds** duas camas

**twist** (tⁱuiçt) v torcer; n torção f

**two** (tuu) num dois

**two-piece** (tuu-piiç) adj de duas peças

**type** (taip) v escrever à máquina, dactilografar; n tipo m

**typewriter** (taip-rai-tă) n máquina de escrever

**typewritten** (taip-ri-tănn) dactilografado

**typhoid** (tai-foid) n tifo m

**typical** (ti-pi-kăl) adj típico, característico

**typist** (tai-piçt) n dactilógrafa f

**tyrant** (taiⁱ-rănnt) n tirano m

**tyre** (taiⁱ) n pneu m; ~ **pressure** pressão dos pneus

# U

**ugly** (a-ghli) adj fcio

**ulcer** (al-çă) n úlcera f

**ultimate** (al-ti-măt) adj último, final

**ultraviolet** (al-tră-vaiⁱ-lăt) adj ultravioleta

**umbrella** (amm-bré-lă) n guarda-chuva m

**umpire** (amm-paiⁱ) n árbitro m

**unable** (a-nei-băl) adj incapaz

**unacceptable** (a-năk-çép-tă-băl) adj inaceitável

**unaccountable** (a-nă-kaunn-tă-băl) adj inexplicável

**unaccustomed** (a-nă-ka-çtămmd) adj desacostumado

**unanimous** (ⁱuu-næ-ni-măç) adj unânime

**unanswered** (a-naann-çăd) adj sem resposta

**unauthorized** (a-nóó-θă-raizd) adj ilícito

**unavoidable** (a-nă-voi-dă-băl) adj inevitável

**unaware** (a-nă-ᵘéⁱ) adj inconsciente

**unbearable** (ann-béⁱ-ră-băl) adj insuportável

**unbreakable** (ann-brei-kă-băl) adj inquebrável

**unbroken** (ann-bro⁰-kănn) adj inteiro

**unbutton** (ann-ba-tănn) v desabotoar

**uncertain** (ann-çăă-tănn) adj incerto

**uncle** (anng-kăl) n tio m

**unclean** (ann-kliinn) adj sujo

**uncomfortable** (ann-*kamm*-fă-tă-băl) *adj* desconfortável

**uncommon** (ann-*kó*-mănn) *adj* insólito, raro

**unconditional** (ann-kănn-*di*-chă-năl) *adj* incondicional

**unconscious** (ann-*kónn*-chăç) *adj* inconsciente

**uncork** (ann-*kóók*) *v* desarrolhar

**uncover** (ann-*ka*-vă) *v* destapar

**uncultivated** (ann-*kal*-ti-vei-tid) *adj* inculto

**under** (*ann*-dă) *prep* debaixo de

**undercurrent** (*ann*-dă-ka-rănnt) *n* ressaca *f*

**underestimate** (ann-dă-*ré*-çti-meit) *v* menosprezar

**underground** (*ann*-dă-ghraunnd) *adj* subterrâneo; *n* metropolitano *m*

**underline** (ann-dă-*lainn*) *v* sublinhar

**underneath** (ann-dă-*niiθ*) *adv* debaixo

**undershirt** (*ann*-dă-chăăt) *n* camisola interior; camiseta *fBr*

**undersigned** (*ann*-dă-çainnd) *n* abaixo-assinado *m*

***understand** (ann-dă-*çtænnd*) *v* compreender, perceber

**understanding** (ann-dă-*çtænn*-dinng) *n* compreensão *f*

***undertake** (ann-dă-*teik*) *v* empreender

**undertaking** (ann-dă-*tei*-kinng) *n* empresa *f*

**underwater** (*ann*-dă-*ᵘóó*-tă) *adj* submarino

**underwear** (*ann*-dă-ᵘé*ă*) *n* roupa interior

**undesirable** (ann-di-*zaiă*-ră-băl) *adj* indesejável

***undo** (ann-*duu*) *v* *desfazer

**undoubtedly** (ann-*dau*-tid-li) *adv* sem dúvida

**undress** (ann-*dréç*) *v* *despir-se

**undulating** (*ann*-dᶦu-lei-tinng) *adj* ondulante

**unearned** (a-*năănnd*) *adj* imerecido

**uneasy** (a-*nii*-zi) *adj* pouco à vontade

**uneducated** (a-*né*-dᶦu-kei-tid) *adj* inculto

**unemployed** (a-nimm-*ploid*) *adj* desempregado

**unemployment** (a-nimm-*ploi*-mănnt) *n* desemprego *m*

**unequal** (a-*nii*-kᵘăl) *adj* desigual

**uneven** (a-*nii*-vănn) *adj* desigual, rugoso; irregular

**unexpected** (a-nik-*çpék*-tid) *adj* inesperado, imprevisto

**unfair** (ann-*féă*) *adj* injusto

**unfaithful** (ann-*feiθ*-făl) *adj* infiel

**unfamiliar** (ann-fă-*mil*-ᶦă) *adj* desconhecido

**unfasten** (ann-*faa*-cănn) *v* soltar, desprender

**unfavourable** (ann-*fei*-vă-ră-băl) *adj* desfavorável

**unfit** (ann-*fit*) *adj* inadequado

**unfold** (ann-*foᵘld*) *v* desdobrar

**unfortunate** (ann-*fóó*-tchă-năt) *adj* desgraçado

**unfortunately** (ann-*fóó*-tchă-năt-li) *adv* infelizmente

**unfriendly** (ann-*frénnd*-li) *adj* antipático

**unfurnished** (ann-*făă*-nicht) *adj* desmobilado

**ungrateful** (ann-*ghreit*-făl) *adj* ingrato

**unhappy** (ann-*hæ*-pi) *adj* infeliz

**unhealthy** (ann-*hél*-θi) *adj* doentio

**unhurt** (ann-*hăăt*) *adj* ileso

**uniform** (*ᶦuu*-ni-fóómm) *n* uniforme *m*; *adj* uniforme

**unimportant** (a-nimm-*póó*-tănnt) *adj* insignificante

**uninhabitable** (a-ninn-*hæ*-bi-tă-băl) *adj* inabitável

**uninhabited** (a-ninn-*hæ*-bi-tid) *adj* desabitado

**unintentional** (a-ninn-*ténn*-chă-năl) *adj*
involuntário

**union** (*i*uu-n*i*ănn) *n* união *f*; confederação *f*, liga *f*

**unique** (*i*uu-*niik*) *adj* único

**unit** (*i*uu-nit) *n* unidade *f*

**unite** (*i*uu-*nait*) *v* unir, reunir

**United States** (*i*uu-*nai*-tid çteitç) Estados Unidos

**unity** (*i*uu-nă-ti) *n* unidade *f*

**universal** (*i*uu-ni-*văă*-çăl) *adj* geral,
universal

**universe** (*i*uu-ni-*văăç*) *n* universo *m*

**university** (*i*uu-ni-*văă*-çă-ti) *n* universidade *f*

**unjust** (ann-*djaçt*) *adj* injusto

**unkind** (ann-*kainnd*) *adj* desagradável,
pouco amável

**unknown** (ann-*no*ᵘnn) *adj* desconhecido

**unlawful** (ann-*lóó*-făl) *adj* ilegal

**unlearn** (ann-*lăănn*) *v* desaprender

**unless** (ănn-*léç*) *conj* a não ser que

**unlike** (ann-*laik*) *adj* diferente

**unlikely** (ann-*lai*-kli) *adj* improvável

**unlimited** (ann-*li*-mi-tid) *adj* ilimitado,
sem fim

**unload** (ann-*lo*ᵘd) *v* descarregar

**unlock** (ann-*lók*) *v* abrir

**unlucky** (ann-*la*-ki) *adj* infortunado

**unnecessary** (ann-*né*-çă-çă-ri) *adj* desnecessário

**unoccupied** (a-*nó*-k*i*u-paid) *adj* desocupado

**unofficial** (a-nă-*fi*-chăl) *adj* oficioso

**unpack** (ann-*pæk*) *v* desempacotar

**unpleasant** (ann-*plé*-zănnt) *adj* desagradável; maçador, aborrecido

**unpopular** (ann-*pó*-p*i*u-lă) *adj* pouco
popular, impopular

**unprotected** (ann-pră-*ték*-tid) *adj* desprotegido

**unqualified** (ann-*k*ᵘó-li-faid) *adj* incompetente

**unreal** (ann-*ri*ă*l*) *adj* irreal

**unreasonable** (ann-*rii*-ză-nă-băl) *adj*
desarrazoado

**unreliable** (ann-ri-*lai*-ă-băl) *adj* indigno de confiança

**unrest** (ann-*réçt*) *n* agitação *f*; desassossego *m*

**unsafe** (ann-*çeif*) *adj* inseguro

**unsatisfactory** (ann-çæ-tiç-*fæk*-tă-ri)
*adj* insatisfatório

**unscrew** (ann-*çkruu*) *v* desaparafusar

**unselfish** (ann-*çél*-fich) *adj* desinteressado

**unsound** (ann-*çaunnd*) *adj* doentio

**unstable** (ann-*çtei*-băl) *adj* instável

**unsteady** (ann-*çté*-di) *adj* vacilante,
instável

**unsuccessful** (ann-çăk-*çéç*-făl) *adj*
mal sucedido

**unsuitable** (ann-*çuu*-tă-băl) *adj* inadequado

**unsurpassed** (ann-çă-*paaçt*) *adj* insuperável

**untidy** (ann-*tai*-di) *adj* desalinhado;
desarrumado

**untie** (ann-*tai*) *v* desatar

**until** (ănn-*til*) *prep* até

**untrue** (ann-*truu*) *adj* falso

**untrustworthy** (ann-*traçt*-ᵘăă-ði) *adj*
indigno de confiança

**unusual** (ann-*i*uu-ju-ăl) *adj* desusado

**unwell** (ann-ᵘé*l*) *adj* indisposto

**unwilling** (ann-ᵘ*i*-linng) *adj* de má
vontade

**unwise** (ann-ᵘ*aiz*) *adj* imprudente

**unwrap** (ann-*ræp*) *v* desembrulhar

**up** (ap) *adv* em cima, acima, para cima

**upholster** (ap-*ho*ᵘl-çtă) *v* forrar, estofar

**upkeep** (*ap*-kiip) *n* manutenção *f*

**uplands** (*ap*-lănndz) *pl* terras altas

**upon** (ă-*pónn*) *prep* sobre

**upper** (a-pă) *adj* superior

**upright** (*ap*-rait) *adj* direito; *adv* em pé

***upset** (ap-çét) *v* transtornar; *adj* transtornado

**upside-down** (ap-çaid-*daunn*) *adv* de pernas para o ar

**upstairs** (ap-çté*ª*z) *adv* em cima; para cima

**upstream** (ap-*çtriimm*) *adv* rio acima

**upwards** (*ap-*ᵘādz) *adv* para cima

**urban** (*ǟ*-bǟnn) *adj* urbano

**urge** (ǟdj) *v* incitar; *n* impulso *m*

**urgency** (*ǟ*-djǟnn-çi) *n* urgência *f*

**urgent** (*ǟ*-djǟnnt) *adj* urgente

**urine** (*'u*ª-rinn) *n* urina *f*

**Uruguay** (*'u*ª-rǟ-ghᵘai) Uruguai *m*

**Uruguayan** (*'u*ª-rǟ-*gh*ᵘai-ǟnn) *adj* uruguaio

**us** (aç) *pron* nós

**usable** (*'uu*-zǟ-bǟl) *adj* utilizável

**usage** (*'uu*-zidj) *n* uso *m*

**use**¹ (*'uuz*) *v* usar; ***be used to ***estar habituado a; ~ **up** *****consumir

**use**² (*'uuç*) *n* uso *m*; utilidade *f*; ***be of** ~ *****servir

**useful** (*'uuç*-fǟl) *adj* útil

**useless** (*'uuç*-lǟc) *adj* inútil

**user** (*'uu*-zǟ) *n* o que usa, utente *m*

**usher** (a-chǟ) *n* arrumador *m*

**usherette** (a-chǟ-rét) *n* arrumadora *f*

**usual** (*'uu*-ju-ǟl) *adj* usual

**usually** (*'uu*-ju-ǟ-li) *adv* habitualmente

**utensil** (*'uu*-*ténn*-çǟl) *n* utensílio *m*, ferramenta *f*

**utility** (*'uu*-*ti*-lǟ-ti) *n* utilidade *f*

**utilize** (*'uu*-ti-laiz) *v* utilizar

**utmost** (at-moᵘçt) *adj* máximo

**utter** (a-tǟ) *adj* completo, total; *v* emitir

# V

**vacancy** (vei-kǟnn-çi) *n* vaga *f*

**vacant** (*vei*-kǟnnt) *adj* vago

**vacate** (vǟ-*keit*) *v* vagar

**vacation** (vǟ-*kei*-chǟnn) *n* férias *fpl*

**vaccinate** (væk-çi-neit) *v* vacinar

**vaccination** (væk-çi-*nei*-chǟnn) *n* vacinação *f*

**vacuum** (væ-kⁱu-ǟmm) *n* vácuo *m*; ~ **cleaner** aspirador *m*; ~ **flask** garrafa termos

**vagrancy** (*vei*-ghrǟnn-çi) *n* vadiagem *f*

**vague** (veigh) *adj* vago

**vain** (veinn) *adj* vaidoso; vão; **in** ~ em vão, inutilmente

**valet** (væ-lit) *n* criado *m*, criado de quarto

**valid** (væ-lid) *adj* válido

**valley** (væ-li) *n* vale *m*

**valuable** (væ-lⁱu-bǟl) *adj* valioso, de valor; **valuables** valores *mpl*

**value** (væ-lⁱuu) *n* valor *m*; *v* avaliar

**valve** (vælv) *n* válvula *f*

**van** (vænn) *n* furgoneta *f*

**vanilla** (vǟ-*ni*-lǟ) *n* baunilha *f*

**vanish** (væ-nich) *v* desaparecer

**vapour** (*vei*-pǟ) *n* vapor *m*

**variable** (vé*ª*-ri-ǟ-bǟl) *adj* variável

**variation** (vé*ª*-ri-*ei*-chǟnn) *n* variação *f*; mudança *f*

**varied** (vé*ª*-rid) *adj* variado

**variety** (vǟ-*rai*-ǟ-ti) *n* variedade *f*; ~ **show** espectáculo de variedades; ~ **theatre** teatro de variedades

**various** (vé*ª*-ri-ǟç) *adj* diversos

**varnish** (vaa-nich) *n* verniz *m*; *v* envernizar

**vary** (vé*ª*-ri) *v* variar; mudar; *****diferir

**vase** (vaaz) *n* vaso *m*

**vast** (vaaçt) *adj* vasto, imenso

**vault** (vóólt) *n* abóbada *f*; casa-forte *f*

**veal** (viil) *n* vitela *f*

**vegetable** (*vé*-djä-tä-bäl) *n* legume *m*

**vegetarian** (vé-dji-té*ä*-ri-änn) *n* vegetariano *m*

**vegetation** (vé-dji-*tei*-chänn) *n* vegetação *f*

**vehicle** (*vii*-ä-käl) *n* veículo *m*

**veil** (veil) *n* véu *m*

**vein** (veinn) *n* veia *f*; **varicose** ~ variz *f*

**velvet** (*vél*-vit) *n* veludo *m*

**velveteen** (vél-vi-*tiinn*) *n* belbutina *f*

**venerable** (*vé*-nä-rä-bäl) *adj* venerável

**venereal disease** (vi-*ni*ä-ri-äl di *ziiz*) doença venérea

**Venezuela** (vé-ni-z*u*ei-lä) Venezuela *f*

**Venezuelan** (vé-ni-z*u*ei-länn) *adj* venezuelano

**ventilate** (*vénn*-ti-leit) *v* ventilar, arejar

**ventilation** (vénn-ti-*lei*-chänn) *n* ventilação *f*; arejamento *m*

**ventilator** (*vénn*-ti-lei-tä) *n* ventilador *m*

**venture** (*vénn*-tchä) *v* aventurar

**veranda** (vä-*rænn*-dä) *n* varanda *f*

**verb** (vääb) *n* verbo *m*

**verbal** (*vää*-bäl) *adj* verbal

**verdict** (*vää*-dikt) *n* sentença *f*, veredicto *m*

**verge** (väädj) *n* borda *f*

**verify** (vé-ri-fai) *v* verificar

**verse** (vääç) *n* verso *m*

**version** (*vää*-chänn) *n* versão *f*

**versus** (*vää*-çäç) *prep* contra

**vertical** (*vää*-ti-käl) *adj* vertical

**vertigo** (*vää*-ti-gho*u*) *n* vertigem *f*

**very** (*vé*-ri) *adv* muito; *adj* preciso, verdadeiro; extremo

**vessel** (*vé*-çäl) *n* embarcação *f*, navio *m*; vasilha *f*

**vest** (véçt) *n* camisa *f*; *nAm* colete *m*

**veterinary surgeon** (*vé*-tri-nä-ri çää-djänn) veterinário *m*

**via** (vai*ä*) *prep* via

**viable** (*vai*ä-bäl) *adj* viável

**viaduct** (*vai*ä-dakt) *n* viaduto *m*

**vibrate** (vai-*breit*) *v* vibrar

**vibration** (vai-*brei*-chänn) *n* vibração *f*

**vicar** (*vi*-kä) *n* vigário *m*

**vicarage** (*vi*-kä-ridj) *n* presbitério *m*

**vicinity** (vi-*çi*-nä-ti) *n* vizinhança *f*, proximidades *fpl*

**vicious** (*vi*-chäç) *adj* vicioso

**victim** (*vik*-timm) *n* vítima *f*

**victory** (*vik*-tä-ri) *n* vitória *f*

**video** (*vi*-di-o*u*) *n* vídeo *m*; ~ **camera** vídeo câmera; ~ **cassette** videocassete; ~ **recorder** videocassete

**view** (v*i*uu) *n* vista *f*; opinião *f*, parecer *m*; *v* observar

**view-finder** (v*i*uu-fainn-dä) *n* visor *m*

**vigilant** (*vi*-dji-lännt) *adj* vigilante

**villa** (*vi*-lä) *n* vivenda *f*; vila *fBr*

**village** (*vi*-lidj) *n* aldeia *f*

**villain** (*vi*-länn) *n* patife *m*

**vine** (vainn) *n* videira *f*

**vinegar** (*vi*-ni-ghä) *n* vinagre *m*

**vineyard** (*vinn*-¹äd) *n* vinha *f*

**vintage** (*vinn*-tidj) *n* vindima *f*

**violation** (vai*ä*-*lei*-chänn) *n* violação *f*

**violence** (*vai*ä-lännç) *n* violência *f*

**violent** (*vai*ä-lännt) *adj* violento; impetuoso

**violet** (*vai*ä-lät) *n* violeta *f*

**violin** (vai*ä*-*linn*) *n* violino *m*

**virgin** (*vää*-djinn) *n* virgem *f*

**virtue** (*vää*-tchuu) *n* virtude *f*

**visa** (*vii*-zä) *n* visto *m*

**visibility** (vi-zä-*bi*-lä-ti) *n* visibilidade *f*

**visible** (*vi*-zä-bäl) *adj* visível

**vision** (*vi*-jänn) *n* visão *f*

**visit** (*vi*-zit) *v* visitar; *n* visita *f*; **visiting hours** horas de visita

**visitor** (*vi*-zi-tä) *n* visitante *m*

**vital** (*vai*-täl) *adj* vital

**vitamin** (*vi*-tä-minn) *n* vitamina *f*

**vivid** (*vi*-vid) *adj* vivo

**vocabulary** (vä-*kæ*-b¹u-lä-ri) *n* vocabulário *m*

**vocal** (*vo*ᵘ-kãl) *adj* vocal

**vocalist** (*vo*ᵘ-kă-liçt) *n* vocalista *m*

**voice** (voiç) *n* voz *f*

**void** (void) *adj* nulo; vazio; *n* vácuo *m*

**volcano** (vól-*kei*-no°) *n* (pl ~es, ~s) vulcão *m*

**volt** (vo°lt) *n* volt *m*

**voltage** (vo°l-tidj) *n* voltagem *f*

**volume** (vó-lⁱumm) *n* volume *m*

**voluntary** (vó-lãnn-tă-ri) *adj* voluntário

**volunteer** (vó-lãnn-*ti*ᵃ) *n* voluntário *m*

**vomit** (vó-mit) *v* vomitar

**vote** (vo°t) *v* votar; *n* voto *m*; votação *f*

**voucher** (*vau*-tchă) *n* vale *m*

**vow** (vau) *n* juramento *m*, voto *m*; *v* jurar

**vowel** (vau°l) *n* vogal *f*

**voyage** (*voi*-idj) *n* viagem *f*

**vulgar** (*val*-ghă) *adj* vulgar; popular, ordinário

**vulnerable** (*val*-nă-rã-băl) *adj* vulnerável

**vulture** (*val*-tchă) *n* abutre *m*

# W

**wade** (ᵘeid) *v* patinhar

**wafer** (*ᵘei*-fă) *n* bolacha de baunilha

**waffle** (ᵘó-fãl) *n* bolacha *f*

**wages** (*ᵘei*-djiz) *pl* salário *m*

**waggon** (*ᵘæ*-ghănn) *n* vagão *m*

**waist** (ᵘeiçt) *n* cintura *f*

**waistcoat** (*ᵘeiç*-ko°t) *n* colete *m*

**wait** (ᵘeit) *v* esperar; ~ **on** *servir

**waiter** (*ᵘei*-tă) *n* criado *m*, empregado de mesa; garçom *mBr*

**waiting** (*ᵘei*-tinng) *n* espera *f*

**waiting-list** (*ᵘei*-tinng-liçt) *n* lista de espera

**waiting-room** (*ᵘei*-tinng-ruumm) *n* sala de espera

**waitress** (*ᵘei*-triç) *n* empregada de mesa; garçonete *fBr*

***wake** (ᵘeik) *v* acordar; ~ **up** despertar, acordar

**walk** (ᵘóók) *v* andar; *passear; *n* passeio *m*; **walking** a pé

**walker** (*ᵘó*-kă) *n* passeante *m*

**walking-stick** (*ᵘóó*-kinng-çtik) *n* bengala *f*

**wall** (ᵘóól) *n* muro *m*; parede *f*

**wallet** (*ᵘó*-lit) *n* carteira *f*

**wallpaper** (*ᵘóól*-pei-pă) *n* papel de parede

**walnut** (*ᵘóól*-nat) *n* noz *f*

**waltz** (ᵘóólç) *n* valsa *f*

**wander** (*ᵘónn*-dă) *v* *vaguear, errar

**want** (ᵘónnt) *v* *querer; desejar; *n* necessidade *f*; carência *f*, falta *f*

**war** (ᵘóó) *n* guerra *f*

**warden** (*ᵘó*-dănn) *n* guarda *m*

**wardrobe** (*ᵘóó*-dro°b) *n* roupeiro *m*, guarda-roupa *m*

**warehouse** (*ᵘéᵃ*-hauç) *n* armazém *m*

**wares** (ᵘéᵃz) *pl* mercadorias *fpl*

**warm** (ᵘóómm) *adj* quente; *v* aquecer

**warmth** (ᵘóómmθ) *n* calor *m*

**warn** (ᵘóónn) *v* *prevenir, avisar

**warning** (*ᵘóó*-ninng) *n* aviso *m*

**wary** (*ᵘéᵃ*-ri) *adj* prudente

**was** (ᵘóz) *v* (p be)

**wash** (ᵘóch) *v* lavar; ~ **and wear** não passar a ferro; ~ **up** lavar a loiça

**washable** (*ᵘó*-chă-băl) *adj* lavável

**wash-basin** (*ᵘóch*-bei-çănn) *n* lavatório *m*

**washing** (*ᵘó*-chinng) *n* lavagem *f*; roupa para lavar

**washing-machine** (*ᵘó*-chinng-mă-chiinn) *n* máquina de lavar

**washing-powder** (*ᵘó*-chinng-pau-dă) *n* detergente em pó

**washroom** (ᵘóch-ruumm) nAm lavabos mpl

**wash-stand** (ᵘóch-çtænnd) n lavatório m

**wasp** (ᵘóçp) n vespa f

**waste** (ᵘeiçt) v desperdiçar; n desperdício m; adj inculto

**wasteful** (ᵘeiçt-fål) adj gastador

**wastepaper-basket** (ᵘeiçt-pei-på-baaçkit) n cesto dos papéis

**watch** (ᵘótch) v observar; vigiar; n relógio m; ~ **for** espreitar; ~ **out** tomar cuidado

**watch-maker** (ᵘótch-mei-kå) n relojoeiro m

**watch-strap** (ᵘótch-çtræp) n correia de relógio

**water** (ᵘóó-tå) n água f; **iced** ~ água gelada; **running** ~ água corrente; ~ **pump** bomba de água; ~ **ski** esqui aquático

**water-colour** (ᵘóó-tå-ka-lå) n tinta de água; aguarela f

**watercress** (ᵘóó-tå-kréç) n agrião m

**waterfall** (ᵘóó-tå-fóól) n queda de água

**watermelon** (ᵘóó-tå-mé-lånn) n melancia f

**waterproof** (ᵘóó-tå-pruuf) adj impermeável

**water-softener** (ᵘóó-tå-çóf-nå) n produto amaciador da água

**waterway** (ᵘóó-tå-ᵘei) n via navegável

**watt** (ᵘót) n watt m

**wave** (ᵘeiv) n onda f, ondulação f; v acenar

**wave-length** (ᵘeiv-lénngθ) n comprimento de onda

**wavy** (ᵘei-vi) adj ondulado

**wax** (ᵘækç) n cera f

**waxworks** (ᵘækç-ᵘääkç) pl museu das ceras

**way** (ᵘei) n maneira f, modo m; caminho m; lado m, direcção f; distância f; **any** ~ de qualquer maneira; **by the** ~ a propósito; **one-way traffic** sentido único; **out of the** ~ afastado; **the other** ~ **round** ao contrário; ~ **back** volta f; ~ **in** entrada f; ~ **out** saída f

**wayside** (ᵘei-çaid) n beira do caminho

**we** (ᵘii) pron nós

**weak** (ᵘiik) adj fraco

**weakness** (ᵘiik-nåç) n fraqueza f

**wealth** (ᵘélθ) n riqueza f

**wealthy** (ᵘél-θi) adj rico

**weapon** (ᵘé-pånn) n arma f

***wear** (ᵘéˀ) v usar, *trazer vestido; ~ **out** gastar

**weary** (ᵘiˀ-ri) adj cansado

**weather** (ᵘé-ðå) n tempo m; ~ **forecast** boletim meteorológico

***weave** (ᵘiiv) v tecer

**weaver** (ᵘii-vå) n tecelão m

**wedding** (ᵘé-dinng) n casamento m

**wedding-ring** (ᵘé-dinng-rinng) n aliança f

**wedge** (ᵘédj) n cunha f

**Wednesday** (ᵘénnz-di) quarta-feira f

**weed** (ᵘiid) n erva daninha f

**week** (ᵘiik) n semana f

**weekday** (ᵘiik-dei) n dia de semana

**weekend** (ᵘii-kénnd) n fim-de-semana m

**weekly** (ᵘii-kli) adj semanal

***weep** (ᵘiip) v chorar

**weigh** (ᵘei) v pesar

**weighing-machine** (ᵘei-inng-måchiinn) n balança f

**weight** (ᵘeit) n peso m

**welcome** (ᵘél-kåmm) adj benvindo; n acolhimento m; v acolher

**weld** (ᵘéld) v soldar

**welfare** (ᵘél-féˀ) n bem-estar m

**well¹** (ᵘél) adv bem; adj bom; **as** ~ também; **as** ~ **as** assim como;

**well!** bem!

**well²** (ᵘél) *n* poço *m*

**well-founded** (ᵘél-faunn-did) *adj* fundamentado

**well-known** (ᵘél-noᵘnn) *adj* conhecido

**well-to-do** (ᵘél-tã-duu) *adj* abastado

**went** (ᵘénnt) *v* (p go)

**were** (ᵘãã) *v* (p be)

**west** (ᵘéçt) *n* ocidente *m*, oeste *m*

**westerly** (ᵘé-çtã-li) *adj* ocidental

**western** (ᵘé-çtãnn) *adj* ocidental

**wet** (ᵘét) *adj* molhado; húmido

**whale** (ᵘeil) *n* baleia *f*

**wharf** (ᵘóóf) *n* (pl ~s, wharves) cais *m*

**what** (ᵘót) *pron* o quê; o que; ~ **for** para quê

**whatever** (ᵘó-té-vã) *pron* tudo o que

**wheat** (ᵘiit) *n* trigo *m*

**wheel** (ᵘiil) *n* roda *f*

**wheelbarrow** (ᵘiil-bæ-roᵘ) *n* carrinho de mão

**wheelchair** (ᵘiil-tchéᵃ) *n* cadeira de rodas

**when** (ᵘénn) *adv* quando; *conj* quando, logo que

**whenever** (ᵘé-né-vã) *conj* sempre que

**where** (ᵘéᵃ) *adv* onde; *conj* onde

**wherever** (ᵘéᵃ-ré-vã) *conj* onde quer que

**whether** (ᵘé-ðã) *conj* se; **whether ... or** quer ... quer

**which** (ᵘitch) *pron* qual; que

**whichever** (ᵘi-tché-vã) *adj* qualquer

**while** (ᵘail) *conj* enquanto; *n* momento *m*

**whilst** (ᵘailçt) *conj* enquanto

**whim** (ᵘimm) *n* capricho *m*, veleidade *f*

**whip** (ᵘip) *n* chicote *m*; *v* bater

**whiskers** (ᵘi-çkãz) *pl* suíças *fpl*

**whisper** (ᵘi-çpã) *v* murmurar, sussurar; *n* sussurro *m*

**whistle** (ᵘi-çãl) *v* assobiar; *n* apito *m*

**white** (ᵘait) *adj* branco

**whitebait** (ᵘait-beit) *n* peixe miúdo

**whiting** (ᵘai-tinng) *n* (pl ~) pescada *f*

**Whitsun** (ᵘit-çãnn) Pentecostes *m*

**who** (huu) *pron* quem; que

**whoever** (huu-é-vã) *pron* quem quer que

**whole** (hoᵘl) *adj* completo, inteiro; intacto; *n* todo *m*

**wholesale** (hoᵘl-ceil) *n* venda por grosso; ~ **dealer** armazenista *m*

**wholesome** (hoᵘl-çãmm) *adj* saudável

**wholly** (hoᵘl-li) *adv* completamente

**whom** (huumm) *pron* a quem

**whore** (hóó) *n* prostituta *f*

**whose** (huuz) *pron* cujo; de quem

**why** (ᵘai) *adv* porquê

**wicked** (ᵘi-kid) *adj* mau

**wide** (ᵘaid) *adj* vasto, largo

**widen** (ᵘai-dãnn) *v* alargar

**widow** (ᵘi-doᵘ) *n* viúva *f*

**widower** (ᵘi-doᵘ-ã) *n* viúvo *m*

**width** (ᵘidθ) *n* largura *f*

**wife** (ᵘaif) *n* (pl wives) esposa *f*, mulher *f*

**wig** (ᵘigh) *n* peruca *f*

**wild** (ᵘaild) *adj* selvagem; feroz

**will** (ᵘil) *n* vontade *f*; testamento *m*

***will** (ᵘil) *v* *querer

**willing** (ᵘi-linng) *adj* disposto

**willingly** (ᵘi-linng-li) *adv* de boa vontade

**will-power** (ᵘil-pauᵃ) *n* força de vontade

***win** (ᵘinn) *v* ganhar

**wind** (ᵘinnd) *n* vento *m*

***wind** (ᵘainnd) *v* serpentear; *dar corda, enrolar

**winding** (ᵘainn-dinng) *adj* sinuoso

**windmill** (ᵘinnd-mil) *n* moinho de vento

**window** (ᵘinn-doᵘ) *n* janela *f*

window-sill (ᵘinn-doᵘ-çil) n peitoril m

windscreen (ᵘinnd-çkriinn) n pára-brisas m; ~ wiper limpa pára-brisas

windshield (ᵘinnd-chiild) nAm pára-brisas m

windy (ᵘinn-di) adj ventoso

wine (ᵘainn) n vinho m

wine-cellar (ᵘainn-çé-lä) n adega f

wine-list (ᵘainn-liçt) n lista dos vinhos

wine-merchant (ᵘainn-mää-tchännt) n negociante de vinhos

wine-waiter (ᵘainn-ᵘei-tä) n sommelier m

wing (ᵘinng) n asa f

winkle (ᵘinng-käl) n búzio m

winner (ᵘi-nä) n vencedor m

winning (ᵘi-ninng) adj vencedor; winnings lucros

winter (ᵘinn-tä) n Inverno m; ~ sports desportos de inverno

wipe (ᵘaip) v limpar

wire (ᵘaiᵃ) n fio m; arame m

wireless (ᵘaiᵃ-läç) n rádio m

wisdom (ᵘiz-dämm) n sabedoria f

wise (ᵘaiz) adj erudito; sensato

wish (ᵘich) v desejar, ambicionar; n desejo m

witch (ᵘitch) n bruxa f

with (ᵘið) prep com

*withdraw (ᵘið-dróó) v retirar

within (ᵘi-ðinn) prep dentro de; adv por dentro

without (ᵘi-ðaut) prep sem

witness (ᵘit-näç) n testemunha f

wits (ᵘitç) pl razão f

witty (ᵘi-ti) adj espirituoso

wolf (ᵘulf) n (pl wolves) lobo m

woman (ᵘu-männ) n (pl women) mulher f

womb (ᵘuumm) n útero m

won (ᵘann) v (p, pp win)

wonder (ᵘann-dä) n milagre m; admiração f; v perguntar a si próprio

wonderful (ᵘann-dä-fäl) adj maravilhoso, estupendo; delicioso

wood (ᵘud) n madeira f; bosque m

wood-carving (ᵘud-kaa-vinng) n talha f

wooded (ᵘu-did) adj arborizado

wooden (ᵘu-dänn) adj de madeira; ~ shoe tamanco m

woodland (ᵘud-lännd) n região arborizada

wool (ᵘul) n lã f; darning ~ linha de passajar

woollen (ᵘu-länn) adj de lã

word (ᵘääd) n palavra f

wore (ᵘóó) v (p wear)

work (ᵘääk) n trabalho m; faina f; v trabalhar; funcionar; working day dia útil; ~ of art obra de arte; ~ permit autorização de trabalho

worker (ᵘää-kä) n trabalhador m

working (ᵘää-kinng) n funcionamento m

workman (ᵘääk-männ) n (pl -men) operário m

works (ᵘääkç) pl fábrica f

workshop (ᵘääk-chóp) n oficina f

world (ᵘääld) n mundo m; ~ war guerra mundial

world-famous (ᵘääld-fei-mäç) adj mundialmente famoso

world-wide (ᵘääld-ᵘaid) adj mundial

worm (ᵘämm) n verme m

worn (ᵘóónn) adj (pp wear) gasto

worn-out (ᵘóónn-aut) adj gasto

worried (ᵘa-rid) adj preocupado

worry (ᵘa-ri) v afligir-se; n preocupação f

worse (ᵘääç) adj pior; adv pior

worship (ᵘää-chip) v adorar; n culto m

worst (ᵘääçt) adj o pior; adv pior

worsted (ᵘu-çtid) n lã cardada

worth (ᵘääθ) n valor m; *be ~ valer; *be worth-while *valer a pena

worthless (ᵘääθ-läç) adj sem valor

**worthy of** (ᵘáắ-ðĭ ắv) digno de
**would** (ᵘud) v (p will)
**wound**¹ (ᵘuunnd) n ferida f; v *ferir, ofender
**wound**² (ᵘaunnd) v (p, pp wind)
**wrap** (ræp) v envolver; embrulhar
**wreck** (rék) n carcaça f; v *destruir
**wrench** (rénntch) n chave-inglesa f; torcedura f; v torcer
**wrinkle** (rinng-kăl) n ruga f
**wrist** (riçt) n pulso m
**wrist-watch** (riçt-ᵘótch) n relógio de pulso
***write** (rait) v escrever; **in writing** por escrito; ~ **down** anotar
**writer** (rai-tă) n escritor m
**writing-pad** (rai-tinng-pæd) n bloco de notas, bloco de papel
**writing-paper** (rai-tinng-pei-pă) n papel para escrever
**written** (ri-tănn) adj (pp write) por escrito
**wrong** (rónn) adj errado, impróprio; n mal m; v lesar; *be ~ *estar errado
**wrote** (roᵘt) v (p write)

# X

**Xmas** (kriç-măç) Natal m
**X-ray** (ékç-rei) n radiografia f; v radiografar

# Y

**yacht** (iót) n iate m
**yacht-club** (iót-klab) n clube náutico
**yachting** (ió-tinng) n vela f
**yard** (iaad) n pátio m
**yarn** (iaann) n fio m

**yawn** (ióónn) v bocejar
**year** (iịå) n ano m
**yearly** (iịå-li) adj anual
**yearn** (iåänn) v ansiar; ter saudades
**yeast** (iiçt) n levedura f
**yell** (iél) v berrar; n berro m
**yellow** (ié-loᵘ) adj amarelo
**yes** (iéç) sim
**yesterday** (ié-çtă-di) adv ontem
**yet** (iét) adv ainda; conj contudo, mas
**yield** (iild) v render; ceder; n rendimento m; produção f
**yoke** (ioᵘk) n canga f
**yolk** (ioᵘk) n gema f
**you** (iuu) pron tu; te; você; o senhor; ao senhor; vocês; os senhores
**young** (iȧnng) adj jovem
**your** (ióó) adj seu; teu; vosso, teus
**yourself** (ióó-çélf) pron te; tu mesmo; você mesmo; o senhor mesmo
**yourselves** (ióó-çélvz) pron se; vocês mesmos; os senhores mesmos
**youth** (iuuθ) n juventude f; ~ **hostel** albergue de juventude

# Z

**zeal** (ziil) n zelo m
**zealous** (zé-lăç) adj zeloso
**zebra** (zii-bră) n zebra f
**zenith** (zé-niθ) n zénite m; apogeu m
**zero** (ziȧ-roᵘ) n (pl ~s) zero m
**zest** (zéçt) n gosto m
**zinc** (zinngk) n zinco m
**zip** (zip) n fecho éclair; ~ **code** Am código postal
**zipper** (zi-pă) n fecho éclair
**zodiac** (zoᵘ-di-æk) n zodíaco m
**zone** (zoᵘnn) n zona f; região f

# Léxico gastronómico

## Comidas

almond amêndoa
anchovy anchova
angel (food) cake bolo fofo à base de claras
angels on horseback ostras envolvidas em bacon, grelhadas e servidas sobre torradas
appetizer aperitivo
apple maçã
~ dumpling espécie de pastel recheado de compota de maçã
~ sauce molho de maçã
apricot alperce (Bras. damasco)
Arbroath smoky arinca fumado
artichoke alcachofra
asparagus espargo
~ tip cabeça de espargo
assorted sortido, variado
aubergine beringela
avocado (pear) abacate
bacon toucinho fumado
~ and eggs ovos estrelados com toucinho fumado
bagel rosca
baked cozido no forno
~ Alaska sobremesa composta duma camada de bolo fino e outra de gelado (Bras. sorvete), recoberta de claras em castelo e açúcar e levada ao forno rapidamente a alourar
~ beans feijão branco guisado

com molho de tomate adocicado
~ potato batata no forno com pele
Bakewell tart tarte de amêndoa com doce (Bras. geléia) de fruta
baloney espécie de mortadela
banana split banana cortada ao comprido com gelado (Bras. sorvete) e nozes e coberta de calda de fruta ou de chocolate
barbecue 1) carne de vaca picada servida com um molho de tomate picante 2) churrasco ao ar livre
~ sauce molho de tomate picante
barbecued grelhado nas brasas
basil manjericão
bass robalo
bean feijão
beef carne de vaca (Bras. boi)
~ olive trouxa, rolinho de vaca
beefburger hamburger, sanduíche de bife de vaca picado
beet, beetroot beterraba
bilberry uva-do-monte
bill conta
~ of fare lista (Bras. cardápio)
biscuit 1) biscoito, bolacha (GB) 2) pãozinho (EUA)

**black pudding** chouriço de sangue, morcela
**blackberry** amora
**blackcurrant** groselha negra
**bloater** arenque salgado e fumado
**blood sausage** chouriço de sangue, morcela
**blueberry** uva-do-monte (Bras. mirtilo)
**boiled** cozido
**Bologna (sausage)** espécie de mortadela
**bone** osso
**boned** desossado, sem ossos
**Boston baked beans** feijão branco guisado com toucinho fumado e melaço
**Boston cream pie** bolo recheado com chantilly ou creme de pasteleiro e coberto com glacé de chocolate
**brains** miolos
**braised** estufado, assado
**bramble pudding** pudim de amoras (geralmente servido com maçãs)
**braunschweiger** chouriço de fígado
**bread** pão
**breaded** panado
**breakfast** pequeno almoço (Bras. café da manhã)
**breast** peito (de aves)
**brisket** peito (de animais)
**broad bean** fava
**broth** caldo
**brown Betty** espécie de pudim de maçã coberto de pão ralado
**brunch** pequeno almoço (Bras. café da manhã) abundante que substitui o almoço
**Brussels sprout** couve-de-bruxelas

**bubble and squeak** batatas e couve fritas como uma omeleta e misturadas, por vezes, com bocados de carne
**bun** 1) pãozinho de leite com frutas secas (GB) 2) pãozinho redondo (EUA)
**butter** manteiga
**buttered** barrado com manteiga
**cabbage** couve
**Caesar salad** salada de alface com alho, anchovas, crostões de pão e queijo ralado
**cake** bolo
**cakes** bolos, pastéis
**calf** vitela
**Canadian bacon** lombo de porco fumado cortado às fatias
**cantaloupe** variedade de melão
**caper** alcaparra
**capercaillie, capercailzie** galo (silvestre)
**carp** carpa
**carrot** cenoura
**cashew** castanha de caju
**casserole** espécie de guisado
**catfish** gata (peixe)
**catsup** ketchup
**cauliflower** couve-flor
**celery** aipo
**cereal** cornflakes
   **hot ~** papas de aveia
**check** conta
**Cheddar (cheese)** queijo de gosto um pouco ácido, parecido com o queijo da ilha
**cheese** queijo
   **~ board** tabuleiro de queijos variados
   **~ cake** tarte de requeijão
**cheeseburger** sanduíche de bife picado com uma fatia de queijo
**chef's salad** salada mista de pre-

sunto, frango, ovos cozidos, tomates, alface e queijo

**cherry** cereja

**chestnut** castanha

**chicken** frango

**chicory** 1) endívia (GB) 2) escarola, chicória (EUA)

**chili con carne** carne de vaca picada com malaguetas e feijão encarnado

**chili pepper** piripiri, malagueta

**chips** 1) batatas fritas (GB) 2) batatas chips (EUA)

**chitt(er)lings** tripas de porco

**chive** cebolinho

**choice** 1) escolha 2) primeira qualidade

**chop** costeleta

~ **suey** prato chinês; tiras muito finas de carne ou de galinha e de legumes variados (feijão, soja, aipo, junça) cortados finos

**chopped** cortado aos bocados pequenos

**chowder** sopa creme de marisco

**Christmas pudding** pudim escuro com frutas cristalizadas e passas, por vezes flamejado com conhaque, e servido com creme de baunilha

**chutney** condimento indiano agridoce que acompanha os pratos à base de caril

**cinnamon** canela

**clam** amêijoa

**club sandwich** sanduíche americana composta de várias tostas intercaladas de frango, toucinho fumado, alface, tomate e maionese

**cobbler** espécie de tarte de frutas

**cock-a-leekie soup** sopa de frango e alho-porro

**coconut** coco

**cod** bacalhau fresco

**Colchester oyster** ostra inglesa muito apreciada

**cold cuts/meat** prato de carnes frias

**coleslaw** salada de couve

**cooked** cozido, cozinhado

**cookie** bolacha, biscoito

**corn** 1) trigo (GB) 2) milho (EUA)

~ **on the cob** espiga de milho, maçaroca

**corned beef** carne enlatada

**cornflakes** flocos de milho

**Cornish pasty** pastel recheado com bocados de batata e de carneiro

**cottage cheese** espécie de requeijão

**cottage pie** empadão de batata

**course** prato

**cover charge** preço do talher

**crab** caranguejo

**cracker** bolacha de água e sal

**cranberry** arando

~ **sauce** molho de arandos

**crawfish, crayfish** 1) lagostim-do-rio 2) lagostim

**cream** 1) natas (Bras. creme de leite) 2) sopa creme 3) creme (sobremesa)

~ **cheese** queijo fresco muito cremoso

~ **puff** espécie de farto recheado com chantilly

**creamed potatoes** batatas cozidas, cortadas aos quadrados e envolvidas em béchamel

**creole** prato muito condimentado, preparado com tomates, pimentos e cebolas e acompanhado de arroz à crioula

**cress** agrião

**crisps** batatas chips
**crumpet** espécie de pãozinho achatado geralmente torrado
**cucumber** pepino
**Cumberland ham** presunto muito apreciado
**Cumberland sauce** molho agri-doce composto de vinho, sumo de laranja, raspa de limão, condimentos e geleia de groselhas
**cupcake** queque
**cured** marinado, salgado e, por vezes, fumado
**currant** 1) passa de uva (GB) 2) groselha (EUA)
**curried** com caril
**custard** creme de baunilha
 ~ **pie** pastel de nata
**cutlet** 1) costeleta 2) posta de peixe 3) escalope (EUA)
**dab** solhão (peixe)
**Danish pastry** pastel folhado
**date** tâmara
**Derby cheese** queijo cremoso e picante de cor amarela pálida
**dessert** sobremesa
**devil(l)ed** com molho muito picante
**devil's food cake** bolo de choco-late
**devils on horseback** ameixas cozi-das em vinho tinto, recheadas de amêndoas e anchovas, en-volvidas em toucinho fumado e grelhadas
**Devonshire cream** natas (Bras. creme de leite) muito espessas
**diced** cortado aos quadradinhos
**diet food** comida dietética
**dill** endro, aneto
**dinner** jantar
**dish** prato
**donut, doughnut** bola de Berlim

**double cream** natas (Bras. creme de leite) muito espessas
**Dover sole** linguado de Dôver, muito apreciado
**dressing** 1) molho para a salada 2) recheio para aves
**Dublin Bay prawn** camarão grande
**duck** pato
**duckling** pato novo
**dumpling** bolinha de massa, por vezes recheada, cozida em água ou caldo
**Dutch apple pie** tarte de maçã polvilhada de açúcar mascava-do ou coberta de melaço
**eel** enguia, eiró
**egg** ovo
 **boiled** ~ semi-cozido (5 min.)
 **fried** ~ estrelado
 **hard-boiled** ~ cozido
 **poached** ~ escalfado (Bras. escaldado)
 **scrambled** ~ mexido
 **soft-boiled** ~ semi-cozido (3 min.) (Bras. ovo quente)
**eggplant** beringela
**endive** 1) escarola, chicória (GB) 2) endívia (EUA)
**entrée** 1) primeiro prato (GB) 2) prato principal (EUA)
**fennel** funcho
**fig** figo
**fillet** lombo de carne ou filete de peixe
**finnan haddock** arinca, pequeno bacalhau fumado
**fish** peixe
 ~ **and chips** filete de peixe com batatas fritas
 ~ **cake** croquete de peixe panada
 ~ **finger** palito de peixe panado
**flan** tarte

**flapjack** crepe (Bras. panqueca) espesso

**flounder** patruça

**fool** mousse de fruta com natas (Bras. creme de leite) batidas

**forcemeat** recheio, picado

**fowl** criação

**frankfurter** salsicha

**French bean** feijão verde (Bras. vagem)

**French bread** cacete (pão)

**French dressing** 1) molho de vinagre para a salada (GB) 2) molho de maionese com ketchup para a salada (EUA)

**french fries** batatas fritas

**French toast** rabanada, fatia dourada

**fresh** fresco

**fried** frito

**fritter** frito

**frogs' legs** pernas de rã

**frosting** glace, cobertura

**fruit** fruta

**fry** fritada

**game** caça

**gammon** carne de porco fumada

**garfish** peixe-agulha

**garlic** alho

**garnish** acompanhamento, guarnição

**gherkin** pickle, pequeno pepino conservado em vinagre

**giblets** miúdos

**ginger** gengibre

**goose** ganso

**gooseberry** groselha verde

**grape** uva
~**fruit** toranja

**grated** ralado

**gravy** molho de carne

**grayling** peixe do lago parecido com a truta

**green bean** feijão verde

(Bras. vagem)

**green pepper** piment(ã)o verde

**greens** legumes verdes, hortaliça

**grilled** grelhado

**grilse** salmão novo

**grouse** galinha-do-mato

**gumbo** 1) quiabo, gombo 2) prato crioula à base de quiabo com legumes, carne, peixe ou mariscos

**haddock** arinca, pequeno bacalhau geralmente salgado e fumado

**haggis** bucho de carneiro recheado de flocos de aveia

**hake** pescada

**half** meio, metade

**halibut** alabote (peixe)

**ham** fiambre (Bras. presunto)
~**and eggs** com ovos estrelados

**hare** lebre

**haricot bean** feijão verde (Bras. vagem)

**hash** restos cortados aos bocadinhos e aquecidos (geralmente carne de vaca e batatas)

**hazelnut** avelã

**heart** coração

**herbs** ervas de cheiros

**herring** arenque

**home-made** caseiro

**hominy grits** milho pilado, cozido em água salgada

**honey** mel

**honeydew melon** melão muito doce, cujo interior é amarelo esverdeado

**horse-radish** rábano silvestre

**hot** 1) muito quente 2) muito condimentado, apimentado
~**cross bun** pãozinho de leite com passas
~**dog** cachorro (Bras. cachorro quente)

**huckleberry** uva-do-monte (Bras. mirtilo)

**hush puppy** frito de farinha de milho com cebolas picadas

**ice-cream** gelado (Bras. sorvete)

**iced** gelado, muito fresco

**icing** glace, cobertura

**Idaho baked potato** batata muito apreciada cozida no forno

**Irish stew** guisado de carneiro com cebolas e batatas

**Italian dressing** molho vinagrete com alho para a salada

**jam** doce (Bras. geléia) de fruta
~ **tart** tartelete de doce de fruta

**jellied** em gelatina

**Jell-O** sobremesa de gelatina

**jelly** geleia de fruta

**Jerusalem artichoke** tupinambo (Bras. topinamba)

**John Dory** peixe-galo, São Pedro

**jugged hare** lebrada

**juniper berry** baga de zimbro

**junket** requeijão com açúcar

**kale** espécie de couve frisada

**kedgeree** arroz de peixe com ovos cozidos e manteiga

**kidney** rim

**kipper** arenque fumado

**Lady Curzon soup** sopa de tartaruga com natas (Bras. creme de leite) e caril

**lamb** borrego

**Lancashire hot-pot** guisado de costeletas, rins de carneiro, batatas e cebolas

**laver** alga marinha comestível

**lean** magro, com pouca gordura

**leek** alho-porro, alho francês

**leg** perna

**lemon** limão
~ **sole** azevia, espécie de linguado

**lentil** lentilha

**lettuce** alface

**lima bean** 1) fava (EUA) 2) feijão encarnado (GB)

**lime** lima, limão verde

**liver** fígado

**lobster** lavagante

**loin** lombo

**Long Island duck** pato de Long Island, muito apreciado

**low-calorie** pobre em calorias

**lox** salmão fumado

**lunch** almoço

**macaroon** bolinho de claras, coco ou amêndoas

**mackerel** sarda

**maize** milho seco

**maple syrup** xarope de ácer

**marinated** marinado

**marjoram** manjerona

**marmelade** marmelada de laranjas

**marrow** 1) tutano 2) variedade de abóbora (GB)
~**bone** osso com tutano

**marshmallow** rebuçado de malvaísco

**marzipan** massa de amêndoas, maçapão

**mashed potatoes** puré de batata

**mayonnaise** maionese

**meal** refeição

**meat** carne
~ **ball** almôndega
~ **loaf** bolo de carne

**medium (done)** mal passado

**melon** melão

**melted** derretido

**Melton Mowbray pie** empadão de carne

**menu** lista (Bras. cardápio)

**meringue** merengue

**milk** leite

**mince** picado
~-**pie** empada de frutas cristali-

zadas cortadas aos bocados
com passas e condimentos
**minced** picado
  ~ **meat** carne picada
**mint** hortelã
**mixed** misto, variado
  ~ **grill** 1) espetada mista (EUA)
  2) prato guarnecido geralmente
  de tomate, cogumelos, ovo
  estrelado, toucinho fumado e,
  por vezes, feijão branco e
  carne grelhada
**molasses** melaço
**morel** funcho, cogumelo muito
apreciado
**mulberry** amora
**mullet** tainha
**mulligatawny soup** canja de
galinha muito condimentada
de origem indiana
**mushroom** cogumelo
**muskmelon** variedade de melão
muito doce
**mussel** mexilhão
**mustard** mostarda (geralmente
agridoce)
**mutton** carneiro
**noodle** nuilha, espécie de massa
às tiras
**nut** noz
**oatmeal** papas de aveia
**oil** óleo
**okra** quiabo (Bras. gombo)
**olive** azeitona
**omelet** omelete
**onion** cebola
**orange** laranja
**ox tongue** língua de vaca
**oxtail** rabo de boi
**oyster** ostra
**pancake** crepe (Bras. panqueca)
**paprika** colorau
**parsley** salsa
**parsnip** pastinaga, cenoura

branca
**partridge** perdiz
**pastry** 1) massa 2) pastel, bolo
**pasty** pastel de carne ou de peixe
**pâté** espécie de pasta de fígado
enformada, também feita com
carnes diversas
**pea** ervilha
**peach** pêssego
**peanut** amendoim
  ~ **butter** manteiga de amendoim
**pear** pêra
**pearl barley** cevadinha
**pepper** pimenta
**peppermint** hortelã-pimenta
**perch** perca
**persimmon** dióspiro, caqui
**pheasant** faisão
**pickerel** lúcio pequeno
**pickled** conservado em vinagre,
em salmoura
**pie** empada, empadão recheado
de carne, legumes ou frutas
**pig** porco
**pigs' feet/trotters** chispe, pé de
porco
**pigeon** pombo
**pike** lúcio
**pineapple** ananás (Bras. abacaxi)
**plaice** solha
**plain** ao natural, simples
**plate** prato
**plum** ameixa
  ~ **pudding** pudim escuro com
frutas cristalizadas e passas,
por vezes flamejado com
conhaque, e servido com creme
de baunilha
**poached** escalfado, cozido ligeiramente
**popcorn** pipoca
**popover** pãozinho de leite
**pork** porco

**porridge** papas (Bras. mingau) de aveia

**porterhouse steak** grande bife de lombo de vaca

**potato** batata

~ **chips** 1) batatas fritas (GB) 2) batatas chips (EU)

~ **in its jacket** cozida com a pele

**potted shrimps** camarões conservados em manteiga condimentada e servidos frios

**poultry** criação

**prawn** camarão

**prune** ameixa seca

**ptarmigan** perdiz da montanha

**pudding** pudim

**pumpernickel** pão de centeio integral

**pumpkin** abóbora

**quail** codorniz

**quince** marmelo

**rabbit** coelho

**radish** rabanete

**rainbow trout** truta arco-íris

**raisin** passa (de uva)

**rare** muito mal passado

**raspberry** framboesa

**raw** cru

**red mullet** salmonete

**red (sweet) pepper** pimentão vermelho

**redcurrant** groselha

**relish** pickles

**rhubarb** ruibarbo

**rib (of beef)** costeleta (de vaca)

**rib-eye steak** bife de lombo

**rice** arroz

**river trout** truta

**roast** assado

~ **beef** rosbife

**Rock Cornish hen** variedade de frango alimentado com grãos

**roe** ovas

**roll** pãozinho

**rollmop herring** filete de arenque marinado em vinho branco e enrolado à volta dum pepino de conserva

**round steak** bife do alto da perna de vaca

**Rubens sandwich** fatia de pão de centeio guarnecida com carne de vaca fumada e chucrute, temperada com molho para salada e alourada no forno

**rumpsteak** bife do alto da perna de vaca

**rusk** tosta

**rye bread** pão de centeio

**saddle** sela, lombo

**saffron** açafrão

**sage** salva

**salad** salada

~ **bar** saladas variadas à descrição

~ **cream** espécie de maionese adocicada

~ **dressing** molho para a salada

**salmon** salmão

~ **trout** truta-das-fontes

**salt** sal

**salted** salgado

**sandwich** sande (Bras. sanduíche)

**sardine** sardinha

**sauce** molho

**sauerkraut** chucrute, couve picada em salmoura

**sausage** enchido

**sautéed** salteado

**scallop** concha de vieira

**scampi** rabo de lagostim descascado

**scone** espécie de pãozinho

**Scotch broth** sopa de legumes com carne de carneiro ou de vaca

**Scotch egg** ovo cozido, enrolado em miolo de salsicha e frito

**Scotch woodcock** torrada com pasta de anchovas e ovos mexidos

**sea bass** robalo

**sea bream** goraz (peixe)

**sea kale** espécie de couve

**seafood** marisco

**(in) season** (da) época

**seasoning** condimento

**service charge** serviço

**service (not) included** serviço (não) incluído

**set menu** ementa fixa (Bras. menu) do dia

**shad** sável

**shallot** chalota

**shellfish** marisco de concha

**sherbet** sorvete (Bras. sorvete com água)

**shortbread** biscoito areado

**shoulder** pá

**shredded** cortado em tiras finas

**~ wheat** espécie de flocos de trigo

**shrimp** camarão

**silverside (of beef)** peça grande de carne de vaca

**sirloin steak** bife de lombo de vaca

**skewer** espetada

**slice** fatia

**sliced** cortado às fatias

**sloppy Joe** picado de vaca com um molho de tomate bem condimentado servido dentro dum pãozinho

**smelt** biqueirão (peixe)

**smoked** fumado

**snack** refeição ligeira

**sole** linguado

**soup** sopa

**sour** azedo

**soused herring** arenque de escabeche

**spare rib** entrecosto de porco

**spice** especiaria

**spinach** espinafre

**spiny lobster** lagosta

**(on a) spit** (no) espeto

**sponge cake** espécie de pão-de-ló

**sprat** espadilha

**squash** espécie de abóbora

**starter** entrada, primeiro prato

**steak-and-kidney pie** empadão de vaca rechcado de carne de vaca e rins

**steamed** cozido ao vapor

**stew** guisado

**Stilton (cheese)** queijo inglês muito apreciado, branco com veios azuis

**strawberry** morango

**string bean** feijão verde (Bras. vagem)

**stuffed** recheado

**stuffing** recheio

**suck(l)ing pig** leitão

**sugar** açúcar

**sugarless** sem açúcar

**sundae** taça de gelado (Bras. sorvete) guarnecida

**supper** ceia

**swede** rutabaga

**sweet** 1) doce 2) sobremesa

**~-corn** milho tenro (Bras. milho doce)

**~ potato** batata doce

**sweetbread** moleja (de vitela ou de borrego)

**Swiss cheese** queijo adocicado com buracos

**Swiss roll** torta enrolada

**Swiss steak** carne de vaca estufada com legumes

**T-bone steak** grande bife de vaca com um osso ao meio

**table d'hôte** ementa (Bras. menu) do dia

**tangerine** tangerina

**tarragon** estragão

**tenderloin** lombo

**Thousand Island dressing** maionese com ketchup, pimentos, azeitonas e ovos cozidos

**thyme** tomilho

**toad-in-the-hole** pudim de massa de crepes (Bras. panquecas) com salsichas

**toast** torrada

**toasted** torrado

~ **cheese** tosta de queijo

~ **sandwich** tosta mista (Bras. misto quente)

**tomato** tomate

**tongue** língua

**treacle** melaço

**trifle** bolo de massa lêveda com doce de fruta, amêndoas raladas, demolhado em vinho e servido com chantilly e creme de baunilha

**tripe** tripas

**trout** truta

**truffle** trufa

**tuna, tunny** atum

**turbot** pregado

**turkey** perú

**turnip** nabo

**turnover** espécie de pastel de massa tenra geralmente recheado de puré de maçã doce

**turtle soup** sopa de tartaruga

**underdone** muito mal passado

**vanilla** baunilha

**veal** vitela

~ **bird** trouxa de vitela

~ **cutlet** escalope

**vegetable** legume

~ **marrow** abobrinha

**venison** caça

**vichyssoise** sopa fria de alhos-porros, batatas e natas (Bras. creme de leite)

**vinegar** vinagre

**Virginia baked ham** presunto (Bras. pernil) assado no forno com cravinhos, guarnecido de ananás (Bras. abacaxi) e cerejas e regado com o sumo (Bras. suco) das frutas

**vol-au-vent** vol-au-vent, pequena forma de massa folhada, recheada com um creme de carne, molejas e cogumelos

**wafer** espécie de bolacha de baunilha

**waffle** panqueca de máquina

**walnut** noz

**water ice** sorvete, gelado feito com água (Bras. sorvete de água)

**watercress** agrião

**watermelon** melancia

**well-done** bem passado

**Welsh rabbit/rarebit** tosta de queijo

**whelk** búzio

**whipped cream** chantilly

**whitebait** espadilha

**Wiener Schnitzel** escalope

**wine list** lista dos vinhos

**woodcock** galinhola

**Worcestershire sauce** molho inglês, condimento líquido picante à base de soja, alho e vinagre

**yoghurt** iogurte

**York ham** presunto de York

**Yorkshire pudding** pudim de massa de crepes (Bras. panquecas) cozido no forno sob uma peça de rosbife

**zucchini** abobrinha

**zwieback** tosta

**ale** cerveja levemente adocicada e fermentada a uma elevada temperatura
   **bitter** ~ cerveja a copo, bastante amarga e pesada
   **brown** ~ cerveja preta de garrafa, ligeiramente adocicada
   **light** ~ cerveja branca de garrafa
   **mild** ~ cerveja preta a copo, de gosto acentuado
   **pale** ~ cerveja branca de garrafa
**angostura** amargo de angustura, essência aromática amarga que se adiciona aos cocktails
**applejack** aguardente de maçã
**Athol Brose** bebida escocesa composta de whisky, mel, água e, por vezes, flocos de aveia
**Bacardi cocktail** cocktail à base de rum, gin, xarope de romã e sumo (Bras. suco) de limão verde
**barley water** refresco aromatizado à base de cevada
**barley wine** cerveja preta de garrafa, muito alcoólica
**beer** cerveja
   **bottled** ~ de garrafa
   **draft/draught** ~ a copo, imperial
**bitters** aperitivos e digestivos, feitos à base de raízes, cascas de frutas ou ervas aromáticas
**black velvet** champanhe misturado com *stout* (bebida que acompanha normalmente as ostras)
**bloody Mary** vodka com sumo

(Bras. suco) de tomate e condimentos
**bottle** garrafa
**bourbon** whisky americano à base de milho
**brandy** 1) nome que designa todas as aguardentes de vinho ou de frutas 2) conhaque
   ~ **Alexander** mistura de conhaque, creme de cacau e natas (Bras. creme de leite)
**British wines** vinhos «ingleses», feitos de uvas ou de sumo (bras. suco) de uvas importados
**champagne** champanhe
**cherry brandy** licor de cereja
**cider** sidra
**claret** vinho tinto de Bordéus
**cobbler** *long drink* à base de sumo (Bras. suco) de frutas misturado com vinho ou licor e servido muito gelado
**cocoa** cacau
**coffee** café
   ~ **with cream** com natas magras (Bras. creme de leite)
   **black** ~ simples
   **caffeine-free** ~ sem cafeína
   **iced** ~ café gelado servido em copo, geralmente com chantilly
   **white** ~ com leite
**coke** coca-cola
**cordial** 1) licor 2) espécie de xarope
**cream** 1) natas (Bras. creme de leite) 2) licor espresso
**cup** 1) chávena 2) refresco à base de vinho, água gaseificada,

aguardente e frutas variadas servido com uma concha

**daiquiri** cocktail de rum, sumo (Bras. suco) de lima e de ananás (Bras. abacaxi)

**double** dose dupla

**Drambuie** licor de whisky com mel

**dry** seco

  **~ martini** 1) vermute seco (GB) 2) cocktail de gin com vermute seco (EUA)

  **medium ~** meio-seco

**egg flip/nog** gemada de bar

**fizzy** gazeificado

**gill** medida utilizada para servir as aguardentes (0,142 litro na GB e 0,118 litro nos EUA)

**gin and it** cocktail de gin

**gin-fizz** gin com sumo (Bras. suco) de limão, açúcar e soda

**ginger beer** limonada de gengibre, ligeiramente alcoólica

**grasshopper** mistura de creme de hortelã-pimenta, de creme de cacau e de natas (Bras. creme de leite)

**Guinness (stout)** cerveja preta ligeiramente adocicada, de gosto acentuado, contendo grande quantidade de malte e de lúpulo

**half pint** medida que corresponde aproximadamente a 3 decilitros

**highball** aguardente ou whisky a que se junta uma boa quantidade de gasosa

**iced** gelado, muito frio

**Irish coffee** café com açúcar e whisky irlandês, coberto de chantilly

**Irish Mist** licor irlandês de whisky com mel

**Irish whiskey** whisky irlandês feito quase exclusivamente de cevada e menos amargo que o escocês

**juice** sumo (Bras. suco)

**lager** cerveja branca e leve, servida muito fresca

**lemonade** limonada

**lime juice** amargo de lima (Bras. suco de limão verde)

**liqueur** licor

**liquor** bebida espirituosa

**long drink** aguardente ou whisky a que se junta uma boa quantidade de gasosa

**Manhattan** cocktail de whisky de milho e vermute com amargo de angustura

**mead** hidromel

**milk** leite

  **~ shake** batido

**mineral water** água mineral

**mulled wine** vinho quente com especiarias

**neat** puro, simples

**old-fashioned** cocktail de whisky e marrasquino com cerejas e amargo de angustura

**on the rocks** com gelo

**Ovaltine** Ovomaltine

**Pimm's cup(s)** bebida alcoólica misturada com sumo (Bras. suco) de frutas ou soda

  **~ No. 1** à base de gin

  **~ No. 2** à base de whisky

  **~ No. 3** à base de rum

  **~ No. 4** à base de aguardente

**pink champagne** champanhe rosé

**pink lady** mistura de claras com aguardente de sidra, sumo (Bras. suco) de limão, xarope de romã e gin

**pint** medida que corresponde

aproximadamente a 6 deci-
litros
**port (wine)** vinho do Porto
**porter** cerveja preta e amarga
**quart** medida que corresponde a
1,14 litro (EUA 0,95 litro)
**red** tinto
**root beer** refresco doce gaseifica-
do, com essências aromáticas
**rye (whiskey)** whisky de centeio,
mais pesado e mais áspero que
o *bourbon*
**screwdriver** mistura de vodka e
sumo (Bras. suco) de laranja
**shandy** *bitter ale* misturada com
limonada ou *ginger beer*
**sherry** xerez
**short drink** expressão que designa
uma bebida espirituosa pura
**shot** dose de licor ou de espirituoso
**sloe gin-fizz** licor de ameixas sil-
vestres com soda e sumo

(Bras. suco) de limão
**soft drink** bedina não alcoólica,
refresco
**spirits** bebidas espirituosas
**stinger** conhaque com creme de
hortelã
**stout** cerveja preta, muito alcoólica
**straight** puro, simples
**sweet** doce
**tea** chá
**toddy** grogue
**Tom Collins** mistura de gin com
sumo (Bras. suco) de limão,
açúcar e água gaseificada
**water** água
   **tonic** ~ água tónica
**whisky sour** whisky com sumo
(Bras. suco) de limão, açúcar e
soda
**white** branco
**wine** vinho
   **sparkling** ~ espumante

# Mini-gramática

## O artigo

O artigo indefinido tem duas formas: *a* emprega-se antes de uma consoante, *an* antes de vogal ou "h" mudo.

| | |
|---|---|
| **a coat** | um sobretudo |
| **an umbrella** | um guarda-chuva |
| **an hour** | uma hora |

O artigo definido tem uma só forma: *the.*

| | |
|---|---|
| **the room, the rooms** | o quarto, os quartos |

*Some* indica uma quantidade ou número indefinido.

| | |
|---|---|
| **I'd like some coffee, please.** | Queria café, por favor. |
| **Please bring me some cigarettes.** | Traga-me cigarros, por favor. |

*Any* emprega-se nas frases negativas e em vários tipos de interrogativas.

| | |
|---|---|
| **There isn't any soap.** | Não há sabão. |
| **Do you have any stamps?** | Tem selos? |
| **Is there any mail for me?** | Há correspondência para mim? |

## O substantivo

O plural da maioria dos substantivos forma-se acrescentando *-s* ou *-es* ao singular.

| | |
|---|---|
| **cup — cups** | xícara — xícaras |
| **dress — dresses** | vestido — vestidos |

*Nota:* Se o substantivo terminar em *-y* precedido de consoante, o plural faz-se em *-ies;* se o "y" for precedido de vogal, junta-se apenas um *-s.*

| | |
|---|---|
| **lady — ladies** | senhora — senhoras |
| **key — keys** | chave — chaves |

Alguns plurais irregulares:

| | |
|---|---|
| **man — men** | homen — homens |
| **woman — women** | mulher — mulheres |
| **child — children** | criança — crianças |
| **foot — feet** | pé — pés |
| **tooth — teeth** | dente — dentes |

## Determinativo de posse (genitivo)

1. Quando o possuidor é uma pessoa e o substantivo não termina em *-s*, junta-se *'s.*

| | |
|---|---|
| **the boy's room** | o quarto do rapaz |
| **Anne's dress** | o vestido de Ana |
| **the children's clothes** | as roupas das crianças |

Se o substantivo acaba em *-s*, acrescenta-se apenas o apóstrofo (').

| | |
|---|---|
| **the boys' rooms** | os quartos dos rapazes |

2. Quando o possuidor não é uma pessoa: empregar a preposição *of*.

**the key of the door**      a chave da porta

*This/That* (este/aquele). *This* (plural *these*) refere-se a uma coisa próxima (no espaço e no tempo). *That* (plural *those*) refere-se a uma coisa mais afastada.

**Is this seat taken?**      Este lugar está ocupado?
**That's my seat.**       Aquele é o meu lugar.
**Those are not my suitcases.**  Aquelas não são as minhas malas.

## O adjetivo

Os adjetivos colocam-se normalmente antes do substantivo.

**a large brown suitcase**     uma grande mala marrom

### Comparativo e superlativo

Há duas maneiras de formar o comparativo e o superlativo dos adjetivos:

1. Os adjetivos de uma sílaba e muitos de duas sílabas acrescentam: *-r* ou *-er* para o comparativo, *-st* ou *-est* para o superlativo.

**small — smaller — smallest**
pequeno — menor — o menor
**busy — busier — busiest***
ocupado — mais ocupado — o mais ocupado

2. Os adjetivos de três ou mais sílabas e alguns de duas sílabas (por ex. os que terminam em *-ful* ou em *-less*) formam o comparativo e o superlativo antepondo respectivamente *more* e *most*.

**expensive** (caro) — **more expensive** — **most expensive**
**careful** (prudente) — **more careful** — **most careful**

Atenção às seguintes formas irregulares:

| | | |
|---|---|---|
| **good** (bom) | **better** | **best** |
| **bad** (mau) | **worse** | **worst** |
| **little** (pequeno) | **less** | **least** |
| **much** (muito) ⎫ | | |
| **many** (muitos) ⎭ | **more** | **most** |

## O pronome

| | Sujeito | Complemento | Possessivo 1 | 2 |
|---|---|---|---|---|
| **Singular** | | | | |
| 1ª pessoa | **I** | **me** | **my** | **mine** |
| 2ª pessoa | **you** | **you** | **your** | **yours** |
| 3ª pessoa (m) | **he** | **him** | **his** | **his** |
| (f) | **she** | **her** | **her** | **hers** |
| (n) | **it** | **it** | **its** | **—** |

*O *y* muda em *i* quando precedido de uma consoante.

|  | Sujeito | Complemento | Possessivo 1 | 2 |
|---|---|---|---|---|
| **Plural** | | | | |
| 1ª pessoa | **we** | **us** | **our** | **ours** |
| 2ª pessoa | **you** | **you** | **your** | **yours** |
| 3ª pessoa | **they** | **them** | **their** | **theirs** |

*Nota:* Em inglês não se emprega o tratamento: "tu". Existe, pois, uma única forma, *you,* significando "tu" ou "vós, você, vocês". O pronome complemento, tanto se emprega para o complemento indireto como depois de preposições:

| | |
|---|---|
| **Give it to me.** | Me dá isto. |
| **He came with us.** | Ele veio conosco. |

A forma um do possessivo corresponde ao adjetivo determinativo possessivo; a forma dois ao pronome.

| | |
|---|---|
| **Where is my key?** | Onde está a minha chave? |
| **That's not mine.** | Não é a minha. |

## Advérbios

Muitos advérbios formam-se juntando *-ly* ao adjetivo.

| | |
|---|---|
| **easy — easily** | fácil — facilmente |
| **slow — slowly** | lento — lentamente |

Note, no entanto:

| | |
|---|---|
| **good — well** | bom — bem |
| **fast — fast** | rápido — rapidamente |

## Verbos auxiliares

Os verbos auxiliares são muito importantes. Deve-se, por isso, aprender o presente do indicativo dos três seguintes:

a. **to be** (ser)

| Afirmativa | Contração | Negativa — Contrações | |
|---|---|---|---|
| **I am** | **I'm** | | **I'm not** |
| **you are** | **you're** | **you're not** | **you aren't** |
| **he is** | **he's** | **he's not** | **he isn't** |
| **she is** | **she's** | **she's not** | **she isn't** |
| **it is** | **it's** | **it's not** | **it isn't** |
| **we are** | **we're** | **we're not** | **we aren't** |
| **they are** | **they're** | **they're not** | **they aren't** |

Interrogação: **Am I? — Is he?** etc.

*Nota:* Na linguagem quotidiana, as formas contractas são mais usadas.

O inglês tem duas formas para traduzir "há" (verbo haver) impessoal: *there is (there's),* seguido de um substantivo no singular; *there are,* seguido de um substantivo no plural.

Negação: **There isn't — There aren't**
Interrogação: **Is there? — Are there?**

b. **to have** (ter)

|  | Contração |  | Contração |
|---|---|---|---|
| **I have** | **I've** | **it has** | **it's** |
| **you have** | **you've** | **we have** | **we've** |
| **he/she has** | **he's/she's** | **they have** | **they've** |

Negação: **I have not (haven't)**
Interrogação: **Have you? — Has he?**

c. **to do** (fazer)

**I do, you do, he/she/it does, we do, they do**

Negação: **I do not (I don't) — He does not (doesn't)**
Interrogação: **Do you? — Does he?**

Os auxiliares obedecem todos ao mesmo modelo:

1. a forma negativa obtém-se acrescentando *not;*
2. as perguntas fazem-se por inversão do sujeito.

## Outros verbos

Presente do indicativo: a mesma forma que o infinitivo, em todas as pessoas, excepto na 3ª do singular. Esta forma-se juntando *s* ou *-es* ao infinitivo.

|  | **(to) speak** falar | **(to) come** vir | **(to) go** ir |
|---|---|---|---|
| **I** | **speak** | **come** | **go** |
| **you** | **speak** | **come** | **go** |
| **he/she** | **speaks** | **comes** | **goes** |
| **we** | **speak** | **come** | **go** |
| **they** | **speak** | **come** | **go** |

A negação faz-se com o auxiliar DO/DOES + NOT + INFINITIVO.
**We do not (don't) like this hotel.**   Não gostamos deste hotel.

## Interrogação

Faz-se também com o auxiliar DO + SUJEITO + INFINITIVO.
**Do you like her?**   Gosta dela?

# Presente contínuo

Este tempo forma-se com o verbo *to be* + o particípio presente do verbo conjugado. O particípio presente forma-se acrescentando *-ing* ao infinitivo (caindo o *-e* final, se o verbo assim terminar). O presente contínuo emprega-se apenas com certos verbos, visto indicar uma ação ou estado que tem lugar no momento em que se fala. Em português corresponde à forma do presente contínuo.

Sendo *to be* um verbo auxiliar, a negação faz-se simplesmente por meio de *not* e a interrogação por inversão do sujeito.

| | |
|---|---|
| **What are you doing?** | Que está fazendo? |
| **I'm writing a letter.** | Estou escrevendo uma carta. |

# Imperativo

O imperativo (singular e plural) tem a mesma forma que o infinitivo (sem *to*). A negação faz-se com *don't*.

| | |
|---|---|
| **Please bring me some water.** | Traga-me água, por favor. |
| **Don't be late.** | Não chegue tarde. |

## Verbos irregulares

Segue-se a lista dos verbos irregulares ingleses. Os verbos compostos ou com prefixo conjugam-se como os verbos principais. Por exemplo: *withdraw* conjuga-se
como *draw* e *mistake* como *take*.

| *Infinitivo* | *Imperfeito* | *Particípio passado* | |
|---|---|---|---|
| **arise** | arose | arisen | *surgir* |
| **awake** | awoke | awoken/awaked | *despertar* |
| **be** | was | been | *ser, estar* |
| **bear** | bore | borne | *trazer; suportar* |
| **beat** | beat | beaten | *bater* |
| **become** | became | become | *tornar-se* |
| **begin** | began | begun | *começar* |
| **bend** | bent | bent | *curvar* |
| **bet** | bet | bet | *apostar* |
| **bid** | bade/bid | bidden/bid | *fazer um lanço; ordena* |
| **bind** | bound | bound | *ligar* |
| **bite** | bit | bitten | *morder* |
| **bleed** | bled | bled | *sangrar* |
| **blow** | blew | blown | *soprar* |
| **break** | broke | broken | *quebrar* |
| **breed** | bred | bred | *criar* |
| **bring** | brought | brought | *trazer* |
| **build** | built | built | *construir* |
| **burn** | burnt/burned | burnt/burned | *queimar* |
| **burst** | burst | burst | *rebentar* |
| **buy** | bought | bought | *comprar* |
| **can\*** | could | – | *poder* |
| **cast** | cast | cast | *lançar; fundir* |
| **catch** | caught | caught | *apanhar* |
| **choose** | chose | chosen | *escolher* |
| **cling** | clung | clung | *agarrar-se* |
| **clothe** | clothed/clad | clothed/clad | *vestir* |
| **come** | came | come | *vir* |
| **cost** | cost | cost | *custar* |
| **creep** | crept | crept | *arrastar-se* |
| **cut** | cut | cut | *cortar* |
| **deal** | dealt | dealt | *tratar; distribuir* |
| **dig** | dug | dug | *cavar* |
| **do (he does\*)** | did | done | *fazer* |
| **draw** | drew | drawn | *puxar; desenhar* |
| **dream** | dreamt/dreamed | dreamt/dreamed | *sonhar* |
| **drink** | drank | drunk | *beber* |
| **drive** | drove | driven | *conduzir* |
| **dwell** | dwelt | dwelt | *morar* |
| **eat** | ate | eaten | *comer* |
| **fall** | fell | fallen | *cair* |

---

\* presente do indicativo

| | | | |
|---|---|---|---|
| **feed** | fed | fed | *alimentar* |
| **feel** | felt | felt | *sentir* |
| **fight** | fought | fought | *lutar* |
| **find** | found | found | *achar, encontrar* |
| **flee** | fled | fled | *fugir* |
| **fling** | flung | flung | *arremessar* |
| **fly** | flew | flown | *voar* |
| **forsake** | forsook | forsaken | *abandonar* |
| **freeze** | froze | frozen | *gelar* |
| **get** | got | got | *obter* |
| **give** | gave | given | *dar* |
| **go (he goes\*)** | went | gone | *ir* |
| **grind** | ground | ground | *moer* |
| **grow** | grew | grown | *crescer* |
| **hang** | hung | hung | *pendurar* |
| **have (he has\*)** | had | had | *ter* |
| **hear** | heard | heard | *ouvir* |
| **hew** | hewed | hewed/hewn | *talhar* |
| **hide** | hid | hidden | *esconder* |
| **hit** | hit | hit | *dar (uma) pancada* |
| **hold** | held | held | *segurar* |
| **hurt** | hurt | hurt | *ferir; doer* |
| **keep** | kept | kept | *guardar* |
| **kneel** | knelt | knelt | *ajoelhar-se* |
| **knit** | knitted/knit | knitted/knit | *tricotar* |
| **know** | knew | known | *saber, conhecer* |
| **lay** | laid | laid | *deitar* |
| **lead** | led | led | *dirigir; levar* |
| **lean** | leant/leaned | leant/leaned | *apoiar-se* |
| **leap** | leapt/leaped | leapt/leaped | *saltar* |
| **learn** | learnt/learned | learnt/learned | *aprender* |
| **leave** | left | left | *partir; deixar* |
| **lend** | lent | lent | *emprestar* |
| **let** | let | let | *deixar (licença); alugar* |
| **lie** | lay | lain | *estar deitado* |
| **light** | lit/lighted | lit/lighted | *acender* |
| **lose** | lost | lost | *perder* |
| **make** | made | made | *fazer* |
| **may\*** | might | – | *poder* |
| **mean** | meant | meant | *significar* |
| **meet** | met | met | *encontrar (pessoas)* |
| **mow** | mowed | mowed/mown | *ceifar* |
| **must\*** | must | – | *ter de* |
| **ought\* (to)** | ought | – | *dever* |
| **pay** | paid | paid | *pagar* |
| **put** | put | put | *pôr* |
| **read** | read | read | *ler* |
| **rid** | rid | rid | *desembaraçar* |
| **ride** | rode | ridden | *montar, andar* |

---

\* presente do indicativo

| | | | |
|---|---|---|---|
| **ring** | rang | rung | *tocar (campainha)* |
| **rise** | rose | risen | *subir, levantar-se* |
| **run** | ran | run | *correr* |
| **saw** | sawed | sawn | *serrar* |
| **say** | said | said | *dizer* |
| **see** | saw | seen | *ver* |
| **seek** | sought | sought | *procurar* |
| **sell** | sold | sold | *vender* |
| **send** | sent | sent | *enviar, mandar* |
| **set** | set | set | *pôr; fixar* |
| **sew** | sewed | sewed/sewn | *coser* |
| **shake** | shook | shaken | *sacudir* |
| **shall\*** | should | – | *dever* |
| **shed** | shed | shed | *despojar-se; derramar* |
| **shine** | shone | shone | *brilhar* |
| **shoot** | shot | shot | *disparar* |
| **show** | showed | shown | *mostrar* |
| **shrink** | shrank | shrunk | *encolher* |
| **shut** | shut | shut | *fechar* |
| **sing** | sang | sung | *cantar* |
| **sink** | sank | sunk | *afundar(-se)* |
| **sit** | sat | sat | *sentar(-se)* |
| **sleep** | slept | slept | *dormir* |
| **slide** | slid | slid | *escorregar* |
| **sling** | slung | slung | *arrojar* |
| **slink** | slunk | slunk | *esquivar-se* |
| **slit** | slit | slit | *fender* |
| **smell** | smelled/smelt | smelled/smelt | *cheirar* |
| **sow** | sowed | sown/sowed | *semear* |
| **speak** | spoke | spoken | *falar* |
| **speed** | sped/speeded | sped/speeded | *acelerar* |
| **spell** | spelt/spelled | spelt/spelled | *soletrar* |
| **spend** | spent | spent | *gastar; passar* |
| **spill** | spilt/spilled | spilt/spilled | *derramar, entornar* |
| **spin** | spun | spun | *fiar; girar* |
| **spit** | spat | spat | *cuspir* |
| **split** | split | split | *rachar(-se); dividir* |
| **spoil** | spoilt/spoiled | spoilt/spoiled | *estragar* |
| **spread** | spread | spread | *espalhar* |
| **spring** | sprang | sprung | *pular; brotar* |
| **stand** | stood | stood | *estar de pé* |
| **steal** | stole | stolen | *roubar* |
| **stick** | stuck | stuck | *colar* |
| **sting** | stung | stung | *picar* |
| **stink** | stank/stunk | stunk | *cheirar mal, feder* |
| **strew** | strewed | strewed/strewn | *espargir* |
| **stride** | strode | stridden | *andar a passos largos* |
| **strike** | struck | struck/stricken | *golpear; fazer greve* |
| **string** | strung | strung | *esticar cordas* |

\* presente do indicativo

| | | | |
|---|---|---|---|
| **strive** | strove | striven | *esforçar-se* |
| **swear** | swore | sworn | *jurar* |
| **sweep** | swept | swept | *varrer* |
| **swell** | swelled | swollen/swelled | *inchar* |
| **swim** | swam | swum | *nadar* |
| **swing** | swung | swung | *balouçar-se* |
| **take** | took | taken | *tomar, pegar* |
| **teach** | taught | taught | *ensinar* |
| **tear** | tore | torn | *rasgar* |
| **tell** | told | told | *contar, dizer* |
| **think** | thought | thought | *pensar* |
| **throw** | threw | thrown | *atirar* |
| **thrust** | thrust | thrust | *empurrar* |
| **tread** | trod | trodden | *pisar* |
| **wake** | woke/waked | woken/waked | *acordar* |
| **wear** | wore | worn | *trazer ou levar (vestido); gastar com o uso* |
| **weave** | wove | woven | *tecer* |
| **weep** | wept | wept | *chorar* |
| **will \*** | would | — | *querer* |
| **win** | won | won | *ganhar* |
| **wind** | wound | wound | *enroscar* |
| **wring** | wrung | wrung | *torcer* |
| **write** | wrote | written | *escrever* |

---

\* presente do indicativo

# Abreviaturas inglesas

| | | |
|---|---|---|
| **AA** | *Automobile Association* | Automóvel Clube da Grã--Bretanha |
| **AAA** | *American Automobile Association* | Automóvel Clube dos Estados Unidos |
| **ABC** | *American Broadcasting Company* | Companhia particular americana de Rádio e Televisão |
| **A.D.** | *anno Domini* | depois de Cristo |
| **Am.** | *America ; American* | América; americano |
| **a.m.** | *ante meridiem (before noon)* | antes do meio-dia (da meia-noite ao meio-dia) |
| **Amtrak** | *American railroad corporation* | Companhia particular americana dos Caminhos-de-Ferro |
| **AT & T** | *American Telephone and Telegraph Company* | Companhia particular americana de Telefones e Telégrafos |
| **Ave.** | *avenue* | avenida |
| **BBC** | *British Broadcasting Corporation* | Companhia nacional britânica de Rádio e Televisão |
| **B.C.** | *before Christ* | antes de Cristo |
| **bldg.** | *building* | prédio, edifício |
| **Blvd.** | *boulevard* | alameda |
| **B.R.** | *British Rail* | Caminhos-de-Ferro Britânicos |
| **Brit.** | *Britain ; British* | Grã-Bretanha; britânico |
| **Bros.** | *brothers* | irmãos |
| **¢** | *cent* | centésima parte do dólar |
| **Can.** | *Canada ; Canadian* | Canadá; canadiano |
| **CBS** | *Columbia Broadcasting System* | Companhia particular americana de Rádio e Televisão |
| **CID** | *Criminal Investigation Department* | polícia judiciária britânica |
| **CNR** | *Canadian National Railways* | Caminhos-de-Ferro Canadianos |
| **c/o** | *(in) care of* | ao cuidado de |
| **Co.** | *company* | companhia |
| **Corp.** | *corporation* | tipo de sociedade americana |
| **CPR** | *Canadian Pacific Railways* | Companhia particular canadiana de Caminhos-de-Ferro |
| **D.C.** | *District of Columbia* | Distrito de Colúmbia (Washington, D.C.) |
| **DDS** | *Doctor of Dental Science* | dentista |
| **dept.** | *department* | repartição; ministério |

| EEC | *European Economic Community* | CEE (Comunidade Económica Europeia), Mercado Commun |
| e.g. | *for instance* | por exemplo |
| Eng. | *England ; English* | Inglaterra; inglês |
| excl. | *excluding ; exclusive* | não incluído, exclusive |
| ft. | *foot/feet* | pé/pés (30,48 cm) |
| GB | *Great Britain* | Grã-Bretanha |
| H.E. | *His/Her Excellency ; His Eminence* | Sua Excelência; Sua Eminência |
| H.H. | *His Holiness* | Sua Santidade |
| H.M. | *His/Her Majesty* | Sua Majestade |
| H.M.S. | *Her Majesty's ship* | navio da marinha real britânica |
| hp | *horsepower* | cavalos-vapor |
| Hwy | *highway* | estrada nacional americana |
| i.e. | *that is to say* | isto é |
| in. | *inch* | polegada (2,54 cm) |
| Inc. | *incorporated* | Sociedade Anónima |
| incl. | *including, inclusive* | incluído, inclusive |
| £ | *pound sterling* | libra esterlina |
| L.A. | *Los Angeles* | Los Angeles |
| Ltd. | *limited* | LDA, (companhia) limitada |
| M.D. | *Doctor of Medicine* | médico |
| M.P. | *Member of Parliament* | membro do Parlamento britânico |
| mph | *miles per hour* | milhas à hora |
| Mr. | *Mister* | Senhor |
| Mrs. | *Missis* | Senhora |
| Ms. | *Missis/Miss* | Senhora/Menina, Senhorita |
| nat. | *national* | nacional |
| NBC | *National Broadcasting Company* | companhia particular americana de Rádio e Televisão |
| No. | *number* | número |
| N.Y.C. | *New York City* | cidade de Nova Iorque |
| O.B.E. | *Officer (of the Order) of the British Empire* | Oficial (da Ordem) do Império Britânico |
| p. | *page ; pence* | página; centésima parte da libra esterlina |
| p.a. | *per annum* | por ano, anual |
| Ph.D. | *Doctor of Philosophy* | doutorado em filosofia |
| p.m. | *post meridiem (after noon)* | depois do meio-dia (do meio-dia à meia-noite) |
| PO | *Post Office* | estação dos correios |

| POO | *post office order* | vale postal |
| P.T.O. | *please turn over* | volte, se faz favor |
| RAC | *Royal Automobile Club* | Automóvel Clube Real da Grã-Bretanha |
| RCMP | *Royal Canadian Mounted Police* | Polícia Real Montada Canadiana |
| Rd. | *road* | estrada, rua |
| ref. | *reference* | veja, confira |
| Rev. | *reverend* | pastor da Igreja anglicana |
| RR | *railroad* | caminho-de-ferro |
| RSVP | *please reply* | responda, se faz favor |
| $ | *dollar* | dólar |
| Soc. | *society* | sociedade |
| St. | *saint ; street* | são, santo; rua |
| STD | *Subscriber Trunk Dialling* | telefone automático |
| UN | *United Nations* | Nações Unidas |
| UPS | *United Parcel Service* | Companhia particular de expedição de encomendas (Bras. pacotes) |
| US | *United States* | Estados Unidos |
| USS | *United States Ship* | navio da marinha de guerra americana |
| VAT | *value added tax* | Imposto de Transacção |
| VIP | *very important person* | personalidade que goza de privilégios particulares |
| Xmas | *Christmas* | Natal |
| yd. | *yard* | jarda (91,44 cm) |
| YMCA | *Young Men's Christian Association* | Associação Cristã de Rapazes |
| YWCA | *Young Women's Christian Association* | Associação Cristã de Raparigas |
| ZIP | *Zip code* | código postal |

# Numerais

| Numerais cardinais | | Numerais ordinais | |
|---|---|---|---|
| 0 | zero | 1st | first |
| 1 | one | 2nd | second |
| 2 | two | 3rd | third |
| 3 | three | 4th | fourth |
| 4 | four | 5th | fifth |
| 5 | five | 6th | sixth |
| 6 | six | 7th | seventh |
| 7 | seven | 8th | eighth |
| 8 | eight | 9th | ninth |
| 9 | nine | 10th | tenth |
| 10 | ten | 11th | eleventh |
| 11 | eleven | 12th | twelfth |
| 12 | twelve | 13th | thirteenth |
| 13 | thirteen | 14th | fourteenth |
| 14 | fourteen | 15th | fifteenth |
| 15 | fifteen | 16th | sixteenth |
| 16 | sixteen | 17th | seventeenth |
| 17 | seventeen | 18th | eighteenth |
| 18 | eighteen | 19th | nineteenth |
| 19 | nineteen | 20th | twentieth |
| 20 | twenty | 21st | twenty-first |
| 21 | twenty-one | 22nd | twenty-second |
| 22 | twenty-two | 23rd | twenty-third |
| 23 | twenty-three | 24th | twenty-fourth |
| 24 | twenty-four | 25th | twenty-fifth |
| 25 | twenty-five | 26th | twenty-sixth |
| 30 | thirty | 27th | twenty-seventh |
| 40 | forty | 28th | twenty-eighth |
| 50 | fifty | 29th | twenty-ninth |
| 60 | sixty | 30th | thirtieth |
| 70 | seventy | 40th | fortieth |
| 80 | eighty | 50th | fiftieth |
| 90 | ninety | 60th | sixtieth |
| 100 | a/one hundred | 70th | seventieth |
| 230 | two hundred and thirty | 80th | eightieth |
| | | 90th | ninetieth |
| 1,000 | a/one thousand | 100th | hundredth |
| 10,000 | ten thousand | 230th | two hundred and thirtieth |
| 100,000 | a/one hundred thousand | | |
| 1,000,000 | a/one million | 1,000th | thousandth |

## As horas

Os Britânicos e os Americanos usam o sistema das doze horas. A expressão «a.m.» (ante meridiem) designa as horas que precedem o meio-dia, «p.m.» (post meridiem) as da tarde e da noite (até à meia--noite). Contudo, na Grã-Bretanha, os horários são progressivamente redigidos segundo o modelo continental.

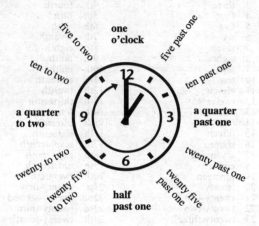

*I'll come at seven a.m.*          Venho às 7 da manhã.
*I'll come at one p.m.*           Venho à 1 da tarde.
*I'll come at eight p.m.*         Venho às 8 da noite.

## Os dias da semana

| | | | |
|---|---|---|---|
| *Sunday* | domingo | *Thursday* | quinta-feira |
| *Monday* | segunda-feira | *Friday* | sexta-feira |
| *Tuesday* | terça-feira | *Saturday* | sábado |
| *Wednesday* | quarta-feira | | |

Notes

Notes

Notes

Notes

**Notas**

**Notas**

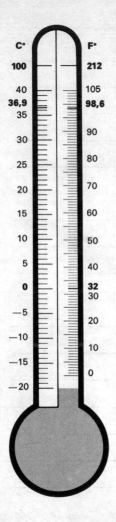

## Conversion tables / Tabelas de conversão

### Metres and Feet
The figure in the middle stands for both metres and feet, e.g. 1 metre = 3.281 ft. and 1 foot = 0.30 m.

### Metros e pés
O algarismo do meio representa, ao mesmo tempo, metros e pés. Por ex.: 1 metro = 3,281 pés e 1 pé = 0,30 m.

| Metres/Metros | | Feet/Pés |
|---|---|---|
| 0.30 | **1** | 3.281 |
| 0.61 | **2** | 6.563 |
| 0.91 | **3** | 9.843 |
| 1.22 | **4** | 13.124 |
| 1.52 | **5** | 16.403 |
| 1.83 | **6** | 19.686 |
| 2.13 | **7** | 22.967 |
| 2.44 | **8** | 26.248 |
| 2.74 | **9** | 29.529 |
| 3.05 | **10** | 32.810 |
| 3.66 | **12** | 39.372 |
| 4.27 | **14** | 45.934 |
| 6.10 | **20** | 65.620 |
| 7.62 | **25** | 82.023 |
| 15.24 | **50** | 164.046 |
| 22.86 | **75** | 246.069 |
| 30.48 | **100** | 328.092 |

### Temperature
To convert Centigrade to Fahrenheit, multiply by 1.8 and add 32.
To convert Fahrenheit to Centigrade, subtract 32 from Fahrenheit and divide by 1.8.

### Temperatura
Para converter os graus centígrados em graus Fahrenheit, multiplique-os primeiro por 1,8 e adicione 32 ao total.
Para converter graus Fahrenheit em graus centígrados, subtraia 32 e divida o resultado por 1,8.